W9-BWT-990

We the People

THE CITIZEN & THE CONSTITUTION
TEACHER'S EDITION

LEVEL 3

CENTER FOR CIVIC EDUCATION
5145 Douglas Fir Road, Calabasas, CA 91302
818.591.9321   www.civiced.org

DIRECTED BY THE
CENTER FOR CIVIC EDUCATION

AND FUNDED BY THE
U.S. DEPARTMENT OF EDUCATION

UNDER THE EDUCATION FOR DEMOCRACY ACT APPROVED BY THE
UNITED STATES CONGRESS

COVER

Howard Chandler Christy, *Signing of the Constitution*,
Architect of the Capitol, House wing, east stairway

COVER + INTERIOR DESIGN

Mark Stritzel

© **2009 CENTER FOR CIVIC EDUCATION**

11 10 09   01 02 03

All rights reserved. Except for use in a review, reproduction or transmittal
of this work in any form or by any electronic, mechanical, or other means,
now known or hereafter invented, including photocopying and recording,
and use of this work in any form in any information storage and retrieval
system is forbidden without prior written permission of the publisher.
Although the contents of this book were developed under a grant from the
Department of Education, they do not necessarily represent the policy
of the Department of Education, and endorsement by the federal government should
not be assumed. The federal government reserves a nonexclusive license to use
and reproduce for government purposes, without payment, excluding copyrighted
content, this material where the government deems it in its interest to do so.

ISBN 10   0–89818–234–4

ISBN 13 978–0–89818–234–7

NATIONAL ADVISORY COMMITTEE

The Honorable Spencer Abraham
The Honorable Les AuCoin
Richard D. Bagin
Richard A. Baker
William G. Baker
The Honorable Max Baucus
The Honorable Bill Bradley
John M. Bridgeland
Anne Bryant
The Honorable John Buchanan Jr.
The Honorable Dale Bumpers
R. Freeman Butts
Mark Cannon
Gene R. Carter
Michael Casserly
The Honorable Thad Cochran
The Honorable William Cohen
John F. Cooke
Philip Crane
The Honorable Mitchell E. Daniels Jr.
Thomas Donohue
Jean Bethke Elshtain
The Honorable Dianne Feinstein
Vincent L. Ferrandino
William Galston
Susan Griffin
Will Harris
The Honorable Orrin G. Hatch
The Honorable Mark O. Hatfield
Charles Haynes
The Honorable Ernest F. Hollings
G. Thomas Houlihan
Paul D. Houston
A. E. Dick Howard

Victoria Hughes
The Honorable James M. Jeffords
The Honorable Edward M. Kennedy
Jack Lockridge
William L. Lucas
Edward J. McElroy
David McIntosh
Glenn Anne McPhee
Joe McTighe
The Honorable Patty Murray
Ralph Neas
Kitty O'Reilley
The Honorable Claiborne Pell
William Pound
The Honorable J. Danforth Quayle
Diane Ravitch
Cheryl Red Owl
Alfred S. Regnery
The Honorable Rick Renzi
Karen M. Ristau, EdD
Robert A. Schadler
The Honorable Philip R. Sharp
The Honorable Gordon H. Smith
John William Smith
Raymond W. Smock
Philippa Strum
Gerald N. Tirozzi
Reg Weaver
Mary Wilson
Paul A. Yost Jr., USCG Ret.

BOARD OF DIRECTORS

PRESIDENT
Thomas A. Craven, Esq.

MEMBERS
Maria Casillas
H. David Fish
C. Hugh Friedman
Ruth M. Gadebusch
Tom Giugni
Janet M. Green
William D. Hatcher
Stanley W. Legro
William L. Lucas
Dale R. Marshall
Ali Mossaver-Rahmani
Laura O'Leary
James D. Otto
James N. Penrod, Esq.
Paul M. Possemato
Clark N. Quinn
M. Carmen Ramirez, Esq.
Clara Slifkin, Esq.
Robert B. Taylor
Jeri Thomson
Jonathan Varat
David Vigilante
Pauline Weaver
Robert Wells
Charles L. Whiteside
Daniel Wong
James W. Ziglar Sr.

MEMBERS EMERITUS
R. Freeman Butts
Joanne M. Garvey
Leland R. Selna

ACKNOWLEDGMENTS

The following staff and consultants have contributed to the development of this text.

PRINCIPAL WRITERS
Margaret S. Branson
Scott E. Casper
Susan M. Leeson
Charles N. Quigley

ADDITIONAL CONTRIBUTORS
Charles F. Bahmueller
Jack Barlow
Stephen E. Frantzich
Will Harris
Robert S. Leming
Kevin Washburn

EDITORIAL DIRECTOR
Mark Gage

EDITORS
Donovan Walling
David Hargrove

CREATIVE DIRECTOR
Mark Stritzel

ILLUSTRATOR
Richard Stein

PRODUCTION DESIGN
Erin Breese
Sean Fay

IMAGE RESEARCH
Mark Stritzel
Donovan Walling

REVIEWERS
William Baker
David Baranow
Erin Braun
Henry Chambers
Erwin Chemerinsky
Tony Corrado
Roger Davidson
Joel Elliott
Ruth Gadebusch
Ellen Grigsby
Sam Hall
David Hudson
John Kaminski
Karl Kurtz
Mark Molli
Jayme Neiman
Michael Simon
Jon Varat
David Vigilante
Tom Vontz

MENTOR TEACHERS
Roger Desrosiers
Elizabeth DeWitt
Abby Dupke
Kevin Fox
Stan Harris
Milton Hyams
Peter Kavouras
Tim Moore
Angela Orr
Beth Ratway
David Richmond
Terri Richmond

SPECIAL THANKS
Robert Meyers for digital scanning,
color correction, and proofing;
Sally Mills, print consultant; and
Robert Sinclair at Sinclair Printing.

We the People: The Citizen & the Constitution

Dear Teacher:

We appreciate your participation in **We the People: The Citizen and the Constitution**. It is our hope that you and your students will find this program an effective means of developing a more profound understanding of and appreciation for the fundamental principles and values of our free society.

The enclosed materials have been carefully designed to help you conduct a successful educational program on the Constitution and Bill of Rights. Several thousand teachers throughout the nation have helped us develop and refine the program. Together, we have attempted to write the text and accompanying materials at a level useful for a wide range of student abilities while providing content challenging to the most academically able. Your experience in using the program with your students will undoubtedly result in the identification of ways it can be improved. We welcome your comments and suggestions regarding the strengths and weaknesses of the program so we can improve it for further use. We are particularly interested in receiving anecdotal information on the effects of the program on students' understanding, skills, attitudes, and behaviors.

We have provided you the best materials we have been able to develop. We realize, however, that the success of the program ultimately depends on you, the classroom teacher. We appreciate your interest in the program and your willingness to use it in your classroom. We want to provide whatever additional help you might need in its implementation.

Additional information, materials, or assistance may be obtained locally by contacting your congressional district coordinator. To contact your district coordinator or to provide feedback on the **We the People** program, go to the Center's website at www.civiced.org or contact our California office at 1-800-350-4223.

Sincerely,

Charles N. Quigley
EXECUTIVE DIRECTOR

Robert S. Leming
WE THE PEOPLE NATIONAL DIRECTOR

THE COMMISSION ON THE BICENTENNIAL OF THE UNITED STATES CONSTITUTION (1985–1992)

WARREN E. BURGER (1907–1995)
CHIEF JUSTICE OF THE UNITED STATES 1969–1986

THE COMMISSION ON THE BICENTENNIAL OF THE UNITED STATES CONSTITUTION

CHAIRMAN
Warren E. Burger

MEMBERS
Frederick K. Biebel
Lindy Boggs
Herbert Brownell
Lynne V. Cheney
Philip M. Crane
Dennis DeConcini
William J. Green
Mark O. Hatfield
Edward Victor Hill
Damon J. Keith
Cornelia G. Kennedy
Edward M. Kennedy
Harry McKinley Lightsey Jr.
William Lucas
Edward P. Morgan
Betty Southard Murphy
Thomas H. O'Connor
Phyllis Schlafly
Bernard H. Siegan
Ted Stevens
Obert C. Tanner
Strom Thurmond
Ronald H. Walker
Charles E. Wiggins
Charles Alan Wright

We the People: The Citizen & the Constitution
Level 3 Teacher's Edition

FOREWORD
BY WARREN E. BURGER
CHIEF JUSTICE OF THE UNITED STATES 1969–1986

The years 1987 to 1991 marked the 200th anniversary of the writing, ratification, and implementation of the basic documents of American democracy, the Constitution and the Bill of Rights. Our Constitution has stood the tests and stresses of time, wars, and change. Although it is not perfect, as Benjamin Franklin and many others recognized, it has lasted because it was carefully crafted by men who understood the importance of a system of government sufficiently strong to meet the challenges of the day, yet sufficiently flexible to accommodate and adapt to new political, economic, and social conditions.

Many Americans have but a slight understanding of the Constitution, the Bill of Rights, and the later amendments to which we pledge our allegiance. The lessons in this book are designed to give the next generation of American citizens an understanding of the background, creation, and subsequent history of the unique system of government brought into being by our Constitution. At the same time, it will help them understand the principles and ideals that underlie and give meaning to the Constitution, a system of government by those governed.

TABLE OF CONTENTS

TABLE OF CONTENTS

TABLE OF CONTENTS

TABLE OF CONTENTS

UNIT AND LESSON LIST

INTRODUCTION

We the People: The Citizen & the Constitution introduces students to the study of constitutional government in the United States. It is not a text on constitutional law. Rather, its intent is to provide students with an understanding of how the Constitution came into existence, why it took the form it did, and how it has functioned for the past two hundred years.

The aim of this text, then, is to provide students with an understanding of the American past and to equip them intellectually to be active participants in the American present and future. It is a text that enables students to learn something about political philosophy, history, politics, and law. In other words, it attempts to provide students with the foundation of a civic education.

TEACHING METHODS

The *We the People: The Citizen & the Constitution* text for high school students employs a conceptually oriented approach that blends expository and inquiry methods, both of which call for active participation by students throughout. The approach stresses the development of analytic and evaluative skills, which will enable students to apply basic substantive knowledge to a wide variety of political questions and controversies. Students are actively involved in their own learning process, acquiring the necessary knowledge for developing an understanding of the American past. They also learn the relevance of the past for an understanding of the American constitutional system in the present.

ASSESSMENT AND CULMINATING ACTIVITY

This curriculum provides many opportunities for assessing student understanding of the concepts, knowledge, and skills emphasized in the text.

STUDENT EDITION:

TERMS AND CONCEPTS TO UNDERSTAND

Each lesson begins with a list of important terms and concepts. Students may be given quizzes—such as multiple-choice, matching, fill-in-the-blank, or using the term or concept correctly in a sentence or statement—to test their knowledge of the terms and concepts.

WHAT DO YOU THINK?

This feature can be used to assess student understanding by having students prepare essays or write position papers.

CRITICAL THINKING EXERCISES

This feature offers another opportunity to assess students' capacity to develop and defend an argument, and to support it with evidence.

REVIEWING AND USING THE LESSON

This feature can be used as a quiz at the end of each lesson to evaluate whether students have learned the material covered in the lesson.

ORAL COMMUNICATION SKILLS

The Terms and Concepts to Understand; What Do You Think?; Critical Thinking Exercises; and Reviewing and Using the Lesson features can also be used to assess students' oral communication skills.

TEACHER'S EDITION:

INTERACTIVE TEACHING STRATEGIES

This section identifies multiple ways to engage students in interactive classroom activities. Their participation can be evaluated using Appendix C 6, the Judges' Score Sheet.

CONGRESSIONAL HEARING

As a culminating activity, teachers are encouraged to have students demonstrate their knowledge and understanding of constitutional principles by participating in simulated congressional hearings. See Appendix C.

MULTIPLE-CHOICE TEST

The teacher's edition contains a 65-question multiple-choice test on the history and principles of the United States Constitution that can be administered after students have completed the text.

The following considerations should be taken into account when designing your evaluation of student achievement:

- Assess how well students can apply what they learned in one situation by asking them to apply similar knowledge and skills in similar situations. Structure situations in which students can construct or create appropriate answers, rather than select from a menu of choices.

- Assess the process and the quality of the performance or product, not the ability to identify correct answers. Stress the thinking and reasoning that supports a quality performance or product.

- Assess how well students see the connections among a variety of related ideas and skills. For example, in preparing for a debate, students should combine reading, research, writing, speaking, and critical thinking skills. Students also should see how knowledge and skills from other disciplines can help them deal with challenging topics.

- Provide the criteria for successful performance in advance and make sure that they are clearly understood. When possible, provide models of exemplary performance.

- Provide criteria for effective and successful group work. Teamwork and group interaction are important skills that are given legitimacy when students know they are being assessed.

- Structure opportunities for students to assess their own progress, to judge for themselves when they have or have not done well. This will help them internalize high standards and learn to judge for themselves when they measure up. Because most learning strategies in this text are used more than once, students will have successive opportunities to reflect on their progress.

- Offer plenty of opportunities for students to receive feedback from the teacher, their peers, and community resource people who participate in activities with the class.

CURRICULUM GOALS

The *We the People: The Citizen & the Constitution* curriculum is designed to promote an increased understanding of the institutions of our constitutional democracy and the fundamental principles and values on which they were founded; develop the skills needed to become effective and responsible citizens; increase understanding and willingness to use democratic processes when making decisions; and manage conflict, in both public and private life.

In studying *We the People: The Citizen & the Constitution*, students develop the ability to identify issues that require political action. They are encouraged through informed inquiry to make a personal commitment to accept the responsibilities associated with the rights we enjoy as citizens—responsibilities essential to the continued existence of a society based on the ideals of freedom, justice, equality, and human rights.

CURRICULUM ORGANIZATION

We the People: The Citizen & the Constitution is about ideas, values, and principles fundamental to understanding our constitutional democracy. The curriculum is organized around ideas that form part of the common core of civic values and concepts that are fundamental to the theory and practice of democratic citizenship in the United States.

We the People: The Citizen & the Constitution may be taught in its entirety, or the teacher may select specific lessons as they relate to general curriculum goals and learning outcomes in a school or district. The lessons need not be taught in any particular order. If a single lesson is selected, only the objectives of that specific lesson will be addressed, not the goals of the unit.

CURRICULUM RATIONALE

A fundamental hypothesis of the *We the People: The Citizen & the Constitution* curriculum is that education can increase a person's capacity and inclination to act knowledgeably, effectively, and responsibly. It follows that the role of educational institutions must be to help students increase their capacity to make intelligent choices for themselves—to learn how to think, rather than what to think. The alternative, indoctrination, is improper for educational institutions in a free society.

The Center for Civic Education was founded on the belief that the learning experiences provided by a curriculum based on this philosophy result in significant progress toward students' development of a reasoned commitment to those principles, processes, and values that are essential to the preservation and improvement of our free society.

We the People high school students display their knowledge of the Constitution in a White House forum titled "American History, Civics, and Service" in Washington, D.C.

SIDEBAR COMMENTS

Each lesson poses questions that are presented in boldface type, such as **Why and How Were the Articles of Confederation Created?** (Lesson 8). Sidebar comments in the margins of the teacher's edition provide additional information about the content covered under most of those questions. Some sidebar comments identify U.S. Supreme Court decisions that help to illuminate a point made in the discussion. Other comments provide quotations from influential thinkers that provide additional perspective. Yet others contain biographical information about important individuals. Some include timelines of significant events. All are intended to help teachers understand the material and to generate ideas about how to host engaging classroom discussions and activities.

WEBSITE REFERENCES

Each lesson contains references to the companion website to the *We the People: The Citizen & the Constitution* student text. These references fall under six categories, which correspond to sections of the website:

wtpcompanion.civiced.org | **LESSON PURPOSE**

Visit the We the People companion website for printable and downloadable Lesson Purpose sections for each lesson. Audio readings of each Lesson Purpose are also available online in MP3 format.

wtpcompanion.civiced.org | **TERMS**

Visit the We the People companion website for printable and downloadable Terms and Concepts to Understand for each lesson. Audio readings of each term and concept are also available online in MP3 format.

wtpcompanion.civiced.org | **BIOGRAPHIES**

Visit the We the People companion website for brief printable and downloadable biographies of the people mentioned in the student and teacher's editions. Audio readings of each biography are also available online in MP3 format.

wtpcompanion.civiced.org | **COURT CASES**

Visit the We the People companion website for links to Supreme Court syllabi and opinions for each of the cases described in the student and teacher's editions. Summaries are provided for selected Supreme Court cases.

wtpcompanion.civiced.org | **PRIMARY SOURCES**

Visit the We the People companion website for links to primary sources. The full text of some primary sources is also provided. Audio readings of selected primary sources are also available online in MP3 format.

wtpcompanion.civiced.org | **LINKS**

Visit the We the People companion website for links to information related to the content of the lesson.

ENRICHMENT ACTIVITIES

In addition to "What do you think?" and "Critical Thinking Exercises" in each lesson, the teacher's edition offers additional activities for many lessons to further engage students in exploring constitutional issues and controversies.

SUGGESTED READING

A brief annotated bibliography appears at the end of the teacher's edition beginning on page 367. The books described will help students and teachers deepen their own knowledge of the content of each unit.

CHARACTERISTICS OF EFFECTIVE CIVIC EDUCATION PROGRAMS

CURRICULUM CHARACTERISTICS

Effective civic education programs are distinguished by at least four characteristics:

EXTENSIVE INTERACTION AMONG STUDENTS

Teaching strategies that foster interactive and cooperative learning among students are keys to development of civic participation skills and responsible citizenship. Examples of these teaching strategies are small-group work, simulations, role-play activities, and moot courts.

REALISTIC CONTENT THAT INCLUDES BALANCED TREATMENT OF ISSUES

Realistic and fair treatment of issues is an essential component of effective civic education. So is critical thinking about all sides to controversies. If our legal and political systems are presented as flawless or infallible, students will doubt the credibility of the teacher and the practicality of the content. By contrast, if only cases in which the system has failed are presented, students will be less likely to view the system as a positive means for maintaining social order, liberty, and justice. A balance should be sought between respect for the legal and political system and constructive criticism about its application in specific cases.

USE OF COMMUNITY RESOURCE PERSONS IN THE CLASSROOM

Interaction with a variety of adult role models who work within our political and legal systems adds credibility and reality to the curriculum and is a powerful influence on development of positive attitudes toward the political and legal systems. Appropriate use of resource persons in the classroom (e.g., government officials from the legislative, executive, and judicial branches; community leaders; and representatives of various interest groups) is strongly associated with increased student interest in issues related to effective citizenship and with positive responses to teachers and the school.

STRONG SUPPORT FOR CIVIC EDUCATION BY THE PRINCIPAL AND OTHER IMPORTANT SCHOOL ADMINISTRATORS

A key to successful implementation of civic education in the schools is strong support by administrators, especially the school principal. Supportive administrators can aid civic education by organizing opportunities for peer support, rewarding teachers for outstanding work, helping teachers explain and justify the program to people in the community outside the school, and providing opportunities for staff development in the knowledge and skills needed to carry out civic education programs. In addition, positive attitudes about civic education on the part of teachers and their colleagues are very important to successful implementation.

Successful citizenship programs involve students in the learning process in ways that reflect a high regard for each person. Reflection, deliberation, and discourse are valued and systematically practiced. The development of knowledge and the cultivation of character are pursued in concert as equally important elements of responsible citizenship in our constitutional democracy. Every attempt has been made to incorporate these essential characteristics in the *We the People: The Citizen & the Constitution* curriculum.

INSTRUCTIONAL METHODOLOGY

CONDUCTING CLASS DISCUSSIONS

The study of the history of ideas includes controversy, debate, evaluation, and reflection. So, too, does the study of *We the People: The Citizen & the Constitution*. Effective civic education presents and discusses controversial subject matter. This approach is what makes the curriculum exciting for both students and teachers. Through the discussion process, students develop knowledge, decision-making skills, conflict management experience, and a commitment to citizenship participation.

To ensure that the experience with this curriculum is stimulating and rewarding for both you and your students, consider the following suggestions for successful classroom discussion of controversial issues and contemporary topics.

Emphasize the legitimacy of controversy, compromise, and consensus. They are the lifeblood of a democratic society.

Try to present the central issues of controversy in tangible form. Make allusions to similar problems and dilemmas students face in their own lives.

Stress historical antecedents so students can see how similar conflicts have been managed in the past. Acknowledge those times when we have not lived up to the ideals and principles on which our nation was founded. Examining the interpretation and application of these concepts over time will help students appreciate the flexibility of our constitutional system and the role individual citizens play in helping our nation better realize its goals.

Emphasize the legitimacy of various viewpoints by encouraging students to examine and present conflicting views in an unbiased fashion. It is incumbent on the teacher to raise any opposing views students may have missed.

Keep students focused on discussing or dealing with ideas or positions, rather than people. Stress that on controversial issues, reasonable people might very well differ.

Encourage students to offer dissenting opinions when they do not agree with the majority—even if they are alone in their dissent.

Help students identify specific points of agreement or disagreement, places where compromise might be possible, and places where it is unlikely to occur. Emphasize that the outcome or the decision that they reach on an issue may not be as important as improving their ability to develop a reasoned position and to express it in a civil manner, respecting the views of others.

Conclude, or debrief, a lesson or discussion by evaluating the arguments presented and exploring the likely consequences of the various alternatives suggested. An effective debriefing involves both the teacher and the students in evaluating the process used for conducting a discussion, preparing group work, or presenting a class activity.

Class discussion and sharing of opinions are critical components to this program; therefore, you may wish to establish a few basic ground rules. For example,

- When expressing an opinion, always be prepared to justify it.

- Listen to the opinions of others politely and respectfully.

- Everyone will get a chance to speak, but only one person will speak at a time.

- Argue with reasons and ideas; do not argue against people.

- As did the delegates to the Philadelphia Convention, you can change your opinion at any time if you are persuaded by a better argument or your own insight deepens or matures. Be prepared to explain your reasons for changing your opinion.

EFFECTIVE QUESTIONING STRATEGIES

Question and response sequences are an important feature of the curriculum. The effective use of questions is critical to the learning process and requires careful planning. Although some questions may be useful to establish how much knowledge students have gained, the primary goal of your questioning strategies should be to help students increase their knowledge, understanding, and ability to reach effective, responsible positions or decisions. Therefore, you will want to choose questioning strategies that help students develop the skills of analysis, synthesis, and evaluation.

There are generally six categories of questions you should consider when planning class discussions. The following is a brief description and example of each, based on Benjamin Bloom's taxonomy of 1956. It has been translated into twenty-two languages and remains one of the most widely applied and often used references by curriculum planners and teachers. After more than fifty years, Bloom's Taxonomy is still considered the de facto standard: [1]

KNOWLEDGE

These questions involve recall of specific facts or information.

Example What are the powers of the legislative branch of government?

COMPREHENSION

This involves the ability to understand the meaning of the material. This may be shown by translating material from one form to another and by interpreting material.

Example What was the constitutional question in *McCulloch v. Maryland*?

APPLICATION

This involves the ability to use learned material in new situations.

Example What examples can you cite from your own experience where these ideas apply?

ANALYSIS

This involves the ability to break down material into its component parts. This includes identifying the parts and establishing the relationship among the parts.

Example What are the central ideas of the Declaration of Independence?

SYNTHESIS

This is the ability to put parts together to form a new whole. The emphasis is on creating new patterns of thought.

Example How does globalization stimulate new thinking about immigration?

EVALUATION

This is the ability to judge the value of ideas, principles, and concepts in different contexts.

Example What basic ideas of American democracy can and should be transmitted to other peoples?

Although others have suggested revisions to Bloom's Taxonomy, the one published in 2001 by Lorin Anderson and David Krathwohl has attracted considerable attention. In this revision, Bloom's six categories were changed from noun to verb forms and some were retitled as illustrated on this page. [2]

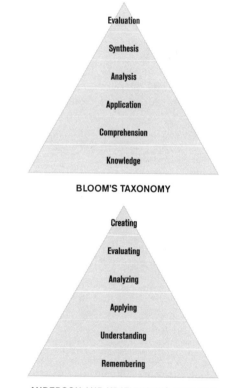

BLOOM'S TAXONOMY

(from top to bottom) Evaluation / Synthesis / Analysis / Application / Comprehension / Knowledge

ANDERSON AND KRATHWOHL'S REVISION

(from top to bottom) Creating / Evaluating / Analyzing / Applying / Understanding / Remembering

1   Adapted from Bloom, Benjamin S., ed. 1956. *Taxonomy of educational objectives; the classification of educational goals, by a committee of college and university examiners.* New York: Longmans, Green.

2   Reprinted with permission from Overbaugh, Richard C., and Lynn Schultz. "Bloom's Taxonomy." http://www.odu.edu/educ/roverbau/bloom/blooms_taxonomy.htm.

The new terms are defined as follows: [1,2]

REMEMBERING

Retrieving, recognizing, and recalling relevant knowledge from long-term memory.

Example What were the major conflicts at the Philadelphia Convention and how were they resolved?

UNDERSTANDING

Constructing meaning from oral, written, and graphic messages through interpreting, exemplifying, classifying, summarizing, inferring, comparing, and explaining.

Example Why did the Founders create America's system of federalism?

APPLYING

Carrying out or using a procedure through executing or implementing.

Example If you were a criminal defendant, would you rather be tried under the adversary or the inquisitorial system of justice? Why?

1 As published in Forehand, M. 2005. *Bloom's taxonomy: Original and revised.* In M. Orey, ed. *Emerging perspectives on learning, teaching, and technology.* http://projects.coe.uga.edu/epltt/. Adapted under Creative Commons attribution-noncommercial-share-alike license. See http://creativecommons.org/licenses/by-nc-sa/3.0/.

2 Adopted from Anderson, L. W., and D. R. Krathwohl, eds. 2001. *A taxonomy for learning, teaching, and assessing: A revision of Bloom's Taxonomy of Educational Objectives.* Complete edition. New York: Longmans, Green.

ANALYZING

Breaking material into constituent parts, determining how the parts relate to one another and to an overall structure or purpose through differentiating, organizing, and attributing.

Example How do the rights found in the U.S. Constitution and the Bill of Rights reflect the influence of classical republicanism and the natural rights philosophy?

EVALUATING

Making judgments based on criteria and standards.

Example Evaluate the Marshall Plan as an American foreign policy using these questions:

- How did the policy seek to advance the interests of the United States?

- How did the policy reflect American values and principles?

- How did other nations respond to the policy?

- What factors led to changes in the policy?

- Was this the right policy for the time it was made? Why or why not?

CREATING

Putting elements together to form a coherent or functional whole; reorganizing elements into a new pattern or structure through generating, planning, or producing.

Example A major issue in the United States is health care reform. Should health care be considered a private or public matter? Create a brief position paper explaining the reasons for your position and the principles involved.

Using either Bloom's Taxonomy or Anderson and Krathwohl's 2001 revision, teachers can formulate questions that encourage students to climb to higher levels of thought and that stimulate their creativity. Encourage students' active participation in the following ways:

- Pose a question and ask students to discuss the answer with a partner.

- Ask students to clarify their responses. This will benefit themselves as well as others.

- Ask students to extend their own or other students' responses by providing additional facts, information, viewpoints, etc.

- Ask students to generate questions of their own on material just presented in class.

- Pause at least seven seconds after asking a question to allow students time to think.

- Ask students to expand on their responses if they provide short or fragmentary answers.

- Call on more than one student per question.

- Encourage students to react to other students' responses.

- Call on nonvolunteers as well as volunteers.

ENCOURAGING SMALL-GROUP LEARNING

The Critical Thinking Exercises in the student text are generally designed as cooperative learning activities with a study partner or in small-group environments. Each individual's participation is essential for the successful completion of an exercise. Students are encouraged not only to contribute academically, but to develop and use appropriate interpersonal skills.

Below are some general recommendations you may want to consider in implementing small-group work in your classroom:

- Make sure the students have the skills necessary to do the work. If they do not, you will quickly know because they will not remain long on task.

- Give clear instructions for completing work and check for understanding of the process or procedures to be followed during an activity.

- Allow adequate time to complete the assigned task. Think creatively about ways to constructively occupy groups that finish ahead of the others.

- Be explicit in dealing with management issues. If someone must report to the class on the group's work, be sure there is a process for selecting a reporter.

- Think about how your evaluation strategies are affected by the use of small groups. Develop methods to reward group efforts.

- Monitor group work and act as a resource to guide your students' development.

- Consider the advantages of the size of groups for specific tasks.

- Consider the advantages and disadvantages of student-selected groups versus teacher-selected groups.

COMMUNITY RESOURCE PEOPLE

Involvement of people from the community who possess appropriate experience or expertise can greatly enhance and extend student understanding of the concepts presented in *We the People: The Citizen & the Constitution*. Community resource people can contribute in the following ways:

- Make the lessons come alive by sharing real-life experiences and applications of the ideas under consideration.

- Help implement activities in the classroom such as role plays, moot courts, and simulated legislative hearings and debates.

- Enrich field experiences by serving as a guide and by responding to questions during visits to places such as courtrooms and legislative chambers.

- Establish an ongoing relationship with a class in which the resource person is available regularly by phone or email to respond to questions or issues that may arise during a particular lesson.

The range of individuals who can serve as resource people is as varied as the community itself. Commonly, this includes government officials from the legislative, executive, and judicial branches, community leaders, and representatives of various interest groups. We the People alumni are often excellent resource people.

Making the involvement of a community resource person as meaningful as possible requires careful planning. Attention should be given to the following considerations:

A resource person's involvement should be relevant to the lesson or concept under consideration.

The principal mode of involvement should be interaction and participation with students. A resource person could be asked to assist students in preparing a role-play or moot court arguments. The resource person can act as a judge, serve on a panel with students, or respond to questions about specific details of a lesson. Also, a resource person should participate in the concluding discussion of a lesson or activity.

A resource person should offer a balanced picture of the topic, including a variety of perspectives. When objectivity is not possible, you might consider inviting a second resource person or a panel to ensure a balanced experience. The guest should avoid professional jargon and speak as simply as possible.

Before a visit by a resource person, students should be well prepared to maximize their thoughtful participation when the visitor is present.

Most resource persons are not trained teachers and should not be responsible for classroom management. The teacher should be in attendance during the entire visit. Sometimes it might be necessary for the teacher to give direction to the guest by asking appropriate questions or offering clues that can help the resource person communicate effectively with students.

For a successful visit, the resource person should receive a copy of the lesson in advance. Usually, a pre-visit meeting or phone call is useful to help clarify what is expected of the guest.

Owing to busy schedules and the limited length of this program, it is advisable to extend invitations as soon as possible. A committee of students should be responsible for hosting the guests on the day of their visit and for the follow-up thank you letter.

INTERACTIVE TEACHING STRATEGIES

INTRODUCTION

An essential feature of *We the People: The Citizen & the Constitution* is the use of instructional methods that actively involve students in developing and presenting positions on related issues. Students learn to apply their knowledge to contemporary issues as well as to a variety of sociopolitical questions. In addition, these learning strategies promote certain dispositions and participatory skills that increase students' capacity to act effectively as citizens in a constitutional democracy. For example, students learn to work cooperatively to reach common goals; to evaluate, take, and defend positions on controversial issues; and to deal with conflicting opinions and positions in a constructive manner. These learning strategies also teach students how government works.

The key learning strategies in this curriculum include, among others, legislative hearings, moot courts, and town meetings. The following material describes these instructional methods and offers specific suggestions for implementation in the classroom.

LEGISLATIVE HEARINGS

Legislative hearings are held by committees of the U.S. Congress and other legislative bodies to gather information on matters of public concern. These hearings are a basic function of legislative branches of government.

Role-playing a legislative hearing provides participants with an opportunity to gain increased understanding of the purpose and procedures of such hearings as well as the roles and responsibilities of committee members. Participants also gain experience in identifying and clarifying the information, interests, and values associated with the subject being discussed.

HOW TO PROCEED

1. CLARIFY TOPICS

Help students understand the topic of the legislative hearing. The topics are clearly identified in the lessons in the student text and in this edition. You also will want to ensure that students understand the role of committees in the legislative process.

2. CONTACT RESOURCE PERSONS

Invite a local legislator, representatives of local groups, or chapters of a national organization to serve as resource people on the topic of the hearing.

3. ASSIGN ROLES

Explain to participants the purpose of a legislative hearing and assign the appropriate roles:

a. **Legislators** Six legislators is a practical number for a committee, but the number may vary according to class needs. Designate one legislator as the chairperson to preside over the hearing.

b. **Witnesses** The number and nature of the witnesses depend on the topic being discussed. The specific roles described in the lessons and in this edition are designed to present differing points of view on the topic.

c. **Recorder** This role is optional. The recorder keeps a record of the proceedings and presents a review or summary of any recommendations that may emerge during the discussions.

d. **Newspaper reporters** This role is optional but is useful in helping students gain insights on the function of the press in the democratic process. Select students to represent newspapers with varying perspectives. Ask them to interview legislators and witnesses, to observe the proceedings, and to write brief articles or editorials about the topic. They should share and discuss their work with the class.

4. PREPARE PRESENTATIONS

Allow time for participants to prepare for the legislative hearing in accordance with their assigned roles.

a. Legislators should identify the key issue(s) and prepare questions to ask each witness.

b. Witnesses should define their position on the issue(s), prepare an opening statement, anticipate questions from the legislators, and formulate possible responses.

c. Witnesses may wish to discuss similarities in positions with other witnesses.

d. When appropriate, have a resource person work with the students or allow students to contact outside resources for assistance in preparing their position on an issue.

5. ARRANGE THE CLASSROOM

Set up the classroom to resemble a legislative chamber. Include a table for the legislators, a desk for the recorder, and a desk or table for the witnesses. Provide a gavel and nameplates with the students' names and their roles. You may want to arrange for the use of a hearing or committee room of a local legislative body.

6. CONDUCT THE HEARING

The following procedures should be used to conduct this activity:

a. The committee chairperson calls the hearing to order, announces the purpose of the hearing, and specifies the order in which the witnesses will be called to testify.

b. The chairperson calls each witness. The witness makes an opening statement, followed by questions from members of the committee. You may want to establish time limits, usually three to four minutes for openings and five to six minutes for questions from the legislators. Appoint a timekeeper to enforce time limitations.

c. The chairperson is the first to question the witness, followed by the other members of the committee. A committee member may interrupt to ask a question or make a comment any time during the proceedings.

d. After the witnesses have been heard, the legislators review the testimony, discuss the issue(s), and make recommendations on what their next step(s) will be.

7. DEBRIEF THE ACTIVITY

Debriefing questions vary according to the topic. Begin by having the legislators announce their decision. Discuss the facts and arguments presented on the topic and evaluate the strengths and weaknesses of the positions taken. Ask students to evaluate their experience with the hearing process itself. Conclude the debriefing by having students discuss the effectiveness of this activity as a tool for learning, including how well they performed their role in it. If a resource person assisted with the activity, that person should be included in the concluding discussion.

LEGISLATIVE DEBATE

Legislative debate is often used productively in the formulation and development of laws. Role-playing a legislative debate provides participants with an opportunity to increase their understanding of the power of legislatures to make laws and to debate matters of public policy.

HOW TO PROCEED

1. CLARIFY TOPICS

Help students understand the topic of the legislative debate. The topics are clearly identified in the lessons in the student text and in this edition. You also will want to ensure that students understand the process whereby bills are enacted into law.

2. CONTACT RESOURCE PERSONS

Contact state and national legislators or their staff assistants to serve as resource persons.

3. ASSIGN ROLES

Consider the entire class as the legislative body with a student or the teacher assuming the role of the presiding officer. Legislators may then be assigned to groups representing various positions on the issue. Groups are clearly identified in the student text and in this edition. You also may want to assign a recorder responsible for tracking key points of discussion during the debate.

4. PREPARE PRESENTATIONS

Allow time for participants to prepare for the legislative hearing in accordance with their assigned roles.

Each group should select a spokesperson and a recorder and then proceed to follow the directions given in the lesson. Students should analyze and evaluate the issue before developing their positions. In some cases, they will be asked to offer amendments to the bills already given in the lesson. In others, they may write a proposed bill designed to alleviate problems raised by the issue.

As each group completes its amendment or proposed bill, the spokesperson reports to the presiding officer asking that the bill be placed on the agenda. Bills should be placed on the agenda in the order in which they are received. Students may wish to discuss any similarities in their proposed amendments or bills with other groups to predetermine whether they can unite behind a common proposal.

5. ARRANGE THE CLASSROOM

Set up the classroom to resemble a legislative chamber. Include a table for the presiding officer, a desk for the recorder, and a podium if you want to have presentations made more formally. Provide a gavel and nameplates with the students' names and their roles. You may want to arrange for the use of a legislative chamber in your community.

6. CONDUCT THE LEGISLATIVE DEBATE

Time limits for the various steps in legislative debates should be decided ahead of time. The presiding officer should be empowered to cut off speakers when the time limit has been reached. Conduct the legislative debate using the following procedures:

a. The presiding officer calls the legislature to order, indicates that all votes will be decided by a simple majority, announces the issue, and opens the debate.

b. The first bill on the agenda is introduced by the group's spokesperson. The spokesperson stands, addresses the presiding officer, and describes the bill the group has written. After presenting the bill, the spokesperson may recognize two other members of the group who may make additional comments on the bill.

c. The bill is discussed and debated by the legislature. Representatives from other groups may ask questions, offer criticisms, or suggest modifications.

d. The steps above are repeated for any additional bills that might be introduced during the session.

e. When the discussion and debate on all proposed bills is completed, legislators may move that one of the bills be voted on or that the session be recessed to enable the groups to consider the bills that have been presented. If the session is recessed, each group meets to decide on a course of action. A group may decide to support one of the bills as presented, suggest amendments to one of the bills presented, or develop a compromise bill.

f. When the session is reconvened, the presiding officer asks for a motion to vote on one of the bills as presented, for a motion to amend one of the bills, or for the introduction of a compromise bill. If amendments or compromise bills are proposed, they are individually debated and voted on.

g. This process is repeated until a bill is passed or the time allotted for the session is up and the legislature is adjourned.

7. DEBRIEF THE ACTIVITY

Debriefing questions vary according to the topic. Discuss the facts and arguments presented on the topic and evaluate the strengths and weaknesses of the positions taken. Also ask students to evaluate their experience with the legislative process itself. Conclude the debriefing by having students discuss the effectiveness of this activity as a tool for learning, including how well they performed their role in it. If a resource person assisted with the activity, that person should be included in the concluding discussion.

PRO SE COURT

A *pro se* (do it yourself) court allows students to role-play a court case using a minimum of participants and simple rules of evidence. The court is organized as a triad consisting of a judge, who will hear the two sides and make the final decision; a plaintiff, who is the person bringing the action before the judge; and the defendant, who is accused of wrongdoing or causing injury.

Pro se courts provide students with a simplified look at judicial decision making and offer an opportunity for all students in a class to be involved in the activity.

HOW TO PROCEED

1. CLARIFY TOPIC

Help students understand the facts and issues in the case. The cases are clearly identified in the lessons.

2. CONTACT RESOURCE PERSON

Invite an attorney or judge to act as a resource person.

3. ASSIGN ROLES

Divide the class into three equal groups—judges, plaintiffs, and defendants.

4. PREPARE PRESENTATIONS

Have the students meet in their respective groups to help each other prepare their presentations. Each student will be actively involved in the role-play, so preparation at this stage is vital to effective participation in the activity.

Instruct the judges to review the case and the issues raised. Ask them to prepare questions that they would like to ask of the plaintiffs and defendants during the presentation phase of the activity. The questions should be designed to clarify positions on the issues that the judges will be called on to decide. Do take some time to review with the judge's group some simple rules of procedure, such as the following:

a. The plaintiff should present first, without interruptions from the defense. The defense presents their case second.

b. Allow brief rebuttals from each side in the case.

c. The judge may interrupt the presentations at any time to pose questions designed to clarify the arguments being made. Instruct the plaintiff and defendant groups to prepare an opening statement and arguments supporting their positions on the issues raised in the case.

5. ARRANGE THE CLASSROOM

You will have multiple courts in session simultaneously; therefore, arrange the desks in the classroom into groups of three, one for each of the roles in the activity.

6. CONDUCT THE COURT HEARING

Before beginning the activity, match one student from the judges' group with one student from the plaintiff and one from the defendant groups. You may want to have the judges seated at a desk in each of the groupings arranged around the room. Then ask one plaintiff and one defendant to join the judge. Identifying role-players may be more easily accomplished by providing role "tags" so students can quickly identify who is a judge, plaintiff, and defendant. Conduct the activity using the following procedures:

a. Instruct the judges that when each has a plaintiff and a defendant, he or she may begin the court session.

b. The judge should first hear opening statements by the participants—first the plaintiff and then the defendant. An appropriate time limit should be imposed on these statements.

c. The plaintiff makes arguments and is questioned by the judge.

d. The defendant presents his or her defense and is questioned by the judge.

e. The judge asks each side for brief rebuttal statements.

f. The judge makes a decision and explains the reasoning that supports it.

7. DEBRIEF THE ACTIVITY

Debriefing questions vary according to the topic. Begin by asking individual judges to share with the class their decision and the reasoning supporting it. Discuss the facts and arguments presented in the case and evaluate the strengths and weaknesses of the positions taken. Also ask students to evaluate the court process itself. Conclude the debriefing by having students discuss the effectiveness of this activity as a tool for learning, including how well they performed their role in it. If a resource person assisted with the activity, that person should be included in the concluding discussion.

MOOT COURT

A moot court is patterned on a Supreme Court hearing. The court, composed of a panel of justices, is asked to rule on a lower court's decision. No witnesses are called, nor are the basic facts in a case disputed. Arguments are prepared and presented on the application of a law, the constitutionality of a law, or the fairness of previous court procedures. In many ways the moot court is like a debate because each side presents arguments for the consideration of the justices.

Because moot courts are not concerned with the credibility of witness testimony, they are an effective strategy for focusing student attention on the underlying principles and concepts of due process.

HOW TO PROCEED

1. CLARIFY TOPIC

Help students understand the facts and the legal or constitutional issues in the case. The cases are clearly identified in the lessons in the student text and in this edition. You may also want to ensure that students understand the purpose and procedures observed for Supreme Court proceedings (optional).

2. CONTACT RESOURCE PERSON

Invite an attorney or judge to act as a resource person.

3. ASSIGN ROLES

Assign students to play the roles of justices of the court. You may establish a court of five, seven, or nine justices. Divide the remaining students into two groups representing the litigants in the case. One group will represent the person or group bringing the challenge before the court, or the petitioner. The other group will represent the person or group defending against the challenge, or the respondent.

4. PREPARE PRESENTATIONS

Each group should meet to prepare arguments for its side of the case. The group should select one or two students to present the arguments.

The justices should meet to discuss the issues involved and any questions they feel need to be addressed for them to reach a decision. The justices should select one student to serve as chief justice. The chief justice will preside over the hearing. He or she will call on each side to present its case, or (more realistically) justices should ask questions without needing to be recognized. The justices should feel free to interrupt lawyers' presentations whenever they want.

Participants should understand that the factual details presented in the summary of the case were established by a trial and are not subject to further dispute.

Arguments should not concentrate on legal technicalities. Any argument that is persuasive from a philosophical, theoretical, conceptual, or practical standpoint can be made. Groups should rely on principles found or implied in the U.S. Constitution.

5. ARRANGE THE CLASSROOM

Set up the classroom to resemble a supreme court.

The justices should be seated at a table at the front of the room. The attorneys for each side should sit on opposite sides of the room facing the justices. Other group members should sit behind their respective attorneys. You may want to take the class to a supreme court's courtroom or to a mock trial room at a law school.

6. CONDUCT THE MOOT COURT

The chief justice should preside over the proceedings and begin by calling the court to order. The chief justice should observe the following procedures:

a. Each side should be allotted five to fifteen minutes for the initial presentation. The chief justice should call for presentations in the following order:

> **Petitioner presentation**
> **Respondent presentation**

b. During or after each presentation, the justices can and should actively question the attorneys in an effort to clarify the arguments. Attorneys may request time to consult with other group members before answering questions. For clarity and continuity, it is suggested that during the presentations, lawyers be given three minutes to present their cases before being interrupted with questions.

c. After arguments have been presented, the justices should organize themselves in a circle. They should consider the arguments and make a decision by a majority vote. Each justice should give reasons for his or her position. The rest of the class may sit outside of the circle and listen, but they may not talk or interrupt the deliberations.

7. DEBRIEF THE ACTIVITY

Debriefing questions vary according to the case. Begin by asking the justices to share with the class their decision and the reasoning supporting it. Discuss the arguments presented in the case and evaluate the strengths and weaknesses of the positions taken. Also ask students to evaluate their experience with the supreme court process itself. Conclude the debriefing by having students discuss the effectiveness of this activity as a tool for learning, including how well they performed their role in it. If a resource person assisted with the activity, that person should be included in the concluding discussion.

If you use a case that has been heard by the Supreme Court, you should share the court's decision with the class during the debriefing. To dispel the notion that there is one "right" answer, also share relevant parts of the dissenting opinion. Help students understand the reasoning that supports both the majority and dissenting opinions.

TOWN MEETING

A town meeting provides members of a community with an opportunity to participate in the decision-making process. A community forum usually considers matters of public policy. A town meeting can serve as a local governing and decision-making body by performing functions similar to those of a representative town or city council. It also can be advisory in nature, providing elected representatives with the views of citizens.

HOW TO PROCEED

1. CLARIFY TOPIC

Help students understand the topic of the town meeting. The topics are clearly identified in the lessons in the student text and in this edition. You also will want to ensure that students understand the nature and purpose of a town meeting.

2. CONTACT RESOURCE PERSON

Invite a member of the city council or a local interest group to serve as a resource person on the topic of the meeting.

3. ASSIGN ROLES

Organize the town meeting by assigning individuals the following roles:

a. chairperson

b. elected officials who represent the entire community in the town or city council

c. representative groups in favor of the proposition

d. representative groups in opposition to the proposition

e. community members at large

f. recorder

4. PREPARE PRESENTATIONS

Allow time for students to prepare for the town meeting in accordance with their assigned roles.

5. ARRANGE THE CLASSROOM

Include a table for the chairperson and for the elected officials, a desk for the recorder, and a podium from which members of interest groups and the community can speak. Provide a gavel and nameplates with the students' names and their roles. You may want to arrange for the use of a hearing or committee room of a local legislative body.

6. CONDUCT THE TOWN MEETING

The following procedures should be used to conduct this activity:

a. The chairperson calls the meeting to order, announces the purpose of the meeting, and introduces the elected officials in attendance. Elected officials may make a brief opening statement about the importance of the issue being considered (not his or her personal views on the topic).

The chairperson also establishes any rules that are to be followed during the meeting, such as time limits for presentations.

b. The chairperson has the authority to cut off debate when time limits have been reached. A person may not speak unless recognized by the chair, and no one may interrupt while another person is speaking. If a speaker wanders from the point, abuses other people, or in any way defeats the purpose of the meeting, the chairperson may declare him or her out of order.

c. The chairperson calls on a representative of the group favoring the proposition to describe that group's position. After the representative has finished speaking, he or she may ask people brought in as witnesses to stand and speak. The chairperson announces that any person in favor of the proposition may stand and speak. They will be recognized in the order in which they stand. Alternatively, you may want to have students sign in and ask the chairperson to recognize speakers by the order in which they signed in.

d. The chairperson calls on a representative of the group opposed to the proposition to speak. After the representative has finished speaking, he or she may ask people brought in as witnesses to stand and speak. The chairperson announces that those people opposed to the proposition will be recognized in the order in which they stand.

e. After all people on both sides of the proposition have had an opportunity to speak, the chairperson opens the question for additional discussion or debate. During this time any person may stand, be recognized, and present his or her point of view, or argue against the point of view of someone else.

f. At the end of the discussion or debate, the chairperson calls for the class to vote on the proposition. The vote is decided by a majority.

7. DEBRIEF THE ACTIVITY

Debriefing questions vary according to the topic. Begin by discussing the results of the vote taken on the proposition. Discuss the facts and arguments presented on the topic. Ask students to evaluate the strength of the positions taken and of the procedures used to develop and support a position. Also ask students to evaluate their experience with the town meeting itself. Conclude the debriefing by having students discuss the effectiveness of this activity as a tool for learning, including how well they performed their role in it. If a resource person assisted with the activity, that person should be included in the concluding discussion.

DEBATE

Debate begins with the assumption that the debater has already found a solution or approach to a specific issue. The intent of the debater is to persuade others that his or her solution or approach is the proper one.

Debate can be an effective device for encouraging students to clearly and logically formulate arguments based on evidence. Debate teaches a means to adequately support a position on an issue. It also develops a sense of efficacy and confidence in a person's ability to sway public opinion or to change public policy.

HOW TO PROCEED

1. CLARIFY TOPIC

Help students understand the topic of the debate. The topics are clearly identified in the lessons in the student text and in this edition. Formulate the topic into a resolution (resolutions always ask for a change from the status quo, e.g., Resolved: that capital punishment should be found unconstitutional by the U.S. Supreme Court).

2. CONTACT RESOURCE PERSON

Invite someone from the community or a local interest group to serve as a resource person on the topic of the debate.

3. ASSIGN ROLES

Select students to take part in the debate. Divide them into two teams, one in support of the resolution, the other opposing it. Make

certain that those participating in the debate are familiar with the procedures to be followed during the debate. Select a moderator and a timekeeper.

4. PREPARE PRESENTATIONS

Allow sufficient time for students to prepare their "constructive arguments" (arguments based on three to five major points logically developed and substantiated by factual evidence in support of a particular position). Help students see the dimensions of the problem and develop clear, logical arguments supported by evidence on the position they defend in the debate. Also, ask them to anticipate the views of the other side in preparation for their "rebuttal arguments."

Help students gain an understanding of some of the implicit values in debate such as learning to make convincing arguments from another frame of reference, as might be the case if one is debating a position that does not correspond with one's own beliefs. This furthers development of students' abilities to understand and respect the right of individuals to hold opinions and beliefs that are different from their own.

5. ARRANGE THE CLASSROOM

The moderator and debaters are seated at the front of the audience, usually with the team in opposition to the resolution to the left of the moderator.

6. CONDUCT THE DEBATE

The form of debate described here is widely used but is rather formalized. You may wish to make the procedures less formal or use some other form of debate.

a. The moderator briefly introduces the subject and the resolution to be debated and establishes the time limits to be observed by the speakers.

b. The moderator introduces the first speaker from the affirmative team and asks the speaker to present his or her constructive argument. The order in which constructive arguments will be given by each member of the team should be determined in advance of the debate. The timekeeper will inform the speaker when the time limit has been reached.

c. The moderator introduces the first speaker from the team in opposition to the resolution and asks the speaker to present his or her constructive argument.

d. The moderator next introduces the second speaker from the affirmative team. This procedure is alternated until each debater on both the affirmative and opposition teams has given a constructive argument.

e. Rebuttal arguments follow the constructive arguments. At this time each debater is given the opportunity to weaken the position of the opponents by attacking their position and by answering attacks that have been made on his or her position. No new issues may be introduced during rebuttal arguments. Rebuttal arguments always begin with the team in opposition to the resolution. Again, follow the same alternating procedures used during constructive arguments.

f. At the conclusion of the debate, the moderator makes a few concluding remarks and the debate is ended.

7. DEBRIEF THE ACTIVITY

You may wish to evaluate the success of the debating teams by informally polling the class to determine how many people agree with the team in support of the resolution and how many agree with the team in opposition to the resolution. You may then ask class members to explain whether their own positions were strengthened or changed as a result of hearing the debate and why. Also ask students to evaluate their experience with the debate process itself. Conclude the debriefing by having students discuss the effectiveness of this activity as a tool for learning, including how well they performed their role in it. If a resource person assisted with the activity, that person should be included in the concluding discussion.

CONTINUUM

The continuum is an exercise in which participants are presented with a range of possible attitudes or approaches on a controversial issue. Participants are asked to determine which element of the continuum (e.g., strongly agree or strongly disagree) most approximates their own attitude. Issues that are clearly controversial positions are suitable for using this method. The issues should have legitimate opposing viewpoints, such as whether equal rights can best be achieved by an amendment or whether gun control is an effective way to stop crime. Issues that are above debate, such as the morality of ethnic cleansing or the sexual abuse of children, are obviously not legitimate topics for a continuum.

The continuum is a useful tool for introducing controversial issues. It can help students see the ranges of values or opinions that exist on a given topic and understand the reasoning that supports those positions. The continuum provides an orderly method for discussing controversy, especially at the early stages of a lesson when students may be expressing "gut-level" reactions rather than informed opinions.

HOW TO PROCEED

1. Identify an issue to be discussed. The issue should be one in which one can identify polar positions, such as the death penalty.

2. Before initiating the activity, it is important to cultivate a classroom atmosphere of trust where opinions can be expressed freely. Being receptive and nonjudgmental is critical to open discussion.

3. The teacher should initiate the activity by describing the issue(s) in enough detail so that the polar positions are clearly understood. These should be written on the board.

4. Students should be asked to write their position on the issue (e.g., strongly agree, agree, disagree, strongly disagree, can't decide) and to list the two most compelling reasons why they believe as they do.

5. While the students are writing their statements, the teacher can draw a continuum across the chalkboard. When the students are finished writing, the teacher can print along the continuum brief versions of some possible polar positions on the issue. Ask a limited number of students to stand at the point on the continuum where they believe their position on the issue falls.

6. At this point, students should be asked to explain or clarify, but not to defend, their positions. They should be encouraged to move their position along the continuum as they listen to others clarify their positions.

7. Students now can be asked to state their reasons for positioning themselves as they have. The teacher may wish to post on the board the different reasons expressed by the students. At this point, students can respond to questions concerning their reasoning, but argumentation should be discouraged.

8. To make sure that students listen to and consider opposing points of view, all students should be asked to present the arguments that, although contrary to their positions, give them pause, make them think twice, or are the most persuasive.

9. Finally, students should be asked to consider the consequences of alternative policy choices. This involves identifying the existing law or policy on the issue being considered, if one exists. The class can then discuss what impact the polar positions presented on the continuum would have on society as a whole and on individuals.

KEEPING JOURNALS

Journal writing provides a systematic way for students to maintain a personal record of summary statements, reflections, or questions about what is being learned in a particular instance. Journal writing encourages students to reflect on the "what," "why," and "how" of their own learning. Taking time to reflect is a good study habit to develop. Journals have the additional benefit of improving writing skills.

Because the content introduced in *We the People: The Citizen & the Constitution* contains many new concepts and experiences, opportunities for students to reflect on what they are learning are especially important. Some opportunities for journal writing are identified in the teacher's edition, but many more exist in this curriculum. You may want to allow a few minutes at the conclusion of a lesson or at the close of an activity for students to complete a journal entry. Encourage students to discuss some aspect of the content studied, to record a personal reaction to the lesson or the outcome of an activity, or to record questions the lesson or activity raised about an issue. Sometimes you may want to assign journal notations as homework.

Whether journals are graded is a personal choice. You should collect journals periodically, however, to offer students some feedback on the content. Writing comments and personal observations in the journals can be an effective tool in establishing a personal dialogue with students. Do encourage students to share their journals with other students and with their parents if they wish. By so doing, students demonstrate to themselves and others what they have learned.

EVALUATING STUDENT ACHIEVEMENT

REFLECTING ON THE LEARNING EXPERIENCE

At the conclusion of the entire curriculum you should have the students reflect on their experiences. Reflections can be of two kinds—as an individual and as a class. Both might be desirable.

You can design a reflection instrument or activity based on your unique experience with this class. An example of a reflective activity appears as the Enrichment Activity "Reflecting on Constitutional Citizenship" in Lesson 39 on page 302 of this teacher's edition.

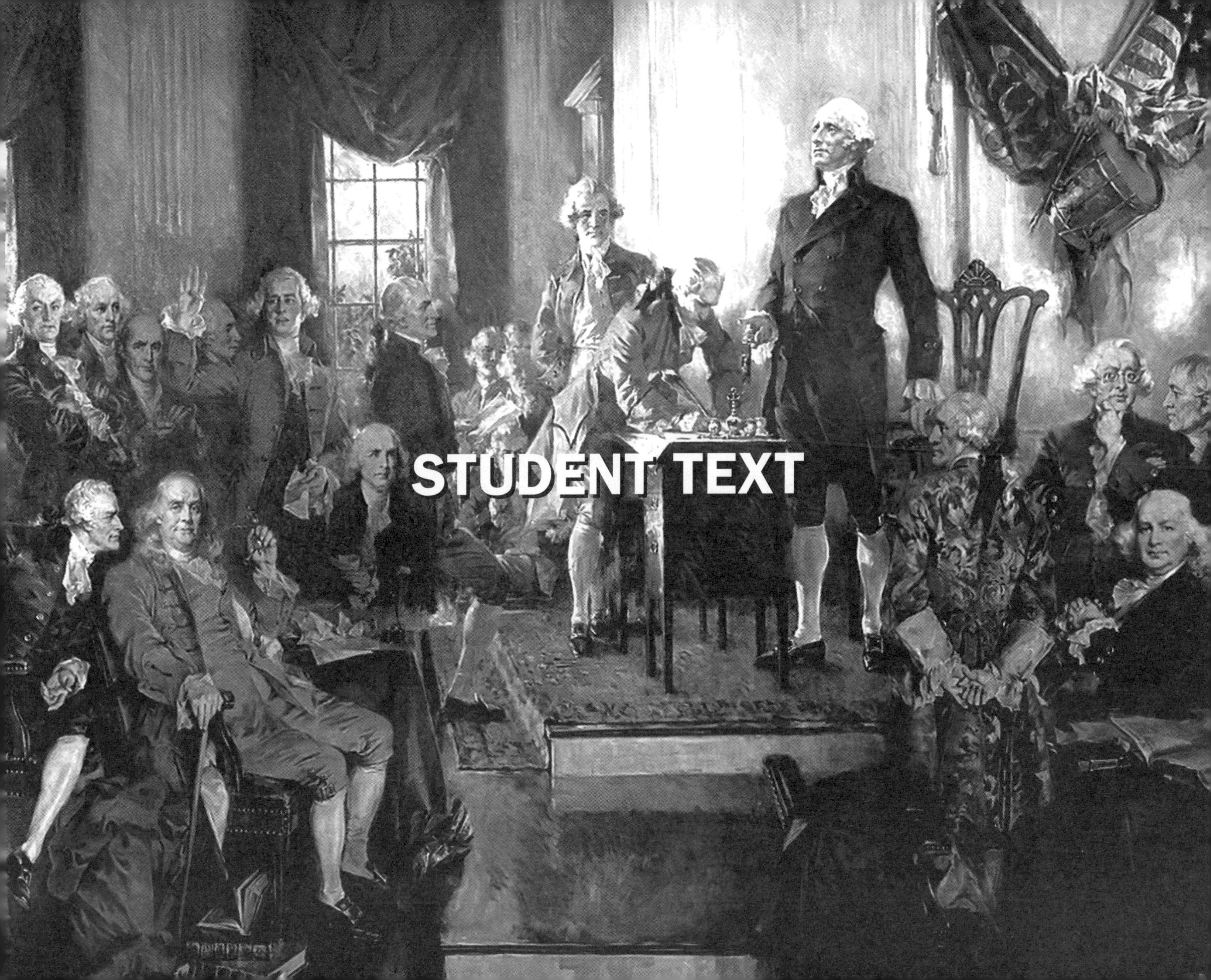
STUDENT TEXT

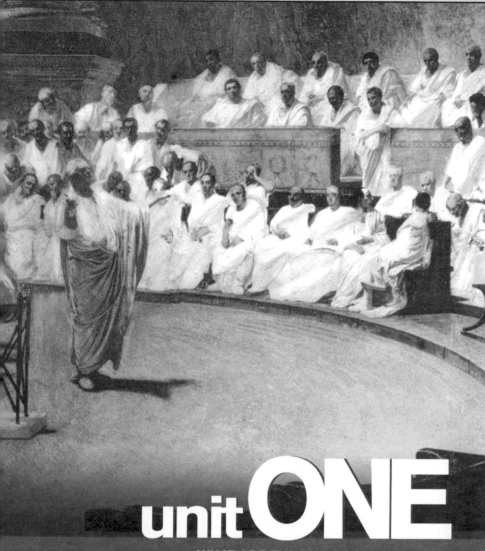

unitONE

WHAT ARE THE PHILOSOPHICAL AND
HISTORICAL FOUNDATIONS OF THE
AMERICAN POLITICAL SYSTEM?

unitONE

The people who led the American Revolution, which separated the American colonies from Great Britain, and who created the Constitution, which established the government we have today, were making a fresh beginning. However, they also were heirs to philosophical and historical traditions as old as Western civilization.

The Founders were well read. "I cannot live without books," Thomas Jefferson once told John Adams. Jefferson's library of approximately 6,500 volumes formed the core of the Library of Congress. Adams reputedly read forty-three books during the year he turned eighty-one years old. These Americans were familiar with the history, philosophy, and literature of the ancient world as well as with the ideas of their own time. They also studied English history and law, from which their constitutional traditions derived. And religion was an important part of the Founders' education. They knew the Bible and its teachings.

Moreover, the knowledge that these people possessed was not limited to what they read in books. In creating the new nation, they drew on their experiences. Many of the Constitution's Framers had fought in the American Revolution and had served in colonial government before America won its independence. They also had experience governing the newly independent states. They used this knowledge and experience when they wrote the Constitution. An understanding of what they learned will help you understand why they wrote the Constitution as they did and why we have the kind of government we have today.

This unit provides an overview of some important philosophical ideas and historical events that influenced the writing of the Constitution and the Bill of Rights. It is particularly important to understand the content of this unit because it provides a frame of reference and a basis for understanding the other units in this text. You will appreciate why our history as a people has been a great adventure in ideas and in trying to make these ideas a reality.

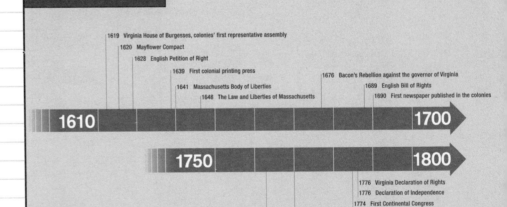

1619 Virginia House of Burgesses, colonies' first representative assembly
1620 Mayflower Compact
1628 English Petition of Right
1639 First colonial printing press
1641 Massachusetts Body of Liberties
1648 The Law and Liberties of Massachusetts
1676 Bacon's Rebellion against the governor of Virginia
1689 English Bill of Rights
1690 First newspaper published in the colonies

1610 ———————————————— 1700

1750 ———————————————— 1800

1776 Virginia Declaration of Rights
1776 Declaration of Independence
1774 First Continental Congress
1765 The Stamp Act
1763 Britain defeats France in the Seven Years' War

1

WHAT DID THE FOUNDERS THINK ABOUT CONSTITUTIONAL GOVERNMENT?

LESSON PURPOSE

This lesson introduces the basic ideas and experiences the founding generation drew on to create the kind of government they believed would best protect the natural rights of individuals and promote the common good. Classical Greek and Roman writers, natural rights philosophy, the Bible, Protestant theology, ancient and modern European history, and the Enlightenment in Europe and America were among the sources of the ideas that influenced the Founders. The Founders also participated in self-government in the American colonies before 1776 and in state and local governments after independence from Great Britain. The Founders' ideas about society and government and their experiences were diverse. The colonies differed widely. This diversity fostered a rich dialogue about the purpose of government and how it should be organized.

When you have finished this lesson, you should be able to describe the diverse features of the early American colonies and states and their populations. You should be able to explain what the Founders learned about government from history and their firsthand experiences of government. How did this knowledge shape their thinking? You should be able to explain the meanings of the terms *constitution* and *constitutional government* and describe the forms of constitutional governments. Finally, you should be able to evaluate, take, and defend positions on the sources that should be consulted if a new constitution for the United States were being written today, whether the Founders' concerns about abuse of government power are still valid today, and the importance of written constitutions.

TERMS AND CONCEPTS TO UNDERSTAND

constitution	limited government	unwritten constitution
constitutional government	Parliament	written constitution
democracy	republic	
forms of government		

3

LESSON 1

UNIT ONE | LESSON 1

WHAT DID THE FOUNDERS THINK ABOUT CONSTITUTIONAL GOVERNMENT?

wtpcompanion.civiced.org | **LESSON PURPOSE + TERMS**

Visit the We the People companion website for printable and downloadable Lesson Purposes and Terms and Concepts to Understand sections for each lesson. Audio readings of each Lesson Purpose and Term are also available online in MP3 format.

student page ▼ 4

WHAT WERE SOME CHARACTERISTICS OF COLONIAL AMERICA?

TREATY OF PARIS Benjamin Franklin led the team to negotiate an end to the war with Great Britain, eventually assisted by John Adams and John Jay. The articles of peace accomplished the following:

- Established boundaries for the newly independent nation
- Resolved prewar debts owed to British creditors
- Provided for evacuating British troops from the thirteen American states
- Restored confiscated property of Americans who had remained loyal to Great Britain

Two treaties were needed, one between America and Great Britain and another between Britain and France. The final articles of peace were signed on September 3, 1783.

LANGUAGES SPOKEN IN COLONIES In addition to English, seventeenth-century colonial languages included Dutch, French, German, Norwegian, Spanish, Swedish, Welsh, Scottish Gaelic and Scots (the Anglic language of Scotland), Finnish, and Irish. Others included native languages spoken by enslaved Africans and many Native American languages.

NATIVE AMERICANS Between ten million and ninety million Native Americans (estimates vary widely) were organized into hundreds of tribes when Europeans arrived in America. Colonists and explorers brought many devastating diseases, such as measles, smallpox, cholera, and yellow fever, which drastically reduced the Native American population, which had little or no immunity. Disease often wiped out entire villages. At various times American policy toward Native Americans has viewed them as peoples to be conquered, as sovereign nations, and as peoples to be assimilated into the national polity.

3

INDENTURED SERVANTS   One-half to two-thirds of all immigrants to colonial America came as indentured servants. In some times and places indentured servants composed as much as three-fourths of the population. The first indentured servants came to Virginia as farm laborers. The colonial government offered fifty acres per servant to landowners as an incentive to import them. Before leaving Great Britain most servants sold themselves to a ship's captain or the agent of a ship for a term of four to seven years in return for passage, food, clothing, and shelter. Their contracts would then be sold to a buyer in the colonies to recover the cost of passage. The following is an example of an indentured servant contract:

I, _____, of _____, do firmly oblige myself as a faithful and obedient servant in all things whatsoever, to serve and dwell with _____ according to the laws and customs and orders for servants in Carolina.

The said _____ providing for his servant all such necessaries in the time of his/her service and at the expiration of the term as the laws oblige masters to perform to their servants.

> Signed   _____ (servant)
> _____ (master)
> Date   _____

---

student page ▾ 5

HOW DID THE FOUNDERS LEARN ABOUT GOVERNMENT?

Aristotle was a student of the philosopher Plato and the teacher of Alexander the Great. Considered one of the great philosophers in the Western intellectual tradition, he wrote treatises on subjects as diverse as government, logic, rhetoric, ethics, poetry, and biology. Aristotle continued an effort begun by Plato to place objects and ideas in categories based on similar properties. After Alexander's death, Aristotle fled Athens, lest "Athens sin against philosophy twice." The first of these sins was the death of Socrates, prescribed by an Athenian jury when Socrates was tried for allegedly introducing new gods, preaching atheism, and corrupting the young.

Cicero was an orator, a lawyer, a politician, and a philosopher whose life coincided with the decline and fall of the Roman Republic. Elected to each of the major offices in Roman government, including senator and consul, Cicero was exiled in 58 BC. During an eleven-year exile he wrote extensively about politics and philosophy, much of his work focusing on the defense and improvement of the Roman Republic. Cicero's

WHAT WERE SOME CHARACTERISTICS OF COLONIAL AMERICA?

The United States was officially recognized as an independent nation in the Treaty of Paris of 1783, nearly two centuries after the first European settlers landed in America. Once colonies were established, one of the first things that the colonists noticed about their new surroundings was their vast size. England and Scotland together were smaller than the present states of New York and Pennsylvania. More than a thousand miles separated the citizens of northern Massachusetts from those of southern Georgia.

Of course, the colonists were not the first people on the North American continent. However, by the end of the Revolutionary War there were relatively few Native Americans living along the Atlantic coast. Encroachment of colonial settlements, disease, and warfare significantly reduced the indigenous population on the eastern seaboard, although many Native Americans remained on the western borders of the colonial frontier and beyond.

More than physical distance separated the colonists. Their backgrounds were diverse. Some, such as the Puritans in Massachusetts and the Quakers in Pennsylvania, came to the New World for religious reasons. Others came for economic reasons. They also differed in social structure and sometimes even in language. Pennsylvania, for example, had a large German-speaking population. French and Dutch were important languages in other colonies.

A few influential families dominated South Carolina, Maryland, and New York. They owned vast estates and tended to replicate European culture and habits as much as they could. By contrast, New England and Georgia had fewer large estates and, partly as a result, had different social and political cultures than those found elsewhere. Most of the colonies also had established or official government religions. Slavery was practiced in all the colonies.

Almost all colonial Americans lived and worked on farms or in rural communities. But farming meant different things in different places. In South Carolina's coastal region, farming meant using slaves to work plantations that produced rice and indigo for export, mostly to England. Virginia's export crop was tobacco. By contrast, farming in New England meant growing crops and raising livestock for a local market. New England farmers relied less on slaves for labor than did Southern colonists, but the New England workforce included thousands of indentured servants, many of whom had entered into work contracts in exchange for transportation to America, food and shelter, or training in various skills.

Colonists who did not work on farms followed various trades, working as sailors, shoemakers, silversmiths, and a host of other occupations. Many dabbled in a favorite American pastime, speculating on land. In many ways colonial America was a society of traditions, in which people played social roles and exercised authority in long-established ways. But more than 300,000 people in 1760 were enslaved. These people, or their ancestors, had been transported to North America as captives from Africa. Later lessons will examine the effect of slavery on American **constitutional government** and culture. Indeed, the British colonies developed a number of different ways of organizing local governments during the century or more of their existence.

What evidence is there in this picture of self-reliance? How might the self-reliance of colonial Americans have influenced their thinking about government?

HOW DID THE FOUNDERS LEARN ABOUT GOVERNMENT?

The Founders learned about government from reading history and philosophy and from their own experience of self-government as colonists within the British Empire. They were as familiar with ancient Greece and Rome as they were with later European history. Many had read classical texts about government and politics by ancients such as Aristotle (384–322 BC), Marcus Tullius Cicero (106–43 BC), and others. They also had read newer theories of government by sixteenth- and seventeenth-century philosophers, such as Thomas Hobbes (1588–1679) and John Locke (1632–1704). By the 1770s some were familiar with the English jurist William Blackstone's explanations of English law, published between 1765 and 1769. Almost all were well read in Protestant theology. The Founders looked to many examples of good and bad government for guidance.

By 1776 Americans also could look back on more than 150 years of local self-government. Free white men from all walks of life had served on juries, attended town meetings, and voted in local elections. In fact, in the colonies and the early states more Americans participated in self-government than did people almost anywhere else in the world.

Why did the Founders read the works of William Blackstone and other jurists and philosophers?

WHAT DID THE FOUNDERS LEARN ABOUT GOVERNMENT?

Not all the sources that influenced the Founders taught the same lessons. Some sources contradicted others. Some did not teach clear lessons at all.

For example, classical (ancient) political philosophers taught that human beings are naturally social creatures with obligations to each other and to their community, without which they could neither survive nor achieve human excellence. To Greek philosophers, such as Plato (c. 428–348 BC), those who govern must be wise. All the classical philosophers agreed that one purpose of government is to help people learn about and perform their civic and moral duties.

Greek and Roman history taught that although democracies may appear to begin well, they tend to end in tyranny when the poor attack the rich. Class warfare breeds chronic disorder. The people then submit to tyrants, who enter the scene promising security.

Natural rights theorists taught that people have natural rights that others must respect. English philosopher John Locke summarized them as rights to "life, liberty, and estate." People agree to form a society and create a government to protect their rights.

British history showed that even a monarchy might evolve into free government. If the people are determined, they can ensure that monarchs respect the rights that the people have gained over time.

American colonial history showed that local self-government could coexist with a distant central authority—in this case, Britain. However, American colonial history also showed that when people believe that the central government is abusing its power, then social and political unrest follows.

The Founders had many examples of government to choose from in designing their state constitutions and the U.S. Constitution. Why did they make the choices they made? From reading their explanations in documents such as the Virginia Declaration of Rights, the Declaration of Independence, and various pamphlets, essays, and letters, it is clear that the Founders had learned at least two important lessons about government:

- Government should be the servant, not the master, of the people.

- A fundamental higher law, or **constitution**, should limit government.

De Officiis, a profound meditation on morality and moral duty, including moral principles as applied to public life, deeply influenced Western civilization since its writing in 44 BC. *De Officiis* was so influential that when the printing press was invented, it was the second book to be printed after the Bible.

Cicero, echoing the views of Stoic philosophy, argued for self-restraint and limits to action for the sake of self-interest. He argued that what is honorable must always be chosen, and some actions, even to save the state, are so morally abhorrent that they must be rejected. In the sixteenth century Machiavelli directly contradicted these ideas and argued that to establish, maintain, and expand their power, rulers must be taught "how not to be good."

Thomas Hobbes, a philosopher of materialism, fled to France during the English civil war (1642–1651, which pitted Parliament against the Crown), where he wrote *Leviathan*. This book argued that humans without government live in a "state of nature," which is a "state of war" against all. Life in such conditions is "solitary, poore, nasty, brutish, and short." Thus in a state of nature all fear violent death, and violent death is what people fear most. To avoid violent death, they agree to set up a state with strict authority and the power to protect life. People agree to leave this state of nature through "social contract" and to give all power to the Leviathan state, which Hobbes characterized as a "mortal god." Hobbes was accused of atheism for the views he expressed in *Leviathan*, where Hobbes pilloried various theological ideas. The English Parliament asserted that *Leviathan* helped cause the plague of 1665 and the Great Fire of 1666. The book was placed on the Index of Forbidden Books by the Catholic Church because it undermined the theory of divine right of kings.

John Locke, a physician and philosopher, worked with famous scientists, including Robert Boyle and Robert Hooke. In contrast to Hobbes, Locke used state of nature and social contract theory to justify limited government and the preservation of individual rights, particularly life, liberty, and property. Locke is sometimes called "America's philosopher" because his *Second Treatise of Government* (1690) was widely read by the colonists, and important ideas found in it—as well as in works of English republican writers—are found in the Declaration of Independence, especially his theories of natural rights and his defense of revolution after "a long train of abuses" of power by rulers. Two verbatim phrases of Locke's are found in the Declaration.

Montesquieu (Charles-Louis de Secondat, Baron de la Brède et de Montesquieu) was a French nobleman and lawyer, recognized as one of the greatest thinkers of the Enlightenment. He first gained fame for a satire, *The Persian Letters*, in 1721, pointing out absurdities of modern European life, especially French life. He also anonymously published *Considerations of the Causes of the Greatness of the Romans and of Their Decline* in 1734. His masterpiece, *The Spirit of the Laws*, published 1748, was placed on the Index of Forbidden Books by the Catholic Church because of its "liberal" views.

William Blackstone (originally pronounced "blextun") was an unsuccessful lawyer who became a lecturer on law at Oxford. He wrote *Commentaries on the Laws of England*, placing the history of English common law into four categories: rights of persons, rights of things, private wrongs (torts), and public wrongs (crimes). Written to be understood by nonlawyers, this work became an important source of legal information for the American colonists. Blackstone, among others, famously articulated "the Rights of Englishmen" held dear by American colonists. Statutory as well as common law, he argued, guarantees the sanctity of an Englishman's life, liberty, and property. These rights include due process of law, attorney-client confidentiality, equality before the law, *habeas corpus*, the right to confront accusers, and the forbiddance of bills of attainder and forced self-incrimination.

wtpcompanion.civiced.org **BIOGRAPHIES**

Visit the We the People companion website for brief printable and downloadable biographies of the people mentioned in the student and teacher's editions. Audio readings of each biography are also available online in MP3 format.

With regard to *history*, in Federalist 9 Alexander Hamilton argued that history is not a good guide for creating government because it provides many bad examples:

> It is impossible to read the history of the petty republics of Greece and Italy without feeling sensations of horror and disgust at the distractions with which they were continually agitated, and at the rapid succession of revolutions by which they were kept in a state of perpetual vibration between the extremes of tyranny and anarchy. If they exhibit occasional calms, these only serve as short-lived contrasts to the furious storms that are to succeed.

Whether history or reason provides a better guide to designing government animated the debates over how best to govern the states and the new nation (see Lessons 13 and 14).

WHAT DID THE FOUNDERS LEARN ABOUT GOVERNMENT?

See Lesson 7 for additional discussion of the Virginia Declaration of Rights.

student page ▾ 6–7

WHAT FORMS OF GOVERNMENT COULD THE FOUNDERS CHOOSE FROM?

MIXED CONSTITUTION In *The Republic*, Plato argued that the best possible form of government would be rule by a philosopher-king. He realized that this is not practical. He identified four other forms of government. Plato's five categories are as follows:

In a nation in which government is the servant of the people, what obligations, if any, do the people have to the government?

WHAT FORMS OF GOVERNMENT COULD THE FOUNDERS CHOOSE FROM?

The Founders were familiar with the writings of the Greek philosopher Aristotle, who observed that every state—meaning "country" or national entity in this sense—must perform three functions. First, states must deliberate about what is to be done and decide what public policy should be. Today we call this the legislative function—deliberating on and enacting law. Second, states must perform an executive function, through which public officials carry out public policy. And third, states must carry out a judicial function, through which disputes about the interpretation of law are managed and applied in everyday life.

Aristotle also distinguished between types of governments on the basis of the number of persons exercising power. Countries may be governed by one person, a few people, or many people. Each of these three **forms of government** has a "right form" and a "corrupt form." Right forms are governed for the common good, whereas corrupt forms are governed for the private interests of the rulers.

The right form of government by a single person is called "monarchy." The right form of government by a few people is called "aristocracy," or the rule of the "best." And the right form of government by many people is called "polity." Aristotle referred to polity as a "mixed" form of government (or "mixed constitution") because it incorporates elements of democracy and oligarchy (see next paragraph). No group of citizens—for example, the rich or the poor—is able to abuse political power. Although a polity is a mixture of social elements, it is most like **democracy**, as we define the concept today.

According to Aristotle, corrupt forms of government are "tyranny," for rule of a single person; "oligarchy," for rule of a few, usually rich, people; and "democracy," for rule of the many, by which he meant the poor.

The following table illustrates right and corrupt forms of government as identified by Aristotle:

RULE OF	RIGHT FORM	CORRUPT FORM
One	Monarchy	Tyranny
Few	Aristocracy	Oligarchy
Many	Polity (mixed constitution)	Democracy

To Aristotle *democracy* meant "direct" democracy, in which the people themselves make decisions, rather than the type of government we call democracy today, which is largely representative. Aristotle's description of democracy as a corrupt form of government refers to what ancient Greece experienced when the poor ("the many") took power. They attempted to seize the property of the rich for themselves, setting off destructive civil wars based on social class. In such cases the poor looked after only their own interests to the exclusion of the common good.

Although Aristotle classified the governments of countries on the basis of their number of rulers, he also focused on economic considerations within countries, which usually are far more important. He was especially concerned with the distribution of wealth and the effects that various distributions have on political stability—specifically on the avoidance of civil strife. He concluded that the dominant group of most stable countries consists of those who are neither rich nor poor but occupy a middle ground of moderate wealth.

According to Aristotle, this middle group is known for moderation. Rule by those who are moderate yields

the most stable form of government because those of moderate means are most likely to behave in accordance with reason. In Aristotle's view the problem with "democracy" is that the poor, who are numerous, attempt to seize the wealth of the rich, who are few. But if a constitution can combine ("mix") the many poor with the lesser number of wealthy persons, then it can achieve stability.

The Founders were familiar with this idea of mixed constitution from reading Aristotle and other writers, such as the Greek historian Polybius (203–120 BC). Polybius popularized the idea in the ancient world that mixed constitution is a combination of monarchical, aristocratic, and democratic elements. This idea, embraced and passed on by the Roman statesman Cicero, then became widespread among scholars in the Middle Ages—roughly the fifth century to the fourteenth century, depending on the country. Through Cicero's great influence in the subsequent period of the Renaissance, the fifteenth through seventeenth centuries, the idea of mixed constitution was incorporated into Renaissance political thought and thus into republicanism. It was then passed on to the Enlightenment in the eighteenth century.

For example, the eighteenth-century French political thinker Charles-Louis de Secondat, Baron de la Brède et de Montesquieu (1689–1755), cited England as a mixed constitution. The British government had a limited monarch, an aristocracy in one house of **Parliament** (the House of Lords), and in theory, the House of Commons for the common people. In fact, the landed aristocracy dominated the House of Commons, though they were of lower rank than members of the House of Lords.

Both the British Parliament and the legislatures of colonies were examples of representative government. Representative government sometimes is called "republican government." The term **republic** comes from the Roman term *res publica*, which is Latin for "thing (or property) of the people." The Roman Republic had an unwritten mixed constitution. Its form of government after 287 BC consisted of executive and legislative branches, in which virtually all classes and tribes in Roman society were represented.

Based on the Founders' reading of history and their personal experiences, they did not believe that direct democracy was the best model for government. It could potentially fail to protect property and other rights, such as rights of minorities. The Founders preferred a representative, or republican, form of government, in which many interests can be represented in the legislature; and those who govern, like ordinary citizens, are required to obey the law.

Which of Aristotle's ideas about government, if any, seem most relevant today?

- Aristocracy (rule by one best)
- Timocracy (rule by the military)
- Oligarchy (rule by the wealthy few)
- Democracy (rule by the *demos*, the common people or the many poor)
- Tyranny (rule by the worst individuals)

Aristotle's typology generally followed Plato. However, Aristotle believed that monarchy can be a good form of government. He eliminated "timocracy" and added a new form, "polity." Aristotle divided the forms into rule of the one, the few, and the many and subdivided them into good and corrupt forms.

student page ▾ 7

Polybius, however, argued for "mixed government" composed of all three elements: rule of the one, the few, and the many. He wrote that the Roman Republic provided a good example of a mixed constitution.

Nearly two millennia later Montesquieu also advocated a mixed constitution, urging the representation of monarchic, aristocratic, and democratic principles in government as well as separating legislative, executive, and judicial functions.

Aristotle studied some 158 constitutions, from which he devised his description of "right" and "corrupt" governments. He also classified governments based on three functions they perform:

- Deliberation
- Execution
- Judging

Aristotle used the same method for classifying governments that he used for classifying animals—by "organs" and "functions."

ROMAN REPUBLIC The Roman Republic began about 500 BC and lasted until almost 1500 AD. This republic had no written constitution, changed over time, and was complicated in its details. However, its essential structure was as follows:

- Consuls (two men) wielded all executive power and controlled the army. Both had to agree in order to take any action.
- Senators (lifetime posts held by men from wealthy families) advised consuls. Initially the senate had about three hundred members, but its size varied.

- Assemblymen—including all free, male Roman citizens— voted on major issues, but the rich patricians had more votes than the poor plebians. Assemblymen elected tribunes to the senate, who were supposed to speak for the poor. Consuls usually followed the senate's advice.

- Prefects (appointed officials) ran the city and heard some court cases.

DEMOCRACY   The word comes from the Greek *demos,* meaning "people" or "many poor," and *kratos,* meaning "rule." Democracies can take many forms. In small societies direct rule is possible. In larger societies the people usually choose representatives, sometimes by lot (random or chance) or by election. Aristotle was one of the first philosophers to explain that democracies can take more than one form.

student page ▼ 8–9

WHAT IS A CONSTITUTION?

The function of a constitution is to establish the principles and rules by which a society is to be governed. Constitutions can be written or unwritten.

Why do you think the Founders wanted to establish a constitutional government?

CRITICAL THINKING EXERCISE
Examining the Founders' Sources of Information

If you were part of a group drafting a new constitution for the United States today, which of the sources the Founders used would you rely on in your deliberations? What other sources might you also consult? Why?

WHAT IS A CONSTITUTION?

As it is understood today, a constitution is a plan that sets forth the structure and powers of government. Constitutions specify the main institutions of government. In so doing, constitutions state the powers of each of these institutions and the procedures that the institutions must use to make, enforce, and interpret law. Usually constitutions also specify how they can be changed, or amended. In the American conception of constitutional government the constitution is a form of higher, or fundamental, law that everyone, including those in power, must obey.

Many controversies surround **written constitutions**, including what the words mean, whether the understanding of the document should evolve or remain unchanged, and who should have the final say about what the document means. Nearly all constitutions are written. Only three of the world's major democracies have **unwritten constitutions**—that is, constitutions that are not single written documents. These are Britain, Israel, and New Zealand. In each of these nations, the constitution consists of a combination of written laws and precedents.

8

Constitutional government means **limited government**—government limited by the provisions of the constitution. Limited government is characterized by restraints on power as specified by the constitution. In democracies, for example, one restraint is the inclusion of free, fair, and regular elections. The opposite is unlimited government, in which those who govern are free to use their power as they choose, unrestrained by laws or elections. Aristotle described the unlimited government of a single ruler as tyranny. Today the terms *autocracy*, *dictatorship*, or *totalitarianism* often are used to describe such governments. Believing that they had been subjected to tyranny by the British king, the Founders also believed that government in the newly independent United States of America should be limited by the higher law of a written constitution.

HOW DID THE FOUNDERS CHARACTERIZE HIGHER LAW?

According to the founding generation a constitution should function as a type of higher law. A higher law differs from a statute enacted by a legislature in these four ways:

- It sets forth the basic rights of citizens.

- It establishes the responsibility of the government to protect those rights.

- It establishes limitations on how those in government may use their power with regard to citizens' rights and responsibilities, the distribution of resources, and the control or management of conflict.

- It can be changed only with the consent of the citizens and according to established and well-known procedures.

9

student page ▾ 10

CRITICAL THINKING EXERCISE

BRIEF BIOGRAPHIES

Alexander Hamilton (1755?–1804)   Hamilton was a senior aide-de-camp to General Washington and an artillery captain during the Revolutionary War. He was a delegate from New York to the Philadelphia Convention and one of three authors of *The Federalist*, written to urge ratification of the U.S. Constitution. He later served as the first secretary of the treasury and advocated a strong national government (see Lesson 10).

Benjamin Franklin (1706–1790)   Franklin was an Enlightenment thinker and inventor. He also was a delegate from Pennsylvania to the Philadelphia Convention. He often was looked to for wisdom and diplomatic experience and often urged delegates to compromise when debates became divisive (see Lessons 10 and 11).

George Mason (1725–1792)   Mason was the author, in 1776, of the Virginia Declaration of Rights (see Lesson 7). He was a delegate from Virginia to the Philadelphia Convention but refused to sign the proposed Constitution because it contained no bill of rights. He argued against ratification for the same reason.

wtpcompanion.civiced.org   **BIOGRAPHIES**

Visit the We the People companion website for brief printable and downloadable biographies of the people mentioned in the student and teacher's editions. Audio readings of each biography are also available online in MP3 format.

ENRICHMENT ACTIVITY

COMPARING A STATE OF NATURE AND A STATE OF WAR

In *Leviathan* Thomas Hobbes described the state of nature as a time of war,

> where every man is Enemy to every man;…wherin men live without other security than their own strength.…In such a condition there is no place for Industry; because the fruit therof is uncertain…no Culture of Earth; no Navigation…no Arts; no Letters; no Society; and which is worst of all continuall feare and danger of violent death; and the life of man; solitary, poore, nasty, brutish, and short.

Students in groups of three or four should consider Hobbes's analogy comparing a state of nature to a state of war. The following questions may be used to guide small-group discussion, and then the groups should share their responses with the class:

❶ In what ways, if any, are a state of nature and a state of war the same or similar? In what ways are they different?

❷ Hobbes claimed that a state of nature—and by analogy a state of war—leaves no place for industry, agriculture, the arts, letters, or society. Do you think this is an exaggerated claim? What evidence from the past or the present can you offer to support your answer?

❸ According to Hobbes "continuall feare" is "worst of all" in a state of nature or war. Do you agree or disagree? Why?

❹ Monitor the news media. Identify current situations in which people might be said to be in a state of nature, where "the life of man [is] solitary, poore, nasty, brutish, and short." What might be done to alleviate those conditions?

CRITICAL THINKING EXERCISE
Examining Why the Founders Feared Government Abuse of Power

Given their knowledge of history and their experiences under British rule, it is not surprising that the Founders feared possible abuses of governmental powers. Read the following three statements by famous American Founders. Then respond to the questions that follow.

> ❝ Give all power to the many, they will oppress the few. Give all power to the few, they will oppress the many.
>
> Alexander Hamilton, 1787

> ❝ There are two passions which have a powerful influence on the affairs of men. These are ambition and avarice; the love of power and the love of money.
>
> Benjamin Franklin, 1787

> ❝ From the nature of man, we may be sure that those who have power in their hands…will always, when they can…increase it.
>
> George Mason, 1787

❶ What view of human nature is expressed in each of these statements?

❷ If you agree with the views of human nature expressed in the statements, what kind of safeguards to prevent abuses of power would you include in a constitution?

❸ Do you think the Founders' concerns about government are as valid today as they were in the 1700s? Why or why not?

WHAT KINDS OF GOVERNMENTS MAY BE CONSTITUTIONAL GOVERNMENTS?

The Founders knew that constitutional government might take many forms. It is possible to have a constitutional government with one ruler, a group of rulers, or rule by the people as a whole as long as those in power must obey the limitations placed on them by the higher law of the constitution. Historically, constitutional governments have included monarchies, republics, democracies, and various combinations of these forms of government.

The problem for any constitutional government is to ensure that those in power obey constitutional limits. History provides many examples of rulers who ignored constitutions or tried illegally to increase their personal power. The Founders believed that direct democracy was more likely to ignore constitutional limits than representative government. Direct democracy makes it easy for momentary passions to inflame people and leads to passionate rather than reasoned judgments. The interests of the community, as well as the rights of individuals in the minority, may suffer as a result.

WHAT DO YOU THINK?

❶ How would you organize a government so that it would be fairly easy to remove and replace officials who violated the constitutional limitations on their powers?

❷ What might happen in a government in which there was no agreed-on or peaceful means for removing officials? Give a recent example to support your answer.

❸ Is it important that a constitution be written? What are the advantages and disadvantages of a written constitution? Of an unwritten constitution?

REVIEWING AND USING THE LESSON

❶ Identify at least three characteristics of the British colonies.

❷ What important lessons did the founding generation learn from political theory and political history?

❸ What is the difference between limited government and unlimited government? Do you think the difference is important? Why or why not?

❹ What is a constitution?

❺ What is a mixed constitution? Explain the advantages and disadvantages of this type of government.

❻ Why is a constitution considered a higher law, and what are the major characteristics of a higher law?

❼ According to Aristotle, what are the differences between right and corrupt forms of government?

2

WHAT IDEAS ABOUT
CIVIC LIFE INFORMED THE
FOUNDING GENERATION?

UNIT ONE | LESSON 2

WHAT IDEAS ABOUT CIVIC LIFE INFORMED THE FOUNDING GENERATION?

---

wtpcompanion.civiced.org **LESSON PURPOSE + TERMS**

Visit the We the People companion website for printable and downloadable Lesson Purposes and Terms and Concepts to Understand sections for each lesson. Audio readings of each Lesson Purpose and Term are also available online in MP3 format.

LESSON PURPOSE

People frequently make judgments about governments or acts of governments, praising them as "good" or criticizing them as "bad." Those judgments may reflect ideas about human nature, the proper function and scope of government, the rights of individuals, and other values. Political philosophers have discussed these matters for thousands of years. This lesson examines concepts such as the common good, civic virtue, the state of nature, natural rights, consent, and the social contract. These concepts are central to discussions about government.

When you have finished this lesson, you should be able to describe how and why natural rights philosophy differs from classical republicanism and how both systems of thought influenced the founding generation in America. You also should be able to explain the kinds of challenges that a society faces when it strives to preserve the rights to life, liberty, property, and "the pursuit of happiness" while at the same time promoting the common good and civic virtue. Finally, you should be able to evaluate, take, and defend positions on the importance of civic virtue today and the role of political philosophy in thinking about government.

TERMS AND CONCEPTS TO UNDERSTAND

civic virtue	inalienable rights	right of revolution
classical republicanism	natural rights	social contract theory
common good	political legitimacy	state of nature
consent of the governed	popular sovereignty	
divine right	pursuit of happiness	

WHAT VALUES FROM ANTIQUITY INFLUENCED THE FOUNDING GENERATION?

MIXED CONSTITUTION OF ROME

The following are some pertinent quotations:

Attributed to Cicero:

- "We are obliged to respect, defend, and maintain the common bonds of union and fellowship that exist among all members of the human race."

- "Everyone has the obligation to ponder well his own specific traits of character. He must also regulate them adequately and not wonder whether someone else's traits might suit him better. The more definitely his own a man's character is, the better it fits him."

Attributed to Aristotle:

- "For as man is the best of all animals when he has reached his full development [within a politically organized society], so he is worst of all animals when divorced from law and justice."

- On his statement that man has a natural social instinct: "But he who is unable to live in society, or who has no need because he is sufficient for himself, must be either a beast or a god."

- "Good habits formed at youth make all the difference."

- "Excellence is an art won by training and habituation. We are what we repeatedly do.... Excellence, then, is not an act but a habit."

WHAT VALUES FROM ANTIQUITY INFLUENCED THE FOUNDING GENERATION?

The men who drafted state constitutions and the U.S. Constitution were familiar with the ideas of antiquity when they thought about government. The Roman Republic, which lasted for almost five hundred years, from the sixth century to the first century BC, was the ancient society that exercised the greatest influence on the Founders. The laws of the Roman Republic established a complex system of offices, in which the common people had a voice but that also provided checks on the people's power. The Roman Republic was described as a mixed constitution because it had elements of monarchical power, aristocracy, and rule of the common people. It fostered and for a time achieved political stability. Many historians during our founding era believed that of all the governments they studied, the Roman Republic had done the best job of promoting the **common good**—that is, doing what was best for the society as a whole.

The devotion of citizens to the common good was a central feature of the political ideas that we now call **classical republicanism**. Classical republicanism placed the needs of people as a community above individual liberty and self-determination. Citizens were taught that they should work together to promote the good of the country, not work for private or selfish interests. Only by working together in a common effort to promote the good of all could citizens maintain their republic and keep it free from the domination of others.

The history of the Roman Republic was both an example and a warning to America's founding generation. For centuries Roman citizens displayed their commitment to the common good. Cicero, a leader of the Roman Republic, viewed public life as the highest calling. Public life required dedicated citizens and leaders willing to make personal sacrifices for the sake of the common good. By Cicero's time, however, Rome had acquired a vast empire. During his lifetime Roman citizens' selfishness and corruption would cost them their political freedom. Civil war ensued. And in 48 BC the Roman people accepted an autocratic master, Julius Caesar (c. 100–44 BC), who was appointed dictator in order to impose order and stability in the aftermath of the civil war.

Three aspects of classical republicanism were particularly influential for the founding generation of Americans:

- **Small, uniform communities** Classical thinkers, such as Aristotle, observed that human beings are not self-sufficient and are always

What were some characteristics of the Roman Republic that might have contributed to its stability?

found living in association with one another in a form of political rule. Man is, he said, "a political animal." Humans need each other. They live together both for security and in order to live well. Good government is possible only in small communities, because in such communities people are able to know and care for one other and to discern the common good. Classical republican thinkers also believed that members of a political community must be fundamentally alike. Great disparities in wealth or differences in culture, religion, or morals cause conflict among people rather than encouraging them to work together for the common good. Classical republicans also feared the corrupting effects of luxury, making them wary of moneymaking and economic growth.

Americans in the eighteenth century experienced many of the advantages of small communities and their devotion to the common good. Survival in early America depended on the ability of neighbors and townspeople to work together to overcome obstacles. Official or established religions also fostered homogeneity and a commitment to the common good as defined by that religion.

- **Citizenship and civic virtue** Classical republicans emphasized the importance of the "office" of citizen and the duties associated with it. In most ancient societies slaves and noncitizens did most of the manual labor, freeing wealthier citizens to participate in civic affairs. Citizens were expected to set aside personal interests to promote the common good. Citizens also were expected to be well informed and engaged in community affairs. Virtuous citizens, classical republicans believed, should have the courage to do what was right even under trying circumstances.

From the classical perspective citizenship should emphasize duties, not rights. Most ancient republics did recognize what today we would call political rights, such as the right to vote, to express opinions about government, and to serve in public office. But most placed limits on the exercise of individual freedoms. For example, there was little concern about protecting an individual's privacy or freedom of conscience or religion.

The founding generation admired the heroes of antiquity, such as the Roman patriot, orator, and writer Cato the Elder (234–149 BC) and the citizen-soldier

What are some advantages of small, homogeneous communities? What are some disadvantages?

13

Why did the Founders consider Cincinnatus a model of civic virtue? What is the importance of civic virtue among leaders and citizens? Is there any relationship between the idea of civic virtue and the ideas expressed in the quotation from Judge Learned Hand on page xviii?

Lucius Quinctius Cincinnatus (519–438 BC). Cincinnatus was twice called on to serve as dictator—in 458 and 439 BC. After defending Rome, each time he voluntarily relinquished political power to resume private life as a farmer. The Founders believed that such men were examples of **civic virtue,** and Americans should emulate them. Indeed, many admired George Washington as "our Cincinnatus," because he sacrificed his private pursuits to lead the nation in war and peace. He then voluntarily relinquished the presidency after two terms in office, though some would have made him an American monarch. Early Americans believed that Washington was an example of the civic virtue that should motivate all citizens.

- **Moral education** Classical republican thinkers believed that civic virtue must be learned. Moral education included instruction in "civil religion"—the symbols, rituals, and values of the society. Moral education also required that children develop proper habits, including generosity, self-control, respect, fairness, and courage—all of which were necessary for speaking and reasoning well. Moral education entailed learning to admire the achievements and civic virtue of the heroes described in history, literature, poetry, and music. Young people also needed to learn the importance of participating in political debate and performing military service.

An important component of moral education was instilling in children the importance of developing and preserving a good reputation. People needed to be able to trust one another in the conduct of their daily affairs, and so they needed to behave morally.

Civic virtue included supervising and nurturing the next generation of citizens. Classical republicans believed that the entire community was responsible for the moral education of the young.

In colonial America small, homogeneous communities and churches assumed responsibility for instilling proper habits and practices. The founding generation believed that if individualism and self-interest were allowed to flourish unchecked, then community life would suffer. Small, uniform communities that emphasized civic virtue and moral education, as the classical republics of antiquity had done, appealed to some of the Founders as means of tempering selfishness and corruption.

14

WHAT DO YOU THINK?

❶ Identify someone living today who you believe shows civic virtue. Explain the reason for your choice.

❷ What did classical republicans believe should be the goal of education? Do you agree? Why or why not?

❸ What civic virtues are important for young people to have today and why?

❹ What similarities and differences are there between your ideas about rights and those of the classical world?

❺ What might be the consequences to individuals and a society of too great an emphasis on the common good at the expense of individual rights?

WHAT IS THE ROLE OF PHILOSOPHY IN THE STUDY OF GOVERNMENT?

Consider these words:

" We hold these Truths to be self-evident, that all Men are created equal, that they are endowed by their Creator with certain unalienable Rights, that among these are Life, Liberty, and the **Pursuit of Happiness**— That to secure these Rights, Governments are instituted among Men, deriving their just Powers from the **Consent of the Governed**, that whenever any Form of Government becomes destructive of these Ends it is the Right of the People to alter or to abolish it, and to institute new Government.

Declaration of Independence, 1776

This excerpt from the Declaration of Independence explains why so many Americans felt justified in separating from Great Britain. It also includes some of the most important philosophical ideas underlying our government. These ideas were familiar to most of the intellectual leaders in the American colonies long before the Revolutionary War. They had been preached in churches, written in pamphlets, and debated in public and private. They had been developed and refined by political philosophers beginning in the 1600s, a century of revolution and civil war in Europe, in an attempt to repudiate the theory of **divine right** of kings. Divine right was the idea that monarchs derive their authority from God. Thus to disobey them or to attempt to replace them or limit their powers is contrary to the will of God. Contrary to divine right, the belief became prominent that self-government is required to lay the foundations for social peace and a just society.

The theory of government set forth in the second paragraph of the Declaration of Independence is from **natural rights** philosophy. This philosophy begins by imagining what life would be like in a **state of nature**. A state of nature is any situation in which there is no government—that is, no recognized authority to make and enforce rules and manage conflicts.

Thinking about what life would be like in a state of nature is a useful way to explore some of the most basic questions of political philosophy. Such questions include

- What is human nature? That is, what traits of personality and character, if any, do all people have in common? Are people selfish? Do they have the capacity to care for the good of others?

- What should be the purposes of government?

- Where should people in positions of power get their authority to govern?

- How should a government be organized?

- What kinds of government should be respected and supported?

- What kinds of government should be resisted and fought?

Why might the ideas of self-government contained in the Declaration of Independence have been considered radical at that time?

15

WHAT IS THE ROLE OF PHILOSOPHY IN THE STUDY OF GOVERNMENT?

The word *philosophy* comes from two Greek words: *philo* (love) and *sophia* (wisdom). Thus it literally means "love of wisdom." Beyond that, the word has many meanings. Philosophy in general involves investigating the nature of existence, the causes of things, principles of reality, values, and logic. The word also is used to describe basic systems of thought. This text, for example, refers to the philosophy of John Locke, among others.

One specialty within the field of moral philosophy is political philosophy, which, broadly speaking, focuses on the nature of justice, political legitimacy, authority, freedom, rights, and laws. Political philosophers ask questions such as, Why is government needed? What are its purposes? What does citizenship mean? What are the rights and responsibilities of citizens? and What is the nature of the Good Life?

STATE OF NATURE   Some observers argue that a good example of a state of nature today is the international arena. Another example is the Internet because users can do more or less as they please. There are no enforceable rules for Internet use, such as limiting what can be written in blogs.

student page ▼ 16–18

WHAT VALUES FROM NATURAL RIGHTS PHILOSOPHY INFLUENCED THE FOUNDING GENERATION?

SOCIAL CONTRACT THEORY The idea that humans are not naturally social and live together in civil society only by agreement is at the core of understanding social contract theory. The degree of limited government that follows from a contract theory of government depends on the nature of the contract. The differences between Hobbes and Locke are a case in point. Thomas Hobbes (1588–1678) was the first modern social contract theorist. In *Leviathan* (1651) he explained that people may agree ("contract") to be ruled by an all-powerful ruler of a state he calls "Leviathan." They agree to an authoritarian government because they fear violent death and want security. The state is established to protect their lives, and their obligations to the state cease if the state ever attacks their lives. "It is the Right of the People to alter or to abolish it, and to institute new Government, laying its Foundation on such Principles, and organizing its Powers in such Form, as to them shall seem most likely to effect their Safety and Happiness." Otherwise, the powers of the state are unlimited.

John Locke, by contrast, used social contract theory to justify the establishment of a far more limited government. The Declaration of Independence, which reflects Locke's view of the matter, states that people consent to government to protect certain natural rights, identified in the Declaration as inalienable rights to life, liberty, and the pursuit of happiness. If government fails to protect these rights, "it is the right of the People to alter or to abolish it, and to institute new government, laying its Foundation on such principles, and organizing its powers in such Form, as to them shall seem most likely to effect their Safety and Happiness."

The second of John Locke's *Two Treatises on Government* (1690) is among the most widely read works on political thought and has been called "the Bible of the American Revolution." This work has seen perhaps a hundred printings in at least fourteen languages. Like the writings of Hobbes and Montesquieu, Locke's writings were placed on the Catholic Church's Index of Forbidden Books. All were seen to undermine the theory of divine right of kings.

With regard to property, a common modern misunderstanding is to regard property as only an inanimate object or thing. Locke insisted that property was a right, not a thing. In his *Second Treatise of Government* he wrote,

> Yet every man has property in his own person; this nobody has any right to but himself. The labour of his body and the work of his hands, we may say, are properly his.

CRITICAL THINKING EXERCISE
Thinking Like a Political Philosopher

Why do people need society and government? If society and government are necessary, what makes them legitimate? What makes them good?

To explore these questions, imagine that you and your classmates have been transported to a place where no one has ever lived. When you arrive, there is no government. There are no laws or controls over how you live. Everyone is free—that is, no one is under an obligation to obey a constituted authority because there is none. You have no means of communicating with people in other parts of the world.

Discuss your responses to the following questions. Think about how your responses reflect your views as a political philosopher.

❶ What would life be like if there were no government, rules, or controls?

❷ Would people in the situation described above have rights or duties? If so, how would those rights and duties be enforced?

❸ What might happen if some people were stronger or smarter than others? Why?

❹ What might weaker or less sophisticated people try to do? Why?

❺ Why might people in the situation described above choose to trade some or all of their freedom to live in society or form a government?

WHAT VALUES FROM NATURAL RIGHTS PHILOSOPHY INFLUENCED THE FOUNDING GENERATION?

The seventeenth century was a period of intellectual and social revolution in England. Classical republican theories about the purpose of society and government seemed unable to provide guidance in a century of rapid change. English philosophers, such as Thomas Hobbes and John Locke, thought that political philosophy needed a fresh start, one that focused on the rights of individuals. They originated the way of thinking about human nature and politics that we know as natural rights philosophy. This philosophy argued that humans are not naturally social and traced government to an imaginary state of nature.

Hobbes argued that a state of nature gives rise to a "war of every man against every man," in which individuals fear violent death at the hands of others. Perpetual war in the state of nature would make life "solitary, poor, nasty, brutish, and short." The ensuing chaos would cause humans to agree to leave the state of nature by entering into a social contract. Through that contract, Hobbes argued, they would consent to an authoritarian state that Hobbes called "Leviathan," named for a mythical sea monster mentioned in several passages in the Hebrew Bible (Old Testament). Thus to maintain order, stability, and peace, according to Hobbes, the Leviathan state must rule largely by fear.

Locke argued that in a state of nature all people are free, equal, and rational. Each individual possesses **inalienable rights** to "life, liberty, and estate [property]." In a state of nature each person also has the right to

Which of Hobbes's ideas do you find most interesting? Why?   Which of Locke's ideas do you find most interesting? Why?

Does this cartoon illustrate Hobbes's or Locke's view of the state of nature? Why?

punish those who do not follow reason and respect the rights of others. People could not survive in the state of nature because most people would seek personal advantage. To secure their natural rights, people would agree through a "social contract" to leave the state of nature and form a civil society. To protect natural rights a second agreement—to form government—also would be needed. Locke argued that if government fails to protect individual rights, then the people are entitled to replace it, if necessary by revolution. This idea became a key argument of the Declaration of Independence.

Natural rights philosophy found fertile ground in early America, where vast resources, huge expanses of land, and the great distance from England allowed freedom and materialism to flourish. Consequently several aspects of natural rights philosophy influenced the founding generation, including the following:

- **Individual rights** Natural rights philosophy emphasizes the existence of inalienable rights of each person, regardless of wealth, social status, or birth. Americans in the founding generation were keenly aware of their rights. Before the Revolution they thought of themselves as British citizens who enjoyed the rights of subjects as those rights had evolved over the centuries in England. During the revolutionary crisis they came to think of their rights more in Lockean terms,

as personal, inherent, and inalienable. As you will learn in more detail in later lessons, social conditions in America contributed to this shift in thinking.

- **Popular sovereignty/government by consent** According to natural rights philosophy, government is created and derives its authority from the agreement of the people, which is called **popular sovereignty**. If people must give their consent to be governed—by agreeing to a social contract or joining a society that already has been established—then it follows that they can withdraw that consent because sovereignty, or ultimate governing authority, rests with the people. Thus natural rights philosophy includes the **right of revolution** and the people's right to create whatever form of government they believe best suits their needs.

- **Limited government** By focusing on the individual and on **social contract theory** as sources of **political legitimacy**, Locke and other writers laid the foundation for limited government. From this new perspective the purpose of government is to serve private ends, especially protection of individual life, liberty, and property. Those who exercise governmental power may not make and

ENRICHMENT ACTIVITY

CHARTING CLASSICAL REPUBLICANISM AND NATURAL RIGHTS PHILOSOPHY

Distribute a blank copy of a graphic organizer or the graphic organizer found at Appendix D 1. Ask students to fill it out by responding to the following questions:

1. What is the primary goal of humans living together?
2. What ought to motivate human behavior?
3. What is the relationship between the public sphere and the private sphere?
4. How important is participation in civic activities?

Below is an example of how the graphic organizer might be filled out in response to these questions.

CLASSICAL REPUBLICANISM	NATURAL RIGHTS PHILOSOPHY
Promote the common good, exercise civic virtue, achieve human "excellence"	Ensure protection of life, liberty, and property
Putting community interest ahead of individual interests	Self-interest, pursuing opportunities
Public sphere most important; therefore, need to limit individual privacy, belief, expression, and opportunities to consider thoughts or ideas incompatible with common good	Public sphere a collection of private individuals and interests; no limits on acquisitions. Government must be limited; public sphere as small as possible
All citizens should participate fully in community to promote common good; civic virtue related to office holding and other contributions to well-being of community	Deciding whether to participate in community or government is up to individual

enforce laws on all subjects or focus on the needs of the community to the exclusion of individuals. Rather, their authority is limited by the purpose for which government is created. The distinction between society, which is formed by the social contract, and government, which is created to reflect the needs of society, further supports the idea that governmental power should be limited. Government is the creature and the creation of society. The sovereign people own their government and control it through elections and other means. Because it is theirs, they can terminate it when it does not guard their interests and meet their expectations.

- **Human equality** Locke argued that in a state of nature all people are free from one another's control and are equal to one another. All are born with equal political rights. Neither God nor nature makes some people rulers and other people subjects. In colonial America more people enjoyed social mobility than they had

possessed in Europe or England. Nonetheless, human inequalities persisted in the colonies. For example, slavery was introduced in Virginia in 1619, and by 1776 every colony legally sanctioned this institution. Women remained legally dependent on men and did not fully participate in political life. However, natural rights philosophy and its commitment to human equality ultimately would become a weapon in the attack on slavery and other inequalities in America.

WHAT DO YOU THINK?

Revisit your responses to the Critical Thinking Exercise earlier in this lesson. How do your answers compare to the values of classical republicans and natural rights philosophers?

REVIEWING AND USING THE LESSON

1. How would you describe the differences between classical republicanism and natural rights philosophy? How are those differences important in thinking about the purposes and goals of government?

2. What is civic virtue? How is it fostered in small, uniform communities? In large, diverse communities?

3. What are the advantages and disadvantages of using the state of nature to explain society and politics?

4. What is meant by *social contract*? How is it connected to the idea that government derives its authority from the consent of the governed? What is the significance of the idea that society and government are based on agreements rather than occurring naturally?

5. If you were asked to create a government that reflects principles of both classical republicanism and natural rights philosophy, which elements of each would you use? Why?

6. What might be the consequences for individuals and society of too great an emphasis on the rights of individuals over the common good?

7. Examine the Preamble to the U.S. Constitution (see Reference section). What influences, if any, of classical republican and natural rights philosophies do you find?

LEVIATHAN
or the
MATTER, FORM
and POWER of
A COMMON WEALTH
ECCLESIASTICAL
and
CIVIL.

Written by
Thos Hobbes

Do Hobbes's ideas about the establishment of authoritarian states to promote order, security, and peace have any relevance today? Why or why not?

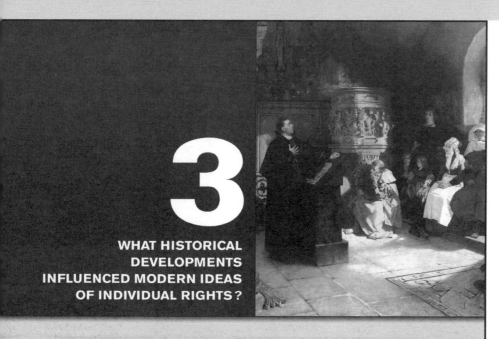

3

WHAT HISTORICAL DEVELOPMENTS INFLUENCED MODERN IDEAS OF INDIVIDUAL RIGHTS?

WHAT HISTORICAL DEVELOPMENTS INFLUENCED MODERN IDEAS OF INDIVIDUAL RIGHTS?

wtpcompanion.civiced.org   LESSON PURPOSE + TERMS

Visit the We the People companion website for printable and downloadable Lesson Purposes and Terms and Concepts to Understand sections for each lesson. Audio readings of each Lesson Purpose and Term are also available online in MP3 format.

LESSON PURPOSE

The previous two lessons explored ideas that shaped the Founders' thinking about constitutional government and civic life. This lesson examines several important historical developments that also influenced their ideas.

When you have finished this lesson, you should be able to explain the differences between classical republican and Judeo-Christian ideas about the importance of the individual. You also should be able to explain how certain historical developments influenced modern ideas about government, constitutionalism, and individual rights. Finally, you should be able to evaluate, take, and defend positions on approaches to theories of morality, the importance of the rise of capitalism, and how the Enlightenment inspired the Founders.

TERMS AND CONCEPTS TO UNDERSTAND

capitalism

city-state

feudalism

Judeo-Christian

nation-state

private morality

public morality

HOW DID THE JUDEO-CHRISTIAN HERITAGE CONTRIBUTE TO THE FOUNDERS' UNDERSTANDING OF HUMAN RIGHTS?

Classical republican ideas and natural rights philosophy influenced the political ideas of the Founders. Another important influence on their thinking was the **Judeo-Christian** religious tradition. The Founders were familiar with the teachings of the Bible, but they also knew that differing religious beliefs had caused serious political conflicts.

Judeo-Christian morality was different from Greek and Roman ideals of civic virtue. Instead of **public morality** (the virtues that are important for acting in the community), it emphasized **private morality**, meaning the virtues of inner faith and obedience to God's law. These were expressed in biblical teachings, such as the Ten Commandments and the Sermon on the Mount. Christian teachings gave special importance to duties such as goodwill and loving others.

The Christian view of the individual also differed from that of classical republicans. Christian teachings stressed the dignity and worth of each human being. Much of the Founders' commitment to liberty and individual rights sprang from their belief in such ideals.

Christianity spread rapidly through the Roman Empire in spite of the government's attempts to suppress it. Christians began receiving relief from persecution when the Roman Emperor Constantine came to power. Within a few years Christianity became the official religion of the Roman Empire. Even after the Roman Empire collapsed in the West near the end of the fifth century, the Christian faith survived to shape European society. In fact, the Roman Catholic Church—often referred to simply as the Church—became an extremely powerful political force during the Middle Ages. Bishops, who were regional church officials, often were as powerful as the princes or barons in their territories. In some places bishops held governmental power.

The Church was the one unifying social institution in Europe during the Middle Ages. Its spiritual leader was the pope, whose seat was the old imperial capital, Rome. Most Europeans identified with this "universal" Church in terms of religion, but political loyalties were local. People looked to local rulers for protection, and they trusted people more than institutions. There were no nations, in the modern sense, to compete for their loyalties.

What evidence is there in this picture of the unequal relationship between lords and vassals? How does this relationship differ from the ideas about relationship between the people and government contained in the Declaration of Independence?

student page ▼ 21

WHAT WERE EUROPEAN CONCEPTS OF THE INDIVIDUAL AND SOCIETY DURING THE MIDDLE AGES?

The term *medieval* often is used to describe the Middle Ages. There is no scholarly consensus on the time period covered by the Middle Ages, but a common reference point is from the fall of the Roman Empire in the fifth century to the fifteenth century.

WHAT WERE EUROPEAN CONCEPTS OF THE INDIVIDUAL AND SOCIETY DURING THE MIDDLE AGES?

Apart from the unifying element of the Church, medieval European society was highly fragmented. Europe was divided into many isolated communities. Communication and travel were dangerous, slow, and difficult. People lived and worked within their own communities and typically had little contact with outsiders. The Church was the authority on all matters.

Government in the Middle Ages generally followed a hierarchical pattern known as **feudalism**. Feudalism was based on the principle of land for service. Those who lived on a lord's land were known as his vassals. They served their lord and in return were entitled to his protection. Feudalism created a political structure in which the feudal contract defined duties and rights. People were loyal to their lord, rather than to a country or to fellow citizens.

Even though Christianity accepted every believer as the equal of all others, certain medieval ideas about society and government were similar to those of classical republicanism. Medieval thinkers borrowed the classical idea of harmony between each individual and the whole of society, which they called *Respublica Christiana*—"Christian Republic." They also borrowed ideas from the Greek philosopher Plato, who compared society to a human body. Plato suggested that some parts of society, like some parts of the human body, are more important than others; but all are necessary for the good of the whole.

In summary, essential ideas of feudalism included the following:

- Society was divided into different classes and groups, such as royalty, nobility, clergy, tradesmen, craftsmen, peasants, and serfs. Each class or group had certain rights and responsibilities.

- Society was hierarchical—that is, classes and groups were ranked from the most powerful, royalty and nobility, at the top to the least powerful, serfs, at the bottom. No equality existed among groups and classes.

- Social relationships were thought to be permanent and hereditary. A person was generally not free to leave the class into which he or she had been born. Property—specifically real estate—could not be freely bought and sold. It could only be obtained or passed on through inheritance. Usually the eldest son was the principal heir. Inheriting property meant inheriting its responsibilities, such as service or protection.

- Rights and duties were tied to group membership or to particular grants of land. There was no concept of natural rights belonging to all individuals.

WHAT DO YOU THINK?

❶ How did Judeo-Christian morality differ from Greek and Roman ideals of civic virtue?

❷ What are the advantages and disadvantages of viewing rights and responsibilities as being possessed by individuals rather than groups?

❸ If the ideas about rights that prevailed during the Middle Ages were dominant today, how would they affect your life?

WHAT WERE THE RENAISSANCE AND THE REFORMATION, AND HOW DID THEY CONTRIBUTE TO IDEAS ABOUT RIGHTS?

The term *renaissance* means "rebirth." The Renaissance is the name given to the period marked by a revival of intellectual life that began in Italy around the fourteenth century and spread throughout Europe. During this period cities developed, commerce began to flourish, and education started to become more widespread. The invention

What was the relationship between the Roman Catholic Church and government during the Middle Ages?

21

student page ▾ 21-23

WHAT WERE THE RENAISSANCE AND THE REFORMATION, AND HOW DID THEY CONTRIBUTE TO IDEAS ABOUT RIGHTS?

RELIGIOUS NAMES

Religious names associated with the Renaissance and the Reformation include the following:

Thomas More (1478–1534)   More was an English barrister and politician who was imprisoned for advocating a decrease in proposed appropriations for King Henry VII. He later helped King Henry VIII refute Martin Luther. As speaker of the House of Commons he also helped establish the parliamentary privilege of free speech. Convicted of treason in 1534 for failing to recognize King Henry VIII as head of the Church of England, More was imprisoned again and beheaded. He was canonized by the Catholic Church in 1886 and declared a saint by Pope Pius XI in 1935. More coined the word *utopia* for his controversial novel of that title, published in 1516.

Martin Luther (1483–1546)   A German monk and theologian considered to be the founder of Protestantism, Luther argued that the Bible, not the pope, was the source of all religious authority and that individuals can attain salvation through faith alone, unmediated by the church. Luther translated the Bible into vernacular German, making it accessible to laypeople. He also wrote hymns that developed the tradition of congregational singing and set the pattern for Protestant clerical marriage.

John Calvin (1509–1564)   Calvin was a French Protestant theologian who also trained as a lawyer. He was a devout Catholic before converting to Protestantism sometime between 1528 and 1533. Calvin published *Institution Christianae Religionis* in 1536, republished as *Institutes of the Christian Religion* in 1541, as an introductory textbook of Protestant faith. He attacked the teachings of Roman Catholicism.

POLITICAL NAMES

Political names associated with the Renaissance and the Reformation include the following:

Machiavelli (1469–1527)   Niccolò di Bernardo dei Machiavelli was an Italian political philosopher and diplomat. A central figure in the political Renaissance, he wrote *Discourses on Livy* and *The Prince* and is most famous for the latter, which describes how political leaders can get, keep, and expand political power. Machiavelli believed that political ends justify whatever means—including cruelty—are required to achieve them. He famously observed that it is safer for a prince to be feared than loved.

Henry VIII (1491–1547)   The second monarch of the house of Tudor, Henry severed the Church of England from the Roman Catholic Church and established the king as head of the Church of England. Famous for six marriages, Henry made the royal court a center of scholarly and musical innovation.

Elizabeth I (1533–1603) The third monarch to follow Henry VIII, she was his daughter and reestablished the Protestant church in England after her half-sister Mary had reverted the kingdom to Catholicism. Elizabeth was a long-lived and immensely popular monarch who sought and took advice to make England one of the most prosperous and powerful countries in the world. Science and culture also flourished during her reign.

SCIENTISTS

Scientists associated with the Renaissance and the Reformation include the following:

Roger Bacon (c. 1214–1294) Bacon was an English empirical philosopher who focused on sensation as the primary method of acquiring knowledge. One of the first advocates of modern scientific method to study the world, he also urged theologians to study science. He advocated reading the Bible and other texts in their original languages.

Nicolaus Copernicus (1473–1543) A Polish astronomer and mathematician, Copernicus advocated the view that Earth rotates on an axis and makes a yearly revolution around a stationary sun. This view marked the beginning of the scientific revolution. The Catholic Church rejected his scientific theories.

Johannes Kepler (1571–1630) A German mathematician and astronomer, Kepler believed that God created the world according to a plan knowable through natural reason. He formulated theories of planetary motion and "laws" built on Copernicus's theories and laid the foundation for Newton's theory of gravity in the next century. Kepler served as imperial mathematician to Emperor Rudolph II and was allowed to practice the Lutheran faith.

Galileo Galilei (1564–1642) Galileo was a Tuscan mathematician, astronomer, and physicist who championed Copernicus and his view that Earth revolves around the sun. His empirical approach to science broke tradition with Aristotle. Albert Einstein called him the "father of modern science." Galileo spent his later years under house arrest on orders of the Italian Inquisition, a Catholic Church tribunal created to protect the church from heresy.

wtpcompanion.civiced.org | **BIOGRAPHIES**

Visit the We the People companion website for brief printable and downloadable biographies of the people mentioned in the student and teacher's editions. Audio readings of each biography are also available online in MP3 format.

of the printing press using movable type in the fifteenth century increased communication and the spread of knowledge. Learned people rediscovered ancient Greek and Roman history, literature, and art, as well as medieval Arabic philosophy and mathematics. These discoveries inspired a view of the world and humanity very different from that of medieval Christianity.

During the Renaissance some people began to place greater importance on the individual than on the class or group into which they had been born. In the volatile **city-states** of Renaissance Italy and later in northern Europe, people found that they could move from one social position to another. Growing possibilities for individual opportunity helped lead to an increased interest among philosophers and jurists in the rights of individuals. This interest contributed to a reexamination of the individual's relationship to religious institutions and governments.

The Protestant Reformation was another powerful stimulus to modern individualism. The Reformation was a religious reform movement that began in the early sixteenth century in western Europe. Religious reformers, studying the Bible and other ancient religious texts, began to challenge the doctrines, traditions, and practices of the Roman Catholic Church. The reform-minded clerics believed that the medieval church had become corrupt and had lost sight of the original truths of Christianity.

Some of these critics attempted to reform the church from within. Other reformers, such as Martin Luther (1483–1546) in Germany and later John Calvin (1509–1564) in France, obtained official government support, or establishment, for their breakaway churches. These reformers and their followers were called Protestants. The word *protestant* is derived from the Latin *protestatio*, meaning "declaration," which Martin Luther made when he and his supporters dissented from an edict against the Reformation in the 1520s. The secular rulers who supported these new churches saw the Reformation as an opportunity to free themselves from the Catholic Church's political influence.

The Reformation was aided by the invention of a printing press using movable type, which allowed for more rapid and economical printing. For centuries the Bible had been available only in Latin, which few people other than priests could read. During the Reformation, Bibles were printed in English, German, French, Italian, and Spanish. Individuals were encouraged to read the Bible in their native language and to determine for themselves what it meant.

Being able to read the Bible for oneself encouraged greater freedom of conscience, or the freedom of individuals to decide about their own religious beliefs. Protestant religious doctrine emphasized a direct relationship between each believer and God. Luther argued

What was the significance of Martin Luther's declaration?

for the "priesthood of all believers," which had the effect of decentralizing religious authority and empowering—and placing responsibility on—individual believers. All individuals were seen as equal in the eyes of God. Individuals were free to interpret the word of God, but God also was viewed as holding individuals accountable for their actions.

The spirit of free inquiry and individual conscience that the Reformation inspired contributed to the development of modern individualism. Ultimately it also posed a threat to most established institutions and authority. Some religious reformers, in fact, began to question the authority of the newly established Protestant churches. In England, for example, certain reformers attacked the Church of England during the Elizabethan period—principally the reign of Queen Elizabeth I from 1558 to 1603—for not being sufficiently Protestant. They were called Puritans, because they wanted to "purify" the church. Many American colonies were settled by people, including Puritans, seeking to worship in their own way, free from the requirements of established Protestant churches.

HOW DID THE NATION-STATE ARISE?

By the end of the Middle Ages rulers were beginning to expand their areas of control and to form new and larger states. The Renaissance and the Reformation helped to speed up this process. But the changes were not easy. During the Reformation Europe was torn apart by religious wars. In some places one-third to one-half the population was killed in this warfare.

In 1648 the Peace of Westphalia ended the Thirty Years' War, which had been fought since 1618 mainly on ground that today is in Germany. The conflict involved most of the continent's powers at one time or another and was one of the bloodiest conflicts that Europe had known. This settlement often is regarded as marking the beginning of the modern system of **nation-states**. The Peace of Westphalia recognized national sovereignty, the right of each nation-state to an independent existence. It also provided that each nation-state would respect the independence or sovereignty of the others. And it confirmed that nation-states could choose their own institutions, including religion.

The rise of the nation-state was important to the development of modern ideas about government and rights. People began to think of themselves as citizens of a particular nation or country, with public rights and duties. In addition to the nation-states there were many independent city-states that practiced self-government by a rising class of merchants, tradesmen, and nobles. This development was in contrast to the old feudal system, in which people's rights and duties were defined in personal terms. Political thought began to focus on the question of what kind of government would be best for these states.

WHAT WAS THE NEW ECONOMIC SYSTEM OF CAPITALISM?

Among the forces that helped to break up medieval society and to pave the way for the Renaissance was the increase in commercial trade and its expansion over greater distances. Eventually this growth produced a new economic system called **capitalism**. Capitalism is an economic system in which the means of producing and distributing goods are privately owned and operated for profit in competitive markets. Unlike in feudal relationships, in capitalism goods and services are freely exchanged.

Capitalism allowed more people to choose their own occupations, to start their own businesses, and to buy and sell property. People also were able to pay more attention to their private interests than to the common good. They were encouraged to work to gain property

How did the Peace of Westphalia contribute to the modern system of nation-states?

---

student page ▾ 23

HOW DID THE NATION-STATE ARISE?

The Peace of Westphalia of 1648 ended the Thirty Years' War. Germany, France, Spain, Sweden, the Dutch Republic, and the Swiss confederacy participated in the pact. A representative of the Holy Roman Empire also participated.

student page ▾ 23–24

WHAT WAS THE NEW ECONOMIC SYSTEM OF CAPITALISM?

The term *capitalism* was coined long after the development of the ideas and behaviors now called "capitalist" and well after Adam Smith's 1776 work, *An Inquiry into the Nature and Causes of the Wealth of Nations* (see below). The word first appeared in an 1854 novel by William Makepeace Thackeray. Capitalism has been defined as

> an economic system characterized by the following: private property ownership; individuals and companies are allowed to compete for their own economic gain; and free market forces determine the prices of goods and services. Such a system is based on the premise of separating the state and business activities. Capitalists believe that markets are efficient and should thus function without interference, and the role of the state is to regulate and protect.

According to the *Oxford English Dictionary* capitalism is defined as "the condition of possessing capital; the position of a capitalist; a system which favors the existence of capitalists." *Capitalist*, referring to "one who has accumulated capital; one who has capital available for employment in financial or industrial enterprises," first appeared in 1792.

Adam Smith (1723–1790) Smith was a Scottish economist who popularized the theory that rational economic self-interest in a free market leads to overall economic well-being. Smith's early works focused on ethics and charity, which Smith argued were part of self-interest. In *An Inquiry into the Nature and Causes of the Wealth of Nations* Smith wrote, "Man has almost constant occasion for the help of his brethren, and it is in vain for him to expect it from their benevolence only." Smith also argued that the American colonies were too expensive for the British Empire to keep.

wtpcompanion.civiced.org   BIOGRAPHIES

Visit the We the People companion website for brief printable and downloadable biographies of the people mentioned in the student and teacher's editions. Audio readings of each biography are also available online in MP3 format.

HOW DID THE ENLIGHTENMENT INSPIRE THE AMERICAN FOUNDERS?

Some Founders, including James Madison and Alexander Hamilton, believed that politics should be studied "scientifically." They were influenced by several thinkers, including the following:

René Descartes (1596–1650)   This French mathematician, who invented analytic geometry, was also a scientist and philosopher—he was considered to be the father of modern philosophy. Descartes sought to discover truth through systematic doubt. He believed that if one were "a real seeker after truth, it is necessary that at least once in your life to doubt, as far as possible, all things." Descartes gave us the famous Latin phrase "cogito ergo sum," or "I think, therefore I am."

Isaac Newton (1643–1721)   An English mathematician and physicist, Newton was one of the greatest thinkers of his or any generation. He was influenced by Descartes, laid the foundation for differential and integral calculus, and is considered the founder of modern physical science. His most notable contributions were in optics and universal gravitation. Newton opposed attempts by King James II to make universities Catholic institutions.

wtpcompanion.civiced.org   BIOGRAPHIES

Visit the We the People companion website for brief printable and downloadable biographies of the people mentioned in the student and teacher's editions. Audio readings of each biography are also available online in MP3 format.

---

and to improve their economic position. As a result in parts of Europe political and economic power began to shift to a newly developing class of successful citizens who gained wealth through commerce and away from the upper classes that derived their wealth from the land.

Natural rights philosophy and Protestant religion both contributed to the rise of capitalism. Natural rights philosophers believed that government existed to secure people's property. Protestant religious groups, especially those in the tradition of John Calvin, saw wealth as a sign of God's grace.

WHAT DO YOU THINK?

❶ How do the new ideas that developed out of the Renaissance and the Reformation still affect our thinking today? Cite some examples of specific effects.

❷ With the development of capitalism people began to view the individual differently than they had in the classical republics or during the Middle Ages. What was this different view and why did it come about?

❸ How were the rise of the nation-state and capitalism related to individualism? What effect did these developments have on the common good?

CRITICAL THINKING EXERCISE
Understanding the Effects of the Renaissance and the Reformation on Ideas about Rights

In previous lessons you studied the ideas of the natural rights philosophers concerning individual rights and the purpose of government. You also learned about classical republican ideas of civic virtue and the common good. Now work in small groups of four or five students to consider what you have learned in this lesson about the Judeo-Christian tradition, the Middle Ages, the Renaissance, the Reformation, and the rise of the nation-state and capitalism.

❶ Were any ideas prevalent during one of these periods with which people who believe in natural rights might not agree? What are these ideas? Why might some people disagree with them?

❷ Do you think that ideas about the importance of the individual, individual rights, and the common good that emerged during these historical periods have influenced your thinking about the nature and purpose of government? If so, explain how.

HOW DID THE ENLIGHTENMENT INSPIRE THE AMERICAN FOUNDERS?

The worldly interests inspired by the Renaissance stimulated natural science—that is, the study of the natural world and the laws that govern it. Commercial expansion and voyages of discovery beyond Europe also encouraged this study. These voyages brought back new knowledge about the natural world and about other cultures.

Science and technology advanced rapidly. People began to believe that humans could solve many problems, such as how to treat diseases, that once had been accepted simply as misfortunes in life. By the eighteenth century this flourishing scientific and intellectual movement would become known as the Age of Enlightenment.

An important early figure in this movement was the English philosopher Francis Bacon (1561–1626). Bacon believed in the power of human reason and observation,

How did advances in scientific thought and reasoning reflected in the work of Francis Bacon and others influence people's ideas about human nature and government?

What are some of the essential elements of capitalism?

not only to understand nature but also to control it for humanity's purposes. The end of scientific study, he said, is the "enlarging of the bounds of human empire, to the effecting of all things possible." His goal was to subdue nature for the benefit of humanity. Discoveries by scientists, such as astronomers Nicolaus Copernicus (1473–1543) from Poland, Galileo Galilei (1564–1642) from Italy, and Isaac Newton (1643–1727) from England, seemed to confirm Bacon's faith in people's ability to understand nature.

This belief in science and reason also influenced the study of human nature and government. Living in the midst of intense scientific research and discovery in seventeenth-century England, philosophers Thomas Hobbes and John Locke, introduced previously, embraced scientific reasoning. Locke himself was an inventive physician. And Hobbes visited French philosopher René Descartes (1596–1650)—often called the Father of Modern Mathematics and the Father of Modern Philosophy—in Paris and Galileo in Florence. Their ideas about the state of nature and the basis for government were founded on the notion that human behavior could be understood, predicted, and controlled.

In the next century came Montesquieu, who was discussed in Lesson 1. This important Enlightenment political philosopher argued that the form of a society's government corresponds to the social, economic, and geographic conditions of that society. Therefore the best government for any nation is one tailored to the unique circumstances of that nation.

The American Founders belonged to the Age of Enlightenment. They believed that reason and observation, complemented by the study of history and writers such as Locke and Montesquieu, would enable them to understand the workings of governmental and social institutions. They thought that this understanding could generate what James Madison (1751–1836), who would become America's fourth president, called the "new science of politics." This new science would help the Founders construct a government for the new United States.

25

REVIEWING AND USING THE LESSON

❶ How would you describe the difference between the classical republican idea of civic virtue and Judeo-Christian ideas of morality?

❷ How did the Judeo-Christian heritage contribute to the Founders' understanding of human rights?

❸ What features of society in the Middle Ages contributed to the view that rights belonged to groups rather than to individuals?

❹ How did feudalism contribute to the idea that government is based on contractual relationships?

❺ What modern ideas about rights were developed during the Renaissance? How did the Reformation contribute to the development of these ideas?

❻ How did the rise of nation-states help to stimulate thinking about principles of government such as constitutionalism, individual rights, and republicanism?

❼ How did the development of capitalism encourage new thinking about the individual and society?

❽ Why was the invention of the printing press with movable type important in promoting the spirit of individualism?

❾ How did the ideas of the Age of Enlightenment influence the Founders?

How might the invention of the printing press with moveable type have influenced intellectual thought during the Renaissance?

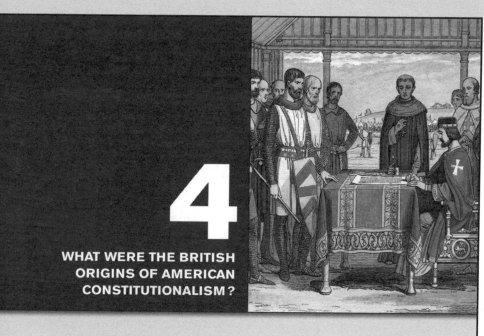

4

WHAT WERE THE BRITISH ORIGINS OF AMERICAN CONSTITUTIONALISM?

WHAT WERE THE BRITISH ORIGINS OF AMERICAN CONSTITUTIONALISM?

wtpcompanion.civiced.org   LESSON PURPOSE + TERMS

Visit the We the People companion website for printable and downloadable Lesson Purposes and Terms and Concepts to Understand sections for each lesson. Audio readings of each Lesson Purpose and Term are also available online in MP3 format.

LESSON PURPOSE

This lesson describes the evolution of British constitutional government. It examines the early stages of English government in the feudal period, concluding with the Magna Carta of 1215. It traces the development of representative institutions in England, English common law, and the relationship between legal and constitutional structures. It also examines some of the differences between British and American constitutionalism.

When you have finished this lesson, you should be able to explain how rights and representative government evolved in England and how this evolution influenced the Founders. You also should be able to identify the origins of some of Americans' most important constitutional rights. Finally, you should be able to evaluate, take, and defend positions on the influence of the Magna Carta on the development of rights and the importance of habeas corpus and trial by jury.

TERMS AND CONCEPTS TO UNDERSTAND

common law

Magna Carta

precedent

redress of grievances

rights of Englishmen

rule of law

stare decisis

writ of habeas corpus

student page ▾ 28

HOW DID ENGLISH GOVERNMENT BEGIN?

Not much is known about the first several hundred years of the Anglo-Saxon, or "English," era after the Romans left England in about 407. Invaders established separate kingdoms, with Saxons settling in the south and west, Angles in the east and north, and Jutes on the Isle of Wight and the mainland opposite. These groups probably thought of themselves as separate peoples, but they shared a common language and similar customs. Kings held power through force, not inheritance, with the result that Anglo-Saxon kingdoms came and went rapidly. Conquered people often became slaves but usually not for life.

After the Norman Conquest in 1066 William the Conqueror established the first strong central administration. He used force to put down rebellions and introduced a system of deference to individual lords, or barons, who were in charge of their own estates. These lords established their own monetary systems, imposed taxes, and administered justice. This system was known as feudalism. Thus central administration and local custom developed together.

The terms *England* and *Britain* (or *Great Britain*) often are incorrectly used interchangeably in the United States. However, they are historically different entities. England refers to the homeland of the Angles (or English) people, the southern part of the island called Great Britain, excluding Wales. The northern part is Scotland, home of the Scots. The southwestern part is Wales, home of the Welsh. The Acts of Union of 1706 and 1707 united England and Scotland, merging their parliaments and creating the Kingdom of Great Britain. Therefore the colonists in North America were British subjects after 1707, although many of them claimed English or Scots ancestry.

HOW DID PARLIAMENTARY GOVERNMENT IN ENGLAND BEGIN?

English monarchs discovered that they could not rule successfully without consulting about their decisions, particularly because they lacked a central army to enforce decisions. Monarchs created advisory councils that evolved into Parliament.

HOW DID ENGLISH COMMON LAW DEVELOP?

Scholars trace the development of the common law to the reign of King Henry II (1154–1189). The term *common law* refers to law that is common to all of England, in contrast to regional customary law that developed during the feudal period. By the end of the Middle Ages royal courts had become the only courts of justice, and judges applied a uniform law throughout the kingdom. The practice of using earlier rulings as the basis for deciding future cases with similar facts (*stare decisis*) evolved into what is now recognized as the system of judge-made law.

HOW DID ENGLISH GOVERNMENT BEGIN?

For several centuries after the fall of the Roman Empire England was divided among a number of tribes. A king or other leader ruled each tribe. Eventually all the tribes of England were united under one king. But unification into a single kingdom did not significantly change most people's lives. England was too large for one person to rule. The English monarch had to let people in local areas tend to their own affairs according to customs they had developed over the years.

A major change in the way England was ruled took place in 1066, when William the Conqueror, the leader of the Normans—people from Normandy in France—invaded England and defeated King Harold II at the Battle of Hastings. As king of England William introduced feudalism into the country, but he and his successors also adopted and adapted many English practices in governing the English. These monarchs recognized that it would help to keep peace in the kingdom if they did not upset people by violating too many local customs.

Originally, English monarchs, either personally or through representatives, made laws, supervised law enforcement, heard cases—thus the term "royal courts"—and defended the kingdom. Frequently monarchs called on advisors to help them, especially when they needed to know local legal traditions and customs, and when they needed money. By the early thirteenth century groups of advisors and assistants were developing into separate institutions. They evolved into Parliament and the royal court.

When Parliament was first established, what benefits did it provide for the English Crown?

HOW DID PARLIAMENTARY GOVERNMENT IN ENGLAND BEGIN?

Even before the Norman Conquest the English monarchs had brought together groups of advisors into councils of leading subjects, whom they relied on to advise them on various matters of state. These councils are the groups that came to be called *parliaments*, from the French word *parler*, which means "to speak."

In 1295 King Edward I summoned what came to be called the Model Parliament. The Model Parliament consisted of two representative parts, or houses. The House of Lords represented the feudal nobility and major church officials. The House of Commons was composed of two knights from each shire, or county; two citizens from each city; and two citizens from each borough, or town. Although called the House of Commons, this body was composed of people who had wealth and status in the kingdom. They were not the common people, as we understand that term today.

Parliament developed into a consistent body over time, in part because the English Crown, or monarchy, found it to be an effective way to raise money. Parliament represented the various interests in the kingdom, thereby providing monarchs with a convenient way of negotiating with all the interests at once. As Edward I said in his summons to the members of the Model Parliament, "What concerns all should be approved by all." In turn, English subjects found Parliament to be an effective way to voice their grievances and to limit or check monarchical power.

HOW DID ENGLISH COMMON LAW DEVELOP?

When William the Conqueror became king of England, there were different systems of law in different parts of the country. This made hearing cases difficult for royal judges, who had to learn about each local system. William and his successors tried to provide a less confusing system of law that would be common to all parts of the kingdom—**common law**—and would be applied consistently by royal judges.

The system of law that William the Conqueror introduced required judges to publish their decisions so that judges in the future would know how earlier cases had been decided. Earlier rulings became **precedents**, or rules to guide future cases. The principle of following precedents is known by the Latin term **stare decisis**—"let the precedent (decision) stand." This system gives predictability and stability to the law. Judges compare the facts of a case with cases decided earlier and attempt to rule in a way that is consistent with the earlier cases. Changes in judge-made law occur incrementally, as judges make minor changes in applying the law to the facts of each case.

HOW DID THE "RIGHTS OF ENGLISHMEN" DEVELOP?

English law and the English constitution gave great importance to tradition, or custom. Once a rule was recognized as the law of the land, it was hard to change. Over the years English monarchs and royal judges came to recognize that subjects had certain personal rights, often referred to as the **rights of Englishmen**. These common law rights were fundamental in the sense that neither the monarch nor Parliament would dare to change or violate them.

Centuries of respect gave these rights a special status. They included the following:

- The right to trial by a jury of one's peers under the law of the land

- Security in one's home from unlawful entry

- Limits on government's power to tax

In 1100 an event occurred in England that was a precedent for a greater event a century later. In this year King Henry I issued a Charter of Liberties, which bound him to obey certain laws regarding the treatment of nobles and church officials. Early in the next century, one of the great charters of liberty in human history, based partly on Henry's charter, was drawn up. This newer charter was written because the king, the pope, and the English barons (the king's feudal vassals) disagreed about the king's rights. This came about after a chain of events in the early 1200s, when King John I tried to take back some rights and powers that his barons had been enjoying. The result was a civil war between the barons and their king. The barons won.

In June 1215, with the support of the Church and others, the barons forced King John to sign a new Charter of Liberties, which later became known as the **Magna Carta**, or "Great Charter." This charter addressed feudal relationships between the Crown and three classes of the population—barons, clergy, and merchants. In the charter the king promised not to increase feudal dues and other money payments to the Crown without consent and to respect various property rights. The charter did not grant new rights. Rather, it confirmed certain traditional rights. At least three principles contained in the Magna Carta were important in the later development of constitutional government:

- **Rule of law** The Magna Carta was perhaps the most important early example of a written statement of law. It expressed the idea that the monarch must respect established

What is the significance of the Magna Carta for the establishment of limited government?

rules of law. The term **rule of law** refers to the principle that every member of society, even rulers, must obey the law. Sometimes the phrase is rendered as "the supremacy of the law" because it means that rulers must base their decisions on known principles or rules instead of on their own discretion. The Magna Carta, for example, stated that no free man could be imprisoned or punished "except by the lawful judgment of his peers" and by the "law of the land." This meant that the government could not take action against the governed unless it followed established rules and procedures. Arbitrary government was outlawed.

- **Basic rights** The barons made King John promise to respect the "ancient liberties and free customs" of the land. The barons did not believe that they were making any drastic change in the position or power of the king. Their goal was to establish a way to secure **redress of grievances**, or compensation for a loss or wrong done to them, should the Crown infringe on their common law rights.

---

student page ▾ 29-30

HOW DID THE "RIGHTS OF ENGLISHMEN" DEVELOP?

King John (1164–1216, reigned 1199–1216), who signed the Magna Carta, later wrote a secret letter to Pope Innocent III asking him to cancel it on the grounds that John had been forced to sign it against his will. The Pope condemned the document and declared it null and void. John violated many provisions of the Magna Carta, and the civil war continued. However, in 1216 John died, probably from dysentery after eating and drinking heavily. His nine-year-old son, Henry, became king. Less than a month later, Henry's supporters confirmed the Magna Carta, this time with the Pope's approval. The Magna Carta was reissued with some revisions in 1216, 1217, and 1225. Copies of the Magna Carta were sent to county courts and cathedrals, where they were read aloud twice yearly, demonstrating the close intermingling of church and state.

wtpcompanion.civiced.org PRIMARY SOURCES

Visit the We the People companion website for a link to the Magna Carta.

Common law rights are the product of a long evolution of social values that are recognized in judicial decisions. Some common law rights have been formally declared, such as the guarantee in the Magna Carta of 1215 that "no free man shall be taken or imprisoned or dispossessed or outlawed, or banished, or in any way destroyed...except by the legal judgment of his peers or by the law of the land." Other laws were recognized by Parliament, including the following:

HABEAS CORPUS ACT, 1641 No man could be put on trial except before the courts "by due process and writ original according to the old law of the land."

HABEAS CORPUS ACT, 1679 A person detained by the authorities was required to be brought before a court of law so that the legality of the detention could be examined.

BILL OF RIGHTS, 1689 The law guaranteed free parliamentary elections and prohibited excessive bail, excessive fines, and cruel and unusual punishments.

wtpcompanion.civiced.org PRIMARY SOURCES

Visit the We the People companion website for links to the Habeas Corpus Act of 1641, the Habeas Corpus Act of 1679, and the English Bill of Rights of 1689.

Some other rights recognized by the common law were the right to be informed of reasons for arrest, the right to a fair trial, and the right to be presumed innocent until proven guilty.

British historian A.V. Dicey described the right to individual freedom as "part of the constitution because it is inherent in the ordinary law of the land" and "one which can hardly be destroyed without a thoroughgoing revolution in the institutions and manners of the nation."

British settlers who cherished their common law rights established them throughout the colonies. Americans departed radically from the British model by putting bills of rights in constitutions, thereby making governmental power subservient to rights, rather than coequal with them as in Great Britain.

student page ▼ 30–32

WHAT IS THE BRITISH CONSTITUTION?

Two basic principles of the British constitution are rule of law and parliamentary supremacy. The primary sources of the British constitution are statutes such as the Magna Carta, laws and customs of Parliament, and case law from courts. Government professor and political commentator Anthony King objects to describing Britain's constitution as unwritten, saying,

> To describe Britain's constitution…as unwritten is simply bizarre. Britain's constitutional legislation runs to hundreds of pages. What Britain's constitution is is uncodified, not both written down and formally gathered all in one place.

wtpcompanion.civiced.org PRIMARY SOURCES

Visit the We the People companion website for a link to the Petition of Right of 1628.

- **Government by agreement or contract**
  The agreement in the Magna Carta was between the king and a limited number of his subjects. It did not include the majority of the English people. However, it did express the feudal principle of drawing up an agreement between parties as a basis for legitimate government.

Later generations would discover in the Magna Carta the seeds of other important constitutional principles. For example, the American colonists found the principle of no taxation without representation and consent in King John's promise not to levy certain feudal taxes without the consent of "our common counsel of the kingdom."

The Magna Carta also brought the law to bear against one law-breaking king. It gave King John's barons the right to go to war with him again if he broke the agreement. Going to war, however, was not a satisfactory method of ensuring responsible government. A better way began to develop in the next century.

What constitutional principles were embodied in the Magna Carta?

WHAT DO YOU THINK?

People have fought and died to establish rights such as those described in this lesson. However, it is difficult to understand the importance of these rights merely by reading about them. Examine the following two articles of the Magna Carta and then respond to the questions about them.

- **Article 39** No freeman shall be taken or imprisoned or disseised [dispossessed] or banished or in any way destroyed, nor will We [the King: this is the "royal We"] proceed against or prosecute him, except by the lawful judgment of his peers or by the law of the land.

- **Article 40** To no one will we sell, to none will we refuse or delay…justice.

❶ What rights, values, and interests are expressed in Articles 39 and 40?

❷ In what ways do these rights limit the monarch? Why would the English nobles want to place such limits on the monarch?

❸ Do you have any of these rights? If so, where are they written?

❹ Do you think a declaration of rights is enough to protect individuals from unfair and unreasonable treatment by their government? Why or why not?

WHAT IS THE BRITISH CONSTITUTION?

The British constitution is not a single written document. It consists of common law, important acts of Parliament, and political customs and traditions. The central principle of the British constitution is respect for established rules and procedures—that is, for the rule of law. Many provisions of the British constitution grew out of a long series of political struggles between monarchs and Parliament.

Three great historical documents are important in the development of the British constitution and the rights of the British people. In addition to the Magna Carta in 1215, these include the Petition of Right in 1628 and the English Bill of Rights in 1689. All three documents were written at times when the struggle for power between monarchs and Parliament was especially intense.

By 1600 Parliament had become so important to English government that it could challenge the Crown's ability to act without its support. But monarchs did not easily give up authority. In the seventeenth century the Crown and Parliament quarreled over a variety of issues,

What was the significance of the Habeas Corpus Act of 1679, passed during the reign of Charles II?

including money, religion, and foreign policy. At the heart of these struggles was the key constitutional issue: Did the Crown have to accept the supremacy of laws made by Parliament?

The first outcome of these struggles was a constitutional document almost as important as the Magna Carta, called the Petition of Right of 1628. King Charles I needed money to fight wars against France and Spain. He sought to raise funds without the consent of Parliament. Parliament responded by forcing Charles to agree to the Petition of Right, which confirmed that taxes could be raised only with the consent of Parliament. The Petition of Right guaranteed English subjects other rights, such as a prohibition against requiring people to quarter soldiers in their homes and the right to *habeas corpus*, which will be explained later in this section. King Charles's acceptance of the Petition of Right strengthened the idea that English subjects enjoyed fundamental rights that no government could violate.

The Petition of Right, however, was not successful in quelling strife between the people and their king. Civil unrest ensued. The English monarchy fell in 1649 and Charles I was executed. Oliver Cromwell instituted the

Commonwealth period, serving as Lord Protector until his death in 1658. He was briefly succeeded by his son Richard, until the monarchy was restored in 1660, and Charles II, the son of Charles I, came to the throne. Thus it was during the reign of King Charles II that the right to habeas corpus gained new authority.

The Habeas Corpus Act of 1679 made consistent a number of previous habeas corpus acts and confirmed the right of British subjects to apply for a legal document called a **writ of habeas corpus**. A writ is a court order to a government official commanding that official to do something. A writ of habeas corpus orders an official to deliver—"habeas"—a person—"corpus," meaning "the body"—who is in custody to a court of law to explain why the person is being held. If the government cannot justify keeping the individual in custody, then the person must be set free. The writ of habeas corpus is one of the most important limitations on government power, because it means that no government official—not even the Crown—can hold someone in prison arbitrarily or indefinitely.

Eventually Parliament became the branch of government that represented the most powerful groups in the

31

What must government do "to preserve all men in their lives, liberties, and Estates [property]"? John Locke contended that government had three major obligations:

- To establish known, or "settled," law, which must accord with the law of nature

- To provide "known and indifferent [impartial] judges," who must have the authority to settle differences according to established law

- To provide power to execute or carry out legal decisions

Ask students in groups of two or three to consider these three criteria and to draw on their personal knowledge and information gleaned from the media to answer the following questions:

❶ How do our national, state, or local governments establish law? How do they make the laws known?

❷ How would you describe "settled law," and why is it important that law be "settled"?

❸ Why must judges be "indifferent," or impartial? Why must they settle differences according to law and not according to their own beliefs or wishes?

❹ In what ways should government exercise its power to carry out its decisions?

kingdom. By the end of the seventeenth century Parliament, not the Crown, was recognized as the highest legal authority in England. Parliament's struggle with the monarchy ended in a bloodless revolution known as the Glorious Revolution of 1688. Under the Revolution Settlement Prince William of Orange of the Netherlands and his wife Mary were invited to be joint monarchs and to preserve the power of Parliament. Among other things Parliament required them to agree to the English Bill of Rights, which in 1689 became a cornerstone of the British constitution.

The English Bill of Rights contained a number of provisions, ranging from limitations on the Crown's power to raise money to guarantees of free speech and debate in Parliament. The Bill of Rights also expressed two important principles that influenced constitutional development in America:

- **Rule of law** The English Bill of Rights restated the idea in the Magna Carta that the rule of law is the foundation of legitimate government.

What events contributed to the shift in power from the Crown to Parliament?

32

- **Representative government** The English Bill of Rights established the idea that only representative government is legitimate. In England that meant the representation of social classes in Parliament, or a mixed constitution, composed of the monarchy (the rule of one), the aristocracy in the House of Lords (the rule of the few), and the House of Commons (the rule of the many).

Debates about who should be represented in government would be taken up in America. In the end the Americans would make a key decision by rejecting the feudal idea of representation by social classes, as the English Parliament did, in favor of the idea of social equality.

CRITICAL THINKING EXERCISE

Evaluating the Importance of Habeas Corpus and Trial by Jury

Work in groups to examine the rights of habeas corpus and trial by jury. Each group should read one of the selections below and then answer the questions that accompany it. Discuss your responses with the entire class.

SELECTION 1: HABEAS CORPUS

The writ of habeas corpus has been called the "Great Writ of Liberty." One constitutional scholar called it the "greatest guarantee of human freedom ever devised by man."

Suppose you were arrested and imprisoned by the English monarch. Although you have the right to be tried by the law of the land, the monarch's jailers keep you in prison. They refuse to bring you before a court and to inform you of the charges against you. How could the right to a writ of habeas corpus protect you from such treatment? How could the jailors be forced to bring you into a courtroom for a fair hearing?

Suppose you had a family member, a friend, or a lawyer who knew you had been arrested and were being kept in prison. That person could go to court and ask the judge to issue a writ of habeas corpus. This writ would be an order by the judge to your jailor to bring you to court and present evidence that you have broken the law. If there were evidence, you would be held for trial. If there were no evidence, you would be set free.

EXAMINING THE RIGHT

❶ What limits does the right to a writ of habeas corpus place on the monarch?

How might the right to habeas corpus protect individuals from the abuse of power by government?

❷ Why would the English Parliament want to place such limits on the monarch?

❸ What arguments can you make for this right today?

❹ What examples of situations in the United States or other nations can you identify that uphold or violate this right?

❺ Under what conditions, if any, do you think this right should be limited?

❻ Is this right included in the Constitution of the United States? If so, where can it be found?

SELECTION 2: TRIAL BY JURY

The right to a trial by jury of one's peers is one of the oldest and most important of the fundamental rights of Englishmen. It has become an essential right in a free society.

Suppose you were arrested and imprisoned by the English king. A judge, appointed and paid by the king, has examined the evidence against you and decided that you should be tried for breaking the law.

The English constitution guarantees you the right to be tried by a jury of your peers. This means that a group of people from your community will listen to the evidence that the king's prosecutor has against you. They also will hear your side of the story. The jury has the authority to decide if you are guilty or innocent of breaking the law. Its verdict must be unanimous to find

you guilty. The jury also has the power to find you not guilty—even if you have broken the law—if the jurors believe that the law is unfair.

EXAMINING THE RIGHT

❶ What limits does the right to a trial by jury place on the monarch?

❷ Why would the English Parliament want to place such limits on the monarch?

❸ What arguments can you make for the right to a trial by jury today?

❹ What examples of situations in the United States or other nations can you identify that uphold or violate this right?

❺ Under what conditions, if any, do you think this right should be limited?

❻ Is this right included in the Constitution of the United States? If so, where can it be found?

REVIEWING AND USING THE LESSON

❶ What is the common law of England? Why is it sometimes called "judge-made law"? How did the common law develop?

❷ What is meant by the phrase "rights of Englishmen"? How were these rights established?

33

How might the right to trial by jury protect individuals from the abuse of power by government?

❸ What is the Magna Carta? How was it created? How did it contribute to the development of constitutional government?

❹ One constitutional scholar called the writ of habeas corpus the "greatest guarantee of human freedom ever devised by man." Why is this right so fundamental?

❺ Among the key documents in the struggle for power between king and Parliament were the Petition of Right of 1628, the Habeas Corpus Act of 1679, and the English Bill of Rights of 1689. Explain how and why each of these documents contributed to the development of constitutional government in England.

❻ How are the ideas in the Magna Carta, the Petition of Right, and the English Bill of Rights related to natural rights philosophy and classical republicanism?

❼ What rights and other principles of government in the U.S. Constitution or in your state's constitution can you trace back to the Magna Carta?

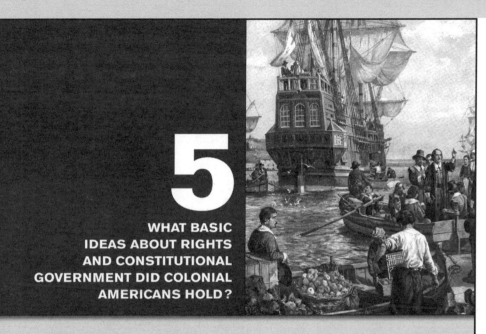

5

WHAT BASIC IDEAS ABOUT RIGHTS AND CONSTITUTIONAL GOVERNMENT DID COLONIAL AMERICANS HOLD?

WHAT BASIC IDEAS ABOUT RIGHTS AND CONSTITUTIONAL GOVERNMENT DID COLONIAL AMERICANS HOLD?

wtpcompanion.civiced.org | **LESSON PURPOSE + TERMS**

Visit the We the People companion website for printable and downloadable Lesson Purposes and Terms and Concepts to Understand sections for each lesson. Audio readings of each Lesson Purpose and Term are also available online in MP3 format.

LESSON PURPOSE

This lesson describes how basic ideas of constitutional government were developed and used in the American colonies before independence from Britain. It explains how social and economic conditions in America sometimes required old ideas about government to be adapted or discarded. Occasionally the colonists needed to create entirely new institutions.

When you have finished this lesson, you should be able to describe the early development of America's traditions of constitutional government. You also should be able to explain why the American colonists attached special importance to such constitutional principles as written guarantees of basic rights and representative government. Finally, you should be able to evaluate, take, and defend positions on the differences between life in colonial America and in England during the same period, the relationship between natural rights theory and slavery in America, and how natural rights philosophy and history help to explain the colonists' views of the proper role of government.

TERMS AND CONCEPTS TO UNDERSTAND

charter	magistrate
constituent	Mayflower Compact
covenant	suffrage
indentured servant	

student page ▾ 36

HOW DID THE COLONIAL SETTLEMENT OF AMERICA INSPIRE NEW EXPERIMENTS IN CONSTITUTIONAL GOVERNMENT?

Two kinds of charters created most of the colonies:

- *Corporate charters* were typically business propositions between Parliament or the Crown and business speculators. Examples include Virginia and Massachusetts.

- *Proprietary charters* usually involved the Crown giving vast tracts of land and full governing authority to "proprietors," usually people owed political or financial debts. Examples include New York, New Jersey, Pennsylvania, Maryland, and the Carolinas.

By the 1690s concern about the colonies' growing independence led to the elimination of proprietary charters and the transformation of most colonies into "royal" colonies subject to British control. In 1776 only two colonies were self-governing, Rhode Island and Connecticut.

HOW DID THE COLONIAL SETTLEMENT OF AMERICA INSPIRE NEW EXPERIMENTS IN CONSTITUTIONAL GOVERNMENT?

More than 150 years elapsed between the time colonists arrived in British North America and 1776, the year when the thirteen colonies gained their independence from Great Britain. This history had a great influence on the Founders.

By the early 1600s England wanted to establish colonies on the North American continent, as Spain and the Netherlands already had done. England had many reasons for wanting colonies in North America. Foremost among these reasons was England's desire to develop a profitable maritime empire. To entice settlers to go to America, the Crown offered various incentives. Two important incentive plans were royal proprietorships and joint-stock companies.

- **Royal proprietorships** One way the Crown encouraged settlements was to create royal provinces in America, called proprietorships. Most proprietors were personal friends of the English king. Proprietors had to find ways to lure settlers to the provinces that the Crown had given them. Eleven of the original thirteen colonies were founded as proprietorships. Perhaps the best-known colonial proprietor was William Penn (1644–1718), the founder of Pennsylvania.

- **Joint-stock companies** The Crown also chartered business ventures called joint-stock companies, giving each company the right to settle certain areas along the East Coast. Each had to attract enough settlers to establish a colony. The Virginia Company of London settled the first successful colony at Jamestown in 1607.

Settlement did not always proceed smoothly. For example, in 1620 after a seven-week voyage from Plymouth, England, under a grant from the Virginia Company of London to settle and establish a government in Virginia, the ship *Mayflower* arrived instead at Cape Cod in what is today the state of Massachusetts, where it had no right to be. Nevertheless, the leaders of the expedition decided before they landed to create a government to serve their needs. The **Mayflower Compact** was an early example of social contract theory put into practice in America. The Compact also laid the foundation for the state of Massachusetts:

❝ We…the loyal subjects of…King James… having undertaken…a Voyage to plant the First Colony in the Northern Parts of Virginia, do by these presents solemnly and mutually in the presence of God and of one another, **Covenant** and Combine ourselves together into a Civil Body Politic, for our better ordering and preservation…and by virtue hereof, to

How did the Mayflower Compact embody the ideas of the social contract and consent?

How did the abundance of cheap and undeveloped land affect economic, social, and political life in colonial America? How might this abundance have resulted in greater economic opportunities for the colonists than for people in Europe?

enact, constitute, and frame such just and equal Laws, Ordinances, Acts, Constitutions, and Offices, from time to time, as shall be thought most meet and convenient for the general good of the Colony, unto which we promise all due submission and obedience.

WHAT WAS UNIQUE ABOUT THE AMERICAN EXPERIENCE?

The special conditions of an undeveloped land profoundly affected economic, social, and political life in colonial America. Land was cheap and especially in New York, Pennsylvania, Virginia, and the Carolinas, readily available. Labor, by contrast, was scarce. Because of the labor shortage indentured servants looked forward to earning their wages and buying land themselves after their period of servitude. An **indentured servant** was a person who sold his or her labor, usually in exchange for the cost of the trip from Europe to the colonies.

Nonindentured and free laborers generally earned higher wages in America than they could earn in Europe. Some of the Southern colonies gave newcomers fifty acres of land if they were able to arrange for their own transportation to the colony.

Cheap land and the high demand for workers meant that American colonists usually had greater opportunities to achieve prosperity than most people in Europe. While some became wealthy, others of course failed, creating a class of American poor. However, over time the great majority of free inhabitants achieved at least moderate prosperity.

Some English practices that protected the landed aristocracy in Great Britain did not survive in the colonies. For example, the English law of entail prohibited the sale or distribution of property beyond male family members. The law of primogeniture required that land be handed down to eldest sons. The colonists paid little attention to these laws, thereby increasing the wide distribution of land in the colonies.

England's rigid class system also was harder to maintain in America. Wealth and family name did not mean automatic success in a land where everyone had to work to survive. Those who came to America without great personal wealth rarely were held back if they were ambitious and hardworking. Carpenters and brick masons, for example, enjoyed only modest social status in England. But the constant demand for new buildings in America allowed such craftsmen to earn a living equal to many of their social superiors. "Well-born" Europeans who considered hard work or manual labor beneath them sometimes had difficulty surviving in the colonies.

The chance to improve one's lot in life became a fundamental ideal of the American experience. Examples abound in colonial America. For instance, one of a candle-maker's seventeen children, Benjamin Franklin (1706–1790), became a great inventor, statesman, and diplomat. An English corset-maker's son, Thomas Paine (1737–1809), arrived in Pennsylvania from England in 1774 and became a famous writer on behalf of the American Revolution. A son of a poor, unwed mother, Alexander Hamilton (1755–1804), became the first secretary of the Treasury of the newly formed United States.

37

student page ▾ 37

WHAT WAS UNIQUE ABOUT THE AMERICAN EXPERIENCE?

Historians take various approaches to the study of colonial America. Some focus on the times when colonies were settled. Others focus on geography, often in terms of regions, such as New England. Geographic groupings highlight the extraordinary diversity among and within the colonies, which in turn sets the stage for understanding the challenges of uniting the states after the Revolution (see the map in the text on page 62).

NEW ENGLAND In 1776 this region included Rhode Island, Connecticut, New Hampshire, and Massachusetts. One of the earliest English settlements was Plymouth, founded in 1620 by Pilgrims fleeing religious persecution in Europe. The Massachusetts Bay Colony was established in 1628 and governed the unsettled territories of Vermont, New Hampshire, and Maine. In 1636 Roger Williams, banished from Massachusetts, founded the Providence Colony in Rhode Island, and the Connecticut Colony also was begun.

Small, independent farming was common in New England. But much of the soil was rocky, the terrain was mountainous, and growing seasons were short. Some colonists traded animal pelts and other items. Harbors and fish were plentiful along the coasts where large trading ports, such as Boston, developed. The first confederation among European settlers occurred in 1649 after a war with the Pequot Indians. The colonies of Massachusetts Bay, Plymouth, New Haven, and Connecticut formed the United Colonies of New England to provide for common defense in wars with Native Americans, Dutch New Netherlands, and Spanish and French colonies to the south and north respectively. The confederation lost its influence when Massachusetts refused to commit to a war against the Dutch.

MIDDLE In 1776 this region included Delaware, New York, New Jersey, and Pennsylvania. First settled by the Dutch and Swedish, this area early housed the most socially diverse population in the colonies, including Scots-Irish, Danes, English Quakers, Portuguese, French, Germans, Welsh, and Italians. More cosmopolitan, commercial, and tolerant than the New England colonies, these middle colonies provided some of the first experiments with religious pluralism as well as utopian experiments, such as William Penn's "holy experiment." Philadelphia and New York were major commercial hubs and ports for international trade. Large-scale farming was common in the region, as was trade and commerce.

SOUTHERN In 1776 this region included Maryland, Virginia, North Carolina, South Carolina, and Georgia. Predominantly rural, these southern colonies had economic and social structures based on a combination of great plantations and yeoman farmers. Owners of plantations supported by slave labor held the most political power. The region's crops included tobacco, indigo, and rice. The last in particular depended on the skills and experience of slaves. Life in the southern colonies was more aristocratic than in other colonies. Some areas—for example, the vicinity of Charleston, South Carolina—complemented farming with trade and commerce. Dense forests provided some of the best shipbuilding materials in the world.

It also should be noted that the enslaved population in the colonies was diverse. A typical slave might meet more Africans from different parts of Africa in a single day in a South Carolina rice field than in a lifetime in Africa.

student page ▼ 38

WHAT RIGHTS BECAME PART OF COLONIAL CHARTERS?

wtpcompanion.civiced.org   **PRIMARY SOURCES**

Visit the We the People companion website for a link to the Massachusetts Body of Liberties of 1641.

WHAT RIGHTS BECAME PART OF COLONIAL CHARTERS?

King James I gave the Virginia Company a royal charter, which granted the company permission to settle Jamestown. A **charter** is a written document from a government or a ruler that grants certain rights. The royal charter granted to the Virginia Company promised that

  ❝ The Persons…which shall dwell…within every or any of the said several Colonies and Plantations, and every of their children… shall HAVE and enjoy all Liberties, Franchises, and Immunities…as if they had been abiding and born, within this our Realm of England, or any other of our said Dominions.

Similar guarantees appeared in the royal charters establishing Massachusetts, Maryland, and other colonies. Such guarantees echoed the ideals of the Magna Carta—that all Englishmen, wherever they went, enjoyed certain basic rights.

This tradition of expressing rights in writing became an essential part of American constitutions. The Massachusetts Body of Liberties of 1641, for example, provided for the rule of law and protection of basic rights of persons living in that colony against any abuse of power by a **magistrate** or judge of the colony. In addition to echoing the Magna Carta in some respects, this document was America's first bill of rights. It provided among other things that

  ❝ No man shall be arrested, restrayned, banished nor anyways punished…unless by vertue of some express laws of the country warranting the same.

The Body of Liberties also guaranteed trial by jury, free elections, and the right of free men to own property. It prohibited government from taking private property without just compensation, from forcing witnesses to testify against themselves (self-incrimination), and from imposing cruel and unusual punishments. Although the Body of Liberties limited **suffrage**, or the right to vote, in Massachusetts, it granted certain political rights to those who did not enjoy the voting franchise, including the right to petition the government for the redress of grievances.

Guarantees of basic rights later appeared in other colonies. Pennsylvania, for example, guaranteed such rights as freedom from arrest except for "probable cause" and trial by a jury of one's peers and the right against taxation without representation, as did other colonies. But Pennsylvania was the first colony to guarantee freedom of conscience—"the rights of conscience."

WHAT DO YOU THINK?

❶ If you had been offered the opportunity to come to America as an indentured servant, do you think you would have done so? Why or why not?

❷ What do you think were the most important differences between life in England and life in the American colonies? How did those differences shape early American governments?

❸ Were the differences between theories of representation in colonial America and England significant? Why or why not?

❹ Social classes developed quickly in the American colonies but were based on wealth rather than birth. Does the distinction matter? Why or why not?

What were some of the basic ideas contained in the Massachusetts Body of Liberties?

WHO DID NOT BENEFIT FROM THE RIGHTS EXPRESSED IN COLONIAL DOCUMENTS?

Not all Americans enjoyed the rights secured in colonial charters and other documents. For example, in some colonies the right to vote or hold office was restricted to Protestant white men. In others such rights were restricted to those who belonged to the colony's official state or established church.

As in England and elsewhere, women were not granted political rights. Colonial laws limited their right to own property and to manage their own legal and personal affairs. Laws varied among the colonies, but married women usually had the legal status of underage children. They lost most of their legal identity to their husbands under a legal doctrine called coverture. According to English law,

  " Husband and wife are one person...
    the very being or legal existence of the
    woman is suspended during the marriage.

Between one-half and two-thirds of all immigrants to the colonies came as indentured servants. Most were bound to masters for periods ranging from a few years to decades. The status of many indentured servants was not much better than that of slaves until their period of indenture ended.

Native Americans also did not enjoy the rights expressed in colonial documents. Like the Spanish and French before them, British settlers treated Indian tribes as foreign entities. They were removed from their lands when necessary for colonial expansion and dealt with through treaties at other times.

The most glaring example of the failure to extend the rights and privileges to all was the institution of racial slavery. African slavery was well established in the American colonies by the eighteenth century. Slaves, who made up twenty percent of the population in 1760, were treated as property and thus were denied basic human rights.

What principles of the Declaration of Independence were violated by slavery?

Why do you suppose the right to vote was usually limited to men who owned property?

CRITICAL THINKING EXERCISE
**Using Natural Rights Philosophy
to Address the Problem of Slavery**

Consider this situation. Some 325,000 of the 1.6 million people living in the colonies in 1760 were enslaved Africans. Slavery flourished in the plantation economy of the Southern colonies, as it did in the British and French West Indies and in South America. Slavery was legally recognized in all thirteen British North American colonies. New York City had a significant slave population, as did New England.

There was some active opposition to slavery among the population of free citizens as well as among the slaves themselves. Some opponents sought its peaceful abolition, while others were willing to use violent or illegal means.

As explained in an earlier lesson, natural rights philosophy emphasizes both human equality and the protection of private property. Both slave owners and abolitionists in the colonies and in Great Britain could point to natural rights philosophy for support. Which side had the stronger argument? Why?

student page ▾ 40–41

WHAT BASIC IDEAS OF CONSTITUTIONAL GOVERNMENT DID THE COLONIAL GOVERNMENTS USE?

Governments in the colonies varied widely. Colonial governors usually represented the Crown or the proprietor, but governors also had responsibilities to the people. Colonial governors typically had extensive powers, which encompassed commanding the militia, convening or dissolving the legislature, and vetoing laws that the governor viewed as unwise. The one significant check on governors' powers was that they could not spend public money without legislative approval.

In all the colonies except Pennsylvania and Georgia the legislature—sometimes called the "general court"—was bicameral, consisting of a council and an assembly. Councils ranged from three members in Maryland to twenty-eight in Massachusetts. The same authority that appointed the governor appointed councilors. Usually councilors were wealthy men residing in the colony. Councils advised governors, served as the upper house of colonial legislatures, and often served as judges.

Qualified voters of the colony elected assemblies, or lower houses of the legislature. Assemblies typically exercised budget and tax powers, but their laws could be vetoed by the governor or set aside by the Crown. As the Revolution neared, issues of taxation led to the greatest conflicts between Britain and the colonies. Starting about 1670 colonies had "agents" in England to look after their interests, including commercial concerns and issues of local government. Some agents, such as Benjamin Franklin, represented more than one colony.

wtpcompanion.civiced.org | **PRIMARY SOURCES**

Visit the We the People companion website for a link to the Fundamental Orders of Connecticut.

What branches of government were established by the Fundamental Orders of Connecticut?

WHAT BASIC IDEAS OF CONSTITUTIONAL GOVERNMENT DID THE COLONIAL GOVERNMENTS USE?

As previously explained, the English colonies originated with charters issued by the Crown. In general the structure of colonial governments consisted of

- A governor, who was the proprietor, or someone else appointed by the Crown

- A council of between three and thirty landholders that advised the governor and in some circumstances served as the highest court of the colony

- An assembly elected by the people that had a say in matters of taxation

Beyond these rudimentary structures Crown charters usually offered few details about how local governments should function. As a result America became a fertile ground for constitution-making and governmental innovation.

In 1636 colonists in several Massachusetts towns received permission to move west into the Connecticut Valley. Three years later those settlers adopted the Fundamental Orders of Connecticut. The Orders derived authority from all free men living in these towns. This colonial constitution helped to establish the American preference for written constitutions. The Fundamental Orders of Connecticut established a central legislative assembly, a governor, and courts. As was the custom, voting was limited to white male property owners. Other colonies also experimented with writing constitutions in the years that followed.

Some of the early written constitutions were successful. Others failed or had to be revised. The forms of colonial government varied from colony to colony. However, all constitutions shared certain basic principles, including the following:

- **Fundamental rights** The colonists were concerned foremost with protecting the common law rights that they brought with them from England. At first colonists understood these rights as the ancient and fundamental rights of Englishmen. As the Revolution neared, the colonists increasingly understood their rights to life, liberty, and property in terms of natural rights philosophy.

- **Rule of law** To protect their fundamental rights, the colonists insisted on the creation of a government of laws under which those responsible for making and enforcing the laws had to obey the laws and could not exercise power arbitrarily.

- **Representative government and the right to vote** One of the most important constitutional developments was the growth of representative government. The first representative assembly in the colonies met in Virginia in 1619. The right of colonists to elect representatives to colonial legislatures was one device for enticing settlers to come to America. Representative assemblies reduced the possibility that royal governors would violate the people's rights. The legislatures would respond to the needs and interests of the people. The creation of representative assemblies also established the principle of no taxation without representation.

- **Separation of powers** Colonial governments typically provided for the exercise of three kinds of governmental power. Separation of powers was evident in the following ways:

  - **Legislatures** All the colonies had legislatures or assemblies that over time assumed greater responsibility for making laws. All but Pennsylvania adopted the structure of Parliament, with "lower" and "upper" houses. Pennsylvania adopted a unicameral, or one-house, legislature. Members of the upper house were either appointed by the governor or elected by the most wealthy property owners of the colony. All the men in the colony who owned a certain amount of property elected members of the lower house. The colonial legislatures eventually became the strongest of the three branches of government.

  - **Governors** Governors were responsible for carrying out and enforcing laws. They also were concerned with ensuring that the colonies were governed in a manner consistent with English law and tradition. The British monarch chose the governors, or the governors were the proprietors. Only in Connecticut and Rhode Island were the governors elected.

  - **Courts** Courts were created to administer local justice and to preside over the trials of those accused of breaking local laws. Judges were required to follow strict rules of procedure. Some colonies created a two-tiered system of trial and appeals courts.

HOW DID COLONIAL GOVERNMENTS BECOME MORE REPRESENTATIVE THAN THE GOVERNMENT IN BRITAIN?

American colonists believed that the security of life and liberty depended on the security of property, which explains in part the property requirement for full political rights, such as voting. If one of the purposes of government was to protect property, it seemed reasonable to many Americans to limit suffrage to those who possessed at least some land.

Owning fifty acres of land was a typical property requirement for voting in the colonies. Land was relatively easy to obtain, and so the body of eligible voters in America was proportionally larger than in England. Colonial legislatures accordingly were more broadly representative.

Unlike in England, colonial elections usually offered the voters a choice of competing candidates for office. Colonial legislators usually served shorter terms than members of Parliament, who faced election only once in seven years.

What were some of the differences between members of colonial legislatures and members of Parliament?

Colonial legislators also were required to live in the districts they represented. They were considered to be the voices, or agents, of the people, or their constituents. A **constituent** is a person represented by an elected official. And so, colonial legislators were responsible for ensuring that the legislature knew about the needs and interests of their constituents. By contrast, in 1776 members of the British Parliament did not have to live in the districts they represented and often had little understanding of the needs of their constituents. Instead, they were charged to represent the interests of the nation as a whole.

What were some of the similarities between colonial legislatures and Parliament?

WHAT DO YOU THINK?

❶ What do you think is the best way to explain the American colonists' views of government? Is social contract theory or historical circumstance more important? Why?

❷ What conflicts, if any, do you see between social contract theory and the status of women, indentured servants, and slaves in eighteenth-century America? What might explain those conflicts?

❸ Does American colonial history help to provide context for understanding any contemporary issues in American politics and government? If so, which ones? If not, why not?

❹ Do you think the same degree of social and economic opportunity exists for immigrants to America today as existed for the colonists? What has remained the same? What has changed?

REVIEWING AND USING THE LESSON

❶ What was the Mayflower Compact? Why was it drafted? How could it be said to reflect the idea that government should be based on consent of the governed?

❷ In what ways were eighteenth-century American and British societies similar and different in terms of the rights of individual liberty, equality of opportunity, suffrage, and property?

❸ How would you describe the economic, social, and political conditions of life in colonial America? How did these conditions affect the development of American ideas about government?

❹ How did the simple governing structures in colonial charters evolve into more comprehensive systems of local government before the Revolution?

❺ What basic features of English constitutionalism were found in the governments of the colonies?

❻ Why was the right to vote in the colonies limited to those who owned a certain amount of property? Why were colonial governments more representative than the British government?

❼ Why were written guarantees of rights in colonial documents important to the development of Americans' ideas about government?

❽ Are written guarantees of rights as important today as they were in colonial times? Why or why not?

6

WHY DID AMERICAN COLONISTS WANT TO FREE THEMSELVES FROM GREAT BRITAIN?

WHY DID AMERICAN COLONISTS WANT TO FREE THEMSELVES FROM GREAT BRITAIN?

wtpcompanion.civiced.org | **LESSON PURPOSE + TERMS**

Visit the We the People companion website for printable and downloadable Lesson Purposes and Terms and Concepts to Understand sections for each lesson. Audio readings of each Lesson Purpose and Term are also available online in MP3 format.

LESSON PURPOSE

The growth of the American colonies raised issues with the parent country, Great Britain, that were difficult to resolve peacefully. This lesson describes the circumstances that produced the Declaration of Independence and the major ideas about government and natural rights included in that document.

When you have finished this lesson, you should be able to describe the British policies that some American colonists believed violated basic principles of constitutional government and their rights as Englishmen. You also should be able to explain why Americans resisted those policies and how that resistance led to the Declaration of Independence. You should be able to evaluate the arguments that the colonists made to justify separation from Great Britain. Finally, you should be able to evaluate, take, and defend positions on violations of colonists' rights before the Revolution and important questions about the meaning and implications of the Declaration of Independence.

TERMS AND CONCEPTS TO UNDERSTAND

compact

law of nature

sovereignty

writs of assistance

`student page ▾ 44`

HOW DID BRITAIN'S POLICY TOWARD THE COLONIES CHANGE?

One of the challenges facing the Crown was how to keep its American colonies loyal. One theory was to let the colonies flourish with as few restrictions as possible. For much of the seventeenth century England did so. It failed to establish and enforce a coherent imperial policy. This was a period of benign or salutary (healthy) neglect, during which the colonies became accustomed to considerable self-government.

The term *salutary neglect* came from a speech by Edmund Burke in the House of Commons in 1775:

> When I know that the colonies in general owe little or nothing to any care of ours, and that they are not squeezed into this happy form by the constraints of watchful and suspicious government, but that, through a wise and salutary neglect, a generous nature has been suffered to take her own way to perfection; when I reflect upon these effects, when I see how profitable they have been to us, I feel all the pride of power sink, and all presumption in the wisdom of human contrivances melt, and die away within me.

SEVEN YEARS' WAR (1756–1763)   Because it was the first war in human history to be fought around the globe, Winston Churchill called the Seven Years' War the first "world war." The beginnings of the war involved the French and Indian War (1754–1763), referring to Britain's two main enemies in North America. The Seven Years' War between France and Britain concluded with the Treaty of Paris in 1763, which ended the dream of a New France in North America and marked the start of British efforts to assert greater control over the colonies.

PROCLAMATION ACT (1763)   The impetus of this act was financial. It did not arise from a desire to protect Native Americans. Indian warfare was costly, and England did not want to deploy troops to the west of its colonies to keep peace. The proclamation also was intended to concentrate colonial settlements on the seaboard, where they could be active in the British mercantile system. If settlements moved west of the Appalachians, they would be more independent and less likely to trade with England.

STAMP ACT (1765)   The Seven Years' War left the British so badly in debt that taxes had to be raised substantially, leading to threats of revolt in England. The Stamp Act was Parliament's first serious attempt to exercise financial control over the colonies by imposing a direct, internal tax. Benjamin Franklin, a colonial agent in Britain, testified about colonial attitudes toward the proposal:

> I never heard any objection to the right of laying duties to regulate commerce; but a right to lay internal taxes was never supposed to be in Parliament, as we are not represented there.

HOW DID BRITAIN'S POLICY TOWARD THE COLONIES CHANGE?

Generations of colonists had grown used to little interference from the British government in their affairs. After 1763, however, several factors caused the British to exert more control over the American colonies than they had done in the previous 150 years. Britain had incurred large debts to gain its victory over the French in the Seven Years' War of 1756–1763. The British government was under heavy pressure to reduce taxes at home. To the British ministers this meant that the American colonists should pay a fair share of the war debt, especially because much of that debt had been incurred in protecting the colonists.

Between 1763 and 1776 Britain tried to increase its control of the colonies. For example, the Proclamation Act (1763) forbade colonial authorities to allow settlement on Indian lands west of the Appalachian Mountains. The act aimed at reducing the costs of protecting colonists from wars that the colonists provoked with Native Americans. To raise revenue the British government also increased its control of trade. The Stamp Act (1765) introduced a new tax on the colonists by imposing duties on stamps needed for official documents. At the same time Parliament passed the first Quartering Act (1765), which required colonists to shelter British troops in their homes—a common practice in England. To the British these measures seemed reasonable and moderate.

WHY DID THE COLONISTS RESIST BRITISH CONTROL?

Although some colonists accepted the new taxes and other controls, many resisted. New trade restrictions and taxes meant that some colonists would lose money. Perhaps more important, the new regulations challenged the colonists' understanding of representative government. In the previous century John Locke had written that

> ❝ The supreme power cannot take from any man part of his property without his own consent…that is, the consent of the majority, giving it either by themselves or their representatives chosen by them.

(Second Treatise, 1689)

The colonists agreed with Locke. They thought that tax laws should be passed only in their own colonial legislatures, in which they were represented. No taxation without representation had become an established belief of settlers in the American colonies.

Small groups in each colony became convinced that only large crowds prepared to act forcefully could successfully resist the Stamp Act. Leaders in Connecticut dubbed their followers the Sons of Liberty. The name spread rapidly, coming to stand for everyone who participated in the popular resistance. Although the Sons of Liberty rarely sought violence, they engaged in political agitation that tended to precipitate crowd action.

Why do you suppose the British government required colonists to shelter troops in their homes?

44

In October 1765 representatives from the colonies met in the Stamp Act Congress to organize resistance—the first such intercolonial gathering in American history. In March 1766 Parliament repealed the Stamp Act but passed the Declaratory Act, asserting Great Britain's full power and authority over the colonies. A little more than a year later, in June 1767, Parliament passed the Townshend Revenue Acts, which levied new taxes on items such as tea, paper, and glass. In response a group of American women calling themselves the Daughters of Liberty led boycotts of English goods and committed themselves to producing cloth and other staples that would help the colonies become economically independent from England.

Parliament also gave new powers to revenue officials. **Writs of assistance,** or general warrants, gave these officials broad authority to search and seize colonial property. Colonists charged with various crimes were transported to Nova Scotia or England for trials that were frequently delayed.

The British sent troops to the colonies to maintain order and facilitate tax collection. In 1770 a conflict broke out between British troops and colonists in Boston, resulting in the so-called Boston Massacre. Five colonists were killed. This incident helped to convince many Americans that the British government was prepared to use military force to coerce the colonists into obedience. Although the Townshend Acts were repealed in 1770, the Tea Act in 1773 reasserted Parliament's right to tax the colonists and led to the Boston Tea Party. This name was given to the event in 1773 when colonists, dressed as Mohawk Indians, boarded

What was the principal argument the colonists made against the Stamp Act and similar acts of the British Parliament?

three British ships and dumped forty-five tons of tea into Boston Harbor. The British government responded with what colonists called the Intolerable Acts, a series of Punitive Acts (as the British called them) that, among other things, closed Boston Harbor to all trade. These measures attacked representative government by altering the Massachusetts charter to give more power to the new royal governor, limit town meetings, weaken the court system, and authorize British troops to occupy the colony.

CRITICAL THINKING EXERCISE
Identifying Violations of Rights

Put yourself in the colonists' shoes. Each of the following situations is based on the experiences of colonists in America. Each has at least one British violation of a right that Americans thought they should have. If you had been an American colonist at the time, what rights would you claim on the basis of such experiences?

❶ Your name is Mary Strong. You have lived in Charlestown most of your life and have definite feelings about how Massachusetts is being governed. When you speak your mind freely, you find yourself arrested and put in an iron device that fits over your head like a mask to prevent you from talking.

❷ Your name is Elsbeth Merrill. While you were baking bread this afternoon and awaiting the return of your husband, an agent of the king arrived to inform you that you must shelter four British soldiers in your home.

❸ Your name is Lemuel Adams. You have a warehouse full of goods near Boston Harbor. The king's magistrate gives British officials a writ of assistance that permits them to search homes, stores, and warehouses near the harbor to look for evidence of smuggling.

❹ Your name is James Otis. You represent colonists who have been imprisoned and are being denied their right to a trial by a jury from their own communities. You argue that denying their traditional rights as Englishmen is illegal because it violates the principles of the British constitution. The royal magistrate denies your request and sends the prisoners to England for trial.

❺ Your name is William Bradford. You have been arrested and your printing press in Philadelphia has been destroyed because you printed an article criticizing the deputy governor. In the article you said the governor was like "a large cocker spaniel about five foot five."

The act set duties (taxes) on "every skin or piece of vellum or parchment, or sheet or piece of paper" used for transacting business and trade—fifty-four kinds of documents in all. To be legally binding, documents affected by the Stamp Act had to be recorded, or stamped, in Britain. Proceeds were earmarked for the support of British soldiers protecting the colonies. Violators were tried in vice-admiralty courts, which did not use jury trials.

QUARTERING ACT (1765) British commanders found it difficult to get colonial assemblies to pay for housing (quartering) and supplying British troops during the French and Indian War. In response Parliament enacted this statute, which provided that Britain would house its soldiers in American barracks and public houses ("pubs"). However, if that was not adequate, then they would be housed in "inns, livery stables, ale houses, victualing houses, and the houses of sellers of wine and houses of persons selling of rum, brandy, strong water, cider or metheglin" and, if numbers required, in "uninhabited houses, outhouses, barns, or other buildings." The act also required colonial assemblies to contribute food and alcohol and to provide for "fire, candles, vinegar, salt, bedding, and utensils" for the soldiers "without paying anything for the same."

student page ▼ 44–45

WHY DID THE COLONISTS RESIST BRITISH CONTROL?

Opposition, in particular to the Stamp Act, arose in three forms. Informal opposition to the Stamp Act included publications, such as James Otis's pamphlet *The Rights of the British Colonies Asserted and Proved*, and agreements among shopkeepers not to import or sell British goods.

Official opposition was stronger. One example is Congress's fourteen-point Declaration of Rights and Grievances. This declaration asserted that only colonial assemblies had the right to tax the colonies, that colonists had a right to trial by jury, that colonists possessed all the rights of Englishmen, and that Parliament could not represent the colonies because the colonies lacked voting rights.

A third form of resistance was crowd action, such as riots to intimidate tax agents and to solidify popular opposition.

The word *congress,* meaning "people's coming together" or "a meeting or interview," first appeared in a 1528 book. As "a formal meeting or assembly of delegates or representatives," the term was first used in 1678. It has the same root as the words *congregation* and *congregational,* familiar religious terms.

Writs of assistance are also known as general warrants. See Lesson 31 for a discussion of writs of assistance.

BOSTON MASSACRE On the night of March 5, 1770, a mob of men and boys in Boston began taunting a British sentry standing guard at the city's customs house. When eight British soldiers came to the sentry's aid, a riot broke out and shots were fired. Four colonists were killed, six were wounded, and another would die four days later. The next day British troops were withdrawn from the center of Boston to a fort on Castle Island in Boston Harbor. The British soldiers who allegedly fired the shots were indicted for murder.

Colonists such as Paul Revere used the Boston Massacre to harden public opinion against the British. Within days he circulated a print depicting the episode as a slaughter of innocent colonists by British tyrants. Samuel Adams called the event "bloody butchery."

Lawyer John Adams, who a year before had defended four American sailors charged with killing a British naval officer, agreed to defend the British soldiers and their captain, Thomas Preston. Preston was acquitted. Six of the soldiers were later acquitted; two were convicted of manslaughter, for which they were branded on their thumbs.

Reflecting on these trials in his later years, Adams wrote,

> The part I took in defense of Cptn. Preston and the Soldiers, procured me anxiety, and obloquy [abusive language] enough. It was, however, one of the most gallant, generous, manly and disinterested actions of my whole life, and one of the best pieces of service I ever rendered my country. Judgement of death against those soldiers would have been as foul a stain upon this country as the executions of the Quakers or Witches, anciently. As the evidence was, the verdict of the jury was exactly right.

`student page ▾ 46`

HOW DID THE COLONISTS ORGANIZE TO RESIST BRITISH CONTROL?

The colonists labeled the acts of Parliament aimed at raising revenue and asserting control over the colonies "Intolerable Acts" or "Coercive Acts." Like the Stamp Act Congress, the First Continental Congress was called to respond to these acts. Some delegates urged reconciliation with Britain. Others contended that relations with Britain were already severed and a new system of government should be created.

The First Continental Congress adopted the Articles of Association, under which colonies agreed to boycott British goods. It also called for a Second Continental Congress to meet in May 1775. The Second Continental Congress adopted the Declaration of Independence and the Articles of Confederation.

HOW DID THE COLONISTS ORGANIZE TO RESIST BRITISH CONTROL?

Colonists formed "committees of correspondence" to publicize colonial opposition and coordinate resistance. In the fall of 1774 each colony except Georgia sent representatives to a meeting in Philadelphia to decide the best response to the actions of the British government. The meeting was the First Continental Congress. Benjamin Franklin drafted a resolution for the congress, which stated that "there is a manifest defect in the constitution of the British Empire in respect to the government of the colonies upon those principles of liberty which form an essential part of that constitution." The delegates to the First Continental Congress voted to impose a ban on colonial trade with Great Britain. Their goal was to force Great Britain to change its policies, but British officials considered the trade ban an irresponsible defiance of authority and ordered the arrest of some of the leading colonists in Massachusetts.

What action by the British led to Paul Revere's famous ride?

46

By this time many of the more radical colonists, especially in New England, were beginning to prepare for war against Great Britain. They believed that it was the right of the people to overthrow the central government because it no longer protected the colonists' rights. These colonists formed a civilian militia, which was called the Minutemen because this force was to be ready at a minute's notice to respond to the British attack that everyone expected.

On April 19, 1775, some seven hundred British troops tried to march to Concord, Massachusetts, where they had heard that the Minutemen had hidden arms and ammunition. Among other things they planned to arrest Samuel Adams and John Hancock, two colonial patriot leaders. Paul Revere and William Dawes alerted the colonists by riding through the countryside, warning people that the British were about to attack. Adams and Hancock escaped. On that day at the towns of Lexington and Concord, war broke out between seventy-five Minutemen and the British troops. The "shot heard round the world" had been fired.

WHAT WAS THE PURPOSE OF THE DECLARATION OF INDEPENDENCE?

The battles of Lexington and Concord began the war between America and Britain. In August 1775 Britain declared the colonies to be in a state of rebellion. In November 1775 the king formally withdrew his protection. That winter Thomas Paine's pamphlet, *Common Sense*, turned colonial opinion toward the idea of independence. And by the spring of 1776 it appeared to many that independence was the only solution to the colonists' problems. On June 7, 1776, Richard Henry Lee (1732–1794) of Virginia introduced a resolution in the Continental Congress asserting "that these United Colonies are, and of right ought to be, free and independent states, that they are absolved from all allegiance to the British Crown, and that all political connection between them and the state of Great Britain is, and ought to be, totally dissolved." The congress appointed a committee of five to prepare a declaration of independence.

Thomas Jefferson (1743–1826) wrote the first draft of the Declaration of Independence. It announced the final, momentous step in the colonists' resistance to the British government by rejecting the **sovereignty**, or authority, of the Crown. Rebelling against the sovereignty of the government to which the colonists and generations of their forebears had sworn allegiance and from which they had sought protection for many years was a serious matter. Members of the Continental Congress believed that it was important to justify this action to other nations and to identify the basic principles of legitimate government to win sympathy and active support. Thus a formal declaration was seen as essential.

How might signing the Declaration of Independence have endangered the Framers?

WHAT WERE THE MAIN IDEAS AND ARGUMENTS OF THE DECLARATION?

The Declaration of Independence is a prime example of the colonists' ideas about government and their complaints about British rule. It does not make an appeal on behalf of the king's loyal subjects to the fundamental rights of Englishmen. Instead, the Declaration renounces the monarchy itself and appeals to those natural rights common to people everywhere. It asserts that sovereignty—the ultimate governing authority—resides with the people, with those who are members of a politically organized community.

The complete text of the Declaration of Independence is in the Reference section. Following are its most important ideas and arguments:

- **Natural rights** The rights of the people are based on a higher law than laws made by humans. The existence of these rights is "self-evident." They are given by "the Laws of Nature and Nature's God" and are "unalienable." In natural rights philosophy the **law of nature** contains universally obligatory standards of justice and would prevail in the absence of man-made law. Neither constitutions nor governments can violate this higher law. If a government deprives the people of their natural rights, then the people have the right to change or abolish that government and to form a new government.

- **Human equality** Humans are equal in the sense that neither God nor nature has appointed some at birth to rule over others. Thus humans are politically equal. To be legitimate, the right to rule must be based on agreement, or a **compact**, among equal civic members.

- **Government by consent** Such a compact once existed between the colonists and Great Britain. By the terms of this compact the colonists consented to be governed by British law as long as the central authority protected their rights to "Life, Liberty, and the Pursuit of Happiness."

- **"A long Train of Abuses"** King George III violated the compact by repeatedly acting with Parliament to deprive the colonists of those rights that he was supposed to protect. These violations and other abuses of power showed a design to reduce government of the colonies to "absolute Tyranny." Specifically, the Declaration charged that the king was

  - Seeking to destroy the authority of the colonial legislatures by dissolving some and refusing to approve the laws passed by others

  - Obstructing the administration of justice by refusing to approve laws for support of the colonial judiciary and making judges dependent on his will alone

student page ▾ 46

WHAT WAS THE PURPOSE OF THE DECLARATION OF INDEPENDENCE?

Several New England colonies advocated separation from Great Britain ahead of the middle and southern colonies. Congress voted against independence on July 6, 1775. Rhode Island was the first to declare independence—on May 4, 1776. The declaration became unanimous only when New York gave its agreement on July 9, 1776.

wtpcompanion.civiced.org PRIMARY SOURCES

Visit the We the People companion website for a link to Jefferson's original draft of the Declaration of Independence and editorial changes made to it.

ENRICHMENT ACTIVITIES

A. DEBATING WHETHER ACTS OF PARLIAMENT VIOLATED COLONISTS' RIGHTS

Divide the class into two or more groups and ask half of the groups to imagine that they are living in the American colonies in the 1770s. Each group should write a speech that could have been delivered in one of the colonial legislatures detailing why the group believes that laws passed by the British Parliament violate their rights.

Ask the other groups to imagine that they are members of the British Parliament. Each of these groups should write a short speech arguing why the laws to which the colonists object are not only necessary but reasonable.

The groups should present their speeches to the class and then engage in debate.

B. EXAMINING THE "SELF-EVIDENT TRUTH" THAT ALL MEN ARE CREATED EQUAL

One of the "self-evident truths" proclaimed in the Declaration of Independence is that "all men are created equal." This assertion not only aroused great controversy at the time it was written but continues to provoke debate today. When the Declaration was first published in England, an indignant member of Parliament sputtered,

> In what way are they equal? Is it in size, strength, understanding, figure, moral or civil accomplishments, or situation in life?

> [The Americans] have…introduced their self-evident truth either through ignorance or by design with a self-evident falsehood, since I will defy any American rebel, or any of their patriotic retainers here in England, to point out to me any two men throughout the whole world of whom it may with truth be said, that they are equal.

Ask students to join with two or three others. Have them consider the questions that follow, then write a short response to the member of Parliament described above that expresses their understanding of the "self-evident truth" that "all men are created equal."

Ask students to consider one or more of the following:

❶ In what ways are all human beings alike? In what ways do or should those similarities affect their equality?

❷ Thomas Jefferson recognized that there was diversity of talents in any society. He insisted, however, that in a republic all men are equally capable of contributing to the good of the community. Do you agree? Why? What examples from your own community can you cite to support your position?

❸ Since the Declaration of Independence was written, various groups have used the "truth" that "all men are created equal" to seize the moral high ground in public debate. Among these groups were women, workers, farmers, abolitionists, and civil rights activists. Choose one of these groups and research how the group used this "truth" to further its cause. Share your findings with the class.

- Keeping standing armies among the people in time of peace without the approval of the colonial legislatures
- Quartering soldiers among the civilian population
- Imposing taxes without consent of those taxed
- Depriving colonists of the right to trial by a jury of their peers
- Altering colonial charters, abolishing laws, and fundamentally changing the constitutions of colonial governments
- **Right of revolution** "Whenever any Form of Government becomes destructive of those Ends" for which government is created, it is the right of the people to "alter or to abolish it" and to create a new government that will serve those ends. The colonists had the right to withdraw their consent to be governed by Great Britain and to establish their own government as "Free and Independent States…absolved from all Allegiance to the British Crown."

How did the colonists justify their revolution against Great Britain?

WHAT DO YOU THINK?

❶ The Declaration of Independence states that people have a right to abolish their government. When is revolution necessary? Are a "long Train of Abuses and Usurpations" required for revolution to be legitimate? Why or why not?

❷ In what ways does the Declaration of Independence reflect John Locke's social contract theory? In what ways does it reflect principles of classical republicanism?

❸ To whom is the Declaration of Independence addressed? Why do you think the drafters of the document would be attentive to "the Opinions of Mankind?"

❹ Despite the fact that Jefferson owned slaves, he denounced slavery and the slave trade in his draft of the Declaration. After Southerners objected, the Congress deleted the passage. Search for the rough draft of the Declaration of Independence on the Internet. What do you think are the most significant differences between the rough draft and the final Declaration, and why do you think changes were made?

REVIEWING AND USING THE LESSON

❶ How would you describe British policies toward the colonies before the 1750s? How and why did those policies change in the 1760s and 1770s?

❷ What were the colonists' major objections to British policies in the 1760s? What rights did the colonists claim that those policies violated?

❸ What is meant by the term *sovereignty*? How was sovereignty a disputed matter between Great Britain and the colonies?

❹ What are the basic ideas and arguments set forth in the Declaration of Independence?

❺ What problems identified in the Declaration would have to be corrected for governments created after American independence to be legitimate?

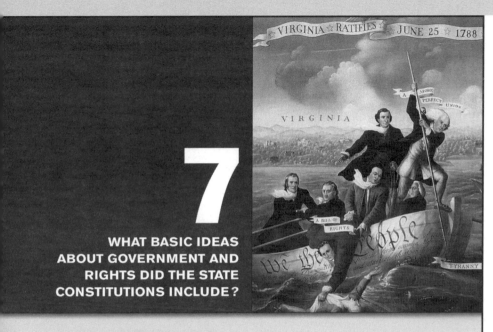

7

WHAT BASIC IDEAS ABOUT GOVERNMENT AND RIGHTS DID THE STATE CONSTITUTIONS INCLUDE?

WHAT BASIC IDEAS ABOUT GOVERNMENT AND RIGHTS DID THE STATE CONSTITUTIONS INCLUDE?

wtpcompanion.civiced.org | **LESSON PURPOSE + TERMS**

Visit the We the People companion website for printable and downloadable Lesson Purposes and Terms and Concepts to Understand sections for each lesson. Audio readings of each Lesson Purpose and Term are also available online in MP3 format.

LESSON PURPOSE

After declaring independence the Founders designed new state governments to protect individual rights and to promote the common good. This lesson shows how the constitution of Massachusetts in particular was designed to achieve these ends. State constitutions also contained bills or declarations of rights. These guarantees of rights, for which Virginia's Declaration of Rights served as a model, had a great influence on the development of the U.S. Bill of Rights.

When you have finished this lesson, you should be able to explain the basic ideas about government and rights that are included in state constitutions. You also should be able to explain how the experiences of the states in developing their constitutions and bills of rights influenced the framing of the U.S. Constitution and Bill of Rights. Finally, you should be able to evaluate, take, and defend positions on the theory of legislative supremacy, the importance of the Virginia Declaration of Rights, and the role of declarations of rights in early state constitutions.

TERMS AND CONCEPTS TO UNDERSTAND

checks and balances

legislative supremacy

veto

student page ▼ 50–51

WHAT BASIC IDEAS DID THE STATE CONSTITUTIONS INCLUDE?

Early state constitutions that allowed free black men to vote included Delaware (1776), Pennsylvania (1776), Maryland (1776), New York (1777), Massachusetts (1780), New Hampshire (1784), and Connecticut (1790).

In Britain universal suffrage was not granted for adult men until 1918 and for adult women until 1930.

CRITICAL THINKING EXERCISE

Jean-Jacques Rousseau (1712–1778), David Hume (1711–1776), and François-Marie Arouet Voltaire (1694–1778) are also examples of Enlightenment thinkers who wrote about the effect of natural rights thinking on government. For example, Hume criticized natural rights thinking; Voltaire embraced it. Rousseau sought to weave classical republicanism and natural rights philosophy by distinguishing between the "will of all" and the "general will." The will of all, he argued, is the collection of individual wills without regard for the interests of the community as a whole. The general will, by contrast, is concerned with the well-being of the entire community. According to Rousseau, good citizens and legislators should engage in reasoned deliberation so that the general will is expressed in legislation.

WHAT WAS THE STATUS OF THE COLONIES AFTER THE SIGNING OF THE DECLARATION OF INDEPENDENCE?

In 1776 the Declaration of Independence proclaimed the colonies to be "Free and Independent States." At the time most Americans would have used the phrase "my country" to refer to their state of residence. The states were united only by their common commitment to fight the war for independence from Great Britain.

In May 1776, shortly before the colonies formally declared their independence, the Second Continental Congress adopted a resolution calling on each state to draw up a new constitution. Between 1776 and 1780 all the states adopted new constitutions. Most kept the basic pattern of their old colonial charters, but they made important modifications. Never before had so many new governments been created using the basic ideas of natural rights, rule of law, republicanism, and constitutional government.

The various meeting places of the Continental Congress. Why do you suppose the congress met in so many different places?

50

WHAT BASIC IDEAS DID THE STATE CONSTITUTIONS INCLUDE?

The states experimented with various models in writing their new constitutions, but all contained the following basic principles:

- **Higher law and natural rights** Every state considered its constitution to be a fundamental, or "higher," law that placed limits on governmental power. Unlike the British Parliament the state legislature did not have the power to change the constitution. Each constitution reflected the idea that the purpose of government is to preserve and protect citizens' natural rights to life, liberty, and property.

- **Social contract** Each state constitution made clear that the state government was formed as a result of a social contract, that is, an agreement among the people to create a government to protect their natural rights as expressed in the constitution's preamble or bill of rights.

- **Popular sovereignty** All the new state constitutions stated that sovereignty, or ultimate governing authority, rests with the people. The people delegate authority to the government to govern in accordance with constitutional requirements.

- **Representation and the right to vote** All the state constitutions created legislatures composed of representatives elected by "qualified" voters, usually white men who owned some amount of property. Because property was relatively easy to acquire in America, about seventy percent of white men could vote. Unlike in Great Britain, representation was not based on fixed social classes. Most state constitutions provided for annual legislative elections. In seven states free African Americans and Native Americans could vote if they met the property requirements.

- **Legislative supremacy** A government in which the legislature has the most power exhibits **legislative supremacy**. Most state constitutions provided for strong legislatures and relied on the principle of majority rule to protect the rights of citizens. This reliance continued a development that had begun during the colonial period, when the legislatures first became strong. It also reflected the former colonists' distrust of executive power, which they believed had been abused under British rule.

The belief in legislative supremacy was based on the following assumptions:

- The legislative branch is most capable of reflecting the will of the people. Voters determine who their representatives will be and can remove them if they believe someone else would better represent them.

- The executive branch is less accountable to the people and should not be trusted with much power. The colonists' greatest problems with the British government had been with its executive branch, that is, with the king's ministers and the royal governors in the colonies.

- Judges also should not be trusted with too much power. Before the Revolution judges had been Crown magistrates who tried the colonists for breaking British laws. Early state constitutions limited judicial power in various ways, including making judges stand for election at regular intervals and giving legislatures the power to reduce judges' salaries. In several states the upper house of the legislature continued to exercise some judicial functions, such as deciding cases involving probate or admiralty matters.

The following examples of a preference for legislative supremacy can be found in state constitutions drafted shortly after the Revolution:

- Executive branches were relatively weak and dependent on legislatures. For example, Pennsylvania's constitution provided for a twelve-member council rather than a governor. Other state constitutions gave legislatures the power to select the governor or to control the governor's salary.

- Governors had short terms of office, usually only one year, to ensure that they would not have time to amass too much power.

- Appointments made by the governor had to be approved by the legislature.

- Governors played virtually no role in lawmaking and had only a qualified, or limited, power to nullify, or **veto**, laws that the legislature had enacted. Some states gave their governors a veto power, but the legislatures in those states could override a veto by re-passing the proposed law.

- **Checks and balances** Most state constitutions placed **checks and balances** on legislative powers, usually within legislatures. For example, every state constitution except those in Pennsylvania and Georgia provided for a check, or limit, on legislative powers by dividing the legislature into two houses. Most important decisions required debate, deliberation, and action by both houses—thus a degree of balance. Each house could check the power of the other by defeating a proposal with which it did not agree. Voters also could check legislators' power by electing new representatives.

CRITICAL THINKING EXERCISE
Evaluating Legislative Supremacy

John Locke and some other natural rights philosophers believed that in a representative government the legislative branch should be supreme because it is the branch closest to the people and reflects the wishes of the people. Accordingly the legislative branch is the least likely to violate the people's rights. Most of the early state constitutions reflected Locke's view and weighted the balance of governmental power in favor of their legislatures. Consider the following questions:

❶ Do you agree with Locke's argument for the supremacy of legislative power? Why or why not?

❷ Does the legislative branch necessarily reflect the people's will? Explain your response.

❸ What might a government be like in which the executive or judicial branch was supreme rather than the legislature?

HOW DID THE MASSACHUSETTS CONSTITUTION DIFFER FROM OTHER STATE CONSTITUTIONS?

Written principally by John Adams (1735–1826), who would later become America's second president, the Massachusetts constitution of 1780 differed from those of the other states. In addition to relying on popular representation in the legislature, it created a strong system of separation of powers and checks and balances. It gave the governor effective checks on the powers of the legislature and provided for a judiciary with judges holding office according to their good behavior, not for limited terms.

The structure of the Massachusetts constitution is more like the U.S. Constitution than the other early state constitutions, and so it is worth examining in some detail. Following are two important characteristics of the Massachusetts constitution:

HOW DID THE MASSACHUSETTS CONSTITUTION DIFFER FROM OTHER STATE CONSTITUTIONS?

In response to a request from the Second Continental Congress, the Council and House of Representatives (General Court) of 1777–1778 met to draft a constitution "for the State of Massachusetts Bay." It was rejected in a popular vote.

In 1779 the voters agreed to call a constitutional convention to draft a constitution. The convention met in Cambridge in September that year. Although John Adams prepared the first draft, some 297 delegates participated in the process. Adams relied on his deep knowledge of Enlightenment political theory, ancient and modern history, including that of Athens, Sparta, and Rome, and his belief that history had presented the new states with a unique opportunity to create their own governments.

Notable features of the constitution include the following:

- A preamble that (a) announces that the purpose of government is to furnish the members of the body politic "the power of enjoying, in safety and tranquility, their natural rights and the blessings of life"; (b) describes the body politic as a "social compact" whereby all agree to be governed by laws designed for the "common good"; and (c) gives the people the right to alter their government

- A declaration of rights derived in part from bills of rights in other state constitutions, with an independent judiciary, is listed as one of the rights

- A commitment to a balanced government of separate powers (legislative, executive, and judicial)

- A government of laws, not men

- A bicameral legislature with representation of people, property, and towns

All free men were eligible to vote on the proposed constitution, which they did in town meetings. An estimated 16,000 men voted, ratifying the document by a two-thirds margin. The constitution went into effect on October 25, 1780.

Eric Foner, a professor of history at Columbia University, contrasts the Massachusetts constitution with the Pennsylvania constitution:

> Widely regarded as the most radical frame of government created during the American Revolution, the Pennsylvania constitution… symbolized the utopian aspects of the Revolution—a radical break with the British past [and] the construction of government from first principles.

The Pennsylvania Constitution of 1776 provided for the following:

- Annual elections
- Rotation of officeholders
- Legislative debates open to the public
- Suffrage for men over age twenty-one who paid taxes
- Elimination of property qualifications for holding office
- A powerful single-house legislature

student page ▾ **52–53**

WHAT WERE THE STATE DECLARATIONS OF RIGHTS?

Virginia was the first state to adopt a declaration of rights, which served as a model for many other states.

wtpcompanion.civiced.org **PRIMARY SOURCES**

Visit the We the People companion website for a link to the Virginia Declaration of Rights.

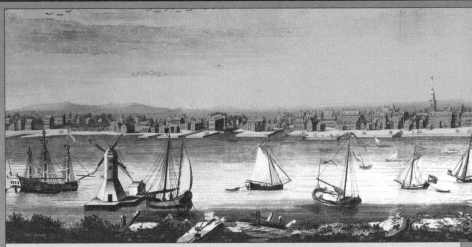

What were some of the problems faced by the newly independent states?

- **Strong executive**
  Qualified voters elected the governor, though for a short term—one year. The writers of this constitution believed that because the governor was popularly elected, it would be safe to trust him with greater power. To enable the governor to be more independent of the legislature and to allow him to check the legislature's use of power, the Massachusetts constitution contained the following provisions:

  - The governor's salary was fixed and could not be changed by the legislature.

  - The governor had the power to revise laws enacted by the legislature, and his revision could be overridden only by a two-thirds vote of the legislature.

  - The governor had the power to appoint officials to the executive branch and judges to the judicial branch.

- **Representation of various economic classes**
  The constitution provided for a complex system of representation to ensure that many groups and interests had a voice. Only electors who owned a large amount of property could vote for the governor. Electors who owned less property could vote for members of the upper house of the state legislature. Electors who owned only a small amount of property could vote for members of the lower house.

By providing for representation of these varied economic classes, the Massachusetts constitution was reminiscent of the classical republican idea of mixed constitution. More classes had a voice in the government, which ensured rich political dialogue and contributed to political stability.

WHAT DO YOU THINK?

❶ In what ways did Americans' colonial experience prepare them to write state constitutions after the Revolution?

❷ How did early state constitutions reflect Americans' fear of centralized political authority?

❸ Which branch of government do you think is most responsive to the will of the people? Should that branch have more power than the other branches? Why or why not?

WHAT WERE THE STATE DECLARATIONS OF RIGHTS?

Most state constitutions began with a preamble and a declaration of rights. For example, the first sentence of the Pennsylvania preamble stated

52

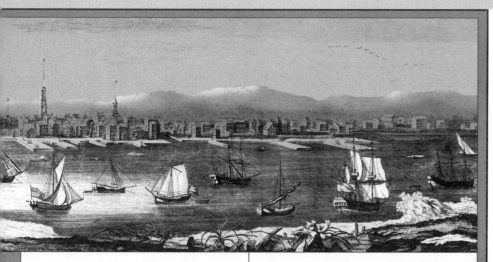

WHAT IMPORTANT IDEAS ARE IN THE VIRGINIA DECLARATION OF RIGHTS?

George Mason wrote the Virginia Declaration of Rights. Later, as a delegate to the Philadelphia Convention (see Lessons 9–12), Mason led the movement against ratification of the U.S. Constitution because it lacked a bill of rights (see Lesson 13). Mason did not want government in America to become like government in England, and he believed declarations of rights as limits on government were one way to prevent this.

Thomas Jefferson was influenced by the Virginia Declaration when drafting the Declaration of Independence. The Virginia Declaration also influenced the French Declaration of the Rights of Man of 1789.

" Whereas all government ought to be instituted and supported for the security and protection of the community as such, and to enable the individuals, who compose it, to enjoy their natural rights, and the other blessings which the Author of Existence has bestowed upon man; and, whenever these great ends of government are not obtained, the people have a right, by common consent, to change it, and take such measures as to them may appear necessary to promote their safety and happiness.

Before allocating any governmental powers, the Pennsylvania constitution first listed the rights of the inhabitants of the state, beginning with the rights of "enjoying and defending life and liberty, acquiring, possessing, and protecting property, and pursuing and obtaining happiness and safety." Writers of early state constitutions attached great importance to guarantees of basic rights. The lists of rights differed somewhat from state to state, but all were based on the idea that people have certain inherent rights that must be protected from governmental interference.

WHAT IMPORTANT IDEAS ARE IN THE VIRGINIA DECLARATION OF RIGHTS?

On June 12, 1776, Virginia became the first state to adopt a declaration of rights. The Virginia Declaration of Rights also was the first protection of individual rights to be adopted by the people acting through an elected convention. The Virginia Declaration of Rights expressed the people's understanding of their funda-mental, inalienable rights and the idea that people create government to protect those rights. It also was the first list of rights to appear in a state's fundamental law, or constitution, thereby insulating those rights from governmental interference.

Both James Madison and George Mason served on the committee appointed to write the Virginia Declaration of Rights. Mason wrote virtually the entire document, and his ideas would later strongly influence Madison's drafting of the U.S. Bill of Rights. In writing the Virginia Declaration Mason relied heavily on the writings of John Locke. He also was influenced by the ideas of classical republicanism and by the American colonial experience.

The Virginia Declaration of Rights listed specific rights, such as freedom of the press and the rights of criminal defendants. It also stated

- All men are by nature equally free and independent, and enjoy the rights of life and liberty, with the means of acquiring and possessing property, and pursuing and obtaining happiness and safety. No governmental compact can deprive them of their rights.

- All power is derived from and kept by the people.

- Government is, or ought to be, instituted for the common benefit, protection, and security of the people, nation, or community. If a government does not serve these purposes, the people have an inalienable right to alter or abolish it.

- All men are equally entitled to the free exercise of religion, according to the dictates of conscience.

The Virginia Declaration ended with a statement based on the ideas of classical republicanism about civic virtue and religious values:

- "No free government, or the blessings of liberty, can be preserved to any people but by a firm adherence to justice, moderation, temperance, frugality, and virtue and by frequent recurrence to fundamental principles.... It is the mutual duty of all to practice Christian forbearance, love, and charity, towards each other."

CRITICAL THINKING EXERCISE
Examining Historical Documents

Work with a study partner to complete the following activities.

❶ Read the Virginia Declaration of Rights in the Reference section. How are the following concepts reflected in this document?

- social contract
- individual rights
- limited government
- civic virtue
- common welfare

❷ Which historical experiences of the colonists seem to have exerted the greatest influence on the authors of state declarations of rights?

❸ Is it significant that most state constitutions began with a list of rights, rather than those rights being included in the body of the constitution or appended as a list at the end of the document? Why or why not?

WHAT RIGHTS DID OTHER STATES PROTECT?

Most states adopted declarations or bills of rights that resembled the Virginia Declaration. The few states that did not have such declarations, such as New York, included guarantees of certain rights in the main body of their constitutions. Like the Virginia Declaration of Rights, the declarations in other constitutions began with statements about natural rights, popular sovereignty, and the purposes of government. Some declarations, such as Delaware's, provided that "all government of right originates from the people, is founded in compact only, and instituted solely for the good of the whole."

Why do you suppose most states chose to place more power in their legislatures than in the other two branches of their governments?

54

What ideas influenced George Mason's writing of the Virginia Declaration of Rights?

Other states' declarations varied in the rights they chose to include or leave out. However, most included political guarantees such as

- The right to vote

- Free and frequent elections

- Freedom of speech and of the press

- The right to petition the government to redress grievances

- No taxation without representation

All state constitutions contained important procedural guarantees of due process such as

- Rights to counsel and trial by a jury of one's peers

- Protection from illegal searches and seizures

- Protection from forced self-incrimination, excessive bail and fines, and cruel and unusual punishment

Most of the state declarations, including the Virginia Declaration, expressed a fear of military tyranny by condemning professional standing armies in time of peace and the quartering of troops in civilian homes. At the same time many declarations endorsed the idea of a "well regulated" civilian militia and the right to bear arms.

These state declarations of rights would have a great influence on the later drafting and adoption of the U.S. Bill of Rights.

Why do you suppose so many state constitutions provided for civilian militia and the right to bear arms?

55

WHAT DO YOU THINK?

1. Why did Americans think that it was important to have written declarations of rights in their state constitutions?

2. Obtain a copy of the bill of rights in the constitution of your state. Are you surprised by any of the rights listed? Why or why not? Do you think all the rights listed in your state constitution also should appear in the Bill of Rights to the U.S. Constitution? Why or why not?

3. In your opinion what is the greatest challenge to individual rights today and what should be done about it?

REVIEWING AND USING THE LESSON

1. What basic ideas about government were contained in the new state constitutions?

2. Explain the meaning and significance of the following concepts:
   * higher law
   * popular sovereignty
   * legislative supremacy
   * checks and balances

3. What were the most significant differences between the Massachusetts constitution and the other state constitutions?

4. What important ideas did the Virginia Declaration of Rights contain? How was this document influential throughout the colonies?

5. Examine the declaration of rights in your state constitution. How does the list of rights limit state government?

What ideas from classical republicanism did George Mason include in the Virginia Declaration of Rights?

56

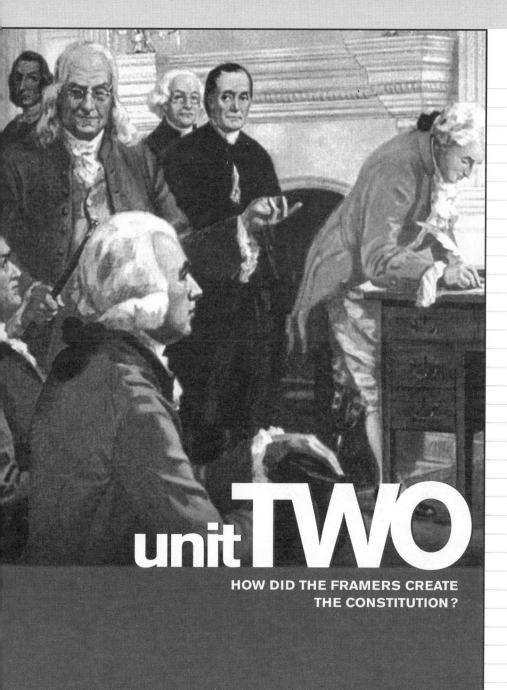

unitTWO

HOW DID THE FRAMERS CREATE THE CONSTITUTION?

unit TWO

After declaring their independence from Great Britain, Americans had to decide how they would govern themselves. The Articles of Confederation, which were the first attempt to establish a national government, proved inadequate in the eyes of many leading citizens. Fifty-five men met in Philadelphia in 1787 and drafted the U.S. Constitution. These men became known as the Framers. The Constitution was not universally acclaimed, and its adoption and ratification provoked discussions of the most basic questions about political life and government institutions.

In this unit you will learn why the Articles of Confederation were replaced by the Constitution. You will learn why the Framers created the United States government as they did. And you will learn how the debates over the adoption of the Constitution raised issues that are debated to this day.

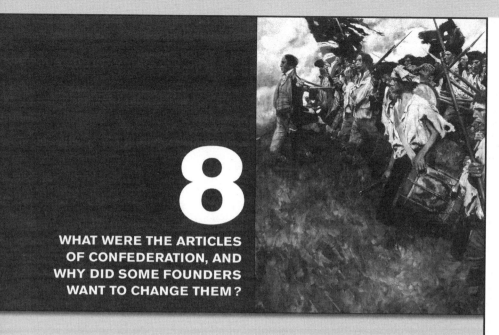

8

WHAT WERE THE ARTICLES OF CONFEDERATION, AND WHY DID SOME FOUNDERS WANT TO CHANGE THEM?

WHAT WERE THE ARTICLES OF CONFEDERATION, AND WHY DID SOME FOUNDERS WANT TO CHANGE THEM?

wtpcompanion.civiced.org | **LESSON PURPOSE + TERMS**

Visit the We the People companion website for printable and downloadable Lesson Purposes and Terms and Concepts to Understand sections for each lesson. Audio readings of each Lesson Purpose and Term are also available online in MP3 format.

LESSON PURPOSE

This lesson examines the government formed by the Articles of Confederation. It was the first of two blueprints for a United States government written between 1776 and 1787. The Articles of Confederation provided the framework of an alliance of states to fight the Revolutionary War. The provisions in this document reflected political realities and divisions among the states as well as the need for unity. Many Founders soon came to believe that this first government of the United States lacked sufficient authority to meet the nation's needs both during and after the war.

When you have finished this lesson, you should be able to describe the United States' first national constitution, the Articles of Confederation. You also should be able to explain why some people thought the government under the Articles of Confederation was not strong enough. Finally, you should be able to evaluate, take, and defend positions on the strengths and weaknesses of the Articles of Confederation, the significance of the Northwest Ordinance, and Americans' mistrust of a strong national government.

TERMS AND CONCEPTS TO UNDERSTAND

Articles of Confederation

confederation

Shays' Rebellion

student page ▾ 60–63

WHY AND HOW WERE THE ARTICLES OF CONFEDERATION CREATED?

While Thomas Jefferson was drafting the Declaration of Independence, other members of the Second Continental Congress were thinking about how to form a government for the confederated colonies. On June 7, 1776, Richard Henry Lee of Virginia introduced a resolution calling for both independence and the drafting of "a plan of confederation" among the colonies. Five days later a committee composed of one delegate from each colony was assigned "to prepare and digest the form of confederation." John Dickinson of Pennsylvania, who argued repeatedly against independence, was chosen to draft the plan. He relied heavily on a plan for confederation that Benjamin Franklin had presented to the Congress almost a year earlier.

wtpcompanion.civiced.org | **PRIMARY SOURCES**

Visit the We the People companion website for a link to Franklin's plan of July 1775.

The debates over the Articles were particularly contentious over issues such as representation in Congress, western land boundaries, and apportionment of taxes. The debates were interrupted by military concerns associated with the Revolutionary War, lack of a quorum of delegates, and the need to relocate Congress from Philadelphia to Baltimore because of the threat of British occupation of Philadelphia. The Articles of Confederation were not ready to go to the states for approval until late November.

Decades later when Southern states seceded from the Union and formed a confederation before the Civil War (see Lesson 17), they also were drawing on a tradition begun in 1643, when a confederation called the United Colonies of New England had been formed as a political and military alliance among the colonies of Massachusetts, Plymouth, Connecticut, and New Haven. This action also echoed Franklin's 1775 call for a confederation of colonies.

WHY AND HOW WERE THE ARTICLES OF CONFEDERATION CREATED?

In addition to writing state constitutions between 1776 and 1780 Americans also considered how to manage economic and political relationships among the states, resolve disputes such as state borders, and conduct relations with the rest of the world. Some kind of union or confederation was necessary to achieve these goals. Therefore the Founders set forth their ideas in a document known as the **Articles of Confederation**. A **confederation** is a form of political organization in which sovereign states delegate power to a central government for specified purposes.

Some leaders had seen the need for a united government for some time. America's elder statesman, Benjamin Franklin, had proposed a colonial government in 1754, and at different times groups of colonies (and then states) had imagined regional confederations to address particular issues. Franklin first submitted a draft for articles of confederation to the Second Continental Congress in July 1775. Several other proposals were made that summer and fall, but the question of independence from Great Britain was more important at that moment than forming a collective government.

On June 7, 1776, Virginian Richard Henry Lee (1732–1794) introduced a set of resolutions to the Second Continental Congress—one for independence, the other for a government. From these resolutions came the Declaration of Independence and the Articles of Confederation.

WHAT PROBLEMS DID THE ARTICLES OF CONFEDERATION ADDRESS?

Two major concerns made it difficult for the Continental Congress and the states to devise a central government: fear of a strong national government and fear that some states would dominate others in the central government.

FEAR OF A STRONG CENTRAL GOVERNMENT

When the war against Great Britain started, each state was like a separate nation with its own constitution and government. To the people their state was their country, and all eligible voters could have a voice in government. They could elect members of their communities to represent their interests in their state legislatures. Especially in smaller states the government was close enough to most citizens that they could participate in some of its activities.

Most members of the Continental Congress agreed that winning the war required a central government. However, they were wary of making one that was too strong. They, like many Americans, believed that the British government had deprived people of their rights, including their right to be represented in government. They thought that this was likely to happen with any central government that was both powerful and far away. They believed that government should be close to the people who could control it and make certain that it did not violate their rights. Their study of history and political philosophy led them to believe that republican government could succeed only in small communities where people shared common ideas and beliefs.

The solution to the problem was to create a "firm league of friendship," not a strong central government. Thus, Article II in the Articles of Confederation stated, "Each state retains its sovereignty, freedoms, and independence, and every power, jurisdiction, and right, which is not by this Confederation expressly delegated to the United States, in Congress assembled." The government created by the Articles strictly defined the authority of the central legislature, or Congress. Article VI

Why didn't the Articles of Confederation create a strong central government?

listed things that states could not do: send or receive ambassadors to foreign nations, lay imposts or duties that conflicted with national treaties, maintain military forces beyond what Congress considered necessary for the state's self-defense, or engage in war (except in case of invasion). Article IX granted Congress "the sole and exclusive right of determining on peace and war," as well as directing military forces, conducting foreign policy, and determining the union's expenses.

The Articles of Confederation left most of the powers of government with the states. For example,

- The Confederation Congress had no authority over any person in any state. Only the state governments had authority over their citizens.

- Congress had no power to collect taxes from the states or from the people directly. It could request money only from the state governments, which were supposed to raise the money from their citizens.

- Congress had no power to regulate trade among the various states.

This is a twenty-shilling note from the colony of Massachusetts. What problems might arise if each of the states could print its own money?

FEAR THAT SOME STATES WOULD DOMINATE OTHERS IN THE CENTRAL GOVERNMENT

The leaders in each state did not want the new national government to threaten their state's interests. Three issues aligned groups of states against one another:

- Representation and voting in Congress: Would each state have one vote, or would states with greater populations or wealth be given more votes than others? This question divided the more populous states (Massachusetts, New York, Pennsylvania, Virginia) from the less populous (Connecticut, Delaware, Georgia, New Hampshire, Rhode Island).

- Apportionment of war expenses among the states: Would each state's contribution to the war effort be based on total population (including slaves) or on free population only? This question divided the states with large enslaved populations (those from Maryland southward) from those with relatively small numbers of slaves (especially New England).

- Territorial claims in the West: Five states (Delaware, Maryland, New Jersey, Pennsylvania, and Rhode Island,) had fixed western boundaries based on their original colonial charters, while others had "sea-to-sea" charters that allowed them to claim vast western territories. Would western lands be transferred to congressional control, creating a common "national domain" that could be sold later to pay off the national debt?

The following solutions to these problems emerged:

- Article V gave each state one vote regardless of its population. The Articles also provided that on important matters (for example, whether to declare war or to admit new states) nine states would have to agree. This way the seven smaller states could not outvote the six larger.

- Article VIII created a formula for requesting funds that was not based on population, free or enslaved. However, this formula (based on the amount of settled, improved land in each state) was impractical because it was difficult to measure the amount of improved land across such a large nation.

In September 1780 Congress requested the "landed" states to grant part of their western lands to the United States. Once New York, Connecticut, and Virginia began the process of ceding those lands, Maryland became the last state to ratify the Articles of Confederation, on March 1, 1781.

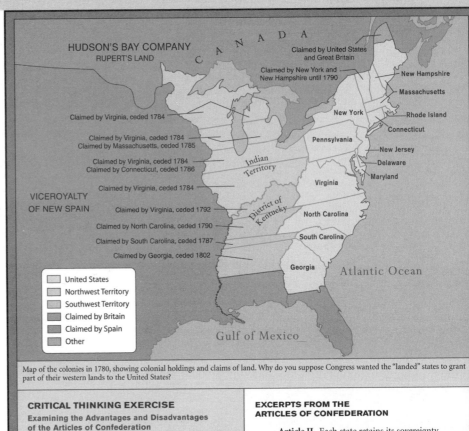

HUDSON'S BAY COMPANY
RUPERT'S LAND

CANADA

Claimed by United States and Great Britain

Claimed by New York and New Hampshire until 1790

New Hampshire

Massachusetts

Claimed by Virginia, ceded 1784

New York

Rhode Island

Connecticut

Claimed by Virginia, ceded 1784
Claimed by Massachusetts, ceded 1785

Pennsylvania

New Jersey

Claimed by Virginia, ceded 1784
Claimed by Connecticut, ceded 1786

Delaware

Indian Territory

Maryland

Claimed by Virginia, ceded 1784

Virginia

VICEROYALTY OF NEW SPAIN

Claimed by Virginia, ceded 1792

District of Kentucky

Claimed by North Carolina, ceded 1790

North Carolina

Claimed by South Carolina, ceded 1787

South Carolina

Claimed by Georgia, ceded 1802

Georgia

Atlantic Ocean

United States
Northwest Territory
Southwest Territory
Claimed by Britain
Claimed by Spain
Other

Gulf of Mexico

Map of the colonies in 1780, showing colonial holdings and claims of land. Why do you suppose Congress wanted the "landed" states to grant part of their western lands to the United States?

CRITICAL THINKING EXERCISE

Examining the Advantages and Disadvantages of the Articles of Confederation

Work with a study partner or in a small group to complete this exercise:

❶ Read the following excerpts from the Articles of Confederation.

❷ For each excerpt create a list of *advantages* to the states or the national government resulting from the particular Article.

❸ Create a second list of the *disadvantages* to the states or the national government resulting from the particular Article.

❹ When you finish, compare your lists and be prepared to share your ideas with the class.

EXCERPTS FROM THE ARTICLES OF CONFEDERATION

Article II Each state retains its sovereignty, freedom and independence, and every Power… which is not by this confederation expressly delegated to the United States, in Congress assembled.

Article V No state shall be represented in Congress by less than two, nor more than seven Members…. In determining questions in the united states, in Congress assembled, each State shall have one vote.

Article VIII All charges of war, and all other expences that shall be incurred for the common defence or general welfare…shall be defrayed out of a common treasury, which shall be supplied by the several states, in proportion to the value of all land within each state…. The taxes for paying that proportion shall be laid and levied by the authority and direction of the legislatures of the several states.

Article IX The united states in congress assembled shall also be the last resort on appeal in all disputes and differences… between two or more states.

Article IX The united states in congress assembled shall also have the sole and exclusive right and power of regulating the alloy [mixture of base metals] and value of coin struck by their own authority, or by that of the respective states.

Article XIII Nor shall any alteration at any time hereafter be made in any of [these articles]; unless such alteration be agreed to in a congress of the united states, and be afterwards confirmed by the legislatures of every state.

WHAT WERE THE ACHIEVEMENTS OF THE NATIONAL GOVERNMENT UNDER THE ARTICLES OF CONFEDERATION?

The first national government accomplished a number of important things. The Revolutionary War was conducted under this government. Through the efforts of its diplomats this government also secured recognition of American independence by European governments.

The Articles of Confederation did not create separate executive or judicial branches. However, Congress did create executive departments to administer finance, foreign relations, and military affairs. These were the beginnings of the later cabinet departments of treasury, state, and war. Although most disputes were to be handled in state courts, Congress could establish courts for certain limited purposes. Thus Congress created admiralty courts to hear appeals from state courts. These courts were the first federal courts in the United States.

Perhaps the most lasting achievement of the Confederation was the Northwest Ordinance of 1787. It defined the Northwest Territory and created a plan for its government. The Northwest Territory encompassed the land north of the Ohio River and east of the Mississippi that would become the states of Ohio, Michigan, Indiana, Illinois, Wisconsin, and part of Minnesota. The ordinance also laid out the process by which a territory could move to statehood and guaranteed that new states would be on an equal footing with existing states. The Northwest Ordinance stated that slavery would be forever prohibited from the lands of the Northwest Territory. It required new states to provide for education by setting aside land that might be sold to fund schools. Congress under the Articles of Confederation could make these regulations for the Northwest Territory because it had complete control over it.

WHAT WERE THE WEAKNESSES OF THE ARTICLES OF CONFEDERATION?

The decision to create a national government with very limited power reflected Americans' fear of a strong national government. Americans believed that power that is not given is power that cannot be misused.

The limitations of the Articles of Confederation and the difficulties that arose under them led some Founders to desire a stronger national government. These limitations included the following:

- **Congress had no power to tax**
  Congress could only request that state governments pay certain amounts to support the costs of the national government. This system did not work. Congress had borrowed most of the money it needed to pay for the Revolutionary War, but it had no way to pay its debts. The state governments and many of the people living in the states also were deeply in debt after the war. When Congress requested ten million dollars from the states to pay for the costs of fighting the war, the states paid only $1.5 million.

- **Congress could make agreements with foreign nations, but it had no power to force state governments to honor these agreements**
  This raised another difficulty. Some citizens imported goods from other nations and then refused to pay for them. Not surprisingly people in foreign countries became reluctant to deal with people in the United States.

What were the consequences of the weakness of the central government under the Articles of Confederation that are portrayed here?

---

student page ▾ 63

WHAT WERE THE ACHIEVEMENTS OF THE NATIONAL GOVERNMENT UNDER THE ARTICLES OF CONFEDERATION?

The Northwest Ordinance of 1787, consisting of six articles, established the means by which states could be created and admitted into the Union. It authorized Congress to appoint governors and judges to rule a territory until it contained 5,000 free male inhabitants of voting age. Then the inhabitants were allowed to elect a territorial legislature, which would send a nonvoting delegate to Congress. When the population reached 60,000, the legislature would submit a state constitution to Congress and, if Congress approved, the state would enter the Union.

wtpcompanion.civiced.org **PRIMARY SOURCES**

Visit the We the People companion website for a link to the Northwest Ordinance.

In addition to settling the policy of prohibiting slavery in the territory, the Northwest Ordinance is important for the following accomplishments:

- Providing an orderly system for settling the West
- Setting the precedent of new states coming into the Union on equal footing with existing states
- Guaranteeing territorial settlers all the rights that had been fought for in the Revolution, including trial by jury, no excessive bail ("all persons shall be bailable") and no "cruel or unusual punishments," habeas corpus, protection of private property and contracts, and religious freedom

student page ▾ 65

WHAT ATTEMPTS WERE MADE TO SOLVE THE PROBLEMS OF THE ARTICLES OF CONFEDERATION?

To calculate a state's population for purposes of representation in the House of Representatives, the number of slaves in a state was multiplied by three-fifths. This ratio was first proposed in 1781 as part of an amendment to the Articles of Confederation. That amendment would have made it simpler for Congress to collect taxes from the states.

However, like every other proposed amendment, it was not enacted because changes to the Articles required unanimous consent. There is no clear historical explanation for why this ratio was suggested at that time, but some delegates to the Philadelphia Convention remembered it six years later. The ratio appeared in the New Jersey Plan (see Lesson 10) and was incorporated into the Constitution.

Prior to the Annapolis meeting in 1786 George Washington and James Madison called a meeting in Annapolis in 1784 to discuss development of the Potomac River as a route to the West. Maryland and Virginia formed the Patowmack Company to improve the waterway and to settle disputes over the upper reaches of the river. Madison, at the urging of Alexander Hamilton, arranged another meeting of the two states the next year, this time to resolve issues about the use of the Chesapeake Bay and its tributaries. The delegates to that meeting agreed to an extended agenda for another meeting in 1786 to discuss commercial issues. The states represented at the Annapolis Convention in 1786 and their delegates were as follows:

- Delaware: Richard Bassett, John Dickinson, and George Read
- New Jersey: Abraham Clark, William C. Houston, and James Schureman
- New York: Egbert Benson and Alexander Hamilton
- Pennsylvania: Tench Coxe
- Virginia: James Madison Jr., Edmund Randolph, and Saint George Tucker

Low turnout prevented the delegates from making progress on their agenda, but they issued a report to the state legislatures and Congress, stating in part

That there are important defects in the system of the Federal Government is acknowledged by the Acts of all those States, which have concurred in the present Meeting; That the defects, upon a closer examination, may be found greater and more numerous, than even these acts imply, is at least so far probable, from the embarrassments which characterize the present State of our national affairs, foreign and domestic, as may reasonably be supposed to merit a deliberate and candid discussion, in some mode, which will unite the Sentiments and Councils of all the States. In the choice of the mode, your Commissioners are of opinion, that a Convention of Deputies from the different States, for the special and sole purpose of entering into this investigation, and digesting a plan for supplying such defects as may be discovered to exist, will be entitled to a preference from considerations, which will occur, without being particularized.

Why weren't the protections of loyalists contained in the Treaty of Paris enforced by the national government under the Articles of Confederation?

In addition, when Great Britain recognized Congress's weakness in controlling foreign trade, it closed the West Indies to American commerce. As a result many Americans, particularly millers and merchants of grain and other foodstuffs, were unable to sell their goods to people in other nations.

- **Congress had no power to make laws regulating trade among the states** Therefore some states levied taxes on goods passing through them to other states. For example, both New York and Pennsylvania taxed goods going to New Jersey, which Benjamin Franklin compared to "a keg tapped at both ends." Such activities hampered efficient and productive trade across state lines.

- **Congress had no power to make laws directly regulating the behavior of citizens** Citizens could be governed only by their state governments. If members of a state government or citizens within a state disobeyed a resolution, recommendation, or request made by Congress, the national government had no way to make them obey.

The inability to make state governments and their citizens obey treaties led to a serious situation. The Treaty of Paris, which ended the Revolutionary War in 1783, included protections for the rights of loyalists (colonists who had remained loyal to Great Britain) and sought to ensure that they would be treated fairly. Some of these loyalists owned property in the states, and some had loaned money to other citizens. However, some state governments refused to respect this part of the Treaty of

Paris. Some states had confiscated loyalists' property during the war. The national government was powerless to enforce its promise to the British government to protect the rights of these citizens.

Moreover, most state governments were controlled by the legislative branch, composed of representatives elected by a majority of people in small districts. In many states divisions emerged between what some historians call "localists" and "cosmopolitans."

Localists were people in relatively isolated rural areas, often in the western parts of states. They belonged to mostly self-sufficient, small communities. Many of these farmers had fallen into debt during and after the Revolutionary War. When representatives of localist districts held a majority in the state legislature, some states passed laws that canceled debts. They also created paper money, causing inflation that benefited debtors at the expense of their creditors.

Cosmopolitans, who lived primarily in seaports and larger towns, often were the creditors. They argued that by canceling debts and issuing paper money, state governments were not protecting their property. They claimed that the state governments were being used by one class of people to deny the rights of others. Many cosmopolitans were involved in international trade as bankers, shipbuilders, and merchants. They also believed that the United States needed to honor its international treaties and foreign debts in order to maintain worldwide credit.

Some people argued that these problems were an example of too much democracy in state governments. They claimed that majority rule in the states did not adequately protect the natural rights of individual citizens or the common good, because majorities pursued their own interests at the expense of the rights of others. They thought this form of tyranny was every bit as dangerous as that of an uncontrolled monarch.

WHAT DO YOU THINK?

❶ The Articles of Confederation demonstrated a distrust of a strong national government. What were the historical and philosophical reasons for this distrust?

❷ What were the positive and negative consequences of a limited national government?

❸ The Northwest Ordinance is considered the most significant measure passed by the Confederation Congress. Why were the policies that it established important?

❹ Many people today continue to distrust the national government. In your opinion is such distrust justified? Explain your position.

WHAT ATTEMPTS WERE MADE TO SOLVE THE PROBLEMS OF THE ARTICLES OF CONFEDERATION?

Recognizing the problems, some members of Congress and other Founders sought to amend the Articles of Confederation to give Congress greater powers of enforcement and taxation. One of these proposals would have changed the formula by which Congress requested money from states. Instead of counting a state's "improved lands," it would have assessed contributions based on each state's population, with five slaves counting the same as three free people. However, Article XIII prevented amendments unless ratified by all thirteen states. No amendment ever won approval from all the states.

By 1783 many of the original members had left Congress and were replaced by others who preferred the limited national government of the Articles of Confederation. Consequently Federalist leaders, such as Alexander Hamilton, James Madison, and others, began to look outside the existing Congress for support for solutions to the weaknesses in the Articles.

A number of prominent leaders suggested holding a meeting of representatives of all the states. This idea of holding a special meeting, or convention, to discuss constitutional changes, instead of using the legislature, was an American invention. Most of the early state constitutions had been written by state legislatures. In 1780 Massachusetts had been the first state to hold a constitutional convention. By 1786 Madison and others decided that if a convention could be used successfully within a state, then it was worth trying at the national level.

In 1786 five states sent representatives to a meeting in Annapolis, Maryland, to discuss commercial problems. Disappointed by the low turnout, Hamilton, Madison, and others wrote a report asking Congress to call a meeting in Philadelphia to suggest ways to change the Articles of Confederation to strengthen the national government. After a delay of several months Congress finally did so. Delegates to the Philadelphia Convention were authorized to propose amendments to the Articles, not to develop an entirely new constitution.

HOW DID SHAYS' REBELLION RESULT IN SUPPORT FOR CHANGE?

Many people realized that the Articles of Confederation were weak, but it took a dramatic event to convince them of the need for a stronger national government. This event, known as **Shays' Rebellion**, occurred in 1786, when a group of several hundred farmers in western Massachusetts gathered under the leadership of Daniel Shays (c. 1747–1825). Shays had

The report requested the states and Congress to call for a convention in Philadelphia in May 1787. Congress issued the call on February 21, 1787, stating that the delegates should meet

> for the sole purpose of revising the Articles of Confederation and reporting to Congress and the several legislatures such alterations and provisions therein as shall, when agreed to in Congress and confirmed by the States, render the federal Constitution adequate to the exigencies of government and the preservation of the Union.

student page ▾ 65–66

HOW DID SHAYS' REBELLION RESULT IN SUPPORT FOR CHANGE?

The Revolutionary War had positive and negative economic consequences in America. Among the positives were the following:

- Trade restrictions ended, leading to the development of a successful merchant marine and trade industry.

- Americans gained the right to expand westward across the Appalachian Mountains.

- Westward expansion attracted new immigrants and stimulated economic growth, particularly for small independent farmers.

Among the negatives were the following:

- America lost its favored position as a trade partner with Great Britain and the protection of the British Navy for maritime trade.

- Agricultural prices fell and unemployment rose.

- Westward expansion led to expensive wars with Native Americans.

Congress had incurred a foreign debt of about $12 million (most of it owed to France), a domestic debt of more than $24 million to individuals who had supplied the revolutionary forces, and a $25 million debt to the states. The combined war debts of the states exceeded that of Congress. In Massachusetts, New York, Virginia, and South Carolina, there were strong movements among settlers, particularly in western regions, to break away from their debt-ridden states to set up their own states. The other states were not eager to devote resources to these four states to help them preserve their authority. States began disputing boundaries and fishing rights, imposed trade barriers against one another, and engaged in trade wars.

In some areas an economic downturn in the mid-1780s resulted in political uproar between creditors and debtors. Farmers from Vermont to Georgia faced ruin from just one bad harvest or, like Daniel Shays, by the refusal of creditors to accept the paper money Congress printed to pay its debt to individuals. In Rhode Island the struggle between debtors and creditors to control the state legislature resulted in frequent changes in the laws and instability of currency. Shays' Rebellion was merely one example of debtors taking the law into their own hands to protect their homes, farms, and families.

ENRICHMENT ACTIVITY

ACHIEVEMENTS OF THE CONTINENTAL AND CONFEDERATION CONGRESSES

Legal historian R.B. Bernstein lists six major accomplishments of the Continental and Confederation Congresses:

❶ They coordinated the colonists' intellectual, political, and military resistance to Britain.

❷ They declared American independence and fostered a creative explosion of state constitution-making.

❸ They launched an American diplomatic corps and secured a place for a fragile new nation in world politics.

❹ They helped General Washington hold together the Continental Army until the final victory in 1783.

❺ They helped secure an advantageous peace treaty from Britain that recognized American independence and doubled the new nation's size.

❻ They devised a series of territorial ordinances that promised to foster the development of an expanded United States without the threat of colonialism (the Northwest Ordinances of 1784, 1785, and 1787).

Ask students to research one of these six statements and then write a short essay explaining why they agree or disagree with Bernstein's claim that it was a major accomplishment.

been a captain in the Revolutionary War. His group called themselves the Regulators, because they sought to regulate the power of the state government.

Massachusetts farmers had serious economic problems. For example, many former soldiers in the Revolutionary War could not pay their debts because Congress had never paid them their wages. They lost their homes and farms. Some were sent to prison. Discontent arose among the people, and crowds gathered to prevent the courts from selling the property of those who could not pay their debts.

None of these tactics was new. Before the Revolutionary War colonists in North Carolina and elsewhere had called themselves Regulators and had attempted to block the actions of British government officials. Crowd action was a longstanding response to perceived injustice. Those who opposed the crowds—including many people in the government—called them "mobs" and "rebels."

What problems led to Shays' Rebellion?

Seeking weapons for their action, Shays and his men tried to capture the arsenal at Springfield, Massachusetts, where arms were kept for the state militia. They failed, and the governor called out the militia to put down the rebellion. The episode frightened many property owners, who feared that similar problems might arise in their states.

The fears generated by such conflicts, combined with the difficulties of raising revenues and regulating foreign trade, convinced a growing number of Americans to strengthen the national government. George Washington, who would not become America's first president for another three years, had long desired such a change. After Shays' Rebellion he wrote to James Madison on November 5, 1786,

❝ What stronger evidence can be given of the want of energy in our governments than these disorders? If there exists not a power to check them, what security has a man of life, liberty, or property?… Thirteen Sovereignties pulling against each other, and all tugging at the federal head, will soon bring ruin on the whole.

REVIEWING AND USING THE LESSON

❶ Why did the Articles of Confederation create only a legislative branch of government? How did the Articles of Confederation deal with fears that some states would dominate others in the national government?

❷ What were some of the achievements of the national government under the Articles of Confederation? What were some of the weaknesses of the Articles of Confederation?

❸ What was Shays' Rebellion? Why did it occur? What was its historical importance?

❹ What were positive and negative consequences of a limited national government? Which Americans were satisfied with government under the Articles of Confederation? Why?

❺ Compare the government under the Articles of Confederation with a contemporary confederation of nations, such as the United Nations, the European Union, the Organization of American States, or the Organization of African States. In what ways are they similar? In what ways are they different?

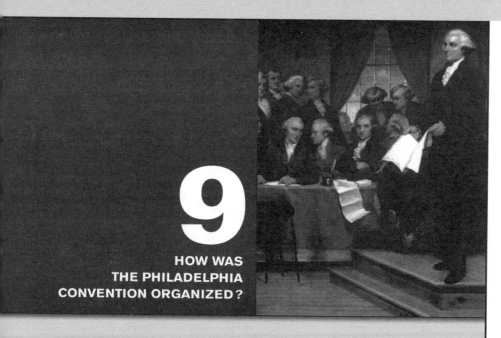

9

HOW WAS THE PHILADELPHIA CONVENTION ORGANIZED?

HOW WAS THE PHILADELPHIA CONVENTION ORGANIZED?

wtpcompanion.civiced.org   **LESSON PURPOSE + TERMS**

Visit the We the People companion website for printable and downloadable Lesson Purposes and Terms and Concepts to Understand sections for each lesson. Audio readings of each Lesson Purpose and Term are also available online in MP3 format.

LESSON PURPOSE

The Constitution of the United States of America was written at a convention held in Philadelphia in 1787. This lesson describes some of the important people who attended and the first steps they took in Philadelphia. The structure and rules they gave to their deliberations played a major role in the outcome by providing a framework for civil discourse, that is, the reasoned discussion of issues. The Virginia Plan, the first blueprint that the delegates considered, created the agenda for subsequent discussions.

When you have completed this lesson, you should be able to describe the organizing phase of the Philadelphia Convention. You also should be able to explain the significance of rules and agendas for effective civil discussion. Finally, you should be able to evaluate, take, and defend positions on determining what interests should be represented in a constitutional convention and the advantages and disadvantages of secrecy in governmental deliberations.

TERMS AND CONCEPTS TO UNDERSTAND

civil discourse

Constitutional Convention

delegate

federal system

national government

proportional representation

student page ▾ 68–69

WHO ATTENDED THE PHILADELPHIA CONVENTION?

In response to the call by the Annapolis Convention the legislatures of Virginia, New Jersey, Pennsylvania, North Carolina, Delaware, and Georgia appointed delegates to the convention in Philadelphia. Several other states, including New York, South Carolina, and Massachusetts, waited to appoint delegates until Congress authorized the Convention. Connecticut and Maryland selected their delegates shortly before the Convention opened. New Hampshire was short of cash and did not send delegates to Philadelphia until July. Rhode Island refused to participate altogether. Fifty-five of the seventy-four appointed delegates attended.

---

wtpcompanion.civiced.org **LINKS**

Visit the We the People companion website for a link to a list of delegates from each state and the population of each state.

WHO ATTENDED THE PHILADELPHIA CONVENTION?

Fifty-five **delegates** attended the meeting that later became known as the Philadelphia Convention or **Constitutional Convention**. This group of men is now often called the Framers of the Constitution.

Delegates were appointed by their state legislatures to represent their states at the convention. States sent as few as two delegates (New Hampshire) and as many as eight (Pennsylvania). However, each state had one vote, just as they did in Congress under the Articles of Confederation.

The delegates ranged in age from twenty-six to eighty-one; the average age was forty-two. About three-fourths of them had served in Congress. Most were prominent in their states, and some had played important roles in the Revolution. Some were wealthy, but most were not.

Contemporary observers were impressed by the quality of the delegates to the Philadelphia Convention. A French diplomat stationed in America observed that never before, "even in Europe," had there been "an assembly more respectable for talents, knowledge, disinterestedness, and patriotism." From Paris Thomas Jefferson wrote to John Adams in London that the convention was "an assembly of demigods."

Perhaps the most balanced view of the men at Philadelphia came later, from early twentieth-century historian Max Farrand, who in 1913 wrote in *The Framing of the Constitution of the United States,*

    ❝ Great men there were, it is true, but the convention as a whole was composed of men such as would be appointed to a similar gathering at the present time: professional men, business men, and gentlemen of leisure; patriotic statesmen and clever, scheming politicians; some trained by experience and study for the task before them; and others utterly unfit. It was essentially a representative body.

Most of the Framers' stories are worth telling in detail. Eight played particularly significant roles.

George Washington (1732–1799) was the most respected and honored man in the country. During the Revolutionary War he had left Mount Vernon, his Virginia plantation, to lead the American army to victory over the British. The difficulties that Congress faced in supplying his army, as well as his experience leading an army composed of men from across the thirteen states, convinced him that the United States needed a strong

What were some of the characteristics of the delegates to the Philadelphia Convention held in Independence Hall?

national government. Washington initially refused the invitation to attend the convention because he wanted to remain in private life. He later agreed to be a delegate from Virginia, fearing that if he did not attend, then people might think that he had lost faith in republican government. Washington was unanimously elected president of the convention. He did not take an active role in the debates. But his presence and support of the Constitution, together with the widespread assumption that he would be the nation's first president, were essential to the success of the Constitutional Convention and the Constitution's ratification by the states.

James Madison probably had the greatest influence on the organization of the national government. Madison was among the youngest of the revolutionary leaders, but by 1787 his talents had long been recognized and admired. In 1776, at the age of twenty-five, he had been elected to the Virginia convention, where he was named to a committee to frame the state constitution. He first displayed his lifelong commitment to freedom of religion when he persuaded George Mason, author of the Virginia Declaration of Rights, to change the clause that guaranteed "toleration" of religion to one that secured its "free exercise." Madison's influence at the convention was great, in part because he spent the previous winter studying ancient and modern political theory in preparation for the deliberations.

Benjamin Franklin of Pennsylvania was eighty-one years old and in poor health. He was internationally respected, and his presence lent an aura of wisdom to the convention. *Alexander Hamilton* of New York, who had been Washington's aide during the Revolution, was among the stalwart supporters of a strong national government. He was outvoted within his own state's delegation and departed Philadelphia in frustration before the convention was half over. However, he returned for a few days and signed the completed document in September. *James Wilson* of Pennsylvania, although not as well known as Madison or Hamilton, also was a major influence, particularly on how the delegates shaped the office of president.

Gouverneur Morris of Pennsylvania was one of the delegates who spoke most often at the convention. He is credited with taking a principal role in drafting the Constitution. *Edmund Randolph*, Virginia's governor, officially headed that state's delegation and introduced the Virginia Plan to the convention. Randolph refused to sign the final document because he said it departed too much from the "Republican propositions" of the Virginia Plan; however, he ultimately supported ratification. Connecticut's *Roger Sherman* was instrumental in forging the Connecticut Compromise on representation in Congress, which helped shape American federalism.

Why was George Washington's attendance at the Philadelphia Convention so important?

WHAT IMPORTANT FOUNDERS DID NOT ATTEND THE CONVENTION?

Several important political leaders did not attend the Constitutional Convention. Thomas Jefferson was in Paris as U.S. minister to France. John Adams (1735–1826), a principal architect of the Massachusetts constitution of 1780 and the author of *Defence of the Constitutions of Government of the United States of America*, was serving as U.S. ambassador to Great Britain. Patrick Henry (1736–1799), the Revolutionary leader, refused to attend the convention, supposedly saying "I smell a rat." He opposed the development of a strong national government and was suspicious of what might happen at the convention. Other leaders who did not attend the Philadelphia Convention included John Hancock, Samuel Adams, and Richard Henry Lee.

Besides these prominent individuals, one state refused to send delegates. Rhode Island's legislature did not want a stronger national government. The Articles of Confederation required the approval of all thirteen states to make amendments. The convention had been appointed to recommend amendments, not to scrap the Articles in favor of a new national constitution. Rhode Island believed that it could exercise veto power over whatever was proposed by simply refusing to participate.

69

student page ▾ 70

WHAT RULES DID THE DELEGATES ADOPT FOR THE CONVENTION?

Each state delegation, regardless of size, was allowed to cast only one vote at the Convention. If a delegation was evenly divided on an issue, then it could not vote. This rule had a substantial effect on important votes, as becomes clear in the next three lessons.

WHAT DO YOU THINK?

❶ What criteria would you use to select a group of people to draft a constitution today?

❷ What would be the advantages and disadvantages of selecting people to represent the interests of their states?

❸ Would you select people to represent other interests? Are there any groups whose interests do not need to be represented? Explain your reasoning.

WHAT RULES DID THE DELEGATES ADOPT FOR THE CONVENTION?

On Friday, May 25, 1787, eleven days after the convention was scheduled to begin, delegations from a majority of the states were present in Philadelphia. After electing George Washington president of the convention, the delegates appointed a committee to draw up the rules for the meeting. The next Monday and Tuesday the delegates adopted the following key rules to govern their debates:

- Delegates from at least seven states had to be present for the convention to do business each day.

- If a delegate's absence would leave a state without representation, then he had to get permission to be absent.

- When rising to speak, a delegate had to address the president. While he was speaking, other members could not pass notes, hold conversations with one another, or read a book, pamphlet, or paper.

- A member was not allowed to speak more than twice on the same question. He could not speak the second time until every other member had had a first opportunity to speak on the subject.

- Committees could be appointed as necessary.

- Any decision made by the convention was subject to reconsideration and change. No decision had to be final until the entire plan was completed.

- The convention's proceedings were to remain secret. No delegate could disclose the substance of the debates, although they were allowed to take notes. (Had it not been for Madison, who attended nearly every session and kept careful notes that would be published after his death, probably little would be known about what happened during the convention.)

The rules established the basis for **civil discourse**, a reasoned discussion in which every member has the opportunity to speak on any question, in which no individual's voice can drown out the ideas of others, and in which listening matters as much as speaking. In this discussion ideas and proposals introduced later had the opportunity to alter decisions already made. This rule was essential, because each provision of a constitution is related to many others. Secrecy allowed for the free exchange of ideas. Many delegates feared that if their debates were made public, then they would not feel free to express their real opinions or to change their minds in response to good arguments. They also thought the new constitution would have a greater chance of being accepted if people did not know about the arguments that occurred while it was being debated.

Over nearly four months these rules guided the convention's debate. At four critical points the delegates appointed committees to suggest solutions to difficult issues: (1) a committee to resolve the problem of representation in Congress; (2) a Committee of Detail to write a draft constitution, including provisions for the executive and judicial branches; (3) a Committee on Postponed Matters to deal with issues such as how to elect the national president; and (4) a Committee on Style to prepare the final language.

Why did Patrick Henry say "I smell a rat" to explain why he refused to attend the Philadelphia Convention?

CRITICAL THINKING EXERCISE

Examining the Advantages and Disadvantages of Secrecy in Governmental Procedures

Opponents of the proposed Constitution criticized the Convention's rule of secrecy. Some of them argued that secrecy alone was a reason to reject the Constitution. They contended that the public's business should be conducted publicly.

Today some governmental deliberations still are held in secret. For example, the Senate and House committees on military intelligence are closed to the public. The deliberations of juries, the Supreme Court, federal courts of appeal, and state appellate courts are not open to the press or the public.

Work in groups of two or three students to answer the following questions. Then be prepared to explain and defend your answers.

❶ What are the advantages and disadvantages of conducting some governmental matters in secret?

❷ In what ways can secret proceedings protect or threaten individual rights?

❸ In what ways can secret proceedings protect or threaten the common good?

❹ What proceedings, if any, do you believe should be conducted in secret?

Why did the delegates decide to hold the Philadelphia Convention in secret?

WHAT WAS THE VIRGINIA PLAN?

Many delegates came to Philadelphia convinced that the Articles of Confederation should be scrapped, not amended. One of these was James Madison. Before the convention he already had drafted a plan for a new national government, which came to be called the Virginia Plan. The Virginia delegates agreed to put Madison's plan forward as a basis for the convention's discussions. Edmund Randolph, Madison's fellow Virginian who later would become the first U.S. attorney general, did so on May 29, 1787.

The most important thing to know about the Virginia Plan is that it proposed a strong national government. The Articles of Confederation authorized the national government to act only on the states, not on the people directly. Under the Virginia Plan the national government would have the power to make and enforce laws and to collect taxes, both actions that would directly affect individuals.

Each citizen would be governed under the authority of two governments, the national government and a state government. Both governments would get their authority from the people. The existence of two governments, national and state, each given a certain amount of authority, is known as a **federal system**. In addition, the Virginia Plan recommended the following:

- The national government would have three branches: legislative, executive, and judicial. The legislative branch would be more powerful than the other branches because, among other things, it would have the power to select people to serve in the executive and judicial branches.

- The national legislature, Congress, would have two houses. A House of Representatives would be elected directly by the people of each state. The House then would elect a Senate from lists of persons nominated by the state legislatures.

- The number of representatives from each state in both the House and the Senate would be based on the size of its population or on the amount of its contribution to the federal treasury. This system of **proportional representation** meant that states with larger populations would have more representatives in the legislature than would states with smaller populations.

- Congress would have power to make all laws that individual states were not able to make, such as laws regulating trade between two or more states.

student page ▼ 71–72

WHAT WAS THE VIRGINIA PLAN?

James Madison brought his political and scholarly talents to the Convention. He was by far the delegate best prepared for the debates. He had been a member of the Virginia Constitutional Convention and served in the Continental Congress. He also read voraciously, many of his books about government being sent to him by Thomas Jefferson from Paris. Madison produced two documents in preparation for the Constitutional Convention. The first, *Notes on Ancient and Modern Confederacies* contained a survey of every available treatise on present and past confederacies. The second, *Vices of the Political System of the United States* built on the *Notes* and led him to conclude that America could succeed only if it were transformed from thirteen independent states into one extended republic.

The plan that Madison drafted—but Edmund Randolph presented—consisted of fifteen "resolutions."

wtpcompanion.civiced.org   **PRIMARY SOURCES**

Visit the We the People companion website for a link to the text of the Virginia Plan.

The prominent features of the Virginia Plan were as follows:

- Three branches of government: legislative, executive, and judicial

- Bicameral legislature

- Lower house based on proportional representation with representatives to serve three-year terms

- Upper house with members elected by the lower house to serve seven-year terms

- Either house able to initiate legislation

- Legislature to have power to "legislate in all cases to which the separate States are incompetent or in which the harmony of the United States may be interrupted by the exercise of individual legislation"

- Legislature to have power to nullify state laws contrary to the Constitution, acts of general government, or treaties

- Legislature to select the executive

- Executive to have qualified veto over legislation and to serve one seven-year term of office and not be eligible for reelection

- Judiciary to be appointed by the legislature to serve during "good behavior"

- Council of revision to be composed of the executive and a "convenient number" of justices to examine and veto all acts of national legislature, subject to extraordinary majority re-passage by legislature

- Ratification of the Constitution by popular vote

wtpcompanion.civiced.org   LINKS

Visit the We the People companion website for a link to material about the Convention prepared by Gordon Lloyd.

James Madison's notes of the proceedings of the Constitutional Convention state: "Mr. Charles Pinckney [of South Carolina] laid before the house the draught of a federal Government which he had prepared, to be agreed upon between the free and independent States of America." Madison made no further reference to Pinckney's plan, and it was not until the early 1900s that Pinckney's plan was discovered in the papers of Pennsylvania delegate James Wilson.

wtpcompanion.civiced.org   PRIMARY SOURCES

Visit the We the People companion website for a link to the text of Pinckney's plan.

The essential elements of Pinckney's plan included the following:

- Three branches of government: legislative, executive, and judicial

- A bicameral legislature

- A lower house, the House of Delegates, to be elected by the people based on proportional representation

- An upper house, the Senate, to be elected by the House of Delegates, four from each of four districts, with four-year terms

- An executive called the president, elected by the legislature

- A council of revision consisting of the president and some or all of his cabinet, with a veto over bills

- National veto power over state legislation

- A national judiciary

- Congress would have power to strike down state laws that it considered to be in violation of the national constitution or the national interest.

- Congress would have power to call forth the armed forces of the nation against a state, if necessary, to enforce the laws passed by Congress.

WHAT DO YOU THINK?

❶ What are the advantages and disadvantages of having two houses of Congress? Why?

❷ Why did the Virginia Plan give Congress the power to strike down laws made by state legislatures? What arguments could you make for or against giving Congress this power?

❸ In what ways did the Virginia Plan correct what the Framers perceived to be weaknesses in the Articles of Confederation?

REVIEWING AND USING THE LESSON

❶ How would you describe the delegates to the Philadelphia Convention? What prominent political leaders attended? Which leaders were absent and why?

❷ Why did Rhode Island refuse to participate in the Philadelphia Convention?

❸ In what ways were the Framers representative of the American people in 1787? In what ways were they not?

❹ How did the Virginia Plan propose to change the structure and powers of the national government under the Articles of Confederation?

❺ Work in small groups to research different states' roles in the Philadelphia Convention. How did each state's delegates respond to the Virginia Plan? Did the delegates from each state always vote the same way? Why or why not? As you study the next lessons in Unit Two, continue to examine each state's responses to proposals for representation, designs for the branches of government, and plans for the balance of power between national and state governments.

What "homework" did James Madison do in preparation for the Philadelphia Convention? What were the consequences of his having done his homework?

10
WHY WAS REPRESENTATION A MAJOR ISSUE AT THE PHILADELPHIA CONVENTION?

WHY WAS REPRESENTATION A MAJOR ISSUE AT THE PHILADELPHIA CONVENTION?

wtpcompanion.civiced.org | **LESSON PURPOSE + TERMS**

Visit the We the People companion website for printable and downloadable Lesson Purposes and Terms and Concepts to Understand sections for each lesson. Audio readings of each Lesson Purpose and Term are also available online in MP3 format.

LESSON PURPOSE

What or whom did the national government represent—the states, the people, or both? This lesson examines that debate at the Philadelphia Convention. It also examines the so-called Great Compromise, which dealt with the makeup of the House of Representatives and the Senate. In addition, it examines two issues that the Great Compromise did not resolve: how population would be counted for representation in the House and how new states might receive representation in Congress.

When you have finished this lesson, you should be able to explain the differences between the Virginia Plan and the New Jersey Plan and the importance of the Great Compromise. You also should be able to explain how the Framers addressed regional issues with the Three-Fifths Compromise and the provision for a periodic census of the population. Finally, you should be able to evaluate, take, and defend positions on why major issues debated at the Philadelphia Convention are still on the national agenda.

TERMS AND CONCEPTS TO UNDERSTAND

Great Compromise

Three-Fifths Compromise

WHAT WERE THE DISAGREEMENTS ABOUT REPRESENTATION?

Luther Martin of Maryland argued in response to the Virginia Plan that the national government should be formed for the states, not for individuals. In speeches that lasted for hours Martin argued that an equal vote for each state in the national legislature "was essential to the federal idea, and was founded in justice and freedom, not merely policy."

On June 28, 1787, Oliver Ellsworth of Connecticut proposed what later would become known as the Connecticut Compromise: proportional representation in the lower house and equal state representation in the upper house. James Madison consistently argued against a constitution that was "partly federal and partly national."

What were the strengths and weaknesses of the Virginia and New Jersey plans?

WHAT WERE THE DISAGREEMENTS ABOUT REPRESENTATION?

The Virginia Plan's proposal to create a two-house Congress was not controversial. Continuing British and colonial practices, all the states except Pennsylvania and Georgia had instituted bicameral legislatures. There also was a widespread belief that a bicameral legislature would be less likely to violate people's rights than a unicameral legislature. Each house could serve as a check on the other.

What was controversial in the Virginia Plan was the principle of *proportional* representation. James Madison, James Wilson, Rufus King, and others believed that the number of members in both houses should be based on the number of people they would represent. They argued that a government that both acted on and represented the people should give equal voting power to equal numbers of people. From Madison's perspective states should not be represented as states in the national government. Rather, each representative should serve a district and connect the people of that district to the national government.

Other delegates argued for *equal* representation of the states, as under the Articles of Confederation. Many of these delegates believed that the United States was a confederation of separate states and that national government derived from and represented the states, not the people as a whole.

The positions of many delegates in this debate reflected the size of their states. Under the Virginia Plan, a state with a larger number of people would have more votes in both houses of Congress. Many delegates from smaller states wanted equal representation. They feared that unless they had an equal voice, the larger states would dominate them.

The delegates agreed on one thing: If the national legislature had two chambers—a House and a Senate—then at least one should be based on proportional representation. This would probably be the House. Thus the debate dealt essentially with representation in the Senate.

By mid-June disagreement over representation created a crisis for the convention. Delegates from several small states, led by New Jersey statesman William Paterson (1745–1806), asked for time to come up with an alternative to the Virginia Plan.

WHAT WAS THE NEW JERSEY PLAN?

On June 15, 1787, William Paterson, who later would become the second governor of New Jersey, presented what has become known as the New Jersey Plan. This plan proposed keeping the framework of the Articles of Confederation, as the delegates had been asked to do. Following are some of the main parts of the New Jersey Plan:

- Congress would have only one house, as in the Confederation, and it would be given the following increased powers:

  - Power to levy import duties and a stamp tax to raise money for its operations, together with power to collect money from the states if they refused to pay

- Power to regulate trade among the states and with other nations

- Power to make laws and treaties the supreme law of the land so that no state could make laws that were contrary to them

- An executive branch would be made up of several persons appointed by Congress. They would have the power to administer national laws, appoint other executive officials, and direct military operations.

- A supreme court would be appointed by the officials of the executive branch. It would have the power to decide cases involving treaties, trade among the states or with other nations, and collection of taxes.

The New Jersey Plan continued the system of government existing under the Articles of Confederation by having the national government represent and act on the states, rather than representing or acting on the people. By the time the New Jersey Plan was presented, after two weeks of debate on the Virginia Plan, many delegates had become convinced that the national government needed new powers and a new organization for exercising those powers.

When the convention voted on the New Jersey Plan four days later, on June 19, it was supported only by the delegations from Connecticut, Delaware, and New Jersey, and a majority of the New York delegation—Alexander Hamilton was always outvoted by his two colleagues—with half the Maryland delegation being divided. Defeat of the New Jersey Plan meant that the Virginia Plan continued to be the basis for the convention's discussion.

The failure of the New Jersey Plan ended the idea of keeping a unicameral national legislature. But it did not mean that all the delegates had abandoned their concerns about large states' power in a bicameral legislature. On July 2 the Framers voted on whether there should be equal representation in the upper house of Congress. The result was a tie, five states to five, with Georgia divided. Neither side in this debate seemed willing to compromise, and delegates began to fear that the convention would end in disagreement and failure.

In response to this impasse a special committee composed of one delegate from each state was formed. This committee was responsible for developing a plan to save the convention. Some supporters of the Virginia Plan, including James Madison and James Wilson, opposed assigning this responsibility to a committee. However, most of the other delegates disagreed with them, and the committee went to work.

What were some of the basic elements of the New Jersey Plan presented by William Paterson?

student page ▾ 75

WHAT WAS THE NEW JERSEY PLAN?

The New Jersey Plan was hastily prepared in response to the Virginia Plan after William Paterson of New Jersey asked for a recess to give some delegates an opportunity to prepare a "purely federal" plan.

wtpcompanion.civiced.org   PRIMARY SOURCES

Visit the We the People companion website for a link to the New Jersey Plan.

The plan consisted of nine resolutions, including the following prominent features:

- Three branches of government: legislative, executive, and judicial
- Unicameral legislature with specified (enumerated) powers, including power of taxation
- Each state to be represented in the legislature
- Legislature to elect a plural executive (number not specified); executives eligible to serve one fixed-year term (length of term not specified)
- Executives to carry out laws, direct military operations, and appoint executive officers
- Executives to appoint "federal judiciary"
- Judges to hold office during "good behavior"
- Original jurisdiction of federal judiciary specified

The Virginia and New Jersey Plans were not the only ones introduced at the Convention. On June 18 Alexander Hamilton, who had been silent until then, introduced a plan consisting of eleven resolutions.

wtpcompanion.civiced.org   PRIMARY SOURCES

Visit the We the People companion website for a link to Hamilton's plan.

The essential elements of the Hamilton Plan were as follows:

- Three branches: legislative, executive, and judicial

- A bicameral legislature to have nearly exclusive sovereignty, with power to legislate on behalf of states

- An assembly to be elected by people (male suffrage) for three-year terms

- A senate to be chosen by electors from states to serve during "good behavior"

- The Senate to have sole power to declare war

- States to exist only as administrative units of national government

- An executive to be elected by electors chosen by people in electoral districts

- The executive to serve during "good behavior" and to have absolute veto over national legislation

- The executive to appoint state governors, who have veto power over state legislation

- Judges to hold office during "good behavior"

Hamilton explained and defended his plan for several hours. However, Madison's notes of the Convention state that after Hamilton spoke, the Convention adjourned without discussing his plan. There is no record that the plan ever was debated.

Hamilton did not participate significantly in the debates and frequently was absent from the Convention because of legal business. During one absence George Washington wrote to him, "I'm sorry you went away. I wish you were back." John Lansing and Robert Yates, New York's other two delegates, left the Convention for good on July 10. Therefore, New York could not vote on matters, giving Hamilton little incentive to attend.

The July 2 vote on Ellsworth's motion to give each state one vote in the upper house was as follows:

- **Yes** New York, New Jersey, Delaware, Maryland, and Connecticut

- **No** Massachusetts, Pennsylvania, Virginia, North Carolina, and South Carolina

- **Divided (could not vote)** Georgia

The result was a tie. New Hampshire delegates did not arrive at the Convention until July 23, and so there was no state to break the tie. This vote led Roger Sherman of Connecticut to comment, "We are now at a full stop."

CRITICAL THINKING EXERCISE
Developing and Defending Plans for Representation

Work in committees of about five students each. Each committee should have some students who represent small states and some who represent large states. The task of each committee is as follows:

❶ The committee should develop a plan for how many representatives each state should be allowed to send to the Senate and the House of Representatives. Your committee may decide that there is no need for a two-house Congress and that a single house will represent the people more effectively.

❷ The group should select a spokesperson to present your committee's plan to the class with all members of the committee helping to defend their plan against criticisms by members of other committees.

❸ Following presentations of all the plans, each committee may revise its original plan if it wishes.

❹ The entire class should then examine the plans made by all the committees and try to reach agreement on a single plan.

Later, individually compare the plans of the committees and the final class plan with the plan that the Framers arrived at, which is described in the next section of this lesson.

WHAT WAS THE GREAT COMPROMISE?

The result of the special committee's work was the Connecticut Compromise. It is now called the **Great Compromise**. The committee adopted a proposal previously suggested by Connecticut delegates Roger Sherman (1721–1793) and Oliver Ellsworth (1745–1807). The Great Compromise contained the following ideas:

- The House of Representatives should be elected by the people on the basis of proportional representation (Article I, Section 2).

- There should be equal representation of each state in the Senate. Each state legislature should select two senators (Article I, Section 3).

- The House of Representatives should have the power to develop all bills for taxation and government spending (Article I, Section 7). The Senate should be limited to accepting or rejecting these bills. This provision later was changed to permit the Senate to amend tax bills developed in the House and to develop appropriations bills.

As in most compromises each side gained a little and lost a little. The small states received the equal representation in the Senate that their delegates wanted in order to protect their interests. Those who believed that the national government derived from and represented the states saw that idea reflected in the Senate. The large states gave up control of the Senate but kept control of the House of Representatives with its important powers over taxation and government spending.

When the committee presented this compromise to the convention, Madison, Wilson, and several other delegates opposed it. They viewed the idea of state equality in the Senate as a step away from a strong national government back toward the system under the Articles of Confederation. Some delegates from small states remained suspicious as well. Two delegates from New York, who had consistently voted with the smaller states, left the convention and did not return. But the crisis was over when the Great Compromise passed by a single vote.

WHAT DO YOU THINK?

Madison argued that the Great Compromise was fundamentally unjust, as his notes of the convention show. Madison "conceived that the Convention was reduced to the alternative of either departing from justice in order to conciliate the smaller States, and the minority of the people of the U. S. or of displeasing these by justly gratifying the larger States and the majority of the people."

Do you agree with Madison that the Great Compromise was not a true compromise but a rejection of the principle of majority rule? Explain your position.

What objections did Madison have to the Great Compromise? Do you agree or disagree with his position? Why?

WHAT WAS THE SIGNIFICANCE OF THE THREE-FIFTHS COMPROMISE?

Settling the question of representation in the Senate did not end the discussion of how representatives would be apportioned in the House of Representatives. What did proportional representation mean? Would each state receive representation based on the entire number of its people, free and enslaved? Would only free people (including indentured servants) be counted? If governments came into being for the purpose of protecting property, then should people or districts with more property receive greater representation than those with less? This debate would result in what is known as the **Three-Fifths Compromise**.

The greatest controversy centered on whether enslaved persons should be counted when apportioning representatives to the states. Delegates from the southern states, which had the most slaves, argued that their slaves should be counted as full persons for purposes of representation. South Carolina delegate Pierce Butler (1744–1822) argued that slaves were the southern equivalent of northern free farmers and laborers. Echoing John Locke, Butler said that "an equal representation ought to be allowed for them in a Government which was instituted principally for the protection of property,

and was itself to be supported by property." Not all southerners agreed. Virginia's George Mason concurred with Butler that slaves were economically valuable, but he "could not however regard them as equal to freemen."

Delegates from the Northern states, where slavery had already been abolished or where it was declining, wondered why slaves should be counted for representation at all. Would not the elected representatives simply serve the interests of the slaves' owners? Those interests were directly opposed to the interests of slaves themselves, who would choose freedom if they could. Should slave states receive extra votes in Congress because of their slaves, votes that they would then use to perpetuate the institution of slavery itself? Also, as Elbridge Gerry of Massachusetts asked on June 11, why should "the blacks, who were property in the South, be in the rule of representation more than the Cattle & horses of the North?"

The delegates ultimately agreed on a compromise that first had been proposed during discussion of the Virginia Plan in June. According to this compromise, the entire population would be periodically counted (a census). For purposes of apportioning representatives a state's population would be equal to its entire population of free persons (including indentured servants) plus three-fifths of "all other persons," meaning slaves—

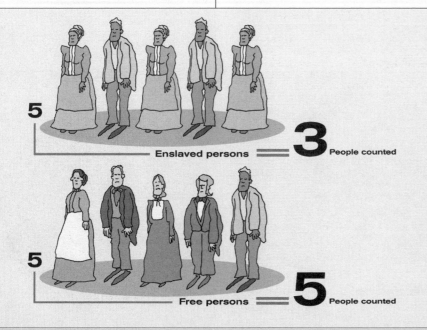

What arguments arose over the Three-Fifths Compromise?

---

student page ▾ 76

WHAT WAS THE GREAT COMPROMISE?

On July 2, the delegates created a committee chaired by Elbridge Gerry. The committee embraced a proposal by Roger Sherman that representation in the lower house be based on population, while giving each state an equal vote in the upper house. James Madison spoke strongly against the proposal, saying that "if the proper foundation of Government was destroyed, by substituting an equality in place of a proportional Representation, no proper superstructure would be raised." Nonetheless, on July 16 the Great Compromise was approved by the following vote:

- **Yes** Connecticut, New Jersey, Delaware, Maryland, and North Carolina
- **No** Pennsylvania, Virginia, South Carolina, and Georgia
- **Divided** Massachusetts

The next day delegates from the large states met to decide whether to call for reconsideration of the vote on the Great Compromise. Gouverneur Morris's motion to reconsider it died for lack of a second.

student page ▾ 77–78

WHAT WAS THE SIGNIFICANCE OF THE THREE-FIFTHS COMPROMISE?

See Lesson 8 for a discussion of the origins of the three-fifths ratio. The number also appeared in the New Jersey Plan on the subject of taxation, stating that

> whenever requisitions shall be necessary, instead of the rule for making requisitions mentioned in the articles of Confederation, the United States in Congress be authorized to make such requisitions in proportion to the whole number of white & other free citizens & inhabitants of every age sex and condition including those bound to servitude for a term of years & three fifths of all other persons not comprehended in the foregoing description, except Indians not paying taxes.

student page ▼ 78

HOW DID THE DELEGATES ADDRESS THE REPRESENTATION OF NEW STATES?

See Lesson 9 for a discussion of the Northwest Ordinance.

student page ▼ 78

ENRICHMENT ACTIVITY

COMPARING PLANS FOR THE U.S. CONSTITUTION

Obtain copies of the Virginia, New Jersey, and Hamilton plans and the summaries of each plan from the We the People companion website. Give a copy of one plan and its summary to each of three groups. Ask each group to prepare a schematic representation, or diagram, of the Constitution and the relationship between the national and state governments that would have resulted if the group's assigned plan had been adopted by the Philadelphia Convention.

> **wtpcompanion.civiced.org** | **PRIMARY SOURCES**
>
> Visit the We the People companion website for a link to the Virginia Plan, the New Jersey Plan, and Alexander Hamilton's plan.

Each group should present its schematic to the class and make the best arguments they can for why the Convention should have adopted it. The other groups should offer critiques. In defending each plan the students should focus on the following:

- The theory of representation contained in its assigned plan
- Whether the plan proposes a strong or weak national government and why
- How the plan envisions the relationship between the national and state governments and why

hence the name Three-Fifths Compromise (Article I, Section 2). Each slave also would be counted as three-fifths of a person when computing direct taxes (taxes owed by states to the national government). The three-fifths ratio was a convenient number, because it had first been proposed in the early 1780s when Congress discussed possible amendments to the Articles of Confederation to raise money from the states.

HOW DID THE DELEGATES ADDRESS THE REPRESENTATION OF NEW STATES?

The Philadelphia Convention considered not only the balance between Southern (slaveholding) and Northern (non-slaveholding) states, but also the balance between existing (eastern) and future (western) states in the makeup of the new nation. The delegates recognized that new states might join the union when western lands owned by the national government attracted settlers. They even thought their neighbor to the north, Canada, might wish to join the United States. A few delegates worried that the population in new states soon would outnumber that of the existing Atlantic seaboard states. Gouverneur Morris argued that the original states should be guaranteed a perpetual majority of the representation in Congress.

However, the Northwest Ordinance had mandated that new states should be admitted on the same terms as the original thirteen, with full representation in Congress. The periodic census, essential for counting free and enslaved persons for purposes of representation, also would allow new states to gain their proportional share of seats in the House of Representatives. The delegates decided to conduct such a census every ten years in order to reapportion, or reallocate, seats in the House based on shifts in America's population.

REVIEWING AND USING THE LESSON

❶ What were the major arguments for and against proportional representation of states in the national government? How did the New Jersey Plan differ from the Virginia Plan?

❷ What were the key elements of the Great Compromise? In what ways did it address the problem of representation, and in what ways did it not?

❸ How did the Three-Fifths Compromise and the census help delegates resolve issues of representation?

❹ How might the history of the United States have been different if the original thirteen states had been guaranteed a perpetual majority of the representation in Congress?

❺ How, if at all, has equal representation in the Senate affected the principle of majority rule?

Why might some delegates from the non-slave states have objected to the slave states counting slaves for purposes of representation?

78

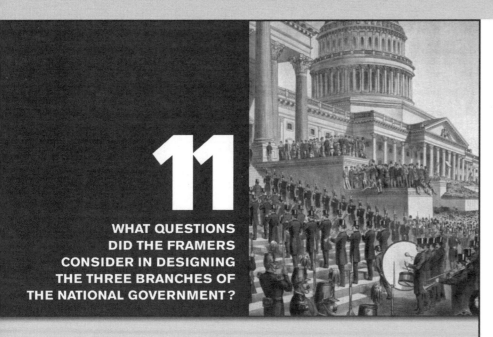

11

WHAT QUESTIONS DID THE FRAMERS CONSIDER IN DESIGNING THE THREE BRANCHES OF THE NATIONAL GOVERNMENT?

WHAT QUESTIONS DID THE FRAMERS CONSIDER IN DESIGNING THE THREE BRANCHES OF THE NATIONAL GOVERNMENT?

wtpcompanion.civiced.org   **LESSON PURPOSE + TERMS**

Visit the We the People companion website for printable and downloadable Lesson Purposes and Terms and Concepts to Understand sections for each lesson. Audio readings of each Lesson Purpose and Term are also available online in MP3 format.

LESSON PURPOSE

Political philosophers since ancient times have written that governments must do three things: make, execute, and judge laws. Unlike the British system, which concentrates power in Parliament, the U.S. Constitution assigns these competing and complementary functions to three separate branches of the national government. This lesson explains how the Framers envisioned the role of each branch.

When you have finished this lesson, you should be able to explain the role of each of the three branches and describe how the Constitution organizes them. You also should be able to explain how and why the system of checks and balances contributes to limited government. Finally, you should be able to evaluate, take, and defend positions on how the president of the United States should be elected and issues relating to the appointment and service of justices of the Supreme Court.

TERMS AND CONCEPTS TO UNDERSTAND

deliberative body   separated powers

Electoral College   shared powers

enumerated powers

necessary and proper clause

student page ▾ 80

WHAT DID THE DELEGATES THINK ABOUT LEGISLATIVE POWER, AND WHAT QUESTIONS DID ORGANIZING THE LEGISLATIVE BRANCH RAISE?

State constitutions gave legislatures power to make laws on any subject by placing legislative authority in an assembly or a bicameral legislature. The Virginia Plan contained a similarly broad grant of legislative authority to the "National Legislature," giving it power "to legislate in all cases to which the separate States are incompetent, or in which the harmony of the United States may be interrupted by the exercise of individual Legislation."

By contrast, the New Jersey Plan followed the Articles of Confederation. Under that plan the United States Congress would continue to hold only those powers "expressly delegated," but the power to tax would be added to the list. The states would retain all other powers.

The difference between the Virginia and New Jersey Plans regarding the scope of national law-making power helps clarify why the decision to give Congress "enumerated powers" was an important compromise. It also helps explain why those opposed to the proposed Constitution were suspicious of vague provisions, such as the "general welfare clause" of Article I, Section 8, Paragraph 1, and the "necessary and proper clause" of Article I, Section 8, Paragraph 18 (see Lesson 13).

See Lessons 21 and 22 on how Congress exercises its legislative powers.

student page ▾ 81

WHAT DID THE DELEGATES THINK ABOUT EXECUTIVE POWER, AND WHAT QUESTIONS DID ORGANIZING THE EXECUTIVE BRANCH RAISE?

By 1776 parliamentary supremacy was well established in Great Britain. Nonetheless, the Declaration of Independence addressed the executive tyranny of King George III. As explained in Lesson 7, most early state constitutions reflected fear of executive power by limiting the powers of governors. The Articles of Confederation also provided for a weak executive, known as the President of the United States in Congress Assembled, who served only a one-year term and whose power was very limited.

Alexander Hamilton later described the problem that the delegates faced in designing the executive branch as finding an appropriate balance among "energy" (efficient power), "stability," and "liberty." A "feeble" executive would not be able to carry out the laws, which would contribute to political instability. An executive with too much "energy" would threaten political liberty, which in turn could destabilize government (see Federalist 70).

wtpcompanion.civiced.org | **PRIMARY SOURCES**

Visit the We the People companion website for a link to Federalist 70.

WHAT DID THE DELEGATES THINK ABOUT THE BALANCE OF POWER AMONG BRANCHES OF GOVERNMENT?

Many Americans thought that an imbalance of power among different branches of government led to tyranny. They believed that the British monarch, through the use of bribes and special favors, had been able to control elections and exercise too much power over Parliament. The British government permitted members of Parliament to hold other offices at the same time, and in the eighteenth century the Crown used its exclusive power to appoint people to office as a reward for friendly members of Parliament.

The Framers believed that these actions upset the proper balance of power between the Crown and Parliament. It was the destruction of this balance to which Americans referred when they spoke of the "corruption" of Parliament by the Crown. They believed that royal governors had tried to corrupt colonial legislatures in the same way.

Given their experiences with the king and his royal governors, it is not surprising that Americans established weak executive branches in most state constitutions. However, this strategy created other difficulties. Weak executives were unable to check the powers of the state legislatures. In many people's opinion these legislatures passed laws that violated basic rights, such as the right to property.

Therefore the challenge that faced the delegates at the Constitutional Convention was how to create a system of government with balanced powers. In order to achieve this balance they created a government of **separated powers** or, as twentieth-century political historian Richard Neustadt called it, "a government of separated institutions sharing powers." This system is familiarly known as "checks and balances," as discussed in Lesson 7.

WHAT DID THE DELEGATES THINK ABOUT LEGISLATIVE POWER, AND WHAT QUESTIONS DID ORGANIZING THE LEGISLATIVE BRANCH RAISE?

Many delegates had considered the organization and powers of Congress long before the convention because of their experiences under the Articles of Confederation and in their state governments. The delegates intended Congress to be a **deliberative body**. This meant that it should thoroughly debate issues and avoid making hasty decisions. The bicameral structure of Congress made it difficult to pass laws, especially at the whim of popular majorities. The delegates agreed with Locke that the power to make laws is the greatest power a government possesses. They

also sought to prevent the sort of "corruption" that Americans remembered from colonial times, when members of Parliament often received additional appointments from the King. Therefore the delegates stipulated that members of Congress are not permitted to hold another national office while serving in the House or Senate.

The Virginia Plan would have given Congress plenary powers—*plenary* meaning "unlimited and undefined"—including a veto over state laws. In contrast, the New Jersey Plan would have more strictly defined legislative powers. With the adoption of the Great Compromise, Congress became a body with **enumerated powers**—that is, powers specifically listed, most of which are in Article I, Section 8, of the Constitution. The Framers also gave Congress the power to make all other laws that are "necessary and proper" for carrying out the enumerated powers. Article I, Section 8, Paragraph 18, is called the **necessary and proper clause** for this reason. Unit Four describes Congress's constitutional powers in detail as well as the tensions between enumerated powers and other kinds of power.

What might be the strengths and weaknesses of a government with separated branches?

WHAT DID THE DELEGATES THINK ABOUT EXECUTIVE POWER, AND WHAT QUESTIONS DID ORGANIZING THE EXECUTIVE BRANCH RAISE?

The Articles of Confederation did not provide for an executive branch, but the Confederation Congress found it necessary to create executive officials for specific purposes, including coordination of foreign affairs and management of the treasury. The Framers wanted to give the executive branch of the new government enough power and independence to fulfill its responsibilities. In contrast to the deliberative nature of Congress, the executive needed "energy"—the capacity to act quickly when necessary for the common defense, to preserve the public peace, and in international relations. However, the delegates did not want to give the executive any power or independence that could be abused.

The Philadelphia Convention did not discuss the executive branch until after it had resolved most issues concerning Congress. No delegate had come with a plan for organizing the executive. The Virginia Plan said only that the national executive should be elected by the national legislature, not what the executive branch should look like or what its powers should be.

To achieve the balance between an energetic executive and limited government, the delegates had to resolve a number of questions. Each question concerned the best way to establish an executive strong enough to check the power of the legislature but not so powerful that it would endanger republican government. Three key matters needed to be decided.

First, should there be more than one chief executive? Many Framers agreed that there should be a single executive to avoid conflict between two or more leaders of equal power. Some delegates also argued that it would be easier for Congress to keep a watchful eye on a single executive. Others argued for a plural executive, claiming that such an arrangement would be less likely to become tyrannical. The Framers agreed that there would be one president of the United States. They also assumed that there would be an executive branch composed of departments.

Second, how long should the chief executive remain in office? The Committee on Detail recommended a seven-year term for the president, but many delegates thought seven years was too long. The Committee on Postponed Matters changed the term to four years, and the convention adopted that proposal.

Third, should the executive be eligible for reelection? Under the Committee on Detail's proposal for a seven-year term of office the president would not have been eligible for reelection. When the term was reduced to four years (Article II, Section 1), the Framers decided to allow the president to serve more than one term. The Constitution originally set no limit on the number of times a president could be reelected.

HOW SHOULD PRESIDENTS BE SELECTED?

The delegates knew that the group with the power to select the president would have great power over the person who held the office. They were concerned that this power might be used to benefit some people at the expense of others. It also might make it difficult for the executive branch to function properly.

The delegates briefly discussed the idea of direct election by the people but rejected it because they believed that the citizens of such a large country would not know the best candidates. As George Mason put it, allowing the people to elect the president directly was like entrusting "a trial of colours to a blind man." Many delegates from small states also feared that direct election would give the most populous states an advantage.

Should presidents be limited to two terms in office? Why or why not?

None of the delegates came to the Convention with a clear vision of executive power in the new national government. James Wilson of Pennsylvania came the closest. On June 1, Wilson proposed a single executive, in opposition to those who feared a unitary executive would be in the best position to pose a threat to state powers. In mid-July Wilson's view prevailed, and the Convention agreed to a single executive without debate.

See Lessons 23 and 24 on how the executive branch functions.

student page ▾ 81–83

HOW SHOULD PRESIDENTS BE SELECTED?

James Wilson believed that the subject of presidential selection was "in truth the most difficult of all on which we have had to decide." The delegates debated selection of the executive many times. By August 24 they still had not reached agreement. That day they defeated direct election of the president (only Pennsylvania and Delaware voted in favor), election by one or both houses of Congress, and a proposal by James Wilson and Gouverneur Morris of Pennsylvania for election by electors.

A major point of controversy was how tie votes for president would be resolved—by the House, representing the people, or by the Senate, representing the states. Eventually the issue of executive selection was assigned to the Committee on Postponed Matters. The committee expanded on suggestions by Wilson and Morris to have delegates of the states make the selection by fashioning the Electoral College. The delegates agreed to it and to giving the House the power to select the president in case of an Electoral College tie vote. The delegates believed they had found an acceptable compromise in agreeing to the Electoral College.

Because states had very different rules regarding suffrage, popular national election of the president was not politically feasible. States with the fewest restrictions on suffrage would have a disproportionately large say over who became president. Only after later constitutional amendments prohibited states from discrimination against particular groups would a system of direct election of the president become a viable alternative.

See Lesson 16 for a discussion of the effect of political parties on presidential elections.

CRITICAL THINKING EXERCISE

Following is information about elections in the exercise.

Elections in which a presidential candidate won the popular vote but did not win the Electoral College vote took place in these years:

1824 Andrew Jackson won 41.3% of the popular vote, John Adams won 30.9%, Henry Clay won 13%, and William Crawford won 11.2%. Because none won a majority of either the popular or electoral votes, the matter was referred to the House of Representatives. In the House, Adams carried 13 states; Jackson carried 7; and Clay carried 4.

1876 Samuel Tilden led the popular vote 51% to 48% and won the electoral vote 184 to 165 with 20 electoral votes undecided. He needed 185 electoral votes to win. An Electoral Commission set up by Congress to resolve disputed electoral votes in Florida, Louisiana, South Carolina, and Oregon awarded all 20 votes to Rutherford Hayes.

1888 Incumbent Grover Cleveland and challenger Benjamin Harrison campaigned on essentially one issue—tariffs. Cleveland received 65% of the popular vote in six Southern states and won the popular vote. But he lost the election to Harrison, who won the popular vote in thirty-six states and won the electoral vote.

2000 Al Gore won 48.38% of the popular vote to George W. Bush's 47.87%. Ralph Nader won 2.75%. Gore won just twenty states and the District of Columbia, allowing Bush to garner 271 electoral votes to Gore's 266.

Elections in which the presidential candidate won the most popular votes but not an absolute majority and then won a significant majority in the Electoral College took place in these years:

1860 Republican Abraham Lincoln won 39.9% of the popular vote and 180 electoral votes to Democrat Stephen Douglas's 29.4% of the popular vote and only 12 electoral votes. Independent Democrat John Breckenridge garnered 72 electoral votes and only 8.1% of the popular vote. Constitutional Union candidate John Bell won 39 electoral votes and 12.6% of the popular vote.

1912 Democrat Woodrow Wilson won the popular vote by 41.8% to Theodore Roosevelt's 27.4%. But Wilson's electoral vote was 435 to Taft's 88. William Taft won 8 electoral votes and 23.2% of the popular vote.

1992 Bill Clinton won 43.3% of the popular vote but 370 electoral votes to George H.W. Bush's 37.7% of the popular vote and 168 electoral votes. Ross Perot won 19% of the popular vote.

Supporters of direct election, including Gouverneur Morris and James Wilson, replied that the populous states were unlikely to agree on the same candidates. They also worried that indirect election—by Congress or by state legislatures, the most common proposals—would lead to "corruption and cabal [cliques or self-serving groups]."

The main methods to be considered involved indirect election of the president. The delegates considered election bodies including Congress, state legislatures, state governors, and a temporary group elected for that purpose.

If Congress were given the power to choose the president, then limiting the term of office to a single, long term—seven years in the initial plan—would be a way to protect separation of the executive and legislative branches. Congress would not be able to manipulate a president who in turn would not have to worry about being reelected. This is why the Framers also decided that Congress could neither increase nor decrease the president's salary once the president was in office. If a president were not to be chosen by Congress, then providing for a shorter term of office would make the president more accountable to the people. But selection by state legislatures or governors might make the president too sensitive to local rather than national matters.

The problem was given to the Committee on Postponed Matters. The committee proposed a clever compromise (Article II, Sections 2, 3, and 4). It did not give any existing group the power to select the president. Instead, it proposed what now is called the **Electoral College**. The main parts of this plan were as follows:

- The Electoral College would be organized once every four years to select a president. After the election the college would be dissolved.

- Each state would select members of the Electoral College, called electors, "in such manner as the legislature thereof may direct." In other words, each state legislature maintained control over how and by whom that state's electors would be chosen.

- Each state would have the same number of electors as it had senators and representatives in Congress. This proposal built both the Great Compromise and the Three-Fifths Compromise into the process of electing a president, as a state got additional electors simply for being a state (having two senators) and for its enslaved population, which increased its representation in the House of Representatives.

- Each elector would vote for two people, at least one of whom had to be a resident of a state other than the elector's state. This forced the elector to vote for at least one person who might not represent his particular state's interests.

- The person who received the highest number of votes, if it was a majority of the electors, would become president. The person who received the next largest number of votes would become vice president, which at the time was a vaguely defined office devised near the end of the convention.

- If the top two candidates received the same number of votes or if no one received a majority vote, then the House of Representatives would select the president by a majority vote, with each state having only one vote. In case of a vice-presidential tie, the Senate would

Why do you suppose the White House is a relatively modest building compared with the palaces of heads of states in many other countries?

select the vice president, with each senator casting one vote.

Although complicated and unusual, this compromise seemed to be the best solution. There was little doubt in the delegates' minds that George Washington would be elected the first president. However, there was great doubt that anyone after Washington would be enough of a "national character" to get a majority vote in the electoral college. The delegates believed that in almost all future elections, the House of Representatives ultimately would select the president.

CRITICAL THINKING EXERCISE
Analyzing the Advantages and Disadvantages of the Electoral College

What arguments can you give for and against the use of the Electoral College to select the president? In thinking about your response, consider the following facts: On four occasions in American history—1824, 1876, 1888, and 2000—the presidential candidate who won the popular vote did not win the Electoral College vote. On other occasions—including 1860, 1912, and 1992—the candidate who won the most popular votes did not win an absolute majority of the popular vote but won a significant majority in the Electoral College.

WHAT DID THE DELEGATES THINK ABOUT JUDICIAL POWER, AND WHAT QUESTIONS DID ORGANIZING THE JUDICIAL BRANCH RAISE?

A national government needed a system for deciding cases involving its laws. This function could be left to state courts, but then the national laws might be enforced differently from state to state.

A judicial branch also would complete the system of separation of powers. The delegates had fewer problems agreeing on how to organize the judiciary than they had with the other two branches. They agreed that judges should be appointed by the president and confirmed by the Senate. They also agreed that all criminal trials should be trials by jury. This was a very important check, they believed, on the power of the government.

The delegates created only the Supreme Court as the head of the national judiciary and left to Congress the power to create lower federal courts (Article III, Section 1). They also reached other important agreements, among them the following:

- Judges should be independent of politics. They would use their best judgment to decide cases free from political pressures.

- Judges should hold office "during good behavior." This meant that they would not be removed from office unless they were impeached (accused) and convicted of "treason, bribery, or other high crimes and misdemeanors."

There also was considerable agreement about the kinds of powers that the judicial branch should have. The judiciary was given the power to decide conflicts between state governments and to decide conflicts that involved the national government.

WHAT DO YOU THINK?

❶ What are the advantages and disadvantages of having judges appointed, not elected, to serve "during good behavior"?

❷ Should the composition of the Supreme Court be required to reflect the political, economic, racial, ethnic, geographical, and gender diversity of our country? Why or why not?

❸ Should the Constitution be amended to require judges to retire at a specific age or after a certain number of years as a judge?

❹ It has been argued that the judiciary is the least democratic branch of our national government. What arguments can you give for and against this position?

Should judges be independent of politics? Why or why not?

student page ▼ 83

WHAT DID THE DELEGATES THINK ABOUT JUDICIAL POWER, AND WHAT QUESTIONS DID ORGANIZING THE JUDICIAL BRANCH RAISE?

Cries about obstruction of justice were raised in the colonies as early as 1761, when judges were appointed to serve only "during the royal pleasure." One of the complaints against King George fifteen years later in the Declaration of Independence was that he had "made Judges dependent on his Will alone" and had "obstructed the administration of justice by refusing his assent to laws for establishing judiciary powers. He has made judges dependent on his will alone for tenure of their offices, and the amount and payment of their salaries."

Article I, Section 3, of the Virginia constitution of 1776 required that "the legislative and executive powers of the State should be separate and distinct from the judiciary." Thus the precedent for an independent judicial branch was set.

All the plans for a national government submitted to the Philadelphia Convention called for a separate judicial branch. The delegates easily agreed to life tenure as a way to prevent judicial dependence on the other two branches. Guaranteeing that judicial compensation "not be diminished during their continuance in office" also meant that legislators could not punish judges for their decisions. Making judges subject to impeachment helped ensure that they would not abuse their office.

How judges should be selected was more controversial. The Virginia Plan called for selection by the National Legislature. The New Jersey Plan called for appointment by the plural executive, which in turn was appointed by the legislature that represented the states. Presidential nomination followed by Senate confirmation was a compromise.

The role that judges ought to play in the proposed system of government was debated primarily in the context of the Virginia Plan's proposal for a Council of Revision. It called for the executive and "a convenient number of the National Judiciary" to examine laws before they went into effect and to reject those they did not believe should become law. Delegates such as Charles Pinckney of South Carolina and Elbridge Gerry of Connecticut strongly opposed "the interference of the Judges in the Legislative business." In mid-August the delegates defeated the proposal for a Council of Revision with only Virginia, Maryland, and Delaware voting for it.

It should be noted that unlike positions held under Articles I and II, Article III does not require judges to be citizens of the United States or to have attained a particular age.

ENRICHMENT ACTIVITIES

A. SEEING THE CONSTITUTION IN COLOR

Ask students to highlight the Constitution using different colors to identify legislative, executive, and judicial powers. For example, Article II gives the president certain executive powers, but Article I gives Congress a say in some executive matters as well. Students should then discuss the color distribution as a demonstration of how separation of powers also involves blending certain powers. Ask students to draw a chart demonstrating how each of the three branches has a major portion of one kind of power but some other kinds of powers as well.

B. DEBATING THE NEED FOR A VICE PRESIDENT

It was not until September 7, 1787, that the Convention even considered the necessity or the desirability of a vice president. Then the Committee on Remaining Matters recommended creating the post. In the occasionally heated debate that followed, a number of positions were taken. Ask students to consider this question:

If you had been a delegate, which of the following positions would you have supported? Which would you have opposed? Why?

❶ The office should go to the person securing the second highest number of votes in the electoral balloting for the president.

❷ The vice president should be given the job of presiding over the Senate to break any legislative deadlocks.

❸ The vice president should not preside over the Senate because it mixes the executive and the legislative too much.

❹ There should be no office of vice president because the president and vice president might conspire against the public good.

❺ Rather than one vice president, there should be a six-person privy council to check the power of the president.

❻ A vice president is needed to serve as a successor to the president in case the president is removed or incapacitated.

Ask students to prepare a short speech that they might have delivered to their fellow delegates to the Philadelphia Convention explaining their position on the vice president.

HOW ARE POWERS DIVIDED AND SHARED AMONG THE THREE BRANCHES?

Implementing their belief in separated powers, the Framers limited the powers of each branch and provided that they had certain **shared powers**. Shared powers, such as the power to make treaties and appoint cabinet members and ambassadors, are powers that are not completely separated between branches of government but are shared among them. This system of separated and shared powers—checks and balances—was accomplished using several strategies, including the following:

● **Veto** The president shares in the legislative power through the veto. Although the president can veto a bill passed by Congress, the bill can still become a law if two-thirds of both houses of Congress vote to override the veto. The veto power appears in Article I, Section 7, although the term *veto* is not used.

● **Appointments** The power to appoint executive branch officials and federal judges is shared with Congress. The president has the power to nominate persons to fill those positions, but the Senate has the power to approve or disapprove the persons nominated (Article II, Section 2).

● **Treaties** The president has the power to negotiate a treaty with another nation, but the treaty must be approved by a two-thirds vote of the Senate (Article II, Section 2).

● **War** Although the president is commander in chief of the armed forces (Article II, Section 2), only Congress has the power to declare war (Article I, Section 8). Congress also controls the money necessary to wage a war. Therefore the power to declare and wage war also is shared.

● **Impeachment** Article I gives Congress the power to impeach the president, members of the executive branch, and federal judges and to remove them from office if they are found guilty of treason, bribery, or other high crimes and misdemeanors. Only the House of Representatives can bring the charges (impeachment). The Senate holds a trial to determine the official's guilt or innocence (conviction or acquittal). If convicted by two-thirds of the Senate, the official is removed from office.

● **Judicial review** The Constitution does not specify that the Supreme Court can decide whether acts of Congress are constitutional. However, many of the Framers assumed that the judicial branch would have this power because the judiciary of many states already played this role.

What are the advantages and disadvantages of the Senate's power to approve or disapprove persons nominated to public office by the president?

84

REVIEWING AND USING THE LESSON

❶ Why did the delegates enumerate the powers of Congress? Why do you think it did not enumerate the powers of the executive and judicial branches in the same detail?

❷ What issues did the delegates have to decide regarding the organization of the executive branch of government, and how did they resolve these issues?

❸ How did the delegates make sure the executive branch would have enough power to fulfill its responsibilities but not so much power that it could dominate the other branches of government?

❹ What is the Electoral College, and why did the delegates decide to create it?

❺ The Framers designed the national judiciary with the goal of making it independent of partisan politics. What constitutional provisions contribute to judicial independence? What constitutional provisions might threaten that independence?

❻ Has the checking and balancing relationship among the three branches intended by the Framers been maintained? Explain your response and support it with evidence.

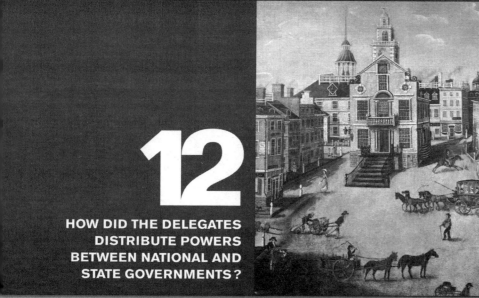

12

HOW DID THE DELEGATES DISTRIBUTE POWERS BETWEEN NATIONAL AND STATE GOVERNMENTS?

HOW DID THE DELEGATES DISTRIBUTE POWERS BETWEEN NATIONAL AND STATE GOVERNMENTS?

---

wtpcompanion.civiced.org | **LESSON PURPOSE + TERMS**

Visit the We the People companion website for printable and downloadable Lesson Purposes and Terms and Concepts to Understand sections for each lesson. Audio readings of each Lesson Purpose and Term are also available online in MP3 format.

LESSON PURPOSE

The relationship between national and state powers, more than any other issue, explains the need for the Constitutional Convention. This relationship was at the core of the first major debate, the one between supporters and opponents of the Virginia Plan. After forging the Great Compromise, the delegates worked out a series of other regulations and compromises that defined what the national and state governments could and could not do. Several of those compromises involved the question of slavery, the most potentially divisive issue among the states.

When you have finished this lesson, you should be able to describe the major powers and limits on the national government, the powers that were specifically left to states, and the prohibitions the Constitution placed on state governments. You also should be able to explain how the Constitution did and did not address the issue of slavery, as well as other questions left unresolved in Philadelphia. Finally, you should be able to evaluate, take, and defend positions on how limited government in the United States protects individual rights and promotes the common good and on issues involving slavery at the Philadelphia Convention.

TERMS AND CONCEPTS TO UNDERSTAND

bill of attainder	supremacy clause
ex post facto	tariff
secede	

student page ▾ 86

WHAT POWERS DID THE NATIONAL GOVERNMENT HAVE OVER STATE GOVERNMENTS AND THE PEOPLE?

The Philadelphia Convention debates focused on both powers and limits of the new national government. The powers listed in this section of the text, in addition to the powers delegated to Congress in Article I, Section 8, reveal the delegates' concerns. Two examples are worthy of further discussion:

ARTICLE IV, SECTION 4   On August 6, 1787, the Committee of Detail presented a draft of the Constitution consisting of twenty-three articles. The eighteenth article provided "that a republican form of government shall be guarantied [*sic*] to each state; and that each state shall be protected against foreign and domestick [*sic*] violence." Although it contains no definition of republican government, the provision apparently was a response to a petition from the delegates from Massachusetts to the Continental Congress on March 9, 1787, regarding Shays' Rebellion (see Lesson 8). On August 30 the delegates agreed without debate to strike the word *foreign* as being implied in the word *violence*. The clause thus guarantees the states a republican form of government, protection against invasion, and protection "against domestic Violence."

ARTICLE VI   The Committee of Detail proposed that all laws and treaties made pursuant to the Constitution be "the supreme law of the several States." On August 23 John Rutledge of South Carolina added the words "This Constitution" to the beginning of the provision. On September 13 the Committee of Style presented a draft of the document that used the phrase "the supreme law of the land" rather than "the supreme law of the several States." There was no objection.

student page ▾ 86–87

WHAT LIMITS DID THE DELEGATES PLACE ON THE NATIONAL GOVERNMENT?

The second through last paragraphs of Article I, Section 9, contain many of the rights considered essential in a bill of rights.

WHAT POWERS DID THE NATIONAL GOVERNMENT HAVE OVER STATE GOVERNMENTS AND THE PEOPLE?

One reason the delegates agreed to meet in Philadelphia was their concern about some things that state governments were doing. They believed that some states were undermining Congress's efforts to conduct foreign relations, and they feared that state governments might threaten individual rights. They also knew that the national government under the Articles of Confederation had no power to enforce its decisions. The delegates all agreed that they had to create a national government with more power than Congress had under the Articles. However, they did not agree about how much power the new national government should have over citizens and the state governments.

The delegates included a number of phrases in the Constitution that set forth the powers of the national government over the states. These include the following:

What section of the Constitution gave President Eisenhower the authority to order troops to Little Rock, Arkansas, in 1957 to enforce desegregation legislation?

- **Article I, Section 4**, grants state legislatures the power to decide the "times, places, and manner" of holding elections for senators and representatives but also grants Congress the power to make or change such regulations at any time.

- **Article I, Section 8**, gives Congress the power to set a procedure for calling the militia into national service "to execute the Laws of the Union, suppress Insurrections, and repel Invasions."

- **Article IV, Section 3**, gives Congress the power to create new states.

- **Article IV, Section 4**, gives the national government the authority to guarantee to each state "a Republican Form of Government." (Virginia delegate Edmund Randolph argued in the convention that no state should have the power to "change its government into a monarchy.")

- **Article IV, Section 4**, also requires the national government to protect the states from invasion or domestic violence.

- **Article VI, Section 2**, also known as the **supremacy clause**, makes the Constitution and all laws and treaties approved by Congress in exercising its enumerated powers the supreme law of the land. It also says that judges in state courts must follow the Constitution, or federal laws and treaties, if there is a conflict with state laws.

WHAT LIMITS DID THE DELEGATES PLACE ON THE NATIONAL GOVERNMENT?

The Constitution also includes several limitations on the powers of the national government. Each of these provisions was designed to prevent a type of abuse that the delegates had seen in British history, in their own colonial and state governments, or in the national government under the Articles of Confederation.

Several provisions protect individual rights against violation by the national government:

- The national government may not suspend the writ of habeas corpus, "unless when in Cases of Rebellion or Invasion the public Safety may require it" (Article I, Section 9).

- The national government may not pass *ex post facto* laws and bills of attainder (Article I, Section 9). An *ex post facto* law changes the legality of an act after it has occurred. A **bill of attainder** is a punishment ordered by a legislature rather than by a court—that is, a law that declares a person guilty of a crime and decrees a punishment without a judicial trial.

- The national government may not suspend the right to trial by jury in criminal cases (Article III, Section 2).

- The Constitution also offers protection from the accusation of treason by defining this crime specifically and narrowly (Article III, Section 3). Congress cannot modify this

definition. It can be changed only
by a constitutional amendment.

Several other limitations protect the political independence and other rights of public officials:

- Members of Congress cannot be arrested "during Attendance at the Session of their respective Houses," unless they commit "Treason, Felony, and Breach of the Peace." Their speech or debate in the halls of Congress also is protected (Article I, Section 6).

- Congress cannot impose a religious test on people who hold national office (Article VI, Section 3). This means that people cannot be required to express certain religious beliefs as a qualification for holding office.

- If members of the executive or judicial branches are accused of misconduct in office, then the impeachment clauses (Article I, Section 3) protect their right to a fair trial.

- The national government cannot take money from the treasury without an appropriation law, nor can it grant titles of nobility (Article I, Section 9).

Why do you think the Constitution prohibits Congress from imposing religious tests on people nominated for public office? Do you agree with this prohibition? Why or why not?

Why do you think the Constitution prohibits states from coining their own money?

WHAT LIMITS DID THE DELEGATES PLACE ON STATE GOVERNMENTS?

The Constitution also limits the powers of state governments but not nearly as much as Madison had hoped for in the Virginia Plan. Many of the Constitution's limitations on state power are in Article I, Section 10, which prohibits states from

- Coining their own money

- Passing laws that enable people to violate contracts, such as those between creditors and debtors

- Making *ex post facto* laws or bills of attainder

- Entering into treaties with foreign nations or declaring war

- Granting titles of nobility

- Laying duties (taxes) on imports or exports, except as necessary to pay for inspections

- Keeping troops or ships of war in times of peace

In addition, Article IV prohibits states from

- Unfairly discriminating against citizens of other states

- Refusing to return fugitives from justice to the states from which they have fled

student page ▾ 87–88

WHAT LIMITS DID THE DELEGATES PLACE ON STATE GOVERNMENTS?

Many of the limitations placed on states also are commonly found in bills of rights. Other provisions protect creditors against debtors. In Federalist 44 Madison defended such provisions as helping to "banish speculations on public measures, inspire a general prudence and industry and give a regular course to the business of society."

student page ▾ 88–89

HOW DID SLAVERY AFFECT THE DISTRIBUTION OF NATIONAL AND STATE POWERS?

ARTICLE I, SECTION 2 (THREE-FIFTHS COMPROMISE) Slavery was one of the most divisive issues at the Philadelphia Convention. It clearly affected the decision about what or who should be represented in Congress. The Virginia Plan, for example, proposed using population as the basis for apportioning representatives. William Paterson of New Jersey (population of about 185,000 to Virginia's population of about 748,000) objected. According to Madison's notes of the Convention,

> He [Paterson] could regard negro slaves in no light but as property. They are no free agents, have no personal liberty, no faculty of acquiring property, but on the contrary are themselves property, and like other property entirely at the will of the Master. Has a man in Virginia a number of votes in proportion to the number of his slaves? And if Negroes are not represented in the States to which they belong, why should they be represented in the General Government?

ARTICLE I, SECTION 9 (LIMITATION ON IMPORTATION OF SLAVES) As originally proposed by the Committee of Detail, the provision prevented Congress from ever prohibiting the slave trade or providing a tax incentive to states to abolish it. Charles Pinckney of South Carolina argued that his state "can never receive the plan [Constitution] if it prohibits the slave trade." Fellow South Carolina delegate John Rutledge argued,

> Religion and humanity had nothing to do with this question. Interest alone is the governing principle with nations. The true question at present is whether the Southern States shall or shall not be parties to the Union.

Opponents of the slave trade, including Maryland's Luther Martin, who argued that slavery was "inconsistent with the principles of the revolution," finally agreed to the compromise contained in this section, which permitted Congress both to eliminate the slave trade in 1808 and to discourage the trade through taxation. Madison wrote of this provision in Federalist 42:

> It were doubtless to be wished that the power of prohibiting the importation of slaves had not been postponed until the year 1808, or rather that it had been suffered to have immediate operation. But it is not difficult to account either for this restriction on the general government, or for the manner in which the whole clause is expressed. It ought to be considered as a great point gained in favor of humanity that a period of

Why do you think the Constitution prohibits state governments from entering into treaties with other nations?

Many of these provisions, including the prohibitions on states making treaties, declaring war, or keeping armed forces in times of peace, were not new. They also had been part of the Articles of Confederation. Other limitations, such as the prohibition on "impairing the obligation of contracts," arose from the delegates' experiences in the 1780s, when some state legislatures attempted to pass laws releasing people from the responsibility to pay their debts.

WHAT DO YOU THINK?

❶ In what ways do the limitations on the national and state governments protect individual rights?

❷ In what ways do the limitations on the national and state governments promote the common good?

HOW DID SLAVERY AFFECT THE DISTRIBUTION OF NATIONAL AND STATE POWERS?

Many delegates opposed slavery, and several northern states had begun to take steps toward abolishing it. Virginian James Madison stated at the convention that he "thought it wrong to admit in the Constitution that there could be property in men." Therefore the words *slave* and *slavery* never appear in the Constitution, even though several provisions clearly protected the institution.

Slaveholders considered their slaves to be personal property. Many delegates, not only Southerners, argued that slavery was fundamentally a state institution, like other matters related to property rights. Oliver Ellsworth of Connecticut stated, "The morality or wisdom of slavery are considerations belonging to the states themselves." If the Constitution interfered with slavery, North Carolina, South Carolina, and Georgia made it clear that they would not become part of the new nation and might instead form their own confederacy.

In addition to the Three-Fifths Compromise described earlier, other provisions in the Constitution reflected the differences between states that depended on slavery and those that did not.

The third paragraph of Article IV, Section 2, often called the "fugitive slave clause," shows how the delegates sought to balance these views. This clause provides that if a person "held to service or labor" in one state escaped into another, he or she had to be delivered back to the person who claimed him or her. In an early draft this clause began with the words "No person legally held to service or labor in one state." On the next-to-last day of the convention the delegates changed this to "No person held to service or labor in one state, under the laws thereof." This alteration was significant because it showed that the delegates did not intend to make slavery legal on a national level or in abstract terms. Instead, this clause reinforced the fact that slavery was a state institution, but it gave slaveholders the right to claim escaped slaves.

Another agreement between Northern and Southern delegates involved the issue of commerce. Congress gained the power to regulate commerce among the states, which the Northern states wanted. The delegates defeated a Southern attempt to require a two-thirds vote of both houses to pass laws regulating commerce. Many Southern delegates feared that Northern congressmen would seek **tariffs** (taxes on imports of manufactured goods). To satisfy the Southern states, the Constitution provided that the national government would not interfere with the importation of slaves to the United States earlier than 1808 (Article I, Section 9). This gave slave owners an additional twenty years to bring new slaves from Africa or the West Indies to the United States.

CRITICAL THINKING EXERCISE
**Understanding Positions on
Slavery at the Philadelphia Convention**

Although the delegates voted to give constitutional protection to slavery, many of them were not proud of having done so. They considered slavery to be a necessary evil at best, and many hoped it would go away by itself if left alone. As we now know, this protection of slavery almost destroyed the United States.

Work in small groups to develop positions for and against the following propositions:

❶ John Locke argued that an essential purpose of government is to protect property. Therefore the value of all property, including enslaved Africans, should be counted in allocating representatives to each state.

❷ The Declaration of Independence asserts that all people are created equal and endowed with inalienable rights. Therefore property in people should not be taken into account in allocating representatives to each state.

❸ The settling of fundamental issues, such as whether or not to allow slavery, should be left up to each state.

WHAT ISSUES DID THE PHILADELPHIA CONVENTION LEAVE UNADDRESSED?

Slavery was not the only issue that the delegates did not directly address. The Constitution they drafted said nothing about national citizenship. Questions of citizenship were implicitly left to each state because the delegates could not agree on the answers. Some Northern states considered free African Americans to be citizens, while Southern delegates objected to that practice.

Similarly the Constitution was mostly silent on the issue of voting rights. Each state had its own laws about who could vote. Usually those laws defined the amount of property a person had to own in order to qualify to vote as well as the amount of property required for a

What provisions of the Constitution protected slavery?

twenty years may terminate forever, within these Sates, a traffic which has so long and so loudly upbraided the barbarism of a modern policy; that within that period it will receive a considerable discouragement from the federal government, and may be totally abolished, by a concurrence of the few States which continue the unnatural traffic in the prohibitory example which has been given by so great a majority of the Union. Happy would it be for the unfortunate Africans if an equal prospect lay before them of being redeemed from the oppressions of their European brethren!

ARTICLE IV, SECTION 2 (FUGITIVE SLAVE CLAUSE) Southern states wanted other states to return escaped slaves, something that the Articles of Confederation did not guarantee. However, the Continental Congress in adopting the Northwest Ordinance had included a clause promising that slaves who escaped to the territory would be returned to their owners. This clause was part of a compromise required to make the Northwest Territory free, not slave territory. At the Philadelphia Convention the Southern states demanded the same provision. New England delegates agreed to it, in part to protect the lucrative slave trade in which several of their states also engaged.

In the years after the Declaration of Independence most Northern states began the process of ending slavery within their borders. They did so by a variety of methods. For example, Vermont abolished slavery in its first constitution in 1777, when it declared itself an independent republic. Vermont would become a state in 1791.

Massachusetts courts heard "freedom suits" from slaves in the late 1770s and interpreted the state constitution to outlaw slavery. In 1783 the Massachusetts chief justice wrote in *Commonwealth v. Jennison* that "there can be no such thing as perpetual servitude of a rational creature."

Five states—Connecticut, Rhode Island, Pennsylvania, New York, and New Jersey—enacted gradual emancipation laws. Pennsylvania's statute in 1780 provided that all slaves born after its passage would become free when they turned age twenty-eight. New York's 1799 law mandated that future-born girls would be free at age twenty-five, boys at twenty-eight. Such laws meant that slavery continued to exist in these states well into the nineteenth century.

person to hold public office. No two states had the same qualifications, which is why the delegates left the "times, places, and manner" of electing members of Congress to the individual states. Only once does the Constitution prescribe voting rights. Article I, Section 2, states that anyone entitled to vote for "the most numerous branch of the state legislature" also is entitled to vote in elections for the House of Representatives.

This clause provoked debate among the delegates when Gouverneur Morris argued that suffrage for the House should be restricted to landowners. Other delegates responded that the states would not be able to agree on such a qualification and that any nationwide qualification would disenfranchise people who already possessed the right to vote in some states. Besides, argued

Benjamin Franklin, many of the sailors who had fought for America's independence were ordinary people who owned no land, and the adult sons of wealthy farmers often did not possess their own land until later in life. If the Constitution disenfranchised these people, Franklin said, it would deny their contributions to the United States. On a practical level Americans were unlikely to ratify a Constitution that stripped them of voting rights.

In practice the powers and limitations on national and state power have proved far more complicated than the provisions in the Constitution. Apart from the specific prohibitions in Article I and elsewhere, the Constitution barely suggests where national power ends and state power begins. In particular, the necessary and proper clause of Article I, Section 8, remains a source of controversy about the extent of national power.

In the seventy years after the Philadelphia Convention it became clear that another fundamental issue had not been resolved. Did states possess the right to **secede**, or withdraw, from the United States once they ratified the Constitution? Under the Articles of Confederation the states made up a "firm league of friendship," a looser confederation than under the Constitution. At several points between the 1790s and 1861 states argued that they retained the right to secede if the national government enacted measures that they considered to be intolerable. A bloody civil war, not the civil discourse of the Philadelphia Convention, would ultimately resolve this question.

How would you respond to the arguments of leaders from slave states such as John C. Calhoun, who believed states should be able to declare federal laws null and void if they thought they were unconstitutional?

90

REVIEWING AND USING THE LESSON

❶ What is the supremacy clause? Why is it important?

❷ How does the Constitution balance state powers with powers granted to the national government? How does it limit each set of powers?

❸ How did the delegates at the Philadelphia Convention deal with the issue of slavery? Why did they choose to take the approach they did?

❹ Examine Article I, Section 8, of the Constitution. List any powers of Congress that are not included that you believe should be and be prepared to explain your choices.

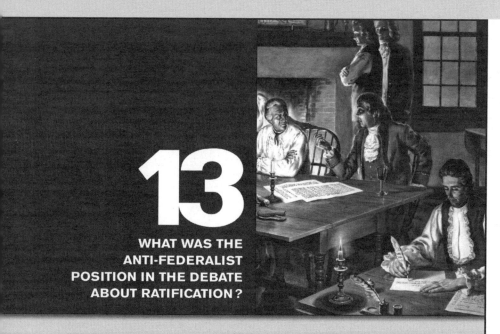

13

**WHAT WAS THE
ANTI-FEDERALIST
POSITION IN THE DEBATE
ABOUT RATIFICATION?**

WHAT WAS THE ANTI-FEDERALIST POSITION IN THE DEBATE ABOUT RATIFICATION?

wtpcompanion.civiced.org | **LESSON PURPOSE + TERMS**

Visit the We the People companion website for printable and downloadable Lesson Purposes and Terms and Concepts to Understand sections for each lesson. Audio readings of each Lesson Purpose and Term are also available online in MP3 format.

LESSON PURPOSE

Most of the delegates at the Philadelphia Convention signed the Constitution on September 17, 1787. Their product would become the law of the land only if ratified by at least nine of the thirteen states. This lesson explains the process of ratification and the opposition that erupted immediately after the draft Constitution became public. Supporters of the proposed Constitution called themselves Federalists and labeled their opponents Anti-Federalists. The names stuck, even though the opponents argued that they—not the Constitution's supporters—were the real believers in a truly "federal" system, a confederation of equal states.

When you have finished this lesson, you should be able to explain why the Anti-Federalists opposed ratifying the Constitution. You also should be able to explain the role of the Anti-Federalists in proposing a bill of rights and to identify other contributions their views have made toward interpreting the Constitution. Finally, you should be able to evaluate, take, and defend a position on the validity and relevance of Anti-Federalist arguments.

TERMS AND CONCEPTS TO UNDERSTAND

Anti-Federalists

bill of rights

ratification

`student page ▼` 92

WHY WAS A RATIFICATION PROCESS REQUIRED?

The proposed Constitution was submitted to Congress, which debated it for three days. On September 28, 1787, Congress sent the Constitution to the states without expressing an opinion about whether it should be ratified. James Madison had urged Congress to endorse ratification.

The original draft of the Preamble stated the following:

> We the People of the States of New-Hampshire, Massachusetts, Rhode-Island and Providence Plantations, Connecticut, New-York, New-Jersey, Pennsylvania, Delaware, Maryland, Virginia, North-Carolina, South-Carolina, and Georgia, do ordain, declare and establish the following Constitution for the Government of Ourselves and our Posterity.

The Committee of Style changed the wording to the Preamble as we know it.

`student page ▼` 92–93

WHERE AND HOW DID AMERICANS DEBATE THE PROPOSED CONSTITUTION?

Benjamin Franklin's speech on the last day of the Philadelphia Convention often is regarded as the beginning of the ratification debates:

> I confess, that I do not entirely approve of this Constitution at present; but, Sir, I am not sure I shall never approve it; for, having lived long, I have experienced many instances of being obliged, by better information or fuller consideration, to change my opinions even on important subjects, which I once thought right, but found to be otherwise. It is therefore that, the older I grow, the more apt I am to doubt my own judgement of others.

All the states except Rhode Island elected ratifying conventions. Rhode Island first used a series of town meetings.

wtpcompanion.civiced.org LINKS

Visit the We the People companion website for a link to the Teaching American History website on ratification prepared by Gordon Lloyd.

WHY WAS A RATIFICATION PROCESS REQUIRED?

Amending the Articles of Confederation required approval by Congress and confirmation by the legislatures of all thirteen states. The Philadelphia Convention originally was conceived only to recommend amendments to the Articles. The convention was expected to submit its work to Congress for approval or disapproval, followed by deliberations in the state legislatures.

Delegates knew that many members of Congress and the state governments would oppose the draft Constitution, largely because it reduced state powers. They also knew that it would be impossible to get all thirteen states to approve the Constitution, because Rhode Island had not sent delegates to Philadelphia.

James Madison developed the plan presented in Article VII of the Constitution: "The **ratification** of the conventions of nine states, shall be sufficient for the establishment of this Constitution between the states." The plan was to go directly to the voters to get them to approve the Constitution. The Constitution would be presented to special ratifying conventions in each state, rather than to the existing state legislatures. Delegates to the conventions would be elected by popular vote for the sole purpose of debating and approving the Constitution. Madison's plan was consistent with the idea in the Preamble to the Constitution, which says, "We the People…do ordain and establish this Constitution…." It also allowed the Constitution to go into effect without ratification in every one of the thirteen states.

The plan for ratification also was an example of social contract theory. The people who were to be governed by the new national government were asked to consent to its creation, consistent with John Locke's natural rights philosophy and the Declaration of Independence: Just governments "derive their…powers from the consent of the governed."

The idea of ratifying conventions also reflected recent history in America. When the states wrote new state constitutions during and after the Revolutionary War, they were submitted to the people for ratification, rather than to the existing state legislatures.

WHERE AND HOW DID AMERICANS DEBATE THE PROPOSED CONSTITUTION?

The debate over adopting the Constitution began within the Philadelphia Convention itself. A week before the convention ended Virginia's George Mason wrote a list of his objections on a draft copy of the Constitution and then departed without signing the finished document.

Ratification was not a foregone conclusion. As soon as the delegates released the proposed Constitution to the public, opposition emerged. In particular, heated debate erupted in the populous states of New York, Massachusetts, Pennsylvania, and Virginia. The United States would have little chance of surviving as a single nation if any of these large, commercially important states failed to ratify the Constitution.

Ratification debates took place largely in the pages of newspapers and pamphlets. The **Anti-Federalists** opened the discussion by stating their objections to the Constitution. Mason's concerns were printed as a pamphlet. Many other distinguished Americans also wrote in opposition. Several, like Mason, had been delegates in Philadelphia, including Maryland's Luther Martin, New York's Robert Yates, and Massachusetts's Elbridge Gerry. Yates wrote sixteen Anti-Federalist essays under the pseudonym, or pen name, Brutus, after Marcus Junius Brutus, who helped assassinate Julius Caesar allegedly in order to preserve the Roman Republic. Other important writers against the Constitution included Mercy Otis Warren, a Massachusetts playwright from a distinguished Revolutionary family, and Richard Henry Lee, a leading Virginia revolutionary and signer of the Declaration of Independence. Lee was once thought to have written Anti-Federalist essays under the pseudonym Federal Farmer. However, most historians now believe that Federal Farmer was Melancton Smith, an Anti-Federalist from New York. As opponents published their criticisms of the Constitution, supporters responded with defenses of the document (discussed in the next lesson).

On both sides writers believed in an essentially republican idea, namely, the use of reasoned discourse to

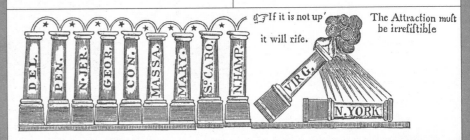

Why do you think Madison suggested having the Constitution ratified by the people in special conventions instead of by state legislatures?

What objections to the Constitution were held by such Anti-Federalists as Mercy Otis Warren?

educate the citizenry. They drew on political philosophy and ancient and recent history to make their arguments. Most of them employed pseudonyms so that their arguments would be read on their merits, rather than on the reputations of the authors. Ordinary Americans read and discussed the arguments in their homes, in coffee-houses and taverns, and in public meetings, thereby creating a truly nationwide debate.

WHAT DO YOU THINK?

❶ Were the delegates justified in creating new rules for the ratification of the proposed Constitution? Why or why not?

❷ If a convention were called today to consider major changes to the United States Constitution or to draft a new constitution, what rules would ensure an informed civic discussion of fundamental issues?

❸ Today most newspapers refuse to publish letters to the editor or opinion statements without identifying the authors. By contrast, many people express opinions on the Internet using pseudonyms. Does the use of pseudonyms today improve or diminish the quality of civil discourse? Explain your reasoning.

WHAT WERE THE KEY ELEMENTS OF THE ANTI-FEDERALISTS' OPPOSITION?

Like many Federalists, Anti-Federalists believed in the basic ideas of republicanism. These ideas included the concept that the greatest governing power in a republic should be placed in a legislature composed of representatives elected by the people.

Anti-Federalists believed in another idea that dated back to classical republicanism, that representative government could work only in a small community of citizens with similar interests and beliefs. Only in such a community can people agree on the common good or their common interest, and only in such a community will representatives truly reflect the beliefs and characteristics of their constituents. A large, diverse state or nation cannot sustain a republic, Anti-Federalists believed. In such a nation a single national government will impose uniform rule over a heterogeneous population of diverse economic pursuits, varied religious and secular beliefs, and differing traditions and customs. In addition, in a large geographical territory many citizens live far away from the seat of government, making it difficult for them to watch over the activities of their representatives.

Once a government operates at a distance from most of its citizens, Robert Yates argued (as Brutus) in the first of his essays, it can no longer reflect those citizens' character or wishes. To maintain its authority, such a government will resort to force rather than popular consent. It will require a standing army, and it will tax the people in order to sustain that army. As a result, truly republican

What principles of classical republicanism did Anti-Federalists such as Richard Henry Lee think would be endangered by the new government created by the Constitution?

93

According to historian Bernard Bailyn,

The initial publication of the Constitution on September 17, 1787, and Congress's call for the states to vote on ratification touched off one of the most extensive public debates on constitutionalism and on political principles ever recorded. The entire political nation was galvanized in the debate. Literally thousands of people, in this nation of only approximately one million eligible voters, participated in one way or another. There were some fifteen hundred official delegates to the twelve state ratifying conventions, where every section, every clause and every phrase of the Constitution was raked over. There was a multitude of newspaper commentaries, sermons, letters, broadsides, and personal debates on the Constitution; they turned up even in the most remote corners of the nation.

The states ratified the Constitution in the following order; vote counts are in parentheses:

Delaware: December 7, 1787 (30–0)

Pennsylvania: December 12, 1787 (46–23)

New Jersey: December 18, 1787 (38–0)

Georgia: January 2, 1788 (26–0)

Connecticut: January 9, 1788 (128–40)

Massachusetts: February 6, 1788 (187–168)

Maryland: April 28, 1788 (63–11)

South Carolina: May 23, 1788 (149–73)

New Hampshire: June 21, 1788 (57–47)

Virginia: June 25, 1788 (89–79)

New York: July 26, 1788 (30–27)

North Carolina: November 21, 1789 (195–77) (The first convention had adjourned August 2, 1788, without voting on ratification.)

Rhode Island: May 29, 1790 (34–32) (Town meetings on March 24, 1788, previously rejected 2,708–237.)

Twenty-nine of the delegates who attended the Convention participated in ratifying debates in their states. Massachusetts was a critical state. The Constitution ran into well-organized opposition there, particularly a demand for amendments before ratification. John Adams and John Hancock eventually negotiated a compromise between opponents who insisted that the document be amended before it was ratified and supporters who insisted that it be accepted or rejected as it was. The compromise was a recommendation that the first Congress under the new Constitution consider amendments.

WHAT WERE THE KEY ELEMENTS OF THE ANTI-FEDERALISTS' OPPOSITION?

Essays by Brutus appeared in newspapers between October 1787 and April 1788, about the same time that the first seventy-seven Federalist papers were written (see Lesson 14). Pamphlets were another common way of circulating opinions. Maryland Farmer—probably John Mercer, a delegate to the Philadelphia Convention who refused to sign the Constitution—wrote so persuasively on issues such as the need for a bill of rights and the virtues of simple versus complex government that his essays attracted wide attention. Other opposition writings remained quite local. For example, the letters of Agrippa, probably written by James Winthrop, the librarian at Harvard University, focused mostly on the proposed Constitution's effect in Massachusetts. Some people opposed to the Constitution, including Patrick Henry of Virginia, gave powerful speeches rather than writing essays.

George Washington later wrote that opposition to the Constitution had been constructive:

> On the whole, I doubt whether the opposition to the Constitution will not ultimately be productive of more good than evil; it has called forth, in its defense, abilities which would not perhaps been otherwise exerted that have thrown new light upon the science of Government, they have given the rights of man a full and fair discussion, and explained them in so clear and forcible a manner, as cannot fail to make a lasting impression.

governments (those at the local or state level) will lose their power. The distant national government's taxation of citizens also will leave little money for local governments.

Anti-Federalists also believed that people living in small, agrarian communities are more likely to possess the civic virtue required of republican citizens. Living closely together, they are more willing to set aside their own interests when necessary and to work for the common good. Moreover, the social and cultural institutions that best cultivate civic virtue—such as education and religion—work most effectively in small, homogeneous communities. Many Anti-Federalists argued that stronger institutions to foster civic virtue, not a stronger central government, would best overcome the problems that America faced in 1787 and in the future.

HOW DID THE ANTI-FEDERALISTS' PHILOSOPHY SHAPE THEIR OBJECTIONS TO THE CONSTITUTION?

Anti-Federalists believed that the Constitution would create a government that the people could not control. The size and diversity of the United States were exactly the opposite of a homogeneous small republic. A strong national government in a large nation, the Anti-Federalists argued, would be prone to the abuses that had destroyed republics since ancient times.

Anti-Federalists believed that each branch of the proposed national government had the potential for tyranny. Their specific arguments against the Constitution included the following:

- The Constitution gives Congress the power to make any laws that Congress believes "necessary and proper" to carry out its responsibilities. There is no adequate limitation on its powers. Congress could grant monopolies in trade and commerce, create new crimes, inflict severe or unusual punishments, and extend its power as far as it wants. As a result, the powers of the state legislatures and the liberties of the people could be taken from them.

- The president of the United States has the unlimited power to grant pardons for crimes, including treason. He could use this power to protect people whom he has secretly encouraged to commit crimes, keep them from being punished, and thereby prevent the discovery of his own crimes.

- The national courts have so much power that they can destroy the judicial branches of the state governments. If this were to happen and the only courts available were national (federal) courts, most people would not be able to

afford to have their cases heard because they would need to travel a great distance. Rich people would have an advantage that would enable them to oppress and ruin the poor.

Anti-Federalists also argued that the celebrated system of checks and balances among the branches could be turned against the people's liberties. Following are two examples:

- The Constitution says that treaties are the supreme law of the land. Treaties can be made by the president with the approval of the Senate, giving the Senate an exclusive legislative power in this area. This means that the Senate can act without the approval of the House of Representatives, the only branch of the legislature that is directly answerable to the people.

- The powers of the executive and legislative branches are more mixed than separated. Rather than check each other, the president and Congress could collude to enact legislation, make war, or pass taxes that would undermine state and local governments.

Anti-Federalists also believed that the Constitution did not create a truly representative national government. The initial House of Representatives would have only sixty-five members from a population of more than three million, roughly one representative for every forty-six thousand citizens. Elected members of Congress would not be able to know, much less reflect the characteristics of, their constituents. An elite, privileged group soon would dominate the national government.

CRITICAL THINKING EXERCISE
Analyzing the Positions of Some Anti-Federalists

Working in small groups, read the following statements by three Anti-Federalist writers. Summarize each writer's concern. What views of republican government are expressed in each statement? How, if at all, do the statements form a chain of reasoning for opposing the proposed Constitution?

> ❝ If respect is to be paid to the opinion of the greatest and wisest men who have ever thought or wrote on the science of government, we shall be constrained to conclude, that a free republic cannot succeed over a country of such immense extent, containing such a number of inhabitants, and these increasing in such rapid progression as that of the whole United States.... History furnishes no example of a

free republic, anything like the extent of the United States.

Brutus (probably Robert Yates of New York), No. 1

" Give me leave to demand, what right had they [the drafters of the Constitution] to say, *We, the People*. My political curiosity, exclusive of my anxious solicitude for the public welfare, leads me to ask who authorized them to speak the language of, *We, the People*, instead of *We, the States*? States are the characteristics, and the soul of a confederation. If the States be not the agents of this compact, it must be one great consolidated National Government of the people of all the States.

Patrick Henry of Virginia

" There is no security in the proffered system, either for the rights of conscience or the liberty of the Press: Despotism usually while it is gaining ground, will suffer men to think, say, or write what they please; but when once established, if it is thought necessary to subserve the purposes, of arbitrary power, the most unjust restrictions may take place in the first instance, and an *imprimatur* on the Press in the next, may silence the complaints, and forbid the most decent remonstrances of an injured and oppressed people.

"A Columbia Patriot" (probably Mercy Otis Warren of Massachusetts)

SHOULD THERE BE A BILL OF RIGHTS?

The lack of a **bill of rights** proved to be the Anti-Federalists' strongest and most powerful weapon. State constitutions listed the rights that state government could not infringe, and the Philadelphia Convention had considered but rejected including a bill of rights.

Not adding a bill of rights proved to be the delegates' greatest tactical error because the omission galvanized Anti-Federalists. The Anti-Federalists often disagreed with one another about specific objections to the Constitution, and they were not a well-organized group. But they soon realized that the best way to defeat the Constitution was to use the issue of a bill of rights.

The Anti-Federalists used the following arguments most often:

● The organization of the national government does not adequately protect rights. Only the House of Representatives is chosen directly by the people. The national government is too far removed from average citizens to understand or reflect their concerns. The national government's power could be used to violate citizens' rights.

● The national government's powers are so general and vague as to be almost unlimited. The necessary and proper and general welfare clauses seem particularly dangerous.

What arguments did the Anti-Federalists make for including a bill of rights in the Constitution?

95

student page ▼ 95

SHOULD THERE BE A BILL OF RIGHTS?

According to historian Bernard Schwartz a total of 124 amendments were offered by the states during the ratification process.

ENRICHMENT ACTIVITY

THINKING BY ANALOGY

Law professor Daniel Farber suggests the following exercise to help students better understand why the Anti-Federalists were alarmed by the powers given to Congress.

Ask students to imagine a proposal to give the United Nations the following:

● Power to tax and spend money for global welfare

● Exclusive power to issue currency

● Control of international commerce

● Jurisdiction over all cases involving the UN Charter

● Jurisdiction over all litigation involving more than one country

● Power to take over national armies to execute UN law

● Power to make any law "necessary and proper"

Add the proviso that the UN's rule will be the "supreme law of the planet," binding all judges notwithstanding the provisions of individual countries' constitutions. Then ask students to respond to the following questions:

❶ In what ways would this proposal affect the sovereignty of member nations of the United Nations?

❷ In what ways did the 1787 Constitution affect the sovereignty of the member states?

❸ Do you agree that the proposed exercise is a valid analogy for understanding the U.S. Constitution? Why or why not?

- There is nothing in the Constitution to keep the national government from violating all the rights that it does not explicitly protect. There is no mention, for example, of freedom of religion, speech, press, or assembly. These are omitted from the Constitution. Therefore, the Anti-Federalists reasoned, the national government is free to violate them.

- State constitutions contain bills of rights. If people need protection from their relatively weak state governments, then they certainly need protection from a vastly more powerful national government.

- A bill of rights is necessary to remind the people of the principles of our political system. As the Anti-Federalist writer Federal Farmer put it in Federal Farmer 16, there is a necessity of "constantly keeping in view…the particular principles on which our freedom must always depend."

Many Anti-Federalist leaders hoped to defeat the Constitution so that a second constitutional convention would be held. There, the Anti-Federalists hoped, they would have more influence in creating a new government.

WHAT DO YOU THINK?

❶ What criticism of the Constitution by Anti-Federalists seems to be the most valid? Why?

❷ What criticism of the Constitution by Anti-Federalists seems to be the least valid? Why?

❸ Which fears of Anti-Federalists do people express today? Are those fears justified? Why?

REVIEWING AND USING THE LESSON

❶ What process did the Philadelphia Convention devise for ratifying the Constitution and why?

❷ Why did many of the writers in the debates over the Constitution use pseudonyms?

❸ What philosophical ideas guided the Anti-Federalists' opposition to a stronger national government? How did those ideas lead them toward specific objections to the Constitution?

❹ What arguments did the Anti-Federalists make with regard to the need for a bill of rights?

Do you agree with the Anti-Federalist position that people living in agrarian communities are more likely to possess republican civic virtue? Why or why not?

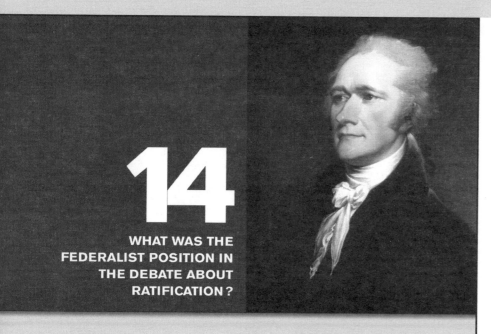

14

WHAT WAS THE FEDERALIST POSITION IN THE DEBATE ABOUT RATIFICATION?

LESSON PURPOSE

The people who supported ratification of the Constitution, which created a stronger national government, called themselves Federalists. This lesson describes the arguments and the strategies that the Federalists used to win support for the Constitution.

When you have finished this lesson, you should be able to explain the key arguments of the Federalists and the process by which the Constitution was finally ratified. You also should be able to evaluate, take, and defend positions on the continuing relevance and validity of the Federalists' arguments.

TERMS AND CONCEPTS TO UNDERSTAND

faction

Federalists

The Federalist

majority tyranny

"new science of politics"

97

UNIT TWO | LESSON 14

WHAT WAS THE FEDERALIST POSITION IN THE DEBATE ABOUT RATIFICATION?

wtpcompanion.civiced.org | **LESSON PURPOSE + TERMS**

Visit the We the People companion website for printable and downloadable Lesson Purposes and Terms and Concepts to Understand sections for each lesson. Audio readings of each Lesson Purpose and Term are also available online in MP3 format.

WHAT STRATEGIES DID FEDERALISTS USE IN THE STRUGGLE FOR RATIFICATION?

Once the Philadelphia delegates agreed on their strategy to use state ratifying conventions, supporters of the Constitution, known as **Federalists**, encouraged their associates in the states to organize as quickly as possible. They knew that the Anti-Federalists had not had enough time to organize their opposition. They believed that if the state conventions acted quickly, then the Anti-Federalists would have little time to oppose ratification.

In Pennsylvania, for example, Federalists knew that significant opposition in the western part of the state might defeat the Constitution. They scheduled the ratifying convention for early December 1787 in Philadelphia, too quickly for westerners to organize or to send many delegates. As a result, many Pennsylvania Anti-Federalists believed that their state had illegitimately ratified the Constitution. Anti-Federalists in New York, Virginia, and Massachusetts would not be defeated so easily.

For Mr. Church from her sister Elizabeth Hamilton

FEDERALIST;

A COLLECTION

OF

ESSAYS,

WRITTEN IN FAVOUR OF THE

NEW CONSTITUTION,

AS AGREED UPON BY THE FEDERAL CONVENTION,
SEPTEMBER 17, 1787.

IN TWO VOLUMES.

VOL. I.

NEW-YORK;

PRINTED AND SOLD BY J. AND A. M^cLEAN,
No. 41, HANOVER-SQUARE.
M,DCC,LXXXVIII.

What was the purpose of the essays contained in *The Federalist*?

The ratification debates in the states lasted ten months. It was an intense and sometimes bitter political struggle, especially in New York. To help the Federalist cause, three men—Alexander Hamilton, James Madison, and John Jay—published a series of essays in three New York newspapers under the pseudonym Publius (in honor of Brutus's friend, the Roman consul Publius Valerius Publicola, whose surname means "friend of the people"). These essays also were used in the contentious Virginia ratification debates and are an important source of information about the conflict over the Constitution. The essays were not intended to be objective. Their purpose was to rebut Anti-Federalist arguments and to convince people to support ratification. Historians and legal scholars consider these essays, now collectively called *The Federalist*, to be the most important work written to defend the new Constitution.

The writers of *The Federalist* were skilled at using basic ideas about government that most Americans understood and accepted. They presented the Constitution as a well-organized, agreed-on plan for national government. They did not stress the conflicts and compromises that had taken place during its development. Instead, they argued that the Constitution reflected a **"new science of politics"** that made the Anti-Federalist critique obsolete.

HOW DID THE FEDERALISTS RESPOND TO THE ANTI-FEDERALISTS' FEARS ABOUT A LARGE REPUBLIC?

Most Americans probably agreed with the main Anti-Federalist argument that a republican government could not be sustained over a large and diverse nation. This argument had support in well-known political theory going back to Aristotle. History supported it as well. No republic had ever survived when the nation grew large. The transformation of ancient Rome from a republic into a monarchical empire seemed like a lesson in the way large republics collapse.

To solve the problem of republican government in a nation as geographically vast and culturally and economically heterogeneous as the United States, the Federalists needed a new political theory. James Madison expressed one most clearly in the tenth *Federalist* essay, which responded to Robert Yates's first Brutus essay.

In Federalist 10 Madison turned classical republican arguments upside down. He began with a central premise that **faction** posed the greatest danger to governments of the people. By *faction* Madison meant any group, majority or minority, within a society that promoted its own self-interest at the expense of the common good. He did not define the common good or explain who decided what the common good was.

What were some of the main arguments for and against the ratification of the Constitution?

- If a faction consisted of a minority, a democracy worked well because the majority could outvote the faction.

- But if the faction consisted of a majority, then the risk of **majority tyranny** arose. Democracy would fail the common good. A republic, in which citizens elected representatives to tend to the people's business, might work better.

- However, in a small, homogeneous republic—the type of society that classical republicanism prescribed—majority tyranny also could arise. Because people were relatively similar in occupations, habits, and manners, there would probably be no more than two sets of ideas on any question. If those opposed to the common good commanded a majority and the representatives simply reflected their constituents' views, then the outcome would still defeat the common good and the people's rights.

Madison next explained the benefits of a large, diverse republic. Such a nation was likely to have so many different factions that none would be able to command a majority. Moreover, in a large nation there were likely to be more "fit characters" for leadership—in other words, more eminent citizens able to see the common good. Unlike Anti-Federalists, who argued that good representatives *reflected* constituents' views and

characteristics, Madison and many other Federalists argued that good representatives "enlarged" or "refined" the public's views by *filtering* out ideas that were based solely on self-interest. A large, diverse republic would therefore defeat the dangers of faction. No single faction would emerge supreme, and elected representatives would be most likely to see beyond the narrow views of ordinary citizens.

CRITICAL THINKING EXERCISE
Examining the Modern Relevance of Federalist 10

Madison wrote Federalist 10 at a time when people in geographically distant states, for example, Georgia and Massachusetts, were unlikely to know one another or one another's "passions and interests." Today modern technologies enable people in distant regions to know and communicate with one another. Working in small groups, respond to the following questions:

❶ Do modern communications technologies promote the formation of "majority factions" in America today? Why or why not?

❷ Have modern communications technologies contributed to a country that is at least as factional as Madison observed in 1787? Why or why not?

❸ How relevant do you think Madison's argument in Federalist 10 remains today?

WHAT WERE THE FEDERALISTS' CENTRAL ARGUMENTS?

Many other prominent leaders helped to win ratification in their states:

- *John Marshall* organized the Virginia ratification convention and spoke eloquently in favor of the Constitution.

- *James Wilson* led the ratification drive in Pennsylvania, where the debates were intense and bitter. He was unable to prevent opponents from sending out a *Pennsylvania Minority Report*, discussed on page 101.

- *John Dickinson*, using the pen name Fabius, wrote several essays supporting the Constitution that were influential in Delaware and Pennsylvania.

- *Roger Sherman* fought for ratification in Connecticut.

- *Oliver Ellsworth* wrote *Letters of a Landholder* in Connecticut.

- *Edmund Randolph*, the delegate from Virginia who introduced the Virginia Plan but refused to sign the final document, eventually changed his mind. By the time the Virginia ratification convention met, eight states already had approved the Constitution. Randolph gave his support because "the accession of eight states reduced our deliberations to the single question of Union or no Union."

WHAT WERE THE FEDERALISTS' CENTRAL ARGUMENTS?

The following chain of arguments helped the Federalists convince a substantial number of people to support ratification:

❶ **Civic virtue can no longer be relied on as the sole support of a government that can protect people's rights and promote their welfare**
Throughout history, the Federalists argued, the greatest dangers to the common good and the natural rights of citizens in republics had been from the pursuit of selfish interests by groups of citizens who ignored the common good. Consequently for almost two thousand years political philosophers had insisted that republican government was safe only if citizens possessed civic virtue. By civic virtue they meant that citizens had to be willing to set aside their own interests in favor of the common good.

Recent experiences with their state governments had led a number of people, including many delegates at the Philadelphia Convention, to doubt that they could rely on civic virtue to promote the common good and to protect the rights of individuals. Many of the state legislatures had passed laws that helped people in debt at the expense of those to whom they owed money. Creditors and others saw these laws as infringing on property rights, which were one of the basic natural rights for which the Revolution had been fought.

The national government created by the Constitution does not rely solely on civic virtue to protect rights and promote the common welfare. Federalists argued that it is unrealistic to expect people in a large and diverse nation, living hundreds of miles apart, to sacrifice their own interests for the benefit of others. At the same time the size and distance of the nation serve as a check on any single interest. So many interests and factions would be represented in the national government that it would be unlikely that any one of them would dominate.

❷ **The way the Constitution organizes the government, including the separation of powers and checks and balances, is the best way to promote the goals of republicanism**
The Federalists argued that the rights and welfare of all are protected by the complicated system of representation, separation of

powers, checks and balances, and federalism that the Constitution created. They also believed that the method of electing senators and presidents would increase the probability that these officials would possess the qualities required for good government. By filtering the people's votes through state legislatures (for senators) and the Electoral College (for the president) the Constitution would help to ensure that the most capable people were elected. The Federalists also argued that this complicated system would make it impossible for any individual or faction—even a majority faction—to take control of the government to serve its own interests at the expense of the common good or the rights of individuals.

Madison rejected the argument that the system was so complicated that it would be difficult to get anything done. One of his criticisms of the state legislatures was that they passed too many laws. Most of the Federalists believed that the best way to prevent a bad law from being passed was to prevent a law from being passed at all.

❸ **The representation of different interests in the government will protect basic rights**
The branches of the national government, the power that the Constitution distributes to each, and the interests each is supposed to represent are as follows:

- **Legislative branch** The House of Representatives protects the people's local interests because representatives are chosen from small congressional districts. The Senate protects the people's state interests because senators are elected by state legislatures.

- **Executive branch** The president safeguards the national interests because electors choose him from among leaders who have achieved national prominence.

- **Judicial branch** The Supreme Court ensures good judgment in the national government because it is independent of political manipulation and therefore responsible only to the Constitution.

To counter Anti-Federalists' demand for a bill of rights, Federalists employed a number of arguments, described by Alexander Hamilton in Federalist 84. Among other things, Hamilton, who later would become the first U.S. secretary of the Treasury, argued

What arguments did Alexander Hamilton make against adding a bill of rights to the Constitution?

that the Constitution allowed the national government to exercise only enumerated powers. Nothing gave the national government authority over individuals. Adding a bill of rights would imply that the national government had powers that the Constitution did not give it. Hamilton also claimed that a bill of rights is unnecessary in a nation with popular sovereignty. Previous bills of rights, such as the English Bill of Rights, protected people from a monarch over whom they had no control. Under the U.S. Constitution the people can remove elected officials who abuse their power.

WHAT DO YOU THINK?

❶ Why did the Federalists believe that they could not rely solely on civic virtue to make the new nation work properly? Do you agree? Why or why not?

❷ How would Anti-Federalists (discussed in Lesson 13) respond to each aspect of the Federalists' philosophy and defense of the Constitution?

❸ Is a good representative one who reflects and directly states his or her constituents' views and characteristics or one who enlarges those views in pursuit of a greater, common good? Explain your response.

HOW DID RATIFICATION SUCCEED?

The Federalists worked hard to overcome Anti-Federalist objections. By June 1788 nine states had voted to ratify the Constitution, enough for it to take effect. But neither New York nor Virginia had ratified. Without them the United States could not survive as a nation. New York and Virginia each had a large population, both were wealthy states, and each occupied a key geographical position. Without either state the nation would be split in two. Moreover, New York was America's primary commercial hub.

Finally a compromise was reached. To get some Anti-Federalists to support the Constitution, or at least to abstain from voting in the state ratifying conventions, the Federalists struck a deal. When the first Congress was held, Federalists would support adding a bill of rights to the Constitution. This agreement reduced support for the Anti-Federalists and deprived them of their most powerful argument against the Constitution.

At that point Anti-Federalist opposition seemed futile, and Virginia ratified the Constitution on June 26, 1788, by an 89 to 79 vote. New York's debate ground on for another month, but ultimately enough Anti-Federalists abstained for the Constitution to be ratified by a vote of 30 to 27.

HOW DID RATIFICATION SUCCEED?

Politics in the founding era was far from sterile. In addition to the intellectual debates in newspapers and pamphlets, other events played a role in ratification, including the following:

- Wide circulation of the inflammatory *Pennsylvania Minority Report* calling for significant changes to Article I regarding representation and Congress's powers

- Claims of biased newspaper reporting, particularly by newspapers owned by Federalist "elites" in urban areas

- Wining, dining, and promises of political benefits for supporting or opposing the Constitution, such as John Hancock being promised the vice presidency to win his support for ratification in Massachusetts

- Manipulation of quorum requirements by postponing sessions or making it impossible for some delegates to attend debates, such as opponents in western Pennsylvania

Some historians contend that the deciding votes in favor of the Constitution came from Westerners in the various states who eventually decided to agree to the union, despite their love of liberty, for the practical reason that they needed help fighting Native Americans on the frontier.

ENRICHMENT ACTIVITY

FEDERALIST/ANTI-FEDERALIST DEBATES

See Appendices D 2 and D 3 for summaries of the Anti-Federalist and Federalist positions on seven issues: republican government, federalism, separation of powers and checks and balances, Congress, the presidency, the judiciary, and the Bill of Rights.

Divide the class into two groups: Federalists and Anti-Federalists. Within each group assign students to each of the seven issues discussed in the summaries. Depending on the size of the class, one to three students should be assigned to each side of each issue. Students should take approximately ten minutes to prepare a brief one- or two-minute position statement on their issue, using the arguments in Appendices D 2 and D 3.

After the preparation period invite the Federalist and Anti-Federalist participants on the first issue (republican government) to the front of the room. The Anti-Federalist participant should present his or her position statement, followed by the Federalist position statement. Then each side should have a brief time (one or two minutes) for rebuttal. Repeat this procedure for each of the other six issues.

Ratification by eleven states still did not end the debate, because North Carolina and Rhode Island refused to approve the Constitution. North Carolina had called a ratifying convention that adjourned without voting. Rhode Island sent the Constitution to town meetings across the state, where it was overwhelmingly rejected. Once the first Congress proposed the ten amendments that became the Bill of Rights, North Carolina ratified the Constitution. Finally, on May 29, 1790, Rhode Island was forced to ratify when its largest city, Providence, threatened to leave the state to join the union and after the United States' first president, George Washington, inaugurated slightly more than a year earlier, had threatened Rhode Island with commercial restrictions as if the state were a foreign country.

WHAT DO YOU THINK?

❶ Explain the Federalists' argument that the Constitution did not need a bill of rights. Do you agree with their position? Why or why not?

❷ Why do you think the delegates in Philadelphia protected some rights in the body of the Constitution but not other rights?

❸ What do you think were the most important reasons put forth by the Federalists to support the Constitution? What do you think were the least important reasons?

REVIEWING AND USING THE LESSON

❶ What strategies did Federalists employ to win the struggle for ratification of the Constitution?

❷ What is *The Federalist*? How and why was it written?

❸ What arguments did Federalists make to support the ratification of the Constitution?

❹ What arguments did Federalists make to resist the demand for a bill of rights? Why did they eventually give in to this demand?

Why did Providence, Rhode Island, threaten to leave the state and join the Union?

102

unit THREE

HOW HAS THE CONSTITUTION BEEN CHANGED TO
FURTHER THE IDEALS CONTAINED IN THE
DECLARATION OF INDEPENDENCE?

EQUAL JUSTICE UNDER LAW

unit THREE

The Constitution of 1787 has been changed in several important ways. The Framers provided mechanisms for some of those changes, including a process for amending the Constitution. Other changes are not explicitly provided for in the text of the Constitution but have played a significant role in the constitutional system. The Civil War produced three amendments that transformed American federalism and moved the Constitution toward the ideals of equality contained in the Declaration of Independence.

In this unit you will learn how judicial review and political parties, neither described in the Constitution, affect American constitutionalism. You also will learn about the constitutional issues that helped cause the Civil War and how that war created what is often called a second American constitution. That transformation emphasized due process of law, equal protection of the laws, and expansion of the right to vote.

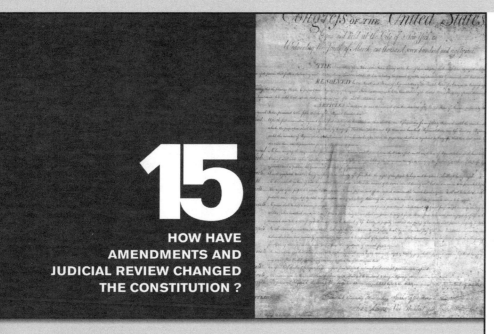

15

HOW HAVE AMENDMENTS AND JUDICIAL REVIEW CHANGED THE CONSTITUTION ?

HOW HAVE AMENDMENTS AND JUDICIAL REVIEW CHANGED THE CONSTITUTION?

wtpcompanion.civiced.org   **LESSON PURPOSE + TERMS**

Visit the We the People companion website for printable and downloadable Lesson Purposes and Terms and Concepts to Understand sections for each lesson. Audio readings of each Lesson Purpose and Term are also available online in MP3 format.

LESSON PURPOSE

This lesson describes the process that the Founders devised for amending the Constitution and the first application of that process: adoption of the Bill of Rights. It also explains the power of judicial review, a process not provided for in the Constitution, and the arguments for and against judicial review.

When you have finished this lesson, you should be able to describe the two ways in which the Constitution can be amended. You should be able to identify major categories of constitutional amendments. You also should be able to explain why James Madison introduced the Bill of Rights. Finally, you should be able to evaluate, take, and defend positions on the amendment process and judicial review.

TERMS AND CONCEPTS TO UNDERSTAND

amendment

judicial review

HOW AND WHY DID THE FRAMERS DEVISE AN AMENDMENT PROCESS?

In the course of more than two hundred years the Constitution has been amended only twenty-seven times. If the Bill of Rights is considered as a "mega-amendment," the number drops to eighteen. When compared to the more than 11,000 amendments introduced or formally recommended to Congress since 1789, the chances for an amendment being added to the Constitution drop to about one in one thousand.

Among the many proposed but rejected amendments are those that sought to accomplish the following:

- Outlaw dueling
- Rename the United States "America"
- Limit, regulate, and prohibit the labor of persons under age eighteen
- Require a balanced budget
- Prohibit desecration of the American flag
- Make English the official language of the United States
- Forbid denial or abridgment of rights on account of sex

HOW AND WHY DID THE FRAMERS DEVISE AN AMENDMENT PROCESS?

The Framers intended the Constitution to be, and to remain, a fundamental framework of law. They did not want the Constitution to become confused with ordinary laws and regulations or to be changed in response to transient whims. However, they also recognized that American society and conditions would change over time in ways they could not predict in 1787. The Constitution that they proposed, George Mason argued, would "certainly be defective," just as the Articles of Confederation had proved to be. Mason said, "**Amendments** therefore will be necessary, and it will be better to provide for them, in an easy, regular, and Constitutional way than to trust to chance and violence."

The Framers made the Constitution difficult to amend but not as difficult as it had been to amend the Articles of Confederation. Under Article V of the Constitution amendments may be proposed by two-thirds of both houses of Congress or by a petition of two-thirds of the states calling for a special convention. Congress has the power to decide how a proposed amendment will be ratified, either by approval of three-fourths of state legislatures or by approval of three-fourths of special state conventions called to consider ratification. Congress also has the power to determine how much time states have to approve an amendment. If a proposal is not ratified within that time, then the amendment fails.

Americans have not been reluctant to suggest changes. Since 1789 more than ten thousand proposed amendments have been introduced in Congress. Only thirty-three amendments have gained enough votes to be submitted to the states for ratification. Of those thirty-three, twenty-seven have been ratified by the required three-fourths of the states. The other process for proposing amendments—by two-thirds of the state legislatures calling a convention—has never been used.

WHAT DO YOU THINK?

❶ Read Article V of the Constitution. What are the advantages and disadvantages of each amendment process described in Article V?

❷ Some critics of the amending process argue that amendments, once proposed, should be put before a national popular referendum. They point out that forty-nine of the fifty states now submit state constitutional amendments to popular vote. Delaware is the only exception. Do you think the amendment process should be revised to bypass state legislatures and allow for a national popular referendum? Why or why not?

WHAT TYPES OF CONSTITUTIONAL AMENDMENTS HAVE BEEN ADOPTED?

The Constitution has been amended twenty-seven times since 1789. These amendments can be grouped into six categories:

- **Bill of Rights** Adopted in 1791, the first ten Amendments are referred to as the Bill of Rights. Many consider this collection of amendments to be part of the original Constitution. James Madison proposed the Bill of Rights in response to debates surrounding the ratification of the Constitution. Congress sent the states twelve amendments for consideration as the Bill of Rights. The states ratified only ten. However, in 1992 another of the original twelve was ratified as the Twenty-seventh Amendment, limiting Congress's power to raise its own salaries. The twelfth proposed amendment, dealing with the number and apportionment of members of the House of Representatives, never became part of the Constitution.

- **Fundamental changes** As later lessons in this unit will explain, the Thirteenth and Fourteenth Amendments made changes that go to the core of the constitutional system. They outlaw slavery, define national citizenship, impose equal protection and due process requirements on the states, and give Congress expansive enforcement powers. Both amendments resulted from the Civil War and resolved issues not settled at the Constitutional Convention. Some scholars argue that the Thirteenth and Fourteenth Amendments are equivalent to a second American constitution because of their effect on the American governmental system.

- **Expansion of suffrage** Also discussed later in this unit are six constitutional amendments that expand the right to vote or increase the opportunity for direct political participation in elections. The Fifteenth, Nineteenth, Twenty-fourth, and Twenty-sixth Amendments prohibit states from denying the franchise based on race, gender, age of persons 18 or older, or failure to pay "any poll or other tax." The Seventeenth Amendment provides for the direct election of senators. The Twenty-third Amendment gives residents of the District of Columbia the right to vote in elections for president and vice president.

Which amendment was passed as a result of such actions as this demonstration for woman suffrage that took place in New York City in 1912? What rights did the amendment establish?

- **Overturning Supreme Court decisions**
  Two Supreme Court decisions proved so controversial that they led to successful efforts to amend the Constitution. The Eleventh Amendment overturned *Chisholm v. Georgia* (1793), which many interpreted as improperly expanding the jurisdiction of federal courts at the expense of state courts. The Sixteenth Amendment overturned *Pollock v. Farmers' Loan & Trust Co.* (1895), which barred Congress from levying an income tax.

- **Refinements** Four amendments address matters affecting Congress and the president that delegates to the Constitutional Convention did not anticipate:

  - The Twelfth Amendment changed Article II, Section 1, by requiring electors to make separate choices for president and vice president.

  - The Twentieth Amendment shortened the time between an election and when the president, vice president, and members of Congress take office. The amendment reflected communications and travel changes that made it possible for officials and the public to know election results sooner and for newly elected officeholders to travel to the nation's capital more quickly.

- The Twenty-second Amendment limits presidents to two terms in office. The amendment gave the force of law to what had been an established custom until President Franklin D. Roosevelt stood for election an unprecedented four times.

- The Twenty-fifth Amendment addresses gaps in Article II about what should happen on the death, disability, removal, or resignation of the president.

- **Morality** In the 1880s the Woman's Christian Temperance Union and the Prohibition Party argued that alcohol consumption had an unhealthy influence on American families and politics. Aided by organizations such as the Anti-Saloon League, these reformers persuaded Congress to propose the Eighteenth Amendment, outlawing the manufacture, sale, and transport of alcohol (private possession and consumption were not outlawed). The amendment was ratified in 1919. However, Americans soon concluded that the amendment was a mistake, and states ratified the Twenty-first Amendment, repealing the Eighteenth, in 1933. The Twenty-first Amendment is the only amendment that has been ratified using the state convention method.

107

student page ▾ 106–107

WHAT TYPES OF CONSTITUTIONAL AMENDMENTS HAVE BEEN ADOPTED?

See Lesson 17 on incorporation, Lesson 20 on expansion of suffrage, and Lesson 16 on political parties.

WHY WAS A BILL OF RIGHTS PROPOSED FOR THE UNITED STATES CONSTITUTION?

On September 12, 1787, as the Philadelphia Convention was winding down, George Mason of Virginia stated that he thought the Constitution should be prefaced with a bill of rights and that "with the aid of the State declarations, a bill might be prepared in a few hours." He feared that without a bill of rights the laws of the United States would "be paramount to State Bills of Right." Elbridge Gerry of Massachusetts moved to have a committee prepare a bill of rights. The motion was defeated.

As explained in Lesson 13, Anti-Federalists argued successfully that a bill of rights needed to be added to the Constitution. The Massachusetts Compromise paved the way for ratification with that condition. In all, the states proposed 124 possibilities for inclusion in a bill of rights, from which James Madison culled his ideas for the list of rights that he offered to Congress.

In his election campaign against James Monroe for a seat in the new House of Representatives, Madison promised to fight for the addition of a bill of rights. Madison won the election. He told the House on May 4, 1789, that he would introduce a bill of rights on May 25. By then Congress was embroiled in a lengthy debate about import duties. Madison tried again on June 8, but other members insisted that Congress had more pressing matters, such as organizing the new government. Madison asserted that he was going to introduce a list of amendments anyway, which he did. The matter was then referred to committee for consideration.

wtpcompanion.civiced.org **PRIMARY SOURCES**

Visit the We the People companion website for a link to Madison's speech proposing a bill of rights and the text of his original proposal.

Madison made clear that he "never considered this provision so essential to the federal constitution, as to make it improper to ratify it, until such an amendment was added; at the same time, I always conceived, that in a certain form, and to a certain extent, such a provision was neither improper nor altogether useless."

WHY WAS A BILL OF RIGHTS PROPOSED FOR THE UNITED STATES CONSTITUTION?

Near the end of the Constitutional Convention George Mason (author of the Virginia Declaration of Rights), Massachusetts delegate Elbridge Gerry, and young South Carolina delegate Charles Pinckney argued unsuccessfully for a bill of rights. Other delegates were not opposed to the idea, but they believed that the Constitution already contained many protections commonly found in bills of rights, such as the right to jury trial in criminal cases, habeas corpus, and prohibitions against bills of attainder, *ex post facto* laws, and religious tests for holding office.

During the ratification debates some opponents argued that the lack of a bill of rights opened the door to tyranny in the national government. Several states directed their delegates to "exert all their influence and use all reasonable and legal methods" to obtain amendments. Eight states wanted a statement that powers not delegated to the national government should be reserved to the states. Seven wanted a guarantee of jury trial in civil cases, while six urged protection for religious freedom.

Several prominent political figures also argued for a bill of rights. Thomas Jefferson, then U.S. minister to France, wrote to James Madison expressing his concern over the "omission of a bill of rights … providing clearly … for freedom of religion, freedom of the press, protection against standing armies, and restriction against monopolies." In his first inaugural address President George Washington urged Congress to amend the Constitution to express the "reverence for the characteristic rights of freemen and a regard for public harmony."

During his campaign for a seat in the House of Representatives in the first Congress under the new Constitution, Madison promised to propose a bill of rights. He made good on that promise by suggesting fourteen amendments to Articles I and III. He also proposed to add the following "prefix" to the Constitution:

> " That all power is originally rested in, and consequently derived from, the people. That Government is instituted and ought to be exercised for the benefit of the people; which consists in the enjoyment of life and liberty, with the right of acquiring and using property, and generally of pursuing and obtaining happiness and safety. That the people have an indubitable, unalienable, and indefeasible right to reform or change their Government, whenever it be found adverse or inadequate to the purposes of its institution.

Madison also recommended other additions to the body of the Constitution in his June 8, 1789, speech to the First Federal Congress. He advocated inserting the following guarantee in Article I, Section 10:

> " No state shall violate the equal rights of conscience, or the freedom of the press, or the trial by jury in all criminal cases.

His proposal was not accepted, but Unit Five will discuss how that guarantee has been accomplished through the Supreme Court's interpretation of the due process clause of the Fourteenth Amendment.

Roger Sherman of Connecticut argued against inserting statements of rights into the body of the Constitution. Sherman believed it was too early to begin rewriting the Constitution itself. He also feared that if amendments were added to the body of the Constitution, then the entire ratification process would have to start over again and might not succeed. Agreeing with Sherman, the House sent a list of seventeen amendments to the Senate to be added at the end of the Constitution as a bill of rights.

The Senate reduced these amendments to twelve. As discussed previously, the states ratified ten of the twelve amendments in 1791.

What arguments did Elbridge Gerry and others make during the Constitutional Convention in their unsuccessful attempt to have a bill of rights added to the Constitution?

108

WHAT DO YOU THINK?

❶ If you had been a member of the first Congress, would you have agreed with Madison that guarantees of rights should be inserted into the body of the Constitution or with Roger Sherman that they should be added as a group at the end? Explain your reasoning.

❷ The Bill of Rights now is viewed as the cornerstone of American government. Do you think the Bill of Rights would be considered as important if the same provisions appeared in the Constitution itself rather than as a separate list? Why or why not? Do you think the Bill of Rights should have been placed at the beginning of the Constitution, as many state constitutions do, rather than at the end? Why or why not?

WHAT IS JUDICIAL REVIEW AND WHY IS IT CONTROVERSIAL?

Another way that the Constitution has developed and expanded is through judicial interpretation. In 1803 in the case of *Marbury v. Madison*, Chief Justice John Marshall (1755–1835) wrote for a unanimous Supreme Court that judges have the power to decide whether acts of Congress, the executive branch, state laws, and even state constitutions violate the United States Constitution. The justices of the Supreme Court have the final say about the meaning of the Constitution. The power to declare what the Constitution means and whether the actions of government officials violate the Constitution is known as the power of **judicial review**.

The Constitution does not mention the power of judicial review. However, both Federalists and Anti-Federalists assumed that the Supreme Court would exercise judicial review. The practice traces its roots to the seventeenth-century English system of law. It was well known and used by most state courts before adoption of the Constitution and even by the Supreme Court before being officially acknowledged in *Marbury*. Alexander Hamilton defended the power in Federalist 78:

❝ A constitution is, in fact, and must be regarded by the judges, as a fundamental law. It therefore belongs to them to ascertain its meaning.

In *Marbury*, Marshall asserted that "it is emphatically the province and duty of the judicial department to say what the law is." According to Marshall, judicial review rests on the following premises:

What arguments can you give for and against the power of judicial review?

- The people exercised their sovereign power when they adopted the Constitution. The Constitution is a superior, paramount law that cannot be changed by ordinary means.

- Particular acts of Congress, the executive, and the states reflect temporary, fleeting views of what the law is.

- Acts of Congress, the executive, and the states that conflict with the fundamental law of the Constitution are not entitled to enforcement and must be disregarded.

- Judges are in the best position to declare what the Constitution means. By striking down laws and acts that conflict with the Constitution, they preserve the nation's fundamental law and the true will of the people.

Judicial review was neither immediately nor universally accepted. Anti-Federalists such as Brutus feared that the Court would use judicial review to eliminate the power of state courts. America's seventh president, Andrew Jackson (1767–1845), argued against it and threatened not to enforce Supreme Court decisions with which he disagreed. Not even all judges accepted the validity of judicial review. In *Eakin v. Raub* (1825) the Pennsylvania Supreme Court decided that the state supreme court had the power to review legislative acts

---

WHAT IS JUDICIAL REVIEW AND WHY IS IT CONTROVERSIAL?

Article III created only the outline of a national judiciary, leaving Congress to fill in the details. Congress adopted the Judiciary Act of 1789. The Judiciary Act did the following:

- Provided for a Supreme Court consisting of a chief justice and five associate justices

- Created thirteen federal district (trial) courts and judgeships

- Created three federal circuit (appellate) courts, staffed by two Supreme Court justices and a district court judge, who traveled throughout the country hearing appeals

- Spelled out the jurisdiction (power) of the lower federal courts

- Spelled out the appellate jurisdiction of the Supreme Court

- Gave the Supreme Court original jurisdiction over cases in which parties requested a writ of mandamus: a directive from the Court compelling government officers to perform a particular act or acts

MARBURY V. MADISON The election of 1800 resulted in Thomas Jefferson becoming president. Before Jefferson took office, the outgoing Federalists made several attempts to make the federal judiciary into a Federalist stronghold, including installing John Marshall, Adams's secretary of state, as chief justice. President Adams also made forty-two "midnight appointments" to judicial posts before leaving office, including justices of the peace. All were confirmed. However, not all the commissions were delivered to the recipients by the time Adams's term expired. Incoming president Thomas Jefferson instructed his acting secretary of state not to deliver them.

Among those not delivered was a commission for William Marbury to be a justice of the peace. Marbury invoked Section 13 of the Judiciary Act of 1789, giving the Supreme Court original jurisdiction over cases in which parties requested a writ of mandamus, asking for an order to compel Secretary of State James Madison to deliver Marbury's commission. Marbury's case, heard in 1803, raised three questions:

- Was Marbury entitled to his commission?

- If he had a right to the commission, did the laws of the United States afford him a remedy?

- If the laws of the United States afforded a remedy, was a writ of mandamus from the U.S. Supreme Court the appropriate remedy?

The court answered the first two questions in the affirmative, the third in the negative. It held that Congress lacked authority to give the Supreme Court original jurisdiction because the Constitution is the only source of the Court's original jurisdiction. Therefore, Section 13 of the Judiciary Act of 1789 was unconstitutional.

Chief Justice Marshall knew that if the court had issued a writ forcing Madison to deliver the commissions, President Jefferson would have ignored the decision, which would have been a severe blow to the authority of the courts. Figuring out how to deny issuing the writ while at the same time asserting the power of judicial review—the authority of the Supreme Court to declare the meaning of the Constitution—was part of Marshall's genius in the case.

wtpcompanion.civiced.org   LINKS

Visit the We the People companion website for a link to two excellent websites about the political and legal background of Marbury v. Madison.

What justification, if any, might be made to support President Andrew Jackson's position that he would not enforce any Supreme Court decisions with which he disagreed?

and, if the acts were contrary to the state constitution, to declare such acts void. In that court decision Justice John B. Gibson dissented and identified several arguments against such judicial review:

- Legislatures are the repository of the people's sovereignty, and the exercise of judicial review is an act of sovereignty, which should reside with the legislatures or the people.

- Judicial review could lead to political turmoil if the other branches of government, or the states, refuse to acquiesce to the Court's interpretation of the Constitution.

- Judicial review makes the judiciary equal or even superior to the legislature, even though judges are not elected.

- All officers of the government take an oath to support the Constitution and therefore all must consider the constitutionality of their actions.

- The judiciary is not infallible. Judges' errors in interpreting the Constitution cannot be corrected at the ballot box, only by constitutional amendment.

CRITICAL THINKING EXERCISE

Evaluating, Taking, and Defending Positions on the Power of Judicial Review

Today judicial review is accepted almost universally in the United States and increasingly throughout the world. Controversy swirls around how the Court uses this power in particular cases, which will be further discussed in both this unit and Unit Five. Work in groups of about five students and respond to the following questions:

1. Which, if any, of Gibson's arguments against judicial review remain relevant today?

2. Should the executive and legislative branches, as well as the judiciary, possess the power to declare what the Constitution means? Why or why not?

3. In what circumstances, if any, should the national judiciary have the power to declare state laws unconstitutional?

REVIEWING AND USING THE LESSON

1. Describe the processes that the Constitution contains for amending the Constitution. What might have been the consequences if the Framers had not provided for an orderly opportunity to amend the document?

2. What were the arguments for and against including the Bill of Rights in the body of the Constitution as opposed to adding these rights at the end of the document?

3. Which of all the amendments to the Constitution have made the country more democratic? In what ways?

4. Describe the doctrine of judicial review. In what ways has judicial review proven to be controversial?

5. Find a recent example of a Supreme Court decision that demonstrates the exercise of the power of judicial review. How does that decision affect individual rights, the common good, the balance of power between the branches of government, or the balance of power between the national government and the states?

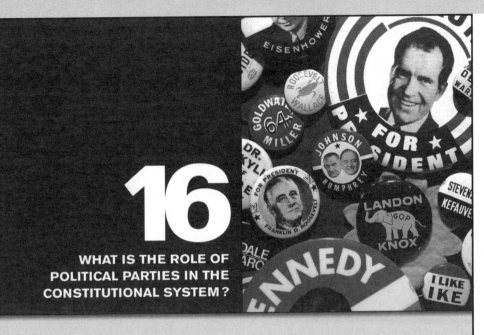

16

WHAT IS THE ROLE OF POLITICAL PARTIES IN THE CONSTITUTIONAL SYSTEM?

WHAT IS THE ROLE OF POLITICAL PARTIES IN THE CONSTITUTIONAL SYSTEM?

wtpcompanion.civiced.org **LESSON PURPOSE + TERMS**

Visit the We the People companion website for printable and downloadable Lesson Purposes and Terms and Concepts to Understand sections for each lesson. Audio readings of each Lesson Purpose and Term are also available online in MP3 format.

LESSON PURPOSE

Soon after the federal government was established, there was an unforeseen development to which most of the Framers were opposed: the formation of political parties. This lesson describes the Framers' views on political parties and how the first parties came to be formed. It also explains how parties became an essential component of the American political system by helping to address challenges that the Constitution left unresolved.

When you have finished this lesson, you should be able to explain why the Framers opposed the idea of political parties. You should be able to describe the other ideas that helped political parties to gain acceptance. You should be able to explain the conflicting points of view that led to the development of parties and the roles that political parties have played in the American constitutional system. You also should be able to evaluate, take, and defend positions on the importance of political parties today.

TERMS AND CONCEPTS TO UNDERSTAND

delegated powers	political party
party system	sedition
patronage	ticket
platform	

`student page ▾` `112`

WHAT DID THE FRAMERS THINK ABOUT POLITICAL PARTIES?

Many colonists were aware of factions and interests, and many colonies produced party-like interest groups. Alignments frequently were based on economics, religion, or nationality. Small merchants, artisans, laborers, and farmers in Massachusetts, for example, came together over proposals to print paper money or charter banks. In New York politicians frequently made appeals in local elections based on economic interests.

Colonial politicians often appealed to religious prejudices, particularly against the Roman Catholic and Anglican Churches. Quakers, Baptists, and Methodists developed particularly effective political strategies. In provincial elections in the late 1730s in Pennsylvania, for example, Quakers put together a slate of candidates for the assembly and urged voters to vote for "none but people of [Quaker] perswaision [sic]." In New York factious disputes often erupted between Dutch and Germans. Influential families and family alliances also competed against one another in contests that took on factional or party dimensions, particularly in New York and Massachusetts.

Factionalism in the Southern colonies was moderated by several factors. European slave owners needed to remain united against slave uprisings because after 1710 captured African slaves outnumbered them two to one—in some rural counties, five to one. Moreover, in colonies such as the Carolinas a very few wealthy planters exercised virtually complete political control.

WHAT DID THE FRAMERS THINK ABOUT POLITICAL PARTIES?

James Madison's argument that the new Constitution would control the effects of factions was part of an ongoing debate within Anglo-American political thought about political parties. Some British writers, as well as Americans such as Alexander Hamilton, used the words *faction* and *party* as synonyms and viewed them as an evil to be eradicated in the society at large. Others, such as the Scottish political philosopher David Hume (1711–1776), had argued that parties were the inevitable result of diverse interests. In fact, James Madison followed this reasoning in Federalist 10 and believed that factions could be controlled. Ireland's Edmund Burke (1729–1797), another important political thinker, contended that open opposition expressed through political parties was a good thing. Without parties, Burke believed, opponents of the ruler would resort to conspiracy and intrigue. Political parties motivated by self-defined guiding principles provided a crucial service to the body politic by fostering open debate.

No major eighteenth-century American leaders echoed Burke's arguments. However, Americans were accustomed to factional politics in their colonial and new state governments, often because of differing regional or economic concerns. Some of the Framers recognized the potential value of political parties. For example, Alexander Hamilton argued in Federalist 70 that parties within a legislature could "promote deliberation and circumspection, and serve to check excesses in the majority." But once a decision was made, Hamilton continued, opposition should cease.

Hamilton, Madison, and the other delegates to the Constitutional Convention had no experience with an ongoing **party system**, that is, a system of organized, relatively durable political parties that accept one another's right to exist and to compete in elections and within government.

WHAT DO YOU THINK?

❶ If political parties had not arisen, how might the constitutional system have accommodated America's tradition of free and open political debate?

❷ In Federalist 10 James Madison described factions. Review his definition of *faction* in Lesson 14. How do political parties differ from factions?

WHAT IDEAS AND EVENTS LED TO THE DEVELOPMENT OF POLITICAL PARTIES IN THE 1790s?

Political parties developed within a decade of the ratification of the Constitution. Ironically Madison and Hamilton became leaders within those parties—on opposite sides. Several issues contributed to divisions within the national government and the nation as a whole. Those divisions became the basis for the first parties. Following are four key issues:

❶ **The power of the national government** Alexander Hamilton, who became secretary of the Treasury in George Washington's presidential administration, argued that the Constitution created a government designed to take on national problems. The national government could address any national issue, whether or not the issue was specifically mentioned in the Constitution. Because the

Federalists   Republicans

What were some of the disagreements that led to the development of political parties?

Constitution stipulated certain **delegated powers** to the national government, those powers could be reduced or eliminated by amending the Constitution. Thomas Jefferson, Washington's first secretary of state, disagreed. He argued that the Constitution's description of national powers was so vague that the government would be able to do whatever it wanted. The "energetic" use of the national government's power was exactly what Jefferson feared.

❷ **Economic vision** To demonstrate the power of the national government and to strengthen the new nation's commercial economy, Hamilton in his treasury role made a number of recommendations to Congress. One was that it pass a law establishing a national bank. Hamilton said that using a national bank was a "necessary and proper" method of carrying out the responsibilities given to Congress by the Constitution, such as collecting taxes and regulating trade. Jefferson, who believed in the virtue of an agrarian society of independent farmers, replied that the necessary and proper clause should be interpreted as if it read "absolutely and indispensably necessary."

❸ **Foreign policy** More than any domestic issue, the Napoleonic Wars between France and Great Britain mobilized American citizens on opposite sides. Jefferson and many of his supporters wanted the United States to help France, which had supported America during the war for independence. Hamilton and his supporters wanted the United States to ally with Britain because Americans had more trade and cultural connection with the British than with the French. Hoping to prevent people from dividing into opposing camps, President Washington declared American neutrality.

However, American supporters of a French alliance created Democratic-Republican Clubs, which held rallies and meetings to oppose the administration's policy. Jefferson, Madison, and other leaders subsidized newspapers that had editors who supported these views. Uniting under the name Republicans, these citizens and leaders forged America's first national **political party**. In response, Hamilton and his followers took the name Federalists.

Federalists and Republicans did not yet constitute a party system. Each party believed

Why did disputes between the Federalists and Republicans arise over the Alien and Sedition Acts?

that the other was a threat to the new nation's very existence. Neither accepted the idea of a long-term, durable "loyal opposition." In the election of 1796 Federalist John Adams became president. But Republican Jefferson received the second-highest number of electoral votes and thus became vice president.

❹ **The Alien and Sedition Acts** Many in the early republic were concerned about foreigners, called aliens, and others who might incite **sedition**, or rebellion, against the authority of the national government. In 1798 President John Adams signed the Alien Act, which gave him the power to force foreigners to leave the country if he considered them dangerous, and the Sedition Act, which made it a crime for editors, writers, or speakers to attack the government. These laws outraged Republicans, especially after Federalist judges fined and jailed several Republican newspaper editors and a member of Congress under the Sedition Act. Madison and Jefferson wrote the Kentucky and Virginia resolutions, which claimed that the states had a right to decide if the national government had exceeded its powers. These resolutions claimed that the state legislatures had the power to declare acts of Congress null and void. Other states did not accept these resolutions. But the Alien and Sedition Acts helped mobilize Republicans for the presidential election of 1800.

student page ▾ 112–113

WHAT IDEAS AND EVENTS LED TO THE DEVELOPMENT OF POLITICAL PARTIES IN THE 1790s?

The division between Federalists and Anti-Federalists in 1787–1788 was not the same as the split between Federalists and Jeffersonian Republicans in the mid-1790s. Remember that Anti-Federalists never called themselves by that name. The Federalists used the label "Anti-Federalists" to describe those opposed to ratification of the Constitution. After the Constitution was ratified, new issues helped realign American political leaders and their constituents. Many of the Anti-Federalists who opposed ratification in 1787 became Federalists in the 1790s, notably Patrick Henry. And many of the Jeffersonian Republicans had supported ratification, most famously James Madison.

ALIEN AND SEDITION ACTS The Alien and Sedition Acts consisted of four pieces of legislation. Two were the Alien Act and the Sedition Act; the other two were the Naturalization Act, which increased from five to fourteen years the residency period for citizenship, and the Alien Enemies Act, which authorized the president to confine or deport aliens of an enemy country during war. The primary goal of the Naturalization Act was to undermine the influence of French and Irish immigrants who were joining the ranks of Jefferson's Republican Party when they came to the United States.

The Alien and Sedition Acts were never challenged before the U.S. Supreme Court and were allowed to expire. After he became president, Jefferson pardoned the ten people convicted under the Sedition Act.

student page ▼ 115–116

WHAT PART DO POLITICAL PARTIES PLAY IN TODAY'S POLITICAL SYSTEM?

Political scientists have described five two-party systems in the history of the United States. By "party systems" they mean coalitions of states and voters making up each party. When these coalitions change—even if the parties' names remain the same—a new party system has emerged.

FEDERALISTS VS. (JEFFERSONIAN) REPUBLICANS, about 1795 to 1815
This party system emerged during debate over American involvement in war between England and France in the 1790s. It collapsed in the 1810s after the War of 1812, when Federalists ceased to be a national party. By 1820 most Americans identified themselves as Republicans.

DEMOCRATS (ANDREW JACKSON, MARTIN VAN BUREN) VS. WHIGS (HENRY CLAY, DANIEL WEBSTER), 1830s to the early 1850s
This party system emerged from a split among the Republicans in the 1820s, especially in the elections of 1824 and 1828. Jackson's policies as president led various opponents to coalesce into the Whig Party by the late 1830s. The Whigs collapsed as a national party after the election of 1852.

WHAT WAS THE "REVOLUTION OF 1800," AND WHAT WAS ITS AFTERMATH?

The presidential election of 1800 was the first to feature candidates for president and vice president who were openly supported by political parties. Federalists supported the reelection of John Adams. Republicans supported Thomas Jefferson. The candidates themselves did not campaign because it was considered undignified for presidential candidates to seek the office actively. But the election heightened the bitter party disagreements.

The election of 1800 was important to the new government. Federalists and Republicans accused each other of wishing to destroy the Constitution, yet both parties accepted the results of the election. On March 4, 1801, the Federalists turned over control of the national government to the Republicans. For the first time in recent history control of a government was given to new leaders as the result of an electoral "revolution," rather than by hereditary succession or violent overthrow.

However, the election of 1800 also exposed a problem in the Constitution. According to Article II, Section 3, each member of the Electoral College was supposed to vote for two candidates. The one receiving the highest number of votes became president, and the one with the second-highest total became vice president. In 1800 every Republican elector voted for Thomas Jefferson and Aaron Burr, resulting in a tie vote. The electors knew that Jefferson was supposed to be the president and Burr the vice president, but the Constitution did not allow electors to specify which candidate belonged in which office. Therefore the tied election had to be decided by the House of Representatives.

By the next presidential election the Twelfth Amendment to the Constitution had been ratified, stipulating that each elector cast one ballot for president and one for vice president. This amendment gave political parties an ongoing role in American politics. Candidates for president and vice president would be a **"ticket"** in the modern sense and would run against the candidates of the opposing party.

Nonetheless, Thomas Jefferson never believed that opposing political parties should be a permanent feature of the American system. In his inaugural address he noted, "We are all republicans—we are all federalists." Beneath this message of unity was another idea—that the Federalists as a political party should wither away because Jefferson's Republicans represented the true common good. Over time, Jefferson hoped, there would be no clash of parties, but instead a national consensus around Republican principles would emerge.

HOW DID POLITICAL PARTIES GROW, AND WHAT FUNCTIONS DID THEY SERVE?

Only in the next generation did American political leaders promote a positive vision of political parties. As supporters of Andrew Jackson mobilized in the 1820s, New York politician Martin Van Buren (1782–1862), who would follow Jackson to become America's eighth president, explained how a new party could serve the public good. Echoing Edmund Burke, Van Buren argued that a political party with clear principles offered voters a clear choice. Van Buren played an important role both in electing Jackson in 1828 and in creating the Democratic Party in the modern sense, which has existed since the 1830s.

Van Buren believed that political parties could serve as a kind of glue within the American constitutional system. Although checks and balances and federalism could prevent tyrants from usurping power, these elements also discouraged the branches of government from working together. There was no mechanism for presidents to amass support for their goals in Congress.

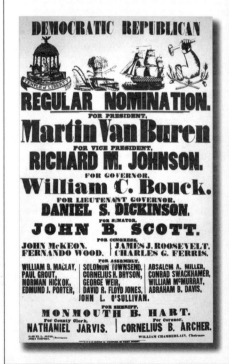

What arguments did Martin Van Buren make in favor of political parties?

In addition, there were great distances between national elected officials and ordinary citizens. Neither senators nor presidents were elected directly by the people, and the national government in Washington also was physically distant from most Americans' lives.

Political parties helped bridge these distances. A president would have allies in Congress, the members of his own party who shared a political vision. Through the **patronage** system of appointing members of his own party to political offices, including local postmaster jobs, the president could build connections between national and local levels of government. Local and state party committees staged elaborate entertainments, such as parades and rallies, to boost support for their candidates and to give citizens a sense of belonging to the party.

Just as revolutionary was Van Buren's idea of a party system in which two parties regularly vied for citizens' allegiance. Unlike Jefferson or Hamilton, who believed that opposition should evaporate once it recognized the true common good, Van Buren and others argued that there were valid, competing notions of the common good. Once a party was elected to power, it installed its supporters in public office and pursued its agenda. The opposing party continued to challenge those in power, holding them accountable. Political parties thus became an additional set of checks and balances alongside the ones that the Constitution had created.

CRITICAL THINKING EXERCISE

Examining the Relationship of Judicial Review and Political Parties to Constitutional Principles

The United States boasts having a written constitution. However, two significant elements of American constitutionalism—judicial review and political parties—are not mentioned in that document. Work in small groups. Each group should choose one the following constitutional principles to examine:

- checks and balances
- federalism
- majority rule
- individual rights
- limited government
- rule of law

Be prepared to explain to the other groups the ways that judicial review and political parties either do or do not support that principle.

WHAT PART DO POLITICAL PARTIES PLAY IN TODAY'S POLITICAL SYSTEM?

Today political parties play an essential role in the American political system. Since the 1860s, the Democratic Party and the Republican Party (founded 1854) have been the two major parties in the United States. However, their agendas and constituencies have changed dramatically over the years as new issues have created new coalitions and new divisions.

Political parties serve several important purposes:

- They mobilize popular participation in the nomination and election of candidates for public office.

- They connect the executive and legislative branches of government. Presidents generally work most closely with members of their own party in Congress, and governors do the same with those in their state legislatures.

- Political parties connect the national government with state governments. However, each major party has enough internal variation to remain viable in states with very different political climates.

- By joining a political party people indicate their support for a particular **platform**, the label given to the priorities and policies of that party.

- Political parties provide forums for deliberating about public policies. In a sense they work in a way that is opposite from what Madison suggested about factions. Rather than fracture the citizenry and promote

What are some of the important purposes served by political parties?

DEMOCRATS VS. REPUBLICANS, about 1856 to 1896

A new Republican Party (founded 1854) became dominant in the North by the late 1850s. Democrats remained a nationwide party, though strongest among white Southerners. The result was a closely divided national electorate and a series of presidential elections decided by narrow margins.

DEMOCRATS VS. REPUBLICANS, about 1896 to 1928

Republicans gained a decisive national majority with a consolidation of Northern workers and Midwestern and Western farmers. Democrats maintained control only in the South.

DEMOCRATS (NEW DEAL COALITION) VS. REPUBLICANS, about 1932 to the 1960s

Democrats won support among the Northern urban working class (white and black) and Midwestern farmers and maintained support among Southern whites, creating a national majority lasting three decades or more.

Some observers argue that a sixth party system emerged in the 1970s and 1980s after passage of the Civil Rights Act (1964) and the Voting Rights Act (1965). Many Southern whites deserted the Democratic Party for the Republican Party, as Southern blacks voted Democratic. Since 1980 Republicans have won the majority of Southern states in every presidential election, and they hold the majority of most Southern congressional delegations. Meanwhile, Democrats are strongest in the Northeast, industrial Midwest, and Pacific states. The result is virtually a mirror image of the third system described above.

wtpcompanion.civiced.org　**LINKS**

Visit the We the People companion website for links to electoral maps of the presidential elections of 1896 and 2004.

The United States has had a stable two-party system since the 1830s, with both parties supporting the U.S. Constitution but interpreting it slightly differently. However, there also have been many other parties that have vied for power, including the Nullifier Party (1830–1839), the Free Soil Party (1848–1855), the Constitutional Union Party (1860), the Populist Party (1892–1908), the Socialist Party of America (1901–1973), the Progressive Party (1913–1930, 1948–1955), the Grassroots Party (1986–2004), and the Green Party (1991–present).

ENRICHMENT ACTIVITY

EXAMINING MINOR POLITICAL PARTIES

Ask students to use the Internet or to consult a library to obtain a list of minor political parties in the United States.

wtpcompanion.civiced.org **LINKS**

Visit the We the People companion website for a link to an example of a website that provides information about various political parties.

Ask students to select a political party. Students can choose a party from the list found on the We the People companion website or they can select any party that interests them. Then ask them to respond to the following questions:

❶ What issues or circumstances gave rise to the party?

❷ Who were its leaders?

❸ To what groups did the party appeal, and what electoral successes did it achieve?

❹ What happened to the party? What are or were the major planks in its platform? If it no longer exists, why?

During a class discussion compare responses among students who analyzed various parties. Ask students to consider what additional insights they have gained into the U.S. party system through this exercise.

passion and interest over reason and the common good, parties can help organize and channel passions and interests into the system. Each major party is like a large tent, under which a variety of interests and issues can coexist. Like the "large republic" that Madison envisioned, political parties actually can work against the most divisive tendencies of faction and passion.

● In times of rapid political change political parties can provide a way of ensuring that people demand a change of government, not a change of constitution. Parties can be an agent of stability.

In recent years many commentators also have observed less favorable aspects of the political party system:

● The longstanding dominance of the Democratic and Republican parties, entrenched through campaign finance laws and other structures, makes it difficult for parties espousing truly alternative views and agendas to gain lasting political support. In most other nations, especially those with parliamentary systems, there usually are many more parties, each representing a particular set of policies and values. Voters in such systems may feel as though they have a wider range of choices.

● American "third parties," such as the Green, Libertarian, or Reform parties, tend to be expressions of discontent with the two major parties. They are generally small and oriented toward a narrow set of issues or are local or state based. They have little chance of becoming new major parties that are long-lasting and competitive nationally with the Republican and Democratic parties.

● If a single set of interests or a particularly passionate interest gains dominant power within a party, then the party is subject to the same threat of majority tyranny that Madison and other Framers feared in small republics and from political factions.

REVIEWING AND USING THE LESSON

❶ What ideas and issues led to the development of political parties in the United States?

❷ How did the election of 1800 contribute to the formation of political parties? Was it a "revolution," as some asserted?

❸ Assess the validity of the following claim: Political parties legitimize government policies by connecting citizens to government.

❹ Are today's political parties factions, collections of factions, or something else? Explain.

❺ In what ways does America's two-party system promote or thwart America's constitutional principles?

Why is it difficult for third parties to compete with the Democratic and Republican parties?

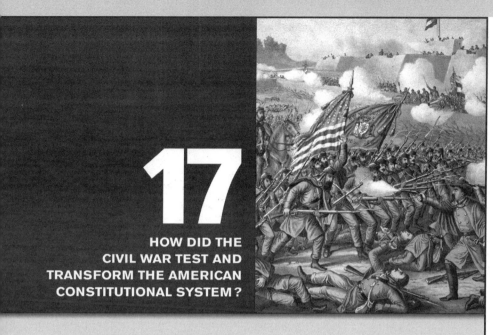

17

HOW DID THE CIVIL WAR TEST AND TRANSFORM THE AMERICAN CONSTITUTIONAL SYSTEM?

HOW DID THE CIVIL WAR TEST AND TRANSFORM THE AMERICAN CONSTITUTIONAL SYSTEM?

wtpcompanion.civiced.org | **LESSON PURPOSE + TERMS**

Visit the We the People companion website for printable and downloadable Lesson Purposes and Terms and Concepts to Understand sections for each lesson. Audio readings of each Lesson Purpose and Term are also available online in MP3 format.

LESSON PURPOSE

Between December 1860 and June 1861 eleven Southern states seceded from the United States and formed the Confederate States of America. The Civil War started in April 1861. The war raised several constitutional issues: the right of states to secede from the union, the president's powers in wartime, the balance between individual rights and national security, and the constitutional status of slavery in the United States. Three constitutional amendments adopted after the war defined American citizenship and transformed the relationship between the national and state governments.

When you have finished this lesson, you should be able to describe several important constitutional issues raised by President Lincoln's actions, including the suspension of the writ of habeas corpus and the Emancipation Proclamation. You should be able to explain the similarities and differences between the United States Constitution and the constitution of the Confederate States of America. You also should be able to explain how the Civil War led to the creation of the Thirteenth, Fourteenth, and Fifteenth Amendments. Finally, you should be able to evaluate, take, and defend positions on the conditions under which the writ of habeas corpus might be suspended and the constitutionality of secession.

TERMS AND CONCEPTS TO UNDERSTAND

abolitionists

grandfather clause

literacy test

poll tax

secession

student page ▼ 118–119

HOW DID CONSTITUTIONAL ISSUES LAY FOUNDATIONS FOR THE CIVIL WAR?

Review Lesson 11 (designing the national government) and Lesson 12 (distributing powers between the national and state governments).

DRED SCOTT V. SANDFORD   Interesting details about the case include the following:

- Sanford's name was misspelled as "Sandford" in court records and never corrected.

- President Andrew Jackson appointed Roger Brooke Taney, author of the Dred Scott decision, to succeed John Marshall. Before his appointment, Taney had been Jackson's attorney general. Jackson wrote of Taney's appointment to the first position, "I have appointed mr Tauney atto. Genl." The President's spelling reflected the correct pronunciation of the nation's fifth chief justice: "taw-nee."

- Because of the public attention that the case had gained and Republican speculation that the Supreme Court would rule against Dred Scott, an editorial in the New York Courier declared that the Supreme Court "is itself on trial."

student page ▼ 119–120

WHAT WAS SECESSION, AND WHAT WERE THE ARGUMENTS FOR AND AGAINST ITS CONSTITUTIONALITY?

wtpcompanion.civiced.org   **PRIMARY SOURCES**

Visit the We the People companion website for a link to the South Carolina Declaration of Causes, 1852, and Abraham Lincoln's First Inaugural.

HOW DID CONSTITUTIONAL ISSUES LAY FOUNDATIONS FOR THE CIVIL WAR?

The constitutionality of slavery, the issue of slavery in new territories, and the new Fugitive Slave Law of 1850 heightened the tensions between Northern and Southern states.

THE CONSTITUTION AND SLAVERY

At the Philadelphia Convention the Framers attempted to avoid the issue of slavery. Unit Two described several provisions of the Constitution reflecting compromise on that issue: The Three-Fifths Compromise (Article I, Section 2) gave slaveholding states additional representation in Congress based on their population of slaves. Article IV, Section 2, provided that enslaved people who fled from one state into another must be returned based on their owners' claims. And Article I, Section 9, prohibited Congress from banning the importation of slaves until 1808. When that ban expired, Congress passed and President Thomas Jefferson signed a law ending the importation of slaves into the United States.

Americans before 1860 debated whether the Constitution was a pro-slavery or an anti-slavery document. Did the Framers intend to allow slavery to continue forever, regulated entirely by states? Advocates of slavery, especially in the Southern states, said yes. The Constitution gave the national government no enumerated power over slavery within states. Many opponents of slavery, known as **abolitionists**, disagreed. They argued that the words *slave* and *slavery* appeared nowhere in the Constitution because the Framers knew that slavery was fundamentally at odds with America's republican ideals. They also cited Article I, Section 9, as evidence that the Framers wanted the importation of enslaved Africans to end within two decades of ratification.

THE CONSTITUTION AND NEW TERRITORIES

The Constitution did not give Congress power over slavery within the states, but it did give Congress power to make rules and regulations respecting territories and to approve the proposed constitutions of new states. The Northwest Ordinance of 1787 banned slavery in the Northwest Territory and in all states created from it. Eventually those new states would be Ohio, Indiana, Illinois, Michigan, and Wisconsin.

The question of slavery emerged anew whenever the United States added new territories and when territories applied for statehood. In 1820 Congress passed the Missouri Compromise to deal with the vast regions of the Louisiana Purchase of 1803. Under the compromise Missouri became a slave state, but other parts of the Louisiana Purchase would be open to slavery only if they lay south of Missouri's southern border. North of that line would be free (non-slave) territory. For the first sixty years under the U.S. Constitution Congress admitted slave and free states in pairs, such as Missouri and Maine in 1820. This way the Senate would always have equal numbers of slave-state and free-state members, even though free-state representatives had a growing majority in the House of Representatives.

Following the U.S. annexation of Texas in 1845 the Mexican-American War of 1846–1848 disrupted that balance. The United States subsequently acquired nearly half of Mexico's territory, stretching all the way to California. Much of this land (including the future states of Utah, Nevada, and parts of Colorado and California) lay north of the Missouri Compromise line. Southerners worried that it would become impossible to maintain the equal number of slave and free states. On the other side increasing numbers of Northerners believed that slavery should not be expanded into new territories. In 1850 Congress crafted another compromise. California, the first state created from the Mexican War territories, would be a free state with no slave state to balance it. But in return the slave states would get a stronger Fugitive Slave Law, which provided mechanisms for the capture and return of alleged runaway slaves.

As settlers organized more of the new territories and envisioned future states, slavery remained a divisive issue. By the mid-1850s there were two major proposals. One, known as "free soil," argued that no new territories should be open to slavery. Another, which became law in 1854 as the Kansas-Nebraska Act, allowed the people of a territory to decide whether it should or should not allow slavery—even though that meant repealing the Missouri Compromise. Each of these concepts was based on ideals in the Declaration of Independence: human liberty in one case, majority rule in the other.

THE FUGITIVE SLAVE LAW AND *DRED SCOTT V. SANDFORD*

An earlier Fugitive Slave Act of 1793 had attempted to enforce a section of the U.S. Constitution that required the return of runaway slaves, but in practice it was rarely enforced. The new Fugitive Slave Law of 1850 was stronger and outraged many Northerners. Anyone— even an abolitionist—could now be forced to help capture African Americans who were claimed as runaway slaves. Using the argument of states' rights, several Northern states passed "personal liberty laws" to circumvent enforcement of the Fugitive Slave Law.

One of the most important and controversial Supreme Court decisions in American history preceding the Civil War was *Dred Scott v. Sandford* (1857). Dred Scott (c. 1800–1858) was an enslaved African American whose master had taken him to the free state of Illinois and the free Wisconsin Territory and then back to

Missouri. In 1846 Scott sued the man who held him in servitude on the grounds that Scott had achieved his freedom by residing in free territory. The Missouri Supreme Court ruled against him. Scott then sued in the federal Circuit Court in Missouri, and that court also ruled against him. Scott's attorney appealed the case to the U.S. Supreme Court.

Chief Justice Roger Taney wrote the Court's majority opinion, which reached several explosive conclusions:

- **African Americans, whether enslaved or free, could not be citizens of the United States** Individual states might grant them state citizenship, but these individuals could not enjoy the rights and protections of national citizenship under the Constitution, such as suing in federal courts. Taney reached this conclusion by reasoning that African Americans were not recognized as U.S. citizens when the Constitution was ratified. Taney's opinion ignored the fact that the Constitution neither defines national or state citizenship nor specifies who does or does not qualify for citizenship.

- **The national government did not have the right to exclude slavery from the territories** Enslaved African Americans were property.

- **The due process clause of the Fifth Amendment protected property rights** Therefore the Constitution protected the right to own slaves, and a slaveholder had the right to own slaves anywhere in the country or its territories.

Taney hoped that the *Dred Scott* decision would peacefully resolve the conflict over slavery and avoid a civil war. The ruling had the opposite effect. Now, it seemed to many people, the Court itself had taken the slaveholders' side in the conflict.

WHAT DO YOU THINK?

❶ How did slavery encourage different interpretations of the Constitution and the nature of the union?

❷ Examine the original Constitution. Do you think it is a pro-slavery document or an anti-slavery document? Cite evidence for your response.

❸ What basic rights were in conflict in the *Dred Scott* case? What are some examples of similar conflicts today?

Why was the decision in the *Dred Scott* case a major defeat for anti-slavery forces?

WHAT WAS SECESSION, AND WHAT WERE THE ARGUMENTS FOR AND AGAINST ITS CONSTITUTIONALITY?

In 1860 Abraham Lincoln was elected president of the United States. Lincoln belonged to the new Republican Party, which was committed to "free soil" principles. Faced with the prospect of a national administration committed to restricting and eventually abolishing slavery, eleven Southern states responded with **secession**. One by one, they voted to leave—secede from—the Union. From December 20, 1860, to June 8, 1861, the eleven states seceded in this order: South Carolina, Mississippi, Florida, Alabama, Georgia, Louisiana, Texas, Virginia, Arkansas, North Carolina, and Tennessee. They formed a new union called the Confederate States of America and adopted a constitution in March 1861 to govern its population of nine million, including 3.6 million slaves.

The states that seceded made two basic arguments for their constitutional right to do so. First, they argued that the Union was a compact of sovereign states. No state gave up its sovereignty when it ratified the Constitution. They wrote that concept into the beginning of their new Confederate constitution: "We, the people of the Confederate States, each State acting in its sovereign and independent character." Second, based on the ideals of the Declaration of Independence and the American Revolution, the leaders of the Confederacy believed that

student page ▼ 120–121

WHAT CONSTITUTIONAL ISSUES DID THE CIVIL WAR PROVOKE?

During the Civil War President Lincoln suspended the writ of habeas corpus (Article I, Section 9, Clause 2) three times: April 27, 1861; September 24, 1862; and September 15, 1863.

TANEY'S RESPONSE TO LINCOLN'S SUSPENSION OF THE WRIT OF HABEAS CORPUS
On May 25, 1861, Union Army forces imprisoned Lt. John Merryman at Fort McHenry as a suspected secessionist. Merryman immediately sought a writ of habeas corpus. Chief Justice Taney issued it. General George Cadwalader, the commanding officer at Fort McHenry, refused to comply with the writ, citing President Lincoln's order of April 27, 1861. Merryman was eventually released. Congress retroactively approved Lincoln's suspension of the writ in the Habeas Corpus Act of 1863.

ABOLITION OF SLAVERY The movement to abolish slavery occurred on many fronts and in many ways, including the following:

DECEMBER 5, 1861	Bills to abolish slavery are introduced in Congress.
MARCH 6, 1862	Lincoln asks Congress for a joint resolution urging compensated emancipation.
MARCH 13, 1862	Congress enacts legislation forbidding the Army and the Navy to forcibly return runaway slaves.
APRIL 14, 1862	Lincoln signs an act of Congress emancipating slaves in the District of Columbia.
MAY 10, 1862	The House adopts a resolution calling for cooperation with any state that would gradually abolish slavery.
JUNE 19, 1862	Lincoln signs legislation abolishing slavery in the territories.
JANUARY 1, 1863	Lincoln signs the Emancipation Proclamation.
MARCH 16, 1864	Arkansas abolishes slavery.
APRIL 8, 1864	The Senate votes for the Thirteenth Amendment.
JUNE 15, 1864	The Thirteenth Amendment is defeated in the House.

SEPTEMBER 5, 1864	Louisiana abolishes slavery.
SEPTEMBER 6, 1864	Maryland abolishes slavery.
JANUARY 6, 1865	The House begins new debate on the Thirteenth Amendment.
JANUARY 31, 1865	The Thirteenth Amendment passes the House.
DECEMBER 18, 1865	The Thirteenth Amendment goes into effect.

wtpcompanion.civiced.org **PRIMARY SOURCES**

Visit the We the People companion website for a link to the text of the Emancipation Proclamation.

During the debates on the Thirteenth Amendment Michigan Senator Jacob Howard noted that the wording of the amendment was "the good old Anglo-Saxon language employed by our fathers in the ordinance of 1787." The Northwest Ordinance, to which Howard alluded, had banned slavery in the area north of the Ohio River.

states and citizens possessed the right of revolution if their fundamental rights—in this case, the right to own slaves, who were regarded as property—were violated. They believed that leaving the Union was a second American Revolution.

President Lincoln and most Northerners denied the constitutional right of any state to secede from the Union. They believed that the Framers had created a perpetual union, a national bond expressing the sovereign authority of the American people as a whole. As Lincoln said in his inaugural address, "No government proper ever had a provision in its organic law for its own termination." Southern states seceded, Lincoln argued, not because any constitutional rights had been violated, but because they feared they would lose the right to own slaves. Secession was therefore an act of rebellion.

The constitution of the Confederate States of America drew most of its provisions and language from the U.S. Constitution. There were the three branches of government, including a bicameral legislature; the enumeration of congressional powers; and the provisions of the Bill of Rights. However, there were several important differences. The Confederate president would serve a single, six-year term. Congress was barred from making tariffs to benefit industry and from appropriating money for most internal improvements. Most important, the Confederate constitution explicitly protected slavery, stating that no "law denying or impairing the right of property in negro slaves shall be passed." Slaveholders were guaranteed the right to take their slaves anywhere in the Confederacy, including new territories; and the fugitive slave clause used the word *slave*.

CRITICAL THINKING EXERCISE
Understanding the Constitution of the Confederate States of America

Obtain a copy of the constitution of the Confederate States of America. Work in small groups. Each group should examine one article of that constitution. The groups should then come together to respond to the following questions:

❶ In what ways did the constitution of the Confederate States of America draw from the U.S. Constitution?

❷ In what ways did the constitution of the Confederate States of America adapt the U.S. Constitution to fit the circumstances of the Confederacy?

WHAT CONSTITUTIONAL ISSUES DID THE CIVIL WAR PROVOKE?

Slavery was the main reason that Southern states seceded from the Union. However, once the Civil War began President Lincoln maintained that his paramount goal was to preserve the Union. Lincoln was opposed to slavery, but he believed his public duty as president was to defend the Constitution, even if that meant allowing slavery to continue. He refused to recognize the right of secession and always called the war a "domestic insurrection." He hoped it would be concluded quickly, but the war became a bloody, four-year conflict that hardened views on both sides.

Lincoln asserted unprecedented presidential powers on behalf of the Union. The Constitution authorized some of his actions, such as calling up the militia. Other actions appeared to contradict congressional powers listed in Article I. For example, Lincoln expanded the regular United States army when Congress was not in session, even though Article I gives Congress the power to "raise and support armies." However, Congress quickly approved Lincoln's action when it convened in the summer of 1861.

Lincoln also exercised extraordinary power in curtailing individuals' rights in wartime. He suspended the writ of habeas corpus. Serving as a federal district judge when the Supreme Court was in recess, Chief Justice Taney held that only Congress had the power to suspend

What arguments can you give for and against the unprecedented powers President Abraham Lincoln took during the Civil War?

the writ. Lincoln defied that order. The result was that at least thirteen thousand civilians were held under military arrest and without judicial hearings during the war, mostly in the rebellious states and in the border states of Delaware, Kentucky, Maryland, and Missouri. These states bordered the Confederacy and permitted slavery but remained within the Union. Another border state, West Virginia, broke away from Virginia and became a new state in 1863. Lincoln also authorized military trials, not only for Confederates in rebel territory and war zones but also for some Union civilians in friendly territory. At various times during the war people were arrested for "treasonable language" and publications that appeared to threaten the Union cause.

The Emancipation Proclamation illustrates the use of the president's power as commander in chief of the armed forces. In the summer of 1862 Lincoln became convinced that abolishing slavery in the rebellious states was a military necessity. Doing so, he believed, would undercut the South's main labor source and consequently its ability to make war. That September Lincoln announced that all persons held as slaves in states or parts of states still in rebellion on January 1, 1863, "shall be then, henceforward, and forever free." The president justified his action as a "fit and necessary war measure." Some critics denounced it as an empty gesture because it left slavery alone in areas under Union control.

For all its limitations the Emancipation Proclamation had profound political and symbolic significance. The fight for the Union was now committed to America's founding principle of liberty. In his annual message to Congress, delivered a month before the Emancipation Proclamation took effect, Lincoln outlined a plan for the total abolition of slavery:

> " Fellow-citizens, we cannot escape history…. The fiery trial through which we pass, will light us down, in honor or dishonor, to the latest generation…. In giving freedom to the slave, we assure freedom to the free—honoring alike in what we give, and what we preserve. We shall nobly save, or meanly lose, the last best hope of earth.

WHAT DO YOU THINK?

❶ What provisions of the Constitution, if any, allow the president to take extraordinary action in wartime?

❷ What do you think should be the limits on the president's authority in wartime? Did President Lincoln exceed those limits? Why or why not?

HOW DID THE CIVIL WAR RESOLVE ISSUES THAT THE FRAMERS LEFT UNANSWERED?

The Civil War resolved the great constitutional and human issue of slavery. Even before the war ended, Congress began considering a constitutional amendment to complete the Emancipation Proclamation. The Thirteenth Amendment, ratified in 1865, abolished slavery "within the United States, or in any place subject to their jurisdiction."

Northern victory also ended the idea of secession as a constitutional right and with it the vision of the Union as a mere federation of states. States continued to enjoy significant power and independence in the system of federalism, but the Civil War marked the beginning of a development that has continued to the present day, namely, the supremacy of the national government.

The Union victory also led for the first time to a definition of national citizenship. Soon after the war, as Union troops withdrew from the defeated states, white Southerners quickly began passing laws called Black Codes. These statutes, which appeared to protect the rights of African Americans, in fact prevented former slaves from developing the political power they might have gained with education and the right to vote. The Black Codes severely limited the rights of African Americans to own property, travel, and work for pay on acceptable terms.

It soon became clear to members of Congress that the Thirteenth Amendment was not enough to protect the rights of former slaves. In an attempt to provide help, Congress passed the Civil Rights Act of 1866—over the veto of President Andrew Johnson, who had succeeded to the presidency on April 15, 1865, following Lincoln's assassination. Despite this legislation, little changed.

As a result of continuing concerns Congress drafted the Fourteenth and Fifteenth Amendments to the Constitution. The Fourteenth Amendment (1868) declared among other things that all persons born or naturalized within the United States are citizens. The amendment thereby nullified the Supreme Court's decision in *Dred Scott*. The Fourteenth Amendment also prohibits states from making or enforcing any law that abridges the privileges or immunities of citizens or denies due process or equal protection of the law.

The Fifteenth Amendment (1870) prohibited both national and state governments from denying citizens the right to vote because of their race, color, or status as former slaves. From the late 1860s and into the 1890s large numbers of African Americans voted. They gained considerable political power and used it to protect their rights. All three amendments gave Congress power to enforce them by "appropriate legislation." That power would transform the relationship between the national government and the states, as later lessons will explain.

student page ▾ 121–122

HOW DID THE CIVIL WAR RESOLVE ISSUES THAT THE FRAMERS LEFT UNANSWERED?

The Joint Committee on Reconstruction, consisting of nine members of the House and six members of the Senate, was formed to draft the Fourteenth Amendment. The committee formed subcommittees to consider various issues, including the status of former slaves, the terms on which states that had seceded would be brought back into the union, and how representation would be determined—based on numbers of citizens or numbers of eligible voters.

When Southern states returned to the Union after the Civil War, former slaves were counted as full persons, not as three-fifths of a person. As a result Southern states were entitled to more representatives in Congress than they had before the war. Northerners, especially abolitionists, worried that this would increase Southern power. Section 2 of the Fourteenth Amendment stipulates that if a state disenfranchises any of its male citizens twenty-one years of age or older, then the state loses representation in Congress in proportion to the percentage of male citizens it disenfranchises. However, Section 2 of the Fourteenth Amendment was not enforced.

The Fifteenth Amendment initially gave African Americans significant political power. They frequently formed coalitions with pro-Union whites to control state legislatures, which in turn were responsible for electing United States senators. In 1870 Hiram Rhodes Revels of Mississippi became the first black member of the Senate. Joseph Rainey of South Carolina became the first black member of the House of Representatives that same year. Thereafter blacks were elected to the House from Alabama, Florida, Georgia, Louisiana, Mississippi, North Carolina, and Virginia. All were members of the Republican Party.

See Lessons 18 and 19 for more detail about how the Supreme Court has interpreted the due process and equal protection clauses. See Lesson 36 for a discussion of civil rights movements.

ENRICHMENT ACTIVITY

COMPARING VIEWS OF THE CONSTITUTION

Separate the class into small groups and give each group a copy of the South Carolina Declaration of Causes (1852) and Lincoln's First Inaugural Address.

wtpcompanion.civiced.org PRIMARY SOURCES

Visit the We the People companion website for a link to the South Carolina Declaration of Causes and Lincoln's First Inaugural Address.

Ask each group to fill out the chart below (Appendix D 4) in response to the following questions:

COMPARING THE SOUTH CAROLINA DECLARATION OF CAUSES AND LINCOLN'S FIRST INAUGURAL ADDRESS

ISSUE	SOUTH CAROLINA DECLARATION OF CAUSES	LINCOLN'S FIRST INAUGURAL ADDRESS
What is the nature of the union formed by the Constitution?		
Who formed the union—the people or the states?		
What are the rights of the states under the Constitution?		
Do states have the right to secede from the union?		
What is the significance of the Declaration of Independence?		

Ask each group to explain to the class how it filled out the chart and why. Conduct a class discussion about the various responses and which document, if either, was "correct" about the issues.

How did laws passed in Southern states in the 1880s and 1890s try to destroy the political power of African Americans?

Eventually public support for protecting the rights of the newly freed people weakened. In less than a decade since their ratification the Fourteenth and Fifteenth Amendments had become ineffectual as tools for protecting these people's rights. In the 1880s and 1890s Southern states began passing laws to destroy the political power of African Americans. These laws included **poll taxes**, which required citizens to pay a tax in order to vote; **literacy tests**, which required citizens to take tests proving they could read or write before they were permitted to vote; and **grandfather clauses**, which allowed people to vote only if their grandfathers had been eligible to vote.

When the U.S. government failed to enforce the Fourteenth and Fifteenth Amendments, African Americans learned to look to themselves and their own community institutions for help. Ministers, teachers, and community leaders became the backbone of a continuing struggle for the rights of African Americans for the next hundred years. By the 1910s and 1920s African Americans would begin to use the Civil War amendments as bases to challenge discrimination authorized by laws.

REVIEWING AND USING THE LESSON

❶ What was the *Dred Scott* case about? Why was the Supreme Court's decision in that case important?

❷ How did Southern states justify their decision to secede from the Union? How did President Lincoln and other Northerners justify treating secession as an act of rebellion?

❸ In what ways did President Lincoln assert presidential powers during the Civil War?

❹ On what constitutional grounds did President Lincoln issue the Emancipation Proclamation? Why did the Emancipation Proclamation not free all the slaves in the United States?

❺ What are the key provisions of the Thirteenth, Fourteenth, and Fifteenth Amendments?

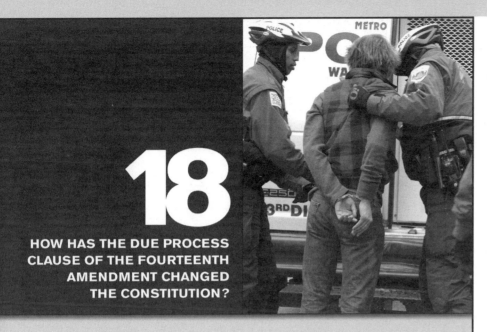

18

HOW HAS THE DUE PROCESS CLAUSE OF THE FOURTEENTH AMENDMENT CHANGED THE CONSTITUTION?

HOW HAS THE DUE PROCESS CLAUSE OF THE FOURTEENTH AMENDMENT CHANGED THE CONSTITUTION?

wtpcompanion.civiced.org **LESSON PURPOSE + TERMS**

Visit the We the People companion website for printable and downloadable Lesson Purposes and Terms and Concepts to Understand sections for each lesson. Audio readings of each Lesson Purpose and Term are also available online in MP3 format.

LESSON PURPOSE

The Fifth Amendment limits only the national government, but the Fourteenth Amendment guarantees that states shall not deprive people of life, liberty, or property without "due process of law." The Constitution does not define "due process of law." However, the concept has deep roots in English history, and it has played a central role in Americans' understanding of whether government actions affecting life, liberty, and property are valid. This lesson explains how the interpretation of due process has changed in American law since the adoption of the Fourteenth Amendment and how the requirement of due process has been used to protect the rights of individuals against actions by state governments.

When you have finished this lesson, you should be able to explain the historical origins of due process. You also should be able to explain the difference between procedural and substantive due process. You should be able to define the concept of incorporation and describe its effect on the powers of the states. Finally, you should be able to evaluate, take, and defend positions on historical and contemporary issues involving due process.

TERMS AND CONCEPTS TO UNDERSTAND

adversary system

due process of law

fundamental rights

incorporation

inquisitorial system

procedural due process

substantive due process

WHAT IS DUE PROCESS OF LAW?

Refer to Lesson 4 and the discussion of the Magna Carta.

WHAT IS DUE PROCESS OF LAW?

Due process of law is an ancient principle. Most scholars trace the idea of due process of law in the Anglo-American tradition to Chapter 39 of the Magna Carta of 1215. King John promised among other things not to imprison, exile, or destroy any free man or his property "except by the lawful judgment of his peers or by the law of the land." The phrase "by the law of the land" meant that government, like the governed, must obey the law. The phrase "due process of law" first appeared in the subsequent 1354 version of the Magna Carta. Both phrases—"due process" and "law of the land"—mean that government must follow known and established procedures and may not act arbitrarily or unpredictably in negatively altering or destroying life, liberty, or property.

As discussed in Unit One, John Locke argued that the purpose of government is to protect life, liberty, and property. Beliefs about what is fair, just, and right when government seeks to affect life, liberty, or property change over time. Therefore due process is both an ancient and an evolving concept.

The Fifth Amendment contains the Constitution's first reference to due process of law. That amendment limits only the national government. Other constitutional provisions also address due process concerns. For example, Article I prohibits Congress and the states from passing *ex post facto* laws. But it is the Fourteenth Amendment that imposes the requirement of due process on the states and gives Congress the power to enforce the requirement through "appropriate legislation." The courts determine whether legislation satisfies the requirements of due process in the Fifth and Fourteenth Amendments.

WHAT IS PROCEDURAL DUE PROCESS?

Historically, due process of law meant that government officials must follow recognized procedures and not act arbitrarily when they make and enforce laws. This is called **procedural due process**, which requires government officials to act in certain ways before they regulate or take life, liberty, or property. In England due process requirements initially focused on the rights of criminal defendants. For a criminal proceeding to be fair, for example, the laws must be clear. The defendant must know the charges that the government seeks to prove and be given a fair trial by a jury of his or her peers and the right to confront witnesses.

In the United States due process guarantees apply to both criminal and noncriminal (civil) matters. For example, the due process clause of the Fourteenth Amendment addresses property, in addition to life and liberty. Property is a broad term. It refers to everything that a person can own, from tangible things such as land and buildings to intangible things such as copyrights and patents. People also have property interests in other intangibles, such as their jobs, welfare or unemployment benefits, and their reputations. In addition to constitutional guarantees, many laws enacted by state legislatures and Congress also contain provisions ensuring due process in matters such as public school discipline. Due process guarantees include the requirement of notice, the opportunity for a fair hearing, the opportunity to present evidence, and the opportunity to appeal an initial decision.

How does the right to due process of law protect an individual's rights to life, liberty, and property?

WHY ARE PROCEDURAL RIGHTS IMPORTANT IN AN ADVERSARY LEGAL SYSTEM?

The legal systems in England and the United States are known as **adversary systems** of justice. This means that there are opposing, or adverse, parties in all cases. This type of system assumes that justice is most likely to result from the clash of positions between contesting parties. The opposing parties are responsible for gathering and presenting evidence and witnesses to support their side and for exposing weaknesses in the other side's case. Both parties seek to persuade a neutral, impartial decision-maker—a judge or a jury—that they should prevail.

In a criminal case, where an individual's life, liberty, or property is at stake, the adversary system assumes that the defendant is innocent until proven guilty. Defendants are not required to prove their innocence. Instead, the prosecution must prove the defendant's guilt and, moreover, must do so "beyond a reasonable doubt," the most rigorous standard of proof in the law. "Reasonable doubt" has been described as a doubt that would cause a prudent person to hesitate before acting on important matters. In civil cases the burden of proof is considerably lower. The side that presents the most credible and persuasive evidence wins. Lawyers, acting as advocates, play a central role in the adversary system. They represent clients in both civil and criminal cases.

The adversary system has been called a "fight theory of justice," because parties are pitted against one another in making their cases. Procedural guarantees ensure that the fight is fair. Both the Constitution and the Bill of Rights place great importance on procedural fairness. The Framers knew that just because a person is accused of a crime does not mean that the person is guilty. Lawyers represent criminal defendants whom they suspect, believe, or even know to be guilty to preserve the integrity of the adversary system.

By contrast, most European countries have an **inquisitorial system** of justice. The inquisitorial system uses specially trained judges to act as both investigators and decision-makers. Parties are expected to answer questions that the judge asks, and the questions usually are based on court-ordered investigations. There are fewer jury trials and fewer lawyers, and court proceedings usually are much shorter.

Supporters of the inquisitorial system argue that the adversary system is based on unjustifiable assumptions: that there will be two adversaries of equal ability and resources and that the clash between these adversaries will yield the truth. Advocates of the inquisitorial system point out that often there is a great disparity in resources and ability between the two sides. They also argue that in the adversary system each side has an interest in presenting what is most likely to win for it; neither side is

What are the basic differences between the adversary system of justice used in the United States and the inquisitorial system used in most European nations?

concerned with ensuring that the truth emerges. The inquisitorial system, by contrast, has courts with the responsibility for full investigation and presentation. Defenders of the inquisitorial system believe that this overcomes the effects of inequalities between litigants and maximizes the chance to discover the truth.

Critics of the inquisitorial system argue that it gives too much unrestrained power to judges and judicial institutions. Some claim that a trial by a jury of one's peers in an adversary system is likely to be far more impartial than a trial by members of a government.

WHAT DO YOU THINK?

❶ The adversary system of justice has been criticized for being inefficient. Should the United States adopt elements of the inquisitorial system in order to make judicial proceedings quicker and less expensive? Why or why not?

❷ Which process, adversary or inquisitorial, is more likely to discover the truth of what happened in a criminal case? Why?

❸ If you were a criminal defendant, would you rather be tried under the adversary system or the inquisitorial system of justice? Why?

WHY ARE PROCEDURAL RIGHTS IMPORTANT IN AN ADVERSARY LEGAL SYSTEM?

The inquisitorial system was first developed by the Catholic Church during the medieval period. Today it is used most often in countries that base their legal systems on civil or Roman codes, such as France, Germany, Spain, Portugal, Italy, and many African, South American, and Asian countries. In the sixteenth century the inquisitorial system in England earned a bad reputation because of the Star Chamber, a court reserved for complex cases that was expanded under the reign of Henry VIII and used torture to compel testimony. The adversary system gradually replaced the inquisitorial system in England. However, with modifications the inquisitorial system is more widely used today than the adversary system. Some countries that use the inquisitorial system, such as Italy, have begun to include some adversary processes in their criminal systems.

student page ▾ 126

WHAT IS SUBSTANTIVE DUE PROCESS?

The idea of substantive due process was expressed well before adoption of the Fourteenth Amendment. In *Calder v. Bull* (1798), for example, Justice Samuel Chase wrote that "an act of the legislature…contrary to the first great principles of the social compact, cannot be considered a rightful exercise of legislative power."

In the 1880s the Supreme Court began holding that one of the liberties protected by the Fourteenth Amendment is liberty of contract, including the right to earn a livelihood, engage in any lawful calling, and enter into "all contracts which may be proper, necessary, and essential to earning money" (*Allgeyer v. Louisiana*, 1897).

In response to the grueling, often abusive conditions in which millions of ordinary Americans labored during the Industrial Revolution, several states and the national government enacted laws limiting the number of hours in a workday or workweek. In *Lochner v. New York* (1905) the Supreme Court declared such laws unconstitutional on the grounds that the right to sell one's own labor is a fundamental right. The so-called Lochner era prohibiting certain economic legislation lasted about thirty years.

In the 1930s the Supreme Court's commitment to economic liberty clashed with President Franklin D. Roosevelt's efforts to revive and transform the economy during the Great Depression. In one of the most important cases involving economic regulation, *West Coast Hotel v. Parrish* (1937), the Court abandoned the view that freedom of contract is a fundamental right.

A year later in *United States v. Carolene Products* (1938) the Court upheld a congressional statute that banned the shipment of imitation milk in interstate commerce. It stated that from then on it would give statutes involving economic regulations minimal judicial scrutiny (asking only whether Congress had a "rational basis" for enacting the legislation). However, in Footnote 4, one of the most famous footnotes in Supreme Court history, the Court stated that it might subject legislation aimed at "discrete and insular minorities" (groups less able to participate in the political process because of a long history of prejudice) to "more searching judicial inquiry." Footnote 4 is the foundation on which today's three levels of equal protection analysis (rational basis, intermediate scrutiny, and strict scrutiny) was built. Lesson 19 examines the equal protection clause and its close relationship to the theory of fundamental rights and due process of law.

wtpcompanion.civiced.org **PRIMARY SOURCES**

Visit the We the People companion website for a link to the complete text of *Carolene Products*, Footnote 4.

WHAT IS SUBSTANTIVE DUE PROCESS?

In the United States due process of law has two meanings. Procedural due process, described earlier, refers to the processes that governments must follow when they make and enforce laws. The second meaning of due process is known as **substantive due process**. It means that the Constitution usually prohibits some kinds of laws altogether, no matter how popular those laws may be with legislatures, executives, or even the people. Substantive due process is based on the idea that some rights are so fundamental that government must have a "compelling," or exceedingly important, reason to regulate or interfere with them. It is the role of the courts, interpreting the Constitution, to determine whether a law is unconstitutional because it violates a fundamental right, and whether a governmental regulation of a fundamental right is justified by a compelling government interest.

The idea of **fundamental rights** traces to natural rights philosophy. As explained in Unit One, social contract theorists such as John Locke argued that people have natural rights that predate government. Some of those rights are so fundamental, or basic, that governments may not interfere with them or regulate them. One of the most difficult roles the Supreme Court plays is to identify which rights are fundamental and which are not. The justices' views of fundamental rights have changed over time.

For many years, for example, the Court held that the right to buy and sell a person's labor is so fundamental that state and congressional laws establishing minimum wages and limiting the number of hours in a workday or workweek were unconstitutional. This was known as the era of economic substantive due process. In 1937 the Court abandoned the view that economic rights are fundamental rights.

However, the Court did not abandon its effort to identify other fundamental rights. It has continued to try to identify rights that are so basic that Congress or states must have a "compelling interest" in order to pass laws that interfere with or regulate such rights. The Court has identified the following rights as fundamental. Note that some but not all such rights are listed in the Constitution or Bill of Rights:

- The right to marry and have children

- The right to purchase and use birth control

- The right to custody of one's own children and to rear them as one sees fit

- The right of mentally competent adults to refuse medical treatment

- The right to free speech

- The right to interstate travel

- The right of legal voters to vote

- The right to associate

- The right to religious freedom

Whether any or all of these rights are indeed fundamental, and thus prohibit most governmental regulations, is a topic of intense controversy in the United States.

Why did the Supreme Court rule early in the twentieth century that laws establishing minimum wages and limiting the number of hours in a workday or workweek were unconstitutional?

WHAT DO YOU THINK?

❶ How is due process related to the principle of limited government? How is it related to the principle of majority rule?

❷ What kinds of controversies might arise in determining whether certain rights are fundamental rights?

❸ Is one branch of government more capable of identifying fundamental rights than the other branches? Explain your reasoning.

WHAT IS THE DOCTRINE OF INCORPORATION?

For the first few decades after ratification of the Fourteenth Amendment the Supreme Court continued to rely on the states to be the principal protectors of individual rights. All the state constitutions contained bills of rights. The Court was leery of interpreting the Fourteenth Amendment in a way that would upset the balance of power between the national government and the states.

However, not all states interpreted their bills of rights to ensure due process and to protect the fundamental rights of everyone within their boundaries. In 1925 the Supreme Court began to examine the due process clause of the Fourteenth Amendment with an eye to identifying the rights in the Bill of Rights that the states, like the national government, must protect. In *Gitlow v. New York* (1925) the Court recognized that the rights of free speech and free press are among the personal rights to liberty protected by the due process clause. States could not infringe on these rights.

Interestingly, the Court upheld the New York Supreme Court's decision that Benjamin Gitlow, a Socialist, was guilty of criminal anarchy after publishing a "Left Wing Manifesto." The U.S. Supreme Court upheld his conviction on the basis that the government may suppress or punish speech when it directly advocates the unlawful overthrow of the government. The Court's ruling on the protected rights in the Fourteenth Amendment was incidental to the decision in this case, but it established a significant precedent.

Gitlow began a process known as **incorporation**—that is, using the due process clause of the Fourteenth Amendment to decide whether various guarantees in the Bill of Rights limit the states as well as the national government. In cases decided in the next two decades the Court ruled that the due process clause prohibits states from infringing on all the rights in the First Amendment. In determining which rights in the rest of the Bill of Rights limit the states through the due process clause, the Court has followed a process called "selective incorporation." This means that the Court has examined rights on a case-by-case basis, rather than holding that all the provisions of the Bill of Rights are limitations on the states. On some occasions it has used a test offered by Justice Felix Frankfurter, who served on the Court from 1939 until 1962. Justice Frankfurter's test involved asking whether it would "shock the conscience" if a particular right were not interpreted to limit the states.

The Court was more reluctant to hold that the criminal procedural guarantees in the Fourth through Eighth Amendments limit the states. Their reasoning reflected a concern for federalism. State governments have a greater responsibility for prosecuting and punishing criminal behavior than does the national government, and procedural guarantees vary from state to state. Unit Five examines, among other things, the Court's approach to identifying rights of the criminally accused that the Supreme Court has held are incorporated through the due process clause of the Fourteenth Amendment to limit the states.

Today, despite the Court's early reluctance regarding criminal procedure, most provisions of the Bill of Rights have been incorporated through the process of selective incorporation. The Court has refused to incorporate, or has not yet considered whether to incorporate, the following rights in the Bill of Rights:

Why do you think the Supreme Court incorporated the right to counsel in criminal trials in the Fourteenth Amendment?

The U.S. Supreme Court has declared the following to be fundamental rights:

- The right to marry and have children (*Loving v. Virginia*, 1967)
- The right to purchase and use birth control (*Griswold v. Connecticut*, 1965)
- The right to custody of one's own children and to rear them as one sees fit (*Santosky v. United States*, 1982)
- The right of mentally competent adults to refuse medical treatment (*Cruzan v. Director*, 1990)
- The right to free speech (*Gitlow v. New York*, 1925)
- The right to travel interstate (*Shapiro v. Thompson*, 1969)
- The right of legal voters to vote (*Dunn v. Blumstein*, 1972)
- The right to associate (*DeJonge v. Oregon*, 1937)
- The right to religious freedom (*Cantwell v. Connecticut*, 1940)

student page ▾ 127–128

WHAT IS THE DOCTRINE OF INCORPORATION?

In *Chicago, Burlington & Quincy Railroad Co. v. Chicago* (1897) the Supreme Court held for the first time that states must honor the requirement in the Fifth Amendment that just compensation be paid to owners if the government takes private property. Although the Fifth Amendment explicitly limits only the national government, the Court held that allowing states to escape the requirement of just compensation would be a denial of due process of law. After *Burlington* the Court began using the Fourteenth Amendment to make states recognize rights in the Bill of Rights.

Review Lesson 13, which discusses Anti-Federalist fears that ratification of the Constitution would mean that the national judiciary would use its powers to destroy the states. Review particularly the essay of Brutus I, in which the author contends,

> It is easy to see, that in the common course of things, these [national] courts will eclipse the dignity, and take away from the respectability, of the state courts. These courts will be, in themselves, totally independent of the states, deriving their authority from the United States, and receiving from them fixed salaries; and in the course of human events it is to be expected, that they will swallow up all the powers of the courts in the respective states.

Some believe that incorporation of the Bill of Rights has realized Brutus's fears. Others argue that it has fulfilled Madison's vision of uniform national policy regarding rights.

NATIVE AMERICANS The Fourteenth Amendment does not apply to Indian tribes. However, in 1968 Congress enacted the Indian Civil Rights Act. Sections 1302 and 1303 provide the following:

§1302. CONSTITUTIONAL RIGHTS

No Indian tribe in exercising powers of self-government shall make or enforce any law prohibiting the free exercise of religion, or abridging the freedom of speech, or of the press, or the right of the people peaceably to assemble and to petition for a redress of grievances; violate the right of the people to be secure in their persons, houses, papers, and effects against unreasonable search and seizures, nor issue warrants, but upon probable cause, supported by oath or affirmation, and particularly describing the place to be searched and the person or thing to be seized; subject any person for the same offense to be twice put in jeopardy; compel any person in any criminal case to be a witness against himself; take any private property for a public use without just compensation; deny to any person in a criminal proceeding the right to a speedy and public trial, to be informed of the nature and cause of the accusation, to be confronted with the witnesses against him, to have compulsory process for obtaining witnesses in his favor, and at his own expense to have the assistance of counsel for his defense; require excessive bail, impose excessive fines, inflict cruel and unusual punishments, and in no event impose for conviction of any one offense any penalty or punishment greater than imprisonment for a term of one year and a fine of $5,000, or both; deny to any person within its jurisdiction the equal protection of its laws or deprive any person of liberty or property without due process of law; pass any bill of attainder or ex post facto law; or deny to any person accused of an offense punishable by imprisonment the right, upon request, to a trial by jury of not less than six persons.

§1303. HABEAS CORPUS

The privilege of the writ of habeas corpus shall be available to any person, in a court of the United States, to test the legality of his detention by order of an Indian tribe.

CRITICAL THINKING EXERCISE

Lessons 31 and 32 focus in detail on the Fourth, Sixth, and Eighth Amendments.

- The Second Amendment right to bear arms

- The Fifth Amendment right to an indictment by a grand jury

- The Seventh Amendment right to a jury trial in civil lawsuits

- The implicit requirement in the Sixth Amendment that the jury in a criminal case must have twelve members and must reach a unanimous verdict

CRITICAL THINKING EXERCISE
Examining the Effects of Incorporation on Your State

Supreme Court decisions that specific rights in the Bill of Rights limit the states as well as the national government have had a significant economic impact on governments throughout the United States. Work in one of these three groups:

- Group 1 will examine the guarantees in the Fourth Amendment.

- Group 2 will examine the guarantees in the Sixth Amendment.

- Group 3 will examine the guarantees in the Eighth Amendment.

Each group should answer the following questions, then explain its responses to the other two groups.

1. What kinds of costs do states incur by having to protect the rights in this amendment?

2. Should the national government assume responsibility for any increased costs to states associated with incorporation of the Bill of Rights? Why or why not?

REVIEWING AND USING THE LESSON

1. Explain the difference between procedural and substantive due process. Is one more important than the other?

2. What are the major differences between the adversary and inquisitorial systems of justice?

3. What is the relationship between substantive due process and fundamental rights?

4. What is the process of selective incorporation?

5. Has incorporation of the Bill of Rights in the states validated the fears of the Anti-Federalists regarding the power of the national judiciary (see Lesson 13)? Explain.

Why do you think the Supreme Court has ruled that the due process clause of the Fourteenth Amendment prohibits states from infringing on all of the rights in the First Amendment?

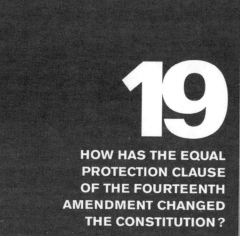

19

HOW HAS THE EQUAL PROTECTION CLAUSE OF THE FOURTEENTH AMENDMENT CHANGED THE CONSTITUTION?

HOW HAS THE EQUAL PROTECTION CLAUSE OF THE FOURTEENTH AMENDMENT CHANGED THE CONSTITUTION?

wtpcompanion.civiced.org | **LESSON PURPOSE + TERMS**

Visit the We the People companion website for printable and downloadable Lesson Purposes and Terms and Concepts to Understand sections for each lesson. Audio readings of each Lesson Purpose and Term are also available online in MP3 format.

wtpcompanion.civiced.org | **COURT CASES**

Visit the We the People companion website for links to Supreme Court syllabi and opinions for each of the cases described in the student and teacher's editions. Summaries are provided for selected Supreme Court cases.

LESSON PURPOSE

The previous lesson explained how the Fourteenth Amendment prohibits state governments from depriving a person of life, liberty, or property without due process of law. This lesson examines how the equal protection clause prohibits state governments from denying people "equal protection of the laws." Like the due process clause, the equal protection clause places limits on America's governments, not private individuals.

When you have finished this lesson, you should be able to define equal protection of the laws. You should be able to explain why neither state governments nor the national government can deprive people of equal protection of the laws. You also should be able to explain the "separate but equal" doctrine of racial segregation and why the Supreme Court abandoned it in *Brown v. Board of Education*. You should be able to describe the categories that the Supreme Court now uses to decide cases challenging governmental actions that treat some people differently from others. Finally, you should be able to evaluate, take, and defend a position on how conflicts between or among rights should be resolved.

TERMS AND CONCEPTS TO UNDERSTAND

equality of condition

equality of opportunity

intermediate scrutiny

rational basis

separate but equal

strict scrutiny

student page ▼ 131

WHAT WAS THE "SEPARATE BUT EQUAL" DOCTRINE, AND WHAT WAS ITS EFFECT?

Despite its otherwise soaring rhetoric on behalf of the Constitution's equal protection clause, Justice Harlan's dissent also contained the following statement:

> There is a race so different from our own that we do not permit those belonging to it to become citizens of the United States. Persons belonging to it are, with few exceptions, absolutely excluded from our country. I allude to the Chinese race. But, by the statute in question, a Chinaman can ride in the same passenger coach with white citizens of the United States, while citizens of the black race in Louisiana, many of whom, perhaps, risked their lives for the preservation of the Union, who are entitled, by law, to participate in the political control of the State and nation, who are not excluded, by law or by reason of their race, from public stations of any kind, and who have all the legal rights that belong to white citizens, are yet declared to be criminals, liable to imprisonment, if they ride in a public coach occupied by citizens of the white race.

student page ▾ 132

WHY DID THE SUPREME COURT ABANDON "SEPARATE BUT EQUAL" IN BROWN V. BOARD OF EDUCATION?

With the permission of the Court individuals or groups who are not parties to a case but wish to have their views on the issue heard are allowed to submit *amicus curiae*, or "friend of the court," briefs. *Brown* involved litigation on behalf of student Linda Brown against the Board of Education of Topeka, Kansas. The United States and the following organizations filed *amicus curiae* briefs supporting Linda Brown: the American Jewish Congress, the American Ethical Union, the American Civil Liberties Union, the American Jewish Committee, the American Federation of Teachers, the American Veterans Committee, Inc., and the Congress of Industrial Organizations.

Some of the briefs submitted in the *Brown* case relied on social science research by Kenneth and Mamie Clark, who studied the negative psychological effects of segregation on African American children. The Clarks also had testified in trial courts about their research in several state cases challenging segregation. The Supreme Court cited the Clarks' work in the Brown decision. The Court's reliance on sociological data about the effect of segregation, rather than on neutral principles of constitutional law, gave the decision only limited value as legal precedent. As explained in the next section, after *Brown* the court developed the legal framework for deciding cases under the equal protection clause.

wtpcompanion.civiced.org | **LINKS**

Visit the We the People companion website for a link to a debate between two legal scholars about the significance of the Court's reasoning in Brown.

student page ▾ 132–133

HOW HAS THE SUPREME COURT'S INTERPRETATION OF THE EQUAL PROTECTION CLAUSE CHANGED SINCE *BROWN*?

The following is background information for moving from the analysis in *Brown* to contemporary equal protection analysis:

Footnote 4 of *Carolene Products* (discussed in Lesson 18) hinted that with the demise of economic substantive due process the Supreme Court might approach the meanings of "liberty" and "equality" under the Fourteenth Amendment differently. World War II thrust equal protection questions to the nation's forefront. On December 7, 1941,

What rights are guaranteed by the equal protection clause of the Fourteenth Amendment?

WHAT IS MEANT BY "EQUAL PROTECTION OF THE LAWS"?

The equal protection clause of the Fourteenth Amendment says that no state may "deny to any person within its jurisdiction the equal protection of the laws." The amendment does not define "equal protection." U.S. Senator Jacob Howard (1805–1871) of Michigan, one of the drafters, explained that the phrase

❝ establishes equality before the law, and it gives, to the humblest, the poorest, the most despised…the same rights and the same protection before the law as it gives to the most powerful, the most wealthy, or those most haughty.

Equal protection of the laws, like due process, is a constitutional guarantee of fair treatment for all persons, regardless of sex, race, national origin, religion, or political views. It is rooted in the truth expressed in the Declaration of Independence that "all Men are created equal."

Equal protection of the laws forbids arbitrary or irrelevant barriers to the full enjoyment of rights by all persons. Two early cases are illustrative of equal protection of the laws in matters of race. *Strauder v. West Virginia* (1880) concerned an African American who had been convicted by an all-white jury. West Virginia law expressly limited jury service to "all white male persons."

On appeal, the Supreme Court declared that law unconstitutional because it violated the equal protection clause of the Fourteenth Amendment.

Six years later the Court ruled in *Yick Wo v. Hopkins* (1886) that a San Francisco city ordinance that discriminated against Chinese laundry businesses violated the equal protection clause. In a unanimous decision the Court held that the ordinance was discriminatory and constituted class legislation prohibited by the Fourteenth Amendment. It also ruled that the equal protection clause applies to all persons, citizens and aliens alike.

Equal protection of the laws means that government must treat all persons as equals without favoritism to any individual or group. It also means that every person is entitled to **equality of opportunity** so that everyone can try to achieve the goals they seek, or as the Declaration of Independence puts it, "the Pursuit of Happiness." Equality of opportunity means that laws must not unfairly disadvantage anyone in his or her opportunity to seek a variety of social goods, such as education, employment, housing, and political rights. It does not mean, however, **equality of condition** or that the results or outcomes of life will be the same for all. Equality of condition means equality in all aspects of life, such as personal possessions, living standards, medical care, and working conditions.

WHAT DO YOU THINK?

❶ What are the differences between equality of condition and equal protection of the laws?

❷ Does inequality of condition undermine the ideal of equality of rights? Explain your response.

WHAT WAS THE "SEPARATE BUT EQUAL" DOCTRINE, AND WHAT WAS ITS EFFECT?

After the end of Reconstruction, when U.S. troops were removed from former Confederate states and white people reasserted control of those states' governments, most Southern states adopted so-called Jim Crow laws. These laws were designed to limit the rights and freedoms of African Americans. By the end of the nineteenth century Jim Crow laws had imposed a system of racial segregation throughout the South and in many other parts of the country.

In the landmark case of *Plessy v. Ferguson* (1896) the U.S. Supreme Court rejected the argument that a Louisiana law requiring blacks and whites to ride in different railroad cars violated the equal protection clause. The Court held that **separate but equal** facilities were constitutional. Justice Henry Billings Brown, writing for the majority in the 7-to-1 decision (one justice did not participate), wrote that if blacks interpreted the "separate but equal doctrine" as a "badge of inferiority," it was "solely because the colored race chooses to put that construction upon it."

Justice John Marshall Harlan, in a strong dissent, argued that allowing state-enforced segregation of the races violated the equal protection clause:

❝ Our Constitution is color-blind…. In respect of civil rights, all citizens are equal before the law…. The judgment this day rendered will prove to be quite as pernicious as… the *Dred Scott* case.

In fact, state-sponsored segregation under *Plessy* lasted almost sixty years. Laws requiring racial separation affected Asian Americans as well as African Americans.

What were the effects of the "separate but equal" doctrine?

Japanese naval and air forces attacked the American fleet at Pearl Harbor, killing 2,335 military personnel and sixty-eight civilians. The next day Congress declared war on Japan. Within a short time anti-Japanese hysteria gripped the West Coast. In February 1942 President Franklin Roosevelt authorized the secretary of war to issue orders regulating the activities and movement of more than 112,000 persons of Japanese descent living on the West Coast, some 70,000 of whom were American citizens.

> **wtpcompanion.civiced.org**   **PRIMARY SOURCES**
>
> Visit the We the People companion website for a link to Executive Order 9066.

Within a few months Lt. General John L. DeWitt, military commander of the Western Defense Command, issued an order requiring all persons of Japanese ancestry to evacuate an area of California and to report to a civil control station. The order also placed curfews on people of Japanese descent.

In 1944 in *Korematsu v. United States* the Supreme Court upheld the validity of the relocation orders, just as it had upheld the validity of the curfew orders a year earlier in *Hirabayashi v. United States* (1943). The Court introduced "strict scrutiny" analysis in *Korematsu* but noted that "pressing public necessity" (such as a war) may sometimes justify the existence of restrictions that courts will subject to "the most rigid scrutiny."

The Supreme Court has held that the term *Indian* does not create a racial classification because Native Americans are not included in the Fourteenth Amendment. See the explanation in *Elk v. Wilkins* (1884). Therefore, Congress can enact laws that create classifications based on the status of being Native American, such as the Indian Child Welfare Act of 1968, which gives preference to tribal jurisdiction over state court jurisdiction in adoption proceedings related to Native American children, even if the children do not live on a reservation.

Until recently the states had virtually exclusive jurisdiction over family matters and children. Most states followed the common law, which viewed children born to an unwed mother as "illegitimate," or *filius nullius* (the child of no one), and therefore having no rights of families. The Supreme Court began making changes in this policy. In *Levy v. Louisiana* (1968), for example, the Court held that an illegitimate child has the right to recover for the wrongful death of his or her mother. In *Stanley v. Illinois* (1972) the Court recognized custody rights of the fathers of illegitimate children. In *Labine v. Vincent* (1971), however, the court refused to strike down a state law that limited the inheritance rights of illegitimate children, reasoning that the states are entitled to promote legally recognized families.

WHAT DO YOU THINK?

This exercise involves examples for which there are not necessarily clear legal or statutory answers. The purpose of the exercise is to encourage students to think about the problem in each example using the levels of analysis that the Supreme Court employs in deciding equal protection cases. Below are resources to help debate the issues:

STRENGTH REQUIREMENTS FOR FIRE FIGHTERS *Berkman v. City of New York*, 906 F2d 209 (Sixth Cir. 1990), certiorari denied, 499 U.S. 936 (1991) (upheld requirements).

DRIVER EXAMS Traditionally the privilege of having a license to drive has been recognized as part of a state's "police power," under which states regulate the public health, safety, welfare, and morals of those within state boundaries. However, suspension of a license can occur only after the state has provided a process—including a hearing—that meets the test of "fairness."

GIRL ON A BOYS' WRESTLING TEAM Many cases claiming discrimination on the basis of sex or gender have been resolved under Title IX, 20 U.S.C. 1681–1688. Regarding athletics that statute provides:

(a) **General** No person shall, on the basis of sex, be excluded from participation in, be denied the benefits of, be treated differently from another person or otherwise be discriminated against in any interscholastic, intercollegiate, club or intramural athletics offered by a recipient, and no recipient shall provide any such athletics separately on such basis.

(b) **Separate teams** Notwithstanding the requirements of paragraph (a) of this section, a recipient may operate or sponsor separate teams for members of each sex where selection for such teams is based upon competitive skill or the activity involved is a contact sport.

The Supreme Court has addressed some sex or gender discrimination cases on constitutional grounds. In *U.S. v. Virginia Military Academy* (1996), for example, the court struck down the academy's longstanding policy of admitting only males. By contrast, in *Bukowski v. Wisconsin Interscholastic Athletic Ass'n*, 726 N.W. 2d 356 (2006), the Wisconsin Court of Appeals upheld a rule that prevented boys from trying out for the girls' gymnastics team.

REFUSING TO PUT ELEVATORS IN A COUNTY COURTHOUSE In *Tennessee v. Lane* (2006) the Supreme Court upheld the "fundamental right" of access to courts.

INCARCERATING HOMELESS PERSONS WITH DOCUMENTED MENTAL DISABILITIES In *City of Cleburne v. Cleburne Living Center* (1985) the Supreme Court declined to use intermediate or strict scrutiny analysis to decide whether a city violated equal protection of the laws in denying a zoning application for a group home for the

WHY DID THE SUPREME COURT ABANDON "SEPARATE BUT EQUAL" IN *BROWN V. BOARD OF EDUCATION*?

The National Association for the Advancement of Colored People (NAACP) was founded in 1909. For its first twenty-five years it appealed to the conscience of all Americans to end racial mob violence and lynching, and it filed lawsuits seeking to end discrimination at the ballot box. The NAACP then turned to ending segregation in education. The association believed that improving educational opportunities and intermingling students of different races in schools would be the most effective way to end long-term patterns of racism in the United States. Under the direction of a legal team that included future Supreme Court Justice Thurgood Marshall, the NAACP argued and proved in case after case that medical, law, and other professional schools maintained for black students were not equal to those maintained for white students.

Those legal victories set the stage to challenge the separate but equal doctrine in segregated public elementary and secondary schools that were the legacy of *Plessy*. In 1952 the NAACP challenged state statutes that authorized "separate schools for the education of white and colored children." The lead case was against the Board of Education of Topeka, Kansas. That school district maintained segregated schools, a situation that sometimes required students to be bused away from their neighborhoods to achieve segregation. Linda Brown, an African American third-grader, was one of the students who had to travel by bus to attend a segregated school. Her father, Oliver Brown, a railroad worker studying for the ministry, worked with the local Topeka NAACP to file a lawsuit seeking to remedy the situation. The trial court applied the separate but equal doctrine, and Brown lost.

On appeal to the U.S. Supreme Court the NAACP emphasized evidence demonstrating the severe and damaging effects of segregated schools on the psychological development of African American children. In *Brown v. Board of Education* (1954) the Supreme Court agreed with the NAACP and unanimously decided that separate education facilities are "inherently unequal." In the field of public education, Chief Justice Earl Warren wrote, "the doctrine of 'separate but equal' has no place." Justice Harlan's dissent in *Plessy* was now the Court's majority view. However, as will be discussed in Unit Six, *Brown* was more difficult to enforce than the Supreme Court anticipated.

HOW HAS THE SUPREME COURT'S INTERPRETATION OF THE EQUAL PROTECTION CLAUSE CHANGED SINCE *BROWN*?

Many laws create classifications, or categories, of people. For example, a state law requiring a person to be at least sixteen years of age to qualify for a driver's license creates two classifications of people—those sixteen and older and those under sixteen. People in one classification qualify to receive licenses or permits. People in the other classification do not. Therefore, the following is an important judicial question: Does a classification that results in different treatment violate the equal protection clause?

The Supreme Court uses at least three levels of analysis to decide whether laws that create classifications violate the guarantee of equal protection of the laws.

● **LEVEL 1: STRICT SCRUTINY**

Laws that create classifications based on race, national origin, religion, or status as a legal alien are subject to the most rigorous judicial scrutiny, called **strict scrutiny**. Laws that deny or dilute the right to vote, impede interstate travel, or appear to restrict access to the courts also are subject to this level of analysis. Judges presume that such laws violate the equal protection clause. The government that adopted the classification can overcome the presumption if it can persuade the Court that there is an extremely strong reason, known as a "compelling state interest," for the law and that the government has imposed the fewest possible restrictions on the disfavored group.

For example, during World War II the U.S. government persuaded the Supreme Court that there was a compelling state interest for racial classifications that resulted in the internment of Japanese Americans and others. All other laws classifying people on the basis of race have been struck down. For instance, in *Loving v. Virginia* (1967) the Court held that the state of Virginia had no compelling state interest for a law prohibiting interracial marriage.

● **LEVEL 2: INTERMEDIATE SCRUTINY**

Classifications based on gender and illegitimacy (birth to an unmarried mother) are subject to **intermediate scrutiny**. Governments that distinguish between groups because of gender or illegitimacy must prove that the laws are "substantially related to an important government purpose."

Using this standard, in *Craig v. Boren* (1976) the Court struck down an Oklahoma law that permitted women to buy 3.2-percent beer at age eighteen but required men to be age twenty-one. It held that the gender-based distinction was not substantially related to the state's interest in promoting traffic safety. However, in *Rostker v. Goldberg* (1981) the Court upheld a federal statute excluding women from the military draft on the ground that women were barred from combat.

● **LEVEL 3: RATIONAL BASIS**

All other laws that create classifications—including classifications based on wealth, disability, and age—are presumed to be constitutional. Courts presume that the deliberative process that legislatures use to enact laws ensures their "rationality"—that is, that such laws have a **rational basis**. The person or group challenging the law must show that the law is not rational, or reasonable.

Only rarely has the Court held that a law was not rational. In *Stanton v. Stanton* (1975), for example, the Supreme Court overturned a Utah statute that required divorced fathers to support their sons to age twenty-one but their daughters only to age eighteen. The state argued that it was rational for divorced fathers to support girls for a shorter time because girls tend

What evidence do you see in this picture of the results of the Supreme Court's decision in the *Brown* case?

to mature and to marry earlier than boys do. The Supreme Court disagreed.

The Fourteenth Amendment's equal protection clause applies only to the states. The Court has held—in *Hirabayashi v. United States* (1943)—that the due process clause of the Fifth Amendment, which limits only the national government, contains an "equal protection component." Both due process and equal protection standards require government to treat people fairly. Therefore individuals or groups who believe the national government has deprived them of equal protection of the laws may challenge their treatment under the Fifth Amendment.

WHAT DO YOU THINK?

What level of judicial scrutiny do you think should apply in the following situations? Explain your reasoning in light of the criteria described regarding each level of scrutiny:

● Rejecting an eighty-five-pound woman from admission to the firefighters' academy.

● Requiring drivers over age seventy-five or male drivers under age twenty-five to take an annual driver's exam.

● Disqualifying a female student in a public high school from participating on the boys' wrestling team.

● Refusing to put elevators in a county courthouse.

● Incarcerating homeless persons with documented mental disabilities.

● Barring the children of illegal aliens from public schools.

WHAT CONTROVERSIES REMAIN IN THE ARENA OF EQUAL PROTECTION OF THE LAWS?

Claims of equal protection raise many difficult issues, including the following:

● Whether laws that give preferences to certain groups that historically have been denied equal opportunities (a practice known as affirmative action) are impermissible "reverse discrimination."

● Whether intermediate scrutiny is the appropriate level for analyzing classifications based on gender.

mentally handicapped. Using the rational basis standard, however, the court struck down the ordinance. The court found that the city's fear of the mentally handicapped was "irrational."

BARRING CHILDREN NOT LEGALLY ADMITTED TO THE UNITED STATES FROM PUBLIC SCHOOLS In *Plyler v. Doe* (1982) the Supreme Court invalidated a Texas statute that prohibited school districts from using state money to educate children not "legally admitted" into the United States. The court applied the intermediate scrutiny test to determine whether denying rights to people based on their status as aliens furthered a substantial state goal.

wtpcompanion.civiced.org	**COURT CASES**

Visit the We the People companion website for links to Supreme Court syllabi and opinions for each of the cases described in the student and teacher's editions. Summaries are provided for selected Supreme Court cases.

student page ▼ 133

WHAT CONTROVERSIES REMAIN IN THE ARENA OF EQUAL PROTECTION OF THE LAWS?

AFFIRMATIVE ACTION Cases involving programs that benefit certain groups based on their race, sex, gender, or alien status currently are subject to strict scrutiny analysis. Most programs have been struck down, beginning with *Regents v. Bakke* (1978). However, in *Grutter v. Bollinger* (2003) the Supreme Court upheld an affirmative action program at the University of Michigan Law School that did not use quotas because the program furthered "a compelling interest in obtaining the educational benefits that flow from a diverse student body."

GENDER Laws treating people differently on the basis of gender are tested under intermediate scrutiny. Some critics describe this level of analysis as "an unworkable half measure." Others argue that for women to receive full constitutional protection an Equal Rights Amendment is needed. Yet others argue that women constitute more than half the population and can hardly be regarded as a "discrete and insular minority" deserving of greater judicial protection than other groups.

"DISCRETE AND INSULAR MINORITY" STATUS under Footnote 4 of *U.S. v. Carolene Products*. Most cases involving the mentally handicapped have been analyzed using rational basis, as in *City of Cleburne v. Cleburne Living Center*, discussed above. Advocacy groups continue to try to persuade the Court to use intermediate scrutiny in analyzing laws that treat the mentally handicapped differently from other groups.

LAWS TREATING CHILDREN OF ILLEGAL ALIENS DIFFERENTLY FROM OTHER CHILDREN
As in *Plyler v. Doe*, discussed above, such cases are analyzed using intermediate scrutiny. Some advocacy groups believe that strict scrutiny is the appropriate level of analysis because the equal protection clause addresses persons, not citizens. Others believe that rational basis is the correct level of review because of the interests of states and localities in preventing immigration of undocumented aliens if possible.

LAWS TREATING GAYS AND LESBIANS DIFFERENTLY THAN HETEROSEXUALS
In *Romer v. Evans* (1996) the Supreme Court struck down a voter-approved initiative that provided:

> Neither the state of Colorado, through any of its branches or departments, nor any of its agencies, political subdivisions, municipalities or school districts, shall enact, adopt or enforce any statute, regulation, ordinance or policy whereby homosexual, lesbian or bisexual orientation, conduct, practices or relationships shall constitute or otherwise be the basis of, or entitle any person or class of persons to have or claim any minority status, quota preferences, protected status or claim of discrimination. This Section of the Constitution shall be in all respects self-executing.

The majority believed that the amendment served "no legitimate government interest." Justice Scalia, in dissent, argued for using a rational basis test in cases challenging laws that treat gays and lesbians differently from other groups.

---

wtpcompanion.civiced.org | **COURT CASES**

Visit the We the People companion website for links to Supreme Court syllabi and opinions for each of the cases described in the student and teacher's editions. Summaries are provided for selected Supreme Court cases.

---

student page ▾ 134

CRITICAL THINKING EXERCISE

Refer to Lessons 31 and 32, which deal in more detail with these amendments.

- Whether groups such as the mentally handicapped, children of illegal aliens, and gays and lesbians should be treated as "discrete and insular minorities" for purposes of equal protection analysis because of prejudice against them.

CRITICAL THINKING EXERCISE
Weighing Equal Protection Against Other Constitutional Rights

Consider the following real-life situation. James Dale was an assistant scoutmaster and an Eagle Scout in New Jersey. In 1990 Boy Scouts of America (BSA) revoked Dale's membership because BSA's standards "forbid membership to homosexuals." Dale sued BSA, arguing among other things that revoking his membership violated his right to equal protection of the laws. BSA responded that the organization was merely exercising its right of association under the First Amendment. It pointed out that the Supreme Court has interpreted associational rights to include control over the political, religious, or cultural messages that an organization wishes to send.

Respond to the following questions:

❶ How should the line be drawn between private organizations (which are not covered by the equal protection clause) and public action when the private organization receives government financial support, as BSA does?

❷ What level of judicial scrutiny should apply to claims of discrimination based on sexual orientation? Why? Compare your responses to the Supreme Court's analysis in *Boy Scouts of America v. Dale* (2000).

❸ What standards should courts apply in resolving conflicts between First Amendment rights and equal protection guarantees?

❹ Identify other situations that also may raise conflicts between equal protection guarantees and other constitutional rights.

REVIEWING AND USING THE LESSON

❶ What was the "separate but equal" doctrine? How did the Supreme Court justify the doctrine in *Plessy v. Ferguson*?

❷ With what arguments did the Court abandon the doctrine in *Brown v. Board of Education*?

❸ How has the equal protection clause been interpreted since 1954?

Should private organizations be free to exclude people upon the basis of such factors as race, gender, ethnicity, or physical characteristics?

134

20

HOW HAS THE RIGHT TO VOTE BEEN EXPANDED SINCE THE ADOPTION OF THE CONSTITUTION?

LESSON PURPOSE

During the colonial period and the early years of the nation, suffrage—the right to vote—was generally restricted to white men who owned property. The majority of adult white men met this requirement, especially in rural areas. Other people—women, Native Americans, African Americans, indentured servants, and members of certain religious groups—usually were denied the right to vote. This lesson examines how the right to vote has been extended since 1787. The expansion of the franchise to include almost all citizens eighteen years of age or older represents one of the great themes in American history, in some respects the most important theme.

When you have finished this lesson, you should be able to describe the extension of the franchise as a result of changes in voting laws in Congress and various states, amendments to the Constitution, and decisions of the Supreme Court. You should be able to evaluate, take, and defend positions on how extending the right to vote is related to fundamental ideas and principles of American constitutional government.

TERMS AND CONCEPTS TO UNDERSTAND

enfranchisement

franchise

135

HOW HAS THE RIGHT TO VOTE BEEN EXPANDED SINCE THE ADOPTION OF THE CONSTITUTION?

wtpcompanion.civiced.org | **LESSON PURPOSE + TERMS**

Visit the We the People companion website for printable and downloadable Lesson Purposes and Terms and Concepts to Understand sections for each lesson. Audio readings of each Lesson Purpose and Term are also available online in MP3 format.

student page ▼ 136

WHY IS THE FRANCHISE IMPORTANT IN THE AMERICAN CONSTITUTIONAL SYSTEM?

Refer to Lesson 5 for a discussion of the right to vote in colonial America. Chief Justice Earl Warren in *Reynolds v. Sims* (1964) commented, "The right to vote freely for the candidate of one's choice is of the essence of a democratic society, and any restrictions on that right strike at the heart of representative government."

student page ▼ 136

HOW WAS SUFFRAGE DETERMINED WHEN THE CONSTITUTION WAS ADOPTED?

Refer to Lesson 12 for a discussion of why the Philadelphia Convention left the question of suffrage qualifications to the states.

student page ▼ 136–137

HOW DID VOTING RIGHTS EXPAND FOR WHITE MEN?

As was true in the states after the Revolution, voting requirements in the colonies varied greatly. Historian Jon Butler reports:

> The property qualification in the colonies reflected the dominant early modern view that voting was a privilege held by orthodox Christian men with property, not a right enjoyed by all. By modern standards, the colonial franchise was narrow, although by eighteenth-century European standards it was generous.

Suffrage in the original states expanded significantly after 1790. Georgia, New Hampshire, and Pennsylvania had no property requirements for voting in 1790. The other original states eliminated property requirements as follows, but they often required payment of taxes and had residency requirements ranging from six months to two years:

- Maryland, 1801
- Massachusetts, 1821
- New York, 1821
- Delaware, 1831
- New Jersey, 1844
- Connecticut, 1845
- Virginia, 1850
- North Carolina, 1854
- South Carolina, 1865
- Rhode Island, 1888

student page ▼ 137

HOW DID AFRICAN AMERICAN MEN WIN–THEN LOSE–THE RIGHT TO VOTE?

The Civil Rights Act of 1868 added some four million former slaves to the voting rolls. The result was that twenty-four African Americans were elected to Congress between 1870 and 1900. In the South Carolina legislature African Americans outnumbered whites eighty-seven to forty.

What changed? In 1876 the Supreme Court held that the Fifteenth Amendment "did not confer the right [to vote] upon anyone" and that "the right of suffrage is not necessarily an attribute of national citizenship" (*United States v. Cruikshank*; *United States v. Reese*). Rather, voting was a privilege conveyed by states. (Refer to Lesson 17 for a discussion of the Civil War and the Fifteenth Amendment.)

POLL TAXES Between 1889 and 1910 eleven states placed taxes averaging about $1.50 on the right to vote. This was enough to prevent poor whites and blacks from voting. Many states made poll taxes cumulative—that is, if a person failed to pay the tax in one election, then the tax would be added to the tax charged for the next election. In *Breedlove v. Suttles* (1937) the Court held that "payment of poll taxes as a prerequisite to voting is a familiar and reasonable regulation long enforced in many states." In 1939 Congress began to discuss a constitutional amendment to abolish poll taxes. By the time the Twenty-fourth Amendment was proposed in 1962, only five states (Alabama,

WHY IS THE FRANCHISE IMPORTANT IN THE AMERICAN CONSTITUTIONAL SYSTEM?

The term **franchise** refers to a right or privilege, in this context specifically the right to vote. Thus **enfranchisement** is the act of giving that right to vote to a person or a group of people. Representative government is based on the principle that the people have a say—either directly or indirectly—in determining who makes, executes, and judges the laws that govern them and in holding those authorities accountable. The most basic way of participating in representative government is to vote in elections.

One of the legacies of the Greek and Roman democracies is that citizens should have an economic "stake" in a community in order to exercise the franchise intelligently. Greeks and Romans believed that property owners were more inclined than others to participate in politics and to act in the public interest because they had a stake in living in a healthy community. The colonists shared that view. In most colonies voting was a privilege limited to Protestant men who owned property. Property qualifications usually were low and land was cheap, which meant that thousands of colonists who would not have been able to vote in Europe were able to do so in America. For example, Virginia required only twenty-five acres of settled land or a hundred acres of unsettled land for enfranchisement. New York allowed otherwise qualified men to vote if they held lifetime leases but did not own the land outright. By European standards in the eighteenth century the franchise in America was generous and far exceeded the scope of the voting franchise in Great Britain. Yet whole classes of Americans—women, Native Americans, religious minorities, slaves, and indentured servants—were still excluded from voting.

HOW WAS SUFFRAGE DETERMINED WHEN THE CONSTITUTION WAS ADOPTED?

The Constitutional Convention could not agree on uniform rules for suffrage. As a result the Constitution stated only that members of the House of Representatives were to be elected by the people in each state who, under state law, were eligible to vote for the lower house of their state legislature.

In other words the Constitution left it to each state to decide who could vote. Because state governments granted or denied the franchise, it follows that many of the early battles over voting rights took place in the states.

An early example occurred in New Jersey. That state's constitution of 1776 granted the franchise to "all inhabitants" who met property and residency requirements. Therefore for the next several years some African American men and women, and many widowed or unmarried women, voted in local elections. Married

women could not meet the property requirement because their property automatically belonged to their husbands. In fact, a 1790 New Jersey election law expressly referred to voters as "he or she." But in 1807 in the name of so-called election reform, women were disenfranchised. African American men were disenfranchised in 1844.

WHAT DO YOU THINK?

❶ Why do you think the Philadelphia Convention declined to establish nationwide qualifications for suffrage?

❷ How might the states' diverse property requirements for suffrage influence citizens' relationships to their governments?

HOW DID VOTING RIGHTS EXPAND FOR WHITE MEN?

The revolutionary intellectual and pamphleteer Thomas Paine identified at least one of the problems with linking the right to vote to property ownership:

❝ You require that a man shall have sixty dollars worth of property, or he shall not vote. Very well, take an illustration. Here is a man who today owns a jackass, and the jackass is worth sixty dollars. Today the man is a voter and goes to the polls and deposits his vote. Tomorrow the jackass dies. The next day the man comes to vote without his jackass and he cannot vote at all. Now tell me, which was the voter, the man or the jackass?

Early in the 1800s Americans became more democratic and less aristocratic in their thinking. For example, American writer James Fenimore Cooper (1789–1851), author of *The Last of the Mohicans*, argued, "Every man who has wants, feelings, affections, and character has a stake in society." It followed that lack of property should not be a barrier to voting.

Some states, such as Massachusetts, retained property requirements out of the fear expressed by former president John Adams that anarchy and mob rule would erupt if men with no property had the right to vote. Virginia did not abolish its property requirement until 1851. But in 1802 Ohio, then a frontier state, gave the vote to almost all white men in an effort to attract settlers. Other western states followed suit, as did the northern "frontier" state of Maine in 1820. Older states gradually amended their election laws to remove property requirements.

Most state voting reforms were accomplished peacefully. An exception was Rhode Island, one of the last states to remove the property requirement. In fact, it was the only state after 1840 not to have universal enfranchisement of white men. The leader for franchise reform there, a lawyer named Thomas Wilson Dorr (1805–1854), convened an extralegal "People's Convention" that drafted a new state constitution enfranchising all white men. This act of rebellion led to a brief, small-scale civil war. But the so-called Dorr Rebellion of 1841–1842 was quickly put down, and Dorr fled the state only to be arrested and imprisoned on his return. Rhode Island subsequently did adopt a new constitution that enfranchised both white and African American men, but the state did not eliminate the property requirement until the 1880s.

Another arena of enfranchisement involved approximately 80,000 free Mexican men residing in the territory that the United States conquered in the Mexican-American War of 1846–1848. The Treaty of Guadalupe Hidalgo that ended the war also enfranchised these men. However, states affected by the treaty resisted recognizing these rights. Violence, fraud, and discrimination forced many Mexican Americans to abandon their lands and return to Mexico. When Texas was admitted into the Union as a slave state in 1845 Mexican Americans who tried to vote risked beating, burning, or lynching. After the Civil War the same tactics used to deny voting rights to African Americans—from physical violence to literacy tests—often were also applied to Mexican Americans.

HOW DID AFRICAN AMERICAN MEN WIN—THEN LOSE—THE RIGHT TO VOTE?

The Fifteenth Amendment was added to the Constitution in 1870, five years after the Civil War. Although the Fifteenth Amendment granted the right to vote to African American men, most states in the South and several outside the South made it almost impossible for them to exercise the right. They were required to take literacy tests and to pay poll taxes. Some states enacted so-called grandfather clauses that permitted citizens to vote only if their grandfathers had been allowed to vote. Physical intimidation and threats of economic reprisals for voting were common. An economic reprisal is an action that limits or eliminates a source of income or makes goods and services more expensive to buy. By 1910 fewer than twenty percent of African American citizens voted across most of the South. In some southern areas fewer than two percent voted.

As Unit Six will explain, the civil rights movement of the 1950s and 1960s galvanized the national government to exercise its power to protect African Americans against voting discrimination. Only then, almost a century later, was great progress made in ensuring the right to vote as guaranteed by the Fifteenth Amendment.

HOW WAS SUFFRAGE EXTENDED TO WOMEN?

During the middle years of the nineteenth century the struggle for freedom and equality for African Americans was closely linked to the campaign for woman suffrage. Many abolitionists worked for woman suffrage, just as many women worked to end slavery. For example, abolitionist Frederick Douglass (1818–1895), who had been born into slavery, participated in the meeting at Seneca Falls, New York, in 1848 that produced the Seneca Falls Declaration of Sentiments. The declaration was crafted by Elizabeth Cady Stanton (1815–1902) and other suffrage leaders. Echoing the Declaration of Independence, this declaration stated:

❝ We hold these truths to be self-evident: that all men and women are created equal.... Such has been the patient sufferance of the women under this government, and such is now the necessity which constrains them to demand the equal station to which they are entitled.

What was Thomas Paine's position on the property requirement for voting?

Arkansas, Mississippi, Texas, and Virginia) still used the tax. North Carolina and Virginia approved the amendment after it had been ratified by the required 38 states, but Alabama, Mississippi, and Texas did not. In *Harper v. Virginia State Board of Elections* (1966) the Supreme Court held that poll taxes violate the equal protection clause of the Fourteenth Amendment.

LITERACY TESTS In 1882 South Carolina adopted the first form of literacy test by putting out eight boxes for ballots and requiring votes for separate offices to go in different boxes. If someone put a ballot for a House seat in a box with ballots for governor, it would be thrown out. Election officials regularly shuffled the order of the boxes so that people who could not read did not know which box was for which elected position. Literacy tests requiring voters to respond correctly to questions were introduced in the 1890s. These tests affected blacks more than whites, because between forty percent and sixty percent of blacks in the South could not read. When illiterate whites complained about literacy tests, some states put in "grandfather clauses," meaning that a voter could vote if his grandfather had the franchise. In 1915 the Supreme Court struck down Oklahoma's grandfather clause as an obvious ruse to evade the Fifteenth Amendment (*Guinn v. United States*).

Other states implemented "understanding clauses," which required voters to interpret the meaning of a constitutional clause read to them by an election official, who also had the authority to determine which responses were correct. Literacy tests were not banned in the South until enactment of the Voting Rights Act of 1965. They were banned nationwide in 1970. (See Lesson 35 for a discussion of civil rights legislation emerging from the civil rights movement.)

student page ▼ 137–138

HOW WAS SUFFRAGE EXTENDED TO WOMEN?

Before women gained the right to vote in all elections, some states allowed them to vote in some elections. For example, beginning in 1847 Kentucky allowed women to vote in school elections, as did Kansas in 1861. Some cities in Ohio allowed women to vote for school boards in the late 1890s. Many arguments were made against allowing women to vote, such as their preoccupation with family and their status in common law as virtual property of their husbands. Women's active roles in abolition and prohibition in the nineteenth century resulted in some people perceiving women as threats to the status quo.

Between 1910 and 1918 twenty-four states had thirty-one referendum elections on whether women should be allowed to vote. The following timeline captures some of the drama of women gaining the vote:

1867–1868	No reference to women is included in Fourteenth and Fifteenth Amendments.
1869	The Territory of Wyoming approves of woman suffrage.
1870	Women are given the vote in Utah territory.
1878	A suffrage amendment is introduced in Congress.
1886	A suffrage amendment is defeated in the Senate.
1887	Women in Utah lose the right to vote.
1893	Colorado gives women the right to vote.
1895	Women regain suffrage in Utah.
1896	Idaho gives women the right to vote.
1910	National Women Suffrage Association submits 404,000 signatures to Congress in favor of woman suffrage.
1912	California, Kansas, Oregon, and Arizona give women the right to vote.
1913	Alaska territory gives women the right to vote.
1917	North Dakota, South Dakota, New York, Oklahoma, Indiana, Michigan, and Nebraska give women the right to vote. President Wilson abandons opposition to woman suffrage. Arkansas allows women the right to vote in primary elections; Illinois allows women to vote in municipal and presidential elections but not in state elections.
1919	A suffrage amendment passes both houses of Congress.
1920	Tennessee is the thirty-sixth state to ratify the Nineteenth Amendment.
1984	Mississippi is the final state to ratify the Nineteenth Amendment.

Newly enfranchised women voted in much smaller numbers than did men, which some sociologists attributed to their being taught as girls that voting was not appropriate for women. In 1980 women surpassed men for the first time in the turnout for a presidential election. In 1984 Geraldine Ferraro was nominated as the Democratic Party's candidate for vice president. In 2007 women held 23.5% of the legislative positions in the states and 24.1% of statewide elected offices. There were seventy-one women in the House of Representatives and sixteen in the Senate. Nancy Pelosi became the first woman to be elected Speaker of the House in 2007.

What reasons were given for denying women the right to vote?

Most people who advocated equal rights for women believed that gaining the right to vote was an essential step toward achieving other rights. When Congress was considering the Civil War amendments, leaders of the women's rights movement tried to get the right to vote extended to women as well as to all men. These leaders, including the prominent suffragist Susan B. Anthony (1820–1906), whose likeness has since been featured on a one-dollar coin, hoped that their long support of the anti-slavery cause would be rewarded in the Fourteenth Amendment. But many male anti-slavery leaders refused to support suffrage for women, fearing that it would set back the cause of former slaves. Instead, they specifically included the term "male citizen" in reference to the right to vote in Section 2 of the Fourteenth Amendment.

In 1872 Anthony and other women went to the polls and insisted that they be allowed to vote. They pointed to Section 1 of the Fourteenth Amendment:

" All persons born or naturalized in the United States, and subject to the jurisdiction thereof, are citizens of the United States and of the State wherein they reside.

They argued that women, as citizens, could not be denied access to the ballot. However, they were denied, and so they took their cause to the courts. In *Minor v. Happersett* (1875) the Supreme Court ruled that being a citizen does not mean that a person has the right to vote and that states therefore could continue to deny the vote to women. The Court noted that citizenship and voting

are not necessarily related, because aliens in the states of Alabama, Arkansas, Florida, Georgia, Indiana, Kansas, Minnesota, Missouri, and Texas who had announced their intention to become United States citizens—but were not yet citizens—enjoyed the franchise.

In 1869 Wyoming, while still a territory, gave women the right to vote. The story is told that subsequently, when considering Wyoming for statehood, certain members of Congress argued against this "petticoat provision." The Wyoming legislature replied that it would rather stay out of the Union for a hundred years than join without allowing women to vote. Wyoming was admitted to the Union. During the next fifty years several other western states extended the vote to women. This was the result of persistent hard work by women in those states and national leaders such as Anthony and Stanton. Eventually some eastern states joined the movement, and by 1918 more than half the states had enfranchised women.

Pressure for a woman suffrage constitutional amendment mounted during World War I, when women entered the workforce in record numbers and the United States fought a war to protect democratic rights in Europe. The uncertainty and slowness of state-by-state victories convinced suffragists to renew the fight for a constitutional amendment. They vigorously lobbied Congress and President Woodrow Wilson until finally, in 1918, Wilson withdrew his opposition. In 1920 after a national campaign that included huge parades, demonstrations, picketing, and civil disobedience in Washington, D.C., Congress passed and sent to the states the Nineteenth Amendment. The amendment forbids states and the United States from denying or abridging the right of citizens to vote on the basis of sex. Within the year enough states ratified the amendment, and women finally gained the franchise.

What amendment to the Constitution did Susan B. Anthony refer to in support of her argument that women should have the right to vote?

HOW WAS THE FRANCHISE EXTENDED TO NATIVE AMERICANS?

The original Constitution mentions Native Americans, as "Indians," twice. Under Article I "Indians not taxed"—those who remained under tribal government—were excluded from state populations for purposes of apportioning taxes and determining representation in Congress. Article I also empowered Congress to "regulate commerce with foreign nations, and among the several states, and with the Indian tribes."

These provisions reflected the position of the Framers, confirmed by opinions of the Supreme Court, that

❝ Native Americans were not citizens of the United States or the states in which they resided. Native American tribes were distinct political entities, separate from states or the federal government, with whom the United States would deal on a basis similar to that with which it dealt with foreign nations.

Native Americans' early relationship with the federal government affected their rights in profound ways. They were "foreigners" and frequently were treated as enemies. The U.S. government often seemed to view them as problematic children. They were not citizens and had no right to vote. The Fourteenth Amendment did not change that status. Section 1 declares that citizenship is reserved for people subject to the jurisdiction of the United States.

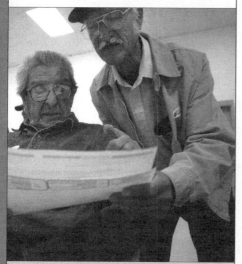

What was the role of Congress in extending the right to vote to Native Americans?

In 1887 Congress enacted the Dawes Act, extending citizenship to Native Americans who were willing to give up their tribal affiliations. One effect of this act was to undermine tribal culture. Three years later the Indian Naturalization Act granted citizenship to Native Americans in an application process similar to immigrant naturalization. Then in 1924 Congress enacted the Indian Citizenship Act, extending the franchise to all "Indians born within the territorial limits of the United States." This stream of legislation reflected a general expectation that tribal governments would wither and that Native Americans gradually would be assimilated into "mainstream" American society.

Many states were slow to comply with the Indian Citizenship Act of 1924. Native Americans encountered obstacles to voting, serving on juries, and giving testimony in courts. For example, New Mexico did not extend the franchise to Native Americans until 1962. Finally, Congress acted to address the problems that Native Americans and other minorities encountered in exercising the franchise by two means.

The first involved proposing the Twenty-fourth Amendment (1964), which prohibited states from denying or abridging the right of any citizen to vote for failure to pay a poll tax or any other tax to vote in elections for national officials.

The second was enacting the Voting Rights Act of 1965, which outlawed discrimination against all minorities by banning voting requirements such as literacy tests, prohibiting the use of English fluency as a requirement for voting, and authorizing the national government to take control of voter registration in states where African Americans and other groups consistently had been denied voting rights.

HOW DID EIGHTEEN-YEAR-OLDS WIN THE RIGHT TO VOTE?

Before 1971 only Alaska, Georgia, Hawaii, and Kentucky allowed persons younger than age twenty-one to vote. In 1970, facing widespread protests against the Vietnam War and resistance to the draft, Congress amended the Voting Rights Act to state that no one age eighteen or older could be denied the right to vote on the grounds of age. This move was not without controversy. In *Oregon v. Mitchell* (1970), in a deeply divided vote, the Supreme Court held that Congress could regulate the voting age in national elections but not in state elections.

In response to the Supreme Court's decision Congress proposed and sent the Twenty-sixth Amendment to the states. Ratified in 1971, this amendment prohibits both the United States and the states from denying or abridging the right to vote of citizens age eighteen or older.

139

---

student page ▾ 139

HOW WAS THE FRANCHISE EXTENDED TO NATIVE AMERICANS?

The two references to Indians in Article I of the Constitution ("Indians not taxed" and "regulate commerce with foreign Nations, and among the several States, and with the Indian Tribes") demonstrate that Native American tribes were viewed as distinct political societies, separate from states or the national government. In *Worcester v. Georgia* (1832) the Supreme Court held that the Cherokee Nation was

a distinct community, occupying its own territory, with boundaries accurately described, in which the laws of Georgia have no force, and which the citizens of Georgia have no right to enter, but with the assent of the Cherokees themselves, or in conformity with treaties, and with the acts of Congress. The whole intercourse between the United States and this nation is, by our constitution and laws, vested in the government of the United States.

Today Native Americans are viewed as an increasingly important voting block in several states. In Alaska, for example, Native Americans constitute nineteen percent of the population; New Mexico, eleven percent; South Dakota, nine percent; Oklahoma, eight percent; Montana, six percent.

ENRICHMENT ACTIVITY

COULD YOU PASS A LITERACY TEST?

Ask students to take Alabama's literacy test of 1965 and then to discuss the following questions:

wtpcompanion.civiced.org **PRIMARY SOURCES**

Visit the We the People companion website for a link to Alabama's literacy test of 1965.

1. How many students received a perfect score?

2. Do the students think the test measured their competence to vote? Why or why not?

3. How many students think some form of literacy test should be required today? Why or why not?

4. If literacy tests were to be required, should they be written by each state, or should there be uniform national standards? Why?

What criteria, if any, should be used for denying a citizen the right to vote?

What reasons can you give for providing the right to vote for citizens eighteen and older?

WHAT DO YOU THINK?

1. What criteria should be used for determining whether changes in the franchise should be made constitutionally or by statute? Why?

2. What principles of American constitutional government are served by expansion of the franchise?

3. What arguments can you make for removing or denying the franchise to particular groups or individuals? Explain your reasoning.

4. Should the voting age be lowered even further? If so, how low and why? If not, why not?

REVIEWING AND USING THE LESSON

1. How have states differed in expanding the franchise?

2. What reasoning supported tying the right to vote to property ownership? Is that reasoning still valid today? Why or why not?

3. What processes did women use to obtain the right to vote? What factors explain why it took women more than three generations to secure the franchise?

4. People between the ages of eighteen and twenty-five vote less often than any other age group. Why do you think this is so?

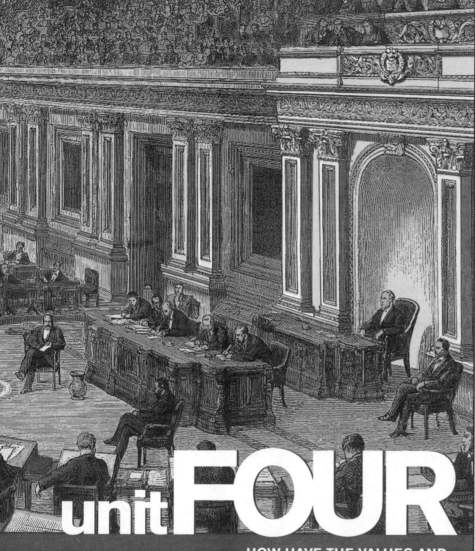

unitFOUR

HOW HAVE THE VALUES AND PRINCIPLES EMBODIED IN THE CONSTITUTION SHAPED AMERICAN INSTITUTIONS AND PRACTICES?

unitFOUR

UNIT PURPOSE

The Constitution was a plan for the new national government. It described the organization of the national government in terms of its powers and limits. The Framers purposely wrote the Constitution as a general framework. They left out many details that they knew would need to be added in the future. They also knew that they needed to reconcile the tension between the national government and the state governments. Therefore they devised a new system called federalism.

In this unit you will learn how the three branches of the national government embody constitutional principles and how they operate. You also will learn how federalism remains a dynamic characteristic of American government.

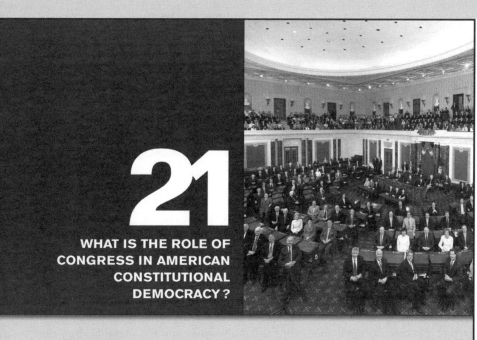

21

WHAT IS THE ROLE OF
CONGRESS IN AMERICAN
CONSTITUTIONAL
DEMOCRACY ?

UNIT FOUR | LESSON 21

WHAT IS THE ROLE OF CONGRESS IN AMERICAN CONSTITUTIONAL DEMOCRACY?

wtpcompanion.civiced.org   **LESSON PURPOSE + TERMS**

Visit the We the People companion website for printable and downloadable Lesson Purposes and Terms and Concepts to Understand sections for each lesson. Audio readings of each Lesson Purpose and Term are also available online in MP3 format.

LESSON PURPOSE

Congress often is called America's first branch of government because of its lawmaking powers and its control over the nation's purse. More than any other branch of the national government, it is the people's branch. Members of Congress are directly accountable to those who elect them. This lesson examines Congress's constitutional powers and how Congress represents both the people and the states.

When you have finished this lesson, you should be able to explain basic differences between Congress and the British Parliament and how Congress reflects America's commitment to representative government and federalism. You should be able to identify several constitutional sources of congressional power. You also should be able to identify some of the challenges that members of Congress face in representing and serving their constituents. Finally, you should be able to evaluate, take, and defend positions on contemporary issues about congressional representation and organization.

TERMS AND CONCEPTS TO UNDERSTAND

delegate theory of representation

enforcement powers

enumerated powers

federalism

gerrymandering

implied powers

inherent powers

trustee theory of representation

143

student page ▾ **144–145**

HOW DOES CONGRESS DIFFER FROM THE BRITISH PARLIAMENT?

Congressional scholars Paul J. Quirk and Sarah A. Binder contend that

> the United States Congress is the most important national legislature
> in the world. That is not because the United States is the most powerful
> country. It is because, among the national legislatures of major countries,
> Congress is the only one that still plays a powerful, independent role
> in public policymaking. In all other cases, the top political executives—
> typically prime ministers and the cabinet—provide all the leadership.
> The legislature debates policies but ultimately, with rare exceptions,
> enacts the executive's bills. Only Congress initiates legislation, makes
> decisions on major provisions, and says "no" to executive proposals.

See Lesson 36 for an additional discussion of federalism in the international context.

HOW DOES CONGRESS DIFFER FROM THE BRITISH PARLIAMENT?

The Founders considered many models of governance—ancient and contemporary—when they designed America's constitutional system. One of those models was the British parliamentary system. Although the Founders drew on one aspect of the parliamentary system by creating a two-house legislature, they proposed a U.S. Congress that would differ from Parliament in four essential ways:

- **Representation** In the eighteenth century each chamber of the British Parliament represented a specific order in society. Members of the House of Lords inherited their seats from ancestors who had been given a peerage, a title of nobility, generations or even centuries earlier. In 1999 the Labor government abolished the hereditary right to a seat in the House of Lords. Today most members hold honorary life peerages. They are appointed because of distinguished service in law, the clergy, business, or the sciences. There are now about twelve hundred members in the House of Lords. It is the final court of appeal for civil cases throughout Britain and for criminal cases in England, Wales, and Northern Ireland.

  The House of Commons is the preeminent body of Parliament. Its members are elected and hold office until Parliament is dissolved or for a maximum of five years. Each member represents a geographic division. Ministers are required to attend Parliament regularly to answer questions about their department, both to the full House and to its committees.

  The Framers of the U.S. Constitution believed that Congress should represent all the people, not particular social classes. Therefore they designed the House of Representatives to express the sentiments and viewpoints of diverse constituencies in electoral districts and to permit frequent turnover if voters choose to replace their representatives at elections that occur every two years. The Framers designed the Senate to be less influenced by popular passions and temporary impulses. Accordingly, senators serve longer terms—six years—than members of the House, and they represent people in states as a whole rather than districts within states.

- **Separation of powers** In parliamentary government there is a close link between executive and legislative functions. When citizens vote in a national election for members of the House of Commons, they are endorsing the platform of a political party. The victorious

How does the placement of Congress on Capitol Hill reflect its place in the Constitution?

144

party thus claims a mandate to govern. Its leader in Parliament becomes the prime minister, the nation's chief executive as well as chief legislative officer. Members of Parliament also hold all other cabinet-level positions. This creates a unified government to legislate and to execute policy. Such a mingling of executive and legislative powers in the U.S. government is prohibited by Article I, Section 6, of the Constitution, which prohibits any member of Congress from occupying any other office in the federal government. This provision prevents the United States from establishing any form of parliamentary system.

In contrast to the British parliamentary system, Congress is one of three coequal branches of government. Congress makes laws, but it does not usually decide who will be president. And it plays an important but limited role in deciding who serves in the president's cabinet and in the federal courts.

For more than a century the House of Commons has been the more powerful house in the British Parliament. The majority party in the House of Commons determines almost everything about the government. By contrast, the House of Representatives and the Senate are equally powerful and frequently check, or limit, one another.

- **Length of terms** Elections for the House of Commons do not occur on a fixed schedule. They must occur at least every five years, but they can occur sooner. The prime minister can call for earlier elections if he or she believes that the party can win an even larger popular mandate, that is, more seats in the House of Commons. If the party in power loses a vote in Parliament on an important national issue, this often is seen as a vote of "no confidence" in the prime minister, which also may trigger a new election.

Members of Congress face elections at times specified in the Constitution, no matter how popular or unpopular they may be. Representatives stand for election every two years, Senators every six. The elections for the Senate are staggered, that is, the Senate is divided as equally as possible into thirds so that one-third of the Senate can be elected every two years, and reelection is possible.

What might be the advantages and disadvantages of mingling executive and legislative powers, such as in the British parliamentary system?

- **Federalism** Federalism is a constitutional arrangement in which power is divided and shared between a central government having nationwide responsibilities and constituent governments having state or local representation. Although cities and towns in Great Britain have their own local governments, these government entities primarily are administrative units of the central government. Most of their powers are delegated to them by the national government. By contrast, Congress is not the only legislature in the United States. State legislatures also wield considerable legislative power, leading to a dynamic and unique system of federalism.

WHAT DO YOU THINK?

❶ Members of Congress can serve unlimited numbers of terms if they are reelected. Is this consistent with the principles of representative democracy and limited government? Why or why not?

❷ What are the advantages of having a representative body such as Congress made up of seasoned and experienced lawmakers? What are the disadvantages of allowing members of Congress to serve as long as their constituents reelect them?

145

student page ▼ 146–147

WHAT ARE CONGRESS'S CONSTITUTIONAL POWERS?

Refer to Lesson 11 for a discussion of the creation of Congress at the Philadelphia Convention.

ENUMERATED POWERS The case in which the Supreme Court first broadly defined Congress's commerce power is *Gibbons v. Ogden* (1824). However, at various times in U.S. history, such as during the era of economic substantive due process discussed in Lesson 18, the Supreme Court has limited Congress's commerce powers. Recently the Court reaffirmed Congress's broad powers of regulation. In *Raich v. Gonzalez* (2005) it held that Congress may prohibit the cultivation and use of marijuana for medical purposes even though the activity occurs entirely within state boundaries. Justice Clarence Thomas wrote in dissent that

> the Framers understood what the majority does not appear to fully appreciate: There is a danger to concentrating too much, as well as too little, power in the Federal Government. This Court has carefully avoided stripping Congress of its ability to regulate interstate commerce, but it has casually allowed the Federal Government to strip States of their ability to regulate intrastate commerce—not to mention a host of local activities, like mere drug possession, that are not commercial.

> One searches the Court's opinion in vain for any hint of what aspect of American life is reserved to the States.

IMPLIED POWERS The meaning of Article I, Section 8, Clause 18, was contested during the debates between Federalists and Anti-Federalists (see Lessons 13 and 14). Federalists argued for "loose construction" of the clause, meaning that courts should interpret it to permit Congress broad discretion in deciding what was "necessary and proper for carrying into Execution the foregoing Powers." Anti-Federalists argued that the provision should be interpreted "strictly" so that the national government would not usurp powers reserved to the states or to the people (Tenth Amendment).

In *McCulloch v. Maryland* (1819) Chief Justice Marshall wrote,

> Let the ends be legitimate, let it be within the scope of the constitution, and all means which are appropriate, which are plainly adopted to that end, which are not prohibited, but consist with the letter and spirit of the constitution, are constitutional.

WHAT ARE CONGRESS'S CONSTITUTIONAL POWERS?

John Locke claimed that the legislature is the most powerful branch of government because it makes laws. Mistrusting any concentration of political power, the Framers carefully limited Congress's powers. The following are three examples:

- **Article I, Section 8** The Constitution limits Congress's lawmaking powers to those "herein granted." In addition to seventeen specific powers Congress has a generalized eighteenth power: "To make all Laws which shall be necessary and proper for carrying into Execution the foregoing Powers, and all other Powers vested by this Constitution in the Government of the United States, or in any Department or Officer thereof."

- **Article I, Section 9** The Constitution identifies several matters on which Congress "shall not" legislate. For example, it cannot tax "Articles exported from any state." It cannot grant titles of nobility. It cannot draw any money from the Treasury "but in Consequence of Appropriations made by Law."

- **Bill of Rights** Added to the Constitution in 1791, the Bill of Rights lists rights on which Congress "shall not" infringe. For example, the First Amendment states that "Congress shall make no law" establishing a national religion or abridging free speech or press. The Eighth Amendment prohibits Congress from levying "excessive fines" and imposing "cruel and unusual punishments" on convicted criminals.

Even with these limitations, Congress today has far-reaching powers. These powers can be clustered under four categories: enumerated, implied, enforcement, and inherent.

- **Enumerated powers** Enumerated powers, or express powers, are those listed in the Constitution. Article I, Section 8, for example, gives Congress power to "regulate Commerce with foreign Nations and among the several States, and with the Indian Tribes." Under the leadership of Chief Justice John Marshall the U.S. Supreme Court defined Congress's commerce power broadly. That broad interpretation has enabled Congress to regulate matters such as manufacturing, child labor, farm production, wages and work hours, labor unions, and civil rights. And Congress is given full power to regulate interstate and foreign commerce.

Other parts of the Constitution also give Congress powers. For example,

- **Article II** The Senate must advise and consent when the president makes treaties and appoints ambassadors, other public ministers, judges of the Supreme Court, and many other public officials.

- **Article III** Congress has complete control over the appellate jurisdiction of the Supreme Court and authority to create lower federal courts.

- **Article IV** Congress can admit new states and adopt all rules and regulations respecting U.S. territories and properties.

- **Article V** Congress, like the states, can propose constitutional amendments. Congress has proposed all twenty-seven amendments to the Constitution and many that have not been ratified.

- **Implied powers** Some express grants of authority to Congress imply, or suggest, other powers. The "necessary and proper" clause in Article I gives Congress power to legislate on at least some subjects not expressly described in the Constitution. The idea of **implied powers** was tested when the first secretary of the Treasury, Alexander Hamilton, proposed the creation of a national bank. In *McCulloch v. Maryland* (1819) the Supreme Court held that the necessary and proper clause and Congress's power to coin and borrow money both implied the power to create a national bank. The Court also held that states could not tax the national bank, a significant blow to the exercise of state power.

Most laws that Congress enacts are written in general terms. They require administrative agencies to formulate rules that more specifically define the laws. The power to create administrative agencies to make rules and execute the laws is implied in Congress's power to legislate. Congress has created hundreds of agencies, ranging from the Internal Revenue Service to the Social Security Administration, to implement its policy mandates.

Most of the agencies and departments that Congress creates are located in the executive branch. One of Congress's most important implied powers is congressional oversight, which includes monitoring and supervising the operations of the agencies it creates.

Committees of Congress frequently question agency heads and administrators about rules and regulations that the agencies have adopted. Congress also examines agency budgets and expenditures. Congress uses the information gained from such oversight to adjust authorizing legislation and the appropriation of funds to federal agencies.

- **Enforcement powers** The Thirteenth Amendment, outlawing slavery, was the first to give Congress the power to enforce it "by appropriate legislation." Since then the Fourteenth, Fifteenth, Nineteenth, Twenty-third, Twenty-fourth, and Twenty-sixth Amendments also have expanded the power of Congress to enforce the provisions of the amendments "by appropriate legislation."

  During the 1960s and 1970s Congress used its **enforcement powers** along with its power to regulate interstate commerce to enact sweeping civil rights, voting rights, and employment laws. For example, Congress used the commerce clause to enforce the Civil Rights Act of 1964 to prevent unfair discrimination against African Americans. The authority to do so was confirmed by the Supreme Court in *Heart of Atlanta Motel v. United States* (1964). In this case the Court ruled that an Atlanta motel that discriminated against African Americans had to comply with the Civil Rights Act because it was in a business that served mostly interstate travelers. Congress's enforcement powers have significantly shifted political power away from the states and to the national government, as you learned in the previous unit.

- **Inherent powers** Some powers are so innate, or ingrained, in an institution that they do not have to be stated in words. These are termed **inherent powers**. Congress's power to investigate is such a power. The next lesson provides examples of Congress's use of this power.

CRITICAL THINKING EXERCISE
Evaluating the Powers of Congress

Article I, Section 8, Clause 18 of the Constitution states that Congress has the power "To make all Laws that are necessary and proper" to carry out the powers that the Constitution gives to the government of the United States. This has been called the "elastic clause" and has been used to establish the implied powers of

Congress. Work in groups to evaluate the effects of this clause by addressing the following questions:

1. How would you define "necessary" and "proper"?
2. Does this clause contradict the principle of enumerated and limited powers? Why or why not?
3. What are the benefits of placing elastic (flexible) power in the hands of a representative body?
4. What are the problems or dangers of placing elastic power in the hands of a representative body?

HOW DOES CONGRESS REPRESENT THE PEOPLE AND THE STATES?

Both the people and the states have voices in Congress. There are no constitutional limitations on how many terms a member of Congress may serve.

Article I, Section 2, provides that the number of representatives "shall not exceed one for every thirty Thousand" and that each state "shall have at Least one Representative." Before 1842 some states elected their representatives "at large," meaning that all qualified voters were eligible to vote for all candidates to fill that state's allotment of representatives. Since 1842 members of the House have been elected from single-member legislative

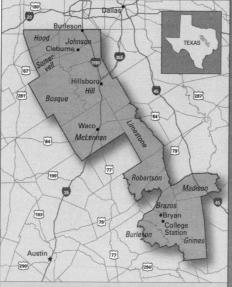

What criteria do you think should be used for establishing the boundaries of congressional districts?

ENFORCEMENT POWERS For examples of cases regarding Congress's enforcement powers see the following cases:

- *Katzenbach v. Morgan* (1966) Congress may use its enforcement powers under the Fourteenth Amendment's equal protection clause (see Lesson 19) to outlaw practices that are not themselves unconstitutional, such as English-language literacy tests.

- *Oregon v. Mitchell* (1970) Congress exceeded its authority when it used the enforcement power in the Fifteenth Amendment to justify a provision in the Voting Rights Act of 1970 lowering the voting age to eighteen in state and local elections. A year later the Twenty-sixth Amendment provided that states cannot set minimum voting ages higher than eighteen (see Lesson 20).

INHERENT POWERS Both the British Parliament and colonial legislatures asserted the right to conduct investigations and compel testimony. The drafters of the Constitution apparently thought it unnecessary to mention these powers explicitly. In *McGrain v. Daughtery* (1927) the Court wrote that

> the power of inquiry—with the process to enforce it—is an essential and appropriate auxiliary to the legislative function.... A legislative body cannot legislate wisely or effectively in the absence of information respecting the conditions which the legislation is intended to affect or change; and where the legislative body does not itself possess the requisite information—which not infrequently is true—recourse must be had to others who possess it. Experience has taught that mere requests for such information often are unavailing, and also that information which is volunteered is not always accurate or complete; so some means of compulsion are essential to obtain what is needed.

See Lesson 24 for a discussion of executive agencies, or "bureaucracy."

student page ▼ 148

WHY IS DISTRICTING CONTROVERSIAL?

The Supreme Court has held that state legislative districts must follow the one person one vote rule (*Reynolds v. Sims*, 1964), thereby prohibiting the representation of counties in the upper houses of state legislatures. In *New York City Board* (1989) the Court extended the rule to all local governments that elect representatives from districts.

In 1812 Jeffersonian Republicans forced through the Massachusetts legislature a bill rearranging district lines to ensure Republicans an advantage in the upcoming senatorial elections. Although Governor Elbridge Gerry, a Massachusetts delegate to the Philadelphia Convention, signed the law reluctantly, a Federalist newspaper editor is said to have exclaimed when he saw the new district lines, "Salamander! Call it a Gerrymander." Elkanah Tinsdale's famous political cartoon depicted the salamander-like shape of the electoral district. The word *gerrymander* has since been used to describe the practice of drawing political district lines for partisan benefit.

wtpcompanion.civiced.org LINKS

Visit the We the People companion website for a link to census data and district sizes as well as examples of modern gerrymandered congressional districts.

student page ▼ 148–149

WHAT THEORIES OF REPRESENTATION GUIDE MEMBERS OF CONGRESS?

The delegate theory is consistent with pure theories of representative government, calling on one person to "present" the views of another or to "re-present" that person's or group's views. Delegates must remain in close contact with those whom they represent in order to remain apprised of their constituents' views and interests and to keep their constituents' confidence.

Edmund Burke (1729–1797), an Irish author and philosopher who served many years in the British House of Commons, explained the trustee theory in a speech in November 1774:

---

districts. That means that each state with a population large enough to entitle it to more than one representative in the House is divided into as many legislative districts as the state has representatives.

In some states the state legislature draws district lines after each ten-year census. In other states independent commissions draw district lines. Groups dissatisfied with the way district lines are drawn can challenge districting maps in court. In those situations judges also have a say in how congressional districts are drawn.

WHY IS DISTRICTING CONTROVERSIAL?

No matter where the lines are drawn, some groups and interests are benefited while others are harmed. For example, after World War I the population of the United States shifted dramatically from farms to cities. Nonetheless, many states continued to draw congressional district lines that favored rural over urban areas. In *Wesberry v. Sanders* (1964) the Supreme Court adopted the rule of "one person, one vote." Congressional district lines now must be drawn on the basis of population after each ten-year census. According to the Court, the population in each district must be mathematically equal to other districts in the state.

The "one person, one vote" requirement has not ended debates over where district lines should be drawn. **Gerrymandering**, or drawing district lines to achieve favorable political results for one political party, remains a fact of American political life.

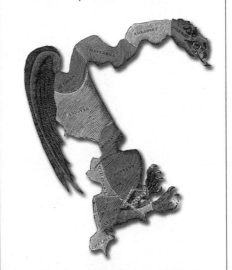

What is the purpose of gerrymandering? What problems does it raise?

148

Drawing district lines is not an issue in the Senate because Article I, Section 3, gives every state two senators no matter how large its population. California and Wyoming, for example, each has two U.S. senators. In 2007 California had a population of about thirty-seven million and Wyoming had a population of about one-half million.

The Constitution originally gave each state legislature authority to decide who would serve as that state's senators. This method of selection ensured that state legislatures would have powerful, though indirect, voices in the Senate. In 1913 the Seventeenth Amendment provided for direct election of senators. Since then senators have been chosen in statewide elections.

In 1913 Congress fixed the size of the House of Representatives at 435 members. When Hawaii joined the Union in 1959, the size of the Senate was fixed at one hundred senators. Congress therefore comprises 535 elected legislators. This large number has significant consequences for how Congress is organized and does its work. In 2004 the average House district approached seven hundred thousand in population. Among the world's legislatures only India has larger constituencies. In addition to the 435 House members, there are five other elected representatives: a resident commissioner for Puerto Rico and four delegates—for the District of Columbia, American Samoa, Guam, and the Virgin Islands. Senators and representatives face formidable challenges simply trying to understand the diverse needs and interests of their many constituents. As explained in Lesson 5, a constituent is a citizen represented by an elected public official.

Other nations have representative bodies that are even larger than the U.S. Congress. In Germany, for example, there are 672 members of the Bundestag, which is the lower house of its parliament, and 69 members of the Bundesrat, the upper house. Mexico's Chamber of Deputies has 500 members, while its Senate has 128 senators. The populations of those countries are considerably smaller than the population of the United States.

WHAT THEORIES OF REPRESENTATION GUIDE MEMBERS OF CONGRESS?

Since the debate over ratifying the Constitution Americans have argued about the role of elected representatives. Should they, as Anti-Federalists believed, be "delegates" of their constituents and mirror their constituents' views in Congress—reflecting the **delegate theory of representation**? Or should they, as Federalists argued, be "trustees" who gain the trust of their constituents and then exercise their own best judgment on matters of public policy—embodying the **trustee theory of representation**? Most representatives say that they try to do both. America's size and diversity make that effort ever more challenging.

What is the difference between the delegate and trustee theories of representation?

In the 1830s French observer and historian Alexis de Tocqueville (1805–1859) identified regional variations in climate, economics, culture, and religion that made it difficult to govern the United States as one nation. Tocqueville's observations are even truer today. The United States has expanded across the continent and beyond, and its population of more than three hundred million reflects the diversity of the world. Members of Congress face an increasingly difficult task representing their constituents and finding common ground with legislators from other states and regions as they participate in their deliberations.

WHAT DO YOU THINK?

❶ What qualifications, other than those listed in Article I, do you think should be used when choosing a member of Congress? Explain your suggestions.

❷ How might members of Congress balance their roles as delegates of their constituents and trustees of the common good?

❸ Does representation by states in the Senate and state-based congressional districts in the House remain a logical basis for selecting congressional representatives today? What are some alternatives? Consider, for example, that southwestern

Virginia has more in common with eastern Kentucky than with eastern Virginia.

❹ Some countries base representation on ethnicity, race, gender, or religious beliefs rather than geography. Would you support such a system of representation in the United States? Why or why not?

❺ Because members of Congress are elected from single-member districts, minorities of whatever kind within a district—racial, ethnic, ideological—might be left unrepresented. Many Western nations have multimember districts in which different representatives are elected to serve the interests of different groups within the districts. This is called proportional representation. What might be the advantages and disadvantages of having such a system in the United States?

HOW DO MEMBERS OF CONGRESS SERVE THEIR CONSTITUENTS?

Members of Congress rely on their constituents to elect and reelect them. It is not sufficient for representatives merely to be perceived as honest, public-spirited individuals committed to enacting good legislation and effectively checking the exercise of executive and judicial powers. Communication and action are essential. Members of Congress use three basic strategies for maintaining positive connections with their constituents:

- **Communications** Members of Congress and their staffs actively communicate with constituents through letters, newsletters, media appearances, websites, blogs, town hall meetings, and other personal appearances in their districts.

- **Casework** Every member of Congress employs staff members in Washington, D.C., and in local offices. These staffers' job, known as casework, is to help constituents solve problems that the constituents have encountered with the national government. They also respond to constituents who want personal favors. Constituents often seek help in dealing with agencies, such as the Internal Revenue Service or the Social Security Administration. Requested favors range from arranging tours of government offices to setting up meetings with government officials. At election time a constituent who has benefited from casework or a personal favor is likely to have a positive view of the representative even if he or she disagrees with the representative's stand on particular issues.

Certainly, gentlemen, it ought to be the happiness and glory of a representative to live in the strictest union, the closest correspondence, and the most unreserved communication with his constituents....But his unbiassed opinion, his mature judgment, his enlightened conscience, he ought not to sacrifice to you, to any man, or to any set of men living. These he does not derive from your pleasure; no, nor from the law and the constitution. They are a trust from Providence, for the abuse of which he is deeply answerable. Your representative owes you, not his industry only, but his judgment; and he betrays, instead of serving you, if he sacrifices it to your opinion....

Parliament is not a congress of ambassadors from different and hostile interests; which interests each must maintain, as an agent and advocate, against other agents and advocates; but parliament is a deliberative assembly of one nation, with one interest, that of the whole; where, not local purposes, not local prejudices, ought to guide, but the general good, resulting from the general reason of the whole. You choose a member indeed; but when you have chosen him, he is not [a] member of Bristol, but he is a member of parliament. If the local constituent should have an interest, or should form an hasty opinion, evidently opposite to the real good of the rest of the community, the member for that place ought to be as far, as any other, from any endeavour to give it effect.

See Lesson 14 for a discussion of theories of representation.

wtpcompanion.civiced.org	**PRIMARY SOURCES**

Visit the We the People companion website for a link to Edmund Burke's speech to the electors of Bristol.

LESSON 21

ENRICHMENT ACTIVITY

WHAT I EXPECT OF MY REPRESENTATIVES AND WHAT THEY CAN EXPECT OF ME

Ask students to work in small groups to draft a letter to their state legislator, congressional representative, or senator. In the letter they should

- explain their expectations of that person, for example, as a delegate or a trustee;

- discuss how they expect the representative to respond to their concerns, interests, or needs; and

- explain how they expect the representative to communicate with constituents.

After writing their letter the groups should be able to explain why they hold such expectations. They should then discuss the expectations they have of themselves as constituents, such as to

- be informed on issues;

- participate in other ways in addition to voting; and

- campaign and contribute time or money.

If there are disagreements within a group that cannot be resolved, ask those who dissent to write separate letters explaining their views. Share each group's letter or letters with the class as a whole.

- **Serving constituents' interests and concerns** Members of Congress also create close ties to their constituents by introducing legislation and sponsoring amendments to legislation that serve constituents' interests and by working to have federal projects located in their district or state. Representatives who are successful in sponsoring legislation that serves constituents' interests—including securing economic benefits for their states or districts in the form of highway projects, dams, military installations, research facilities, or other public projects—are more likely to be viewed favorably by their constituents than those who do not.

REVIEWING AND USING THE LESSON

1. In what ways does the U.S. Congress differ from the British Parliament?

2. How would you explain the following terms?
   - enumerated powers
   - implied powers
   - enforcement powers
   - inherent powers

3. Why has the creation of congressional districts been controversial throughout American history? Why did the "one person, one vote" rule fail to end the controversy?

4. Should representatives be "delegates" of their constituents and mirror their views or should they be "trustees" who exercise their own best judgment on matters of public policy? Explain your answer.

5. Describe ways that members of Congress try to maintain positive connections with their constituents.

6. Find and examine your representative's and senators' websites. What can you learn about your members of Congress from the information presented there? Is there an interactive feature on the website that enables you to convey your views to the legislator? What additional information would you like to have found on the site?

What are some of the ways members of Congress serve their constituents' interests?

150

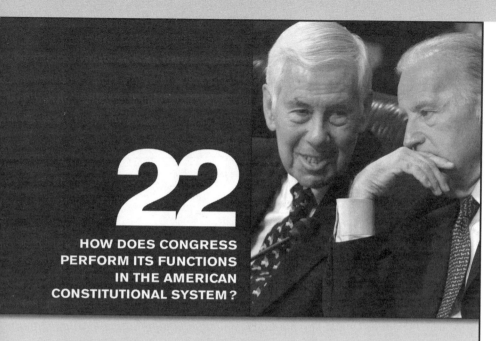

22

HOW DOES CONGRESS PERFORM ITS FUNCTIONS IN THE AMERICAN CONSTITUTIONAL SYSTEM?

HOW DOES CONGRESS PERFORM ITS FUNCTIONS IN THE AMERICAN CONSTITUTIONAL SYSTEM?

wtpcompanion.civiced.org | **LESSON PURPOSE + TERMS**

Visit the We the People companion website for printable and downloadable Lesson Purposes and Terms and Concepts to Understand sections for each lesson. Audio readings of each Lesson Purpose and Term are also available online in MP3 format.

LESSON PURPOSE

The United States Congress is one of the few national assemblies in the world with the power to initiate legislation rather than simply vote on bills proposed by the executive. Congress also conducts important investigations that can lead to changes in public policy and even the removal of federal judges and the president. From its earliest days Congress has relied on rules and leadership structures to facilitate its work. Today, with 535 members, Congress faces a variety of organizational challenges in its effort to represent growing and diverse constituencies.

When you have finished this lesson, you should be able to describe the role of rules, committees, and political parties in the organization and operation of Congress. You should be able to describe the process through which proposed legislation becomes law. You should be able to identify the primary sources on which members of Congress rely for information in the lawmaking process and to explain the importance of Congress's inherent power to investigate. You also should be able to explain why compromise is required in the deliberative process. Finally, you should be able to evaluate, take, and defend positions on how Congress functions and whether it should streamline its procedures.

TERMS AND CONCEPTS TO UNDERSTAND

bill	pocket veto
cloture	power to investigate
filibuster	resolution
impeachment	seniority
lobbying	

student page ▾ 152–153

HOW DO COMMITTEES AND RULES HELP CONGRESS DO ITS WORK?

Historian Anna K. Nelson observes,

> Of the three branches of government, only the legislative branch consistently provides the public with a running account of its business. The gathering and publication of information begins in the committee rooms. Hearings and reports are printed with all pertinent inserts and additions. Even closed executive sessions usually leave a transcript. From the *Congressional Record* the public receives a verbatim account of every sentence spoken on the floor of both chambers and quite a few sentences that weren't. Television now adds a new dimension to the account of current information available to the public.

Examples of how television makes the actions of Congress available to the public include televising committee hearings, floor debates, and votes and covering special events such as presidential addresses to Congress.

The word *congress* often is used to refer to the two-year cycle of activities of the legislative branch. For example, the 110th Congress was scheduled for January 3, 2007, to January 3, 2009. Legislation introduced during the two-year period may be taken up at any time. However, measures "die" if they are not enacted into law during that time and must be introduced anew in the next Congress.

During the 110th Congress the House had the following standing committees, each with its own website:

- Agriculture
- Appropriations
- Armed Services
- Budget
- Education and Labor
- Energy and Commerce
- Financial Services
- Foreign Affairs
- Homeland Security
- House Administration
- Judiciary
- Natural Resources
- Oversight and Government Reform
- Rules
- Science and Technology
- Small Business
- Standards of Official Conduct
- Transportation and Infrastructure
- Veterans' Affairs
- Ways and Means

Why do congressional committees hold public hearings?

HOW DO COMMITTEES AND RULES HELP CONGRESS DO ITS WORK?

The Constitution says little about how the House or the Senate should function. Article I, Section 5, states only that each chamber "may determine the Rules of its Proceedings." The first Congress (1789–1791) set a precedent that is followed to this day by creating committees and adopting rules that govern how each house functions.

- **Committees** Both the House and the Senate have standing, or permanent, committees. Each committee, such as the House Agriculture Committee or the Senate Appropriations Committee, has jurisdiction over particular subjects and appoints subcommittees to examine proposals within specific areas. In committees and subcommittees proposals can be examined carefully and various perspectives heard. It is common for these committees and subcommittees to hold public hearings to receive testimony from individuals and groups on matters of interest to them. Oversight hearings also may be held during which members of administrative agencies may be called on to testify regarding how they carry out laws enacted by Congress. In these committees and subcommittees the careful, deliberative work of Congress occurs. Committee assignments shape members' careers within Congress, enable them to serve their constituents' interests, and sometimes provide them national prominence.

  Both chambers also use select committees and task forces, which usually have specific assignments and exist for a limited time. For example, a select committee was created to review James Madison's proposal for a Bill of Rights during the first session of Congress because members feared that using the regular committee process might take too long. Individual members of committees, such as the Senate Foreign Relations Committee, conduct personal investigations and make on-site visits related to their committee assignments.

- **Rules** House rules, which are adopted by each Congress, specify the size of committees. House rules also specify the jurisdiction of committees. That is, they specify the kinds of draft proposals for legislation, known as **bills**, such as education, energy, or defense bills, that should be handled by each committee.

House rules also place limits on the number of members on committees and subcommittees, how many committees a member can serve on, and term limits for the chairpersons of the committees. House rules also govern the form and structure of debates on the floor of the House. For important bills the Rules Committee of the House, which is controlled by the majority party, creates "special rules." Committees also make rules that specify committee procedures, such as the order in which members ask witnesses questions at hearings, how long each member may ask questions, how proposals are amended or "marked up" in committee, and the form in which bills are reported from committees.

The Senate also operates according to rules, but the rules are treated more informally in the Senate than in the House. Traditionally, members of the Senate have been more independent than members of the House, perhaps because senators originally were regarded as "ambassadors" from their states. A single senator can use the **filibuster**, a practice of refusing to surrender the floor during a debate, to prevent a vote on a proposal. In 1917 the Senate adopted a rule that allows a vote of 60 members to cut off debate, known as **cloture** vote, and thus bring a proposal to a vote by the full Senate. Senators also have the opportunity to amend bills on the floor, something that the House rules forbid.

Political parties also have organizations and leaders within Congress whose job is to encourage members to adhere to party policies and platforms. Party control traditionally has been stronger in the House than in the Senate. Under political party control, committee chairs are appointed not only according to **seniority**, or length of service, but also on the basis of party loyalty. At this time, chairs of committees are limited to three two-year terms.

WHAT DO YOU THINK?

❶ Throughout American history deliberative bodies have used committees to facilitate their work. How does the use of committees in Congress promote or undermine the principles of representation, majority rule, and limited government?

❷ What principles and values do rules and strict adherence to them serve in a representative deliberative body such as the United States Congress?

WHO LEADS THE HOUSE AND SENATE?

The Constitution states that members of the House "shall choose their Speaker and other Officers." The House selects one of its own members to be Speaker. Leadership in the House has taken essentially three forms:

- **Strong institutional Speaker** At many times in America's history the Speaker of the House has been one of the most powerful political figures in the country and has wielded tight control over the organization and the legislative agenda of that chamber. Speakers typically control committee appointments and chair the powerful Rules Committee, called the "traffic cop" of the House because it decides which bills will come to the floor and what the rules of debate will be. In the 1890s Speaker Thomas B. Reed was so powerful that he was known as "Czar Reed."

- **Decentralized committee leadership** Sometimes leadership in the House has been decentralized. In the early twentieth century, for example, members of the House rebelled against the Speaker's centralized leadership by placing power in the hands of committee chairs. During periods of decentralized leadership committee chairs frequently are selected

What are some of the powers of the Speaker of the House of Representatives?

153

wtpcompanion.civiced.org **LINKS**

Visit the We the People companion website for links to each of these committees.

The House also had three joint committees with the Senate—on economics, printing, and taxation—and two select committees—on intelligence and global warming.

During the same Congress the Senate had the following standing committees, each with its own website:

- Agriculture, Nutrition, and Forestry
- Appropriations
- Armed Services
- Banking, Housing, and Urban Affairs
- Budget
- Commerce, Science, and Transportation
- Energy and Natural Resources
- Environment and Public Works

- Finance
- Foreign Relations
- Health, Education, Labor, and Pensions
- Homeland Security and Governmental Affairs
- Judiciary
- Rules and Administration
- Small Business and Entrepreneurship
- Veterans' Affairs

wtpcompanion.civiced.org **LINKS**

Visit the We the People companion website for links to each of these committees.

student page ▾ 152

CONGRESSIONAL RULES The Constitution (Article I, Sections 4 and 5) gives each house the right to establish its own rules. Each house is to be the judge of the "elections, returns, and qualifications of its own members." Each house also "may determine the rules of its proceedings, punish its members for disorderly behavior, and with the concurrence of two-thirds, expel a member."

In the First Congress both houses appointed special committees to propose rules. The rules adopted by the House favored majority rule, while those adopted by the Senate protected the rights of the minority. That difference between the two bodies persists and serves as an additional check and balance on the powers of government.

House rules deal with the Speaker's powers, the behavior of members, and procedures for debate. The House also has established a powerful standing committee, the Rules Committee, which functions as a valve or sifting device. Because more bills are reported out of standing committees than the House has time to consider, the Rules Committee functions as a legislative-control officer. It can establish special rules under which specific bills will be debated, amended, and considered in the House.

Senate rules have differed from House rules from the time of the First Congress. The Senate values unlimited debate and exhaustive consideration of legislation. Amendments are an important means of refining legislation and so the Senate has placed few restrictions on them. Members can offer amendments on virtually any subject, regardless of whether it is germane to the legislation at hand. Although various revisions of the Senate's rules have strengthened the majority's ability to act, the Senate remains a body of equals. The most junior member of the minority may speak at length on any proposed bill and attempt to influence its final wording.

Rules of both the House and Senate remain few in number. Some outmoded rules have been dropped, while a few new ones have been added. But whenever either body applies or interprets a rule, it establishes a precedent. These accumulating precedents allow Congress to function and to meet changing needs without constantly having to change the rules.

---

wtpcompanion.civiced.org LINKS

Visit the We the People companion website for links to the House and Senate.

---

student page ▾ 153

FILIBUSTER The House Rules Committee has placed limits on how long a measure can be debated. The Senate does not limit debate. It uses the filibuster (from a Dutch word meaning "pirate") to make it possible for one or a few members to debate endlessly to prevent a vote. The filibuster became popular in the United States in the 1850s. Before that, both houses of Congress followed the practice of the Continental Congress and the British House of Commons, in which a simple majority could vote to end debate on a measure.

Invoking cloture is not easy. The senator seeking to do so must wait two days after a filibuster begins, obtain sixteen signatures on a motion to invoke cloture, wait two more days for a vote, make sure that two-thirds of the senators will vote in favor of the motion, and then wait an additional thirty hours before a final roll call vote. Therefore a filibuster—or the threat of one—remains a viable debate tactic.

---

on the basis of seniority. Powerful committee chairs often compete with one another to control the legislative agenda.

- **Political party control** A third model of House leadership is a strong Speaker who represents the majority party more than the institution as a whole. For example, in the 1990s Republican Speaker Newt Gingrich championed his party's "Contract with America," an agenda to reform many aspects of American national government. Committee chairs were appointed on the basis of party loyalty rather than seniority.

Leadership in the Senate always has differed from leadership in the House. The Constitution provides that the "Vice President of the United States shall be President of the Senate." However, the vice president is not a member of the Senate and often is not a member of the majority party in the Senate. (Recall that since the adoption of the Twelfth Amendment in 1804 the vice president always has been a member of the same political party as the president.) As Senate president, the vice president's only real power is to cast tie-breaking votes. In the absence of a constitutionally recognized leader, senators have elected majority and minority party leaders to guide their operations. However, leadership in the Senate never has been as formal as in the House, largely because of the tradition of individual independence in that chamber.

WHAT ROLES DO MAJORITY RULE AND COMPROMISE PLAY IN CONGRESSIONAL DELIBERATIONS?

Enacting a law is one of the most complicated processes in American politics. Only about one in ten proposals survives and rarely without significant changes. The process begins when a member, either alone or with cosponsors, introduces a proposal for a law. Most proposals take the forms of bills, but they also can be **resolutions**. A simple resolution addresses procedural rules or expresses sentiments in each chamber. A joint resolution, introduced in both chambers at the same time, is a device for proposing constitutional amendments or other matters. If signed by the president or passed over his or her veto, a joint resolution has the force of law. A concurrent resolution usually expresses the "sentiment" of Congress but is not law. However, since the 1974 Congressional Budget Act a concurrent resolution has bound Congress to budget limitations.

A bill can be introduced into either or both chambers. However, the Constitution requires revenue bills, which raise money, to originate in the House. When a bill or a joint resolution is introduced, it is assigned a number (with the prefix H in the House and S in the Senate). In general terms, the process then unfolds as follows:

- **Committee assignment** All bills are assigned to at least one committee. The committee chair usually refers bills to subcommittees. Most bills are subjected to rigorous scrutiny,

Why do you think the Constitution requires that revenue bills originate in the House of Representatives?

In what ways have organized groups used the political process to establish rights not explicitly contained in the Constitution?

and their sponsors must agree to compromises in the form of amendments.

- **Hearings** Once a bill has been assigned, the committee schedules a hearing, which usually is open to the public and often announced in newspapers and other forums. (See Reference section for a description of a congressional hearing.) People such as representatives of interest groups and outside experts may present testimony. Testimony also may be presented by governmental organizations that support the legislative branch, such as the Congressional Budget Office, the Congressional Research Service, and the Government Accountability Office.

- **Deliberations** If a committee wants to try to get a bill enacted into law, it will schedule what are called "mark-up" sessions in which committee members review the bill, modify it as they wish, approve of their final version, and then recommend the bill to the full House or Senate for approval. Bills developed by subcommittees are referred to full committees for approval before being submitted to the full House or Senate. Committee chairs determine whether the full committee will consider bills reported out of a subcommittee. During committee or subcommittee deliberations, amendments to bills can be

offered and debated. If a bill is assigned to more than one committee and is defeated or significantly amended in at least one, then it is not likely to survive.

- **Report** If the bill wins a favorable committee vote, then it is reported to the full chamber either in its original form or with recommended amendments. The written report that accompanies the bill explains why the committee acted as it did. Committee reports always are made available to the public.

- **Floor vote** When a bill is reported out of committee, it is placed on a calendar for consideration and a vote by the full House or Senate.

- **Referral to the other chamber** Bills or resolutions passed by one chamber must be sent to the other chamber, and the process begins again. The other chamber may defeat proposals, amend them, or approve them without amendment.

- **Conference committee** Few bills that survive in one chamber emerge from the other chamber without being amended. When Senate and House versions of a bill differ, a conference committee, composed of members of both chambers, usually is appointed to try to reach a compromise. If the conference

155

student page ▼ 153–154

WHO LEADS THE HOUSE AND SENATE?

SPEAKER OF THE HOUSE One definition of the word *speaker* is a person "who presides over and speaks for a deliberative assembly." In England the office of speaker originated in the fourteenth century. The speaker was the spokesman for the Commons in dealings with the Crown. At first the office was highly political and carried with it great political and personal risk because of fierce disagreements between the Crown and Parliament. By the end of the seventeenth century the speaker was relatively free of royal pressure.

Article I, Section 2, which says, "The House of Representatives shall chuse [sic] their Speaker and other Officers," was proposed by the Committee of Detail at the Philadelphia Convention and adopted unanimously without discussion. Therefore it is not known whether the drafters intended the Speaker of the House to be a nonpartisan official like the Speaker of the House of Commons or the kind of legislative speakers who emerged as fierce political partisans in the colonies and early state legislatures.

Perhaps because of the lack of broad-based political parties, the first Speakers of the House acted in a nonpartisan manner. The rise of political parties and the use of parties to organize the House later gave a distinctly partisan flavor to the role. However, it was not until Kentucky's Henry Clay became Speaker in 1812 that the Speaker began to use the position to push a party agenda in presiding over legislative proposals.

PRESIDENT OF THE SENATE Article I, Section 3, states, "The Vice President of the United States shall be President of the Senate, but shall have no Vote, unless they be equally divided." This provision also was recommended by the Committee of Detail and adopted by the Philadelphia Convention without debate. Shortly before the Convention ended, the Committee of Style suggested adding the provision, "The Senate shall chuse [sic] their other Officers, and also a President pro tempore, in the absence of the Vice President." This provision has contributed to speculation about how the drafters envisioned the role of Senate president.

Leadership in the Senate has followed a different path than in the House. Until the Seventeenth Amendment was ratified in 1913 senators were selected by state legislatures and viewed themselves more as "ambassadors" to the national government than as members of the national government. Moreover, with ratification of the Twelfth Amendment in 1804 the vice president became politically tied to the president, losing any aura of being a member of the legislative branch. Since well before the turn of the twentieth century vice presidents have rarely presided over Senate sessions except to break tie votes. By the end of 2007 forty-six vice presidents had voted to break ties in the Senate 243 times. John Adams broke the most ties, twenty-nine, between 1789 and 1797.

The president pro tempore (*pro tempore* meaning "for the time being") presides over the Senate in the place of the vice president. The president pro tempore position evolved into a permanent position and today is the most senior member of the majority party in the Senate.

WHIP   In 1899 the majority in the House selected the first Whip, a position patterned after one of the same name in the British Parliament. The term derived from foxhunting, in which it was used to describe the person whose job was to keep the hounds from straying. The most important function of both Majority and Minority Whips is to inform political party leaders about which members are or are not following party lines as floor votes approach.

student page ▼ 154–156

WHAT ROLES DO MAJORITY RULE AND COMPROMISE PLAY IN CONGRESSIONAL DELIBERATIONS?

wtpcompanion.civiced.org   **PRIMARY SOURCES**

Visit the We the People companion website for a link to an example of a concurrent resolution (No. 76 of the 100th Congress, September 16, 1987) and an example of a simple resolution (SR 145 of the 84th Congress).

VETOES AND VETO OVERRIDES   As of late 2007, presidents had vetoed 2,556 laws enacted by Congress. Congress had overridden the veto only 107 times. Franklin D. Roosevelt used the veto 635 times, far more than any other president. Only seven presidents never used the veto power: John Adams, Jefferson, John Quincy Adams, Harrison, Taylor, Fillmore, and Garfield.

What is the role of conference committees in resolving differences between the House and Senate?

committee reaches agreement, then it issues a conference report that is submitted to both chambers for a vote. A conference report may not be amended, although it may be the subject of a filibuster in the Senate.

- **Referral to the president**   Bills approved by both chambers are sent to the president. If the president signs a bill, then it becomes law. If the president vetoes the bill, it will become law only if it is passed again by a two-thirds majority of those present and voting of each chamber. If the president does not sign within ten days and Congress adjourns, the bill is dead. This last action is known as a **pocket veto**.

A bill must win majority support at every stage of the process. It is not enough to win a majority vote just once. The bill also must be acceptable to those who manage the process, including party leaders. Members of Congress who sponsor bills must be persistent and willing to compromise if they are to build winning coalitions at each stage.

By the time a proposal becomes a law, many groups and individuals with different interests and perspectives usually have scrutinized and debated it. The lawmaking process demonstrates America's system of representative government, limited government, and checks and balances at work.

CRITICAL THINKING EXERCISE

Examining the Role of Congress in Promoting the Protection of Individual Rights

Attention to landmark cases in which Supreme Court decisions have resulted in the protection of the rights of minorities often has overshadowed the role of Congress and the active engagement of citizens in the political process. *Brown v. Board of Education* is an example of such a case. Congress drafted the Bill of Rights and all the subsequent amendments that protect individual rights and extend rights to those deprived of them in the past. Congress also has passed landmark legislation that not only has given support to these amendments but also has established rights not explicitly contained in the amendments. The results have been significant changes in American life. Landmark legislation significantly changes public policy or the relationship between the national government and the states. Another example is the National Labor Relations Act of 1935 that protects the rights of workers to form and join labor unions. When the amendments to the Constitution have not been sufficient to protect individual rights, Congress has passed facilitating legislation. In the area of civil rights, for example, Congress passed the Civil Rights Acts of 1866, 1871, 1875, 1957, 1960, 1964, 1968, and 1991.

The passage of such legislation is a result of using democratic political processes made possible by our Constitution. Members of government have used these processes, as have private citizens, many affiliated with interest groups and movements. The abolition movement and the woman suffrage movement are examples.

Work in groups of three to five students. Each group should select one piece of landmark legislation from the list below and research what rights the legislation was designed to protect and how Congress and interest groups used the political process to pass the legislation. Each group should then develop answers to the questions that follow and prepare a short presentation for the class.

- Civil Rights Act (1866)
- National Labor Relations Act (1935)
- Servicemen's Readjustment Act (G.I. Bill) (1944)
- Civil Rights Act (1964)
- Voting Rights Act (1965)
- Freedom of Information Act (1966)
- Indian Civil Rights Act (1968)
- Pregnancy Disability Act (1978)
- Americans with Disabilities Act (1990)
- Homeland Security Act (2002)

❶ What historical circumstances led to the legislation?

❷ What are the major provisions of the legislation?

❸ What rights does the legislation promote or protect?

❹ How does the legislation reflect a major shift in American public policy?

❺ How has the legislation changed the course of private and public action?

❻ How was the political process used to pass this legislation?

- Was this legislation initiated by one or more members of Congress? If so, who were they and why did they initiate the legislation?

- Was this legislation the result of members of Congress working cooperatively with interest groups? If so, what were the groups and how did they help get the legislation passed?

- Was this legislation the result of members of Congress being pressured by other members or by interest groups? If so, who applied the pressure and what methods did they use?

- Was this legislation the result of pressure put on Congress by an administration supported by coalitions of civil rights organizations and activists?

- What other factors contributed to the passage of the legislation?

Patriot Act.

How did disabled Americans use the political process to encourage the creation of the Americans with Disabilities Act of 1990?

157

What are the principal functions of the State of the Union address?

158

WHERE DO MEMBERS OF CONGRESS GET IDEAS FOR LEGISLATION AND INFORMATION IN DECIDING WHICH BILLS TO SUPPORT?

Members of Congress often initiate legislation based on campaign promises to constituents, responses to problems or crises, or their own analysis of what laws are needed. They also introduce legislation at the request of others and must decide whether to support bills that are submitted by others. The Library of Congress through its Congressional Research Service frequently assists Congress by providing information and analyzing issues. The Congressional Budget Office will provide an analysis of the budget for a bill and its projected costs. In addition, information and requests for legislation often come from the following sources:

- **The executive branch** Article II, Section 3, instructs the president to give Congress information on the "State of the Union" and to "recommend to their Consideration such Measures as he shall judge necessary and expedient." The president delivers an annual State of the Union address to Congress that outlines the president's legislative agenda, among other things. This agenda can include creating, consolidating, or eliminating departments or agencies. Members of the president's party in Congress usually sponsor the president's legislative proposals.

  Executive departments and agencies are another regular source of legislative proposals. Most proposals from the executive branch are aimed at improving the functions of the departments or agencies that Congress already has created. These proposals usually are carefully crafted and ready for a member of Congress to introduce.

- **Constituents** Many of those who live in a representative's district or a senator's state communicate with their elected officials, recommending the enactment of new laws or the repeal of existing laws. Constituents make telephone calls, respond to public opinion polls, send faxes and email, write personal letters, participate in letter-writing campaigns, and use blogs to inform their elected representatives and to persuade them about the need for particular legislation. Sometimes constituents ask their representative to introduce special legislation to address an individual problem or situation.

- **Interest groups** Thousands of individuals and groups seek to influence members of Congress and legislation through **lobbying**, the practice of trying to affect legislation on behalf of organizations, industries, or interest groups through contact with legislators. Groups that participate in lobbying include businesses, civic organizations, professional associations, and nongovernmental organizations. The Lobbying Disclosure Act of 1996 requires some lobbyists to disclose the interests they represent, the issues in which they are interested, and how much they spend annually. The act does not limit the amount of lobbying in which any individual or group may engage. The activity of lobbying reflects the First Amendment rights to speak, assemble, and petition. Effective lobbyists, whether individuals or groups, must be

- **Well informed** Members of Congress must be able to rely on the information they receive from lobbyists. Information must be able to withstand scrutiny, and it must be timely.

- **Knowledgeable** Lobbyists need to know not only their own issues but also the intricacies of the legislative process, key players, and which groups support and oppose particular proposals.

- **Organized** Interest groups must convey a consistent message and must be persistent. They must be able to explain how an issue affects their members and clients. And they must use various forms of communication effectively, including personal contact with members of Congress.

- **Cooperative** Successful interest groups, like members of Congress, must be able to build coalitions with other interest groups in the search for workable majorities.

HOW DOES CONGRESS USE ITS POWER TO INVESTIGATE?

Legislative bodies have claimed the **power to investigate** since at least the seventeenth century. Congress has conducted hundreds of investigations since 1792. The purposes of investigations include the following:

- Finding facts on which to base legislation
- Discovering or influencing public opinion
- Overseeing administrative agencies
- Probing into questionable activities of public officials
- Securing partisan political gain

Congress began making full use of its inherent power to investigate only in the twentieth century. For example, a congressional investigation into labor practices in the 1930s resulted in federal labor legislation. Standing congressional committees most often conduct investigations. Recently, however, Congress has made greater use of special investigative commissions, such as to examine the explosion of the *Challenger* space shuttle in 1986 and the terrorist attacks on the United States in 2001. Today Congress's investigations rival its lawmaking powers and have helped Congress maintain its power in relation to the executive branch.

Congress uses its power to investigate as part of its power to impeach, or to put federal officials on trial. Any member of the House may initiate **impeachment** proceedings by introducing a resolution. The type of resolution determines which committee will investigate the charges. For example, a resolution calling for the impeachment of a federal judge will be referred to the Judiciary Committee. If the committee finds that there are grounds for impeachment, then it reports "articles of impeachment"—accusations of misconduct—to the full House for debate. If a majority of those present and voting agree on impeachment, then the matter is sent to the

IMPEACHMENT PARADE

©1999 HERBLOCK

"Impeachment Parade," a 1999 Herblock Cartoon, copyright by The Herb Block Foundation

What evidence, if any, is there for the opinion about the impeachment process conveyed in this cartoon?

159

student page ▼ 159–160

HOW DOES CONGRESS USE ITS POWER TO INVESTIGATE?

The Constitution does not explicitly give Congress the power to investigate. However, at the Philadelphia Convention George Mason described members of Congress as being "not only Legislators, but they possess inquisitorial powers. They must meet frequently to inspect the Conduct of the public offices."

The first House investigation occurred in 1791 and inquired into Robert Morris's conduct as Superintendent of Finance under the Continental Congress. In 1821 in *Anderson v. Dunn* the Supreme Court recognized the power of Congress to investigate and held that either branch could punish a person other than a member of Congress for contempt of its authority. In *McGrain v. Daugherty* (1927) the Court reaffirmed the power to investigate as "an essential and appropriate auxiliary to the legislative function."

The powers to issue subpoenas and to hold those who do not comply in contempt are the two means of implementing the power to investigate. However, Congress must provide notice and an opportunity to be heard before a person may be held in contempt and sentenced (*Groppi v. Leslie*, 1972). Usually a simple request to appear before a committee to provide information is all that is required for Congress to obtain the information it needs.

The House and Senate use their powers of investigation most actively when the majority of their members are of a different political party than the president. Examples of other famous investigations include the following:

1792	Defeat of the Army force by confederated Indian tribes
1860	John Brown's raid on Harper's Ferry, Virginia
1912	Campaign contributions during the presidential elections of 1904 and 1908
1923	Leasing of government oil reserves in Wyoming to private companies
1936	Allegations of anti-union practices
1950	Charges of disloyalty by State Department employees
1963	Whether favoritism was involved in defense contracting
1973	Break-in at Democratic campaign headquarters ("Watergate")
1987	Secret selling of American arms to Iran to fund Nicaraguan "Contras"

LESSON 22

1999 Acquisition by China of U.S. nuclear weapons information

2002 Joint Inquiry into Intelligence Community Activities before and after the terrorist attacks of September 11, 2001

ENRICHMENT ACTIVITY

DEBATE THE QUESTION, SHOULD THE IMPEACHMENT CLAUSE BE AMENDED?

The original impeachment proposal submitted to the Philadelphia Convention on June 13, 1787, included the possibility of Congress voting to remove the president "on impeachment and conviction of malpractices or neglect of duty." On September 17 George Mason of Virginia moved that "or maladministration" be added to the list of impeachable offenses. James Madison protested that "so vague a term will be equivalent to a tenure during pleasure of the Senate," and Mason withdrew his motion. Pennsylvania's Gouvernor Morris said he believed that "an election every four years will prevent maladministration."

Recently debate has rekindled about whether "maladministration" or "incompetence" should be added to the list of reasons for which Congress may impeach a president in Article II, Section 4: Treason, Bribery, or the High Crimes and Misdemeanors.

Three possibilities for change suggested by constitutional scholar James L. Sundquist are listed below. Ask students to consider these possibilities in small groups and be prepared to support or oppose each of them in a class debate.

- **POSSIBILITY 1** Congress must declare by a two-thirds vote of the entire Congress meeting in joint session that it has "no confidence" in the president. It then schedules a special election to take place within a month to pick a successor to the discredited president. The current president could choose to run as a way of testing whether Congress actually spoke for the people.

- **POSSIBILITY 2** If by a two-thirds vote Congress expresses "no confidence," the president must immediately resign and be succeeded by the vice president.

- **POSSIBILITY 3** Upon a vote of "no confidence" by two-thirds of Congress in joint session, the members of Congress who are of the same political party as the now deposed president shall meet and select someone to serve as president for the remainder of the term.

Senate for a trial. Conviction requires a two-thirds majority vote. If the person convicted is an executive officer, then removal from office is automatic.

The House does not often use its impeachment power. Only seventeen national officers have been impeached:

- Presidents Andrew Johnson (1868) and Bill Clinton (1998) (both acquitted)
- Secretary of War William Belknap (1876) (acquitted after resignation)
- Senator William Blount (1799) (charges dismissed after expelled from Senate)
- Thirteen federal judges (seven found guilty, four acquitted, two resigned), including Supreme Court Justice Samuel Chase (1805) (acquitted)

The threat of impeachment alone can be powerful. President Richard Nixon (in office, 1969–1974) and Supreme Court Justice Abe Fortas (in office, 1965–1969), as examples, each resigned when it appeared that he would be impeached.

Should members of the public be allowed to observe impeachment proceedings? Why?

CRITICAL THINKING EXERCISE
Restoring Congressional Power

Congress is the lynchpin of the American constitutional system. However, several scholars and even former members of Congress believe that it is now a "broken branch." Among other things they criticize members of Congress for not effectively using the power to investigate, for ceding power to the executive, and for using the institution for personal advancement rather than promotion of the common good. Work in small groups to respond to the following questions. Then share your responses with other groups.

1. What organizational changes might make Congress work more effectively?

2. How might Congress's processes for reviewing and debating proposed legislation be streamlined? Should they be? What values are served by streamlining or by not streamlining these processes?

3. How could Congress make the most effective use of its power to investigate?

REVIEWING AND USING THE LESSON

1. How do committees, rules, and political parties help Congress organize to do its work?

2. What values are served by using seniority to determine committee leadership positions in Congress? What values are served by using party loyalty to determine leadership positions? Is one method more consistent with constitutional ideals? Why?

3. How has the role of Speaker of the House evolved since 1900?

4. Describe the responsibilities of the House, the Senate, and the president in the law-making process.

5. Explain the roles of interest groups in making laws.

6. How does landmark legislation differ from ordinary legislation?

7. Congress uses its power to investigate to assess blame for government acts in the past and to acquire information to help it enact laws. Is one use of the power to investigate more justifiable than the other? Why or why not?

8. Research the committees on which your congressional representatives serve. How do those committees address the interests and concerns of your district or state and the nation as a whole?

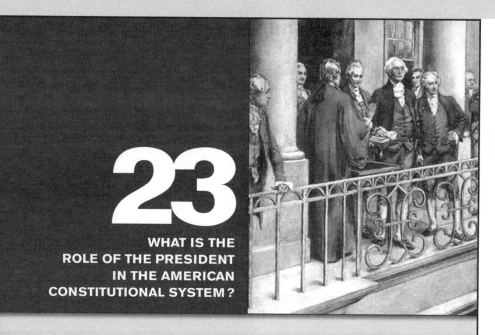

23

WHAT IS THE ROLE OF THE PRESIDENT IN THE AMERICAN CONSTITUTIONAL SYSTEM?

WHAT IS THE ROLE OF THE PRESIDENT IN THE AMERICAN CONSTITUTIONAL SYSTEM?

wtpcompanion.civiced.org | **LESSON PURPOSE + TERMS**

Visit the We the People companion website for printable and downloadable Lesson Purposes and Terms and Concepts to Understand sections for each lesson. Audio readings of each Lesson Purpose and Term are also available online in MP3 format.

LESSON PURPOSE

The president of the United States is among the most powerful political figures in the world. In the international realm the president speaks for the country and is the symbol of America. At home the president suggests the policy agenda for Congress and is the leader of his or her political party. Americans look to the president for leadership, while at the same time fearing the concentration of political power in the executive branch. This lesson examines sources of presidential power and ways that checks and balances limit presidential power.

When you have finished this lesson, you should be able to explain the president's constitutional responsibilities and how the office of president has evolved. You also should be able to identify various constitutional and political checks on the president's power. You should be able to explain fundamental differences between the office of prime minister in a parliamentary system and the American presidency. Finally, you should be able to evaluate, take, and defend positions on issues involving the exercise of presidential power and the relationship between the president and the other branches of government.

TERMS AND CONCEPTS TO UNDERSTAND

commander in chief

executive order

executive power

student page ▼ 162

WHAT ARE THE PRESIDENT'S CONSTITUTIONAL RESPONSIBILITIES?

POWER TO PARDON Article II gives the president the power to grant reprieves, postpone punishment, and issue pardons. The power to pardon is both absolute (a complete pardon) and conditional (a partial pardon) (*Illinois Central Railroad v. Bosworth*, 1890). The power to commute sentences is effective without a convict's consent (*Ex parte William Wells*, 1856).

| **wtpcompanion.civiced.org** | **COURT CASES** |

Visit the We the People companion website for links to Supreme Court syllabi and opinions for each of the cases described in the student and teacher's editions. Summaries are provided for selected Supreme Court cases.

ANALYZING PRESIDENTIAL POWER In a concurring opinion in *Youngstown Sheet and Tube v. Sawyer* (1952) Justice Robert Jackson set forth the framework that is widely used to assess presidential power, particularly when the president's actions have the effect of making public policy:

❶ When the President acts pursuant to an express or implied authorization of Congress, his authority is at its maximum, for it includes all that he possesses in his own right plus all that Congress can delegate. In these circumstances, and in these only, may he be said (for what it is worth), to personify the federal sovereignty….

❷ When the President acts in absence of either a congressional grant or denial of authority, he can only rely upon his own independent powers, but there is a zone of twilight in which he and Congress may have concurrent authority, or in which its distribution is uncertain. Therefore, congressional inertia, indifference or quiescence may sometimes, at least as a practical matter, enable, if not invite, measures on independent presidential responsibility. In this area, any actual test of power is likely to depend on the imperatives of events and contemporary imponderables rather than on abstract theories of law.

❸ When the President takes measures incompatible with the expressed or implied will of Congress, his power is at its lowest ebb for then he can rely only upon his own constitutional powers minus any constitutional powers of Congress over the matter.

Like Congress, the president has inherent powers that are not mentioned in the Constitution. What these powers are continues to be a source of controversy. It is uncontested that the president has the inherent power to seek the advice of cabinet officers (see Lesson 24). More controversial are issues such as whether the president has the power to take the following actions:

WHAT ARE THE PRESIDENT'S CONSTITUTIONAL RESPONSIBILITIES?

Article II of the Constitution places "the **executive Power**," the powers of the executive branch of government, in the president of the United States. Unlike Article I, which gives Congress those powers "herein granted," Article II does not define executive power. The Constitution lists some of the president's powers, but those listed have never been thought to be the president's only powers. The listed powers include the following:

● Commanding the army and navy as **commander in chief**

● Heading the executive department (cabinet and executive departments)

● Granting reprieves, or postponement of punishment, and pardons

● Making treaties, subject to the advice and consent of the Senate

● Nominating ambassadors, public ministers, consuls, and judges of the Supreme Court and other federal courts

● Recommending legislation to Congress

● Reviewing legislation passed by Congress and returning bills to which the president objects

● Receiving ambassadors and other public ministers (chief diplomat)

The Constitution further directs the president to "take Care that the Laws be faithfully executed." It also requires the president to take an oath that includes a promise to "faithfully execute the Office of President and…preserve, protect, and defend the Constitution of the United States."

Presidents have asserted many reasons to justify a broad definition of executive powers, particularly in times of national emergency, such as the Great Depression, and war. The Constitution has proven flexible enough to adapt to changing understandings of presidential power.

Should the president have the power to veto bills passed by majorities of both houses of Congress? Why?

WHAT DO YOU THINK?

❶ Article II, Section 1, gives the president "executive Power" but does not define what that power is. What other provisions of Article II give an indication of what the Framers meant by executive power?

❷ What additional insights into the nature of executive power are provided in Article I?

HOW DID THE FRAMERS ENVISION THE PRESIDENCY?

The Framers envisioned the president as an official above partisan politics, that is, a person not devoted to a particular political party. Publius explained in Federalist 68 that they wanted the president to be a person who had earned the esteem and confidence of the entire nation, with a character "preeminent for ability and virtue." They designed the Electoral College to identify people of such character. There was no expectation that candidates would campaign for the office. The Framers thought that the president should remain above partisan politics. But their expectations were unmet even during President Washington's administration, when factions arose that led to the development of political parties.

The Framers did not want the president to have the powers of a monarch. But they did want the president to be "energetic," a quality they contrasted with legislative "deliberation." "Energy" refers to the capacity of one person to act efficiently and vigorously on behalf of the nation. The Framers feared what they called a "feeble executive." As Alexander Hamilton argued in Federalist 70, "A feeble execution is but another phrase for a bad execution; and a government ill executed, whatever it may be in theory, must be, in practice, a bad government."

HOW HAS THE PRESIDENCY EVOLVED?

Occupants of the office of president have varied in stature and achievements. Some have been undeniably great, others have been mediocre, and still others are regarded as failures. The precedents for the modern presidency are the powerful figures who took a broad view of their authority under the Constitution.

Early examples of powerful presidents are our first and third presidents, George Washington and Thomas Jefferson. However, some scholars trace the rise of the powerful modern presidency to Andrew Jackson. Before Jackson presidents used the veto power sparingly to aid Congress in the performance of its deliberative functions. They returned bills to Congress for "reconsideration," or further reflection. Jackson used the

power differently. He vetoed the recharter of the Second Bank of the United States. In the resulting battle between the president and Congress, Jackson appealed directly to the public to support his position on the bank. During his two terms in office President Jackson used the veto twelve times, more than all his predecessors combined. He used it not only against bills that he considered unconstitutional but also against those he viewed as bad policy.

Abraham Lincoln contributed significantly to the growth of the office, even though he rarely used the veto power. Confronted with the Civil War (discussed in Unit Three), Lincoln asserted unprecedented, unilateral executive power. He justified actions such as imposing a blockade on southern ports, suspending the writ of habeas corpus, nationalizing the militia, and expanding the size of the army and the navy as exercises of what he called an "inherent executive power" in times of emergency. Congress ultimately authorized most of Lincoln's actions.

Theodore Roosevelt and Woodrow Wilson also helped transform the presidency into the powerful institution it is today. Roosevelt used the office as a "bully pulpit" to shape public opinion and frame debates on domestic legislation that he proposed to Congress. A bully pulpit is a position of visibility and influence, often a political office, from which to advocate a particular point of view. The word *bully*, in this case, means "very good" or "excellent." Wilson similarly carried issues directly to the public, notably in his unsuccessful fight for America's entry into the League of Nations after World War I.

The most influential president in the twentieth century was Franklin D. Roosevelt. Roosevelt was elected during the Great Depression and served until nearly the end of World War II. He used both crises to consolidate presidential power. At home Roosevelt took direct control of the policy process, submitting a wide range of reforms to Congress as part of his New Deal. These included Social Security, employment programs, and extensive reforms of executive agencies. As commander in chief during World War II Roosevelt helped to establish America's preeminence in the international arena. He also was the first president to make extensive use of public opinion polls, which informed him about how Americans were responding to his proposals. He talked directly to the people through radio "fireside chats," using a conversational, personal style to establish trust and confidence.

Presidents since Roosevelt have served in his shadow. Some have agreed with Roosevelt's domestic policies. Others have sought to dismantle them. However, all effective presidents have relied on strategies that Roosevelt used to bolster presidential power. Ronald Reagan, for

- Issue a "signing statement" when signing a bill into law, reserving the right not to enforce particular provisions of legislation

- Engage in wars or warlike activities without congressional authorization

- Authorize foreign and domestic surveillance in the name of national security

- Hold "enemy combatants" captured abroad and on American soil without access to recognized judicial proceedings

- Authorize coercive interrogation, including torture, when deemed necessary

- Assert "executive privilege" in refusing to respond to requests for information from Congress

HOW DID THE FRAMERS ENVISION THE PRESIDENCY?

Review Lessons 11 and 16.

student page ▾ 163–164

HOW HAS THE PRESIDENCY EVOLVED?

America's early presidents—Washington, John Adams, Jefferson, Madison, Monroe, and John Quincy Adams—were all part of the founding generation. Therefore, they brought to the office a keen awareness of helping to shape the institution for future generations. However, presidential historian Gleaves Whitney argues that it is hard to stereotype presidents with respect to their views of the presidency as an institution. He notes, for example, that

Thomas Jefferson seemed to have every intention of wearing the presidency with humility. From the start he threw off monarchical tendencies that John Adams especially had displayed. He understood the importance of symbolic gestures and wanted to make the office fitting for a republic. Determined to be the model of republican simplicity, Jefferson walked to his inauguration in the Capitol, did away with formalities, and abandoned the precedent of delivering annual reports to Congress in a speech. In fact, Jefferson gave only two speeches during eight years in office. The reason? He did not want to mimic the British monarch's Address to Parliament....

However,…our third president was not above stretching the powers of the office when it suited his purposes. He knew, for instance, that the Constitution provided for the admitting [of] new states to the Union, not acquiring new territories in the hinterland, yet he was determined to see the Louisiana Purchase through, even though the action was technically unconstitutional.

BULLY PULPIT   Presidential biographer Hugh Sidney contends that "the presidency had been transformed from a bully pulpit on Pennsylvania Avenue to a stage the size of the world."

WHAT IS THE PRESIDENT'S ROLE IN FOREIGN POLICY?

The president's power is at its zenith in foreign affairs. In *United States v. Curtiss-Wright Export Corporation* (1936) Justice George Sutherland wrote the following:

> In this vast external realm [of foreign affairs], with its important, complicated, delicate and manifold problems, the President alone has the power to speak or listen as a representative of the nation. He *makes* treaties with the advice and consent of the Senate; but he alone negotiates. Into the field of negotiation the Senate cannot intrude; and Congress itself is powerless to invade it.…
> (emphasis in original)

The Court distinguished between domestic and foreign powers, reasoning that "the two classes of powers are different, both in respect of their origin and their nature."

wtpcompanion.civiced.org   COURT CASES

Visit the We the People companion website for links to Supreme Court syllabi and opinions for each of the cases described in the student and teacher's editions. Summaries are provided for selected Supreme Court cases.

example, established himself as the Great Communicator, whereas John F. Kennedy and Bill Clinton used their personal charisma to win political allies and to persuade the American people to support their policies.

CRITICAL THINKING EXERCISE
Examining Presidential Qualifications

The Constitution lists three formal requirements for the office of president: natural born citizen, resident of the United States for fourteen years, and at least thirty-five years of age. Work in small groups to make a list of the *informal* qualifications that you think a president should possess. For example, should a president be well educated? Have previous government or military experience? Be charismatic, articulate, and personable? Why? Compare your list with the lists prepared by other groups. Are there informal qualifications that appear on everyone's list? How does your list compare with the qualifications the Founders believed were important?

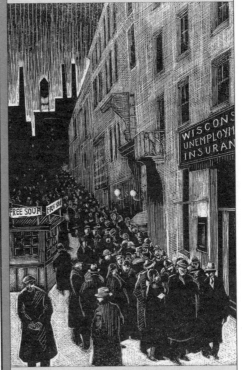

What responsibility, if any, should government take regarding unemployment?

WHAT IS THE PRESIDENT'S ROLE IN FOREIGN POLICY?

Article II grants four powers that, taken together, establish the president as the nation's leader in foreign policy. Congress also has enormous powers over foreign policy because it establishes and collects taxes, declares war, pledges the credit of the United States, and regulates foreign commerce. Congress also funds the armed forces, makes rules governing them—the Uniform Code of Military Justice—and makes rules related to "Captures on Land and Water," as contained in Article I, Section 8, of the Constitution. However, Congress's role is largely one of reacting to the president. The president's powers in foreign relations include the following:

- **Commanding the armed forces**
  The nation's military power can be used both to protect the nation from hostile powers and as a threat to help persuade other countries to comply with America's policies. Congress has declared war only five times. However, every president after Roosevelt has used the commander in chief's power to send American troops to countries abroad—including Korea, Vietnam, Lebanon, Grenada, Kuwait, Somalia, Kosovo, Afghanistan, and Iraq—without declarations of war.

- **Making treaties**   Treaties are agreements with other nations and international organizations. They can address matters ranging from economics to defense. The president has sole authority to negotiate and make treaties on behalf of the United States. However, the treaties must be approved by a two-thirds vote of the Senate. In 1949, for example, President Harry Truman made the United States one of the founding members of the North Atlantic Treaty Organization, a military alliance. The Senate approved. But other treaties, notably the Treaty of Versailles after World War I, have not been ratified.

- **Appointing ambassadors and consuls**
  The president decides who represents the United States within other countries. The president's appointees, who must be approved by a majority vote in the Senate, help to shape the image of the United States overseas and to advise on foreign policy, including monetary assistance to other countries, or foreign aid.

- **Receiving ambassadors and other public ministers**
  President Thomas Jefferson helped to establish the principle that this provision of the

What are some of the checks on the president's powers in foreign relations?

Constitution means that the president is "the only channel of communication between the United States and foreign nations." The right to receive ambassadors and other public ministers from abroad includes the right not to recognize them. Withholding recognition can be used as a policy tool. For example, in 1913 President Woodrow Wilson's refusal to recognize the provisional government of Mexico contributed to the downfall of that government.

HOW DO THE PRESIDENT'S POWERS EXPAND IN WAR AND EMERGENCY?

During wars and emergencies presidents commonly exercise powers not granted by the Constitution. President Grover Cleveland deployed federal troops without congressional authorization in 1894 to put down a strike among Pullman train car workers. President Franklin Roosevelt transferred destroyers to Great Britain in 1940, a year before the United States entered World War II. And President Truman ordered the secretary of commerce to operate the nation's steel mills during a strike to ensure an adequate supply of steel during the Korean War.

On occasion Congress and the Supreme Court have tried to rein in the president. In 1952 the Supreme Court held that President Truman had exceeded his authority in seizing the steel mills. In the 1970s, Congress also debated withdrawing funding for the Vietnam War as the war continued to lose public support. In 2006 the Court held that President George W. Bush's creation of special military commissions to try alleged terrorists violated the Uniform Code of Military Justice passed by Congress in 1950 and the 1949 Geneva Convention, an international treaty that the United States had signed. These examples aside, during wars and national emergencies both Congress and the Court tend to defer to the president.

HOW AND WHY HAS PRESIDENTIAL POWER EXPANDED HISTORICALLY?

It sometimes is argued that the two-plus centuries of American experience have been characterized by a general drift of authority and responsibility toward the executive branch. In fact, the preponderance of power has flowed over time from one branch to another. During most of the nineteenth century Congress predominated. In the twentieth century as the role of the United States in world affairs grew, so did the formal and informal powers of the president. The administrations

---

HOW DO THE PRESIDENT'S POWERS EXPAND IN WAR AND EMERGENCY?

The Constitution contains no express provision regarding the exercise of power in "emergency" or "crisis," but the Supreme Court held in *Ex parte Milligan* (1866) that no written provision is necessary: "The government, within the Constitution, has all the powers granted to it which are necessary to preserve its existence."

Presidents Lincoln, Wilson, and Franklin Roosevelt stand out as chief executives who exercised extraordinary powers during wars and emergencies. Lincoln launched the Civil War without congressional action. He sought congressional authorization, and Congress gave it, only after the war had begun. Wilson asked Congress for almost unlimited powers after Germany attacked American ships and submarines, taking the United States into World War I. Congress gave him everything he requested.

During Franklin Roosevelt's first one hundred days Congress gave him virtually every power he asked for to respond to the Great Depression. After the Japanese attack on Pearl Harbor in 1941 Roosevelt asked Congress for power to wage World War II but also asserted, "In the event the Congress should fail to act, and act adequately, I shall accept responsibility, and I will act." He argued that the president has the power "to take measures necessary to avert a disaster which would interfere with winning of the war."

Only rarely do Congress and the courts attempt to rein in the president during wars and emergencies. The 1952 and 2006 Supreme Court cases attempting to do so are as follows:

Youngstown Sheet and Tube v. Sawyer (1952) arose out of the Korean War, after President Truman sent air and naval forces to Korea in 1950 at the request of the United Nations Security Council. In 1951 contracts between the Youngstown Sheet and Tube Company and the United Steelworkers Union expired. Workers went on strike in April 1952 when negotiations for a new contract collapsed. President Truman issued Executive Order 10340 authorizing Secretary of Commerce Charles Sawyer to take command of the steel mills and operate them so that the country would not lose the steel it needed for the Korean military effort. The Supreme Court held that President Truman improperly invaded Congress's "exclusive constitutional authority to make laws necessary and proper to carry out the powers vested by the Constitution."

Hamdan v. Rumsfeld (2006) involved Salim Hamdan, a former driver for wanted terrorist Osama bin Laden, who was being held at Guantanamo Bay, Cuba, since his arrest in 2001. President Bush ordered that Hamdan be tried by a special military commission rather than an ordinary military court. The Supreme Court held that Congress had not authorized special military commissions for trying suspected terrorists and that presidential creation of such commissions violated both the Uniform Code of Military Justice and the Geneva Convention. In late 2006 Congress passed a law that authorized military tribunals.

In *Boumediene v. Bush* (2008), the Supreme Court held that detainees being held at Guantanamo Bay have a constitutional right to go to federal court to challenge their detention. Unlike *Youngstown* and *Hamdan*, *Boumediene* involved a challenge to a statute, the Military Commissions Act, that Congress enacted in 2006 at the president's request, giving the president authority to suspend the writ of habeas corpus in some circumstances.

wtpcompanion.civiced.org   COURT CASES

Visit the We the People companion website for links to Supreme Court syllabi and opinions for each of the cases described in the student and teacher's editions. Summaries are provided for selected Supreme Court cases.

student page ▼ 165–166

HOW AND WHY HAS PRESIDENTIAL POWER EXPANDED HISTORICALLY?

Scholars frequently observe that presidential power has increased dramatically in the United States since the early 1930s. Factors contributing to the growth of power include the following:

- The Great Depression
- World War II
- The Cold War
- Terrorism
- Increased (some say disproportionate) media focus on the executive compared to the other branches of government

wtpcompanion.civiced.org   LINKS

Visit the We the People companion website for a link to the American Presidency Project, which contains archives of executive orders and signing statements.

of Franklin Roosevelt, Lyndon Johnson, Richard Nixon, and George W. Bush were marked by increased assertions of presidential authority.

There are several reasons for the increase in the powers of the presidency. One reason is that Americans have always expected their chief executives to act vigorously and to address the nation's problems. Alexander Hamilton in Federalist 70 claimed, "Energy in the executive is a leading character in the definition of good government." Thomas Jefferson contended that circumstances "sometimes occur" when the president must assume authorities beyond the law when necessity or self-preservation require. Interestingly, however, public opinion polls taken since the 1930s reflect two unchanging popular attitudes toward the presidency. The first is that people want strong, activist presidents. The second is that people fear and distrust activist presidents. Americans want and expect the other two branches of government to act as checks and balances on the executive.

A second reason for the enlargement of executive authority is that the constitutional powers of the president are stated in broad terms. It is possible to interpret them in ways that have permitted an expansion of presidential influence.

A third reason for the growth of executive power is the president's role in recommending legislation to Congress (Article II, Section 3). The executive branch proposes most of the bills that Congress considers. Enforcing decisions of the Supreme Court and carrying out and enforcing laws enacted by Congress also have led to a more central role for the executive. Moreover, the executive has played an increasingly active role in the development of federal regulations. Federal regulations are rules created by executive agencies to elaborate the often general laws passed by Congress to make them operational. They are printed in the *Federal Register*, a daily government publication of notices, rules, and other information, and are open to public comment for 30 days before they are approved and become law. As such, they are an example of the shared power of lawmaking.

A fourth reason for the growth of executive authority is the use of executive orders. An **executive order** is a rule or regulation issued by the president. The use of executive orders by presidents has greatly increased in recent years as a result of the tendency of legislative bodies to leave the details of laws they pass to be filled in by the executive branch. All executive orders issued by the federal government must be published in the *Federal Register*. Some states have similar publications.

Finally, presidential and executive power has increased as the federal government has assumed responsibilities that formerly were seen as the responsibilities

of individuals or of local and state governments. Examples of responsibilities shifted to the national government range from education to health care, transportation, and product safety.

HOW ARE PRESIDENTIAL POWERS LIMITED?

Despite the president's immense powers, the system of checks and balances limits presidents in a number of ways. For example, the Twenty-second Amendment limits the president to two elected terms in office. This amendment was adopted after Franklin Roosevelt abandoned the tradition begun by George Washington of stepping down after two terms. Even though Roosevelt had been immensely popular, Americans feared a president who remained in power too long.

Congress can check the exercise of the president's power by

- **Rejecting the president's legislative agenda or modifying it in ways that make it unacceptable to the president** Examples include the rejection of Franklin Roosevelt's proposal to increase the number of justices on the Supreme Court and his plans to reorganize the executive branch.

What opportunities does the Federal Register provide for citizens to monitor and influence government?

- **Asserting its constitutional authority**
An example is the 1973 War Powers Resolution intended to reinforce the constitutional power of Congress to declare war. Among other things it requires the president to consult with Congress before initiating any foreign hostilities and regularly thereafter until American armed forces no longer are engaged in hostilities.

- **Refusing to ratify treaties**
For example, in 1996 Bill Clinton signed a comprehensive nuclear test ban treaty with 137 other nations. Ten years later the Senate had neither ratified nor held major hearings on it.

- **Refusing to confirm presidential nominees to the judiciary or top administrative posts**
Examples are the Senate's refusal to confirm Richard Nixon's nominations of G. Harrold Carswell and Clement Haynsworth to the Supreme Court and George H. W. Bush's nomination of John Tower to be secretary of the Department of Defense.

- **Refusing to fund the president's programs**
By cutting off or reducing funds, or by threatening to do so, Congress can abolish agencies, curtail programs, or obtain requested information. An example is the refusal of Congress to provide funding for emergency aid for Vietnam as requested by President Lyndon B. Johnson.

- **Removing the president from office by impeaching, trying, and convicting him**

The Supreme Court also can check the exercise of presidential power. Examples include the following:

- *Humphrey's Executor v. United States* (1935)
Congress must approve the president's decision to remove an official of an independent regulatory agency.

- *United States v. Nixon* (1974)
The president is not entitled to automatic immunity from the legal process (reaffirmed in *Clinton v. Jones*, 1997).

- *Train v. City of New York* (1975)
The president cannot refuse to spend money that Congress has appropriated unless Congress gives the president discretion to do so.

What are some of the principal means by which the powers of the president can be limited?

The executive branch itself also can limit the president, as will be discussed in the next lesson. Executive agencies and bureaus develop their own change-resistant traditions and styles of performing their jobs. Career civil service employees—many of them experts in their fields—may resist the president's political priorities without fear of losing their jobs.

Finally, public opinion limits the exercise of presidential power. A president who lacks public support is handcuffed in his efforts to carry out his policy agendas at home and abroad. President Truman once lamented, "I sit here all day trying to persuade people to do the things they ought to have sense enough to do without my persuading them…. That's all the powers of the president amount to."

Which branch of government was responsible for the integration of the military?

CRITICAL THINKING EXERCISE

Examining the Role of the Executive Branch in Promoting the Protection of Individual Rights

The actions of the executive branch in developing federal regulations and executive orders are subject to the same democratic political processes made possible by our Constitution. Private citizens and interest groups and movements have used these processes to influence executive branch decisions.

Work in groups of three to five students. Each group should select one of the regulations or executive orders listed below and determine what rights it was designed to protect and how the political process was used to influence the actions of the government. Each group should answer the questions following the list and prepare a short presentation for the class.

- **Emancipation Proclamation (1863)**
  Freedom of slaves in territory of the Confederate States of America that did not return to Union control by January 1, 1863

- **Executive Order 8802 (1941)**
  Nondiscrimination in employment

- **Executive Order 9981 (1948)**
  Integration of the military

- **Executive Order 10730 (1957)**
  Integration of schools in Little Rock, Arkansas

- **Executive Order 11246 (1965)**
  Enforcement of affirmative action

- **Philadelphia Plan (1969)**
  Affirmative action in federal employment

- **Code of Federal Regulations, Title 34 (C.F.R. 34) (2000)**
  Implementation of parts of the Civil Rights Act of 1964 regarding nondiscrimination in education, as follows:

  - **Part 100**
    Prohibits discrimination on the basis of race, color, or national origin

  - **Part 104**
    Prohibits discrimination on the basis of disability

  - **Part 106**
    Prohibits discrimination on the basis of sex

  - **Part 110**
    Prohibits discrimination on the basis of age

- **Code of Federal Regulations, Title 28, Part 35 (1991)**
  Prohibits discrimination on the basis of disability

What are some of the differences between the roles of prime minister and president?

❶ What were the historical circumstances that led to the executive action?

❷ What are the major provisions of the executive order or federal regulation?

❸ What rights does the order or regulation promote or protect?

❹ How does the order or regulation reflect a major shift in American public policy?

❺ How has the order or regulation changed the course of private and public action?

❻ How was the democratic political process used to influence the executive branch to issue this order or regulation?

● Was this order or regulation a result of congressional action? If so, what was the cause of the action?

● Was this order or regulation the result of the influence of civil society interest groups? If so, what were they and how did they help get the order or regulation enacted?

● What other factors contributed to the enactment of this order or regulation?

HOW DOES THE AMERICAN PRESIDENT DIFFER FROM A PRIME MINISTER?

In a parliamentary system the majority party or coalition in Parliament appoints the prime minister, the highest-ranking member of the executive branch of a parliamentary government. Cabinet ministers usually are the leading parliamentary figures in the majority party. In Britain the prime minister must have served in Parliament so that he or she comes to the office of prime minister with extensive government experience. Legislative and executive powers are integrated in parliamentary systems. That integration is believed to make government more efficient and better able to reflect the popular will. A prime minister who submits a list of measures to Parliament can be confident that Parliament will enact the proposals. However, if the prime minister loses the confidence of Parliament, he or she can be removed immediately.

In the United States the legislative, executive, and judicial branches are not integrated. The country as a whole chooses the president. Congress usually has no say in who is elected, and the Constitution does not require a president to have any prior experience in national government. Neither must the majority in either the House or the Senate be of the same political party as the president. The Constitution does not require Congress to adopt legislation that the president proposes, approve treaties that the president negotiates, confirm the president's judicial or other nominees, or

student page ▼ 169–170

HOW DOES THE AMERICAN PRESIDENT DIFFER FROM A PRIME MINISTER?

Congress can have a role in who is elected president under the following circumstances:

● *A tie vote in the Electoral College.* This has happened only once, in the election of 1800. Thomas Jefferson and Aaron Burr each received 73 electoral votes. The House voted 10 to 4 (with two abstentions) for Jefferson after 36 successive votes.

● *If no candidate wins an Electoral College majority.* In 1825 neither Andrew Jackson nor John Quincy Adams received a 131-vote majority of Electoral College votes, the number then needed to win the presidency. Adams won in the House vote on the first ballot.

In the United States having separate elections for every office means that unlike in Great Britain, it is possible for one party to control Congress—or for one party to control the House and another the Senate—while a member of another party is president. So-called divided government is common in the United States.

wtpcompanion.civiced.org | **LINKS**

Visit the We the People companion website for a link to a chart on party affiliations of the President, House and Senate between 1945 and 2007.

ENRICHMENT ACTIVITY

HOW MUCH AUTHORITY SHOULD A PRESIDENT HAVE IN TIMES OF CRISIS?

The proper scope of presidential power remains vigorously debated not only by Congress and presidents but also by the courts and the public. Debate is particularly heated during a time of crisis. Law professor Daniel Farber has summarized five major arguments for presidents taking unauthorized action to meet emergency situations. Each of the arguments has appealing features and significant shortcomings.

Ask students to work in groups of two or three to identify those appealing features as well as the shortcomings of each argument. The groups should then share their views with the class.

- **ARGUMENT 1** As chief executive the president has inherent power to preserve society and protect the nation. When the nation is faced with disaster, the people expect the president to take decisive action with or without specific legal authority.

- **ARGUMENT 2** The vesting clause declares, "The executive power shall be vested [entrusted or granted] in a President of the United States of America" (Article II, Section 1). This means that the president possesses vast and general powers that have never been defined in the Constitution. The president may take whatever action is required under the circumstances so long as it is not solely within the jurisdiction of another branch or prohibited by the Constitution.

- **ARGUMENT 3** The president is required to take the following oath before entering office (Article II, Section 8):

    I do solemnly swear (or affirm) that I will faithfully execute the office of the President of the United States, and will to the best of my ability, preserve, protect and defend the Constitution of the United States.

    No other official is required to take this oath. This language does not grant any additional powers, but it requires the president to use whatever powers he does have as needed to achieve certain ends.

- **ARGUMENT 4** Article II, Section 3, requires that the president "shall take care that the Laws be faithfully executed and shall Commission all the Officers of the United States." This is phrased as a duty rather than a grant of power, but it does make the president responsible for seeing that his or her subordinates faithfully enforce the laws. The words "take care" presumably give the president some discretion in implementing the laws.

- **ARGUMENT 5** In the president's role as commander in chief (Article II, Section 2) the president exercises a vast array of "war powers" during periods of war or threat of war. The president also is supreme commander of the state National Guard units when they are called into federal service. Under his war powers the president may employ U.S. forces anywhere in the world. As has happened many times in American history, the president may order them into action against a foreign foe without a declaration of war by Congress.

fund wars. The president's actions also are subject to review by the judiciary and may be declared unconstitutional. Unlike a prime minister, the president serves a fixed four-year term and does not lose office merely because of low public opinion or failure to persuade Congress to enact proposed legislation.

If the president of the United States has become the preeminent figure in domestic and international politics, it is because presidents have used their constitutional and discretionary powers to advantage. Presidential power depends on the ability to persuade, to navigate through the complexities of separation of powers, to garner trust, and to shape public opinion. History also shows that the president's roles in foreign affairs and as commander in chief are great sources of power. However, as Lyndon Johnson discovered during the Vietnam War, if public opinion turns against the president's foreign policies, that president's power is in jeopardy. Finally, since the United States has become a world power, the president's standing in the eyes of the public and, in the words of the Declaration of Independence, in the "Opinions of Mankind," may enhance or detract from the international reputation of the nation.

Why might presidents be less vulnerable to public opinion than prime ministers?

WHAT DO YOU THINK?

1. Would you support a constitutional amendment to change the president's tenure in office from a fixed term to a vote-of-confidence system as in Great Britain? Why or why not?

2. What are the advantages and disadvantages of having the president chosen by the people rather than the legislature?

3. Should the president be required to appear before Congress from time to time to answer direct questions, as prime ministers are required to do in parliamentary systems? Why or why not?

REVIEWING AND USING THE LESSON

1. What factors explain the growth of presidential power during our nation's history?

2. Has Congress relinquished too much power to the president? Explain your view.

3. How is the system of checks and balances designed to limit the exercise of presidential power?

4. How well does the system of checks and balances work? Why?

5. How can public opinion affect presidential power?

6. How would you define a "feeble" executive? In what ways might a feeble executive be as dangerous as an overly "energetic" executive?

7. What are the differences between a president and a prime minister?

24

HOW ARE NATIONAL LAWS ADMINISTERED IN THE AMERICAN CONSTITUTIONAL SYSTEM?

LESSON PURPOSE

Departments, agencies, and bureaus that administer the laws, often referred to as the bureaucracy, touch every aspect of American life. For example, the Environmental Protection Agency sets standards for water and air quality. The Department of Transportation adopts rules for the development and operation of the interstate highway system. The Federal Aviation Administration oversees air traffic safety. The Food and Drug Administration approves medications. This lesson examines the role of administrative departments and agencies in America's national government.

When you have finished this lesson, you should be able to explain why Congress creates administrative units, the circumstances that contribute to their creation, and the range of governmental functions that administrative units perform. You also should be able to identify some of the checks on the exercise of administrative power. Finally, you should be able to evaluate, take, and defend positions on public administration in the United States.

TERMS AND CONCEPTS TO UNDERSTAND

bureaucracy	patronage
cabinet	quasi-judicial powers
civil service	quasi-legislative powers
independent agencies	

171

171

24

HOW ARE NATIONAL LAWS ADMINISTERED IN THE AMERICAN CONSTITUTIONAL SYSTEM?

student page ▾ 172–173

WHAT KINDS OF ADMINISTRATIVE UNITS EXIST IN THE AMERICAN NATIONAL GOVERNMENT?

Article I, Section 6, provides that "no person holding any Office under the United States, shall be a Member of either House during his Continuance in office." This provision helps to protect the principle of separation of powers and emphasizes one of the differences between the American constitutional system and the British parliamentary system. U.S. cabinet officers, "secretaries," are nominated by the president and confirmed by the Senate.

One definition of *secretary* is "an official who presides over an administrative department of state." In the fourteenth century the term referred to "one who is entrusted with private or secret matters; a confidant; one privy to a secret."

The word *bureaucracy* refers to the workplace where officials do their jobs. The term came into use before the French Revolution of 1789 and frequently had a negative connotation. In a letter of July 1764 the French Baron de Grimm, for example, wrote the following:

> We are obsessed by the idea of regulation, and our Masters of Requests refuse to understand that there is an infinity of things in a great state with which a government should not concern itself. The late Monsieur de Gournay…sometimes used to say: "We have an illness in France which bids fair to play havoc with us; this illness is called bureaumania."

From this perspective the purpose of administrative agencies was not to carry out the laws in the public interest but to preserve jobs for public officials. The term *bureaucracy* continues to have a negative connotation for many today.

WHAT KINDS OF ADMINISTRATIVE UNITS EXIST IN THE AMERICAN NATIONAL GOVERNMENT?

The Founders understood that Congress would need to create organizations to execute the laws. Several of the *Federalist* essays discussed the importance of "good administration" as a condition of good government. The first Congress under the Constitution created the first administrative units: the Departments of State, War, and Treasury. It also created the Office of the Attorney General, which later merged into the Justice Department. Over the years Congress has created other administrative agencies. Today there are basically three categories of administrative organizations, each with distinct responsibilities:

- **Executive departments** At present there are fifteen primary administrative units, or departments, in the executive branch. Congress directs each department to administer particular laws. The president appoints the secretaries, or heads, of each department. The secretaries of the departments serve in the president's **cabinet**, which advises the president. The secretaries also are in the line of presidential succession if the vice president, Speaker of the House, and president pro tempore of the Senate are unable to serve. Some departments, such as the Departments of Defense and Justice, are the result of combining older departments or offices. Others, such as the Department of Health and Human Services and the Department of Education, are the result of dividing older departments. Every department contains various divisions and bureaus, each with a particular area of expertise.

- **Executive Office of the President (EOP)** President Franklin Roosevelt complained that he lacked the necessary administrative "machinery" to execute the laws. In 1939 Congress created the Executive Office of the President to help with matters such as budgeting, personnel management, and natural resources planning. The EOP has grown into an umbrella organization with more than a dozen staff agencies. These agencies include the White House Office—including Homeland Security staff—the Office of Management and Budget, the Council of Economic Advisors, the National Security Council, and the Office of the United States Trade Representative. Some presidents rely on the EOP primarily for technical and managerial advice. Others use it to try to gain greater political control over the national **bureaucracy**.

- **Independent agencies** Since 1887 Congress has created many **independent agencies** that are located outside the structure of executive departments. These agencies do more than merely implement congressional statutes. The first independent agency was the Interstate Commerce Commission. Congress directed the commission to decide whether the rates that states imposed on interstate commerce were "reasonable"—a partial, or "quasi," legislative power—and to order the states to stop

2000	2002 Department of Homeland Security
	1988 Department of Veterans Affairs
1975	1979 Department of Health and Human Services
	1979 Department of Education
	1977 Department of Energy
	1966 Department of Transportation
	1965 Department of Housing and Urban Development
1950	
	1947 Department of Defense
1925	
	1913 Department of Labor
1900	1903 Department of Commerce
	1889 Department of Agriculture
1875	
	1870 Department of Justice
1850	
	1849 Department of the Interior
1825	
1800	
	1789 Department of State
	1789 Department of Treasury
1775	

What, if anything, does this chart portray about changes in interests and priorities and the role of government throughout history?

imposing "unreasonable" charges. Congress also empowered the commission to go to court to enforce its orders. In 1894 the Supreme Court held that the authority Congress had given to the commission was a "necessary and proper" exercise of its power to regulate commerce. Since then Congress has created more than fifty other independent agencies. These agencies include the Social Security Administration, the Environmental Protection Agency, the Peace Corps, and the Federal Energy Regulatory Commission.

Not all administrative organizations fit into these three categories. For example, the Federal Emergency Management Agency was created as an independent agency. It is now officially located in the Department of Homeland Security, but it retains much of the autonomy that it established while it was an independent agency. The United States Postal Service is an example of a government corporation, created to replace the Post Office Department. The Federal Communications Commission and the Occupational Safety and Health Review Commission are examples of organizations created to make and enforce regulations affecting regulated industries.

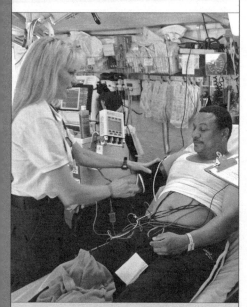

What kinds of events might justify the establishment of the Federal Emergency Management Agency?

CRITICAL THINKING EXERCISE
What Is "Good Administration"?

Federalist 68 argued that the "true test of a good government is its aptitude and tendency to produce good administration." Work in small groups to respond to the following questions and then compare your responses with other groups.

❶ What are the characteristics of "good administration"? Have the characteristics changed since the creation of the first administrative agency in 1789? If so, in what ways?

❷ What powers do Congress, the president, and the courts have to help ensure "good administration"?

WHY DOES CONGRESS CREATE ADMINISTRATIVE ORGANIZATIONS AND WHAT POWERS DO THEY EXERCISE?

Laws are often written in general terms. Congress cannot anticipate and does not have the expertise to resolve problems that arise when general laws are applied to specific circumstances. Almost from the beginning Congress has had to delegate some of its law-making powers to those who administer the laws. Administrative units exercise **quasi-legislative powers** by adopting rules to implement broad congressional mandates. Rules are published in the *Federal Register*. Many administrative units also exercise **quasi-judicial powers** by holding hearings to resolve disputes that involve parties claiming to have been injured by administrative policies or procedures.

The Internal Revenue Service (IRS) provides an example. The Sixteenth Amendment gives Congress the power to "lay," or establish, and collect taxes on income. Congress enacts general income tax laws. It has delegated to the IRS the responsibility to make and enforce rules about tax collection, including income tax forms, deadlines, and penalties for late filing. The IRS holds quasi-judicial proceedings, including hearings and opportunities to present evidence to a neutral hearings officer, for taxpayers who are accused of violating tax rules.

In 1946 Congress adopted the Administrative Procedure Act, which established guidelines for administrative units to follow when they make rules to implement laws. Among other things, the act requires public notice and an opportunity for the public to be heard before a rule goes into effect. The act also permits judicial review of the decisions of administrative units in federal court after someone has gone through, or exhausted, all quasi-judicial proceedings within the administrative unit.

student page ▾ 173

WHY DOES CONGRESS CREATE ADMINISTRATIVE ORGANIZATIONS AND WHAT POWERS DO THEY EXERCISE?

All executive departments publish the rules and regulations they adopt in the *Federal Register* (see the photograph of the cover of the *Federal Register* in the student text, page 166).

wtpcompanion.civiced.org LINKS

Visit the We the People companion website for a link to the *Federal Register*.

Although the Constitution creates three branches of government, some argue that in practice administrative agencies—particularly those that have quasi-legislative or rule-making as well as quasi-judicial or dispute-resolution powers—have in fact become a fourth branch of American government that exercises all three governmental powers and is not adequately accountable to the people.

student page ▼ 174

WHAT FACTORS HAVE CONTRIBUTED TO THE NUMBER OF ADMINISTRATIVE ORGANIZATIONS?

The size of the federal bureaucracy decreased between 1968 and 1994, and it also declined as a percentage of the civilian workforce. In part that decrease reflected a policy of decentralization embraced by both political parties under the umbrella of "new federalism," which returned to the states responsibilities that the national government had assumed during the Great Depression and World War II (see Lesson 26). However, terrorist attacks on the United States in 2001 and natural disasters such as Hurricane Katrina in 2004 reversed that trend.

student page ▼ 174

HOW ARE ADMINISTRATIVE AGENCIES STAFFED?

The tension between patronage and civil service staffing has resulted in litigation raising speech and association issues under the First Amendment (see Lessons 29 and 30). In *Elrod v. Burns* (1976) and *Branti v. Finkel* (1980) the Supreme Court held that the First Amendment forbids government officials from discharging or threatening to discharge public employees for the sole reason that they did not support the political party in power unless party affiliation is an appropriate requirement for the position involved. In *Rutan v. Republican Party of Illinois* (1990) the Court extended that rule, holding that promotion, transfer, recall, and hiring decisions involving low-level public employees may not be based on party affiliation and support. Justice Antonin Scalia wrote in dissent,

> As the merit principle has been extended and its effects increasingly felt; as the Boss Tweeds, the Tammany Halls, the Pendergast Machines, the Byrd Machines and the Daley Machines have faded into history; we find that political leaders at all levels increasingly complain of the helplessness of elected government, unprotected by "party discipline," before the demands of small and cohesive interest groups. The choice between patronage and the merit principle—or, to be more realistic about it, the choice between the desirable mix of merit and patronage principles in widely varying federal, state, and local political contexts—is not so clear that I would be prepared, as an original matter, to chisel a single, inflexible prescription into the Constitution.

WHAT FACTORS HAVE CONTRIBUTED TO THE NUMBER OF ADMINISTRATIVE ORGANIZATIONS?

The national bureaucracy has grown in response to demands placed on the national government. To establish greater control over the nation's natural resources, Congress created the Departments of Agriculture and the Interior. In response to problems that arose during the Industrial Revolution, Congress created the Departments of Commerce and Labor, the Interstate Commerce Commission, and the Federal Trade Commission.

The Great Depression and President Franklin Roosevelt's New Deal caused another significant growth of the national bureaucracy. The Tennessee Valley Authority, the Small Business Administration, the Federal Communications Commission, and the Social Security Administration trace their origins to the economic crisis of the 1930s and 1940s. Many programs also were added to existing agencies and departments during that time, such as a commodity support program in the Department of Agriculture.

The Cold War spawned the creation of the Department of Defense, the National Security Council, the Central Intelligence Agency, and the National Science Foundation. Programs such as the War on Poverty in the 1960s and energy crises in the 1970s led to the creation of more agencies, including the Department of Housing and Urban Development and the Department of Energy.

Beginning in the 1970s presidents and many members of Congress sought to reduce the size of the national government. The Civil Aeronautics Board, which regulated commercial aviation, was abolished in 1984. The Interstate Commerce Commission and the Resolution Trust Corporation, created to respond to bankruptcies of hundreds of savings and loan institutions, were abolished in 1995. The national bureaucracy also was scaled back when greater responsibility for welfare was returned to the states. The terrorist attacks on New York and Washington in 2001, however, led President George W. Bush to agree to the creation of a Department of Homeland Security, which Congress created in 2002.

HOW ARE ADMINISTRATIVE AGENCIES STAFFED?

Today the vast majority of administrative civilian employees are selected through a **civil service** program or merit system. Congress created the system in 1883 following the assassination of President James Garfield by a disappointed office seeker. In passing the nation's first civil service law Congress substituted merit for **patronage**, or the practice of rewarding supporters by giving them permanent jobs in the civil service.

By law Congress continues to exercise broad control over administrative employees. Congress can establish special requirements for holding office. It can set employee performance standards, wages, benefits, and cost of living adjustments. Congress also can provide protection for "whistle blowers," employees who expose waste or corruption.

When the civil service system was developed, it was intended to create a class of administrative employees

What factors have contributed to the establishment of new administrative organizations?

who were insulated from politics. Thus Congress passed the Hatch Act of 1939, which prohibited political parties from pressuring administrative employees to make financial contributions or to work for their candidates as a condition of job security or promotion. Some people complained that the Hatch Act deprived administrative employees of opportunities to participate in the political life that other Americans enjoyed. Finally, in 1993 President Clinton signed the Hatch Act Reform Amendments into law. These measures encourage civil servants to participate in political activity in accordance with regulations prescribed by the Office of Personnel Management.

Title 5 of the United States Code governs the merit principle in today's administrative agencies. However, a growing number of administrative jobs are being exempted from the provisions of Title 5. Individual agencies and departments have received authority to create their own personnel services outside standard civil service laws. The United States Postal Service, the Department of Defense, the Federal Aviation Administration, and the new Department of Homeland Security are examples.

Presidents also make appointments to federal agencies. These political appointees serve at the pleasure of the president, and their numbers have been growing. Through these appointments presidents have been able to place their own people in key leadership and support positions in all the federal agencies. Such appointments include the secretaries, or heads, of the departments that constitute the president's cabinet. By means of this network of political appointees the president can exercise considerable control over the federal bureaucracy to ensure that it furthers his or her policy priorities and agenda.

Whenever a new administration takes office, most political appointees lose their positions. There may be an almost complete change in the leadership of some of the administrative agencies. However, civil service employees retain their jobs and remain available to assist the new president and his or her cabinet in implementing the new administration's policies. By contrast, only a small number of senior civil service positions change hands in Britain when a new prime minister is chosen.

WHAT DO YOU THINK?

❶ What are the advantages and disadvantages of patronage? Of civil service?

❷ Should individual agencies or departments be able to create their own personnel service standards outside the civil service laws? Why or why not?

HOW DO CHECKS AND BALANCES AFFECT ADMINISTRATIVE AGENCIES?

Administrative agencies are subject to many checks on the exercise of their powers. Those who exercise checks include the following:

● **The president** Presidents use their appointment power to reward political loyalists and advance their policy agendas. Presidential appointees usually are required to pursue the president's policies in administering government programs, thereby checking the power of civil service career employees.

Presidents also check the exercise of administrative power through the use of executive orders, which direct agency heads and cabinet members to take particular actions. Executive orders have become more common in recent years as a means of forcing agencies to adjust administrative policies and procedures. For example, soon after he took office President George W. Bush issued executive orders creating Centers for Faith-Based and Community Initiatives offices in several departments and agencies to help ensure that faith-based groups would receive government contracts to provide social services. (See the Reference section for an example of an executive order.)

● **Congress** Congress can control the bureaucracy in many ways. It is responsible for the creation, consolidation, and elimination of administrative agencies. The Senate must confirm high-level presidential appointees. Many statutes direct agencies to undertake certain actions and refrain from others. Congress also must appropriate the money required for agencies to operate. Congressional committees are responsible for overseeing the actions of administrative agencies. They review agency budgets, require administrators to justify expenditures, hold investigative hearings about agency activities, and require agencies to submit their proposed rules, which Congress has the power to veto. Although the Supreme Court declared the congressional veto unconstitutional in 1983, Congress has continued to use it and has found other ways, including joint resolutions, to prohibit agencies from implementing rules with which Congress disagrees.

● **Courts** Courts decide whether agency operations follow the Fourteenth Amendment requirements of due process and

How can citizens monitor and check the use of power by administrative agencies?

equal protection. Courts also determine whether Congress has delegated too much legislative authority to administrative agencies. The Supreme Court has never questioned Congress's power to permit administrative agencies to "fill in the details" of statutes, but the Court has insisted that Congress clearly identify the standards that agencies must meet.

- **Federalism** If a state policy differs from a national policy—as has occurred in areas such as education, welfare, and environmental protection—then national bureaucrats can encounter resistance or refusal to comply with the national standards. Sometimes acting alone, and almost always when acting with others, states can have a significant effect on the national bureaucracy.

- **Citizens, interest groups, and the media** Those who are directly affected by administrative policies or who are interested in particular areas of public policy also check the exercise of administrative power. Many Social Security recipients, for example, monitor actions of the Social Security Administration and report complaints to the agency or to members of Congress. Environmental activists, welfare recipients, and many other individuals and groups keep close watch over various administrative agencies. Media investigations also can alert the public and elected officials to problems and miscarriages of justice in the bureaucracy.

CRITICAL THINKING EXERCISE
Administrative Agencies and Limited Government

James Madison argued in Federalist 47 that the

" accumulation of all powers, legislative, executive and judiciary in the same hands… may justly be pronounced the very definition of tyranny. Were the federal Constitution, therefore, really chargeable with this accumulation [of power], or with a mixture of powers, having a dangerous tendency to such an accumulation of power, no further arguments would be necessary to inspire a universal reprobation of the system.

Some administrative agencies exercise all three types of governmental powers to some degree. In addition to executing the laws, they exercise quasi-legislative powers by making rules and quasi-judicial powers by holding hearings on whether those rules have been violated. However, administrative agencies also are subject to checks and balances. Work in small groups to respond to the following questions and then compare your responses.

❶ In what ways is the exercise of all three kinds of powers by administrative agencies inconsistent with theories of separation of powers and limited government?

❷ What checks on the exercise of administrative authority are available to prevent agencies from coming within Madison's definition of tyranny?

❸ What might be some alternatives to agencies exercising all three kinds of governmental powers? Are those alternatives realistic?

REVIEWING AND USING THE LESSON

❶ How would you define the term *bureaucracy*?

❷ How and why do Congress and the president rely on administrative agencies?

❸ How does the national bureaucracy affect your everyday life and the lives of other Americans?

❹ Why are there ongoing debates about whether the bureaucracy should be staffed by civil service employees or by political appointees?

❺ Describe the sources of limits on the exercise of administrative power.

❻ Find an example of how the media or a citizens group in the United States or in your community has brought to light a problem in the bureaucracy.

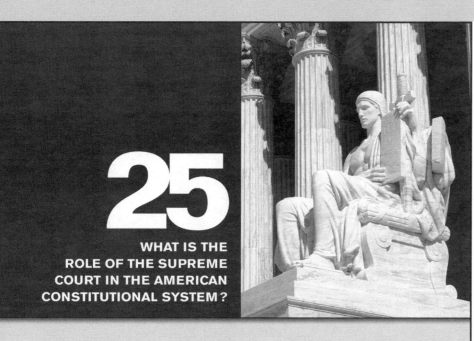

25

WHAT IS THE ROLE OF THE SUPREME COURT IN THE AMERICAN CONSTITUTIONAL SYSTEM?

LESSON PURPOSE

The U.S. Constitution provides for an independent judiciary, a significant departure from the English tradition of formally placing judicial power in the legislative branch. Alexander Hamilton predicted that the Supreme Court would be the "least dangerous branch" because it depends on the other two branches to enforce its decisions. This lesson examines how the U.S. Supreme Court has become a coequal branch of the national government and describes some of the institutional checks on its power.

When you have finished this lesson, you should be able to explain the difference between the Supreme Court's original and appellate jurisdictions. You should be able to explain four methods of constitutional interpretation. You also should be able to explain how America's system of checks and balances limits the power of the Supreme Court. Finally, you should be able to evaluate, take, and defend positions on issues relating to the role of the Supreme Court in the constitutional system.

TERMS AND CONCEPTS TO UNDERSTAND

advisory opinion

appeal

appellate jurisdiction

jurisdiction

landmark decision

litigant

methods of constitutional interpretation

original jurisdiction

writ of certiorari

177

LESSON 25: WHAT IS THE ROLE OF THE SUPREME COURT IN THE AMERICAN CONSTITUTIONAL SYSTEM?

wtpcompanion.civiced.org | **LESSON PURPOSE + TERMS**

Visit the We the People companion website for printable and downloadable Lesson Purposes and Terms and Concepts to Understand sections for each lesson. Audio readings of each Lesson Purpose and Term are also available online in MP3 format.

student page ▼ | **178–179**

WHAT ARE THE CONSTITUTIONAL POWERS OF THE SUPREME COURT?

The U.S. Supreme Court always has assumed that Article III regarding original jurisdiction is "self-executing," which means that it does not require any action by Congress to implement. However, in 1940 Congress adopted 28 U.S.C. Section 1251, establishing original jurisdiction that is exclusive to the Supreme Court and original jurisdiction that exists *concurrently* with lower courts:

❶ The Supreme Court shall have original and exclusive jurisdiction of all controversies between two or more States.

❷ The Supreme Court shall have original but not exclusive jurisdiction of:

* All actions or proceedings to which ambassadors, other public ministers, consuls, or vice consuls of foreign states are parties;

* All controversies between the United States and a State;

* All actions or proceedings by a State against the citizens of another State or against aliens.

As a result the only cases that the Court hears under its original jurisdiction are disputes between two or more states, usually regarding boundaries, water claims, or other property issues. The Court typically is asked to decide only one or two such cases each term. Examples are *Louisiana v. Mississippi* (1995), a boundary dispute, and *Arizona v. California* (2006), concerning tribal water rights to the Colorado River.

In exercising its original jurisdiction the Court usually appoints a Special Master, often a district or circuit court judge, to hear the evidence and make factual findings. The Court then reviews the facts and announces the law.

The Supreme Court has adopted rules to govern matters such as submission of *amicus curiae* briefs (Rule 21). Supreme Court Rule 10 states, "Review on a writ of certiorari is not a matter of right, but of judicial discretion. A petition for a writ of certiorari will be granted only for 'compelling reasons.'" One of those reasons is a conflict among the federal circuits concerning the meaning of a congressional statute or a provision of the Constitution. (Appendix D 5 is a map showing the geographical jurisdiction of twelve of the United States Courts of Appeal, or circuit courts.) The additional circuit court is the United States Court of Appeals for the Federal Circuit, which is a specialized court with national jurisdiction, thus ensuring a uniform interpretation of the law in areas including patents, international trade, and veterans' claims.

wtpcompanion.civiced.org   PRIMARY SOURCES

Visit the We the People companion website for a link to Appendix D 5, a map showing the geographical jurisdiction of twelve of the United States Courts of Appeal, or circuit courts.

student page ▼ 180–181

WHAT METHODS ARE USED TO INTERPRET THE CONSTITUTION?

The Supreme Court is both the guardian and interpreter of the Constitution. In *Democracy in America* Alexis de Tocqueville wrote the following:

> When we have examined in detail the organization of the Supreme Court and the entire prerogatives which it exercises, we shall readily admit that a more imposing judicial power was never constituted by any people. The Supreme Court is placed higher than any other known tribunal, both by the nature of its rights and the class of justiciable parties which it controls.

It is not surprising that methods of constitutional interpretation are highly contested. In 2005 Justice Antonin Scalia captured the controversy in a speech to scholars at the Wilson Center. Describing himself as an "originalist" who believes judges should "give the text the meaning it had when it was adopted," he said,

> If you think the Constitution is some exhortation to give effect to the most fundamental values of the society as those values change from year to year;…if you think it is simply meant to reflect the evolving standards of decency that mark the progress of a maturing society— if that is what you think it is, then why in the world would you have it interpreted by nine lawyers?

What arguments can you make for and against the Supreme Court's power of judicial review?

WHAT ARE THE CONSTITUTIONAL POWERS OF THE SUPREME COURT?

Article III of the Constitution created the Supreme Court and gives Congress power to create other courts that are inferior to, or below, the Supreme Court. The Constitution gives all judges whose authority comes from Article III, called federal judges, life tenure. It gives courts created under the authority of Article III, called federal courts, **jurisdiction**, or power to decide only certain cases. These are cases arising under national laws and involving citizens from more than one state. Finally, the article guarantees trial by jury in all criminal cases except impeachment. As explained in Unit Three, the Supreme Court also exercises the power of judicial review, deciding whether acts of Congress, the executive, state laws, and even state constitutions violate the U.S. Constitution.

The Constitution gives the Supreme Court jurisdiction to decide two categories of cases: original and appellate.

- ***Original jurisdiction*** refers to the power of a court to pass judgment on both the facts of a case and the law. The Supreme Court has original jurisdiction in "Cases affecting Ambassadors, other public Ministers and Consuls,... [and]...Controversies to which the United States shall be a Party." When the Supreme Court hears a case in its original jurisdiction, it is the only court to hear the case. The Court hears very few cases under its original jurisdiction. Those cases typically involve foreign diplomats or disputes between states over land, boundaries, or water and mineral

rights. The U.S. Supreme Court has held that Congress cannot add to or subtract from the Court's original jurisdiction.

- ***Appellate jurisdiction*** refers to the power of a superior, or higher, court to review and revise the decision of an inferior, or lower, court. To **appeal** means to ask for a new hearing from a higher court in the hope that it will overturn or modify a lower court's decision. The Supreme Court has appellate jurisdiction in all cases not in its original jurisdiction "with such Exceptions and under such Regulations as the Congress shall make." Beginning with the Judiciary Act of 1789 Congress created a three-tiered system of national courts. Today there are trial courts in each state, known as federal district courts, and thirteen courts of appeal, known as federal circuit courts. Congress frequently debates whether to limit the Supreme Court's appellate jurisdiction in areas such as school prayer and the rights of criminal defendants. Historically, however, Congress has made relatively few exceptions to the Supreme Court's appellate jurisdiction.

A **litigant**—a party involved in a lawsuit—who loses in a lower federal court or the highest court of a state can ask the Supreme Court to review the case. The party does so by filing a document called a petition, or request, for a **writ of certiorari**. The Court is not required to issue a writ. The Court's rules currently state that the justices are more likely to allow review if there is disagreement among the federal courts of appeal on a legal matter. If four Supreme Court justices vote to allow review of a case, then the Court issues the writ, which commands the lower court to send the record of the case to the Supreme Court. The Court traditionally does not explain its rationale for accepting or rejecting cases for review.

Each year the Supreme Court receives thousands of petitions asking it to issue a writ of certiorari. The justices accept only a small fraction. The number of cases that the Court decides has steadily decreased in recent years. For example, in 1980 the Court decided 232 cases. In 1995 the number was 95, and in 2006 it was 72. Most of the cases that the Court decides require it to interpret only the meaning of statutes or administrative rules, not their constitutionality.

CRITICAL THINKING EXERCISE
Examining Landmark Supreme Court Decisions

Some Supreme Court decisions have such profound effects on the meaning of separation of powers, checks and balances, individual rights, and federalism that they become known as **landmark decisions**. Like landmark legislation, described in Lesson 22, these decisions have far-reaching effects on how American constitutional government functions. Work in one of six groups, with each group taking a different case from the list below. Each group should study the case and then prepare a brief following the format for briefing Supreme Court decisions in the Reference section. Each group should then present its brief to the other members of the class.

- *McCulloch v. Maryland* (1819)
- *Gibbons v. Ogden* (1824)
- *Gideon v. Wainwright* (1963)
- *Reynolds v. Sims* (1964)
- *Nixon v. United States* (1974)
- *United States v. Lopez* (1995)

❶ What are the implications of the case for the way American constitutional government should function?

❷ How did the Court's decision in this case clarify the meaning of the Constitution?

❸ What additional constitutional challenges might arise in response to this decision?

❹ Should the decision in this case be considered a landmark decision? Why or why not?

What is the relationship between the right to appeal and the protection of individual rights?

179

Justice Hugo Black agreed:

> I realize that many good and able men have eloquently spoken and written, sometimes in rhapsodical strains, about the duty of this Court to keep the Constitution in tune with the times. The idea is that the Constitution must be changed from time to time and that this Court is charged with a duty to make those changes. For myself, I must with all deference reject that philosophy. The Constitution makers knew the need for change and provided for it. Amendments suggested by the people's elected representatives can be submitted to the people or their selected agents for ratification. That method of change was good for our Fathers, and being somewhat old-fashioned I must add it is good enough for me. (Dissenting opinion, *Griswold v. Connecticut*, 1965)

Justice Stephen Breyer, speaking at Princeton University in 2006, characterized Justice Scalia's approach as "wooden" and apparently also disagreed with the late Justice Black:

> Wooden means looking at phrases in the statute or the Constitution as if they set up a matrix and you could deduce the answer from some kind of logical determination based on language and history alone....

> I think we'll do a better job of taking into major account the purpose and consequences so that the Constitution, which was written in 1789, can work today to impose the values which are enduring upon facts which change every minute. In other words, it works in today's world.

student page ▼ 181–182

WHAT CHECKS EXIST ON THE SUPREME COURT?

The Virginia Plan introduced at the Philadelphia Convention would have involved the judiciary in the law-making process by having some number of judges, along with the president, constitute a "council of revision" to decide the validity of laws before they went into effect. That proposal was rejected. The delegates also rejected the suggestion that the chief justice be an advisor to the president and that the executive or legislative branches be able to request advisory opinions from the Supreme Court. These votes are evidence that the majority of Framers wanted to limit the role of judges to that of resolving issues raised in lawsuits.

In order to decide a case a court must have jurisdiction, or authority. Federal courts are courts of limited jurisdiction. Litigants must plead and prove their right to have their lawsuit tried in federal court, citing either the constitutional or statutory basis for jurisdiction. State courts, by contrast, are courts of general jurisdiction; parties are presumed to have the right to have their lawsuits resolved in state court. The limited jurisdiction of federal courts is one constraint on the Supreme Court's power.

The term *justiciable* refers to the propriety of examining a dispute in a particular forum. Justiciability rules are another limit on the Supreme Court's power. Five rules of justiciability are particularly important:

- **NO ADVISORY OPINIONS** In 1793 President Washington asked Thomas Jefferson, his secretary of state, to write a letter to Chief Justice John Jay asking the Supreme Court to advise the president on twenty-nine questions of international law and neutrality. Jay declined, establishing the rule that courts will not give opinions except in actual cases or controversies between parties.

- **NO "POLITICAL QUESTIONS"** If a court believes that a case raises issues that are more appropriate for the legislative or executive branches, it will declare the case "nonjusticiable." In *Gilligan v. Morgan* (1973), for example, the Court held that questions involving the training and discipline of National Guard troops are nonjusticiable, reasoning that Congress and the executive are responsible for organizing, arming, and disciplining the military.

- **PARTIES MUST HAVE STANDING TO SUE** To be involved in a lawsuit the parties must have adverse legal interests and one party must claim to have been "injured." With rare exceptions third parties cannot assert the rights of others. In *Sierra Club v. Morton* (1972) the Supreme Court dismissed a challenge by the Sierra Club, an environmental interest group claiming to have a "special interest in the conservation and sound maintenance of the national parks, game refuges, and forests of the country," against a skiing development in the Mineral King Valley in California. The Court held that the Sierra Club lacked standing to sue because it could not show that it had suffered or would suffer injury.

- **CASES MUST BE "RIPE" FOR ADJUDICATION** The Court will not decide a case if it believes it would be premature to do so or if there are other avenues for resolving the dispute, such as an administrative proceeding. Generally the Court will not decide cases that have become "moot," which occurs if a party drops out of the lawsuit for some reason or the parties settle the case or no longer have a controversy. An example of "mootness" is *DeFunis v. Odegard* (1974). In 1971 Marco DeFunis challenged the University of Washington's

WHAT METHODS ARE USED TO INTERPRET THE CONSTITUTION?

Since its inception the Supreme Court has issued written opinions explaining its decisions. Initially each justice wrote an opinion in each case. Chief Justice John Marshall changed that practice, and since his era the Court has issued only majority, concurring, and dissenting opinions. Written opinions serve several functions. An important one is that they hold the Court accountable to the people by making a public record of the decision and its rationale. Written opinions also establish a record that can serve as precedent for future cases. (See the Reference section for suggestions about how to read and brief a Supreme Court opinion.)

Some parts of the Constitution are very specific. For example, Article I states, "The Senate of the United States shall be composed of two Senators from each State." Many provisions are not as clear as this one and so require interpretation. Examples include the following:

- "The Congress shall have Power...To make all Laws which shall be necessary and proper for carrying into Execution the foregoing Powers, and all other Powers vested by this Constitution in the Government of the United States, or in any Department or Officer thereof." (Article I, Section 8)

- "The United States shall guarantee to every State in this Union a Republican Form of Government." (Article IV, Section 4)

- "No State shall...deprive any person of life, liberty, or property, without due process of law." (Amendment XIV)

The following are four common **methods of constitutional interpretation**. All interpretation, regardless of method, begins with the words of the Constitution.

- **Textualism, literalism, or strict construction** This method involves looking at the meaning of words in the Constitution and giving each word, phrase, or clause its ordinary meaning. Advocates of this method argue that interpreting the Constitution according to its plain meaning keeps the Supreme Court neutral and helps justices avoid imposing their values on the Constitution. Relying on the plain meaning of words also makes the law certain and predictable.

- **Original intent or original history** This method is related to the method described above, but it addresses the question of how to interpret words, phrases, or clauses that are not clear. Advocates of this method seek to understand what the Founders meant

What rights and responsibilities do citizens have regarding the interpretation of the Constitution?

180

when they wrote the words. They argue that the Founders debated and chose the words of the Constitution carefully, with the goal of producing an enduring constitutional framework. Seeking and applying the original intent of the Founders helps to maintain stability and neutrality in the law.

- **Fundamental principles**
This method looks to principles—such as natural rights, republican government, or limited government—to interpret the meaning of words, phrases, and clauses that may not be clear. Advocates of this method argue that identifying the fundamental principles embodied in the Constitution is a useful way to determine the meaning of words, phrases, or clauses that may not be clear.

- **Modernism or instrumentalism**
This method starts from the premise that the Constitution should be interpreted and interpretation should adapt to changing circumstances and contemporary needs. Otherwise, advocates of this method argue, the Constitution will have to be amended frequently or new constitutional conventions will need to be held. Advocates of this method further argue that justices should not hold back social progress by adhering to outmoded understandings of the Constitution.

What means might be used to determine the original intent of the Framers of the Constitution?

WHAT DO YOU THINK?

❶ What are the advantages and the disadvantages of each method of interpreting the Constitution?

❷ Which method or methods do you prefer? Why?

WHAT CHECKS EXIST ON THE POWER OF THE SUPREME COURT?

The Supreme Court exercises immense power when it interprets the Constitution. However, there are many checks on the exercise of judicial power, including limitations that the Supreme Court has imposed on itself. The following are checks on the Court's power:

- **Self-imposed limits** The Court avoids partisan politics by refusing to decide "political questions," or questions that it believes should properly be decided by other branches or levels of government. The Court decides only cases in controversy. The Supreme

Court does not issue an **advisory opinion**. That is, the Court will not offer an opinion about how a law should be interpreted unless there is a specific case before the Court in which the interpretation of that law is actually in dispute. The Court will decide cases by interpreting statutes if possible, thereby avoiding interpreting the Constitution. Written opinions also constrain future Courts.

- **Presidential appointments** Presidents seek to influence future Supreme Court decisions with their nominees to the Court. By changing Court personnel, presidents seek to change approaches to constitutional interpretation and attitudes about the role of the Court in the constitutional system.

- **Executive enforcement** Presidents and administrative agencies are responsible for enforcing the Court's decisions. Occasionally presidents have threatened to refuse to enforce Supreme Court decisions or have enforced them only reluctantly. For example, in 1974 Americans anxiously waited to see if Richard Nixon would comply with the Supreme Court's order in *United States v. Nixon*. The Court had ordered the president to turn over White House tape recordings to prosecutors. Once revealed, the tapes implicated Nixon and his aides in the Watergate scandal.

affirmative action plan as reverse discrimination. By the time the case reached the Supreme Court DeFunis had been admitted to the law school. The Court dismissed his case, reasoning that he was no longer an injured party.

- **AVOIDING CONSTITUTIONAL DECISIONS** If a case can be resolved by interpreting a statute or a rule rather than interpreting the Constitution, then the justices will do so. In 1965, for example, in *United Mine Workers v. Pennington* the Supreme Court was asked to resolve a matter involving restraint of trade under the First Amendment. The Court concluded that the controversy could be resolved under the Sherman Anti-Trust Act and refused to address the constitutional question.

EXAMPLES OF OTHER CHECKS ON THE SUPREME COURT In *Kelo v. City of New London* (2005) the Supreme Court upheld the power of a city to use its power of eminent domain—permitting government to take private property for public use if it provides "just compensation"—under the Fifth Amendment to take private property and then sell it to private developers. Within a few days the House of Representatives passed a bill denying federal funds to any city or state project that uses eminent domain to force people to sell their property to make way for a profit-making enterprise. The Senate considered less sweeping legislation. (See Lesson 37 for state responses to *Kelo*.)

In his confirmation hearing before the Senate future chief justice John Roberts said that the public reaction to *Kelo* shows that Congress and state legislatures "are protectors of the people's rights as well" and "can protect them in situations where the Court has determined, as it did...in *Kelo*, that they are not going to draw [the] line."

The number of justices is another check. In 1801 Congress reduced the size of the Supreme Court from six to five to make it more difficult for President Jefferson to nominate new justices. In 1863—in the midst of the Civil War—Congress increased the size of the Court to ten, giving President Lincoln an additional appointment at a critical time. In 1866, when the war was over, Congress reduced the size of the Court to seven, thereby depriving President Andrew Jackson of an opportunity to appoint justices who might disagree with Congress's Reconstruction plans. In 1869, the year Ulysses S. Grant became president, Congress increased the size of the Court to nine justices, as it has remained.

Congress likewise determines the appellate jurisdiction of the Supreme Court and the time and place of sessions of the Court. In 1801 it changed the terms so that for fourteen months the Court could not convene.

As explained in Lesson 15 three constitutional amendments—Eleven, Fourteen, and Sixteen—have overturned Supreme Court decisions.

ENRICHMENT ACTIVITY

SHOULD THE SUPREME COURT SPEAK WITH ONE VOICE?

In some cases the Supreme Court issues unanimous opinions. In other cases the justices express their individual views through concurring opinions—stating agreement with the result in the case but not the reasoning of other justices or the rule of law announced in the case—or dissenting opinions—stating disagreement both with the result in the case, the rule of law announced, and usually with its reasoning. Recently the Supreme Court has issued several plurality opinions: those in which there is not a majority of justices in agreement on the rule of law or the reasons supporting it.

Divide the class into four groups and distribute the following reading assignments:

- **GROUP 1** *Brown v. Board of Education of Topeka, Kansas* (1954) (unanimous opinion)

- **GROUP 2** *Gideon v. Wainwright* (1963) (two concurring opinions)

- **GROUP 3** *Kyllo v. U.S.* (2001) (5–4 split)

- **GROUP 4** *Rapanos v. U.S.* (2006) (4–1–4 split)

| **wtpcompanion.civiced.org** | **COURT CASES** |

Visit the We the People companion website for a link to Supreme Court syllabi and opinions for each of the cases described above.

After reading the decision, the groups should respond to the following questions:

❶ What are the advantages and disadvantages of a Supreme Court opinion containing the kind of voting block reflected in the case you read?

❷ Do you think the Supreme Court better serves the country when it speaks with one voice or expresses the divergent views of its individual members? Explain.

❸ Under what circumstances, if any, do you think a justice should compromise his or her views in order for the court to issue a unanimous opinion? Why?

- **Congressional powers** Congress determines the Supreme Court's appellate jurisdiction and controls its budget. Congress has threatened to use those powers in response to Supreme Court decisions with which it disagrees. If the Supreme Court declares a congressional statute unconstitutional, Congress may pass the statute in another form to demonstrate its resolve on the issue. Congress also can alter the size of the Court, as it has done several times over the years. It can even determine when the Court meets or suspend a term of the Court, as it did in 1802. Finally, Congress can initiate constitutional amendments in response to unpopular Court decisions, such as a decision in 1895 that struck down an income tax statute. The Sixteenth Amendment, ratified in 1913, subsequently gave Congress the power to lay and collect taxes on income.

- **Federalism** States, like the executive branch, are responsible for implementing Supreme Court decisions. Sometimes state enforcement is lax. For example, fifty years after the Supreme Court ordered public school desegregation, several states still have found ways to evade that ruling.

REVIEWING AND USING THE LESSON

❶ Explain the difference between original and appellate jurisdiction. What is the role of Congress in determining the Supreme Court's appellate jurisdiction?

❷ Identify four approaches to interpreting the Constitution. Which approach do you think is best? Why?

❸ What criteria do you think should be used to determine whether a Supreme Court decision is a landmark decision?

❹ Describe checks on the power of the Supreme Court and provide an example of each.

What can Congress do to pass a law after it has been declared unconstitutional by the Supreme Court?

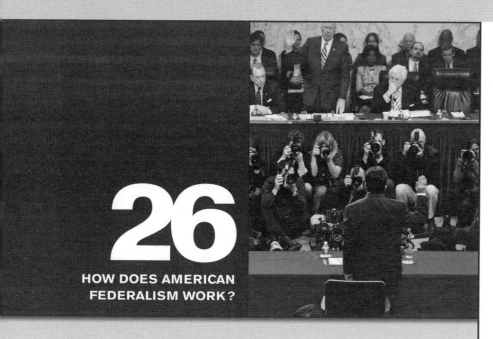

26

HOW DOES AMERICAN FEDERALISM WORK?

HOW DOES AMERICAN FEDERALISM WORK?

wtpcompanion.civiced.org **LESSON PURPOSE + TERMS**

Visit the We the People companion website for printable and downloadable Lesson Purposes and Terms and Concepts to Understand sections for each lesson. Audio readings of each Lesson Purpose and Term are also available online in MP3 format.

LESSON PURPOSE

The American constitutional system is made up of two levels of government: national and state. The system is called federalism. The powers of and the boundaries between the national and state governments never have been clear. Sometimes the national and state governments seem to work in harmony. Sometimes they seem locked in a struggle for power. This lesson examines constitutional provisions affecting the states in their relationship to the national government. It explains how state governments are organized, including their creation of units of local government. Finally, it describes the role of states as "laboratories of democracy."

When you have finished this lesson, you should be able to explain how American federalism involves divided sovereignty and an ongoing effort to balance power between the national and state governments. You also should be able to explain the function of three basic kinds of local governmental units—counties, municipalities, and special districts. You should be able to give examples of governmental innovations at the state and local levels. Finally, you should be able to evaluate, take, and defend positions on continuing issues related to America's unique system of federalism.

TERMS AND CONCEPTS TO UNDERSTAND

initiative

local governments

police powers

recall

referendum

reserved powers

student page ▼ 184

WHAT IS THE CONSTITUTIONAL STATUS OF STATE GOVERNMENTS?

Political scientist Charles Stewart III observes,

> The Constitution that was crafted in Philadelphia...created an integrated system of government that was predicated on balancing power horizontally and vertically. The vertical balance was between a national government, with newly enhanced capacities, and state governments, which had operated under considerable latitude ever since independence. We now call this balance federalism. The horizontal balance was between the various components of the new national government itself, which had hitherto been organized around a unitary structure. We now call this *separation of powers*.

American federalism has been described as an ongoing negotiation about the vertical balance between the states and the national government.

The police powers of states have never been precisely defined and probably never will be. They encompass the inherent powers of states as America's basic units of government to control people and property for the common good, limited only by express provisions in state constitutions or the U.S. Constitution. The term *police* derives from the Greek *polis*, meaning "small, self-contained political community," a term associated with classical republicanism (see Lessons 1 and 2 on classical republicanism; Lesson 26 on federalism). The term is often misunderstood today, because law enforcement agencies have used the word *police* to describe their activities since the early nineteenth century.

States and local governments exercise their police powers by enacting laws that regulate private interests for the protection of the public safety, health, welfare, and morals. Police powers include the power to prevent fraud and oppression and to promote the public convenience and prosperity. In practice police powers include maintaining the peace, licensing some trades and professions, regulating work hours and conditions, enacting health regulations (including quarantines) and compulsory vaccinations, and setting minimum wages.

The national government has no police powers as such, because its authority comes from the Constitution. However, provisions of the Constitution, such as the power to regulate interstate commerce in Article I, Section 8, have been interpreted so broadly that the national government has assumed powers akin to the police power of the states, particularly since the Supreme Court abandoned substantive economic due process (see Lesson 18).

WHAT IS THE CONSTITUTIONAL STATUS OF STATE GOVERNMENTS?

As explained in Lesson 7, states were the only units of government in the United States after the Revolution. They had complete governing authority over the people within their boundaries. Under the Articles of Confederation states retained their "sovereignty, freedom, and independence" and all powers not "expressly delegated" to the United States.

The Constitution created a new national government, but it left, or "reserved," many governmental powers to the states. James Madison argued in Federalist 45 that the powers of the states would "extend to all the objects which, in the ordinary course of affairs, concern the lives, liberties, and properties of the people, and the internal order, improvement, and prosperity of the State."

States play an important role in the structure and operation of the national government. Article VII, for example, required the votes of "nine States" to ratify "this Constitution between the States." Article I provides that the House of Representatives will be elected by voters who have the same qualifications as are required to vote for the "most numerous Branch of the State Legislature," usually called a "house" or "assembly." States are represented equally in the U.S. Senate. States also have a role in the Electoral College.

The Constitution suggests, but does not plainly identify, many governing powers left to the states. Article I, Section 9, lists eight powers that the states do *not* have. For example, no state can place taxes or duties on articles exported from that state, and states cannot grant titles of nobility. The list of what states cannot do implies that the states can do what is not prohibited. Article I describes the powers of Congress as those "herein granted," again suggesting that governing powers not granted to Congress remain with the states. Moreover, the Tenth Amendment, added to the Constitution in 1791, states, "The powers not delegated to the United States by the Constitution, nor prohibited by it to the States, are reserved to the States respectively, or to the people."

The **reserved powers** referred to in the Tenth Amendment often are called **police powers**, a term that refers to the inherent power of a government to enact legislation protecting the health, safety, welfare, and morals of those within its jurisdiction. Examples of police powers are laws creating and operating public schools, making and executing criminal and civil laws, and making and enforcing land use regulations, or "zoning."

Although the states retain considerable governing powers, the Constitution, the laws made under it, and treaties made under the authority of the United States are the "supreme Law of the Land." Since the beginning there has been tension between the Constitution's supremacy clause and the powers of the states. Some constitutional scholars believe that ambiguities about which level of government has the power over matters of domestic politics are part of the genius of the American constitutional system. These ambiguities mean that both levels of government always must strive to win the confidence and support of the American people.

WHAT DO YOU THINK?

❶ Read the supremacy clause in Article VI, Section 2, and the Tenth Amendment to the Constitution. How do these two provisions help to explain why the national and state governments seem to be locked in a perpetual struggle for power?

❷ How would you explain American federalism to a non-American?

HOW ARE STATE GOVERNMENTS ORGANIZED?

All fifty states have constitutions. The following are some common features of the state constitutions:

● **Bill of rights** All the state constitutions have bills of rights, and in most states they appear at the beginning of the constitution. The preamble of most state constitutions declares that the purpose of government is to protect those rights. State bills of rights include many of the same rights as in the U.S. Constitution, such as rights to freedom of speech, press,

Why did the Framers provide that some powers of the government should be reserved to the states?

and assembly and the right to a jury trial. Some state constitutions contain other rights, such as the right to work or the right to an education.

- **Three branches of government**
  All state constitutions create legislative, executive, and judicial branches:

  - **Legislative** The lawmaking branch usually is called the legislature, but some states use the term *assembly*. Most legislatures meet annually; some meet only biennially—that is, every other year. Most legislatures are bicameral, or two-house, although Nebraska has a unicameral, or one-house, legislature. The Supreme Court has ruled that the legislative districts for both houses of state legislatures must be based on population. Unlike the U.S. Senate, therefore, the upper house of the state legislatures must reflect population, not geography. State legislatures enact laws on subjects ranging from speed limits and crimes to health care, education, land use, environmental protection, and licensing of professionals, including teachers, doctors, lawyers, beauticians, and morticians.

  - **Executive** The chief executive officer of each state is the governor. Most governors serve two- or four-year terms and may be reelected for at least one additional term. Most states also have a lieutenant governor, whose role is much like the vice president of the United States. State administrative agencies collectively employ far more people than the national administrative bureaucracy. In 2003, for example, almost three million people worked for the U.S. government, while more than fifteen million people worked for state and **local governments** (see the explanation on page 186).

  - **Judicial** The judicial systems of each state consist of trial and appellate courts. Many states elect judges, although some states use an appointment process. Some courts are local and specialized, such as justice-of-the-peace and municipal courts, with jurisdiction over matters such as traffic offenses. States also have a full range of trial and appellate courts. The state court of last resort, usually called the state supreme court or the court of appeal, has the final say about the meaning of the state constitution.

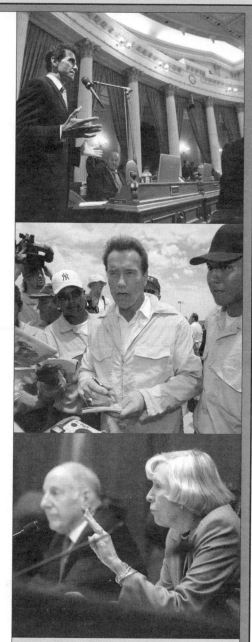

What arguments can you make to support certain powers being given to state governments instead of the federal government?

185

HOW ARE STATE GOVERNMENTS ORGANIZED?

wtpcompanion.civiced.org | **PRIMARY SOURCES**

Visit the We the People companion website for links to state constitutions.

The following are examples of rights in state constitutions that differ from the U.S. Constitution:

NEW JERSEY, ARTICLE I, SECTION 3

No person shall be deprived of the inestimable privilege of worshipping Almighty God in a manner agreeable to the dictates of his own conscience; nor under any pretense whatever be compelled to attend any place of worship contrary to his faith and judgment; nor shall any person be obliged to pay tithes, taxes, or other rates for building or repairing any church or churches, place or places of worship, or for the maintenance of any minister or ministry, contrary to what he believes to be right or has deliberately and voluntarily engaged to perform.

NEW HAMPSHIRE, ARTICLE 13

No person, who is conscientiously scrupulous about the lawfulness of bearing arms, shall be compelled thereto.

MASSACHUSETTS, ARTICLE VI

No man, nor corporation, or association of men, have any other title to obtain advantages, or particular and exclusive privileges, distinct from those of the community, than what arises from the consideration of services rendered to the public; and this title being in nature neither hereditary, nor transmissible to children, or descendants, or relations by blood, the idea of a man born a magistrate, lawgiver, or judge, is absurd and unnatural.

LIEUTENANT GOVERNORS The term *lieutenant governor* traces to the practice during colonial times of Great Britain requiring a lieutenant governor to live in each of the thirteen colonies. Royal governors, by contrast, could rule from Great Britain.

In 2008 forty-two states had lieutenant governors as constitutional officers. West Virginia provided for a lieutenant governor by statute. Arizona, Maine, New Hampshire, Tennessee, Oregon, Wyoming, and New Jersey did not have lieutenant governors. However, New Jersey voters approved creation of the office beginning in 2009. Twenty-five lieutenant governors were elected to office with the governor—so they are of the same political party—whereas eighteen were elected separately.

For many years lieutenant governors were considered the "fifth wheels" of American politics. Today they are playing a more important role as the only state leaders with both executive and legislative powers in many states. In twenty-three states the lieutenant governor is the acting governor when the governor is out of the state or otherwise unable to serve. Many preside over their state senates, and more than half are allowed to cast tie-breaking votes. In 2005 the North Carolina lieutenant governor cast the tie-breaking vote to create a state lottery. In some states, including Hawaii and Utah, the lieutenant governor exercises the same powers as a secretary of state.

student page ▼ 186

LOCAL GOVERNMENTS Americans inherited from England a tradition of local self-government on many matters even though local governments legally are creatures of the state. However, in the nineteenth century state legislatures in many states dominated by rural interests neglected the needs of rapidly growing cities. Political corruption in major cities became rampant, with officials providing services based on patronage. An example was the Tammany Hall "machine" in New York City controlled by the Democratic Party. The rule of William "Boss" Tweed in the 1870s was particularly notorious.

In *City of Clinton v. Cedar Rapids and Missouri RR Co.* (1868) Iowa judge John Dillon adopted a view of local government that has come to be known as "Dillon's Rule." It holds that local governments are merely political subdivisions of the state, which exist only to carry out administrative duties delegated by the states. In *Hunter v. Pittsburgh* (1907) the Supreme Court adopted Dillon's view, upholding the power of the state of Pennsylvania to consolidate two cities against the wishes of a majority of the residents.

The counter to this view is seen in the "home rule" movement, one of the reforms of the Progressive Era, under which local governments draft and adopt their own charters. Advocates of home rule believed that local control of local matters made governments more responsive to citizens. Opponents argued that few issues are truly local in nature and that most matters should be resolved by states.

By the year 2000 all states except Alabama, Hawaii, Nevada, and New Hampshire had provided some form of home rule for municipalities, and thirty-seven had authorized home-rule charters for counties.

wtpcompanion.civiced.org   COURT CASES

Visit the We the People companion website for links to Supreme Court syllabi and opinions for each of the cases described in the student and teacher's editions. Summaries are provided for selected Supreme Court cases.

What is the relationship between state and local governments?

186

- **Creation of local governments**
State constitutions give legislatures power to create local governments, which receive charters, or grants of authority, to carry out a wide range of governmental responsibilities. The laws that local governments enact usually are called ordinances. Most local government officials are elected. There are three broad categories of local governments, although there is considerable diversity among the states:

- **Counties** (called parishes in Louisiana and boroughs in Alaska) Counties usually occupy large geographic areas within states. Their functions include recordkeeping, such as births, deaths, and land transfers; administration of elections, including voter registration; construction and maintenance of roads; collection of state and local taxes; and maintenance of courts, courthouses, and jails. In 2004 there were 3,034 counties in the United States.

- **Municipalities** (cities and townships) Cities and townships usually serve urban areas, ranging from small towns of only a few hundred people to cities of many millions. They provide services such as police and fire protection, water and sewer systems, zoning and building-code enforcement, hospitals, libraries, streets, and parks. According to the 2002 Census of Governments, there were 35,933 municipalities in the United States.

- **Special districts** Special districts operate independently of other local governments and usually are created to provide only one or a few services within a specific geographic area. Special districts usually operate schools or provide water and natural resource conservation; fire protection, usually in rural areas; libraries; transportation; cemeteries; and emergency services. Most special district officials are elected. In 2004 there were 13,506 school districts in the United States and 35,052 other special districts.

WHAT DO YOU THINK?

❶ Read the preamble to your state's constitution. How does it compare with the Preamble to the U.S. Constitution?

❷ Read the bill of rights in your state's constitution. How does it compare with the national Bill of Rights?

❸ How does the way in which your state's government is organized contribute to achieving the goals set forth in the preamble to your state's constitution?

HOW HAVE STATE CONSTITUTIONS CHANGED?

Since the first state constitutions were adopted in 1776, state constitutional conventions have resulted in new constitutions being adopted some 144 times. Louisiana, for example, has had eleven constitutions. Most other states have had two or three. Only eighteen of the fifty states still use their original constitutions.

State constitutions also have been amended thousands of times. Nearly every state election ballot contains proposals for constitutional amendments, either referred by the state legislature or placed on the ballot through the **initiative** process, which is explained later in this lesson. Some state legislatures, such as that of Massachusetts, regularly hold legislative sessions called constitutional conventions to consider whether to submit constitutional amendments to voters.

State constitutional amendments often reflect state responses to policy debates occurring throughout the United States. For example, beginning in the late twentieth century Americans have debated whether same-sex couples should be allowed to marry. Several states have adopted constitutional amendments banning marriage between same-sex couples, whereas others have adopted provisions or statutes granting same-sex couples a wide range of rights short of marriage.

Frequent amendments have made state constitutions much longer than the U.S. Constitution. The average length of a state constitution is 26,000 words, compared to about 8,700 words in the U.S. Constitution.

WHAT DO YOU THINK?

What are the advantages and disadvantages of a constitution being a concise document stating fundamental principles, such as the U.S. Constitution, compared to a document that spells out in greater detail the powers and limits of government, such as many state constitutions?

CRITICAL THINKING EXERCISE
Preparing a "Biography" of Your State's Constitution

❶ Describe the historical circumstances under which your state's constitution was written, who wrote it, and how it was ratified.

❷ How does your state constitution reflect principles of classical republicanism and natural rights philosophy? Provide examples.

❸ Has your state had more than one constitution? Why or why not?

❹ How many times has your state's constitution been amended? How have those amendments been made? Have any of those amendments made fundamental changes to your state's government? If so, in what ways?

❺ How does the bill of rights in your state's constitution compare with the national Bill of Rights? Are there rights in your state constitution that do not appear in the Bill of Rights or vice versa? What are they?

❻ How is your state's constitution similar to and different from the U.S. Constitution with respect to separation of powers and checks and balances?

HOW DOES AMERICAN FEDERALISM WORK IN PRACTICE?

Since the adoption of the Constitution Americans have debated whether the national government, state governments, or both have governing authority over certain matters. Regulation of commerce and grant-in-aid programs demonstrate the kinds of issues that are common in America's system of shared governmental authority.

● **Regulation of commerce** The Constitution (Article I, Section 8) gives Congress the power to regulate interstate commerce. However, the states retain the power to regulate commerce within their own borders as part of their police powers. The two powers often come into conflict. In an early example the state of New York passed a law requiring ship captains to post bonds to pay for the care of impoverished passengers who came into the Port of New York. The purpose was to prevent an influx of foreigners who might become paupers, exhaust the state's resources, and cause crime and vagrancy. From one perspective the law was an exercise of New York's police power. From another perspective it infringed on Congress's power to regulate interstate commerce.

Occasionally the Supreme Court has limited Congress's regulatory powers over commerce out of deference to the states. In contrast in 2005 the Court reasserted Congress's power to regulate even purely local activities if those

187

LESSON 26

student page ▼ 187

HOW HAVE STATE CONSTITUTIONS CHANGED?

Alabama has the longest state constitution at more than 172,000 words. It also has been amended the most times: more than 770 as of 2005. The shortest state constitution is Vermont's at 8,295 words. The oldest state constitution still in effect is that of Massachusetts, from 1780; the newest is the Georgia constitution, ratified in 1983.

wtpcompanion.civiced.org | **PRIMARY SOURCES**

Visit the We the People companion website for links to state constitutions.

As of the beginning of 2008 the state of Massachusetts had legalized same-sex marriage, and the California Supreme Court had held that prohibiting same-sex marriages violated the guarantee of equal protection in the California constitution (*In re Marriage* Cases, S 147999, 2008). Same-sex domestic partnerships or civil unions were permitted by statute in Connecticut, New Hampshire, New Jersey, Vermont, California, Hawaii, Maine, and Oregon. Hawaii and Vermont had adopted statutes allowing same-sex couples to be reciprocal beneficiaries. Same-sex marriage was prohibited by statute in Arizona, Connecticut, Delaware, Florida, Illinois, Indiana, Iowa, Maryland, Minnesota, New Hampshire, New York, North Carolina, Pennsylvania, Washington, West Virginia, and Wyoming. Twenty-seven states had adopted constitutional provisions prohibiting same-sex marriage.

187

`student page ▼ 187-188`

HOW DOES AMERICAN FEDERALISM WORK IN PRACTICE?

GRANTS IN AID The national government established the precedent of grants in aid to the states in 1790 by assuming the states' Revolutionary War debts. Anti-federalists (see Lesson 13) strongly opposed the program but eventually agreed to the national government assuming state war debts in exchange for moving the national capitol, now known as Washington, D.C., to the Potomac River in the South.

After the Great Depression the next big growth in grants in aid came during the administration of President Lyndon Johnson. His "Great Society" program included massive grants to cities and metropolitan areas and programs to assist the poor and minorities. More grant programs came into existence during the five years of Johnson's administration than any other time in American history.

President Richard Nixon declared the Johnson grant programs a "terrible tangle" and sought to decentralize decision making as well as to improve efficiency. He implemented a new program, revenue sharing, designed to combine the national government's capacity to raise money and the state's discretion over spending. Contrary to Nixon's plan, revenue sharing resulted in a greater direct national impact on state and local governments because federal money always had strings attached.

President Ronald Reagan also pushed for grant reform, primarily to reduce the amount of national government money being spent on state and local programs. There was little effort to reform grants after Reagan until President George W. Bush created the White House Office of Faith-Based and Community Initiatives in 2001. Its purpose was to strengthen the capacity of faith-based and community organizations to provide federally funded social services.

In *South Dakota v. Dole* (1987) the Supreme Court upheld Congress's attempt to regulate the drinking age by tying receipt of national highway funds to adoption of a uniform minimum drinking age of twenty-one. The Court also approved of Congress's use of its spending power—and the threat to withhold funds for failure to comply with its requirements—as an indirect way to promote the general welfare. However, in 1995 in *United States v. Lopez* the Court considerably curtailed Congress's powers to regulate state and local activities by relying on the Commerce Clause of Article I, Section 8, Clause 3. It struck down the Gun-Free School Zones Act of 1990 as exceeding Congress's regulatory powers under the commerce clause.

`wtpcompanion.civiced.org`   **COURT CASES**

Visit the We the People companion website for links to Supreme Court syllabi and opinions for each of the cases described in the student and teacher's editions. Summaries are provided for selected Supreme Court cases.

Should the federal government or state governments have the power to regulate immigration? Why? Illegal immigration? Why?

activities "have a substantial effect on interstate commerce."

The case was *Gonzalez v. Raich*, in which the Court upheld Congress's authority to regulate the interstate market in drugs, even small quantities of marijuana grown and consumed by patients on their physicians' advice under California's Compassionate Use Act of 1996. The ruling did not overturn laws in California and ten other states that permit medical use of marijuana for pain control. But it does mean that anyone who uses marijuana as a medical treatment risks legal action by the U.S. Drug Enforcement Administration or other federal agencies. In a strong dissent Justice Clarence Thomas argued that if the "majority is to be taken seriously, the Federal Government may now regulate quilting bees, clothes drives, and potluck suppers throughout the 50 states."

- **Grant-in-aid programs** In the mid-1800s the national government began giving money grants to states to help them with programs ranging from transportation to welfare. States had to submit plans for the use of the money and often had to match the monies with funds raised through state taxes. For many years grant-in-aid programs permitted the states and the national government to work in relative harmony (known as "cooperative federalism"). The states performed their traditional functions with financial help from the national government.

The Great Depression of the 1930s and 1940s changed federalism profoundly, as people looked to the national government to solve problems such as unemployment and to help in areas such as job services and old-age assistance. Previously people had looked to private charitable organizations or to their state governments. The Social Security Act of 1935, for example, established a number of grant-in-aid programs —but with strings attached. In return for money from the national government, the states had to comply with congressional policies and rules adopted by the national bureaucracy.

Grants-in-aid have grown over the years and so have the conditions attached to them. They have become a device for the national government to influence state policymaking by giving or withholding money. For example, the national government lacks constitutional authority to set state speed limits. However, if a state wants grants for highway construction, then the Federal Highway Administration requires it to comply with a "national" speed limit. States such as Montana have debated whether it is worth losing the power to make decisions about speed limits to receive the grants.

Similar questions have swirled around education grants. The national government has no constitutional authority to set school policy. But for decades the national government has offered grant-in-aid programs designed to improve education from preschool through college. An example is the 2002 No Child Left Behind Act (NCLB). The Department of Education has issued rules about testing and state standards for measuring student proficiency. School districts that do not meet the proficiency targets set by the Department of Education risk losing federal funds, among other penalties. In 2005 the state of Utah risked losing its NCLB funding by subordinating NCLB requirements to state policies. Connecticut and other states filed lawsuits challenging the legality of some elements of NCLB.

HOW ARE THE STATES "LABORATORIES OF DEMOCRACY"?

Supreme Court Justice Louis D. Brandeis observed that one of the principal values of American federalism is that a "single courageous State may, if its citizens choose, serve as a laboratory; and try novel social and economic experiments without risk to the rest of the country." There are many examples of governance experiments in states and localities. Some innovations catch on in other states or in the nation as a whole. For instance, many states, starting with Wyoming, began permitting women to vote at least in local and state elections well before 1900. Those experiments set the stage for adoption of the Nineteenth Amendment in 1920, which guaranteed women the right to vote in all elections. The following are other examples of states as "laboratories of democracy":

- **Initiative, referendum, recall** This trio of methods, begun during the Progressive era of the late nineteenth and early twentieth centuries, allows citizens to participate in direct democracy in their states. Initiative, referendum, and recall describe discrete actions, but they are related by their direct involvement of citizens. South Dakota was the first state to permit the **initiative**. There are two forms of initiative: direct and indirect. In a direct initiative an individual or a group proposes and drafts a law or a state constitutional amendment. Then the initiator gathers a prescribed number of signatures to place the proposal on the ballot for approval or rejection by the voters. In the indirect process

proposals first go to the legislature. If legislators reject the proposal or take no action on it, then the proposal goes on the ballot. Twenty-four states today use the initiative.

The **referendum** involves placing a measure that has been approved by a legislature on the ballot for popular vote. Some state constitutions require the legislature to refer certain kinds of measures to the people. Others permit citizens to demand a vote on a law that has been passed by the legislature by gathering a prescribed number of signatures. Twenty-four states now use the referendum.

Recall is a process of removing elected officials from office. In the eighteen states that permit recall it is used most frequently at the local level. However, in 2003 enough California voters signed petitions to call an election to recall their governor and elect a new one.

- **Environmental protection** Since 1997 some 165 countries have ratified or accepted the Kyoto Accords, an international treaty aimed at reducing the level of carbon dioxide and five other greenhouse gases in the air. President Bill Clinton signed the treaty, but the U.S. Senate did not ratify it. When President George W. Bush took office, he

What might be the advantages and disadvantages of establishing the processes of initiative, referendum, and recall?

189

student page ▾ 189

HOW ARE THE STATES "LABORATORIES OF DEMOCRACY"?

In addition to agreeing to cooperate with one another on energy and environmental initiatives, states also have joined forces to pursue litigation agendas. In September 2005, for example, the states of Pennsylvania, California, Connecticut, Illinois, Iowa, Maine, Massachusetts, New Hampshire, New Jersey, New Mexico, New York, North Carolina, Rhode Island, Vermont, and Wisconsin (and the City of New York) sued, claiming the Department of Energy was violating congressionally enacted standards for reducing air pollution.

withdrew the United States from the Kyoto Accords. In 2006 seven northeastern states entered into the Regional Greenhouse Gas Initiative aimed at achieving most of the emission standards set by the Kyoto Accords. The coalition of states also hoped to put pressure on the national government to commit the United States to the Kyoto Accords.

Also in 2006 California became the first state to impose a cap on the emission of carbon dioxide and other gases. The Global Warming Solutions Act aims to cut California's emissions by twenty-five percent by 2020. Many of the nation's cities, from Seattle to New York, also are adopting measures aimed at reducing air pollution and global warming.

- **Health care** By the mid-1990s soaring health-care costs and increasingly large numbers of people without health insurance

had become a major issue of public concern. Congress had not adopted legislation to address the problem. However, by 2006 several states had adopted programs seeking to offer nearly universal access to health insurance for all their residents, regardless of ability to pay. Several other states were considering programs at that time. A former Oregon governor, John Kitzhaber, initiated the Archimedes Movement in 2006, which aimed at mobilizing people at the grassroots level to find a solution to the health-care problem that eventually would be accepted nationwide.

What responsibility, if any, should state and federal governments have regarding health care?

WHAT DO YOU THINK?

❶ If your state has adopted the initiative process, do you think it has been used to serve the common good or to advance special interests? Explain. If your state has not adopted the initiative process, what arguments can you make for and against doing so?

❷ What arguments might be made for or against adoption of initiative, referendum, and recall at the national level?

REVIEWING AND USING THE LESSON

❶ Why does each state have its own constitution?

❷ What are local governments? Why do state governments create them?

❸ Identify the local governments where you live and the functions they perform.

❹ What are initiative, referendum, and recall? How do they reflect principles of popular sovereignty? How do they undermine the concept of representative government?

❺ Has your state served as a "laboratory of democracy"? If so, how? Is it considering innovations that might serve as models for other states or the national government?

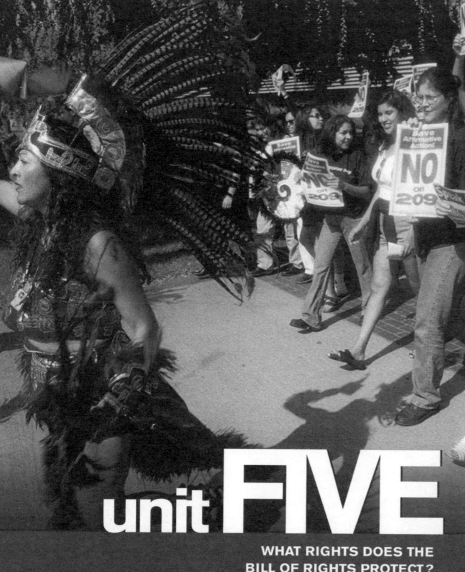

unit FIVE

WHAT RIGHTS DOES THE BILL OF RIGHTS PROTECT?

unit FIVE

UNIT PURPOSE

The Bill of Rights commonly refers to the first ten amendments to the U.S. Constitution. The Bill of Rights contains twenty-seven provisions that protect a variety of rights and freedoms. Originally the Bill of Rights protected individuals only from the misuse or abuse of power by the national government. Through the process of selective incorporation (see Lesson 18) the U.S. Supreme Court has ruled that most of the rights in the Bill of Rights also protect individuals from the misuse or abuse of power by state governments.

A few provisions of the Bill of Rights no longer seem very important. The Third Amendment protection against the involuntary quartering of soldiers in civilian homes in time of peace is one example. Other provisions, such as First Amendment protection of freedom of expression and procedural protections of individuals in the Fourth and Fifth Amendments, have become more important since 1791, when they took effect.

A number of important rights also are included in the body of the Constitution and in constitutional amendments added after the Bill of Rights, as discussed in Lessons 15 and 17. Together, these rights sometimes have been called the "extended Bill of Rights."

After studying this unit, you should have a better understanding of why the rights contained in the body of the Constitution, the Bill of Rights, and subsequent amendments are so important to Americans, and why the interpretation and application of these rights often is controversial.

27

WHAT ARE BILLS OF
RIGHTS AND WHAT KINDS
OF RIGHTS DOES THE U.S.
BILL OF RIGHTS PROTECT?

LESSON 27

UNIT FIVE | LESSON 27

WHAT ARE BILLS OF RIGHTS AND WHAT KINDS OF RIGHTS DOES THE U.S. BILL OF RIGHTS PROTECT?

wtpcompanion.civiced.org | **LESSON PURPOSE + TERMS**

Visit the We the People companion website for printable and downloadable Lesson Purposes and Terms and Concepts to Understand sections for each lesson. Audio readings of each Lesson Purpose and Term are also available online in MP3 format.

LESSON PURPOSE

This lesson provides a foundation for examining many of the rights contained in the U.S. Constitution, the Bill of Rights, and subsequent amendments to the Constitution that are discussed in earlier lessons. It also examines four provisions of the Bill of Rights that usually do not receive as much attention as others: the Second, Third, Ninth, and Tenth Amendments.

When you have finished this lesson, you should be able to explain what bills of rights are and how they have evolved. You should be able to examine the Constitution and its amendments and identify which of the rights they contain are (1) held by individuals, classes, or categories of individuals, or institutions; (2) personal, economic, or political rights; and (3) positive or negative rights. You also should be able to identify possible conflicts among these rights. You should be able to describe various interpretations of the Second, Third, Ninth, and Tenth Amendments. Finally, you should be able to evaluate, take, and defend positions about the kinds of rights protected by the U.S. Constitution and Bill of Rights.

TERMS AND CONCEPTS TO UNDERSTAND

autonomy

classes or categories of individuals

economic rights

negative rights

personal rights

political rights

positive rights

rights

193

193

student page ▾ 194–195

WHAT ARE BILLS OF RIGHTS AND HOW HAVE THEY EVOLVED?

A copy of the Virginia Declaration of Rights appears in the Reference section. As introduced by James Madison the Bill of Rights contained a preamble that included the following sentences:

> The conventions of a number of the States having at the time of their adopting the Constitution, expressed a desire, in order to prevent misconstruction or abuse of its powers, that further declaratory and restrictive clauses should be added: And as extending the ground of public confidence in the Government, will best insure the beneficent ends of its institution.

The text of the amendments submitted to the states for ratification did not include the preamble.

wtpcompanion.civiced.org   PRIMARY SOURCES

Visit the We the People companion website for a link to the text of the Bill of Rights Madison proposed where he argued each provision should be placed in the Constitution, as well as a copy of the Bill of Rights as it was submitted to the states for ratification.

In a letter to Thomas Jefferson in 1789 James Madison wrote,

> The following [addition to the Bill of Rights] would have pleased me: The people shall not be deprived or abridged of their right to speak, to write, or otherwise to publish anything but false facts affecting injuriously the life, liberty or reputation of others, or affecting the peace of the [United States] with foreign nations.

WHAT ARE BILLS OF RIGHTS AND HOW HAVE THEY EVOLVED?

The struggle between the **rights** of people and groups and the power of government to interfere with or violate those rights is one of the great themes of human history. The Magna Carta, discussed in Lesson 4, is one example of efforts to protect rights against government abuse. It is sometimes referred to as the Great Charter of Freedoms, or the *Magna Carta Libertatum*.

The English Bill of Rights of 1689, also discussed in Lesson 4, is another example of listing the rights of individuals and groups in relationship to their government. Among other things, the English Bill of Rights guaranteed free speech and debate to Parliament, permitted English subjects to petition the Crown, prohibited the imposition of excessive bail and cruel and unusual punishments, and prohibited the Crown from keeping a standing army in peacetime. The English Bill of Rights also established that the rule of law is the foundation of legitimate government and that the People are entitled to be represented in legislative institutions.

The English Bill of Rights is important in understanding the evolution of bills of rights in the United States, but it is significant that the English Bill of Rights was enacted by Parliament. Therefore, Parliament can repeal it because it is merely an act of ordinary legislation that is subject to change at any time. By contrast the drafters of America's first state constitutions included bills of rights that would bind all branches of government and could not be easily changed. The first state to do so was Virginia.

The Virginia Declaration of Rights of June 1776 states that its purpose is to form "the basis and foundation of government." The first three sections of the Virginia Declaration of Rights explain the relationship between rights and government authority:

- **Section 1** That all men are by nature equally free and independent, and have certain inherent rights, of which, when they enter into a state of society, they cannot, by any compact, deprive or divest their posterity; namely, the enjoyment of life and liberty, with the means of acquiring and possessing property, and pursuing and obtaining happiness and safety.

- **Section 2** That all power is vested in, and consequently derived from, the People; that magistrates are their trustees and servants, and at all times amenable to them.

- **Section 3** That Government is, or ought to be, instituted for the common benefit, protection, and security of the people, nation or community; of all the various modes and forms of Government that is best which is capable of

producing the greatest degree of happiness and safety and is most effectually secured against the danger of maladministration; and that, whenever any Government shall be found inadequate or contrary to these purposes, a majority of the community hath an indubitable, inalienable, and indefeasible right to reform, alter, or abolish it, in such manner as shall be judged most conducive to the publick weal.

The next fourteen sections of the Virginia Declaration of Rights of 1776 explain how representative government should be organized. These sections also place limits on the government, such as prohibiting excessive bail and the suspension of laws without the consent of representatives of the people. The declaration also identifies rights that should be free from government interference, including freedom of the press, and a prohibition on general warrants (see Lesson 31). The last section of the

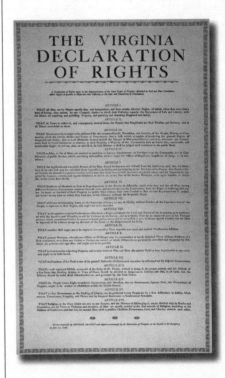

What ideas in the Virginia Declaration of Rights are also found in the Declaration of Independence?

Virginia Declaration of Rights includes principles of classical republicanism:

- **Section 15** That no free Government, or the blessing of liberty, can be preserved to any people but by a firm adherence to justice, moderation, temperance, frugality, and virtue and by frequent recurrence to fundamental principles.

Each state adopted a constitution after the Declaration of Independence was issued. All states except New York, which embedded its bill of rights in the constitution, began their constitutions with bills or declarations of rights. As discussed in Lesson 13, the Anti-Federalists used the lack of a bill of rights in the U.S. Constitution as a rallying cry against ratification. Lesson 15 explained how James Madison made good on the promise to introduce a bill of rights into the First Federal Congress. Today the constitutions of all fifty states, as well as the U.S. Constitution, contain bills or declarations of rights. As explained in Lesson 26, states typically place bills or declarations of rights at the beginning of the constitution.

WHAT QUESTIONS ARE USEFUL IN EXAMINING AND UNDERSTANDING BILLS OF RIGHTS?

When analyzing bills of rights, certain questions can help clarify an understanding of rights:

- Who holds the right? Is it held by individuals, **classes or categories of individuals,** or institutions?

- What kind of right is it— personal, economic, or political?

- Does the right require government to act, or does it require government to refrain from acting?

The following information should be useful in answering these questions.

WHO MAY HOLD RIGHTS?

Rights may be held by individuals, classes or categories of individuals, or institutions.

- **Individuals** The idea that individuals can hold rights reflects the belief that humans should be considered autonomous and self-governing. This includes the belief that each individual should possess certain fundamental rights, such as those to freedom of thought and conscience, privacy, and movement.

This emphasis on the rights of individuals is reflected in natural rights philosophy, exemplified in the Declaration of Independence by the statement that "all Men are created equal, that they are endowed by their Creator with certain unalienable Rights, that among these are Life, Liberty, and the Pursuit of Happiness."

- **Classes or categories of individuals** Under most legal systems members of certain classes or categories of individuals within a society are recognized in the law as holding certain rights. For example, laws may grant such rights to children, the mentally ill or disabled, veterans, and those who hold professional qualifications, such as teachers, doctors, attorneys, building contractors, and airplane pilots.

- **Institutions** Institutions such as schools; governmental institutions at local, state, and national levels; unions; universities; business partnerships; and corporations also hold certain rights.

WHAT ARE COMMON CATEGORIES OF RIGHTS?

Three common categories are personal rights, economic rights, and political rights:

- **Personal rights** These rights provide for individual **autonomy,** including, among other rights, freedom of thought and conscience, privacy, and movement. The idea that humans are autonomous, self-governing individuals with fundamental rights is central to natural rights philosophy, as discussed in Unit One. The rights to life, liberty, property, and the pursuit of happiness often are said to be "God-given" or based on nature. Every person is believed to possess such rights at birth. The purpose of government is to protect those rights.

- **Economic rights** These rights include choosing the work one wants to do, acquiring and disposing of property, entering into contracts, creating and protecting intellectual property such as copyrights or patents, and joining labor unions or professional associations. Like political rights, such rights can be created and protected by statutes, national or state constitutions, or both. Many people consider economic rights to be associated with ownership.

195

student page ▾ 196–197

WHAT KINDS OF RIGHTS DOES THE BILL OF RIGHTS PROTECT?

In *District of Columbia v. Heller*, 2008, the Supreme Court ruled by a vote of 5–4 that the Second Amendment protects the individual's right to own a gun for personal use. The Court struck down the District of Columbia's ban on handguns, but left open the question of whether states and localities can impose reasonable restrictions on handgun ownership. Legal scholars predict years of litigation over the constitutionality of particular restrictions.

wtpcompanion.civiced.org | **COURT CASES**

Visit the We the People companion website for links to Supreme Court syllabi and opinions for each of the cases described in the student and teacher's editions. Summaries are provided for selected Supreme Court cases.

What economic rights do workers have?

- **Political rights** These are rights of individuals that address political participation and can be created and protected by statutes, national or state constitutions, or both. Examples are the rights to vote and to engage in political activities, such as supporting particular candidates for office or running for office.

DO RIGHTS REQUIRE GOVERNMENT TO ACT OR REFRAIN FROM ACTING?

Another common distinction made in discussions of rights is between **positive rights** and **negative rights**. In this context, the terms *positive* and *negative* do not refer to "desirable" and "undesirable." Rather, they usually refer to the relationship of individuals and classes or categories of individuals to their government.

Positive rights require government to act in specified ways. They include, for example, the rights of individuals to receive certain services from government, such as protection of their persons and property from criminal acts, protection from aggression from other nations, public education, and in some cases food, housing, or medical care.

Some provisions of the Bill of Rights also require government action. The Sixth Amendment, for example, guarantees criminal defendants the right to speedy and public trials. That guarantee requires government to establish and fund systems of open courts and to prosecute crimes without delay. The Seventh Amendment guarantees individuals the right to a jury trial, which requires government to ensure that judges and juries are available to hear cases.

Negative rights restrict government action. Many of the individual rights protected by the U.S. Constitution and the Bill of Rights are stated as negative rights. For example, the First Amendment states that "Congress shall make no law" that violates fundamental rights to freedom of religion, speech, press, assembly, and petition.

WHAT KINDS OF RIGHTS DOES THE BILL OF RIGHTS PROTECT?

The Bill of Rights appended to the U.S. Constitution is commonly understood to contain specific guarantees of individual rights. In fact, the situation is more complicated because the Bill of Rights involves the kinds of rights described above.

For example, the Second Amendment provides that "A well regulated Militia, being necessary to the security of a free State, the right of the people to keep and bear Arms, shall not be infringed." The amendment requires the government to refrain from infringing upon the "right of the people to keep and bear Arms" and, as such, is a negative right. Some people argue that this amendment refers to the institutional rights of states to maintain militia units. Others contend that it refers to the individual right to keep and bear arms that is permitted by law in most states. The Supreme Court seemed to side with the institutional view in 1939 in *United States v. Miller*, but lower federal courts have continued to debate the issue. In 2007, however, the Court agreed to revisit the question by agreeing to rule on a case challenging the constitutionality of a District of Columbia ban on the possession of handguns by individuals.

Another example is the Third Amendment, which states, "No Soldier shall, in time of peace be quartered in any house, without the consent of the Owner, nor in time of war, but in a manner to be prescribed by law." This amendment, which embodies the centuries-old Anglo-Saxon legal principle that "a man's home is his castle," addresses the individual right not to be required to house soldiers. The amendment does acknowledge, however, the federal government's institutional right, or power, in time of war to set aside this right on behalf of the right of the nation to security.

CRITICAL THINKING EXERCISE
Identifying Different Kinds of Rights in the Bill of Rights and Potential Conflicts among Them

Work in groups of three to five students to examine one of the following amendments: First, Fourth, Fifth, Sixth, Seventh, or Eighth. For each amendment, identify whether the rights protected are

- Held by individuals, classes or categories of individuals, or institutions

- Personal, economic, or political rights

- Positive or negative rights

Each group should report its conclusions to the class as a whole. Then the class should discuss how and in what ways the rights protected in the Bill of Rights might conflict with one another.

What other rights are protected by the right to privacy?

197

student page ▼ 197

The Third Amendment was written in response to the Quartering Act of 1765, discussed in Lesson 6. Pennsylvania was the only colony that complied with the act. There have been no Supreme Court cases addressing the Third Amendment. However, the Court of Appeals for the Second Circuit ruled on the amendment in a case in 1982. That court held that members of the National Guard qualify as soldiers under the Third Amendment and that the amendment applies to the states as well as the national government (*Engblom v. Carey*, 1982).

wtpcompanion.civiced.org   COURT CASES

Visit the We the People companion website for links to Supreme Court syllabi and opinions for each of the cases described in the student and teacher's editions. Summaries are provided for selected Supreme Court cases.

student page ▼ 198

WHAT ARE THE MEANING AND IMPORTANCE OF THE NINTH AND TENTH AMENDMENTS?

NINTH AMENDMENT   In presenting the Bill of Rights to the House James Madison said,

It has been objected also against a bill of rights, that, by enumerating particular exceptions to the grant of power, it would disparage those rights which were not placed in that enumeration; and it might follow by implication, that those rights which were not singled out, were intended to be assigned into the hands of the General Government, and were consequently insecure. This is one of the most plausible arguments I have ever heard against the admission of a bill of rights into this system; but, I conceive, that it may be guarded against. I have attempted it, as gentlemen may see by turning to the last clause of the fourth resolution [the Ninth Amendment].

Some see this statement as an endorsement of the second bullet point on page 198 of the student text regarding interpretation of the Ninth Amendment. In 1965, the Court's decision in *Griswold v. Connecticut* unleashed new debate about the meaning of the Ninth Amendment. In that case, the court struck down a state statute prohibiting married couples from using contraceptives. The majority reasoned that the law infringed on the right of marital privacy, a right that is not mentioned in the Constitution. Justice William O. Douglas reviewed several cases in which the Supreme Court had recognized freedoms—including the right to associate (*DeJonge v. Oregon*, 1937) and the right to educate one's child (*Pierce v. Society of Sisters*, 1925)—not explicitly mentioned in the Constitution. He then wrote the following:

> The foregoing cases suggest that specific guarantees in the Bill of Rights have penumbras [implied guarantees], formed by emanations from those guarantees that help give them life and substance. Various guarantees create zones of privacy. The right of association contained in the penumbra of the First Amendment is one, as we have seen. The Third Amendment in its prohibition against the quartering of soldiers "in any house" in time of peace without the consent of the owner is another facet of that privacy. The Fourth Amendment explicitly affirms the "right of the people to be secure in their persons, houses, papers, and effects, against unreasonable searches and seizures." The Fifth Amendment in its Self-Incrimination Clause enables the citizen to create a zone of privacy which government may not force him to surrender to his detriment. The Ninth Amendment provides: "The enumeration in the Constitution, of certain rights, shall not be construed to deny or disparage others retained by the people."

In his concurrence, Justice Goldberg focused on the Ninth Amendment. His opinion appeared to endorse the ideas in the first and third bullet points on page 198 of the student text regarding the interpretation of that amendment. In dissent, Justice Black criticized the Court for recognizing a right not found in the text in the Constitution. He argued that the justices were verging on restoring substantive due process (discussed in Lesson 18), which the Court had long rejected.

TENTH AMENDMENT   As noted in Lesson 26 the precise meaning of American federalism regarding the powers of the states in relation to the national government has never been resolved. Therefore it is to be expected that the Supreme Court's jurisprudence on the meaning of the Tenth Amendment has been inconsistent.

In *McCulloch v. Maryland* (1819), for example, Chief Justice Marshall gave an expansive interpretation to the necessary and proper clause of Article I, Section 8, Clause 18, in upholding the right of the national government to incorporate a national bank and rejecting the right of a state to tax the bank. Marshall held that the Tenth Amendment did not limit the national government's power under the necessary and proper clause, thereby rekindling worries that Anti-Federalists had expressed during the ratification debates (see Lesson 13).

By contrast, in *National League of Cities v. Usery* (1975) the Court struck down the 1975 amendments to the Fair Labor Standards Act of 1938 that sought to regulate minimum wage and overtime pay for state and local government employees. The Court held that the Tenth Amendment prohibits Congress from enacting legislation that would "directly displace the States' freedom to structure integral operations in areas of traditional

WHAT ARE THE MEANING AND IMPORTANCE OF THE NINTH AND TENTH AMENDMENTS?

The first eight amendments to the U.S. Constitution contain specific guarantees of rights. By contrast, the Ninth and Tenth Amendments do not. There is ongoing debate about the meaning of these amendments.

The Ninth Amendment provides that "the enumeration in the Constitution of certain rights shall not be construed to deny or disparage others retained by the people." Theories about the Ninth Amendment include the following:

- It is simply an admission that it would be impossible to list all the rights and liberties that should be protected from government interference.

What is the importance of the constitutional protection of the right of members of Congress to speak and debate freely in either house without fear of prosecution?

- It confirms that the Bill of Rights does not increase the powers of the national government in areas not mentioned in the first eight amendments. It does not guarantee any rights or impose any limitations on the national government.

- It commands judges and Congress to affirm rights not mentioned in the Constitution.

The Tenth Amendment states, "The powers not delegated to the United States by the Constitution, nor prohibited by it to the States, are reserved to the States respectively, or to the people." Of all the amendments the Anti-Federalists demanded in state ratifying conventions, one designed to reserve powers to the states was the most common. Two views of the Tenth Amendment are the following:

- It states the nature of American federalism but adds nothing to the Constitution as originally ratified.

- It protects the powers of the states against the national government.

CRITICAL THINKING EXERCISE
Assessing the Meaning and Importance of the Ninth and Tenth Amendments

Work in groups of three to five students and develop responses to the following questions regarding the Ninth and Tenth Amendments.

❶ What do you think is the meaning of the Ninth Amendment? Of the Tenth Amendment?

❷ What do you think is the importance of the Ninth Amendment to you personally and more generally to the preservation of individual rights and a democratic political system? Of the Tenth Amendment?

WHAT RIGHTS ARE PROTECTED IN THE BODY OF THE CONSTITUTION?

In addition to those rights protected in the first ten amendments—known as the Bill of Rights—the body of the U.S. Constitution and subsequent amendments also protect many rights. Alexander Hamilton argued in Federalist 84 that the Constitution itself is a bill of rights. Each provision is aimed at preventing the type of abuse that the Framers had seen in British history, their own colonial governments, their state governments, or the national government under the Articles of Confederation. Since the adoption of the Bill of Rights in 1791, seventeen other amendments have been added to the Constitution, one of which was repealed. Many of these also protect rights. However, the following exercise will focus on those rights protected in the body of the Constitution because the rights contained in the Eleventh through Seventeenth Amendments have been discussed in other lessons.

CRITICAL THINKING EXERCISE
What Kinds of Rights Are Protected in the Body of the Constitution?

Work in small groups and examine Articles I, II, III, and IV of the U.S. Constitution. Then respond to the following questions:

❶ How does Article I protect the political rights of those serving in Congress?

❷ How does Article I protect individual rights from infringement by Congress? By the states?

❸ How does Article I protect economic rights?

❹ How does Article II protect the political rights of the president?

❺ How does Article III protect the political rights of judges? Of individuals?

❻ How does Article IV protect political rights of individuals? Of classes or categories of individuals?

❼ Are the rights protected in Articles I through IV of the Constitution positive rights, negative rights, or some of each? Explain.

Compare each group's response to these questions with the responses of other groups. Are there differences? If so, how do you explain the differences?

HOW HAVE ATTITUDES ABOUT THE BILL OF RIGHTS CHANGED SINCE 1791?

Many Federalists criticized James Madison for pushing the Bill of Rights through Congress. At best, they considered it of little importance. Madison himself, tired of the disagreement and dissent associated with the debates on the Bill of Rights, described the process as a "nauseous project."

Ironically, several Anti-Federalists who had based much of their opposition to the Constitution on the lack of a bill of rights also were unhappy. They had hoped to use the movement for a bill of rights as an opportunity to rewrite the Constitution. Some predicted that the Bill of Rights

What have polls shown about the public's knowledge of the Bill of Rights?

would do more harm than good by giving the national government power over the states in enforcing those rights.

The initial reaction of most Americans to the Bill of Rights was lukewarm. Its passage had little effect on the average person, who had closer ties to a particular state than to the national government. In *Barron v. Baltimore* (1833) the U.S. Supreme Court ruled that the Bill of Rights applied only to the national government. The Fourteenth Amendment and many Supreme Court decisions thereafter were required to incorporate most of the provisions of the Bill of Rights as limits on the states as well as on the national government.

In the twentieth century the Bill of Rights achieved a significance never dreamt of in the eighteenth century. Today the Bill of Rights is recognized throughout the world as one of the most important single documents that expresses and delineates fundamental individual rights.

Despite this fame, public opinion polls during the bicentennial of the Bill of Rights in 1991 revealed shortcomings in Americans' knowledge of this important document. Polls did show that a high percentage of Americans knew that the first ten amendments to the Constitution are called the Bill of Rights. But most of those interviewed knew little or nothing about the meaning, history, and application of key concepts in the Bill of Rights. A recent poll showed that sixty-nine percent of respondents knew that the First Amendment protects freedom of speech, but only twenty-four percent knew that it also protects the free exercise of religion.

governmental functions." The Court held that the Tenth Amendment limits Congress's power under the commerce clause of Article I, Section 8, Clause 3, because the function of the amendment is to protect the states' traditional activities. In *Fry v. United States*, (1975), decided that same term, the Court held that the Tenth Amendment "expressly declares the constitutional policy that Congress may not exercise power in a fashion that impairs the States' integrity or their ability to function effectively in a federal system."

In 1985 in *Garcia v. San Antonio Metropolitan Transit Authority* the Court overruled *Usery*. The Court rejected as "unsound in principle and unworkable in practice" the *Usery* rule that focused on whether a particular function of government was "traditional." The Court acknowledged that the states "unquestionably" retain "a significant measure of sovereign authority" but "only to the extent that the Constitution has not divested them of their original powers and transferred those powers to the Federal Government."

wtpcompanion.civiced.org　**COURT CASES**

Visit the We the People companion website for links to Supreme Court syllabi and opinions for each of the cases described in the student and teacher's editions. Summaries are provided for selected Supreme Court cases.

student page ▼ 198–199

WHAT RIGHTS ARE PROTECTED IN THE BODY OF THE CONSTITUTION?

In Federalist 84 Alexander Hamilton argued that a bill of rights was unnecessary for a variety of reasons, including the following:

- Bills of rights are stipulations between kings and subjects, whereas the people have surrendered nothing under the proposed Constitution.

- It would be dangerous to list the rights people retain, because that would imply that the rights not listed do not exist.

- Various provisions of Article I protect essential rights.

- The Constitution is a "bill of rights of the Union," declaring the political privileges of citizens in the structure and administration of the national government.

ENRICHMENT ACTIVITY

EXAMINING CLAIMS ABOUT RIGHTS

It is popular in the United States for groups to assert "rights" ranging from animal rights to the rights of airplane passengers. Ask students to conduct research to find at least five more examples of claims of rights made by various groups. Then ask them to explain which, if any, of the claimed rights are embraced by the Bill of Rights or the rights protected in the body of the Constitution. Finally, ask students to consider whether any of the claimed rights should be added to the Bill of Rights. Why or why not?

Moreover, only eleven percent knew that in addition it protects freedom of the press; ten percent that it protects freedom of assembly; and just one percent that it protects the right to petition government for a redress of grievances. More than half believed that the First Amendment guarantees the right to trial by jury and the right to vote.

WHAT DO YOU THINK?

❶ In response to public opinion polls revealing Americans' ignorance of the Bill of Rights, one commentator argued that "the less Americans know about freedoms, the more they are likely to erode without our notice." Do you agree or disagree with this statement? Why?

❷ Reread the Bill of Rights. Do you think some rights are more important than others? If so, which ones? Explain your reasoning.

REVIEWING AND USING THE LESSON

❶ How do the rights found in the U.S. Constitution and the Bill of Rights reflect the influence of classical republicanism and natural rights philosophy?

❷ How do American bills of rights at national and state levels differ from the 1689 English Bill of Rights as limitations on government? Is the difference significant? Why?

❸ How do the rights of institutions and classes of individuals, such as doctors or the disabled, differ from the rights possessed by all individuals under the U.S. Constitution? Under what circumstances, if any, should such rights be given preference over individual rights? Why?

❹ What are "positive rights" and "negative rights"? Provide examples of each.

❺ Why has it been difficult to resolve the meaning of the Second, Third, Ninth, and Tenth Amendments to the U.S. Constitution?

Do you agree or disagree with the quotation attributed to Voltaire, "I disapprove of what you say, but I will defend to the death your right to say it"? Why?

28

HOW DOES THE FIRST AMENDMENT AFFECT THE ESTABLISHMENT AND FREE EXERCISE OF RELIGION?

HOW DOES THE FIRST AMENDMENT AFFECT THE ESTABLISHMENT AND FREE EXERCISE OF RELIGION?

wtpcompanion.civiced.org | **LESSON PURPOSE + TERMS**

Visit the We the People companion website for printable and downloadable Lesson Purposes and Terms and Concepts to Understand sections for each lesson. Audio readings of each Lesson Purpose and Term are also available online in MP3 format.

LESSON PURPOSE

The first two clauses in the First Amendment prohibit Congress from making laws regarding the establishment of religion or prohibiting the free exercise of religion.

The exact meaning of the establishment and free exercise clauses has been a topic of fierce debate. Did the Founders intend to build "a wall of separation between Church and State" as Thomas Jefferson asserted? Or did they merely intend to prevent religious persecution and the establishment of one national religion?

When you have finished this lesson, you should be able to explain the importance of religious freedom in the United States and to identify primary differences between the establishment and free exercise clauses. You should be able to describe how the Supreme Court has interpreted the religion clauses, ongoing issues involving those clauses, and how conflicts can arise between the establishment and free exercise clauses. Finally, you should be able to evaluate, take, and defend positions on issues arising from guarantees relating to the establishment and free exercise of religion clauses of the Constitution.

TERMS AND CONCEPTS TO UNDERSTAND

compelling state interest

established church

establishment clause

free exercise clause

separation of church and state

WHAT IS AN ESTABLISHED RELIGION?

Thomas Jefferson called America's constitutional protections of religion a "bold" and "novel" experiment. Some fifty-seven independent countries around the world have official state, or established, religions. The following are among the represented religions as of the year 2000.

- Twenty-one Catholic countries, including Bolivia, Spain, and Italy
- Twenty-two Muslim countries, including Yemen, Saudi Arabia, and Iraq
- Nine Protestant countries, including the United Kingdom, Denmark, and Tonga
- Four Buddhist countries, including Bhutan and Sri Lanka
- One Hindu country, Nepal

Several other countries, though lacking an official religion, support religion in general, including Australia, Belgium, Brazil, Cyprus, the Philippines, South Africa, and Switzerland.

WHY DOES THE FIRST AMENDMENT PROHIBIT CONGRESS FROM ESTABLISHING A NATIONAL RELIGION?

According to the *World Fact Book* in 2002 the approximate religious affiliation in the United States was as follows: fifty-two percent Protestant, twenty-four percent Roman Catholic, two percent Mormon, one percent Jewish, one percent Muslim, ten percent other, and ten percent none.

wtpcompanion.civiced.org LINKS

Visit the We the People companion website for a link to a list of self-identified religious affiliations in the United States in 2001.

Why was Roger Williams exiled from the Massachusetts Bay Colony?

WHAT IS AN ESTABLISHED RELIGION?

In the seventeenth century, when the first English colonies were being settled in America, Europe was in the throes of religious wars. This period was part of the era known as the Reformation, which began in the sixteenth century. The period led to more than a century of bloodshed as Catholics and Protestants struggled for political power. As various groups came to power, they often attempted to eliminate others by outlawing their religions or banishing, torturing, jailing, or killing adherents to religions other than their own.

Despite the turmoil caused by religious struggles, most Europeans continued to accept the legitimacy of an established, or official, religion. It was generally believed that religion and morality formed the necessary foundation of a successful government. Almost every nation in Europe had an **established church**. In France and Spain it was Roman Catholicism. In some German states and in Sweden it was Lutheranism. In England the Act of Supremacy of 1534 made the Church of England, or the Anglican Church, the established church.

People fleeing religious persecution settled many American colonies. However, most colonies followed the tradition of having established churches, and there was little patience with those who did not belong to the established church. Religious intolerance and persecution of those with nonconforming religious beliefs was commonplace in Anglican Virginia and Congregational, or Puritan, Massachusetts. People were taxed against their will to support state religions and punished for failing to attend public worship and sometimes for heretical or nonconformist opinions.

However, religious intolerance did not remain universal in the colonies for long. Intolerance of religious dissent and an unwillingness to separate church and state led to the exile of the dissenting theologian Roger Williams (c. 1603–1683) from Massachusetts Bay Colony. In 1636, together with a few friends, Williams secured land from the Indians in what is now Rhode Island. There he founded a new society based on freedom of conscience, religious toleration, and **separation of church and state**. This phrase refers to the lack of an established church or the state supporting one religion over others. Members of Williams's new colony had to promise to obey the majority, but "only in civil things." In 1663 the colony of Rhode Island and Providence Plantations was formally established.

WHY DOES THE FIRST AMENDMENT PROHIBIT CONGRESS FROM ESTABLISHING A NATIONAL RELIGION?

A religious revival in the mid-eighteenth century known as the Great Awakening drew many into new religious groups, such as Methodists and Baptists. Diverse religious groups often existed within the same community, and people became used to living and working with others who had different beliefs. The growing number of religious groups made it unlikely that one particular church could dominate all others. Increased religious diversity also made it difficult for only one church to claim special privileges from the government. Government support began to go to several Protestant churches in the effort to support religion in general. Catholics, Jews, and other religious groups were not supported and frequently were the subjects of discrimination.

Eighteenth-century Americans generally thought that religion was important in developing the character of individuals needed to maintain a free society. By the closing years of the century, when the Constitution was written, most Americans also thought that freedom of belief was an essential right that needed protection. Americans considered freedom of religion to be something that strengthened both church and state.

Although most Americans believed that the nation should not have an established religion, some, such as James Madison, also believed that individuals in a free society should be able to decide for themselves what to believe. The religion clauses of the First Amendment address both concerns:

❝ Congress shall make no law respecting an establishment of religion, or prohibiting the free exercise thereof.

WHAT DO YOU THINK?

❶ Do you think it is important to keep church and state separate? Why or why not?

❷ What are the advantages and disadvantages of religious diversity in society? What role, if any, should government play in fostering or limiting religious diversity? Why?

❸ The First Amendment is stated in absolute terms: "Congress shall make no law respecting an establishment of religion." Does that wording reflect hostility toward religion? Why or why not?

HOW DOES THE ESTABLISHMENT CLAUSE AFFECT THE STATES?

The **establishment clause** prohibits Congress from establishing a national religion. In 1791 some people supported the First Amendment because they thought it would leave the states free to maintain established religions. However, as new sects developed throughout the United States, religious groups learned to coexist in the same community. People became accustomed to working and associating with others of different beliefs. States began to abandon the practice of established churches. By 1833, when Massachusetts changed its constitution to require the separation of church and state, there were no longer established state churches in the United States.

The disappearance of established religions in the states did not end controversy about the meaning of the establishment clause. Debate shifted to other issues. For example, some states passed laws providing aid to religious organizations or requiring prayer and Bible reading in public schools. In 1947 the Supreme Court held that the due process clause of the Fourteenth Amendment incorporates the establishment clause against the states (*Everson v. Board of Education*). The establishment clause therefore limits both the states and the national government.

HOW HAVE THE COURTS INTERPRETED THE ESTABLISHMENT CLAUSE?

There is general agreement that the establishment clause means that government may not sponsor an official church. What else the establishment clause means is subject to much disagreement. The disagreement can be summarized as three types of interpretation.

- **Broad interpretation** People holding this position argue that the First Amendment prevents the government from providing any aid to any religion. They believe that no tax money can be used to support any religious activity, practice, or institution. However, the government may give religious groups the same services that everyone else receives, such as police and fire protection. The government may provide assistance that makes it easier for people to exercise their religion. For example, schools may excuse students from classes during religious holidays.

- **Narrow interpretation** People holding this position argue that government is prohibited from giving one religious group preferential treatment. They believe that the First Amendment does not prohibit government from supporting religion as long as it does so impartially. This group supports placing the

---

student page ▾ 203

HOW DOES THE ESTABLISHMENT CLAUSE AFFECT THE STATES?

Review Lesson 18 for a discussion of incorporation of the Bill of Rights to the states through the due process clause of the Fourteenth Amendment.

student page ▾ 203–204

HOW HAVE THE COURTS INTERPRETED THE ESTABLISHMENT CLAUSE?

The Supreme Court has not addressed all the questions concerning the relationship between religion and the state. Consider, for example, the following statement from the website of the United States Mint:

> From Treasury Department records it appears that the first suggestion that God be recognized on U.S. coinage can be traced to a letter addressed to the Secretary of Treasury from a minister in 1861. An Act of Congress, approved on April 11, 1864, authorized the coinage of two-cent coins upon which the motto first appeared.
>
> The motto was omitted from the new gold coins issued in 1907, causing a storm of public criticism. As a result, legislation passed in May 1908 made "In God We Trust" mandatory on all coins on which it had previously appeared.
>
> Legislation approved July 11, 1955, made the appearance of "In God We Trust" mandatory on all coins and paper currency of the United States. By Act of July 30, 1956, "In God We Trust" became the national motto of the United States.
>
> Several years ago, the appearance of "In God We Trust" on our money was challenged in the federal courts. The challenge was rejected by the lower federal courts, and the Supreme Court of the United States declined to review the case.

In his dissent in *Wallace v. Jaffree* (1985) Chief Justice William Rehnquist reviewed the history of the religion clauses in the First Amendment seeking the intent of the drafters and wrote regarding James Madison,

> It seems indisputable from these glimpses of Madison's thinking, as reflected by actions on the floor of the House in 1789, that he saw the Amendment as designed to prohibit the establishment of a national religion, and perhaps to prevent discrimination among sects. He did not see it as requiring neutrality on the part of government between religion and irreligion.

Two examples of cases decided on a broad interpretation of the establishment clause are *Engle v. Vitale* (1962) and *Stone v. Graham* (1982).

Three examples of cases decided on a narrow interpretation of the establishment clause are *Reynolds v. United States* (1878), *Everson v. Board of Education* (1947), and *Employment Division v. Smith* (1990).

Two examples of cases decided on a literal interpretation of the establishment clause are *Sherbert v. Verner* (1963) and *Lynch v. Donnelly* (1984).

It is not possible to predict how the justices on the Supreme Court will decide cases or to stereotype their views on complex issues surrounding the religion clauses of the First Amendment. In *Rosenberger v. University of Virginia* (1995) Justice Sandra Day O'Connor explained, "The need for careful judgment and fine distinctions presents itself even in extreme cases. When bedrock principles collide, they test the limits of categorical obstinacy and expose the flaws and dangers of a Grand Unified Theory that may turn out to be neither grand nor unified."

Justice O'Connor identified three "bedrock principles" from which to begin the analysis of establishment clause cases. The First Amendment

- prevents any government endorsement or support of religion;
- allows governments to "accommodate" religion by providing support to religion so long as all are treated equally and none is given special preference; and
- permits governments to "endorse" religion generally.

CRITICAL THINKING EXERCISE

The examples in this exercise are derived from court cases that students may wish to read to compare with their responses:

- **GROUP 1** *Zorach v. Clauson* (1952)
- **GROUP 2** *Mueller v. Allen* (1983)
- **GROUP 3** *Stone v. Graham* (1980); *Doe v. Harlan County School District* (6th Cir. 2000) (The Supreme Court denied review in 2005.)
- **GROUP 4** *Wolman v. Walter* (1977)

wtpcompanion.civiced.org **COURT CASES**

Visit the We the People companion website for links to information about each of the cases described above.

---

words "In God We Trust" on currency and allowing nondenominational school prayer. People using a broad interpretation of the First Amendment often oppose these kinds of actions.

People who hold either the broad or the narrow interpretation agree that the First Amendment prohibits government acknowledgment of Christmas as a holiday if the holidays of other religious groups are not recognized.

- **Literal interpretation** People holding this position suggest that the First Amendment prohibits only the establishment of an official government religion. They would not prohibit the government's participation in particular religious practices. For example, the government may participate in Christmas celebrations as long as Christianity is not declared an official established religion.

Since 1947 the Court has heard many cases involving freedom of religion. These cases have involved issues such as prayer in schools, Christmas displays of nativity scenes on government property, and various kinds of support for religious education. Although most people agree that church and state should be separate, Americans are no closer today to defining that separation than the country was in 1791.

CRITICAL THINKING EXERCISE
Taking and Defending a Position on the Establishment Clause

Work in one of four groups. Each group should read one situation and answer the questions that follow. Be prepared to present and defend your position to the class as a whole.

GROUP ❶
New York City arranged a voluntary program permitting its public schools to release students during school hours to receive religious instruction off campus.

GROUP ❷
A Minnesota statute allowed state taxpayers to deduct from their income taxes the costs of providing tuition, textbooks, and transportation for their children who attended religious schools.

GROUP ❸
A Kentucky statute required a copy of the Ten Commandments, purchased with private funds, to be posted on the wall of every public school classroom in the state.

GROUP ❹
An Ohio statute authorized the state department of education to provide students at religious schools with books, standardized testing and scoring, diagnostic services, and therapeutic and remedial services.

❶ Do you think the law or program violates the establishment clause? Why or why not?

❷ Does your position reflect a broad, narrow, or literal interpretation of the establishment clause? Explain your answer.

WHAT RIGHTS DOES THE FREE EXERCISE CLAUSE PROTECT?

Another important clause is called the **free exercise clause**. There are two parts to the constitutional guarantee of free exercise of religion. One is the freedom to believe. The other is the freedom to practice religious beliefs. The Supreme Court has held that individuals have an absolute right to freedom of belief or conscience. No government may interfere with this right by prescribing religious beliefs. However, the right to practice one's religion is not absolute. The practice of religious beliefs may be limited to protect other important values and interests. The problem is deciding which religious practices should be protected and which practices government may limit.

CRITICAL THINKING EXERCISE
Examining Tensions between Establishment and Free Exercise

The establishment and free exercise clauses frequently are in tension. Work in small groups to consider the following examples. Be prepared to take and defend a position in each of the three situations.

- If the government pays to provide for chaplains in the armed forces and in prisons, does it violate the establishment clause? If the government refuses to provide chaplains, does it limit the free exercise of beliefs by persons in the armed forces or in prison?

- If public school officials excuse Jewish students from attending classes on Yom Kippur to attend religious services, do they give preference to a particular religious group in violation of the establishment clause? If they deny students the right to be absent, are they prohibiting the free exercise of religion?

- If schools provide meeting facilities for student religious groups that want to meet after school, do they violate the establishment clause? If they do not, are they limiting students' rights to the free exercise of religion?

HOW IS THE RIGHT OF FREE EXERCISE BALANCED AGAINST OTHER INTERESTS OF SOCIETY?

The justices of the Supreme Court often have held differing opinions on these issues. Sometimes they have overruled earlier decisions. The justices have continually attempted to refine the "tests," or criteria, they use to make a decision.

The Court has considered some issues several times. For example, when the health of the community must be balanced against the religious beliefs of an individual or group, public health is considered to be more important.

By contrast, when the life, health, or safety of individuals, rather than the community, is involved, the Court has upheld the right of mentally competent adults to make their own decisions based on their religious beliefs. For example, an adult may refuse to receive a blood transfusion even if his or her life is at risk. But parents may not refuse a transfusion for their child in similar circumstances. The courts may step in to protect the rights of minors.

The Court also has protected the right of students to refuse to salute the flag or to attend high school if doing so is against their religious beliefs. In deciding such cases the Court asked whether the government had a **compelling state interest**, one that was great enough to

Should tax money be used to pay for military or prison chaplains? Why or why not?

justify limiting the individual's free exercise of religion. For example, the justices held that reasons the government might have to require a student to salute the flag are not strong or compelling enough to require the student to violate his or her religious beliefs.

In deciding cases involving the free exercise clause the Supreme Court usually asks two questions, which together compose the Court's current test for deciding cases arising under the free exercise clause:

- Is the law to which religious adherents object neutral and does it apply to everyone? If the law is neutral and it applies to everyone, then the law does not violate the free exercise clause, even if it hinders religious practices.

- If the law is not neutral and does not apply to everyone, did the government have a compelling interest for enacting it, and did the government adopt the least restrictive means for furthering that compelling interest?

The government has the burden of proving that its interest in the law is compelling—such as protecting public health or safety—and that it satisfied its interest in the least intrusive way possible. If the government can meet its burden of proof, then the law does not violate the free exercise clause. Two cases demonstrate how the justices have applied the free exercise test.

- ***Smith v. Oregon*** (1990) An Oregon statute outlaws the use of peyote, a drug that has hallucinogenic effects. Peyote use is a felony, a serious crime. The Native American Church uses peyote in religious ceremonies. A member of the Native American Church contended that the Oregon law violated his rights under the free exercise clause. The Supreme Court upheld the law, because it was a neutral law outlawing drug use that applies to everyone.

- ***Church of the Lukumi Babalu Aye, Inc. v. City of Hialeah*** (1993) The City of Hialeah, Florida, prohibited the slaughter of animals in religious ceremonies. Animal sacrifice is a central part of the Santería religion, a combination of traditional African religion with elements of Roman Catholicism. The Court held that the prohibition violated the free exercise clause. Seven justices reasoned that the prohibition did not apply to everyone because it did not outlaw all animal slaughter. They also held that the city failed to show that it had a compelling interest in outlawing the religious practice. Two justices believed the prohibition targeted the Santería religion.

CRITICAL THINKING EXERCISE

The examples in this exercise come from the following court cases:

- **MILITARY CHAPLAINS** *Cutter v. Wilkinson* (2005)

- **EXCUSING STUDENTS FOR RELIGIOUS OBSERVANCES** *Church of God v. Amarillo Independent School District* (N.D. Texas 1981, aff'd 5th Cir. 1982)

- **AFTER-SCHOOL USE OF SCHOOL FACILITIES BY RELIGIOUS GROUPS** *Good News Club v. Milford Central School* (2001)

wtpcompanion.civiced.org LINKS

Visit the We the People companion website for links to information about each of the cases described above.

student page ▾ 205

HOW IS THE RIGHT OF FREE EXERCISE BALANCED AGAINST OTHER INTERESTS OF SOCIETY?

The Supreme Court's test for resolving free exercise cases is explained in *Agostini v. Felton* (1997). *Agostini* modified the three-prong test the Court had adopted in *Lemon v. Kurtzman* (1971). To be constitutional under the *Lemon* test a statute had to satisfy all three prongs:

- Have a "secular legislative purpose"

- Have principal effects that would neither "advance nor inhibit religion"

- Not foster "an excessive government entanglement with religion"

Lemon was extremely controversial and difficult to apply.

Agostini reduced the three prongs to the two-prong test explained in the text, essentially eliminating the "entanglement" prong. Doing so required the Court to overrule *Aguilar v. Felton* (1985). In *Felton* the Court had struck down a New York statute that allowed public school teachers to teach in parochial schools. The court believed that this statute led to excessive "entanglement" between church and state.

CRITICAL THINKING EXERCISE

The group tasks are derived from Supreme Court cases. Students may wish to compare their responses with the Court's reasoning.

- **GROUP 1, DOORBELL RINGING** *Martin v. City of Struthers* (1943)

- **GROUP 2, UNEMPLOYMENT BENEFITS** *Thomas v. Review Board of the Indiana Employment Security Division* (1981)

- **GROUP 3, SCHOOL ATTENDANCE FOR THE AMISH** *Yoder v. Wisconsin* (1942)

wtpcompanion.civiced.org **LINKS**

Visit the We the People companion website for links to information about each of the cases described above.

WHAT DO YOU THINK?

The questions are based on Supreme Court decisions as follows:

❶ **EXEMPTION FROM MILITARY SERVICE FOR CONSCIOUS OBJECTORS** *Arver v. United States* (1918)

❷ **EXCUSING PEOPLE FROM WORKING ON THEIR SABBATH** *Sherbert v. Verner* (1963)

❸ **EXCUSING STUDENTS FROM FLAG SALUTE** *West Virginia State Board of Education v. Barnette* (1943); compare with *Minersville School District v. Gobitis* (1940)

❹ **EXCUSING STUDENTS FROM MILITARY SCIENCE CLASSES** *Hamilton v. Regents of California* (1934)

wtpcompanion.civiced.org **COURT CASES**

Visit the We the People companion website for a link to Supreme Court syllabi and opinions for each of the cases described above.

wtpcompanion.civiced.org **LINKS**

Visit the We the People companion website for a link to a summary of the Supreme Court's leading religion cases as of the year 2000.

CRITICAL THINKING EXERCISE
Taking and Defending a Position on the Free Exercise Clause

Work in one of three groups. Each group should read one situation and answer the questions that follow. Each group should be prepared to explain and defend its positions to the class.

GROUP ❶

A local ordinance makes it illegal for anyone who distributes literature to ring a doorbell or otherwise summon a resident to the door to receive the literature. Mormon missionaries are instructed to ring doorbells and to engage residents in conversation while handing out church literature. They contend that the ordinance violates their right to free exercise of religion.

GROUP ❷

A Jehovah's Witness, whose religion opposes war and all activities associated with war, is ordered by his company to work on an assembly line that makes parts for the military. He quits his job and applies for unemployment benefits. His application is denied because he did not quit "for good cause." He contends that being denied unemployment benefits violates his right to free exercise of religion.

GROUP ❸

A state law requires all school-age children to attend school through the tenth grade. The Amish religion values a simple life of labor in communities that are insulated from materialism and modern life. Amish parents refuse to send their children to school past the eighth grade and contend that forcing their children to attend school through the tenth grade violates the free exercise clause.

What considerations, if any, should be used to limit the free exercise of religion?

❶ What values and interests support the law or government action?

❷ What values and interests might be endangered by the law or government action?

❸ What decision would you make in each of the three situations described using the two types of questions from the previous Critical Thinking Exercise? How useful were those questions in making your decision?

WHAT DO YOU THINK?

The following are questions that have been raised in cases before the Supreme Court under the religion clauses of the First Amendment. If you were a Supreme Court justice, how would you go about answering each question? Which provisions of the Constitution or constitutional principles support your responses? Explain your reasoning.

❶ Should conscientious objectors be exempt from military service in times of mandatory conscription (the draft)?

❷ Should persons whose religious Sabbath falls on a day other than Sunday be excused from working on their Sabbath?

❸ Should public school students whose religious beliefs prohibit worshiping "graven images" be excused from saluting the American flag?

❹ Should a student whose religious beliefs oppose war be excused from attending mandatory classes in military science and tactics at a public university?

REVIEWING AND USING THE LESSON

❶ What is an "established church"? Why is the establishment clause important even though there have not been established churches in America for nearly two centuries?

❷ How would you explain the principle of separation of church and state?

❸ Why have disagreements arisen over the meaning of the establishment clause?

❹ What is the free exercise clause?

❺ How might the establishment clause and the free exercise clause come into conflict? Give examples.

❻ What tests has the Supreme Court used in deciding cases under the establishment clause and the free exercise clause?

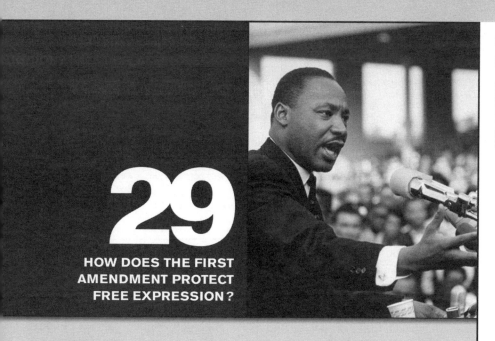

29

HOW DOES THE FIRST AMENDMENT PROTECT FREE EXPRESSION?

HOW DOES THE FIRST AMENDMENT PROTECT FREE EXPRESSION?

wtpcompanion.civiced.org   **LESSON PURPOSE + TERMS**

Visit the We the People companion website for printable and downloadable Lesson Purposes and Terms and Concepts to Understand sections for each lesson. Audio readings of each Lesson Purpose and Term are also available online in MP3 format.

LESSON PURPOSE

The First Amendment says that "Congress shall make no law…abridging the freedom of speech, or of the press; or the right of the people peaceably to assemble, and to petition the Government for a redress of grievances." Together these four rights may be considered as one—the right to freedom of expression.

This lesson examines the benefits that freedom of speech and freedom of the press offer to the individual and society, why they were important to the Founders, and the circumstances under which the government should be able to limit them.

When you finish this lesson, you should be able to explain the importance of freedom of expression to both the individual and society and its historical significance. You should be able to explain considerations useful in deciding when the government should be able to place limits on freedom of speech and the press and be able to evaluate, take, and defend positions on issues involving the right to freedom of expression.

TERMS AND CONCEPTS TO UNDERSTAND

libel

seditious libel

time, place, and manner restrictions

student page ▼ 208

WHY IS PROTECTING THE RIGHT TO FREEDOM OF EXPRESSION IMPORTANT?

Walter Lippmann, a twentieth-century American writer, columnist, and political commentator, wrote, "A free press is not a privilege, but an organic necessity in a great society."

James Madison's original draft of the Bill of Rights contained two proposed amendments regarding free speech:

- The people shall not be deprived or abridged of their right to speak, to write, or to publish their sentiments; and the freedom of the press, one of the great bulwarks of liberty, shall be inviolable.

- No *state* shall violate the equal rights of conscience, or of the press. (emphasis added)

Congress rejected Madison's effort to impose free speech protections on the states, even though Madison called that amendment the "most valuable amendment on the whole list." Madison's wish to limit the states' rights to restrict speech was fulfilled in 1925, when the Supreme Court held that the First Amendment limits the states as well as the national government through the due process clause of the Fourteenth Amendment (*Gitlow v. New York*; see Lesson 18).

wtpcompanion.civiced.org **LINKS**

Visit the We the People companion website for a link to a chart listing how the provisions of the First Amendment have been incorporated as limitations on the states through the due process clause of the Fourteenth Amendment.

student page ▼ 208–209

HOW WAS FREEDOM OF EXPRESSION PROTECTED IN EARLY AMERICA?

Free expression was not highly valued in the early colonies. Slander, a spoken or written statement that ruins a person's reputation, was a serious crime. So was blasphemy, which included believing in more than one god or denying the Holy Trinity. It was not until the eighteenth century and the trial of John Peter Zenger (below) that free speech came to be valued as a tool for resisting despotic government.

The law of seditious libel in England traces to the 1606 case *De Libellis Famosis* in Star Chamber, a special court that sat between 1487 and 1641 to hear cases of libel and treason against the Crown. Attorney General Edward Coke (pronounced "cook") prosecuted the publisher of poems that made fun of two archbishops of Canterbury.

WHY IS PROTECTING THE RIGHT TO FREEDOM OF EXPRESSION IMPORTANT?

The First Amendment was written because the Founders believed that the freedom to express personal opinions is essential to free government. The Founders knew from their own experience and knowledge of history that the freedom to write and publish must be protected from government interference.

It is not easy for people to tolerate the speech or writings of those with whom they strongly disagree. In a democracy the danger to freedom of speech comes not only from government officials but also from majorities intolerant of minority opinions.

The pressures to suppress freedom of expression are widespread and powerful in any society. It is important therefore to reaffirm constantly the benefits of freedom of expression to the individual and society. Among the arguments that favor free speech are the following:

- **Freedom of expression promotes individual growth and human dignity** The right of people to think about issues and to arrive at their own conclusions concerning morality, politics, or anything else is part of individual freedom. That right would be meaningless without the freedom to speak and write about opinions and without the freedom to test those opinions by comparing them to the views of others.

- **Freedom of expression is important for the advancement of knowledge** New ideas are more likely to be developed in a community that allows free discussion. As the British philosopher John Stuart Mill (1806–1873) said, progress is possible only when all points of view can be expressed and considered. This way, scientific or other discoveries can form the basis for future discoveries and inventions.

- **Freedom of expression is a necessary part of representative government** In the United States governments respond to the will of the people. If the people are to instruct government properly, then they must have access to information, ideas, and various points of view. Freedom of expression is crucial both in determining policy and in monitoring how well governments carry out their responsibilities.

- **Freedom of expression is vital to bringing about peaceful social change** The right to express one's ideas freely provides a safety valve for strongly held opinions. Freedom of expression allows a person or a group to try to influence public opinion through persuasion rather than by resorting to violence.

- **Freedom of expression is essential for the protection of all individual rights** The free expression of ideas and the right to speak against the violation of one's rights by others or by the government are essential for the protection of all the other rights of the individual.

HOW WAS FREEDOM OF EXPRESSION PROTECTED IN EARLY AMERICA?

Many ideas about the importance of freedom of speech and of the press were brought to America from England. In the seventeenth century the English won the right to speak and publish without prior censorship. But they could still be prosecuted afterward for what they said or wrote under the common law of **seditious libel**. This law made it a crime to publish anything that might injure the reputation of the government. And there were other restrictions on what

Art © Estate of Ben Shahn / Licensed by VAGA, New York, NY

What are some of the benefits of the right to freedom of expression?

could be published, such as **libel** directed at individuals, indecent expression, and blasphemy.

There is no indication that the Framers intended the Constitution or the Bill of Rights to prevent prosecution for seditious libel. The common view in both America and Britain was that no one should be able to make false or malicious accusations against the government.

However, the Constitution made no mention of a free press because the Framers believed, as Roger Sherman of Connecticut declared, "The power of Congress does not extend to the Press." The First Amendment was designed to quiet fears that Congress might interfere with the press anyway. These fears seemed to be confirmed by the passage of the Sedition Act of 1798. This act, passed by some of the same people who approved the Bill of Rights, indicates that some Americans still had a narrow view of free expression.

Many people opposed such limitations. One reason that the Republicans won the election of 1800 was that they were viewed as supporters of political freedom. By 1800 freedom of speech and press were beginning to be considered an essential part of free government. As Jefferson put it, "Our liberty depends on freedom of the press, and that cannot be limited without being lost."

HOW DID THE TRIAL OF JOHN PETER ZENGER HELP ESTABLISH FREEDOM OF THE PRESS?

What is "seditious libel"? The common law definition was vague. In general it meant defaming or ridiculing officers of the government, the constitution, laws, or government policies in a way that might jeopardize "public peace." This included publishing not only things that were false and malicious but also things that were true.

In 1735 John Peter Zenger (1697–1746), a New York printer, was charged with seditious libel by the colonial authorities. Zenger's lawyer argued that what Zenger had published was true and therefore could not be libelous.

The judge told the jury that the common law did not permit truth as a defense. It was the judge's prerogative to decide, as a matter of law, whether the articles met the definition of seditious libel. He instructed the jury that the only thing they could decide was the "fact" of whether Zenger was the publisher of the articles in question. If he was the publisher, which Zenger did not deny, then he was guilty pure and simple.

The jury ignored the judge's instructions and found Zenger not guilty because the information he reported in the articles was true. Many Americans believe that this case not only established an important right of freedom of the press but also proved the importance of the jury as a check on arbitrary government.

What principles were established by the trial of John Peter Zenger?

The court held that libel is punishable because "libels, regardless of what actual damage results to the reputation of the defamed…tend to create breaches of the peace when the defamed or his friends undertake to revenge themselves on the defamer." Today a common defense against a claim of libel is that the words were true. English law did not recognize truth as a defense to libel until 1842.

During the seventeenth and eighteenth centuries the British Crown prosecuted hundreds of cases of seditious libel, often imposing severe penalties. In 1664, for example, William Twyn refused to reveal the name of an author of a book asserting the right of the people to rebel against a government. He was convicted of sedition and of "imagining the death of the King." The court sentenced him to be hanged, emasculated, disemboweled, quartered, and then beheaded.

student page ▾ 209

William Blackstone's *Commentaries on the Laws of England*, published in 1769, had a major influence on thinking about free speech and press in the United States. According to Blackstone, freedom of the press consisted of "laying no previous restraints upon publications, and not in freedom from censure for criminal matter when published."

student page ▾ 209

HOW DID THE TRIAL OF JOHN PETER ZENGER HELP ESTABLISH FREEDOM OF THE PRESS?

The jury's verdict in Zenger's case is one of the most famous examples of what is known as "jury nullification." Jury nullification means a verdict of not guilty, despite overwhelming proof that the defendant committed a particular act, because the jury believes that the law making the act a crime is immoral or wrong.

Zenger was charged with printing seditious libels of William Cosby, the highly unpopular governor of the New York colony, in the *New York Weekly Journal*, a newspaper founded to oppose Cosby. At trial Zenger did not dispute that he had written allegedly libelous words. The judge therefore instructed the jury that it must return a guilty verdict based on the facts. The jury disregarded the judge's instructions. Instead it returned a verdict of not guilty, as Zenger's lawyer had urged it to do. The jury apparently was influenced by the story of a courageous jury in London in 1670 that had refused to find William Penn guilty for preaching Quaker religious doctrine even though the Quaker faith was then illegal in England.

wtpcompanion.civiced.org **LINKS**

Visit the We the People companion website for a link to historian Douglas Linder's excellent account of the Zenger trial.

Other examples of jury nullification in American history include Northern juries declaring defendants prosecuted for harboring slaves in violation of fugitive slave laws not guilty and not guilty verdicts during Prohibition, when defendants were prosecuted for violating laws against manufacturing or possessing alcohol. The possibility of jury nullification exists to this day.

student page ▾ 210

WHEN HAS FREEDOM OF EXPRESSION BEEN SUPPRESSED?

See the discussion in a later section of this lesson about how wars and emergencies affect free speech and press.

student page ▾ 210–211

WHAT ARE COMMONLY ACCEPTED LIMITATIONS OF FREEDOM OF EXPRESSION?

Acceptable limits on speech and press are seen in the following ways:

- **REGULATIONS** The Federal Communications Commission regulates what may be said on the public airways, including radio and television. States and local governments may enact regulations on noise and public gatherings as long as those regulations are not "content based" and are applied in a nondiscriminatory manner.

- **PROHIBITIONS** The Supreme Court has held that the right of speech and press in the First Amendment is not absolute. For example, the First Amendment does not protect obscenity (*Roth v. United States*, 1957).

- **PUNISHMENTS** Courts can impose sanctions on people who speak falsely under oath (perjury) or speak in a manner that is disrespectful to the court (contempt). As discussed previously, punishment also is possible for defaming another's reputation or engaging in "hate" speech, using "fighting words," or violating another's copyright.

WHEN HAS FREEDOM OF EXPRESSION BEEN SUPPRESSED?

There has been pressure at many times throughout history to suppress unpopular ideas. Restrictions generally have been imposed during times of war or when the government has felt threatened. Before the Civil War, for example, Congress made it a federal offense to send abolitionist literature through the mail. The early years of the twentieth century were marked by fears of the growing labor movement, socialism, communism, and anarchy. From World War I through the McCarthy era of the 1950s state and federal governments prosecuted many suspected anarchists, socialists, and communists for advocating draft resistance, mass strikes, or violent overthrow of the government. These actions raised serious questions about the right of free speech and led to a number of Supreme Court cases. However, since the 1960s there have been fewer attempts to prosecute those who advocate their beliefs, including belief in the benefits of a different form of government.

CRITICAL THINKING EXERCISE
Evaluating and Developing Positions on the Scope and Limits of Freedom of Expression

Judges, professors of constitutional law, and other students of the Constitution have tried to develop standards for deciding when freedom of expression may be limited. The following are two positions that judges and others have proposed. Work in one of two groups to debate the opposing positions described below. Make sure your position addresses the questions at the end of the exercise.

GROUP ❶

The freedom of expression of groups that advocate antidemocratic ideas may be limited. The rights of certain groups to express their ideas should not be protected by the First Amendment. Typically, these are groups that advocate overthrowing our representative government. They also may be groups that express malicious ideas that violate the dignity and hurt the feelings of other people in the community.

Advocates of this viewpoint often conclude by arguing that only people who agree to abide by the rules of our society, such as those in the Constitution and the Bill of Rights, should be allowed to participate in free and open discussion.

GROUP ❷

All people should be allowed freedom of expression no matter how dangerous or obnoxious their ideas. People holding this position say that rarely, if ever, should government be allowed to limit freedom of expression. For example, if public order is jeopardized, limitations on free expression could be justified. They claim that even totalitarian, racist, and other unpopular ideas may serve to make people defend and better understand their own values. To suppress such expression only makes those people who were denied the right to express their ideas more hostile. It eliminates the safety-valve function of free speech and weakens society.

Advocates of this viewpoint also argue that to give government the power to suppress the expression of ideas that some people find unacceptable is too dangerous. It gives government the power to decide what beliefs and opinions are acceptable and unacceptable. A statement often attributed to Voltaire (1694–1778), the eighteenth-century French philosopher noted for his criticism of tyranny and bigotry, summarizes this position: "I disapprove of what you say, but I will defend to the death your right to say it."

❶ What rights, values, and interests of individuals and society might be promoted or endangered by the position that advocates limiting the freedom to express antidemocratic ideas?

❷ What rights, values, and interests of individuals and society might be promoted or endangered by the position that advocates limiting freedom of expression rarely, if ever, no matter how dangerous or obnoxious the expressed ideas may be?

❸ After the debate, reflect on whether your own opinions on this issue were changed. Explain why or why not.

WHAT ARE COMMONLY ACCEPTED LIMITATIONS ON FREEDOM OF EXPRESSION?

Despite the statement in the First Amendment that "Congress shall make no law…abridging the freedom of speech," most people argue in favor of limiting freedom of expression in certain situations.

Suppose the First Amendment were interpreted to mean that there could be no laws at all limiting speech. People would be able to say anything they wanted at any time they wanted. People could lie in court and deprive others of their right to a fair trial. People could scream in libraries, give political speeches in the middle of church sermons, or speak through loudspeakers in neighborhoods in the middle of the night.

Most judges and legal scholars believe that the First Amendment should not be interpreted to protect freedom of expression in situations such as these examples. Liberty is not license to do anything one pleases. In some situations limiting freedom to speak may actually increase a person's ability to be heard. For example, there are rules governing when someone may talk at a meeting or a debate. A person may have the right to protest a government policy that person does not like, but that person doesn't have the right to do so with a loudspeaker in a residential area in the middle of the night.

HOW MAY GOVERNMENTS LIMIT EXPRESSION?

The Supreme Court always has permitted some regulation of speech and press. The Court's approach to analyzing restrictions on speech and press has been described as both "dynamic" and "unpredictable." That is because the Court's rulings change with changes in the Court's membership. Generally the following rules apply to laws and rules restricting free speech and press:

- **Laws may not discriminate unfairly on the basis of the content of the expression or the speaker** For example, a city council could not permit some religious organizations to pass out literature on public streets but forbid other religious organizations from doing so.

Laws and regulations also cannot single out people who hold unpopular views and prevent only them from speaking. However, no one has the right to publish secret military information or the names of U.S. intelligence agents working overseas.

- **Time, place, and manner restrictions must be content-neutral and applied fairly** Speech can be limited by **time, place, and manner restrictions** on when, where, and how it can occur. For example, a city council can restrict public speeches to certain parts of the day or require organizations to obtain permits for large public gatherings. Such regulations may not affect the content of expression or favor some individuals, groups, or opinions over others.

- **Regulations on expression cannot be vague** Restrictions on expression must be clear so that people know what is permitted and what is forbidden. For example, an administrative rule prohibiting "disrespectful speech that interferes with the public good" would be too vague. Neither a person wanting to speak in a lawful manner nor a police official charged with enforcement would know what the rule permits or prohibits.

What considerations, if any, should be used to limit freedom of expression?

student page ▼ 211

HOW MAY GOVERNMENTS LIMIT EXPRESSION?

The following Supreme Court cases show how the justices approach laws and rules restricting free speech and press discussed in this section:

- *Chaplinsky v. New Hampshire* (1942) ("fighting words")

- *Frisby v. Schultz* (1988) (picketing outside a private home)

- *Grayned v. City of Rockford* (1976) (picketing in violation of an anti-noise ordinance)

- *Madsen v. Women's Health Center* (1994) (picketing that blocks entrance to a clinic)

- *Cox v. Louisiana* (1965) ("disturbing the peace" ordinance and peaceful gathering)

- *Clark v. Community for Creative Non-Violence* (1984) ("symbolic" homeless tents in a national park)

- *Smith v. Goguen* (1974) (vagueness in a statute regarding treatment of the American flag)

- *Bible and Tract Society v. Stratton* (2002) (door-to-door canvassing regulation)

wtpcompanion.civiced.org   COURT CASES

Visit the We the People companion website for a link to Supreme Court syllabi and opinions for each of the cases described above.

- **Regulations must not be overly broad and must be implemented by the "least restrictive means"** Regulations must be written narrowly so that they solve a specific problem without limiting more expression than is necessary. Regulations also must employ the "least restrictive means" of achieving their goals. For example, violence sometimes erupts during political protests. Banning all political protests would be broader than necessary to solve the problem of occasional violence, therefore such a ban would not be the least restrictive means for reducing the risk of violence.

WHAT DO YOU THINK?

❶ The Supreme Court has held that the First Amendment does not protect obscene material. However, the Court also has been unable to agree on a definition of obscenity. In 1973 the Court held that "contemporary community standards" should provide the basis for deciding what is obscene and therefore subject to prohibition. How might a community go about deciding what is obscene? Who ought to be involved in making that determination? Is leaving the definition of obscenity to local communities a better solution to the problem than attempting to establish a national standard? Explain your reasoning.

❷ Do you think that a law restricting the amount of money that an individual or group is allowed to give to a political party or candidate violates freedom of expression? Why or why not?

❸ Consider the following examples that raise contemporary issues involving free speech and press. Which, if any, do you think should be subject to (a) regulation, (b) prohibition, (c) punishment, or (d) more speech or press expressing different opinions? Explain your reasoning.

- A newspaper publishes an editorial cartoon calling on opposing religious sects to attack one another so that we can finally know "which side God is on."

- A student places a statement on the school's website falsely accusing a teacher of reading obscene magazines at home.

- A website targeted at children ages nine to twelve contains much information of interest to children but also allows pornographic pictures to pop up without warning.

- A newspaper editorial compares a popular political figure to Adolf Hitler and claims that Americans are too complacent to find out the truth about him.

What considerations, if any, should be used to limit the right to freedom of expression of students at universities?

212

CRITICAL THINKING EXERCISE

Taking and Defending Positions on an Issue of Freedom of Expression

Read the following description of issues regarding freedom of expression on college and university campuses and then follow the directions for this exercise.

Colleges and universities are places where free inquiry, debate, and expression are highly valued. Professors and students are supposed to have freedom to explore, express, debate, and discuss both popular and unpopular ideas. The university is a place where all ideas are worthy of exploration.

In years past most students at major colleges and universities were white. Today student bodies of colleges and universities better reflect the diversity of our nation.

Despite the increased understanding of diversity in the United States, conflicts among students along racial, ethnic, and religious lines have occurred on college campuses. As a result, university administrators and student governments have attempted to promote civility and understanding on campus by various means.

Recently at more than two hundred colleges and universities across the nation student codes of conduct or "speech codes" were established. They are designed to prevent statements or comments about race, gender, religion, national origin, or sexual orientation that might offend some people. The goal of such codes is to discourage prejudice and to create a more comfortable learning environment for all students.

Supporters of the codes explain that "freedom of expression is no more sacred than freedom from intolerance or bigotry." Critics charge that the result has been to violate students' and teachers' right to free expression. They refer to various instances in which students have been suspended or expelled for comments that were offensive to others.

Work in small groups and assume that you and the people in your group are college students. You have been asked to determine what policy should be established to deal with the issue of what limitations, if any, should be placed on freedom of expression for students on campus. Develop a proposed policy and be prepared to present it to the class. Explain whether your position is based on philosophical principles, constitutional principles, specific circumstances, or on some or all of these. If your proposed policy is different from the current policy for society at large, justify the difference.

WHAT DO YOU THINK?

❶ Should any limits be placed on the freedom of expression of professors whose courses are required of all students for graduation? Explain your position.

❷ Should any limits be placed on the freedom of expression of professors of elective courses? Explain your position.

❸ Should any limits be placed on which guest speakers can be invited to address students at a university? Explain your position.

HOW DO WARS AND EMERGENCIES AFFECT FREE SPEECH AND PRESS?

During wars and emergencies free speech and press frequently are curtailed. Government officials seek to limit dissent or criticism in the name of defense. Early examples, discussed in previous units, include the Alien and Sedition Acts of the 1790s and restrictions on expression imposed during the Civil War.

From World War I through the McCarthy era of the 1950s states and the national government enacted laws punishing suspected anarchists, socialists, and communists for advocating draft resistance, mass strikes, or the violent overthrow of the government. Many people were prosecuted for violating the laws.

In 1969 the Supreme Court adopted an approach to free speech and press that was much more tolerant of provocative, inflammatory speech than past approaches. The Court explained that its decisions had

> ❝ fashioned the principle that the constitutional guarantees of free speech and free press do not permit a State to forbid or proscribe advocacy of the use of force or of law violation *except where such advocacy is directed to inciting or producing imminent lawless action and is likely to incite or produce such action.* (Emphasis added.)
>
> *Brandenburg v. Ohio* (1969)

Between 1969 and 2001 the Court heard very few cases involving this *Brandenburg* test. However, in 2001 terrorist attacks on the United States rekindled public debate about whether the *Brandenburg* test is too lenient in times of war and emergency.

student page ▾ 213

HOW DO WARS AND EMERGENCIES AFFECT FREE SPEECH AND PRESS?

In *Ex parte Milligan* (1866) the Supreme Court upheld President Lincoln's suspension of the writ of habeas corpus during the Civil War. However, it also ruled that military tribunals could not be used to try citizens in states whose civilian courts were still operating. The Court wrote the following:

> The Constitution of the United States is a law for rulers and people, equally in war and in peace, and covers with the shield of its protection all classes of men, at all times, and under all circumstances. No doctrine, involving more pernicious consequences, was ever invented by the wit of man than that any of its provisions can be suspended during any of the great exigencies of government. Such a doctrine leads directly to anarchy or despotism.

However, during times of war and emergency that soaring rhetoric has given way to a variety of restrictions on speech and press. Examples of cases between World War I and the McCarthy era include the following:

- *Schenck v. United States* (1919)
- *Gitlow v. New York* (1925)
- *Whitney v. California* (1927)
- *Dennis v. United States* (1951)

wtpcompanion.civiced.org COURT CASES

Visit the We the People companion website for a link to Supreme Court syllabi and opinions for each of the cases described above.

WHAT DO YOU THINK?

Do you think that in times of war and emergency the government should be able to place greater limitations on freedom of expression than at other times? Why or why not?

REVIEWING AND USING THE LESSON

❶ How does freedom of expression contribute to individual liberty and good government?

❷ What forms of expression does the First Amendment protect?

❸ What are time, place, and manner restrictions?

❹ How might new forms of communication, such as the Internet, give rise to important First Amendment issues?

What limits, if any, should be placed on freedom of the press during times of war and emergency?

214

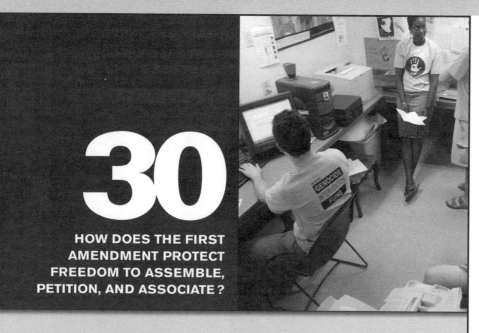

30

HOW DOES THE FIRST AMENDMENT PROTECT FREEDOM TO ASSEMBLE, PETITION, AND ASSOCIATE?

UNIT FIVE | **LESSON 30**

HOW DOES THE FIRST AMENDMENT PROTECT FREEDOM TO ASSEMBLE, PETITION, AND ASSOCIATE?

wtpcompanion.civiced.org | **LESSON PURPOSE + TERMS**

Visit the We the People companion website for printable and downloadable Lesson Purposes and Terms and Concepts to Understand sections for each lesson. Audio readings of each Lesson Purpose and Term are also available online in MP3 format.

LESSON PURPOSE

The previous lesson examined the First Amendment protection of speech and press. This lesson focuses on "the right of the people peaceably to assemble, and to petition the Government for a redress of grievances." It examines the importance and historical background of these rights. It also discusses an important related right— the freedom to associate.

When you have finished this lesson, you should be able to explain the importance of the rights to assemble, petition, and associate. You also should be able to describe the history of these rights and when they can be limited. Finally, you should be able to evaluate, take, and defend positions relating to the exercise of these three rights.

TERMS AND CONCEPTS TO UNDERSTAND

gag rule	right to associate
public forum	right to petition
right to assemble	

WHAT IS THE IMPORTANCE OF THE RIGHTS TO ASSEMBLE, PETITION, AND ASSOCIATE?

ASSEMBLE Historically the right to assemble peaceably was considered merely a means of exercising the right to petition the government for a redress of grievances. However, in *De Jonge v. Oregon* (1937) the Supreme Court held that the right to assemble peaceably limits state governments as well as the national government. The Court wrote the following:

> Freedom of speech and of the press are fundamental rights which are safeguarded by the due process clause of the Fourteenth Amendment of the Federal Constitution [citations omitted]. The right of peaceable assembly is a right cognate to those of free speech and free press, and is equally fundamental…. It is one that cannot be denied without violating those fundamental principles of liberty and justice which lie at the base of all civil and political institutions—principles which the Fourteenth Amendment embodies in the general terms of its due process clause

PETITION The right to petition for a redress of grievances traces to Chapter 61 of the Magna Carta (1215), which provided that

> if we or our justiciar [the head of the royal judicial system], or our bailiffs, or any of our servants shall have done wrong in any way toward any one, or shall have transgressed any of the articles of peace or security; and the wrong shall have been shown to four barons of the aforesaid twenty-five barons, let those four barons come to us or to our justiciar, if we are out of the kingdom, laying before us the transgression, and let them ask that we cause that transgression to be corrected without delay.

Today the rights to assemble and petition, along with the speech and press clauses, tend to be treated under the broad umbrella of "expression."

ASSOCIATE Recognition of a right to associate, which is not mentioned in the First Amendment, arose out of cases in the 1950s and 1960s, challenging the efforts of some states to limit the activities of civil rights groups such as the National Association for the Advancement of Colored People, or NAACP (see Lesson 35). In *NAACP v. Alabama ex rel Patterson* (1958) the Supreme Court wrote,

> It is beyond debate that freedom to engage in association for the advancement of beliefs and ideas is an inseparable aspect of the "liberty" assured by the Due Process Clause of the Fourteenth Amendment, which embraces freedom of speech…. Of course, it is immaterial whether the beliefs sought to be advanced by association pertain to

WHAT IS THE IMPORTANCE OF THE RIGHTS TO ASSEMBLE, PETITION, AND ASSOCIATE?

The First Amendment protects people's right to form their own opinions, including those about politics and religion. It also protects the right to communicate those opinions to others. These rights would not mean very much if the government had the power to prevent people from getting together to express their views. To petition means to ask the government to take action or change its policies, or to ask for a redress of grievances—that is, for the government to grant a remedy for a perceived wrong. The people's freedom to assemble and to petition the government enhances the First Amendment protection of political rights.

A related right that has been recognized by courts is the **right to associate.** People are free to associate with others who share their opinions. These associations include political groups, church groups, professional associations, social clubs, and community service organizations. The right to associate freely protects all such groups.

WHY WERE THE RIGHTS TO ASSEMBLE AND PETITION IMPORTANT TO THE FOUNDERS?

The rights of assembly and petition were part of English common law for hundreds of years and were seen by Americans as fundamental to a constitutional democracy. Historically these two rights have been associated with each other. People thought that the purpose of the **right to assemble** was to petition the government. The right of petition was recognized in the Magna Carta. In fact, the Magna Carta itself was a petition addressed to the king demanding that he correct certain wrongs. A century before the American Revolution, a resolution of the House of Commons in 1669, along with the English Bill of Rights of 1689, guaranteed English subjects the **right to petition** both the House of Commons and the monarch.

The American colonists considered the right to petition a basic right of Englishmen and used it often. They could not send representatives to Parliament, and so they saw the right to petition as an important means of communication with the British government. One of the colonists' frustrations in the years before the Revolution was the feeling that Parliament was ignoring their petitions.

During and after the Revolution most states protected the rights of assembly and petition, either in their state constitutions or in their state bills of rights. Today the rights of assembly and petition have been included in all but two of the fifty state constitutions.

Why is the right to assemble fundamental to constitutional democracy?

HOW HAVE THE RIGHTS TO ASSEMBLE AND PETITION BEEN USED?

From the beginning Americans have felt free to ask the government for action on issues that were important to them. In the 1790s one task that faced the first Congress was acting on hundreds of petitions for pensions or back pay promised to the widows and orphans of soldiers in the Revolutionary War.

In the 1830s Congress received numerous petitions urging that slavery be abolished in the District of Columbia. The feeling against abolitionists was so strong that in 1836 the House of Representatives—but not the Senate—passed a **gag rule**, which is a rule prohibiting debate on certain topics, to prevent petitions against slavery. This rule not only prevented any discussion of ending slavery in the House of Representatives, it also limited an important way that nonvoters could express their views on the issue. The use of the right to petition was an important way for women, African Americans, and others who were denied the right to vote to communicate with public officials. The gag rule was finally repealed in 1844, thanks to the leadership of former president John Quincy Adams, a member of Congress at that time.

The U.S. government has tried to silence its critics at other times. For example, during the Great Depression a group of World War I veterans known as the Bonus Army converged on the nation's capital in the summer of 1932 to petition Congress for early payment of their military bonuses. Congress refused to support the bill, and half the veterans returned home. However, several thousand remained in a camp outside the city. President Herbert Hoover ordered General Douglas MacArthur, who is remembered as commander of the World War II allied invasion of Japan, and the army to drive the veterans out of the camp. MacArthur did so with tanks, guns, and tear gas, killing two veterans and wounding several others.

American women made extensive use of petition and assembly in their long struggle to win the vote, to serve on juries, to own property, and to gain opportunities for education and employment. For example, in the early 1800s women and girls who worked in textile mills organized the Lowell Female Labor Reform Association. They presented petitions with more than two thousand signatures to the Massachusetts legislature urging laws limiting the workday to ten hours and requiring safety devices on dangerous machinery. They did not succeed, but they adopted the motto Try Again. Other women's associations did just that. Women in New York gathered ten thousand signatures to petition their state legislature for the right to vote and the right of married women to own property. In 1865 women's groups sent a petition with four hundred thousand signatures to

Why is the right to petition fundamental to constitutional democracy?

Congress asking for a Thirteenth Amendment to the Constitution to abolish slavery.

The importance of the right to assemble is nowhere better illustrated than in the civil rights movement of the 1950s and 1960s. Under the leadership of the Reverend Martin Luther King Jr. (1929–1968) thousands participated in the March on Washington for Jobs and Freedom in 1963.

political, economic, religious or cultural matters, and state action which may have the effect of curtailing the freedom to associate is subject to the closest scrutiny.

wtpcompanion.civiced.org   COURT CASES

Visit the We the People companion website for a link to the Supreme Court syllabus and opinions for *NAACP v. Alabama ex rel Patterson* (1958).

student page ▾ 216

WHY WERE THE RIGHTS TO ASSEMBLE AND PETITION IMPORTANT TO THE FOUNDERS?

The English Parliament obtained the right of petitioning the Crown for a redress of grievances as a tradeoff for the Crown's demands for taxes. In 1669 the House of Commons asserted that every commoner in the realm had "the inherent right to prepare and present petitions" to it "in case of grievance," and claimed the power "to receive the same" and to judge whether they were "fit" to be received. In 1689 the English Bill of Rights included the provision "That it is the right of the subjects to petition the king, and all commitments and prosecutions for such petitioning are illegal."

Petitioning played an important role in politics in the American colonies. Virginia, for example, encouraged the use of petitions to propose legislation or to seek redress of grievances. Petitions provided an orderly mechanism for bringing problems of colonial administration to Parliament's attention. Petitions frequently dealt with defense issues, land disputes, or problems with royal charters. As the Revolution neared, colonists made increasing use of petitions, as noted in the Declaration of Independence: "In every stage of these Oppressions we have Petitioned for Redress in the most humble Terms: Our repeated petitions have been answered only by repeated Injury."

After the Revolution states began including the guarantee of the right to petition for a redress of grievances in their new constitutions. Later, in *Adderley v. Florida* (1966) the Supreme Court explained that the right to petition encompasses a broad range of activities constituents use to communicate with government officials:

> The right...has an ancient history, and is not limited to writing a letter or sending a telegram to a Congressman; it is not confined to appearing before local city council, or writing letters to the President or Governor or Mayor. Conventional methods of petitioning may be, and often have been, shut off to large groups of our citizens. Legislators may turn deaf ears, formal complaints may be routed endlessly through a bureaucratic maze; courts may let the wheels of justice grind very slowly. Those who

do not control television and radio, those who cannot afford to advertise in newspapers or circulate elaborate pamphlets may only have a limited type of access to public officials. Their methods should not be condemned as tactics of obstruction and harassment as long as the assembly and petition are peaceable.

student page ▼ 217–218

HOW HAVE THE RIGHTS TO ASSEMBLE AND PETITION BEEN USED?

In 1840 the House adopted a standing rule in place of the special "gag rule" providing

> that no petition, memorial, resolution, or other paper praying the abolition of slavery in the District of Columbia, or any State or Territories of the United States in which it now exists, shall be received by this House, or entertained in any way whatever.

House rules now recognize petitions as one way to communicate with the House. Rule XII (3) of the 110th Congress (2006–2008) states the following:

> If a Member, Delegate, or Resident Commissioner has a *petition*, memorial, or private bill to present, he shall endorse his name, deliver it to the Clerk, and may specify the reference or disposition to be made thereof. Such petition, memorial, or private bill (except when judged by the Speaker to be obscene or insulting) shall be entered on the Journal with the name of the Member, Delegate, or Resident Commissioner presenting it and shall be printed in the Congressional Record. (emphasis added)

Today the right to petition government often is associated with the activity of lobbying (see Lessons 21 and 22 on Congress, Lessons 23 and 24 on the executive, and Lesson 26 on federalism). Petitions to Congress cover a wide range of topics, from requests for immigration and visa assistance to recognition of Native American tribes and statements about American foreign policy.

student page ▼ 218

WHAT LIMITATIONS MAY GOVERNMENT PLACE ON THE RIGHT TO ASSEMBLE?

Examples of the Court's approach to whether legislative attempts to place restrictions on assembly are valid in particular circumstances include the following:

Today the right to petition is widely used at the local, state, and national levels. Groups that do not have the money to buy advertising often use the right to assemble and petition to make their views known by attracting the attention of the news media. In 2006 millions of Latin American immigrants sponsored marches throughout the United States to draw attention to the plight of undocumented workers.

The right to petition includes much more than formal petitions. Faxes, emails, phone calls, and letters to public officials also are methods of petitioning the government. The right to petition is not limited to people wishing the government to correct wrongs. Individuals, groups, and corporations lobby government officials to try to persuade them to adopt policies that will benefit their interests or the interests of the country as a whole.

WHAT LIMITATIONS MAY GOVERNMENT PLACE ON THE RIGHT TO ASSEMBLE?

The Supreme Court has emphasized the importance of the right to assemble in a free society, but it has approved certain restrictions. For example, in 1939 the Court held in *Hague v. Congress of Industrial Organizations* that people have the right to assemble in a **public forum**, such as in the street, in parks, and on sidewalks. But government is responsible for ensuring that demonstrations remain peaceful and do not endanger community safety or unreasonably inconvenience the public. The justices have struggled with how to balance the right to assemble against other rights and the needs of the public. The Court generally has held that time, place, and manner restrictions—which affect when, where, and how assemblies occur—are permissible if two conditions are satisfied:

- The government imposing the restriction identifies a legitimate government interest, such as preventing riots or keeping streets clear during rush hour, and does not impose the regulation with the purpose of suppressing free speech or assembly.

- The restriction is precisely worded and is applied in a nondiscriminatory manner. That is, the restriction must apply to all groups and cannot be imposed because of the theme or subject of the assembly.

What considerations, if any, should be used to limit the right to freedom of assembly?

CRITICAL THINKING EXERCISE

Taking and Defending a Position on the Right to Assemble

The following are examples that illustrate the difficulty of balancing the right to assemble with the obligation of government to protect the public. Work in small groups to examine the following situations and then answer the questions that follow for each situation.

- Demonstrators plan to march on a public sidewalk in front of a private home to protest the investment decisions of the corporate executive who lives there. A city ordinance prohibits gatherings on public sidewalks that are "intended to harass or upset" others.

- People plan to assemble in a park across the street from a shopping mall to protest the sale of animal-fur coats by one of the stores. A county law permits people to gather in public parks only for picnics.

- Several students plan to march through a public school during their lunch hour—while other students are in class—to protest a new dress code. A school rule requires students to remain in the cafeteria during their lunch hour.

- A group of striking workers demanding health-care benefits as part of their union contract plans to block the sidewalk in front of the entrance to a grocery store. A state statute prohibits members of unions from blocking public sidewalks.

❶ What constitutional arguments can you make on behalf of allowing those participating in the assemblies described above to do so without restriction?

❷ What constitutional arguments can you make on behalf of the government official defending the restriction in each situation described above?

❸ How does each situation illustrate the difficulty of balancing the right to assemble against the government's obligation to protect the public?

HOW IS THE RIGHT TO ASSOCIATE PROTECTED?

The right of association is not mentioned in the Constitution, but the courts have said that it is implied by the other rights in the First Amendment—in particular by the rights of free speech and assembly. The right to associate freely with other citizens is part of living in a free society. The government should not interfere with

- *Feiner v. New York* (1951)
- *City Council v. Taxpayers for Vincent* (1984)
- *Ward v. Rock Against Racism* (1989)
- *Forsyth County v. Nationalist Movement* (1992)
- *City of Ladue v. Gilleo* (1994)
- *Madsen v. Women's Health Center* (1994)
- *Watchtower Bible v. Stratton* (2002)

wtpcompanion.civiced.org   **COURT CASES**

Visit the We the People companion website for a link to Supreme Court syllabi and opinions for each of the cases described above.

student page ▾ 219–220

HOW IS THE RIGHT TO ASSOCIATE PROTECTED?

Examples of the Court's approach to whether organizations must comply with nondiscrimination laws include the following:

- *Roberts v. United States Jaycees* (1984)
- *Board of Directors of Rotary International v. Rotary Club of Duarte* (1987)
- *Hurley v. Irish-American GLIB Society* (1995)
- *Boy Scouts of America v. Dale* (2000) (see Lesson 19)

wtpcompanion.civiced.org   **COURT CASES**

Visit the We the People companion website for a link to Supreme Court syllabi and opinions for each of the cases described above.

Should private organizations be required to make lists of their members public? Why or why not?

ENRICHMENT ACTIVITY

ASSESSING CONSTITUTIONAL PROTECTIONS OF FREEDOM TO ASSEMBLE

Ask students to study the following provisions regarding the right to assemble in three state constitutions.

MASSACHUSETTS CONSTITUTION, 1780

> The people have a right, in an orderly and peaceable manner, to assemble to consult upon the common good; give instructions to their representatives; and to request of the legislative body, by the way of addresses, petitions, or remonstrances, redress of the wrongs done them, and of the grievances they suffer.

OHIO CONSTITUTION, 1803

> That the people have a right to assemble together, in a peaceable manner, to consult for their common good, to instruct their Representatives, and to apply to the Legislature for a redress of grievances.

ALASKA CONSTITUTION, 1956

> The right of the people peaceably to assemble, and to petition the government shall never be abridged.

Ask students to compare the wording of each provision with the wording of the provision in the First Amendment to the Constitution and then to respond to the following questions:

❶ Is it important that the guarantees regarding assembly appear in separate provisions of the state constitutions rather than in the same amendment that addresses rights of speech, press, and petition as in the Constitution? Why or why not?

❷ What is the significance, if any, in the change of wording over time in the states' constitutions? Explain.

---

people's right to join with others, it is argued, whether such association takes place in private clubs, college fraternities or sororities, political parties, professional organizations, or labor unions.

The first time that the Supreme Court dealt with an issue regarding the right to associate was in 1958. The state of Alabama had ordered the National Association for the Advancement of Colored People (NAACP) to disclose its membership list. During this time the NAACP was engaged in a bitter civil rights struggle. The Supreme Court thought that if the NAACP membership list was made public, then this disclosure might lead to hostile acts against NAACP members. The Court ruled in *NAACP v. Alabama* (1958) that the First Amendment protects the right to associate and that Alabama's demand for the membership list violated this right.

However, soon after the Alabama ruling the Court upheld laws that required disclosure of membership lists of the Communist Party. In *Barenblatt v. United States* (1959) the Court justified this decision on the ground that the organization advocated violent overthrow of the government.

One question that arises is whether the right to associate means that one has the right not to associate with certain people. Should private organizations be able to prohibit some people from becoming members? For example, should the government be able to require private golf courses to admit African Americans or private men's clubs to admit women? This question involves the right of equal protection as well as that of association.

In cases involving this question the Supreme Court has ruled that the government cannot interfere in a person's choices about whom to associate with in private life. On the other hand, the Court has ruled that in some situations that go beyond close personal relationships and involve larger social purposes, the government may require private organizations not to discriminate on the basis of race, gender, or ethnic background. For example,

- Some associations are so large and their purposes are so diverse and focused on social policy that they must comply with antidiscrimination laws. The Rotary Club and the Junior Chamber of Commerce are examples of such organizations.

- Some private clubs operate much like restaurants, providing regular meals to members and their guests. Such clubs must comply with laws that prohibit discrimination.

- Some employers pay their employees' memberships in associations. In general, if members do not pay the dues themselves,

then the association must comply with laws that prohibit discrimination.

These issues can be very difficult. The difficulties reflect the tension between two important ideals:

- Eliminating unfair discrimination in American life

- The right of each individual to live his or her own life as free as possible from government interference

One hundred fifty years ago French political thinker Alexis de Tocqueville commented on Americans' habitual practice of joining together to solve common problems. The exercise of freedom of association was, Tocqueville believed, one of the outstanding characteristics of American citizenship. It is difficult to imagine the development of labor unions, political parties, and a host of other organizations that play important roles in American civic life without the exercise of this right.

Tocqueville believed that the right to associate was essential for preserving free government in the United States given the country's social equality. Americans did not need to rely on government to solve all their problems because private groups could organize themselves quickly to respond to common concerns or needs. Tocqueville thought that this capacity helped to make Americans more public spirited. Americans were aware that they were responsible for helping to achieve the common good, and each citizen could do something to help achieve it.

What did Alexis de Tocqueville believe were some of the most outstanding qualities of American society?

WHAT DO YOU THINK?

❶ Should the right to associate be interpreted to mean that organizations may not impose any limits on their membership? Explain your position.

❷ Do you think that the actions by some cities and towns to prohibit certain groups from peacefully gathering in public parks violate the rights to assemble and associate? Why?

❸ What conflicts might occur between the right to assemble and other values and interests of society? How should these conflicts be managed?

CRITICAL THINKING EXERCISE
Taking and Defending a Position on a First Amendment Issue

Board of Education of the Westside Community Schools v. Mergens (1990) involved most of the First Amendment rights you have been studying—religion, speech, and association. Read the summary of the case below. Then to complete this exercise, work in one of three groups. All groups should be sure to address the questions that follow the case summary.

In 1984 Congress passed the Equal Access Act, which prohibits any public secondary school that receives federal funds and provides facilities for extracurricular organizations from discriminating against student clubs because of their religious or philosophical orientation.

Westside High School is a public school in Omaha, Nebraska, with about fifteen hundred students. Students have the opportunity to participate in a number of groups and clubs, all of which meet after school on school premises. Among these groups are the Creative Writing Club, the Math Club, and the Future Medical Assistants. School board policy requires that each group have a faculty sponsor, and no group may be sponsored by any organization that denies membership based on race, color, creed, gender, or political belief.

In January 1985 student Bridget Mergens met with the Westside principal to request permission to form a Christian Club, the purpose of which would be to "permit students to read and discuss the Bible, to have fellowship, and to pray together." The club would be open to all students, regardless of religious beliefs. There would be no faculty sponsor.

Both the principal and the district superintendent denied the request. They said, first of all, that the sponsor requirement was not met. More important, permitting the religious

Should religious clubs be able to meet on public school property? Why or why not?

club to meet on school property would be unconstitutional. The school board upheld the denial.

Mergens and her parents sued the school for violating the Equal Access Act and the First Amendment protections of speech, association, and exercise of religion. The trial judge ruled in favor of the school saying that the Equal Access Act did not apply because all the other clubs at school were related to the school curriculum and linked to the school's educational function.

The U.S. Court of Appeals reversed the lower court ruling, noting that there were other school clubs, such as the Chess Club and the Surfing Club, that were not directly related to the school's educational function. The school district appealed to the Supreme Court.

GROUP ❶

Develop arguments for the Westside High School position.

GROUP ❷

Develop arguments for the position of Bridget Mergens.

GROUP ❸

Act as judges, listen to both arguments, and decide whether the Christian Club should be able to meet after school. The judges should be able to explain the basis for their decision and defend it before the class.

Be sure to consider the following questions:

❶ What First Amendment issues are raised in this case?

❷ What values and interests are in conflict in this case?

❸ What arguments can you make for allowing the group to meet?

❹ What arguments can you make for prohibiting the group from meeting?

REVIEWING AND USING THE LESSON

❶ How would you explain the rights to assemble, petition, and associate?

❷ How would you describe the historical origins of the rights to assemble and petition?

❸ How and why have the rights to assemble and petition been important in American history?

❹ What restrictions have been imposed on the right to assemble, and how have these restrictions been justified?

❺ Although the right to associate is not mentioned in the First Amendment, how have courts justified treating it as a constitutional right?

What criteria should be used to determine what type of clubs can meet on school campuses?

222

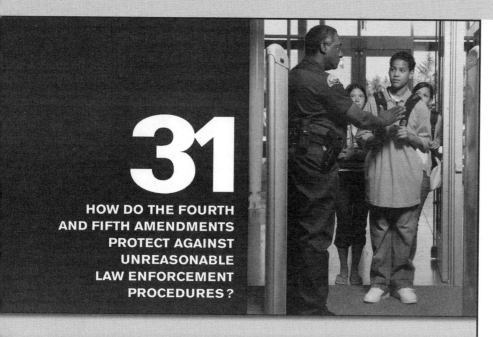

31

HOW DO THE FOURTH AND FIFTH AMENDMENTS PROTECT AGAINST UNREASONABLE LAW ENFORCEMENT PROCEDURES?

UNIT FIVE | LESSON 31

HOW DO THE FOURTH AND FIFTH AMENDMENTS PROTECT AGAINST UNREASONABLE LAW ENFORCEMENT PROCEDURES?

wtpcompanion.civiced.org | **LESSON PURPOSE + TERMS**

Visit the We the People companion website for printable and downloadable Lesson Purposes and Terms and Concepts to Understand sections for each lesson. Audio readings of each Lesson Purpose and Term are also available online in MP3 format.

LESSON PURPOSE

The Fourth Amendment limits the powers of government officials to search and seize individuals, their homes, their papers, and other property. The Fifth Amendment contains several other important protections for criminal defendants, including protection from self-incrimination. This lesson focuses on the Fourth Amendment and the protection from self-incrimination in the Fifth Amendment. It examines the history of these protections and why they were important to the Framers.

When you have finished this lesson, you should be able to explain the purpose and history of the Fourth Amendment and issues raised by its interpretation. You also should be able to explain the importance of the Fifth Amendment provision against self-incrimination. Finally, you should be able to evaluate, take, and defend positions on contemporary issues involving the Fourth Amendment and self-incrimination.

TERMS AND CONCEPTS TO UNDERSTAND

affidavit

exclusionary rule

probable cause

reasonableness

search

seizure

self-incrimination

use immunity

warrant

student page ▾ **224**

WHAT IS THE HISTORY OF THE FOURTH AMENDMENT?

The idea that "a man's home is his castle" traces to the opinion of Sir Edward Coke in *Semayne's Case* in 1604. Coke wrote that "the house of everyone is to him as his castle and fortress." It followed, Coke reasoned, that defending one's house from thieves by either injuring or killing them was not a felony.

The British believed that smuggling in the colonies in violation of various trade acts was so serious that general writs commonly allowed customs officials to enter any house or other place to search for and seize "prohibited and uncustomed" goods. The writs also allowed custom officials to command the assistance of any British subject in carrying out the searches and seizures.

General writs issued during the life of a king or queen remained in effect through the lifetime of that monarch and six months after the monarch's death. When King George II died in 1760, British authorities had to request new writs for the colonies. James Otis (1725–1783), who once had been an advocate general in vice admiralty courts charged with prosecuting smugglers, represented Boston merchants in the effort to prevent the writs from being reissued. In a five-hour speech in February 1761 Otis argued that general writs violated the colonists' natural rights and that any act of Parliament contrary to those rights was void. In his speech he said,

> A man's house is his castle; and whilst he is quiet, he is as well guarded as a prince in his castle. This writ, if it should be declared legal, would totally annihilate this privilege. Custom-house officers may enter our houses when they please; we are commanded to permit their entry. Their menial servants may enter, may break locks, bars, and everything in their way; and whether they break through malice or revenge, no man, no court may inquire.

Otis lost and the writs were reissued.

John Adams, then a young lawyer, later said that Otis's argument was the first act of colonial resistance to British policies. Otis became an instant celebrity and was elected to the Massachusetts legislature (called the general court). He played a prominent role in revolutionary politics until 1769, when a British custom official beat him on the head with a cane in retaliation for an offensive newspaper article that Otis had written. Otis's head injuries left him mentally unstable and ended his political career.

John Adams later drafted the Massachusetts Constitution of 1780. Regarding searches and seizures Article XIV of the Declaration of Rights provided the following:

> Every subject has a right to be secure from all unreasonable searches, and seizures, of his person, his houses, his papers, and all his possessions.

WHAT IS THE HISTORY OF THE FOURTH AMENDMENT?

Americans inherited from British history the principle that "a man's home is his castle." The right to privacy and its importance to a free society have been understood at least since the Magna Carta. One way English common law protected the right to privacy was by prohibiting judges from giving law enforcement officials general warrants, also known as writs of assistance. A **warrant** is a document given to a police officer or other government official giving permission to intrude into a person's privacy —**search**—or interfere with a person's property or freedom of movement—**seizure**. A general warrant does not describe in detail the places to be searched or the things or persons to be seized. General warrants have been referred to as open-ended "hunting licenses" because they allow government officials to search people, businesses, homes, and property indiscriminately.

Despite the common law prohibition against general warrants, Parliament and royal commissions sometimes allowed their use. General warrants were used to harass and persecute individuals who were critical of the government or who, like Puritans, dissented from the Church of England.

Should police be able to search school lockers without a warrant or a student's permission? Why or why not?

In the eighteenth century Parliament also approved the use of general warrants in the American colonies. British officials used such warrants to collect taxes, to recover stolen goods—including slaves—and to prosecute persons they believed to have violated British trade restrictions by smuggling tea and other products into the colonies. The British were not entirely wrong in suspecting the colonists of smuggling. John Hancock's father, for one, made a great deal of money smuggling tea into Boston. A general warrant enabled the British to discover that John Hancock himself was smuggling wine.

The colonists' strong objections to British trade laws and the use of general warrants contributed to the American Revolution. After the Revolution state declarations of rights typically outlawed general warrants. Anti-Federalists later criticized the Constitution for not placing similar limitations on the national government. Abraham Holmes, a delegate to the Massachusetts ratifying convention, said, "There is no provision made in the Constitution to prevent...the most innocent person...[from] being taken by virtue of a general warrant...and dragged from his home."

WHAT IS THE PURPOSE AND IMPORTANCE OF THE FOURTH AMENDMENT?

Few provisions in the Bill of Rights grew so directly out of colonial experience as the Fourth Amendment. The amendment protects persons, houses, papers, and other personal effects from "unreasonable searches and seizures." In particular the amendment

- Prohibits general warrants
- Requires applications for warrants to be supported by probable cause (discussed later in this lesson)
- Requires a judge or magistrate, not the official who will serve the warrant, to decide whether probable cause exists
- Requires applications for warrants to "particularly" describe the "place to be searched, and the persons or things to be seized"

Soon after he served as a judge at the Nuremberg trials of Nazi war criminals in 1949, Supreme Court Justice Robert Jackson stressed the importance to a free society of the protections against unreasonable searches and seizures. He said,

> " Among the deprivations of rights, none is so effective in cowing a population, crushing

All warrants, therefore, are contrary to this right, if the cause or foundation of them be not previously supported by oath or affirmation; and if the order in the warrant to a civil officer, to make search in suspected places, or to arrest one or more suspected persons, or to seize their property, be not accompanied with a special designation of the persons or objects of search, arrest, or seizure: and no warrant ought to be issued but in cases, and with the formalities prescribed by the laws.

student page ▼ 224–225

WHAT IS THE PURPOSE AND IMPORTANCE OF THE FOURTH AMENDMENT?

The terms *search* and *seizure* refer to methods that law enforcement officers use to investigate crimes, locate evidence, question witnesses, and arrest suspects. To implement the Fourth Amendment Congress has adopted Federal Rules of Criminal Procedure. All state constitutions also contain provisions regarding searches and seizures, and state legislatures have adopted statutes to implement those provisions.

The Supreme Court has held that the Fourth Amendment protects only a "reasonable expectation of privacy" (*Katz v. United States*, 1967). Moreover, the Fourth Amendment limits governments in criminal, not civil, cases (*Murray v. Hoboken Land & Improvement Company*, 1856). Today the protections of the Fourth Amendment bind the states as well as the national government through the due process clause of the Fourteenth Amendment (*Wolf v. Colorado*, 1961).

Not all expectations of privacy are considered reasonable. For example, one has no reasonable expectation of privacy while in plain public view, and police may seize evidence that is in plain view without a warrant (*Horton v. California*, 1990). There is no reasonable expectation of privacy in public places, such as on a thoroughfare (*United States v. Knotts*, 1983) or in a prison cell (*Hudson v. Palmer*, 1984).

There have been vast technological changes since the adoption of the Fourth Amendment. Photography, radio, television, and digital imagery have affected how police officers do their work. State and lower federal courts have been ahead of the Supreme Court in being asked to interpret the significance of ever-changing technology and surveillance techniques.

Leading cases on wiretapping and other forms of eavesdropping include the following:

- *Olmstead v. United States* (1928)
- *Berger v. New York* (1967)
- *Katz v. United States* (1967)
- *United States v. United States District Court* (1972)

Why did Parliament approve the use of general warrants to allow searches in the American colonies?

the spirit of the individual and putting terror in every heart as uncontrolled search and seizure. It is one of the first and most effective weapons in the arsenal of every arbitrary government.

Courts have interpreted the Fourth Amendment as protecting reasonable expectations of privacy, although the amendment does not specifically state that it protects privacy. However, protecting privacy against intrusion by government officials is a deeply held value in the United States. Privacy also is an important component of the rights to freedom of conscience, thought, religion, expression, and property. The rapid growth of surveillance and other technology makes concerns about privacy particularly acute today.

WHAT DO YOU THINK?

❶ What powers should be given to law enforcement officers in order for them to be able to enforce the law? Is the Fourth Amendment's prohibition against general warrants still desirable in light of ongoing threats of terrorism? Explain.

❷ What values are served by requiring law enforcement officers to get permission from a judge to arrest someone or search his or her property?

❸ In 2007 the deputy director of national intelligence stated, "Protecting anonymity isn't a fight that can be won. Anyone [who has] typed in their name on Google understands that." Privacy, he argued, has basically become what the government and the business community say it is. Do you agree or disagree? Why?

WHAT ISSUES ARISE IN INTERPRETING AND APPLYING THE FOURTH AMENDMENT?

The Fourth Amendment protects against "unreasonable" searches and seizures. It seeks to strike a balance between society's need for order and safety and the individual's right to autonomy and privacy. Achieving the proper balance under ever-changing circumstances is the ongoing challenge in interpreting the Fourth Amendment.

The Fourth Amendment raises three important questions:

- When is a warrant required?
- What is probable cause and when is it required?
- How should the Fourth Amendment be enforced?

225

- *United States v. Kahn* (1974)
- *Waller v. Georgia* (1984)
- *Kyllo v. United States* (2001)

wtpcompanion.civiced.org   **COURT CASES**

Visit the We the People companion website for a link to Supreme Court syllabi and opinions for each of the cases described above.

student page ▼ 225

WHAT ISSUES ARISE IN INTERPRETING AND APPLYING THE FOURTH AMENDMENT?

The Fourth Amendment eliminates any doubt about the acceptability of general warrants or writs of assistance. However, its wording creates many difficult interpretive issues:

- What is the meaning of *unreasonable*?
- What is the meaning of the terms *search* and *seizure*?
- With how much "particularity" must a request for a warrant describe the place to be searched or the person or things to be seized?
- What is "probable cause?" Does the Fourth Amendment require it in all circumstances?
- What is encompassed by the terms *house*, *paper*, and *effects*?

Courts never have definitively answered these questions and probably never will. Technology changes quickly. Photographs, telephones, microphones, radios, televisions, and electronic surveillance techniques did not exist when the amendment was adopted. Thus judicial interpretation of the Fourth Amendment seems to be a constant feature of American jurisprudence. Changes in social circumstances—terrorist attacks and threats of attacks—also affect judicial interpretations.

student page ▼ 226

WHEN IS A WARRANT REQUIRED? WHAT IS PROBABLE CAUSE?

The Supreme Court has ruled that the Constitution expresses a "preference" that searches, seizures, and arrests be conducted pursuant to a lawfully executed warrant (*Mincey v. Arizona*, 1978).

WHEN IS A WARRANT REQUIRED? WHAT IS PROBABLE CAUSE?

Requiring police officers and other officials to get warrants before they can search, arrest, or seize evidence is a means of checking their power and protecting individuals from arbitrary and unlawful government actions. Government officials who want a warrant must submit an **affidavit**, or sworn statement, to a judge. **Probable cause** means that there is enough evidence for a reasonable person to believe that it is likely that an illegal act is being or has been committed. The official requesting a warrant must describe facts and circumstances in sufficient detail to persuade the judge that probable cause exists to issue a warrant.

Probable cause requires more than a hunch or a vague suspicion, but it does not require absolute certainty. Determining whether probable cause exists requires careful analysis of the facts of each case and is somewhat subjective. The Supreme Court continually refines the specific criteria for probable cause in light of experience. This process reveals a commitment to protecting the rights of individuals while also protecting society from those who break the law.

During the 1960s the Supreme Court held that searches conducted without warrants are inherently unreasonable. By the 1970s the Court had recognized a number of exceptions to the warrant requirement. There are times when law enforcement officers cannot wait for a warrant. For example, police may be on the scene of a violent crime or a robbery in progress. If they do not arrest the suspect immediately, then the person might injure a police officer or others or escape. Under these emergency circumstances it is necessary for officers to be able to arrest a person or search property without a warrant.

The Court has also held that in some circumstances warrants are never required. For example, vessels may be boarded and searched randomly for purposes of inspecting documentation. No warrant is required if a person consents to being searched or arrested or to having his or her property seized.

HOW DOES THE EXCLUSIONARY RULE ENFORCE THE FOURTH AMENDMENT'S WARRANT REQUIREMENT?

What should be done if law enforcement officers or other government officials break the law by not showing probable cause and obtaining warrants for searches and seizures?

In 1914 the Supreme Court held that the national government could not introduce papers belonging to a defendant in court as evidence because officers had seized the papers from the defendant's home without a

What purposes are served by requiring law enforcement officers to get a warrant from a judge before conducting a search?

warrant (*Weeks v. United States*). Preventing the government from using illegally obtained evidence at trial is known as the **exclusionary rule**. Judges created the exclusionary rule to discourage law enforcement officers from breaking the law. The courts have argued that the rule is the most effective way of preventing violations of individual rights during arrests, searches, seizures, and interrogations.

In 1961 the Supreme Court extended the exclusionary rule to criminal trials in state courts (*Mapp v. Ohio*). This resulted in considerable controversy and widespread criticism of the Court's action. Criminal defendants in state courts often have committed dangerous crimes. Public sympathy for the rights of such defendants usually is not as high as it is for so-called white-collar criminals, who more often are prosecuted in federal courts. The use of the exclusionary rule in state courts sometimes resulted in defendants being set free or retried if the evidence against them was not allowed to be used at their trials. Some critics claim that the Court has "tied the hands of the police." They argue that the exclusionary rule is too high a price to pay for government violations of the Fourth Amendment. Others believe that the Supreme Court's decision in *Mapp* is inconsistent with principles of federalism and exceeds the national government's power over the states.

Since 1961 the Supreme Court has modified the exclusionary rule in several ways. For example, if government officials relied in good faith on a defective search warrant, then they can introduce at trial evidence that they obtained in an illegal search. If government officials can show that they would have discovered the evidence as a routine matter—the "inevitable discovery" rule—then they can introduce at trial evidence they obtained in violation of the Fourth Amendment.

WHAT ARE SOME ALTERNATIVES TO THE EXCLUSIONARY RULE?

Americans continue to debate other ways to check the abuse of power by law enforcement officers and other government officials, rather than losing valuable evidence against criminals at trial. Proposals include

- **Departmental discipline**
  Some law enforcement agencies have created independent boards that investigate claims that an officer violated a right of a criminal defendant. A board conducts hearings and if it finds that the officer violated the Fourth Amendment, then it imposes discipline.

- **Civilian review boards**
  A civilian review board appointed by local government officials sometimes supervises law enforcement agencies. Such boards investigate charges against officers accused of breaking the law or violating rules and procedures. If a board concludes that an officer broke the law, then it recommends appropriate action to the law enforcement agency or suggests criminal prosecution.

- **Civil suits**
  Persons who believe that their rights have been violated by government officials sometimes have the right to sue individual officers or their agencies for money damages in a civil court or under the Civil Rights Act of 1964. Some argue that awarding money damages to criminal defendants whose Fourth Amendment rights were violated would be better than excluding evidence in a criminal trial.

EXCEPTIONS TO THE WARRANT REQUIREMENT

Exceptions that the Supreme Court has recognized include the following:

- Consent given voluntarily by someone who appears to have the authority to do so (*Schneckloth v. Bustamonte*, 1973)

- Search incident to arrest, including the area around the person taken into custody (*United States v. Robinson*, 1973; *Chimel v. California*, 1969)

- Hot pursuit of "fleeing targets" that can escape the jurisdiction before a warrant is obtained (*Chambers v. Maroney*, 1970; *California v. Acevedo*, 1991; *United States v. Johns*, 1985)

- Limited pat-downs of anyone suspected of participating in criminal activity (*Terry v. Ohio*, 1968)

- Officer safety, such as ordering people out of a car after a lawful traffic stop and conducting a "safety sweep" for weapons (*Pennsylvania v. Mimms*, 1977; *Maryland v. Buie*, 1990)

- Inventory search of possessions worn or carried by a person lawfully arrested (*Illinois v. Lafayette*, 1983)

- Administrative searches for municipal code violations under some circumstances (*Camara v. Municipal Court*, 1967; cf. *James v. Valtierra*, 1971)

- Automobile searches, if there was probable cause to stop the car (*United States v. Ross*, 1982)

- Routine customs searches (*United States v. Montoya de Hernandez*, 1985)

The USA Patriot Act, passed by Congress in 2001, created several additional exceptions to the warrant requirement.

wtpcompanion.civiced.org **PRIMARY SOURCES**
Visit the We the People companion website for a link to the text of the USA Patriot Act.

Exceptions to the warrant requirement raise as many questions as they answer. For example, if a person consents to a search of a car, does that include the trunk? Can voluntary consent be obtained from someone who is in custody? How extensive can a "search incident to arrest" be? How "contemporaneous" to the arrest must the search be?

Under what conditions, if any, should a law enforcement officer be able to arrest someone without a warrant?

student page ▼ 226–227

HOW DOES THE EXCLUSIONARY RULE ENFORCE THE FOURTH AMENDMENT'S WARRANT REQUIREMENTS?

The exclusionary rule is based on a theory of deterring police misconduct rather than on the rights of criminal defendants. The rule allows defendants to challenge the admissibility of evidence by bringing a pretrial motion to suppress evidence that allegedly was obtained illegally.

In *Arizona v. Evans* (1995) the Court held that the exclusionary rule does not require suppression of evidence that a police officer obtained through good-faith reliance on a search warrant that was issued erroneously.

student page ▼ 228

CRITICAL THINKING EXERCISE

The examples in the exercise are hypothetical cases and so there are no judicial answers.

WHEN ARE WARRANTS AND PROBABLE CAUSE NOT REQUIRED?

When juveniles are involved in cases that would be considered criminal if the defendant were an adult, the courts generally refer to the juvenile only by initials, not by name. In addition to *T.L.O.* the leading Supreme Court cases on searches in public schools are

- *Vernonia School District v. Acton* (1995)
- *Board of Education v. Earls* (2002)

wtpcompanion.civiced.org COURT CASES

Visit the We the People companion website for a link to Supreme Court syllabi and opinions for each of the cases described above.

CRITICAL THINKING EXERCISE
Deciding Whether to Apply the Exclusionary Rule

Work in groups of three to five students. Consider the following situations in which government officials illegally obtained evidence of a crime. Then answer the questions that follow and be prepared to present and defend your positions.

- A chief executive officer (CEO) of a major corporation that employs hundreds of thousands of workers faces criminal charges for stealing millions of dollars from employee pension funds. Government officials obtained evidence of the crime by hacking into the CEO's home computer.

- A high school junior faces criminal charges for selling marijuana. Police suspected that the student was involved in drug trafficking, went to the student's home without a warrant, and broke in after they determined that no one was home. They found receipts for drug sales and other incriminating evidence.

- A person faces criminal conspiracy charges for planning to blow up an office building in a major American city. Government officials obtained evidence of the plot by illegally wire-tapping the defendant's home telephone.

- A person faces criminal charges for tax evasion, a crime that government officials had suspected for many years but never been able to prove. They obtained evidence to support the charges by paying the defendant's accountant to give them records of the defendant's income for the past fifteen years.

❶ Should the evidence obtained in each situation be allowed in or excluded from the trial of each of the defendants? Explain your reasoning.

❷ If you think the exclusionary rule is not appropriate in any of the situations described above, what alternative would you suggest and why?

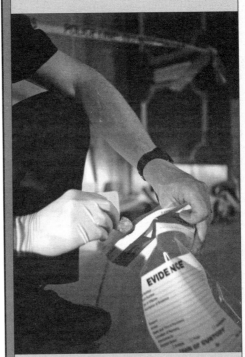

If law enforcement officers obtain evidence illegally, what should be done with it? Why?

WHEN ARE WARRANTS AND PROBABLE CAUSE NOT REQUIRED?

The Supreme Court has held that warrants are never required in certain circumstances. For example, the warrant requirement is "unsuited to the school environment" because school officials are guardians of students, not law enforcement officers. Searches conducted at schools are reviewed to determine if the search was "reasonable." The Court has held that a search is reasonable if

- Specific facts, together with rational inferences from those facts, justified the intrusion

- The search was reasonably related in scope to the circumstances justifying it (*T.L.O. v. New Jersey*, 1985)

Safety and health are primary considerations used for determining whether a search is reasonable in the public school setting. The court has approved the **reasonableness** standard in two other settings:

- Random drug testing of public and transportation employees and students who participate in extracurricular activities in public schools

- Searches of homes of people who are on probation

Under what conditions, if any, should a law enforcement officer be able to enter a person's home without a warrant?

CRITICAL THINKING EXERCISE

Evaluating, Taking, and Defending Positions on Reasonableness and Probable Cause

Work in one of three groups:

GROUP ❶

Make your best arguments for abandoning the probable cause requirement and using a reasonableness standard to evaluate all searches after they have occurred.

GROUP ❷

Make your best arguments for always requiring probable cause before a search.

GROUP ❸

Make your best arguments for using a reasonableness standard in some circumstances but requiring probable cause in others.

After each group has compiled its arguments, the groups should compare their responses. In evaluating the positions each group has developed, the class as a whole should consider how each group's arguments balance the government's interest in combating crime with the individual's interest in being free from government intrusions. Did any group's argument change your personal views on this issue? Why or why not?

WHAT IS THE PURPOSE OF THE FIFTH AMENDMENT PROVISION AGAINST SELF-INCRIMINATION?

The right not to incriminate oneself, or the right against **self-incrimination**, means that a criminal defendant cannot be forced to take the stand to testify at trial. However, if a criminal defendant decides to testify, that person has to answer all questions that are asked. Anyone else who testifies cannot be forced to answer questions that would tend to implicate him or her in a criminal act unless the prosecution offers the witness **use immunity**. This kind of immunity means that neither the witness's testimony nor evidence subsequently uncovered by the government because of the witness's testimony can ever be used to prosecute that person as a criminal.

student page ▾ 229–230

WHAT IS THE PURPOSE OF THE FIFTH AMENDMENT PROVISION AGAINST SELF-INCRIMINATION?

James Madison's proposal for the self-incrimination clause was, "nor shall be compelled to be a witness against himself." The House of Representatives added the phrase "in any criminal case," thereby limiting the scope of the protection.

In inquisitorial systems of justice accused wrongdoers can be compelled to incriminate themselves by being sworn to tell the truth before they are informed of the charges against them. This approach was used in Star Chamber proceedings (see Lesson 18) to uncover political heresies.

In *Tehan v. United States ex rel. Shott* (1966) the Supreme Court explained the basic purpose behind the privilege against self-incrimination as "preserving the integrity of a judicial system in which even the guilty are not to be convicted unless the prosecution 'shoulder the entire load.'"

In *Malloy v. Hogan* (1964) the Supreme Court held that the privilege against self-incrimination is a limitation on the states as well as on the national government. (Review Lesson 18 on incorporation doctrine.)

wtpcompanion.civiced.org   **COURT CASES**

Visit the We the People companion website for a link to Supreme Court syllabi and opinions for each of the cases described above.

An incriminating statement is one that tends to establish a person's guilt or to connect the person to criminal activity. The Fifth Amendment limits the government's power to obtain incriminating statements. It states, "No person…shall be compelled in any criminal case to be a witness against himself." The source of the self-incrimination clause is the Latin maxim, *nemo tenetur seipsum accusare*—no man is bound to accuse himself. The clause underscores the principle that in an adversary system of justice the government carries the burden of proof in a criminal proceeding. It cannot shift that burden to the defendant by forcing the defendant to reveal incriminating facts.

The right to remain silent does not mean that suspects cannot make statements voluntarily after they acknowledge that they understand their rights. However, if police violate the *Miranda* rule, explained in the next section, and a defendant makes incriminating statements, then the statements are generally excluded at trial. Statements made by a defendant after a *Miranda* violation may be admitted at trial only if the defendant subsequently testifies in court and says something that is inconsistent with the statements made after the *Miranda* violation.

Protection against self-incrimination applies in any public proceeding in which information obtained could tie a person to criminal activity. For example, in the 1950s when the House Committee on Un-American Activities asked for information about links to the Communist Party—which could subject witnesses to prosecution under the 1940 Alien Registration Act—some people "took the Fifth." That means they sought refuge in the Fifth Amendment's right against self-incrimination to avoid answering the questions.

The right against self-incrimination is personal. Individuals can refuse to incriminate themselves. However, unless they have some special privilege that the law respects, such as a doctor-patient relationship, no one can refuse to testify on the grounds that the testimony might incriminate someone else.

CRITICAL THINKING EXERCISE

Identifying Violations of the Protection against Self-Incrimination

Work in groups of three to five students. Examine the following situations and develop your responses to the questions that follow. Be prepared to present and defend your positions.

- A state statute makes it a crime for anyone under age eighteen to own a gun. A different statute requires gun owners to register their guns with a state agency. The registration form asks the gun owner's age. A sixteen-year-old received a gun for his birthday and plans to use it for target shooting. He claims that the gun registration law violates his right against self-incrimination.

Do you think the privilege against self-incrimination should apply to governmental hearings other than trials? Why?

- Federal tax laws require taxpayers to report and pay taxes on income earned the previous year from "any source." Failure to list income can result in a fine. A taxpayer earned more than $200,000 from illegal gambling. The taxpayer objects to listing the income on her tax returns, asserting that doing so would violate her right against self-incrimination.

- A county ordinance requires convicted sex offenders to register with the county. Names and addresses of registered individuals are then posted on a county website. Failure to register carries a fine of $100 and can be used as evidence in any future prosecutions. An individual who wishes to establish residency in the county was convicted of sex abuse twenty years ago, has had no subsequent convictions, and contends that the registration requirement violates her right against self-incrimination.

- A city ordinance requires all city employees to live inside the city limits. Employees must disclose their home addresses annually. Failure to reside within the city can result in job loss. A sanitation worker has been employed by the city for more than ten years but no longer can afford to pay the high rental rates in the city. He has moved to an affordable apartment in the suburbs and contends that requiring him to give the city his new address violates his right against self-incrimination.

- A congressional statute requires all persons to maintain and make public records of corporate activities. Violation of the statute can result in a fine and imprisonment. A member of the Communist Party refuses to disclose the contents of the party's corporate records on the grounds that it will violate his right against self-incrimination.

❶ Which, if any, of the laws described above do you think violate the Fifth Amendment provision against self-incrimination? Explain your reasoning.

❷ Do you think the right against self-incrimination should be interpreted to apply in noncriminal as well as criminal cases? Why or why not?

What are the purposes of the *Miranda* rule?

WHAT IS THE *MIRANDA* RULE?

In 1966 the Supreme Court held that police officers must tell all people taken into police custody about their right against self-incrimination (*Miranda v. Arizona*, 1966). Under *Miranda*, law enforcement officers must warn suspects that

- They have the right to remain silent

- They have the right to have an attorney with them when they are being questioned

- Anything they say may be used against them in court

- If they cannot afford an attorney, one will be appointed for them

As mentioned earlier the right to remain silent does not mean that suspects cannot make statements voluntarily after they acknowledge that they understand their rights. However, if police violate the *Miranda* rule and a defendant makes incriminating statements, then the statements are excluded at trial.

231

student page ▾ **231–232**

WHAT IS THE *MIRANDA* RULE?

The Court's statement in *Dickerson* came as a surprise to many because the Court previously had held that evidence obtained in an interrogation in which the defendant had not properly been apprised of *Miranda* rights was nonetheless admissible (*Oregon v. Elstad*, 1985; *New York v. Quarles*, 1984; *Harris v. New York*, 1971).

In 2004 in *United States v. Patane* the Court allowed statements obtained in violation of *Miranda* to be used to impeach (contradict) statements a defendant made at trial.

Some critics argue that the *Miranda* decision "hand-cuffs" police. Others believe the decision is inconsistent with principles of federalism because it interferes with state processes for fighting crime. In 1968 Congress attempted to overturn the decision by passing a statute that declared that all voluntary statements are admissible at trial. However, in 2000 the Supreme Court reaffirmed *Miranda*, holding that it was a constitutional decision that could not be overruled by an act of Congress (*Dickerson v. United States*).

WHAT DO YOU THINK?

❶ What is the basic purpose of the *Miranda* rule?

❷ What means other than the *Miranda* rule might be used to serve its basic purpose?

❸ Do you think the *Miranda* rule should be maintained, modified, or eliminated? Why?

REVIEWING AND USING THE LESSON

❶ What historical experiences led to adoption of the Fourth Amendment? Which, if any, of those conditions exist today?

❷ What rights does the Fourth Amendment protect?

❸ What is a warrant? When are warrants required? What are some exceptions to the warrant requirement?

❹ Explain the term *probable cause*.

❺ What is the *Miranda* rule?

❻ How does the exclusionary rule reinforce the principles of the Fourth Amendment?

❼ How would you explain the right against self-incrimination? How is that right related to principles of limited government and rule of law?

WARNING AS TO YOUR RIGHTS

You are under arrest. Before we ask you any questions, you must understand what your rights are.

You have the right to remain silent. You are not required to say anything to us at any time or to answer any questions. Anything you say can be used against you in court.

You have the right to talk to a lawyer for advice before we question you and to have him with you during questioning.

If you cannot afford a lawyer and want one, a lawyer will be provided for you.

If you want to answer questions now without a lawyer present you will still have the right to stop answering at any time. You also have the right to stop answering at any time until you talk to a lawyer.

P-4475

What arguments can you make for and against the *Miranda* rule?

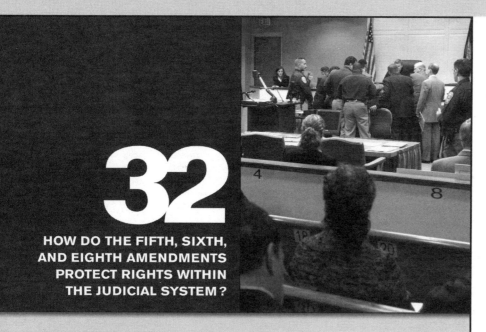

32

HOW DO THE FIFTH, SIXTH, AND EIGHTH AMENDMENTS PROTECT RIGHTS WITHIN THE JUDICIAL SYSTEM?

HOW DO THE FIFTH, SIXTH, AND EIGHTH AMENDMENTS PROTECT RIGHTS WITHIN THE JUDICIAL SYSTEM?

wtpcompanion.civiced.org | **LESSON PURPOSE + TERMS**

Visit the We the People companion website for printable and downloadable Lesson Purposes and Terms and Concepts to Understand sections for each lesson. Audio readings of each Lesson Purpose and Term are also available online in MP3 format.

LESSON PURPOSE

Four of the first eight amendments in the Bill of Rights address the rights of criminal defendants. The previous lesson examined how the Fourth and Fifth Amendments protect accused persons from unreasonable law enforcement practices. This lesson explores how the Fifth, Sixth, and Eighth Amendments protect the rights of accused criminals before and during trial and the rights of those who have been convicted of crimes.

When you have finished this lesson, you should be able to explain the Fifth and Sixth Amendment guarantees regarding indictments, double jeopardy, and due process of law. You should be able to identify the rights protected by the Sixth Amendment, particularly the right to counsel. You should be able to describe the Eighth Amendment provisions about bail and punishment. Finally, you should be able to evaluate, take, and defend positions on the death penalty.

TERMS AND CONCEPTS TO UNDERSTAND

bail	indictment
capital punishment	plea agreement
cruel and unusual punishment	right to counsel
double jeopardy	
grand jury	

233

student page ▾ 234

WHY IS PROCEDURAL JUSTICE IMPORTANT?

> "The history of American freedom is, in no small measure, the history of procedure."
>
> Justice Felix Frankfurter,
> *Malinski v. New York*
> (1945, concurring opinion)

> "It is significant that most of the provisions of the Bill of Rights are procedural, for it is procedure that marks much of the difference between rule by law and rule by fiat."
>
> Justice William O. Douglas,
> *Wisconsin v. Constantineau* (1971)

The majority of rights in the Bill of Rights focus on people who are accused of crime. The rights are procedural, which means that they establish rules that government must follow in prosecuting criminal defendants. Defining what constitutes a crime is largely a matter of state and local law. However, Congress has identified some acts that invoke the jurisdiction of federal trial courts because they involve activities extending beyond state boundaries or have a special impact on the operation of the national government. States as well as the national government have adopted codes of criminal procedure to implement the rights in state constitutions and the Bill of Rights.

Historian Leonard Levy wrote the following:

> An exact duplication of English common-law criminal procedure did not exist anywhere in the colonies in the seventeenth century, especially not in the earlier decades. Nor was the procedure the same in the various colonies. Significant variations existed among them.... Great distances, frontier conditions, political and religious dissimilarities, and a scarcity of lawyers and law books required improvisation that resulted in some indigenous legal developments from colony to colony.

Levy's statement helps to explain the diversity of criminal laws and procedures that has developed among the states.

wtpcompanion.civiced.org **LINKS**

Visit the We the People companion website for a link to an American Bar Association diagram of how a criminal case typically moves through the criminal justice system.

WHY IS PROCEDURAL JUSTICE IMPORTANT?

The fundamental premise of the American criminal justice system is that a person accused of a crime, no matter how horrible the alleged offense, is innocent until the government proves guilt beyond a reasonable doubt. That means that the prosecution must eliminate doubts about guilt in the mind of a reasonable, ordinary person about every element of the crime.

The procedural rules contained in the Bill of Rights are designed primarily to protect the innocent. Sometimes people who are accused of crimes use the rules to prevent government from obtaining convictions, as can happen when prosecutors are not allowed to introduce illegally obtained evidence at trial. Many observers have argued that allowing some guilty people to remain free is a small price to pay to avoid mistakenly convicting innocent persons. Above all, they argue, it is a reminder of America's commitment to the rights of each individual and to the rule of law.

The Fourth, Fifth, Sixth, and Eighth Amendments contain guarantees ensuring that police, prosecutors, judges, and juries will follow fair procedures when dealing with people accused of crimes. Procedural rights are important because criminal law pits the power of the government against the individual.

HOW DO THE FIFTH, SIXTH, AND EIGHTH AMENDMENTS PROTECT AN INDIVIDUAL'S RIGHTS BEFORE TRIAL?

The period between arrest and trial is very important to prosecutors and people accused of crimes. Judges rule on pretrial motions, or requests for rulings on legal points, over issues such as whether the accused should be released on bail pending trial. Both sides gather evidence, interview witnesses, and develop trial strategies. Criminal defendants must decide whether to enter into a **plea agreement**—pleading guilty to a lesser crime—or to proceed to trial.

The Fifth, Sixth, and Eighth Amendments protect the people accused of crimes between arrest and trial in three ways:

● **Indictment** Government prosecutors have many choices about whether to charge an individual with a crime and which crime or crimes to charge. The Fifth Amendment requires them to issue an **indictment,** or a formal statement of charges, so that the defendant knows how to prepare a defense. Indictments also limit the range of evidence that the government may present at trial.

In what ways do the procedural rules in the Bill of Rights protect individuals from the power of the government?

234

The Fifth Amendment states that indictments must be by grand jury. A **grand jury** is a special panel of jurors who listen to the evidence that prosecutors have obtained and decide whether the government has a strong enough case to proceed to trial. If the grand jury concludes that there is enough evidence for an indictment, it issues a "true bill." If it does not issue a true bill, then the government may not proceed with the case.

The grand jury requirement applies only to cases in federal courts. The Supreme Court has held that states may use other indictment processes as well. Some states rely mostly on preliminary hearings. These hearings resemble trials but judges, not juries, evaluate whether the government has enough evidence against the accused to issue formal charges. Some states indict by information, a less formal process that also requires a judge to determine whether the prosecution has enough evidence to proceed to trial.

- **Bail** Permitting criminal defendants to be released on bail and free before trial helps them prepare their defense and avoids punishing innocent suspects by holding them in jail without a conviction. **Bail** refers to the sum of money that a court requires a defendant to deposit with the court. Not all criminal suspects can be trusted to appear in court when they are supposed to, and some may be so dangerous that a judge will require them to remain in custody between arrest and trial.

If a judge allows a criminal suspect to be free on bail before trial, then the Eighth Amendment prohibits the government from requiring "excessive bail." A defendant who fails to appear forfeits the bail deposit. Bail is excessive when it is higher than an amount reasonably calculated to ensure the government's interest in having the defendant appear for trial.

- **Counsel** The Sixth Amendment guarantees criminal defendants the assistance of counsel for their defense. The **right to counsel** includes having a lawyer present during police interrogation, while preparing for trial, and during the trial. Both state governments and the national government are required to permit criminal defendants to hire lawyers and to provide counsel for defendants at government expense if they cannot afford to pay (*Gideon v. Wainwright*, 1963).

What is the importance of the right to counsel?

The American criminal justice system is an adversary system as opposed to the inquisitorial system used in some countries. In an adversary system there are two sides that present their positions before an impartial third party—a jury, a judge, or both. The prosecuting attorney presents the government's side; the defense attorney presents arguments for the accused person.

The complexity of the adversary system requires the use of lawyers to represent defendants. Even well-educated people and many lawyers who do not specialize in criminal law are not competent to conduct an adequate defense in today's courts.

The Supreme Court and Congress have extended the right to counsel to people for whom it had not been provided in the past. This right is now interpreted to guarantee that

- Every person accused of a felony—a major crime—may have a lawyer.
- Those too poor to afford to hire a lawyer will have one appointed by the court.

235

---

student page ▾ 234–235

HOW DO THE FIFTH, SIXTH, AND EIGHTH AMENDMENTS PROTECT AN INDIVIDUAL'S RIGHTS BEFORE TRIAL?

In *Escobedo v. Illinois* (1964) the Supreme Court explained the importance of pretrial protections for criminal defendants:

> Our Constitution strikes the balance in favor of the rights of the accused to be advised by his lawyer of his privilege against self-incrimination…. No system worth preserving should have to fear that if an accused is permitted to consult with a lawyer, he will become aware of, and exercise, these rights. If the exercise of constitutional rights will thwart the effectiveness of a system of law enforcement, then there is something very wrong with that system.

PLEA AGREEMENTS As important as pretrial procedures are for those who go to trial, more than ninety percent of all criminal cases filed in state and federal courts are resolved before trial through a plea of guilty to a lesser offense. Plea agreements, also known as plea bargains, are negotiated between the prosecutor and the accused and must be approved by a judge to ensure that the plea is made knowingly and voluntarily. Trials involve significant risks for both the prosecution and the defense, creating incentives to come to agreements. In *Brady v. United States* (1970) the Supreme Court explained that the plea agreement process benefits both sides as long as guilty pleas are made voluntarily and with full understanding. In *Santobello v. New York* (1971) the Court stated that plea agreements are "an essential component of the administration of justice" and should be "encouraged" as long as the process of arriving at guilty pleas is properly administered.

INDICTMENT In *Hurtado v. California* (1884) the Court held that the Constitution requires indictment by grand jury only in federal criminal cases. Only about half the states now use grand juries.

student page ▾ 235

BAIL In *Roper v. Simmons* (2005) the Supreme Court stated that the Eighth Amendment's provision regarding bail is applicable to the states through the Fourteenth Amendment.

RIGHT TO COUNSEL *Gideon v. Wainwright* (1963) spawned more litigation about when criminal defendants have the right to counsel. The Court has held that the guarantee attaches to a pretrial proceeding that is a "critical stage" (*United States v. Wade*, 1967). The Court has not defined "critical stage," choosing instead to determine on a case-by-case basis whether a defendant has made a compelling argument for the need for counsel. A criminal defendant can waive, or forgo, the right to counsel, but any waiver must be knowing and intelligent (*Argersinger v. Hamlin*, 1972).

wtpcompanion.civiced.org   COURT CASES

Visit the We the People companion website for a link to Supreme Court syllabi and opinions for each of the cases described above.

student page ▼ 236–237

HOW ARE THE RIGHTS OF CRIMINAL DEFENDANTS PROTECTED DURING TRIAL?

Review Lesson 18, which explains how various provisions of the Bill of Rights have been made applicable to the states ("incorporation doctrine") through the due process clause of the Fourteenth Amendment. The following is a summary:

student page ▼ 236

SPEEDY TRIAL See *Klopfer v. North Carolina* (1967). The right to a speedy trial traces to the Magna Carta (1215) and appeared in the Virginia Declaration of Rights of 1776.

PUBLIC TRIAL See *In re Oliver* (1948). In this case the Court stated,

> The traditional Anglo-American distrust for secret trials has been variously ascribed to the notorious use of this practice by the Spanish Inquisition, to the excesses of the English Court of Star Chamber, and to the French monarchy's abuse of the lettre de cachet [letters from French kings to cabinet ministers to enforce arbitrary decisions from which there was no appeal].… Whatever other benefits to the guarantee to an accused that his trial be conducted in public may confer upon our society, the guarantee has always been recognized as a safeguard against any attempt to employ our courts as instruments of persecution.

wtpcompanion.civiced.org   COURT CASES

Visit the We the People companion website for links to Supreme Court syllabi and opinions for each of the cases described in the student and teacher's editions. Summaries are provided for selected Supreme Court cases.

CRITICAL THINKING EXERCISE

Free Press versus Fair Trial

Many have questioned whether it is possible for criminal defendants in high-profile cases to receive fair trials because of pretrial publicity. The United States and Britain have adopted considerably different approaches.

In Britain when someone has been arrested on criminal charges, members of the press face contempt of court if they publish much more than the name of the accused, the name of his or her counsel, a summary of the offense charged, and where and when the trial will take place. Only rarely do judges lift these restrictions.

In the United States, media coverage, speculation, and expression of opinions about guilt or innocence are common in high-profile cases, even at the early stages of a criminal investigation. Judges have some tools for responding to pretrial publicity, such as

- Changing the venue, or location, of the trial
- Postponing the trial to permit publicity to die down
- Restricting what prosecution and defense attorneys can say publicly
- Questioning prospective jurors about the effect of pretrial publicity

These tools may not be effective, leading some observers to contend that in high-profile cases, criminal defendants in the United States face two trials—trial by jury and trial by the media.

Work in groups of three to five students and discuss the following questions. Be prepared to report and defend your positions before the class.

❶ Identify a recent high-profile case that has received extensive pretrial publicity. Were your views of the defendant's guilt or innocence affected by the publicity? Why or why not? Do you think the media coverage before the trial was appropriate or inappropriate? Explain.

❷ Should the United States adopt the British approach to media coverage of criminal cases? Why or why not? What constitutional principles inform your response?

HOW ARE THE RIGHTS OF CRIMINAL DEFENDANTS PROTECTED DURING TRIAL?

A criminal trial is a carefully planned presentation of witnesses and evidence. Proof of guilt beyond a reasonable doubt is the most rigorous level of proof that the law requires. The judge ensures that both the prosecution and the defense obey the rules of evidence and procedure. The Fifth and Sixth Amendments give criminal defendants the following procedural rights:

- **A speedy, public trial** The requirement for a speedy trial prevents the government from holding a defendant in jail for a long time without trial. A speedy trial contributes to procedural fairness by diminishing the possibility that evidence will disappear and that witnesses' memories will fade.

The requirement of a public trial safeguards against courts being used as instruments of persecution. This requirement also provides ordinary citizens the opportunity to see the justice system in action and to become more informed about issues in their community and the performance of their elected officials, including prosecutors and judges in many states.

The requirement of a public trial does not prevent judges from imposing regulations to preserve a defendant's right to a fair trial. For example, a judge can order some proceedings to be closed if having the press or public present would make it impossible for the defendant to receive a fair trial. Judges also decide whether television cameras should be permitted in the courtroom.

What limits, if any, should be put on the press in high-profile trials?

236

What purposes are served by the right to be tried by a jury of one's peers?

- **Right to counsel** As discussed earlier in this lesson, this right includes having a lawyer at trial. Indigent, or poor, defendants are entitled to court-appointed counsel at public expense if they risk loss of life or liberty if convicted. A defendant can waive, or give up, the right to counsel if the waiver is informed, intelligent, and voluntary.

- **Compulsory process and confrontation** The right to "be confronted by the witnesses against" them means that defendants can require accusers to appear in court and be cross-examined, or questioned, by the defense. This requirement prevents prosecutors from establishing a defendant's guilt through written statements from witnesses who are not subject to cross-examination to test the truth of those statements.

- **Trial by an impartial jury in the state and district where the crime was committed** The jury trial guarantees help in protecting accused persons against unfounded criminal charges and biased, complacent, or eccentric judges. The guarantee also reflects trust in average community members to hear evidence and make decisions about guilt or innocence.

Although it is revered, the guarantee of a jury trial has raised several questions. Among them are the following:

- **Is trial by jury required in all criminal cases?** Jury trials are expensive and time-consuming. The Supreme Court has held that jury trials are not required for petty offenses, those for which the maximum penalty for conviction is six or fewer months in jail.

- **Must all juries have twelve jurors?** Juries need to be large enough to provide a cross-section of the community and to encourage group deliberation. Historically, juries had twelve members. The Supreme Court held that fixing the jury size at twelve was a "historical accident" (*Williams v. Florida*, 1970). The Court has permitted juries to be as small as six in cases not involving the death penalty.

- **Does proof beyond a reasonable doubt require a criminal jury to be unanimous?** English common law required unanimous jury verdicts in criminal cases. The Supreme Court has upheld state laws permitting less-than-unanimous verdicts by twelve-person juries if the defendant does not face the death penalty. However, juries must be unanimous to convict in capital, or death penalty, cases or if the jury consists of only six people.

- **Who is qualified to serve on a jury?** For many years only men were allowed to serve on juries in the United States. More than half a century after women gained the right to vote the Supreme Court held that laws that automatically exclude women from juries violate a criminal defendant's right to trial by a jury drawn from a representative cross-section of the community (*Taylor v. Louisiana*, 1975). The court also has struck down laws discriminating against prospective jurors on the basis of race and religion.

student page ▾ 237

RIGHT TO COUNSEL See *Powell v. Alabama* (1932) in cases carrying the possibility of a death penalty; *Gideon v. Wainwright* (1963) for extending *Powell* to all felony cases.

COMPULSORY PROCESS TO OBTAIN WITNESS TESTIMONY See *Washington v. Texas* (1967).

CONFRONTATION OF ADVERSE WITNESSES See *Pointer v. Texas* (1965).

TRIAL BY AN IMPARTIAL JURY IN THE STATE AND DISTRICT WHERE CRIME WAS COMMITTED See *Duncan v. Louisiana* (1968). A defendant may move for trial in a different location (change of venue) if the judge is persuaded that the defendant cannot receive a fair trial where the crime was committed. The right to trial by jury does not extend to juveniles in juvenile proceedings (*McKeiver v. Pennsylvania*, 1971). In *Duncan* the Court explained,

> The guarantees of jury trial in the Federal and State Constitutions reflect a profound judgment about the way in which law should be enforced and justice administered. A right to jury trial is granted to criminal defendants in order to prevent oppression by the Government. Those who wrote our constitutions knew from history and experience that it was necessary to protect against unfounded criminal charges brought to eliminate enemies and against judges too responsive to the voice of higher authority. The framers of the constitutions strove to create an independent judiciary but insisted upon further protection against arbitrary action.

IMPARTIALITY HAS TWO COMPONENTS First, the pool from which the jury is selected must represent a cross-section of the community (*Taylor v. Louisiana*, 1965). Second, the jurors chosen to serve must be unbiased and willing to decide the case based on the evidence presented (*Remmer v. United States*, 1956).

JURY SIZE AND UNANIMITY REQUIREMENTS A twelve-member jury need not be unanimous in noncapital cases—that is, when the death penalty is not a possibility (*Apodaca v. Oregon*, 1972; a vote of 10 to 2 to establish guilt was upheld). Six-member juries must vote unanimously to convict (*Burch v. Louisiana*, 1979). In *Williams v. Florida* (1970) the Court stated that fixing the size of a jury at twelve was "a historical accident." The Court determined that the appropriate focus was on the function a jury serves, not an arbitrary size. It concluded that a jury of between six and twelve members could accomplish the goals of community cross-section, group deliberation, and freedom from outside intimidation.

wtpcompanion.civiced.org   **COURT CASES**

Visit the We the People companion website for a link to Supreme Court syllabi and opinions for each of the cases described above.

student page ▾ 238–239

HOW DO THE FIFTH AND EIGHTH AMENDMENTS PROTECT CRIMINAL DEFENDANTS AFTER TRIAL?

The Supreme Court has incorporated the following provisions as limitations on the states:

NO DOUBLE JEOPARDY See *Benton v. Maryland* (1969). The double jeopardy prohibition does not prevent a defendant from being tried once in a criminal court (prosecution by the government with a "beyond reasonable doubt" standard of proof) and again in a civil case (brought by a member of the public with a "preponderance of the evidence" standard of proof) for the same conduct. Penalties in civil cases do not include the possibility of loss of life or liberty.

NO EXCESSIVE FINES As explained in the text the Court has not addressed this provision directly in a criminal case. However, in *Cooper Industries v. Leatherman Tool Group, Inc.* (2001) the Court suggested that it may be willing to consider whether the Eighth Amendment provision limits the amount of punitive damages (damage awards aimed at punishing or deterring behavior) that may be imposed in civil cases.

NO CRUEL AND UNUSUAL PUNISHMENT See *Robinson v. California* (1962). In *Kennedy v. Louisiana* (2008), the Court held that the Eighth Amendment prohibits imposing the death penalty as a punishment for the crime of rape of a child.

In *Baze v. Rees* (2008), the Court held that carrying out the death penalty by use of a three-drug lethal injection does not violate the Eighth Amendment.

wtpcompanion.civiced.org COURT CASES

Visit the We the People companion website for a link to Supreme Court syllabi and opinions for each of the cases described above.

WHAT DO YOU THINK?

The requirement that courts appoint counsel for indigent defendants who risk losing their life or liberty if convicted has proven very costly to the states because most criminal defendants in state courts cannot afford to pay a lawyer. States have devised a variety of ways to meet the requirement. Some states have created public defender offices staffed by lawyers whose job is to represent indigent defendants. A public defender is a lawyer paid by the government and appointed by a court to represent a person accused of a violation of criminal law who cannot pay for legal representation. Other states maintain lists of lawyers willing to represent indigent defendants. Study each situation below and then respond to the questions. In formulating your responses, consider the constitutional right to counsel, the expense associated with providing counsel, and the values underpinning the American criminal justice system described in this unit.

❶ The county in which a defendant will be tried has a public defender's office, but the defendant does not like the lawyer who has been assigned to represent her. She claims the lawyer refuses to visit her in jail to learn the details of the case and does not return her telephone calls. Should the judge order another lawyer to take over the case? Explain your reasoning.

❷ The state in which a defendant is being tried maintains a list of lawyers who have volunteered to represent indigent criminal defendants at no charge. The defendant has been charged with a drug crime and faces six years in prison if convicted. The lawyer who has volunteered to represent the defendant has no experience with criminal cases. Should the judge permit the volunteer lawyer to represent the defendant? Why or why not?

❸ A defendant is on trial for murder and faces the death penalty if convicted. The defendant received court-appointed counsel but asked the court to appoint someone else because of a "personality conflict." The court did so. The defendant complained about the second appointed attorney, contending that the attorney was not preparing adequately and developing the defense that the defendant wanted to present. The court appointed a third attorney. The defendant asserts that his current counsel has not had enough trial experience to represent him adequately. Should the judge appoint another lawyer to represent the defendant? Why or why not?

HOW DO THE FIFTH AND EIGHTH AMENDMENTS PROTECT CRIMINAL DEFENDANTS AFTER TRIAL?

Criminal defendants have three important rights after trial:

● **No double jeopardy** If a defendant is acquitted—that is, found not guilty of a crime—then the government cannot again prosecute the person, or put him or her in jeopardy of conviction, for the same crime. This right of criminal defendants ensures that prosecutors cannot wear someone out with repeated charges and trials for the same conduct.

There is an important exception to the protection against **double jeopardy** that reflects American federalism: A defendant can be charged for the same conduct in both federal and state courts, if the conduct violated both state and federal laws.

● **No excessive fines** If a criminal defendant is convicted or pleads guilty, then one penalty might be a fine. The prohibition of excessive fines ensures that fines are reasonable in relation to the crime. The Supreme Court has not interpreted this prohibition directly, because the Court has focused instead on whether a particular fine deprives a defendant of the equal protection of the laws guaranteed by the Fourteenth Amendment.

What is the purpose of the Eighth Amendment's prohibition of excessive fines?

What criteria should be used to determine if a punishment is cruel and unusual?

- **No cruel and unusual punishment**
  The prohibition against **cruel and unusual punishment** reflects the belief that society should treat with dignity even those who have committed the most horrible crimes. The prohibition also reflects the history of torture and barbarous punishment in the eighteenth century. Punishments such as drawing and quartering, the rack, and public dismemberment have never been acceptable forms of punishment in the United States. However, neither the Supreme Court nor the American people have been able to agree on a precise definition of the prohibition. The Court has held that taking away the citizenship of a natural-born citizen is cruel and unusual punishment because it results in the "total destruction of the individual's status in organized society" (*Trop v. Dulles*, 1958).

CRITICAL THINKING EXERCISE
Examining Early Positions on Punishment

The French philosopher Montesquieu, discussed in previous lessons, greatly influenced Americans' views on law and punishment. Below is a quotation from his writings, followed by an excerpt from a letter by Thomas Jefferson. Read these selections and then answer the questions that follow.

> Experience shows that in countries remarkable for the lenity of their laws the spirit of the inhabitants is as much affected by slight penalties as in other countries by severer punishments.... Mankind must not be governed with too much severity.... If we inquire into the cause of all human corruptions, we shall find that they proceed from the impunity [exemption from punishment] of criminals, and not from the moderation of punishments.... It is [also] an essential point, that there should be a certain proportion in punishments.... It is a great abuse amongst us to condemn to the same punishment a person that only robs on the highway and another who robs and murders.
>
> Baron de Montesquieu, "Of the Power of Punishments," *The Spirit of the Laws,* 1748

> The fantastical idea of virtue and the public good being a sufficient security to the state against the commission of crimes, which you say you have heard insisted on by some, I assure you was never mine. It is only the sanguinary [bloodthirsty] hue of our penal laws which I meant to object to. Punishments I know are necessary, and I would provide them, strict and inflexible, but proportioned to the crime.... Let mercy be the character of the lawgiver, but let the judge be a mere machine. The mercies of the law will be dispensed equally and impartially to every description of men.
>
> Thomas Jefferson to Edmund Pendleton, August 26, 1776

❶ What position does Montesquieu take on the effects of lenient and severe punishments?

❷ What does Montesquieu say is a major cause of crime?

❸ In what ways do Montesquieu and Jefferson appear to be in agreement?

❹ What idea is expressed in Jefferson's statement that is not found in the statement by Montesquieu?

❺ Do you agree or disagree with the positions stated by Montesquieu and Jefferson? Explain your position.

239

student page ▾ 240

WHAT IS CAPITAL PUNISHMENT AND WHY IS IT CONTROVERSIAL?

wtpcompanion.civiced.org | **LINKS**

Visit the We the People companion website for a link to the Bureau of Justice Statistics, which publishes information and opinions about the death penalty.

WHAT IS CAPITAL PUNISHMENT AND WHY IS IT CONTROVERSIAL?

The Supreme Court has ruled that **capital punishment**, or the death penalty, is a constitutionally acceptable form of punishment. At one time death was the automatic penalty for conviction of murder or other serious crimes. By the early twentieth century most states had passed laws that allowed juries a choice between the death penalty and other forms of punishment, including life in prison. However, in most states juries were not given much guidance in making these decisions.

In 1972 the Supreme Court held that states and Congress had to enact new laws containing standards to avoid arbitrarily imposing the death penalty (*Furman v. Georgia*, 1972). Five years later the Court held that imposing the death penalty in rape cases is unconstitutional because the sentence is disproportionate to the crime (*Coker v. Georgia*, 1977). In 2005 the Court held that it is unconstitutional to sentence anyone to death who was younger than eighteen years of age when the crime occurred (*Roper v. Simmons*, 2005).

States are not required to have the death penalty. Some states have abolished it. Others have abolished it, only to reinstate it years later. Public debate continues over whether the death penalty should be abolished altogether.

CRITICAL THINKING EXERCISE

Taking and Defending a Position on the Death Penalty

Work in one of two groups to complete the exercise described below.

GROUP ❶

Prepare a list of reasons why your state and the national government should allow the death penalty. Identify the values that are served by each reason. For example, one reason commonly advanced in support of the death penalty is public safety. Once a convicted murderer is executed, there is no chance that he or she will break out of prison and kill or injure someone else.

GROUP ❷

Prepare a list of reasons why the death penalty should be abolished. Identify the values that are served by each reason. For example, one reason commonly advanced in opposition to the death penalty is that it is not applied equitably. The poor, men, and racial minorities are over-represented among those executed.

The groups should compare lists and then, as a class, identify the strongest and weakest arguments on each side of the death penalty debate. Explain your reasoning.

Explain whether your personal position on the death penalty is the same as the position you were assigned to represent in your group. Why or why not? When and how did you develop your views about the death penalty?

What evidence or argument might convince you to change your position on the death penalty? Why?

REVIEWING AND USING THE LESSON

❶ What rights does the Sixth Amendment guarantee? How do these rights ensure a fair trial for those who are accused of crimes?

❷ What is the right to counsel? Why is it important?

❸ Explain the terms *indictment, grand jury, information, bail, double jeopardy,* and *plea agreement.*

❹ Why is it important for criminal defendants to have rights before, during, and after trial?

❺ What limitations has the Supreme Court placed on states that use the death penalty?

What arguments can you make for and against the death penalty?

unit SIX

**WHAT CHALLENGES MIGHT FACE
AMERICAN CONSTITUTIONAL
DEMOCRACY IN THE
TWENTY-FIRST
CENTURY?**

unitSIX

The U.S. Constitution has proven to be remarkably resilient. It has survived more than two centuries because it has been able to accommodate massive transformations in American life, including the increasing diversity and size of the nation and a traumatic civil war. The constitutional system provides Americans many opportunities to participate in local, state, and national affairs. At home and abroad its principles and ideals have inspired people. In this, the twenty-first century, its resilience will continue to be tested.

In this unit you will learn about American citizenship and opportunities for participation in local, state, and national government. You also will learn how the American constitutional model has influenced other countries and international organizations. Finally, you will consider some challenges facing American constitutionalism in the future.

33

WHAT DOES IT MEAN TO BE A CITIZEN?

WHAT DOES IT MEAN TO BE A CITIZEN?

---

wtpcompanion.civiced.org   **LESSON PURPOSE + TERMS**

Visit the We the People companion website for printable and downloadable Lesson Purposes and Terms and Concepts to Understand sections for each lesson. Audio readings of each Lesson Purpose and Term are also available online in MP3 format.

LESSON PURPOSE

Justice Louis D. Brandeis once remarked that "the only title in our democracy superior to that of president is the title citizen." Brandeis was acknowledging one of the oldest principles of American democracy, part of the nation's legacy of classical republicanism. America's experiment in self-government depends foremost not on presidents, members of Congress, or justices, but on each of us as citizens. This unit begins with a discussion of influences of classical republicanism and natural rights philosophy on Americans' ideas about citizenship. It concludes by offering you the opportunity to discuss some of the most fundamental questions of citizenship. This lesson examines the concept of "citizen," how the concept has changed in American history, how one becomes a citizen, and the moral and legal rights and obligations of citizens.

When you have finished this lesson, you should be able to explain the meaning of citizenship in the United States, the ways Americans become citizens, and why all American citizens are citizens both of their states and their nation. You also should be able to identify essential rights and responsibilities of citizens, and why citizenship is particularly complicated for Native Americans. You should be able to describe the process of naturalization, differences between citizens and resident aliens, and how citizenship can be lost. Finally, you should be able to evaluate, take, and defend positions on the legal and moral rights and obligations of citizens.

TERMS AND CONCEPTS TO UNDERSTAND

alien	enlightened self-interest	naturalization
citizen	*E pluribus unum*	resident alien
denaturalization	*jus sanguines*	
dual national citizenship	*jus soli*	

student page ▾ 244–245

HOW HAVE AMERICANS THOUGHT OF CITIZENSHIP?

Unit One discussed classical republicanism and natural rights philosophy. Both have consequences for citizenship.

CLASSICAL REPUBLICANISM   Aristotle described citizens as those "who share in the civic life of ruling and being ruled in turn" and defined the excellence of a citizen as the capacity to rule and to be ruled. Aristotle argued that good education was essential to good citizenship.

Cicero echoed Aristotle's views. Cicero argued that a republic could be sustained only by virtuous citizens who engage in morally upright civic conduct. He believed that a sound education is a prerequisite for good citizenship and should emphasize the study of philosophy, history, law, and rhetoric.

NATURAL RIGHTS PHILOSOPHY   Locke argued that government exists to protect life and property—and that government has "nothing to do with the good of men's souls." Nonetheless, Locke agreed with classical republicans on the importance of education to instill virtue in children. In *Some Thoughts Concerning Education* (1693) he wrote, "I think I may say that of all the men we meet with, nine parts of ten are what they are, good or evil, useful or not, by their education." Locke understood virtue to be a combination of self-denial and rationality. Good people, as well as good citizens, must "follow what reason directs as best, though the appetite lean the other way."

Rousseau also emphasized the importance of education for citizenship. He wrote the following:

> You will have everything if you train citizens, and that training
> is not just a day's work. Liberty depends upon the virtue that only
> a very complex and structured schooling can produce.

Rousseau believed that in addition to instructing the young in the traditions and goals of the community, education must arouse people to passion. He saw emotion as essential to good citizenship because it is the fierce love that one bears for his compatriots that makes the association of citizens into a community. Like classical republicans, Rousseau believed that education is "the most important business of the state." Obedience to the laws, a sense of the group, history, an appetite for service to the community—all are the result of a "public education…in the bosom of equality."

COMMONWEALTH   Some colonies used *commonwealth* to mean a government based on the common consent of the governed rather than on royal charters issued by the Crown. Four states today retain the term, the commonwealths of Massachusetts, Pennsylvania, Virginia, and Kentucky. There is no legal difference between a commonwealth and a state.

HOW HAVE AMERICANS THOUGHT OF CITIZENSHIP?

As discussed in Unit One, America has been strongly influenced by the ideas of classical republicanism and natural rights philosophy. Each tradition continues to affect Americans' thinking about what it means to be a **citizen**. Citizenship, broadly defined, refers to the rights and responsibilities of people who owe allegiance to a particular government and are entitled to that government's protection.

The early American colonies of the seventeenth century were small, self-contained political communities in which Americans personally experienced their dependence on one another and the need to put the common good ahead of selfish interests. Many of these colonies were called *commonwealths*, a word that meant something like a republic—that is, a self-governing community in which members are expected to help serve the good of all. The spirit of devotion to a common cause also was reflected in the Mayflower Compact, when the Pilgrims declared their intent to "covenant and combine ourselves together into a civil Body Politick." Admiration for civic virtue and public spiritedness remained important to the Founders because they knew that America's strength would be found primarily in its citizens.

The natural rights philosophy of John Locke, found prominently in the Declaration of Independence, also influenced the Founders. Natural rights philosophy differs in several important ways from the ideals of classical republicanism. It stresses the importance of individual rights and self-interest. Human communities exist to protect the individuals who belong to them, each of whom is free to pursue his or her own interests as long as those interests do not interfere with the rights of others. The Founders counted on citizens who viewed themselves as self-sufficient individuals capable of meeting most of their own needs. Such citizens were most likely to thrive in a system of limited government.

The Founders realized that the classical republicanism of the ancient city-states could not be easily adapted to a country as large and diverse as the America of their day. They also realized that republican self-government requires a greater measure of civic virtue than other forms of government require. How can civic virtue and self-interest coexist?

The Founders looked in general to two solutions: religion and education. The Founders held various religious beliefs, and many were wary of the dangers of any one religion becoming dominant in the United States. Nonetheless, the Founders knew that religion helps to promote moral integrity and civic virtue. In addition, religious instruction helps people learn the importance of obeying authority and participating with others to pursue a common goal.

Why did the Founders believe religion and education were important for republican self-government?

244

The Founders also knew the importance of education. For the American experiment in republican government to succeed, the country's citizens had to be schooled in the ideas and principles of popular sovereignty, limited government, individual rights, and how to exercise those rights responsibly. Public, or "common," schools rapidly developed to prepare Americans not only to work in the country's growing economy but also to exercise their citizenship, committed to the principles of self-government. Nineteenth-century American educator Horace Mann later would observe that "schoolhouses are the republican line of fortifications."

HOW DID TOCQUEVILLE CONNECT GOOD CITIZENSHIP WITH SELF-INTEREST IN THE UNITED STATES?

French historian Alexis de Tocqueville explained another way that Americans could embrace both civic virtue and self-interest. In his widely hailed two-volume work *Democracy in America* (*De la démocratie en Amérique*), Tocqueville wrote that he was impressed by the equality of opportunity in American democracy, but he wondered how a society so devoted to materialism and the pursuit of individual self-interest could produce the civic spirit needed for self-government. Tocqueville

found the answer in traditions of local self-government and habits of free association.

Tocqueville believed that New England townships were examples of classical republicanism in practice, where residents developed the habits of good citizenship. According to Tocqueville, participating in small, local governments helped people see the nature of both their rights and their duties. The American tradition of local self-government also encouraged people to join voluntary associations to solve problems without depending on government. Lesson 34 examines the ongoing importance of voluntary associations in America.

Like the Founders, Tocqueville realized that the civic virtue of the ancients was not practical in the United States and that self-interest is a powerful motivator. However, Tocqueville argued that Americans had found a way to bridge the gap between classical republican virtue and natural rights self-interest. Americans, he argued, demonstrated that

    " an enlightened regard for themselves constantly prompts them to assist each other, and inclines them willingly to sacrifice a portion of their time and property to the welfare of the state.

How might participating in local government help people understand their rights and responsibilities?

student page ▼ 245

PUBLIC SCHOOLS Horace Mann is credited with founding the American public school system. He believed that public schools, which he claimed are indispensable, free, universal, nonsectarian institutions, are the pillars of American democracy. In 1852 Mann, a steadfast abolitionist, lost the election for governor of Massachusetts. He then became president of a new coeducational college, Antioch College in Ohio. During his presidency Mann insisted on the admission of students irrespective of race, creed, or gender.

student page ▼ 245–246

HOW DID TOCQUEVILLE CONNECT GOOD CITIZENSHIP WITH SELF-INTEREST IN THE UNITED STATES?

Tocqueville's theory of enlightened self-interest merges classical republicanism and the natural rights views of citizenship.

student page ▼ 246–247

HOW HAVE IDEAS ABOUT CITIZENSHIP CHANGED IN THE UNITED STATES?

Unlike national citizenship, state citizenship is flexible and no government approval is required to move from state to state, except for convicts on parole.

student page ▼ 247–248

WHO ARE NATURALIZED CITIZENS AND WHAT SHOULD THE CRITERIA BE FOR NATURALIZATION?

The current Oath of Allegiance was adopted in 1952. In some instances the agreement to bear arms is waived. In 1997 the U.S. Commission on Immigration Reform found that the average person did not understand words such as *abjure* and *potentate* and that the oath needed to be updated. The commission proposed the following wording:

> Solemnly, freely, and without any mental reservation, I hereby renounce under oath all former political allegiances. My sole political fidelity and allegiance from this day forward is to the United States of America. I pledge to support and respect its Constitution and laws. Where and if lawfully required, I further commit myself to defend them against all enemies, foreign and domestic, either by military or civilian service. This I do solemnly swear, so help me God.

The proposal was met with strong opposition, including from some members of Congress who sponsored legislation to retain the present oath. As of 2008 the oath remains as written in 1952.

NATURALIZATION CRITERIA Immigration and naturalization rules are closely related. The assumption is that those who come to the United States do so with the goal of becoming citizens. The following brief timeline highlights U.S. immigration policy:

1790 The Naturalization Act provided that any free, white, adult alien, male or female, who had resided within the limits and jurisdiction of the United States for a period of two years was eligible for citizenship. Application for citizenship was made to a court of record in the state in which the alien had resided for at least one year.

1795 Congress increased the residency requirement to five years. Aliens seeking citizenship had to renounce any foreign allegiance and give up any hereditary title of nobility.

The realization that one can fulfill private ambitions only if one also contributes to the common good is known as **enlightened self-interest**. To this day Americans are willing to devote themselves to public ends because they realize that the success of their private ambitions depends in large part on the success of American democracy.

WHAT DO YOU THINK?

❶ Some people claim that the best way to achieve the common good is for each person to work only for his or her self-interest. Do you agree? Why or why not?

❷ Some argue that enlightened self-interest must be learned. What are some effective ways of teaching about and experiencing enlightened self-interest?

❸ The idea of the common good is a principle originally associated with small, homogeneous societies. Do you think there is a common good in a nation as large and diverse as the United States? Why or why not?

HOW HAVE IDEAS ABOUT CITIZENSHIP CHANGED IN THE UNITED STATES?

For many years American colonists thought of themselves as British subjects. As explained in Unit Two, many later began to think of themselves as Americans. However, they initially thought of themselves as Americans who were citizens of particular colonies.

After the Revolution each of the original thirteen states was an independent, sovereign political community. When Americans talked about "my country," they usually meant their particular states. Most states welcomed the foreign-born because immigrants brought financial and human resources. However, some states imposed property and religious qualifications for citizenship. Most also imposed residency requirements, typically ranging from one to two years. Many states permitted only "free whites" to become citizens. Native Americans usually were regarded as members of foreign nations.

Although the "United States of America" had existed since July 4, 1776, the tension or ambiguity between the "united" portion of the equation (singular) and the "states" portion (plural) was plain for all to see. Americans felt themselves bound more to their states than to the Union, which was a central problem of the Articles of Confederation period (1781–1788). One of the primary goals of leaders such as James Madison at the Philadelphia Convention was to create a national government that would lead Americans to think of their country as the United States, not their individual states.

One way the tension between state and national identity surfaced at the Philadelphia Convention was in debates over the requirements for holding public office under the proposed Constitution. The delegates eventually agreed that to serve in the House of Representatives, a person must be "seven Years a Citizen of the United States." To serve in the Senate, a person must be "nine Years a Citizen of the United States." To be president, a person must be a "natural born Citizen" or a "Citizen of the United States at the time of the Adoption of this Constitution." However, it was significant that the delegates could not agree on the definition of national citizenship. To do so would have required deciding whether slaves, former slaves, and free African Americans were citizens of the United States. The delegates were so deeply divided on that issue that they left the definition of citizenship to the states. Thus, under the 1787 Constitution the definition of national citizenship depended on state definitions.

Lessons in Unit Three explained why it took a civil war and an amendment to the Constitution to define national citizenship. The Fourteenth Amendment, ratified in 1868, provides that

> ❝ All persons born or naturalized in the United States and subject to the jurisdiction thereof, are citizens of the United States and of the State wherein they reside.

What is the meaning and significance of the nation's motto, *E pluribus unum*?

This clause defines national citizenship and says that national citizens also are citizens of the states in which they live. As citizens of both the United States and the states in which they reside, citizens have authority over and responsibility for the proper functioning of their state and local governments as well as the national government.

The Fourteenth Amendment uses the principle of *jus soli*, a Latin phrase meaning "law of the soil" or "right of birthplace." This means that any child born in the United States is a citizen of the United States, even if the child's parents are not citizens, which includes persons who are merely visiting the country. Congress has declared that the soil of the United States includes Puerto Rico, Guam, the Virgin Islands, and the Northern Mariana Islands.

The tension between national unity and some degree of state sovereignty remains even today as Americans continue to negotiate the meaning of the country's unique system of federalism. This is not surprising. After all, the idea expressed in the nation's motto, *E pluribus unum*—Out of Many, One—does not mean that the plurality of *pluribus* is eliminated by the unity of the *unum*. Rather, the two live side by side, finding a degree of unity *within* diversity.

WHAT DO YOU THINK?

❶ What tensions, if any, between national unity and state sovereignty exist today? How does the Constitution provide for dealing with such tensions?

❷ What were the implications of the Fourteenth Amendment for racial and other barriers to citizenship included in the laws of many states before this amendment was passed?

❸ What limitations does the Fourteenth Amendment place on states in regard to citizenship? Would these limitations be adequate to protect the rights of citizens? Why or why not?

❹ What are the advantages and disadvantages of using the *jus soli* principle of national citizenship today? Does simply being born in the United States establish a foundation for good citizenship? Why or why not?

❺ Should the Fourteenth Amendment be changed to reflect additional or different criteria for national citizenship? Explain.

WHO ARE NATURALIZED CITIZENS AND WHAT SHOULD THE CRITERIA BE FOR NATURALIZATION?

Naturalization is the legal process by which a foreign citizen becomes a citizen of the United States. Citizenship through naturalization may be granted to individuals or entire populations by statute or treaty, as has occurred in Alaska, Hawaii, Texas, Puerto Rico, Guam, the Northern Mariana Islands, and the Virgin Islands.

Naturalization is tied to U.S. immigration policy, because only those who are lawfully admitted to the United States can become citizens. Article I of the Constitution gives Congress the power to establish uniform rules for naturalization. The Immigration and Naturalization Service administers naturalization laws. The criteria for naturalization have changed over time, but today individuals qualify for naturalization if they

● Are at least 18 years old

● Have been lawfully admitted to the United States for permanent residence

● Have resided continuously in the United States for at least five years

Should all children born in the United States automatically become citizens? Why or why not?

1802	Records of entry into the United States were begun.
1855	Alien wives of U.S. citizens were granted citizenship automatically.
1870	The naturalization process was opened to persons of African descent.
1882	The Chinese Exclusion Act prohibited Chinese laborers from entering the country for ten years. This was the first act specifically targeting an ethic group. The act was extended several times before being repealed in 1943.
1892	Ellis Island, a processing depot for immigrants, opened in New York. It was closed in 1954, marking an end to mass European immigration.
1906	The Bureau of Immigration and Naturalization was put in charge of "all matters concerning the naturalization of aliens." It was made part of the Department of Justice in 1940.
1924	The first immigration quotas were imposed. The quota for each country was based on the ratio of the number of citizens of that nationality already residing in the United States to the total U.S. population in 1920. As a result immigrants from the United Kingdom, Germany, and Ireland made up more than two-thirds of those eligible for U.S. citizenship. In 1952 the quota was changed to one-sixteenth of one percent of the population in 1920.
1929–1945	Immigration to the United States virtually stopped during the Great Depression, World War II, and the beginning of the Cold War.
1965	National origin quotas were abolished and replaced by regional quotas (such as the Western Hemisphere or the Eastern Hemisphere).
1986	Penalties were imposed on employers who knowingly hire aliens who lack proper documentation.
1996	Categories of criminal activity as grounds for deportation were increased.

wtpcompanion.civiced.org **LINKS**

Visit the We the People companion website for a link to a more comprehensive timeline of immigration policy and a link to an engaging website on immigration.

MILITARY SERVICE Beginning in World War I Congress began making it easier for aliens to become citizens through military service.

wtpcompanion.civiced.org **LINKS**

Visit the We the People companion website for a link to information about current rules on naturalization through military service.

student page ▼ 248–249

HOW HAS THE CITIZENSHIP STATUS OF NATIVE AMERICANS EVOLVED?

Before passage of the Indian Citizenship Act, the Dawes Severalty Act of 1887 had encouraged Native Americans to integrate into mainstream America by, among other things, giving tribal lands to individuals in 160-acre parcels. Native American land deemed "surplus" was sold, and the money was used to establish Indian schools. By 1932 an estimated 138 million acres of former tribal lands had been sold.

In 1928 the Rockefeller Foundation funded a study of the conditions of Native Americans in twenty-six states. Its report, "The Problem with Indian Administration," commonly is called the Meriam Report after director Lewis Meriam. The report documented problems associated with efforts to assimilate Native Americans.

wtpcompanion.civiced.org **LINKS**

Visit the We the People companion website for a link to the Meriam Report.

Several hundred tribes in the United States are seeking official tribal recognition, a process that often takes decades to complete. Federal recognition is important for tribes because it formally establishes a government-to-government relationship. Status as a sovereign entity carries with it significant privileges, including exemptions from state and local jurisdiction. These exemptions generally apply to lands that the federal government has taken into trust for a tribe or its members. Additionally, federally recognized tribes are eligible to participate in federal assistance programs. Through these programs tribal governments may receive funds that they can then use to provide community services, such as health clinics.

- Show that they are of good moral character

- Demonstrate a belief in and a commitment to the principles of the Constitution of the United States

- Are able to read, write, speak, and understand words of ordinary usage in the English language

- Take the following Oath of Allegiance:

> I hereby declare, on oath, that I absolutely and entirely renounce and abjure all allegiance and fidelity to any foreign prince, potentate, state, or sovereignty of whom or which I have heretofore been a subject or citizen; that I will support and defend the Constitution and laws of the United States of America against all enemies, foreign and domestic; that I will bear true faith and allegiance to the same; that I will bear arms on behalf of the United States when required by the law; that I will perform noncombatant service in the Armed Forces of the United States when required by the law; that I will perform work of national importance under civilian direction when required by the law; and that I take this obligation freely without any mental reservation or purpose of evasion; so help me God.

Recent changes in the laws now make it easier for noncitizens serving in the U.S. military to become naturalized citizens.

WHAT DO YOU THINK?

❶ Review the list of criteria for naturalization today. Are there other or different criteria you think Congress should adopt? Explain.

❷ Should all Americans be required to take the Oath of Allegiance to the United States when they register to vote? Why or why not?

❸ Should the wording of the Oath of Allegiance be changed in any way? Explain. Should the oath be enforced? Explain.

❹ Should all Americans be required to demonstrate a belief in and a commitment to the principles of the Constitution in order to be able to vote? If so, how should that belief and commitment be demonstrated?

HOW HAS THE CITIZENSHIP STATUS OF NATIVE AMERICANS EVOLVED?

Native American tribes were self-governing communities long before Europeans arrived in what is now the United States. As explained in Unit One, the overall number of Native Americans was markedly reduced as American colonies, then states, and eventually the United States expanded its territory westward. Defining the legal status of surviving Native Americans proved to be difficult well into the twentieth century.

The Constitution does not contain a clear statement of the relationship between Native American tribes and the United States. Article I gives Congress the power to regulate commerce with foreign nations and "with the Indian tribes," suggesting that Native American tribes are separate, sovereign nations. However, in 1831 the Supreme Court defined Native American tribes as "domestic dependent nations" (*Cherokee Nation v. Georgia*, 1831). National government policy vacillated between respecting the sovereignty of Native American tribes and seeking to dismantle tribal governments and to integrate their members into the United States.

In 1924 Congress enacted the Indian Citizenship Act, making Native Americans citizens of the United States and of the states in which they reside. Some viewed the act as a tribute for the heroic service of many Native Americans in World War I. Others viewed it as the final step in assimilating Native Americans into the so-called

What is the United States' "trust responsibility" for Native Americans?

mainstream of American life. But even though Native Americans were declared American citizens in 1924, many were excluded from voting by state laws.

The Indian Civil Rights Act of 1968 affirmed that the United States' "trust responsibility" for Native Americans includes protecting the "sovereignty of each tribal government." Thus today Native Americans are members of their tribe, citizens of the United States, and citizens of the state in which they reside. More than a million Native Americans qualify for membership in more than one tribe. The U.S. government recognizes more than 560 tribes within its boundaries.

WHAT IS DUAL NATIONAL CITIZENSHIP?

Dual national citizenship, as the phrase implies, means being a citizen of two or more countries. This may occur because the United States recognizes as citizens those born within its boundaries, even if they also are citizens of another country. The United States also recognizes as citizens the children born abroad to American citizens, even though those children may also be citizens of the country in which they were born. *Jus sanguines*, "law of the blood," is a principle in which citizenship is determined by parentage rather than place of birth, or *jus soli*.

Increased mobility of people and business throughout the world has resulted in greater acceptance of dual national citizenship in various countries. Countries that now permit dual national citizenship include Australia, Canada, France, Mexico, Spain, Switzerland, and the United Kingdom. Other countries, including China, Germany, India, Japan, Uganda, and Venezuela, do not permit dual national citizenship.

Current citizenship and immigration laws of the United States do not specifically address dual national citizenship. The State Department acknowledges the status but does not encourage dual citizenship, believing that it may cause problems, such as conflicting loyalties. However, many citizens believe that dual citizenship is not an issue to be resolved solely by the State Department.

Those who favor allowing dual citizenship often cite hardships to immigrants if dual nationality were not available to them. They argue that dual citizenship is accepted by a number of other democracies and that some dual nationals would lose important benefits if they gave up their original citizenship. They also argue that dual citizenship facilitates commerce.

Opponents argue that dual citizenship dilutes American citizenship and establishes a legitimacy of dual loyalties that is inconsistent with loyalty to the United States. Critics say that dual citizenship weakens the nation. Naturalized citizens have taken an "oath of allegiance and renunciation" of competing political loyalties that is incompatible with dual citizenship.

The issue is bound to remain controversial, with strong views expressed on both sides.

HOW MAY UNITED STATES CITIZENSHIP BE LOST?

The Supreme Court has held that the Eighth Amendment prohibition on cruel and unusual punishment means that natural-born citizens cannot be stripped of their citizenship. The justices explained that taking away citizenship is a "form of punishment more primitive than torture, for it destroys for the individual the political existence that was centuries in development" (*Trop v. Dulles*, 1958).

Nonetheless, Congress has recognized that giving up U.S. citizenship is a "natural and inherent right of the people."

What arguments can you make for and against dual citizenship?

249

student page ▾ 250-251

WHAT ARE THE RIGHTS OF CITIZENS AND PERMANENT RESIDENTS?

The Supreme Court has rejected the proposition that a person's unlawful immigration status places that person beyond the protective bounds of the Constitution. In *Wong Wing v. United States* (1896) the Court held that even aliens who are in the country illegally enjoy the protections of the Fifth and Sixth Amendments.

In *Plyler v. Doe* (1982) the Court declared unconstitutional a Texas statute that effectively excluded the children of undocumented aliens from public schools. The statute violated the Fourteenth Amendment's equal protection clause. The guarantee of equal protection extends to each person regardless of citizenship or immigration status. Justice Louis Powell wrote, "A legislative classification that threatens the creation of an underclass of future citizens and residents cannot be reconciled with one of the fundamental purposes of the Fourteenth Amendment."

student page ▼ 252

WHAT ARE THE RESPONSIBILITIES OF CITIZENS AND RESIDENT ALIENS?

During the late colonial and early statehood periods the right to vote often rested solely on the ability of voters to meet standards such as holding property, being a resident, and paying taxes. The sense of nationalism that strongly influences the debate about whether resident aliens should be allowed to vote began to be felt during the War of 1812. Suspicion of foreigners typically surges during times of war and emergency.

Some states today permit resident aliens to vote in some local elections, such as school board elections. These states and locales include the following:

- **MARYLAND** Montgomery County and six cities in the county—Garrett Park, Takoma Park, Somerset, Chevy Chase, Martin's Additions, and Barnesville

- **MASSACHUSETTS** Amherst and Cambridge

Among the cities that recently have debated allowing resident aliens to vote are New York City, San Francisco, and Washington, D.C.

In 2005 Indiana adopted a law requiring registered voters to show a government-issued photo identification card, such as a driver's license, a state I.D., or a passport, in order to vote. Opponents challenged the law before it went into effect seeking a declaration that it was unconstitutional "on its face." (To prevail on a facial challenge, plaintiffs must show that there are no circumstances under which the law could be constitutional.) In *Crawford v. Marion County Election Board* (2008), the Supreme Court upheld the law, on the ground that the I.D. requirement was "neutral and nondiscriminatory" and was closely related to Indiana's legitimate interests in preventing voter fraud.

Most states require that jurors be United States citizens. However, if a noncitizen is summoned for jury duty, the person must appear to explain his or her citizenship status or risk facing sanctions that could include deportation.

All male residents of the United States must register with the Selective Service.

The following voluntary acts may result in loss of U.S. citizenship:

- Becoming a naturalized citizen of another country

- Swearing an oath of allegiance to another country

- Serving in the armed forces of a nation at war with the United States

- Working for the government of another nation in a capacity that requires becoming naturalized in that country or swearing an oath of allegiance

- Renouncing citizenship formally

- Being convicted of the crime of treason

Voluntarily renouncing citizenship has serious implications. A person cannot seek to retain some of the privileges of citizenship while surrendering others. A person who gives up United States citizenship cannot get it back.

Naturalized citizens can lose their citizenship in the same ways as natural-born citizens. They also can have their citizenship revoked through **denaturalization**. The most common ground for denaturalization is fraud, or willful misrepresentation, when applying for citizenship. Denaturalization is a legal process in which the government has the burden of proof, and the citizen is entitled to due process of law.

WHAT ARE THE RIGHTS OF CITIZENS AND PERMANENT RESIDENTS?

Most rights in the United States belong to everyone who lives here. Like citizens, permanent residents who have been lawfully admitted to the United States can live and work anywhere in the country. They qualify for Social Security, Supplemental Security Income, and Medicare benefits. They can own property and qualify for state driver's licenses, attend public schools and colleges, join the armed forces, and purchase and own a firearm if they satisfy the requirements. The guarantees of equal protection and due process in the Fourteenth Amendment apply to all persons, not just citizens. The guarantees in the Bill of Rights similarly apply to persons, not just citizens. All persons have the right to assemble peaceably, speak, and petition government for a redress of grievances.

For the most part only citizens can hold public office. Residency requirements usually accompany citizenship requirements for holding office, whether for governor or member of Congress. Only the president must be a "natural born" citizen of the United States.

Being a citizen did not always mean that one was allowed to vote. For many years women and free African Americans were not permitted to vote, even though they unquestionably were citizens. Citizens living in the District of Columbia could not vote for president until passage of the Twenty-third Amendment in 1961. Congress has extended citizenship to residents of territories,

Should convicted felons be allowed to vote upon release from prison? Why or why not?

Should resident aliens be allowed to vote? Why or why not?

such as Puerto Rico, but these citizens cannot vote in national elections when they live in their territorial homes and so, like residents of the District of Columbia, they are not represented in Congress. Age requirements for the franchise—the right to vote—still apply to all citizens. Since ratification of the Twenty-sixth Amendment in 1971 voters must be at least eighteen years old. Many states also prohibit citizens who have been convicted of felony crimes from voting.

A contemporary issue regarding the right to vote is whether **aliens**—people who are not citizens—should be allowed to vote in American elections. Many states and a number of territories allowed noncitizen voting during some portion of the eighteenth and nineteenth centuries. Vermont, for example, originally permitted aliens to vote if they met the state's property, race, sex, and age requirements. Some states allowed such voting for relatively few years and others for several decades and in a few cases longer.

Defenders of alien voting today argue that **resident aliens** are affected by local public policies as much as citizens are, and such residents should have a say in how they are governed. Aliens pay taxes just as citizens do. The children of aliens attending schools are affected by school policy as much as the children of citizens. Therefore, alien children's parents should also have the opportunity to play a role in governing schools.

Opponents argue that alien voting makes American citizens and aliens all but indistinguishable. Alien voting, they say, is a step toward the loss of sovereignty and self-government by the nation and its citizens. If aliens wish to vote, then becoming American citizens allows them to do so.

WHAT DO YOU THINK?

❶ Should the United States allow dual national citizenship or does it undermine American citizenship? Explain your response.

❷ Is the Oath of Allegiance compatible with dual citizenship? Why or why not? If it is incompatible, should the oath be changed to accommodate dual citizenship? Why or why not?

❸ Should the practice of permitting resident aliens to vote in school board or other local elections be allowed, or should it be eliminated? Explain your response.

❹ Should resident aliens have the right to be elected to local government office? Why or why not?

ENRICHMENT ACTIVITIES

A. EXAMINING THE NEW NATURALIZATION EXAMINATION

Beginning in October 2008 the U.S. Immigration and Naturalization Service (INS) adopted a new naturalization examination with one hundred questions on American government, history, and civics, any ten of which an applicant may be required to answer. The applicant must respond correctly to six of the ten to pass the exam. Below are examples that the INS provided to demonstrate the differences between the old and new tests.

Ask students to work in small groups to study the two sample tests and consider two questions:

❶ Do you think one test is superior to the other? Why?

❷ How well do the tests achieve their goal of assessing understanding of the concepts of democracy and the rights and responsibilities of citizenship?

Pre-2008 U.S. Citizenship Test, Sample Questions

- How many stars are there in our flag?
- How many states are there in the Union?
- What color are the stars on our flag?
- What do the stars on the flag mean?
- How many stripes are there in the flag?
- What date is the Day of Independence?
- Independence from whom?
- What country did we fight during the revolutionary war?
- Who was the first president of the United States?
- What do we call a change of the constitution?

Redesigned U.S. Citizenship Test, Sample Questions

- Name one war fought by the United States in the 1900s.
- What did Susan B. Anthony do?
- What is one thing Benjamin Franklin is famous for?
- There were thirteen original states. Name three.
- What is one responsibility that is only for United States citizens?
- What does the judicial branch do?
- Name your U.S. Representative.

- Who makes federal laws?
- What does the Constitution do?
- What is the supreme law of the land?

B. CONSENTING TO BE A CITIZEN

Some Americans argue that they did not consent to the Constitution written in 1787 and have no duty to be "ruled by the dead." Political scientists Walter Murphy, James Fleming, and Sotirios Barber respond that Americans today owe allegiance to the Constitution for at least three reasons:

People who are legally free to expatriate themselves but choose not to give their consent to be governed by the Constitution and the laws enacted pursuant to it.

Most people, at some time in their lives, will take an oath to support and defend the Constitution; for example, as a member of the military, as a juror, in some professional capacities such as lawyers, or as one of the millions of America's government officials.

People who participate in the electoral process give their tacit agreement to be governed by the Constitution.

Ask students to consider the following questions:

❶ Are there additional reasons why Americans today should consider themselves bound by the Constitution even though they did not participate in its writing or ratification?

❷ Should everyone be required to take an oath to support and defend the Constitution as a condition of (a) voting, (b) graduating from high school, or (c) receiving government benefits? Why or why not?

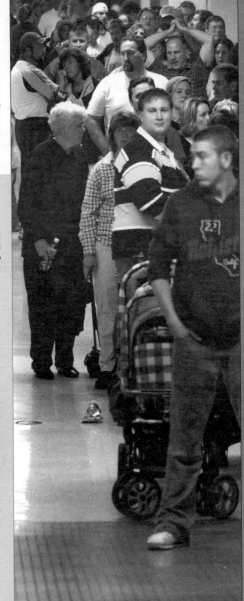

WHAT ARE THE RESPONSIBILITIES OF CITIZENS AND RESIDENT ALIENS?

Citizens and resident aliens share many responsibilities. For example, everyone has a duty to obey the laws and pay taxes. Men must register with the Selective Service when they turn eighteen years of age.

Citizens have additional responsibilities, including casting informed ballots in elections and serving on juries. Some people find jury duty burdensome because it takes them away from work, home, or leisure. However, the constitutional right to trial by a jury of one's peers depends on the willingness of citizens to serve as jurors when called. Juries also help to ensure that government officials who initiate criminal prosecutions do not abuse their power.

CRITICAL THINKING EXERCISE

What Are Some of the Rights and Obligations of Citizenship?

This lesson has described ways in which people can become American citizens and some of the rights and responsibilities of citizenship. Work in groups of three to five students to respond to the following:

❶ List what you think are some of the most important legal rights and obligations of citizens.

❷ List what you think are some of the most important moral rights and obligations of citizens.

❸ Be prepared to explain and defend your responses.

REVIEWING AND USING THE LESSON

❶ How was citizenship defined in the United States before and after the Fourteenth Amendment?

❷ Explain how *jus soli*, *jus sanguines*, and residency differ as principles for defining citizenship.

❸ How does the Constitution define national and state citizenship?

❹ How is citizenship through naturalization different from citizenship by birth?

❺ Should all Americans be required to demonstrate their knowledge of American government and history as naturalized citizens must do in order to become citizens? Explain.

❻ How do the rights and responsibilities of citizens differ from those of resident aliens?

What obligations accompany the right to vote?

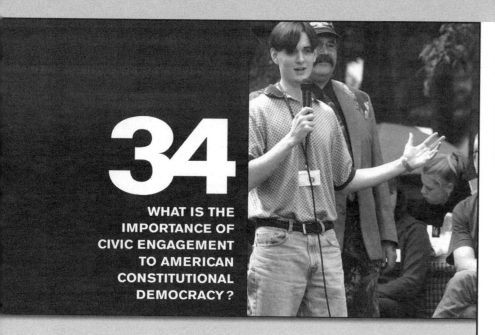

34

WHAT IS THE IMPORTANCE OF CIVIC ENGAGEMENT TO AMERICAN CONSTITUTIONAL DEMOCRACY?

UNIT SIX | LESSON 34

WHAT IS THE IMPORTANCE OF CIVIC ENGAGEMENT TO AMERICAN CONSTITUTIONAL DEMOCRACY?

wtpcompanion.civiced.org   **LESSON PURPOSE + TERMS**

Visit the We the People companion website for printable and downloadable Lesson Purposes and Terms and Concepts to Understand sections for each lesson. Audio readings of each Lesson Purpose and Term are also available online in MP3 format.

LESSON PURPOSE

America's founding principles assume the active involvement of its people in civic life. Popular sovereignty, for example, means that the people have ultimate governing authority, which carries with it the responsibility to exercise that authority knowledgeably to balance individual interests and the common good. Protection of individual rights requires people to be guardians of their own rights and to be willing to defend the rights of others.

This lesson describes ways that Americans can participate in civic life to help achieve the ideals they have set for themselves and their nation, ideals that were examined in Units One and Two. It explains how civic engagement can advance both self-interest and the common good. It also discusses issues related to voting and voter turnout.

When you have finished this lesson, you should be able to explain why Americans need to be engaged in civic affairs. You also should be able to identify opportunities for civic engagement through voluntary associations and nongovernmental organizations and participation in local, state, and national politics. Finally, you should be able to evaluate, take, and defend positions on challenges associated with voting and other forms of participation in civic life in the United States.

TERMS AND CONCEPTS TO UNDERSTAND

nongovernmental organization

voluntary associations

voter registration

student page ▾ 254

WHY SHOULD AMERICANS PARTICIPATE IN THE CIVIC LIFE OF THE COUNTRY?

The following are observations about the importance of civic participation.

Athenian statesman Pericles:

> We do not say that a man who takes no interest in politics is a man who minds his own business; we say that he has no business here at all.

Political scientist Michael X. Delli Carpini and public affairs analyst Scott Keeter:

> Although political participation can be seen as a good in and of itself, its primary value is as a means of translating individual and collective interests into public action.

Law professor Toni Marie Massaro:

> The quality of our public debates depends not only on the right of all to express their ideas freely, but also on a community willing to listen to their views. That is, meaningful participation in the constitutional conversation involves both speech and reflective silence.

Education reformer Joseph Tussman:

> The democrat turns his back resolutely on the temptation to divide men into pursuers of happiness and bearers of responsibility. He summons every man to his place in the public forum.

student page ▾ 254–255

HOW DO VOLUNTARY ASSOCIATIONS CONTRIBUTE TO CIVIC ENGAGEMENT?

The following are observations about the role of voluntary associations.

Tocqueville:

> It is the duty as well as the interest of men to be useful to their fellows.... What had been calculation becomes instinct. By working together for the good of his fellow citizens, he in the end acquires a habit and a taste for serving them.

Political scientists Theda Skocpol and Morris P. Fiorina:

> Voluntary associations have always rivaled voting as pathways Americans follow into community and public affairs. Organized voluntary groups

---

WHY SHOULD AMERICANS PARTICIPATE IN THE CIVIC LIFE OF THE COUNTRY?

American constitutional democracy often has been called an experiment in self-government. Sovereignty resides with the people. How the people use their power directly affects the society in which they live and the vibrancy of their civic institutions. The people also determine which problems they can solve for themselves and which problems require governmental responses.

Participation in civic life does more than address problems. Participation helps individuals become attached to their communities, regions, and states as well as the country as a whole. Such attachment is necessary for Americans to develop pride in their communities and country and to understand that they share a common destiny. For many people civic engagement includes recommitting to the ideals that they have set for themselves and understanding how those ideals relate to the fundamental principles of American constitutional democracy.

Those who participate actively in civic life are more likely to vote. They also are more likely to become well-informed voters.

What are some of the benefits of voluntary associations?

HOW DO VOLUNTARY ASSOCIATIONS CONTRIBUTE TO CIVIC ENGAGEMENT?

When the French historian Alexis de Tocqueville visited the United States in the 1830s, he observed greater equality of opportunity and condition among people and social classes in America than anywhere else he studied. Tocqueville admired much of what he saw and was especially impressed that Americans sought to rely on their own efforts to solve problems and to resist what he called "the evils and the difficulties of life." He also observed that Americans formed many **voluntary associations**, or unpaid groups, to solve community problems and take care of one another.

Voluntary associations still thrive in the United States. Associations engaged in civic projects are motivated by a commitment to making their communities and the world better places to live. They depend on their members for ideas, volunteer time, and money to carry out their activities. In turn, members experience the satisfaction of working with others toward a common goal.

Most of the thousands of voluntary associations in the United States fit into the following categories:

- **Religious organizations** Churches and other religious organizations are one type. Americans in general have shown relatively high levels of religious commitment and participation in religious organizations. In addition to addressing their members' spiritual needs, religious groups commonly perform community services, such as caring for the sick, the elderly, and the poor. Many sponsor youth activities. Religious organizations have been leaders on issues as diverse as maintaining the integrity of the nuclear family, protecting the environment, advancing civil rights in the United States and elsewhere, and advocating for world peace and international human rights.

- **Social organizations** Millions of Americans have joined groups that provide opportunities to socialize with others and to assist one another in times of need. Many of these groups also perform community service by sponsoring athletic events for youth, collecting books for public libraries, and offering scholarships to needy students or adults who were unable to complete high school. Book clubs, sports clubs, assistance leagues, and women's organizations are examples.

- **Service and business organizations** Early in the twentieth century service and business organizations, such as Kiwanis, Lions, Jaycees, and Rotary, sprang up across the country. These organizations address a variety of interests, from business networking to community service. For example, Kiwanis International "serves the children of the world" by promoting child safety, building safe playgrounds, and offering programs to discourage drinking and smoking among young people. Lions Clubs International supports vision and health screenings, provides disaster relief, and awards scholarships. The United States Junior Chamber, also known as the Jaycees, raises money for cancer research.

- **Nongovernmental organizations** In the past fifty years thousands of nonprofit organizations have formed. They depend primarily on charitable donations and volunteer service to address particular issues of concern to their members. **Nongovernmental organizations** (NGOs) often are classified by their focus, such as disaster relief, economic development, health care, or environmental protection. Many of the organizations described above as social or service groups satisfy the definition of an NGO. Other examples are the League of Women Voters, the Carter Center, Athletes for Peace, and Family Health International. NGOs are becoming increasingly significant in world affairs. They also influence domestic policy through lobbying and public education.

WHAT DO YOU THINK?

❶ To what, if any, voluntary associations do you or your parents belong? Why?

❷ What are the benefits of participating in voluntary associations? The costs?

❸ Review the discussion of "factions" in Lesson 14. Do NGOs and other voluntary associations with "value-based" agendas fit James Madison's definition of faction? Explain.

HOW CAN AMERICANS PARTICIPATE IN LOCAL AND STATE GOVERNMENTS?

Tocqueville believed that New England townships were models of classical republicanism, where the habits of citizenship and self-government were developed. By practicing the art of government in small spheres, he argued, Americans learned the nature of their responsibilities and the extent of their rights. Americans continue to have many opportunities for political involvement. Local and state government are examples.

- **Local government** There are thousands of local governments in the United States, ranging from those in townships and cities to counties and special districts. Local governments touch the lives of every American by providing the essential governmental services people need to live together day to day. As explained in Unit Four, there are many forms and varieties of local government. Each depends on citizens taking an active role in determining appropriate tax bases, electing and overseeing those who hold local government office, and being willing to hold office themselves. Many city councils, county commissions, school districts, and other special districts do not pay elected officials a salary. Those officials are volunteers. In addition to elected positions local governments rely on citizen advisory boards and commissions. Examples are police review boards, civil rights advisory committees, and library advisory boards. Students often hold elected or appointed positions on advisory boards.

What are some of the benefits of participating in local government?

mediate between government and society, empower participating citizens, and embody relationships between leaders and supporters. Associations are, moreover, sites where citizens learn—and practice—the "knowledge of how to combine" so vital to democracy.

Theda Skocpol:

> Voluntary action is educational, and those who take part become in many ways better human beings—more independent, efficacious and competent, larger in their capacities for thought, greater in their respect for others and their willingness to take responsibility, better able to appraise their own interests and those of the community.... What matters is not only the amount of civic activity but also its distribution, not just how many people take part but also who they are.

The Ford Foundation's Michael Edwards:

> In their social role, civil societies are seen as a reservoir of caring, cultural life and intellectual innovation, teaching people…the skills of citizenship.

> In their political role, voluntary organizations are seen as a crucial counterweight to states and corporate power and an essential pillar in promotion of transparency, accountability and other aspects of good governance.... It is civil society that provides the channels through which most people can make their voices heard in government decision-making, protect and promote their civil and political rights, and strengthen their skills as future political leaders.

By some estimates there were more than a million nongovernmental organizations (NGOs) in the United States in the year 2000 and thousands more international NGOs (commonly known as INGOs). Many are incorporated entities, often with nonprofit status. It is not uncommon for NGOs to receive state or federal funding as well as support from for-profit entities.

NGOs play an important role in influencing public policy. One example is the American Legion, which worked toward drafting and lobbying for enactment of the "G.I. Bill of Rights" in 1944. Another example is Mothers Against Drunk Driving, founded in 1980 by Candy Lightner, a mother whose child was killed by a drunk driver.

LESSON 34

student page ▼ 255–256

HOW CAN AMERICANS PARTICIPATE IN LOCAL AND STATE GOVERNMENTS?

Longtime Speaker of the House Thomas "Tip" O'Neill argued that "all politics is local." By that he meant that problems and issues close to home quickly affect what happens in Washington, D.C. Moreover, state and local government is the "training ground" for higher political posts. Some observers therefore argue that learning about American government from a local perspective is more important than learning about American government from a national perspective.

wtpcompanion.civiced.org   LINKS

Visit the We the People companion website for a link to information about *We the People: Project Citizen.*

- **State government** All fifty states have representative governments with structures that are like the system of separated and shared powers at the national level. Voters must make informed decisions about who should be governor, who should hold other executive offices, and who should serve in the legislature. Many states also elect their judges, including justices of the peace, municipal judges, county trial judges, and state appellate judges. Like local governments, state governments also rely on residents to serve on boards and commissions to study and make recommendations to elected officials about matters such as child welfare, drug and alcohol programs, and environmental protection.

Most Americans who are active in local and state politics take pride in their accomplishments. Their involvement broadens their understanding of issues facing their community and the country, making them more thoughtful and informed than most of those who are not involved.

CRITICAL THINKING EXERCISE

Understanding and Participating in State and Local Government

There are approximately five hundred thousand elected officials in the United States. Fewer than eighty-five hundred are national officials. The vast majority of elected officials serve in state and local offices. Americans have many opportunities to make important governmental decisions by electing state and local officials and by serving on boards and commissions or running for state and local offices.

Work in one of three groups to respond to the following questions and then compare your group's responses with the rest of the class. If there are significant differences among the groups' responses, discuss what might account for those differences.

❶ How many elected officials are there in your state?

❷ Where can you obtain information about the elected officials in your state and a description of their responsibilities?

❸ What are the five most important issues facing the state and local governments where you live? How can you become informed about those issues?

❹ What considerations would persuade you to run for a state or local office or to work on a state or local political campaign? Explain.

What are some of the benefits of working together to solve community problems?

What opportunities do constituents have to communicate with their members of Congress?

HOW CAN AMERICANS PARTICIPATE IN THE NATIONAL GOVERNMENT?

Opportunities for direct participation in the national government are more limited than at state and local levels, but they do exist. Political parties play a central role in shaping the national policy agenda. Party participation is open to all interested Americans, regardless of age or background. America's two major parties, as well as other, or third, parties, have grassroots organizations that encourage and welcome participation. Political parties offer opportunities to work on political campaigns, to help get out the vote, and to have a voice in shaping party platforms, or statements of policy goals.

Congressional representatives rely on constituent groups to advise them on issues of public policy. Members of Congress often host "town hall" meetings in their districts to discuss issues with their constituents. They pay careful attention to communications from constituents expressing opinions on issues. Constituents can communicate with national officials in many ways, such as by using email, letters, and telephone calls and by visiting their representatives' offices in their home districts or in Washington, D.C.

Presidents also seek the advice of members of the public by appointing citizen commissions and committees to investigate problems and make recommendations. An example is the Safe and Drug-Free Schools and Communities Advisory Committee created in 2006 in response to school shootings. Other examples are commissions on education reform, immigration policy, and scientific matters, such as stem cell research and global warming.

One of the ways that Americans can influence the national government is by joining voluntary associations and NGOs that lobby. Americans also can influence national politics by having their views reflected in public opinion polls. As explained in Lesson 23, public opinion can have a significant effect on legislation and even on presidential decisions.

WHAT NEEDS TO BE DONE TO ENCOURAGE VOTER TURNOUT?

Popular sovereignty and representative government mean that voters have both the authority and the responsibility to decide who will serve as elected officials in all of America's governments.

Elections in the United States are administered at the state and local levels with some assistance from the Federal Election Commission. All states except North Dakota require those who wish to vote to establish eligibility by registering with county officials. **Voter registration** lists, or lists of qualified voters maintained by state and local election officials, help these officials decide how many polling places, or voting locations, they will

257

student page ▼ 257

HOW CAN AMERICANS PARTICIPATE IN THE NATIONAL GOVERNMENT?

Political scientist Jeffrey Berry comes to the following conclusion:

> Citizen groups are "heard" in many important ways in the policymaking process. They are singularly impressive in their rate of participation before congressional committees and in their disproportionate share of network news stories featuring interest group opinions.... Citizen groups prove to be strong and successful advocates in Congress, both in getting their issues on the agenda and in getting legislation passed.

Political scientist Michael X. Delli Carpini and public affairs analyst Scott Keeter argue as follows:

> Campaigns and elections are intended as periods of public deliberation and as broad referenda on the state of American society.... The quality and range of this dialectic depends on the quality of the periodic national conversations.... The public's knowledge of politics sets up the parameters of public discourse. The less informed citizens are, the more likely that campaigns will devolve into sensationalism and demagoguery, as the media and political leaders play for the public's lesser instincts or seek to capitalize on their inability to distinguish between fact and fiction.

student page ▾ 257–258

WHAT NEEDS TO BE DONE TO ENCOURAGE VOTER TURNOUT?

In 2002 President George W. Bush signed into law the Help America Vote Act (HAVA), which called for three changes in how states conduct elections:

- Elimination of punch card voting systems
- Creation of the Elections Assistance Commission
- Establishment of minimum election administration standards

Each state must decide how it will implement the law. North Dakota does not have a voter registration requirement. The state eliminated the voter registration requirement in 1951 because local election boards know the voters who enter the polls on election day. Thus North Dakota is exempt from the HAVA requirement that states implement centralized voter registration systems and adopt voter identification requirements.

wtpcompanion.civiced.org   PRIMARY SOURCES

Visit the We the People companion website for a link to the text of the Help America Vote Act.

student page ▾ 258

CRITICAL THINKING EXERCISE

HOW CAN GREATER VOTER PARTICIPATION BE ENCOURAGED?

wtpcompanion.civiced.org   LINKS

Visit the We the People companion website for a link to the U.S. Census Bureau.

---

need and where polling places should be located. In 1993 Congress adopted the National Voter Registration Act to establish uniform standards for voter registration and to make it easier for voters to register. Today voters can register by mail, at state motor vehicle departments, or at other government offices.

In the past voters had to go to a polling place on Election Day to cast their ballots. Most polling places were in neighborhood schools or other civic buildings. Today early voting and absentee ballots are common. By filling out a form, voters can request a ballot that they can mail in before the close of Election Day. The growing use of absentee ballots led the state of Oregon to adopt a vote-by-mail system for all elections. And in some states voters can cast ballots in person days and even weeks before Election Day.

Americans are considering other ways to make it easier to vote. Some observers argue that at least presidential elections should be declared national holidays so that many voters would not have to take time off from work to vote. Others argue for keeping polling places open up to twenty-four hours. Still others contend that voting should occur over a period of several days to give voters more opportunities to vote and to minimize long lines at polling places.

- Young adults had the lowest voting rate in 2004 but the greatest increase in rate since 2000.

Work in small groups to respond to the following questions and then discuss your responses as a class:

1. What factors might account for higher rates of turnout among older, better-educated, wealthier voters than among other types of voters?

2. What might be done to improve voting rates among younger voters?

3. To encourage voting many counties throughout the United States are printing ballots in languages other than English if their area has large numbers of registered voters for whom English is not their first language. Is this a good policy? Why or why not?

4. What factors might explain why voter turnout is lowest for the units of government closest to the people? What steps could be taken to increase voter turnout in state and local elections?

5. Some localities permit resident aliens to vote in local elections. What are the advantages and disadvantages of doing so?

CRITICAL THINKING EXERCISE

How Can Greater Voter Participation Be Encouraged?

The United States Census Bureau compiles voting statistics. According to the Bureau,

- Between 1960 and 2004 turnout of voting-age citizens in elections for national officials ranged from a low of 36.4 percent (1998 and 1986) to a high of 63.1 percent (1960). Turnout typically was lower in state elections and dramatically lower in local elections.

- Non-Hispanic whites had the highest level of voter turnout in the November 2004 election (67 percent), followed by African Americans (60 percent), Hispanics (47 percent), and Asian Americans (44 percent). More native-born citizens vote than naturalized citizens.

- At each successive level of educational attainment, voting rates increase.

- The voting rate is highest among citizens age fifty-five and older and among those with annual household incomes greater than $50,000 per year.

HOW IS CIVIC PARTICIPATION CONNECTED TO SELF-INTEREST?

Many Americans engage in civic activities and vote because they realize it is in their self-interest to do so. Business people, for example, serve on local boards and commissions or run for county commission or city council because they know that healthy communities are good for business. Parents volunteer their time to create and maintain parks because they want safe places for their children to play. Homeowners join neighborhood associations because they care about the value of their property.

Civic engagement has other personal benefits, including the following:

- Acquiring skills, such as speaking and debating in public, organizing groups, and writing letters
- Becoming more self-confident
- Learning how to affect decisions
- Building a reputation as an important member of the community
- Making new friends
- Developing important contacts

Self-interest is not necessarily a narrow concept. Tocqueville observed that Americans often demonstrate "enlightened" self-interest as well as narrow self-interest. Many Americans sacrifice time, money, and effort to strengthen their communities and their country because they realize that the good of the whole benefits them as individuals.

HOW IS CIVIC PARTICIPATION RELATED TO ADVANCING THE COMMON GOOD?

Working with others in civic activities frequently makes people aware of other perspectives and leads to a concern for the common good. Commitment to the common good is a central feature of classical republicanism. Concern for the common good requires individuals to see themselves as part of a larger whole and to modify their behavior to serve the needs of the whole.

Civic participation is one of the ways Americans strengthen the network of interdependence and contribute to the common good. Sometimes acting on behalf of the common good simply requires providing opportunities for others to have a voice in their community.

At other times acting on behalf of the common good requires a more significant action, such as voting to increase taxes even though one receives no personal benefit from the increase.

WHAT DO YOU THINK?

Assume that there is an upcoming election in your community. One of the measures on the ballot asks property owners to agree to an increase in their property taxes to fund schools and playgrounds. Explain how an appeal to self-interest, enlightened self-interest, or the common good might influence the following groups of voters to support the tax increase:

- Parents of school-age children
- Senior citizens who have no children in school
- Members of a civic organization with a community service focus on homelessness
- Small-business owners whose profit margins are small

How can civic participation serve one's interests and the common good?

259

ENRICHMENT ACTIVITIES

A. A "DEMANDING SORT OF CITIZENSHIP"

Political scientist Rogers M. Smith argues for a "demanding sort of citizenship" that requires citizens to be skeptical of "flattering civic myths advanced by aspiring leaders," to look "unblinkingly" at the realities of their history and their present, and to retain an awareness that the United States merits citizens' loyalty and sacrifices despite its flaws. Smith concludes that American patriotism must be "at once profound and qualified, recognized as something both necessary and dangerous, and thus as an allegiance that is deepest when it harbors searching doubts."

Ask students to form small groups and discuss the following questions:

❶ Do you agree or disagree with Smith's call for a "demanding sort of citizenship"? Why?

❷ What about Smith's views of patriotism? Can one be patriotic while harboring searching doubts? Explain.

❸ Are there other views of citizenship that you think better capture what is required of patriotic Americans? If so, what are they?

B. EVALUATING AN ARGUMENT ABOUT DEMOCRACY

Ask students to work in pairs to study the following argument recently advanced by legal philosopher Ronald Dworkin, and then use the questions that follow to prepare an evaluation of Dworkin's argument.

There is no genuine democracy, even though officials have been elected in otherwise fair elections, unless voters have access to the information they need so that their votes can be knowledgeable choices rather than only manipulated responses to advertising campaigns. Citizens of a democracy must be able to participate in government not just spasmodically, in elections from time to time, but constantly through informed and free debate about their government's performance between elections.

❶ What do you think voters need to know in order to make "knowledgeable choices"?

❷ How serious is the problem of voters' choices being manipulated by advertising campaigns? What evidence gathered from the media or other sources can you offer as evidence?

❸ How can voters stay informed and evaluate their government's performance between elections?

❹ Do you agree with the author's basic premises? Why or why not?

CRITICAL THINKING EXERCISE

Evaluating the Relationship between the Ideals of Classical Republicanism and Civic Engagement

Some of today's observers worry about the future health of America's experiment in self-government. They believe that Americans have focused too much on the self-interested aspects of natural rights philosophy and not enough on the public-spirited aspects of classical republicanism. These critics see America as a fragmented society in which individuals are preoccupied with the pursuit of economic self-interest. They note that fewer Americans now participate in voluntary associations and local government than did so in the past. They believe that civic life is disconnected from people's private lives and that too many Americans fail to engage with others in pursuit of the common good.

Work in small groups to develop positions on the following questions. Be prepared to present and defend your positions before the class.

❶ Do you agree with those who are worried about the future health of America's experiment in self-government? Why or why not?

❷ Do you think the classical republican sense of community is possible in American society today? What forces work for and against it? How might a greater sense of community be promoted in the neighborhood or city where you live?

❸ What ways can you think of to involve more Americans in civic life? What reforms would you propose to the education system? To the political process? To the Constitution?

REVIEWING AND USING THE LESSON

❶ Describe opportunities for participation in civic life afforded by
  - Voluntary associations
  - Nongovernmental organizations
  - Service and business organizations
  - Voting

❷ Explain the difference between self-interest, enlightened self-interest, and the common good. Provide examples of each as related to civic engagement.

❸ Voting is mandatory in more than sixty countries in the world, many of them democracies. Should it be made mandatory in the United States? Explain your response.

❹ The most common reason people offer for not voting is lack of time. What suggestions do you have for solving that problem?

❺ Describe ways to contact the following officials from the area in which you live:
  - City councilor
  - State legislator
  - U.S. representative
  - U.S. senator
  - U.S. president

What is the importance of volunteerism to America?

35

HOW HAVE CIVIL RIGHTS MOVEMENTS RESULTED IN FUNDAMENTAL POLITICAL AND SOCIAL CHANGE IN THE UNITED STATES?

HOW HAVE CIVIL RIGHTS MOVEMENTS RESULTED IN FUNDAMENTAL POLITICAL AND SOCIAL CHANGE IN THE UNITED STATES?

wtpcompanion.civiced.org | **LESSON PURPOSE + TERMS**

Visit the We the People companion website for printable and downloadable Lesson Purposes and Terms and Concepts to Understand sections for each lesson. Audio readings of each Lesson Purpose and Term are also available online in MP3 format.

LESSON PURPOSE

The Declaration of Independence is celebrated for its commitment to the principles of human liberty and equality. The Fourteenth Amendment guarantees equal treatment under the law. This lesson focuses on political and social movements that have used and continue to use the Declaration and the Fourteenth Amendment to effect fundamental political and social change in the United States.

When you have finished this lesson, you should be able to explain why African Americans, women, and other groups found it necessary to take concerted action to ensure recognition of their civil rights. You should be able to describe some of the goals and tactics that civil rights movements have used. You should be able to describe and explain the importance of the Civil Rights Act of 1964 and the Voting Rights Act of 1965. You also should be able to identify some ongoing issues involving civil rights. Finally, you should be able to evaluate, take, and defend positions on landmark legislation involving civil rights and the role of civil disobedience in America's constitutional democracy.

TERMS AND CONCEPTS TO UNDERSTAND

civil disobedience

civil rights

de facto segregation

de jure segregation

261

student page ▾ 262–263

WHAT WAS THE STATUS OF CIVIL RIGHTS IN MID-TWENTIETH CENTURY AMERICA?

The Ku Klux Klan originally was organized in Pulaski, Tennessee, in 1866. It was so effective in using force and intimidation to curtail black voting that Congress enacted Force Acts in 1870 and 1871 designed to protect the right to vote.

A second KKK was founded in 1915 in Stone Mountain, Georgia. It added "white supremacy," anti-Catholicism, anti-Semitism, and nativism (opposition to newcomers) to its agenda, which allowed it to spread its influence to the North. During World War I the KKK was an outlet for militant patriotism. Its membership dwindled during the Great Depression. After World War II the KKK was revived in response to the civil rights movement. Members committed violent attacks on blacks as well as on white civil rights workers in Florida, Alabama, and Mississippi. Its membership dwindled once again in the late 1960s. It was revived by Louisiana politician and self-described "white nationalist" David Duke in the early 1990s. Its latest focus has been opposing gay rights and illegal immigration, with a growing membership in many Northern states.

wtpcompanion.civiced.org **LINKS**

Visit the We the People companion website for a link to a website offering videos and study guides to assist student understanding of the history of the civil rights movement in the United States and civil rights movements around the world.

WHAT WAS THE STATUS OF CIVIL RIGHTS IN MID-TWENTIETH CENTURY AMERICA?

Discrimination in the United States has affected African Americans and other groups, including Native Americans, Hispanic Americans, Asian Americans, women, and members of religious minorities. Discrimination based on race has its roots in racial separation, known as segregation. There are two kinds of segregation:

- **De jure segregation** refers to separation required by law. For example, before the Supreme Court's 1954 decision in *Brown v. Board of Education* several states had laws requiring school districts to maintain separate schools for white and nonwhite students. These laws always affected African Americans but sometimes affected other racial minorities as well, including Asian Americans.

- **De facto segregation** refers to racial separation caused by the actions of private individuals and groups. For example, before passage of the Civil Rights Act of 1964 (discussed later in this lesson) some restaurants, hotels, and theaters served only white customers. Some landlords refused to rent houses, apartments, or businesses to racial minorities.

The *Brown* decision addressed only *de jure* segregation in public schools. However, that decision clearly implied that all laws compelling separation of the races violate the guarantee of equal protection of the laws. When little was done to implement the *Brown* decision, the NAACP brought a follow-up case. In *Brown II* (1955) the Supreme Court authorized federal district courts to issue such orders "as are necessary and proper to admit to public schools on a racially nondiscriminatory basis with all deliberate speed the parties to these cases."

Some school districts found ways to implement the *Brown* decisions. But in some parts of the country the decisions were extremely unpopular. To understand why, it is necessary to recall that slavery was legal in America for almost 250 years, from 1619 to 1865. After the Civil War and Reconstruction the Jim Crow system maintained racial separation for more than a half century. Soldiers in the U.S. Army were segregated by race until after the end of World War II. The army was officially desegregated in 1948 by an executive order of President Harry Truman.

Still, in the 1950s racial segregation and discrimination were deeply entrenched. African Americans and other nonwhites were treated as second-class citizens. A web of state laws and local ordinances mandated *de jure* segregation in almost every aspect of public life, including schools, streetcars and buses, toilets, and drinking fountains. In some

What democratic principles are violated by *de jure* and *de facto* segregation?

places the courts kept separate Bibles for administering oaths to whites and nonwhites, prisoners were segregated based on race, and laws prevented interracial marriage.

Such discrimination was not limited to the South, but Southern leaders promised "massive resistance" to the *Brown* decisions. Some states refused to desegregate their schools and waged legal battles to maintain segregation. Other states passed laws making it possible for white students to attend private schools with state financial support. Some school districts closed their schools altogether rather than desegregate.

For the most part the national government deferred to state governments in matters of race. The Ku Klux Klan, an organization created after the Civil War to advocate the supremacy of the white race, was reconstituted and revitalized in 1955. The next several years saw an increase in racially motivated murders, assaults, death threats, cross burnings, and attacks on private homes. President Dwight Eisenhower, who had been reluctant to intervene in state matters, finally sent National Guard troops into Little Rock, Arkansas, in 1957 to open public schools that had been closed in protest to *Brown* and to enforce order.

WHAT DO YOU THINK?

❶ Is *de facto* segregation more difficult to change than *de jure* segregation? Why or why not?

❷ Does *de facto* segregation occur today based on race, ethnicity, gender, or other characteristics? Explain.

❸ Is there ever such thing as permissible segregation? Why or why not?

WHAT WERE THE ORIGINS OF THE MODERN CIVIL RIGHTS MOVEMENT FOR AFRICAN AMERICANS AND WHAT WERE ITS GOALS?

African Americans, leaders and ordinary men and women alike, challenged and resisted Jim Crow laws from the beginning. They had organized cooperative associations to assert community economic rights, and they had armed themselves against violence from the Klan and other white-supremacy organizations. In segregated public schools they had taught and learned black history. Their religious, social, and political associations had nurtured networks of communication and resistance by the time the Supreme Court issued the *Brown* decision.

Organizations such as the NAACP, founded in 1909, helped keep **civil rights** issues on the national agenda after *Brown*. The NAACP was joined by several religious

What are the principles of nonviolent direct action as practiced by Mohandas Gandhi and leading organizations of the civil rights movement?

organizations, including the Alabama Christian Movement for Human Rights, the Southern Christian Leadership Council, and the Fellowship of Reconciliation, an interfaith organization founded in 1914 to promote peace and justice. Many civil rights leaders also were influenced by principles of nonviolent direct action used by the Indian leader Mohandas Gandhi, commonly known as Mahatma Gandhi, in winning independence for India from Great Britain in 1947. Nonviolent direct action sometimes included **civil disobedience**, or the open violation of unjust laws together with a willingness to accept the consequences of violating those laws.

Preparation and education were central to the civil rights campaigns of the 1950s and 1960s. Many civil rights participants were trained in political organization and nonviolent social action at the Highlander Folk School in Tennessee. After petitioning local, state, and national leaders to repeal laws allowing racial segregation and discrimination, leaders organized direct actions, including sit-ins at restaurants and other public facilities, protests, marches, boycotts, and demonstrations. They were met with hostility and often violence.

In December 1955 as part of a planned protest, NAACP member and chapter secretary Rosa Parks refused to give up her seat to a white man on a city bus in Montgomery, Alabama. She was arrested for violating an ordinance requiring segregated seating on public transportation. The NAACP used Parks's case to test the constitutionality of the ordinance and called for a

263

student page ▾ 263–264

WHAT WERE THE ORIGINS OF THE MODERN CIVIL RIGHTS MOVEMENT FOR AFRICAN AMERICANS AND WHAT WERE ITS GOALS?

wtpcompanion.civiced.org   LINKS

Visit the We the People companion website for a link to an online encyclopedia providing information about people, events, and actions taken on behalf of civil rights in the United States.

student page ▼ 264–265

WHAT IS THE CIVIL RIGHTS ACT?

wtpcompanion.civiced.org | **PRIMARY SOURCES**

Visit the We the People companion website for a link to the Civil Rights Act of 1964.

The Civil Rights Act of 1964 was preceded by three other major civil rights acts:

- **CIVIL RIGHTS ACT OF 1866** Passed over the veto of President Andrew Johnson (who claimed it would "operate in favor of the colored and against the white race"), it protected the rights of blacks to make contracts, sue, be a witness in court proceedings, and own private property. The legislation did not contain effective enforcement mechanisms.

- **CIVIL RIGHTS ACT OF 1957** President Dwight Eisenhower proposed this legislation, which created the Civil Rights Section in the U.S. Department of Justice and gave federal prosecutors authority to seek court orders (injunctions) to prohibit interference with the right to vote. The act also created the Civil Rights Commission to investigate discrimination in the United States and recommend corrective measures.

- **CIVIL RIGHTS ACT OF 1960** Also proposed by President Dwight D. Eisenhower in response to bombings of black churches and schools in the South, it extended the life of the Civil Rights Commission and contained penalties against those who interfered with or sought to interfere with the right to vote. Debates on the bill paved the way for enactment of the Voting Rights Act in 1965.

In 1991 Congress enacted another Civil Rights Act, primarily in response to a series of Supreme Court decisions in 1989 that made it more difficult for employees to sue their employers for discrimination.

wtpcompanion.civiced.org | **PRIMARY SOURCES**

Visit the We the People companion website for a link to the Civil Rights Act of 1991.

Among other things the law gave plaintiffs the right to a jury trial on discrimination claims and opened the door to damages for emotional distress. Four of the Supreme Court decisions that sparked the legislation were as follows:

- *Patterson v. McLean Credit Union* (1989)
- *Price Waterhouse v. Hopkins* (1989)

What were the results of the refusal of Rosa Parks to give up her seat to a white man on a city bus in Montgomery, Alabama in 1955?

boycott of the Montgomery bus system. Martin Luther King Jr., a young minister in Montgomery, helped lead the year-long boycott, which ended when the Supreme Court ordered Montgomery city officials to end segregation on city buses.

Civil rights activists also worked for passage of laws to protect their right to vote. King, like Gandhi, an advocate of nonviolent direct action, believed that the *Brown* decision could be implemented "without rancor or bitterness" if everyone had access to the ballot.

WHAT DO YOU THINK?

❶ Explain the importance of the following for civil rights movements to succeed today:

- Support of religious groups
- Leadership and organization
- Preparation
- Public education
- Patience
- Links to principles in the Declaration of Independence or the Constitution

❷ What factors would influence your decision to organize, join, or support a civil rights movement today? What factors would influence your decision to refrain from joining such a movement?

WHAT IS THE CIVIL RIGHTS ACT?

In the spring of 1963 civil rights leaders organized public demonstrations throughout the South in which young people often were prominent. Some protests were met with violence. In Birmingham, Alabama, local police used powerful fire hoses and dogs to break up marches. Television cameras captured scenes of confrontations, and newspapers around the world carried pictures and stories. These images aroused sympathy and outrage throughout the United States.

In August that same year more than two hundred thousand people, mostly African Americans, converged on Washington, D.C., to demonstrate for a full and speedy program of civil rights and job opportunities. President John F. Kennedy announced that he would ask Congress to enact major new civil rights legislation. Kennedy was assassinated three months later. The task of pushing for the legislation fell to his successor, Lyndon B. Johnson. Congress passed the Civil Rights Act of 1964, using its constitutional power under Article 1 to regulate interstate commerce so that it could regulate private activities as well as state action. The act remains the most far-reaching civil rights legislation in American history, outlawing both *de jure* and *de facto* segregation and many forms of discrimination. The central provisions of the act

- Outlaw discrimination in hotels, restaurants, theaters, gas stations, airline terminals, and other places of public accommodation

What events led to President Johnson signing the Voting Rights Act of 1965?

Why was the Voting Rights Act of 1965 needed to enforce the provisions of the Fifteenth Amendment?

- Give the national government additional authority to end school desegregation

- Prohibit job discrimination by businesses and labor unions

- Authorize the United States Justice Department to file lawsuits against states that discriminate against women and minorities

WHAT IS THE VOTING RIGHTS ACT?

The Civil Rights Act did not address problems that minorities encountered when they tried to vote. In March 1965 civil rights protesters met in Selma, Alabama, to march from there to Montgomery to protest voting discrimination. Alabama's governor sent state troopers to stop the march. Several demonstrators were clubbed and beaten. One was killed. The event was covered on national television. Five days later President Johnson announced that he would send Congress a voting rights bill. Using its authority to enforce the provisions of the Fifteenth Amendment, Congress quickly passed the Voting Rights Act of 1965. Amended several times since its passage and extended to 2031, the Voting Rights Act now

- Prohibits discrimination based on race

- Eliminates literacy tests, poll taxes, and discriminatory registration practices

- Requires states, counties, and cities with significant numbers of voters who do not speak English to provide voting materials and assistance in appropriate languages

- Requires states and counties with a history of discrimination to be monitored by the Justice Department

When President George W. Bush signed the 2006 extension of the Voting Rights Act, he acknowledged both progress in the area of civil rights and the need for continued efforts:

> In four decades since the Voting Rights Act was first passed, we've made progress toward equality, yet the work for a more perfect union is never ending. We'll continue to build on the legal equality won by the civil rights movement to help ensure that every person enjoys the opportunity that this great land of liberty offers.

CRITICAL THINKING EXERCISE
Examining the Civil Rights and Voting Rights Acts

Work in one of two groups. One group should obtain a copy of the Civil Rights Act (1964) and all amendments to it. The other group should obtain a copy of the Voting Rights Act (1965) and all amendments to it.

First, each group should review the criteria for landmark legislation in Lesson 22. Then each group should study its statute and amendments and do any additional research to enable the group to respond to the following questions. Finally, each group should share its responses with the class as a whole.

❶ Does the statute you examined qualify as landmark legislation? Explain your reasoning.

❷ What are the significant features of amendments to the statute your group examined? Why were they added?

❸ Have there been obstacles to implementing the statute or its amendments? If so, explain what they have been and what has been done to overcome them.

- *Martin v. Wilkes* (1989)
- *Wards Cove Packing v. Antonio* (1989)

wtpcompanion.civiced.org   COURT CASES

Visit the We the People companion website for a link to Supreme Court syllabi and opinions for each of the cases described above.

student page ▼   265

WHAT IS THE VOTING RIGHTS ACT?

wtpcompanion.civiced.org   PRIMARY SOURCES

Visit the We the People companion website for a link to the Voting Rights Act of 1965.

President Lyndon Johnson's special message to Congress proposing this act is considered to be one of his best speeches. In part he said,

> Our fathers believed that if this noble view of the right of man was to flourish, it must be rooted in democracy. The most basic right of all was the right to choose your own leaders. The history of this country, in large measure, is the history of the expansion of that right to all of our people.

wtpcompanion.civiced.org   PRIMARY SOURCES

Visit the We the People companion website for a link to the entire text of President Johnson's speech.

The Voting Rights Act marked the most significant change in the relationship between the national government and state governments regarding voting since the aftermath of the Civil War. It was challenged on several grounds, including as a violation of states' rights. Two significant Supreme Court decisions sustained the legislation and the increased power of the national government over the states: *South Carolina v. Katzenbach* (1966) and *Allen v. State Board of Elections* (1969).

wtpcompanion.civiced.org   COURT CASES

Visit the We the People companion website for links to Supreme Court syllabi and opinions for each of the cases described above.

WHAT IS THE ROLE OF CIVIL DISOBEDIENCE AS A FORM OF POLITICAL PARTICIPATION?

Mohandas K. ("Mahatma," or "great soul") Gandhi identified nine essential steps in a nonviolent campaign for social change. Known as a *satyagraha* ("force or firmness of truth") campaign, the steps are as follows:

❶ Start with negotiation and arbitration. Make every effort to resolve conflict through existing channels.

❷ Prepare the group for direct action by examining motives and initiating exercises in self-discipline. Launch full group discussions on the issues at stake, appropriate procedures to be undertaken, circumstances of the opponent, the climate of public opinion, etc. At times use purificatory fasting.

❸ Use agitation and undertake an active propaganda campaign together with demonstrations such as mass-meetings, parades, and slogan shouting.

❹ Issue an ultimatum that makes a final strong appeal to the opponent, explaining what further steps will be taken if no agreement is reached. Its wording should offer the widest scope for agreement, allowing for face-saving by the opponent, and offering a constructive solution to the problem.

❺ Undertake economic boycott and forms of strike, possibly including picketing, demonstrations, education of the public, *dharna* (sit-down strike), nonviolent labor strike, and general strike.

❻ Use non-cooperation, possibly including nonpayment of taxes, boycott of schools and other public institutions, etc.

❼ Undertake civil disobedience. Great care should be given to selection of laws to be contravened.

❽ Usurp the functions of government. Create substitute services and processes.

❾ Institute a parallel government.

WHAT IS THE ROLE OF CIVIL DISOBEDIENCE AS A FORM OF POLITICAL PARTICIPATION?

Participants in the struggles against slavery, the woman suffrage movement, and the civil rights movement all used civil disobedience to advocate change. They did so only after the use of their First Amendment rights of petition, free speech, and assembly proved futile. In his "Letter from Birmingham City Jail" Martin Luther King Jr. wrote,

> " I submit that an individual who breaks a law that his conscience tells him is unjust, and willingly accepts the penalty by staying in jail to arouse the conscience of the community over its injustice, is in reality expressing the very highest respect for the law.

King's words echoed those of American philosopher Henry David Thoreau (1817–1862), who in 1849 set forth some of the basic ideas about civil disobedience in his essay "On the Duty of Civil Disobedience." Thoreau argued that individuals should obey their conscience. When conscience and law conflict, individuals have a moral responsibility to promote justice by disobeying the law. Thoreau and others who have written about civil disobedience, such as Russian novelist Leo Tolstoy and India's Gandhi, agree that civil disobedience must be nonviolent and that those who participate in civil disobedience must be willing to identify themselves and accept legal sanctions. Civil disobedience does not attempt rebellion or revolution. But it does put conscience above the law.

Justification for this viewpoint has ancient roots. Antigone, the title character and tragic heroine of the Greek playwright Sophocles' drama, justified disobedience to royal authority in the name of law higher than civil authority. For Sophocles (c. 496–406 BC) that higher law was an objective morality rooted in law made by the gods, not by human beings, as Antigone defies the tyrant Creon to secure a respectable funeral for her brother.

Critics argue that civil disobedience is never justified because it is an attack on constitutional democracy. American democracy's legal system, they argue, often has protected minority rights in the face of majority oppression, as in *Brown v. Board of Education* and in many other instances. They add that when democratic decisions appear to go amiss, they can be challenged in court. American constitutional democracy does not leave fundamental individual rights at the mercy of majorities. The practice of civil disobedience makes individual conscience absolute, the final judge of obedience or disobedience. Thus it weakens respect for law and is an invitation to social chaos, a state of gross disorder where no rights or values are safe.

Defenders of civil disobedience counter that, in fact, there can be no other final judge of obedience to law than individual conscience. Each person must make his or her own decision whether to obey particular laws. After all, the defenders contend, laws are not necessarily just. They can be unjust. Defenders therefore argue that there are higher moral laws than the laws of any state, however democratic and constitutional. These higher laws shape the moral conscience of individuals. An unjust social situation breeds disorder. Seeking a more just society through civil disobedience may promote order rather than undermine it.

WHAT DO YOU THINK?

❶ Under what circumstances, if any, do you think a citizen in a representative democracy has the right to engage in civil disobedience? Explain your position.

❷ Read Martin Luther King Jr.'s "Letter from Birmingham City Jail." How might King respond to the charge that those who followed their consciences to defy local segregation laws were no different from white protesters who defied court orders to integrate?

Should people be allowed to demonstrate by holding sit-ins in public buildings? Why or why not?

What civic purposes are served by public demonstrations?

HOW HAS THE MOVEMENT FOR CIVIL RIGHTS CHANGED SINCE THE MID-TWENTIETH CENTURY?

The Civil Rights and Voting Rights Acts were major legal achievements of the civil rights movement of the 1950s and 1960s. Unfortunately King was assassinated in 1968 while helping to organize a protest supporting sanitation workers in Memphis, Tennessee, who needed better pay and working conditions. His murder led to riots in cities throughout the United States. Other riots occurred in American cities during the 1960s protesting perceived economic discrimination and alleged police brutality.

After passage of the laws in the 1960s organizations such as the NAACP turned their attention to other issues affecting minorities and the poor, including

- Voter registration
- Laws increasing the minimum wage
- Better health care for people with HIV/AIDS
- Health services for minority populations in urban and rural areas
- High-quality public education for all minority children

Other groups also have been active in pursuing rights for their members and other minorities. The following are merely three examples:

- **Farm workers** In the early 1950s Mexican American Cesar Chavez began to register minority voters and to organize farm workers to demand better conditions in the fields of California. He and Dolores Huerta later founded the United Farm Workers Union. It and similar organizations have lobbied Congress for better pay and working conditions for farm workers, organized consumer boycotts of farm products such as grapes and lettuce, challenged the hiring of illegal aliens during farm-worker strikes, and protested the use of dangerous pesticides.

- **Native Americans** In 1968 several hundred members of Native American tribes met to discuss issues affecting their communities. Conversations focused on substandard housing, an eighty percent unemployment rate, discrimination in education and other areas, and claims of police brutality. The American Indian Movement (AIM) emerged out of this meeting. AIM gained national and international attention in the 1970s when some of its members seized the headquarters of the Bureau of Indian Affairs in Washington, D.C., and participated in standoffs with public authorities at Wounded Knee and Pine Ridge, South Dakota, in

Gandhi also required his followers to agree to certain fundamental rules, including the following:

- Self-reliance at all times
- Ongoing education of the opponent, the public, and your own participants
- Constant reassessment/adjustment as truth requires
- Advancing the movement progressively through steps and stages
- Launching direct action only when all other steps have failed
- Persistently seeking avenues of cooperating with the adversary on honorable terms
- Seeking to achieve agreement with the adversary, not triumph over the adversary

Finally, Gandhi insisted that volunteers in social movements adhere to a strict code of discipline that included the following:

- Harboring no anger
- Refusing to return the assaults of the opponents
- Not swearing or making insults
- Not resisting arrest
- Always behaving in an exemplary manner, especially if arrested

These rules and steps in a nonviolent social-change campaign help to distinguish civil disobedience from mere lawlessness.

ENRICHMENT ACTIVITY

ATTEMPTING TO EXPAND RIGHTS THROUGH CONSTITUTIONAL AMENDMENT: WHEN HAS AN AMENDMENT FAILED?

Some expansions of rights have been achieved through amendments to the Constitution, such as suffrage amendments (Amendments 15, 19, and 26). Article V specifies the manner in which the U.S. Constitution may be amended, but it is silent about when or if the ratification process has failed.

Beginning with the Eighteenth Amendment (but excluding the Nineteenth) Congress has included a requirement that amendments must be ratified within seven years. The proposed Equal Rights Amendment is an example of controversies that can arise regarding the ratification process. That amendment was not ratified within seven years of being proposed in 1972.

Ask students to work in small groups and develop positions on the following questions:

❶ Should states have the right to withdraw ratification of an amendment during the ratification period specified by Congress? Why or why not?

❷ Does Congress have the power to extend the ratification period for an amendment? Why or why not?

❸ If Congress does not place a time limit on ratification, should an amendment be allowed to go into effect many years later, without requiring states that originally voted for ratification to revote on the matter? (The Twenty-seventh Amendment, for example, was originally the second amendment on the list of twelve submitted to the states for ratification in 1789. Only Delaware, Maryland, South Carolina, North Carolina, Rhode Island, and Virginia voted in favor of ratification, short of the eleven then required. The proposal lay dormant until 1992, when it was finally ratified 202 years after it had been proposed.)

Follow up by asking students to compare their views with those of the Supreme Court in two cases:

- *Dillon v. Gloss* (1921)   Congress is entitled to set a reasonable deadline so that ratification of an amendment is "sufficiently contemporaneous… to reflect the will of the people in all sections at relatively the same time period."

- *Coleman v. Miller* (1939)   Whether a state may ratify an amendment it previously has rejected and whether a state may ratify an amendment thirteen years after Congress proposed it with no time limit are "political questions" within the sole discretion of Congress to decide.

wtpcompanion.civiced.org   **COURT CASES**

Visit the We the People companion website for links to Supreme Court syllabi and opinions for each of the cases described above.

disputes over land and mineral rights. Today AIM's focus includes cultural renewal, monitoring police treatment of Native Americans, opposing the use of Native American caricatures as mascots for sports teams, such as the Atlanta Braves and Florida State University Seminoles, and creating employment programs for Native Americans. AIM also supports the efforts of indigenous groups outside the United States.

- **Women** Women worked for generations to win the right to vote, which they achieved through the Nineteenth Amendment, ratified in 1920. In the 1960s and 1970s women's organizations turned their attention to issues such as reproductive rights, equal pay for equal work, and harassment in the workplace. The National Organization for Women, formed in 1966, lobbied for the Equal Rights Amendment (ERA), which Congress submitted to the states in 1972. The proposed amendment provided that

  " Equality of rights under the law shall not be denied or abridged by the United States or any State on account of sex.

Only thirty-five of the required thirty-eight states ratified the ERA. Although the amendment failed, Congress has passed laws that achieve some of the goals of the proposed amendment, such as the Pregnancy Discrimination Act, making it unlawful to fire, not hire, or otherwise discriminate against a woman because of pregnancy or intent to become pregnant, and the Equal Credit Opportunity Act, making it unlawful to discriminate on the basis of gender or marital status in making loans. The Supreme Court also has held that sexual harassment is a form of illegal discrimination (*Meritor Savings Bank v. Vinson*, 1986). Legislative and judicial triumphs have led some to believe that the ERA is not necessary.

CRITICAL THINKING EXERCISE

Evaluating Contemporary Civil Rights Movements

Work in one of three groups. Each group should select a contemporary civil rights movement and then respond to the following questions. The groups should compare responses.

❶ How is the movement you studied organized? Who are its leaders?

❷ What are the stated objectives of the movement? How are those objectives related to

principles in the Declaration of Independence and the Constitution?

❸ What role does public education play in the movement?

❹ Has the movement used civil disobedience or supported civil disobedience to achieve its goals? Why or why not?

REVIEWING AND USING THE LESSON

❶ What is the difference between *de jure* and *de facto* segregation?

❷ Why has the Civil Rights Act of 1964 been called the most far-reaching civil rights legislation in American history?

❸ Why was it necessary to extend the Voting Rights Act of 1965 in 2006?

❹ How is civil disobedience different from merely breaking the law?

What changes have been made due to the movement for women's rights?

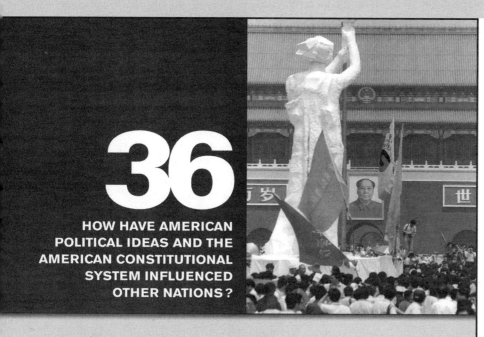

36

HOW HAVE AMERICAN POLITICAL IDEAS AND THE AMERICAN CONSTITUTIONAL SYSTEM INFLUENCED OTHER NATIONS?

UNIT SIX | LESSON 36

HOW HAVE AMERICAN POLITICAL IDEAS AND THE AMERICAN CONSTITUTIONAL SYSTEM INFLUENCED OTHER NATIONS?

wtpcompanion.civiced.org **LESSON PURPOSE + TERMS**

Visit the We the People companion website for printable and downloadable Lesson Purposes and Terms and Concepts to Understand sections for each lesson. Audio readings of each Lesson Purpose and Term are also available online in MP3 format.

LESSON PURPOSE

The ideas in the Declaration of Independence, the Constitution, and the Bill of Rights have inspired other countries seeking to create independent, democratic governments. This lesson examines some of the challenges associated with using the American constitutional model in other parts of the world.

When you have finished this lesson, you should be able to identify which aspects of the American constitutional system have been influential elsewhere. You should be able to explain why some countries and international organizations have chosen to modify the American system or to use other types of democratic systems. You also should be able to explain how the Bill of Rights has influenced other countries and how some countries have adopted bills of rights that are considerably different. Finally, you should be able to evaluate, take, and defend positions on why some aspects of American constitutional democracy that have been effective in the United States have not been used in other countries.

TERMS AND CONCEPTS TO UNDERSTAND

human rights

Universal Declaration of Human Rights

student page ▼ 270

HOW HAVE AMERICAN IDEAS ABOUT GOVERNMENT AND HUMAN RIGHTS INFLUENCED OTHER PARTS OF THE WORLD?

Thomas Jefferson was aware that the Declaration of Independence would have far-reaching appeal and consequences. He wrote that the Declaration was

> an appeal to the tribunal of the world…. This was the object of the Declaration of Independence. Not to find out new principles, or new arguments never before thought of, not merely to say things which had never been said before; but to place before mankind the common sense of the subject, in terms so plain and firm as to command their assent.

Since 1776 more than one hundred declarations of independence have been issued throughout the world on behalf of regional or national groups. Many more local declarations also have appeared in places such as Central America in the 1820s, China after the Revolution of 1911, and Korea in 1918–1919. Some of these declarations stated a desire for independence yet to come; most marked a fait accompli. Many, like the American Declaration, listed grievances to justify the independence they claimed. However, relatively few contained a declaration of individual rights that paralleled the second paragraph of the American Declaration.

Political scientist Jeremy A. Rabkin adds the following:

> The American Declaration of Independence does affirm that men are "endowed by their Creator with certain unalienable rights." But it immediately goes on to say that to secure these rights, governments are instituted among men, deriving their just powers from the consent of the governed. Individual rights may derive their moral impetus from a prior or higher claim—the "Law of Nature and Nature's God," perhaps. But the Declaration is quite clear that rights are not secure without an actual government to enforce them.

Poland's Constitution of 1791 was the world's second written constitution. Like the U.S. Constitution it was a product of the Enlightenment. The similarity to the U.S. Constitution is particularly evident in the preamble, which states in part "desirous, moreover, to deserve the blessing and gratitude, not only of our contemporaries, but also of future generations…for the sake of the public good…for securing our liberty…we do solemnly establish the present constitution." Unlike the U.S. Constitution, however, the Polish Constitution of 1791 never went into effect.

Political scientist Linda Camp Keith reports that more than two-thirds of the world's constitutions have been written since 1970.

HOW HAVE AMERICAN IDEAS ABOUT GOVERNMENT AND HUMAN RIGHTS INFLUENCED OTHER PARTS OF THE WORLD?

America's constitutional principles—including popular sovereignty, individual rights, limited government, and rule of law—are perhaps this country's greatest contribution to the world. Few other documents in history have had the impact of the Declaration of Independence and the Constitution. Many other charters of freedom have copied or paraphrased the words of both documents.

American constitutional democracy grew out of the world's first democratic revolution. America's experiment in self-government has influenced many other countries. For example, the American Revolution inspired the French Revolution of 1789. The French Constitution of 1791 copied many elements from America's first state constitutions. The Polish Constitution of 1791 also drew on the American example. When Latin American countries won their independence from Spain in the early nineteenth century, they looked to the United States as a model for republican government. In Russia in 1825 the first demands for constitutional government, even though they were unsuccessful, were inspired by American ideas.

The influence of American constitutionalism abroad expanded during the twentieth century, in part because the United States was by then a major world power. During the American occupation of Germany after World War II the German Constitution of 1949 incorporated elements of the American model, guaranteeing rights including freedom of religion, assembly, speech, press, and other forms of expression.

While the United States celebrated the bicentennial of its Constitution in 1987–1991, other nations were writing new chapters in the history of constitutional government. The 1980s and early 1990s saw the collapse of Soviet communism and the emergence of democratic governments in Eastern Europe and other parts of the world. Among the more than twenty countries that have adopted new constitutions since then are Afghanistan, Bosnia and Herzegovina, East Timor, Eritrea, Iraq, Poland, South Africa, and Venezuela. In different ways all these countries drew on the American constitutional system and experience for inspiration in writing constitutions that reflect democratic ideas.

The aftermath of the Cold War witnessed renewed interest in American constitutionalism. Many former communist states began to experiment with their own forms of constitutionalism. The leaders of these newly independent countries have delivered some of the most eloquent tributes to the Constitution of the United States. During the bicentennial of the U.S. Constitution, Václav Havel, then president of Czechoslovakia, said in a speech to Congress,

> Wasn't it the best minds of your country, who wrote your famous Declaration of Independence, your Bill of Rights, and your Constitution?… Those great documents… inspire us all, they inspire us despite the fact they are over 200 years old. They inspire us to be citizens.

Following the breakup of Czechoslovakia, Havel served ten years (1993–2003) as the first president of the new Czech Republic.

WHAT DO YOU THINK?

1. In what ways has the Declaration of Independence influenced other peoples and nations?

2. Has it influenced you? If so, how?

3. Why do you think the principles in the Declaration of Independence, the Constitution, and the Bill of Rights have inspired people on every continent in the world?

4. In what ways are the principles in America's founding documents as relevant today as they were more than two centuries ago?

According to President Václav Havel of the Czech Republic, what has been the influence in the world of American founding documents?

What are the similarities and differences between the Philadelphia Convention and the European Convention of 2004?

WHAT ELEMENTS OF AMERICAN CONSTITUTIONALISM HAVE INFLUENCED OTHER COUNTRIES?

As the world's first written framework for national government, the U.S. Constitution set an important standard. Today nearly all countries undergoing democratic reforms believe in the importance of a written constitution. Even totalitarian regimes, such as North Korea, call themselves "democratic" and have written constitutions. However, those documents have not restricted the exercise of government power.

The American experience also set a standard for using conventions to draft constitutions that are then submitted to the people for ratification. For example, in 2004 the European Convention met in Brussels to draft a constitution for a European Union consisting of twenty-five member countries. In 2005 France and the Netherlands rejected the proposed European Constitution, leading to new debates about whether ratification by all member countries is necessary for the document to go into effect.

Other features of the U.S. Constitution have attracted attention, including the following:

- **Presidential government** A main feature of the U.S. Constitution is the office of president, which separates the executive from the legislative branch. The president is both the symbolic head of state and the head of government. Presidents in the American system are elected separately from the legislature and hold office for a fixed period. They cannot be removed from office by the legislature simply by a vote of no confidence, as in parliamentary systems. Parliamentary systems, by contrast, separate the head of state—a monarch or president, largely symbolic and ceremonial offices—from the head of government, who is the prime minister and is elected by the legislature. Legislatures can remove prime ministers simply by passing a vote of no confidence, making prime ministerial power entirely dependent on parliamentary approval.

Presidential government—with separation of powers and checks and balances—was instituted in several cases in Latin America during the nineteenth century. Notable is Brazil's 1891 constitution, which adopted many features of

---

WHAT ELEMENTS OF AMERICAN CONSTITUTIONALISM HAVE INFLUENCED OTHER COUNTRIES?

CONSTITUTIONALISM Constitution writing tends to occur in the wake of momentous political events:

- **WAR** The constitutions of Germany and Japan were written in the wake of their defeat in World War II.

- **REVOLUTION** The U.S. Constitution was written after the American Revolution of 1776, the French constitution after the French Revolution of 1789.

- **INDEPENDENCE** Usually nations write constitutions when they break from colonial status, as was the case with all the countries in the British Commonwealth that gained independence in the twentieth century.

- **COLLAPSE OF AN EXISTING SYSTEM** Examples in this case include the fall of the Soviet Union and the dramatic change in South Africa after apartheid.

Although the cultural roots of Latin America are in Iberia (Spain), the institutional roots of Latin America are in Philadelphia. The influence of the U.S. Constitution on the new republics of the Western Hemisphere is easily one of the best-documented cases of institutional diffusion in modern history. All the Spanish colonies adopted presidential forms of government and nearly all opted for bicameral legislatures. But the broad similarities between the U.S. and Latin American constitutional frameworks, so compelling on paper, have proved to be very different in practice. Dictatorship and revolution have been commonplace in Latin American countries.

Constitutional scholars Tom Ginsburg, Zachary Elkins, and James Melton have studied all the constitutions adopted since 1789. They calculate the average lifespan of a written constitution to be sixteen years.

PRESIDENTIAL GOVERNMENT Political scientist Mark Kesselman makes the following observation:

> The Republic of France is usually described as a semi-presidential system. It combines elements of presidential and parliamentary systems. In a wholly presidential system, as in the United States, the executive and the legislature are chosen separately and neither is answerable to the other.... Moreover, both institutions have fixed terms of office and neither the government nor the legislature can force the other to resign and face new elections....

The president of France, who is elected for a seven-year term, combines the independent powers of the U.S. president—notably command of the executive branch and independence from legislative control—with the powers that accrue to the government in a parliamentary regime—namely, control over parliament's agenda and the ability to dissolve parliament and force new elections.

student page ▾ 272

FEDERALISM A federal state can be defined as a nation-state that distributes power vertically between a national government and state or provincial units. It is the opposite of a unitary or completely centralized nation-state. Federal systems are now found mainly in large states and those that have extremely diverse populations. Only about twenty of the world's nations have federal organizations, but about half of the world's population lives in countries with federal systems.

Political scientist Gabriel A. Almond writes the following:

> Federalism has been widely praised as one of the great American contributions to the art of government. A number of nations have adopted it as a way of enabling different regions with sharply different cultures and interests to form together as one nation. The clearest examples of such nations today are Australia, Canada, Germany, and Switzerland, but significant elements of federalism are also found in systems as disparate as those of Brazil, India, and Mexico.

When Nigeria became independent in 1954, it established a decentralized federal system. Both the 1979 and the 1989 constitutions of Nigeria describe a three-level federalism. In the United States, Canada, and Australia the constitutions focus on the federal-state relationship with local government principally in the domain of the state or province.

JUDICIAL POWER AND HUMAN RIGHTS Protection of human rights in many countries of the world must begin with protection against slavery, arbitrary arrest and detention, political torture, imprisonment, and disappearance. In 1985 the United Nations adopted standards for achieving judicial independence, a goal deemed important because of the close link between an independent, impartial judiciary and the effective protection of human rights.

wtpcompanion.civiced.org **LINKS**

Visit the We the People companion website for a link to "Basic Principles on the Independence of the Judiciary."

Why have European countries tended to avoid strong presidential governments?

the U.S. Constitution. Versions of the American separation of powers system also have been adopted more recently, for example in Argentina.

The current French constitution features a strong president but combines the office with parliamentary government, making it quite unlike the U.S. system. Many countries, especially in Europe, have shied away from strong presidential government because of their experience with Napoleon Bonaparte (1769–1821) and his successors in the nineteenth century. A general during the French Revolution, Napoleon staged a *coup d'état* in 1799 and five years later crowned himself emperor. Some countries therefore have been wary of the possibility of positions of executive power and leadership turning into dictatorship. Countries that composed the former Soviet Union, freed from communist rule and mistrustful of executive power, have provided for weak executives in their constitutions.

The office of president in the U.S. Constitution is set in the context of a federal system that substantially limits presidential power, making it far less dangerous to constitutional government. Even so, after 1891 Brazil's presidential government evolved into dictatorship. This instance, together with similar dangers seen by observers in modern Venezuela, illustrates what one scholar termed the "perils of presidentialism."

- **Federalism** America's system of federalism, which establishes two sets of governments with separate and overlapping powers, also has been of great interest and influence in other parts of the world. Scholars have argued that of all the features of American constitutionalism, federalism has had the greatest effect. The American system in 1787 was something new and very different from the ways that governments had been organized in the past.

  Among the notable aspects of federalism is that it provides powerful support for maintaining limited—constitutional—government by dispersing power. By so doing it helps protect both the state governments and individuals from abuse of power by the central government.

  Many countries have adopted federal systems influenced to varying degrees by the American model. Among them are Argentina, Australia, Austria, Belgium, Brazil, Canada, Germany, India, and Switzerland. For example, both Australia and Canada have federal systems that give important power to states or provinces. However, federalism has many variants. Countries such as Bosnia and Herzegovina and Iraq have considered adopting models of federalism that ensure representation of ethnic and religious groups in the country's governing structure.

- **Judicial power and human rights** The Bill of Rights in the U.S. Constitution is probably the single greatest contribution of American constitutionalism to the world. Building on the experience of the states after the Revolution, the Bill of Rights provided a prominent example of incorporating fundamental guarantees of individual rights into written constitutions. But the bills of rights in the state constitutions, written in the 1780s, also made their own important contributions to the spread of universal rights ideas. They did so not only by their effects on the 1791 Bill of Rights.

The Bill of Rights became especially important during the second half of the twentieth century, when interest in basic **human rights** increased around the world. Human rights are rights held by individuals simply because they are human beings. Human rights, therefore, are rights shared equally by everyone, regardless of gender, race, or nationality. It was not until after World War II that many people realized how important the process of constitutional amendment is to the protection of human rights. The amendment process makes it difficult to change constitutional protections of human rights. If laws protecting human rights were easily changed, as in traditional parliamentary systems, then human rights guarantees could be altered overnight.

Furthermore, what distinguishes the Bill of Rights from other bills of rights, such as the French Declaration of Rights, is that it has an enforcement mechanism. This mechanism is judicial review, the power of the judiciary to void any law that contradicts constitutional provisions. This key connection between human rights as part of a national constitution and judicial review by an independent judiciary should not be overlooked. The spread throughout the world not only of the ideas of human rights but also of the enforcement mechanism of judicial review by an independent judiciary is among the principal achievements of American constitutionalism abroad.

About three-quarters of the countries in the world today recognize some form of judicial review. The American judicial review model has been adopted in at least fifty countries, including Denmark and Estonia in Europe; Botswana, Ghana, Kenya, and Nigeria in Africa; Israel in the Middle East; India and Japan in Asia; New Zealand in Australasia; Canada in North America; and Argentina, Belize, and Bolivia in Central and South America.

Emerging constitutional governments in Central and Eastern Europe have embraced judicial review as a means of promoting the supremacy of constitutional principles and protecting fundamental rights. However, unlike in the United States, where all courts have the power of judicial review, European countries have given this power only to specialized constitutional courts. American courts do not give advisory opinions about the constitutionality of acts or statutes prior to enactment. By contrast, European constitutional courts rule on the constitutionality of statutes before they go into effect.

WHAT DO YOU THINK?

❶ What features of American history and culture have contributed to the effectiveness of the presidential system, separation of powers, and federalism in the United States?

❷ For what reasons might those features of American constitutional democracy be a good fit or a poor fit for other constitutional democracies?

❸ What features of American constitutionalism have been most influential in other countries? Why have some been more influential than others?

HOW DO OTHER GUARANTEES OF RIGHTS DIFFER FROM THE BILL OF RIGHTS?

The Bill of Rights was written in the eighteenth century and in many ways reflects colonists' concerns about government based on their experience with the English. Most of these concerns, which reflect mistrust of governmental power, are universal and relevant today. The Bill of Rights primarily guarantees individual personal, economic, and political rights. A number of the rights guaranteed in the Bill of Rights are stated as negative rights. That is, they describe what government "shall not" do and how individuals are to be protected from wrongful government acts.

Contemporary charters of human rights, such as the 2000 Charter of Fundamental Rights of the European Union and the 1981 African Charter of Human and Peoples' Rights, reflect changes that have occurred in government and society during the past two hundred years. In addition to protecting rights such as freedom of religion, thought, and conscience, those charters assert positive rights, such as the rights to health care, education, equal pay for equal work, and fair and just working conditions.

HOW DO OTHER GUARANTEES OF RIGHTS DIFFER FROM THE BILL OF RIGHTS?

Bills of rights in other countries are not necessarily the same as the U.S. Bill of Rights. For example, Chapter III of the 1946 Constitution of Japan lists the "Rights and Duties of the People." Article 13 provides the following:

> All of the people shall be respected as individuals. Their right to life, liberty, and the pursuit of happiness shall, to the extent that it does not interfere with the public welfare, be the supreme consideration in legislation and in other governmental affairs.

Chapter III guarantees rights such as academic freedom, the right of marriage, the right to "maintain the minimum standards of wholesome and cultured living," and the right of all people to receive an equal education "correspondent to their ability." Chapter III imposes on all people the obligation to work and to hold property "in conformity with the public welfare."

Some nations, such as Australia, New Zealand, and Israel, have followed the British practice of adopting statutes rather than protecting rights in constitutions, in part in deference to the principle of parliamentary sovereignty. Others, including Australia, have debated whether a separate national bill of rights is needed in light of that country's ratification of the Universal Declaration of Human Rights (see the Reference section).

Political scientist Ran Hirschl notes that

> the constitutionalization of rights has recently become a booming industry. Many countries and several supranational entities (e.g., the European Union) have engaged in fundamental constitutional reform over the past three decades. Significantly nearly every recently adopted constitution or constitutional revision contains a bill of rights and establishes some form of active judicial review....

> The global trend has been described by scholars of constitutional rights as... one of the most significant trends in late twentieth and early twenty-first century government.

student page ▾ 274–275

HOW IS THE UNITED NATIONS' UNIVERSAL DECLARATION OF HUMAN RIGHTS SIMILAR TO AND DIFFERENT FROM THE BILL OF RIGHTS?

Political theorist Amy Gutmann wrote the following:

> The rampant violation of the practice of human rights also illustrates what calling human rights universal cannot mean. It cannot mean that human rights are universally accepted or even close to it. Calling human rights universal means that rights should apply not parochially, to a few groups, but to all persons, variously but similarly considered our equals, dignified beings, free and equal persons, or simply human agents who should be able to live a decent life, regardless of their cultural membership.

Which rights among the "aspirational goals" of the Universal Declaration are protected by laws in the United States?

HOW IS THE UNITED NATIONS' UNIVERSAL DECLARATION OF HUMAN RIGHTS SIMILAR TO AND DIFFERENT FROM THE BILL OF RIGHTS?

Before the twentieth century individual rights generally were regarded as matters to be left to each state or nation to decide for its own population. The worldwide economic depression of the 1930s and human rights violations by totalitarian governments before, during, and after World War II gave the issue of human rights a new urgency.

In his 1944 State of the Union address President Franklin Roosevelt asked Congress to adopt laws that would amount to a "Second Bill of Rights." The laws that he proposed contained economic guarantees, ranging from medical care and adequate housing to jobs and education. After Roosevelt's death in 1945 his widow, Eleanor Roosevelt, used his proposal to help the United Nations craft the **Universal Declaration of Human Rights**.

The Universal Declaration and the charter of the United Nations proclaim universal standards of human rights considered to be essential to the dignity of every person. In 1948 the United States was one of forty-eight nations that agreed to the thirty articles of the Universal Declaration of Human Rights. The preamble to this declaration asserts that

> the inherent dignity and…the equal and inalienable rights of all members of the human family is the foundation of freedom, justice and peace in the world.

The influence of the Declaration of Independence, the U.S. Constitution, and the Bill of Rights is apparent in the Universal Declaration. Provisions in the Universal Declaration of the right to life and equality echo the U.S. Declaration of Independence of 1776. The prohibition of *ex post facto* laws, the affirmation of the equivalent of habeas corpus, and the equal protection of the law reflect the body of the U.S. Constitution and amendments in addition to the Bill of Rights. Other guarantees in the Universal Declaration, such as those related to freedom of religion, speech, assembly, and association as well as property rights, prohibition of torture, and the sanctity of home and correspondence, reflect the Bill of Rights.

In some instances the Universal Declaration strengthens or elaborates rights that are expressed more generally in the American documents. For example, freedom of religion is to include the right to change one's religion or beliefs. The right to personal liberty is to include the right not just to marry but to marry only if both parties consent, eliminating coerced or "arranged" marriages. Slavery is outlawed.

In addition to provisions found in the American founding documents, or that might be considered extensions of them, the Universal Declaration contains other concepts. A novel departure for a declaration or charter of rights is the inclusion of a statement of universal "duties to the community," and among the limits to freedom are the "just requirements of morality."

The Universal Declaration also contains provisions that have been interpreted as "aspirational goals," including the following rights:

- To work, join trade unions, and receive equal pay for equal work

- To rest and leisure, including reasonable work hours and periodic paid holidays

- To a standard of living adequate for the health and well-being of families and individuals, including food, clothing, housing, medical care, and necessary social services

- To an education

- To seek, receive, and impart information and ideas through any media, regardless of frontiers

Regional agreements have expanded the concepts of the Universal Declaration in the decades since its adoption. For example, in 1950 as one of the preliminary steps toward formation of the European Union, the countries of Western Europe agreed to a European Convention on Human Rights. They established a European Court of Human Rights to which the citizens of member countries can appeal when they believe their rights have been violated. In practice, however, individual nations remain responsible for guaranteeing rights. Charters such as the Universal Declaration remain largely statements of guiding ideals.

In 1976 the United Nations sponsored a Covenant on Civil and Political Rights and a Covenant on Economic, Social, and Cultural Rights. Both were ratified by enough nations to become international law obligating all signatories. President Jimmy Carter signed both covenants on behalf of the United States in 1977. Fifteen years later, in 1992, the U.S. Senate ratified most of the Covenant on Civil and Political Rights. However, it specified that people have no right to sue in U.S. courts to enforce the civil or political rights listed in the covenant. The Senate has not ratified the Covenant on Economic, Social, and Cultural Rights.

What problems of national sovereignty might result from the establishment of the European Court of Human Rights?

ENRICHMENT ACTIVITY

HOW LONG SHOULD A CONSTITUTION LAST?

The average longevity of constitutions written since 1789 is sixteen years, according to research by constitutional scholars Tom Ginsburg, Zachary Elkins, and James Melton. The U.S. Constitution, of course, is more than 215 years old. Ask students to work in small groups to respond to the following questions. Then compare each group's responses.

❶ What factors do you think account for the longevity of the U.S. Constitution? Do you think it is relevant that the U.S. Constitution is a relatively short document compared to the constitutions of most other countries? Why or why not?

❷ What are some advantages and disadvantages of constitutional longevity?

❸ In 1816 Thomas Jefferson made the following argument:

> Let us provide in our constitution for its revision at stated periods.... Each generation is as independent as the one preceding.... It has, like them, a right to choose for itself the form of government it believes most promotive of its own happiness; consequently, to accommodate to the circumstances in which it finds itself...and it is for the peace and good of mankind that a solemn opportunity of doing this every nineteen or twenty years should be provided by the constitution, so that it may be handed on with periodical repairs from generation to generation to the end of time, if anything human can so long endure.

Do you think the world's constitutions should provide for revision "at stated periods"? Why or why not?

The protection of rights has become an important diplomatic issue among nations. The United States and other countries have restricted trade with countries considered to be violating human rights, including South Africa before the abolition of racial apartheid, Iraq, North Korea, and Sudan.

CRITICAL THINKING EXERCISE

Examining the Universal Declaration of Human Rights

Read the Universal Declaration of Human Rights in the Reference section of this book and then respond to the following questions:

❶ What rights does the Universal Declaration of Human Rights proclaim that are in the U.S. Constitution and the Bill of Rights?

❷ What rights in the Constitution and the Bill of Rights are not included in the Universal Declaration of Human Rights?

❸ What rights in the Universal Declaration of Human Rights are not included in the Constitution and the Bill of Rights?

❹ How, if at all, can the rights in the U.S. Constitution be effectively enforced? If they can be enforced, what are the enforcement mechanisms?

❺ How can the rights in the Universal Declaration of Human Rights be effectively enforced? What are the enforcement mechanisms?

❻ How do the rights listed in the Constitution, the Bill of Rights, and the Universal Declaration of Human Rights reflect the history and experiences of the times in which they were written?

REVIEWING AND USING THE LESSON

❶ Which aspects of American constitutional democracy have been particularly influential in other countries? Which have not been influential? Why?

❷ What are some important differences between the Bill of Rights and the Universal Declaration of Human Rights?

❸ Why do you think federalism, an American invention, has proved especially popular in other countries?

Under what conditions, if any, should the United States and other nations intervene in the affairs of other sovereign nations to stop them from violating human rights?

37

WHAT KEY CHALLENGES DOES THE UNITED STATES FACE IN THE FUTURE?

WHAT KEY CHALLENGES DOES THE UNITED STATES FACE IN THE FUTURE?

---

wtpcompanion.civiced.org | **LESSON PURPOSE + TERMS**

Visit the We the People companion website for printable and downloadable Lesson Purposes and Terms and Concepts to Understand sections for each lesson. Audio readings of each Lesson Purpose and Term are also available online in MP3 format.

LESSON PURPOSE

From the beginning Americans have looked to the future. This lesson examines some of the challenges that might affect Americans as individuals and in their civic lives in coming years. It also explores issues that might lead to proposals for additional changes to the United States Constitution.

When you have finished this lesson, you should be able to discuss the effects of diversity and technology on the lives of Americans. You also should be able to explain the importance of civil discourse in debating divisive issues. Finally, you should be able to evaluate, take, and defend positions on the changing expectations of America's governments and potential constitutional amendments.

TERMS AND CONCEPTS TO UNDERSTAND

eminent domain

immigration

student page ▾ 278

HOW MIGHT THE UNITED STATES LOOK IN THE FUTURE?

In 1860 the average life expectancy in the United States was 39.5 years for whites and 23 years for blacks. By 2000 the numbers were up to 77.4 years for whites and 71.7 years for blacks. Women tend to live longer than men. In 2007 it appeared that obesity and obesity-related diseases might result in a declining life expectancy in the United States.

In the year 2000 more than half of the population of the United States lived in ten states: California, Texas, New York, Florida, Illinois, Pennsylvania, Ohio, Michigan, New Jersey, and Georgia. California was the most populous state with 33.9 million residents.

wtpcompanion.civiced.org **LINKS**

Visit the We the People companion website for a link to the U.S. Census Bureau for the most recent U.S. population data, plus a database that tracks population distribution in the United States.

wtpcompanion.civiced.org **LINKS**

Visit the We the People companion website for a link to worldwide life expectancy tables.

student page ▾ 278–279

HOW DOES DIVERSITY CREATE NEW CHALLENGES?

The Census Bureau estimates that today there are at least 311 languages spoken in the United States. At least 149 of those are immigrant languages, while 162 are indigenous, including those spoken in particular regions or by indigenous peoples. In more than fourteen million households people speak a language other than English; one in five people in the United States speaks a language other than English.

wtpcompanion.civiced.org **LINKS**

Visit the We the People companion website for a link to a site for more information about languages spoken in the United States.

HOW MIGHT THE UNITED STATES LOOK IN THE FUTURE?

The U.S. Census Bureau predicts significant changes in the United States by the year 2050. Warning that predictions are always uncertain because world events, such as political decisions, new policies, wars, diseases, and global economic factors, always can change things, the forecasters estimate the following:

- The population of the United States will exceed four hundred million.

- Most of the increase in population will result from **immigration**, that is, from people coming from other countries with the intent of remaining in the United States.

- The United States will be more racially and ethnically diverse than ever. Probably twenty-four percent of the population will be Hispanic; fifteen percent, African American; and eight percent, Asian. The Native American population will double, reaching approximately four million.

- Racial lines will blur as people intermarry.

- Medical advances will help Americans live longer. At least one in four Americans will be over the age of sixty-five.

- The typical American neighborhood will be in the South or West.

- The cost of water, oil, and natural gas will soar.

- Communications and information technologies will offer new kinds of telephones, televisions, and computers, bringing new ways to acquire information and to communicate.

As they have needed to do in the past, America's social and political institutions will have to adapt continually to a society very different from the one that existed in the late 1700s—or even the late 1900s.

HOW DOES DIVERSITY CREATE NEW CHALLENGES?

America has been a land of immigrants and their descendants for four centuries. The American goal of *e pluribus unum*—out of many, one—usually has been achieved by balancing the benefits of a diverse society with the unifying influence of a common civic culture and constitutional ideals. One of the major challenges now and for the future is to sustain that balance.

When the first census was taken in 1790, the United States consisted of thirteen states along the East Coast. The U.S. population was almost four million, including more than half a million slaves. The white people were mostly northern European in ancestry and overwhelmingly Protestant. By 2007 the population of the United States exceeded three hundred million and was spread across the continent and beyond. The United States has become a nation composed of immigrants and the descendants of immigrants from virtually every country on earth. Those whose ancestors were not native to Europe compose about a third of the nation's citizenry. Evidence of America's diversity is seen in its public schools, where it is not uncommon to find students from diverse ethnic groups, races, and religions. In the Los Angeles school district, for example, more than two hundred languages are represented.

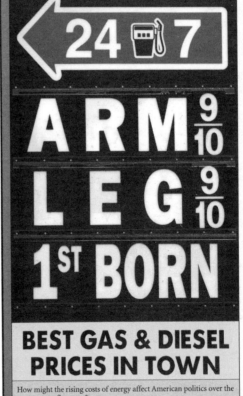

How might the rising costs of energy affect American politics over the next twenty-five years?

Americans disagree about the significance of this increasing diversity. Some argue that recent immigration patterns are not substantially different from what has happened throughout American history. They maintain that most recent immigrants, like their predecessors, enrich the nation's economy, culture, and educational institutions. Others worry that there are limits to how much diversity the country can absorb, particularly if large groups of immigrants do not learn to speak English and continue to adhere to cultural practices that conflict with fundamental American principles.

What might be some of the challenges caused by the increasing diversity of the United States?

WHAT DO YOU THINK?

❶ What advantages and disadvantages does the American political system gain from diversity of people and ideas? Is there such a thing as too much diversity? Explain.

❷ Early in the twentieth century President Woodrow Wilson argued that a person whose primary identity is with a particular group in America "has not yet become an American." Do you agree or disagree? Why?

❸ What obligations, if any, do Americans have toward people who hold social, religious, or political beliefs with which they strongly disagree? Explain.

CRITICAL THINKING EXERCISE

Tracing a Family's Journey to the United States

Write as complete a history as possible of one family in the United States. The family may be your biological, adopted, or foster family, the family of a close friend, or the family of a famous person in American history about whom you can locate information.

❶ When did the family or its ancestors come to the United States? Where did they settle? Why?

❷ What was U.S. policy on immigration when the family or its ancestors came to the United States? Has the policy changed? Explain.

❸ In what ways, if at all, does the experience of this family affect your understanding of what it means to be a citizen of the United States and of the state in which you reside?

If the family has Native American roots, the history should include responses to the following questions:

❶ Where was the tribe located before the arrival of immigrants from other countries? How did those immigrants affect the tribe?

❷ What have been the migration patterns, if any, of the tribe since the eighteenth century? Where is it located today?

❸ What is the status of the tribe today? What connections does the family have with the tribe? How have tribal membership or tribal connections affected the family's views of the United States and state citizenship?

After you have prepared the family history, use a world map to trace the various journeys the family made on its way to the United States. Then use a map of the United States to trace the journeys the family has made within this country. Discuss as a class how such research affects students' views on U.S. immigration policy today.

In surveys conducted in 2001 Americans reported association with some 313 religions or religious denominations.

wtpcompanion.civiced.org **LINKS**

Visit the We the People companion website for a link to more information about religions currently practiced in the United States.

wtpcompanion.civiced.org **LINKS**

Visit the We the People companion website for a link to the Statistical Abstract of the United States maintained by the U.S. Census Bureau since 1878 containing social, economic, and political statistics.

student page ▼ 280

HOW IS MODERN TECHNOLOGY AFFECTING AMERICA'S CIVIC LIFE?

Recent studies suggest that young people today may think about civic life differently than previous generations and that technology may play a role in those differences.

wtpcompanion.civiced.org   LINKS

Visit the We the People companion website for a link to studies analyzing the effects of technology on civil participation and a link to a database on worldwide Internet use.

CRITICAL THINKING EXERCISE

HISTORICAL BACKGROUND   After the Revolution of 1776 it was common for state legislatures to enter into partnerships with private corporations to develop infrastructure such as streets, highways, canals, and bridges. Another common practice was for state legislatures to incorporate businesses and grant them charters to build public facilities, such as roads and bridges. The famous case of *Charles River Bridge v. Warren Bridge* (1837) demonstrates the kinds of conflicts that erupted as states debated how best to provide certain services.

The Charles River Bridge Company was granted a charter to build the Charles River Bridge in 1786 and operate it as a toll bridge. In 1828 the Massachusetts legislature responded to the demands of urban growth and granted a charter to the Warren Bridge Company to build a bridge parallel to the Charles River Bridge that would become the property of the state and provide free river crossing. The owners of the Charles River Bridge argued that granting the charter to the Warren Bridge Company violated Article I, Section 10, of the U.S. Constitution, which prohibits states from passing laws that impair the obligations of contracts. The Supreme Court rejected that argument, giving states authority to foster economic development.

States relied heavily on private philanthropy to provide services such as hospitals, schools, youth reformatories, "poor houses," and services to the elderly and handicapped until well into the nineteenth century. Some facilities, such as the New York House of Refuge, which cared for poor children, received charters from the state legislature to provide services.

Slave patrols and night watches were the early forerunners of public police departments. Even when urban police forces were created beginning in the 1830s, they usually were staffed by nonprofessionals and administered informally and police officers did not wear uniforms.

HOW IS MODERN TECHNOLOGY AFFECTING AMERICA'S CIVIC LIFE?

Improvements in electronic communications are transforming how Americans acquire political information and participate in constitutional democracy. Advocacy groups now use the Internet, databases, and email to inform and organize their members. Americans with access to cable or satellite television can watch congressional hearings and debates. Many state legislatures and local governments broadcast government proceedings on community-access television. Witnesses wishing to testify at public hearings increasingly can do so on closed-circuit television or through computer-based communication, rather than traveling to the public meeting. Even some judicial proceedings are conducted through electronic communication. These advances allow Americans to participate and to become informed as never before.

But advances in technology do not guarantee that Americans are better informed. So much information is available on the Internet that many people feel overwhelmed. Often it is difficult or impossible for Internet users to determine the reliability of what they read. Radio, television, and print media target increasingly specialized audiences. Political messages frequently are aimed at specific audiences. If people receive news from only one source, then they do not hear all sides of issues. Writing on diary-like blogs is an increasingly common practice. Blogging allows people with similar views to exchange messages, often avoiding opposing opinions. One challenge of modern technology is that Americans must devise ways to use such technology to enhance their knowledge and civic participation, not to insulate themselves from genuine interaction and political discourse.

CRITICAL THINKING EXERCISE

Assessing the Effect of Technology on America's Civic Life

Work in small groups to respond to the following questions and then compare the groups' responses.

❶ In what ways, if at all, might the unrestricted use of technology—the Internet, electronic databases, cellular telephones, and other devices—threaten or enhance the following fundamental principles of American constitutional democracy?

  • Individual rights (especially privacy)
  • Limited government
  • Rule of law
  • Equality of opportunity

❷ In what ways, if any, do advances in technology make America's fundamental principles outmoded? Explain your response.

❸ What suggestions can you make to ensure that technology will have a positive effect on American civic life?

HOW MIGHT AMERICANS' EXPECTATIONS OF THEIR GOVERNMENTS CHANGE?

Tocqueville observed that Americans are trained from infancy to rely on themselves and private associations to meet many of their needs. Tocqueville believed that Americans, unlike Europeans, "look upon social authority with an eye of mistrust and anxiety" and turn to government only when they are unable to do without it.

Since the beginning of the twentieth century and especially since World War II, Americans increasingly have looked to government to provide a social safety net. Today the U.S. government spends far more on health and human services—including Social Security, Medicare, and Medicaid—than it does on defense. However, the

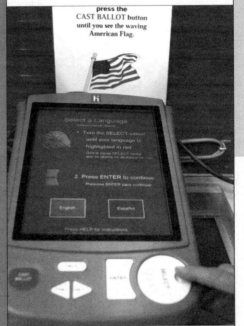

What are the implications of advances in technology for citizen participation in government?

Horace Mann crusaded for public "common schools" in the 1830s. Before that, even though many states made education "compulsory," instruction was provided privately, often by churches or philanthropic organizations.

What are the benefits of direct participation in meetings and hearings?

greatest growth in government has occurred at state and local levels, not the national level.

Some people believe that Americans are becoming too dependent on government to solve social problems. They lament inefficiencies, costs, and loss of privacy associated with government provision of services. Others believe that the growth of government, particularly at state and local levels, is a sign that the private sector is not capable of providing many of the services required as the United States grows and matures as a nation.

CRITICAL THINKING EXERCISE

Taking and Defending Positions on Public and Private Sector Provision of Services

Below is a list of the most common services provided by state and local governments today. Work in one of six groups. Each group should conduct research on one of these services and then respond to the questions that follow.

- Schools (preschool through university)
- Public safety (police, crime investigation, and fire)
- Prisons (including jails)
- Welfare (services to low-income, disabled, and elderly people)
- Hospitals
- Highways, streets, and roads

❶ How, if at all, was the service provided before it became a state or local function?

❷ What were the historical circumstances leading to the service being provided at public expense?

❸ To what extent, if at all, are state and local governments today contracting the service to private sources? Has private contracting been successful?

❹ Is this a service that could or should be provided privately or through some combination of the public and private sectors? Explain your position.

HOW CAN CIVIL DISCOURSE HELP TO ADDRESS THE CHALLENGES FACING AMERICANS?

Local, state, national, and international matters—from education reform to immigration and foreign policy—call up deeply held values that generate spirited debates. This is nothing new. The robust exchange of ideas and opinions by an engaged citizenry is a hallmark of a vibrant democracy. Civil discourse—the respectful, thoughtful exchange of ideas in the search for workable solutions to problems—is essential in a democracy.

Personal attacks, deliberate falsehoods, and negativity have become commonplace in political life. Simplistic phrases, or "sound bites," are offered as solutions to complicated problems. Many Americans, including opinion leaders such as talk show hosts and other media personalities, shout their disagreement with others and do not listen to opposing viewpoints. One of the most important

student page ▼ 282–284

WHAT ADDITIONAL CONSTITUTIONAL CHANGES MIGHT AMERICANS DEBATE?

In terms of property rights, by 2006 Alabama, Delaware, Ohio, Michigan, and Texas had amended their constitutions to prohibit the use of eminent domain to acquire property to sell to private developers. The National Conference of State Legislatures tracks state responses to decisions such as *Kelo v. New London, Connecticut* (2005).

wtpcompanion.civiced.org | **LINKS**

Visit the We the People companion website for a link to the National Conference of State Legislatures.

---

challenges of the twenty-first century has become the fostering of civil discourse. The civil exchange of ideas and perspectives increases the chances of finding mutually acceptable solutions to problems. It also permits people to live together even when they disagree.

The Constitutional Convention of 1787 provides one model of civil discourse. As explained in Unit Two, the delegates to the convention were deeply divided politically and economically. In order to debate the issues that separated them they adopted and followed rules for debate, including

- Giving everyone the opportunity to speak and no one the opportunity to dominate debate

- Addressing issues without making personal attacks or interrupting other speakers

- Giving full attention to the debates by not reading or engaging in other activities at the same time

Delegates who occasionally violated the rules apologized. The delegates socialized with one another during evening recesses to get to know and understand one another better. They realized that everyone would have to compromise if they were going to succeed in writing a constitution for a country as diverse as the United States.

What is civil discourse and what are its benefits?

282

No delegate departed the convention completely satisfied, but most agreed with Benjamin Franklin, who said,

> I confess that there are several parts of this constitution which I do not at present approve, but I am not sure I shall never approve them: For having lived long, I have experienced many instances of being obliged by better information, or fuller consideration, to change opinions even on important subjects, which I once thought right, but found to be otherwise. It is therefore that the older I grow, the more apt I am to doubt my own judgment, and to pay more respect to the judgment of others.

WHAT DO YOU THINK?

Americans always will face issues that divide them along economic, social, religious, cultural, and political lines. Developing the capacity to learn from, debate, disagree with, and get along with those who hold other points of view remains a challenge. What suggestions can you offer for developing the skills of civic engagement for yourself and others? Explain.

WHAT ADDITIONAL CONSTITUTIONAL CHANGES MIGHT AMERICANS DEBATE?

Americans have proposed thousands of changes to the U.S. Constitution and to their state constitutions. In addition to debating the merits of new proposals, Americans will have to decide if constitutional changes or legislation at the state or national level are appropriate ways to respond. The following are some examples of issues that may generate debates about constitutional amendments:

- **Life and death** Modern science is making it possible to sustain life across a broader age spectrum, beginning with the fetus and extending to advanced old age. Life support systems make it possible to sustain life that would not be tenable without such support.

  - Should the Constitution be amended to define when life begins and to identify a right to be born?

  - Should the Constitution be amended to define when life ends and to identify a right to die?

  - Should the Constitution be amended to include the right to use modern medical advances to transform and improve lives?

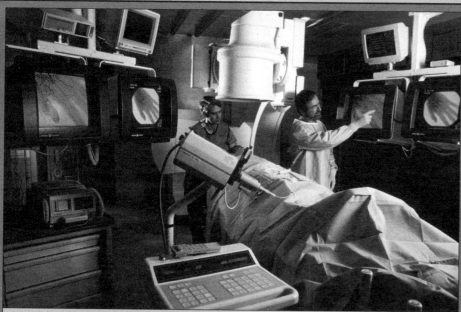

What are some of the legal and ethical issues raised by advances in medical science?

- **Term limits** The Twenty-second Amendment, ratified in 1951, limits presidents to two terms in office. There are no similar restrictions on members of Congress or federal judges.

  - Should the Twenty-second Amendment be repealed so that the people, not the Constitution, determine how many terms a president may serve?

  - Should the Constitution be amended to limit the number of terms a person can serve in the House or Senate? If so, how many terms? See *U.S. Term Limits v. Thornton* (1995), holding that states cannot add to the qualifications for serving in Congress stated in Article I.

  - Should the Constitution be amended so that judges holding office under Article III of the Constitution, including Supreme Court justices, serve limited terms instead of serving during "good behavior"?

- **Property rights** The "takings clause" of the Fifth Amendment to the Constitution permits the federal and state governments to "take" private property for public use,

if the owner is paid "just compensation." Governments long have used this power, known as **eminent domain**, to force owners to sell their property for projects such as highways, urban renewal, and water treatment facilities. In recent years governments have used eminent domain to buy property and then sell it to private individuals or corporations that promise to build something that will create jobs, bring more money into the community, and generate more taxes. The Supreme Court held in *Kelo v. New London, Connecticut* (2005) that taking private property to promote economic development is a "public use." Several states amended their constitutions to prohibit state governments from using eminent domain in the manner approved in *Kelo*.

  - Should the Constitution be amended to set aside *Kelo v. New London, Connecticut*?

- **Campaign finance** Money always has played a role in political campaigns. At this time no limits are placed on how much money candidates can spend to get elected or on how much money interest groups or others can

ENRICHMENT ACTIVITY

HOW IMPORTANT IS LITERACY TO DEMOCRACY?

Renaissance scholar Walter J. Ong believed that modern technology might be taking Americans into an era of "secondary orality," by which he meant renewal of an oral tradition somewhat akin to the oral tradition that existed before the advent of the written word. Writer and essayist Caleb Crain argues that "oral" and "literate" people understand the world differently. For example, he notes that "literates" tend to think abstractly, like to debate ideas, and can reconcile inconsistencies in arguments and historical events. "Oralists," by contrast, make sense of the world through stories, clichés, myths, and stereotypes.

Ask students to work in small groups to discuss the following questions:

❶ Does modern technology, including the Internet, make book and newspaper reading less attractive as a way of obtaining information, acquiring knowledge, and enjoying leisure time? Why or why not?

❷ Think about the way you absorb information from (a) books or newspapers, (b) television, and (c) videos. Are there differences? What are they? Are the differences significant? Why?

❸ What advantages might literate citizens have over those who get their information chiefly from oral sources?

❹ Do you think American democracy depends on having a literate citizenry, or can democracy flourish in an age of "secondary orality"? Explain.

spend on behalf of candidates. In *Buckley v. Valeo* (1976) the Supreme Court held that laws limiting campaign expenditures violate the First Amendment rights to free speech and association.

- Should the Constitution be amended to set aside *Buckley*?

- Should the Constitution be amended to set limits on how much money candidates can spend to get elected?

- **Immigration** In the last decades of the twentieth century some Americans became concerned about the millions of people illegally entering the country or entering legally but remaining after their visas expired. Critics question whether such immigrants should be allowed to receive government services and other legal protections.

  - Should the Fourteenth Amendment be changed so that children of aliens do not acquire citizenship merely by being born in the United States?

  - Should the equal protection and due process clauses be amended to substitute *citizen* or *legal resident* for the word *person*?

REVIEWING AND USING THE LESSON

❶ What are the five most significant challenges posed by increasing social and cultural diversity in the United States? What opportunities do these changes present?

❷ Identify ways in which technology might or might not be consistent with the fundamental principles of American constitutional democracy.

❸ How might technology improve opportunities for civic engagement in the United States?

❹ Explain what is meant by civil discourse. Why is it important? How might civil discourse be promoted in schools, the media, and political life?

❺ What issues in addition to those discussed in this lesson might lead to proposals for constitutional change? Which would you favor or oppose? Why?

Should local governments be able to use the power of eminent domain to take people's property for private development for the good of the community? Why or why not?

38

WHAT ARE THE CHALLENGES OF THE PARTICIPATION OF THE UNITED STATES IN WORLD AFFAIRS?

LESSON PURPOSE

The United States is involved in a system of international relations in which sovereign nations compete to achieve and maintain strategic positions in world affairs. The challenges facing the United States and its citizens in world affairs are complex and difficult. They will continue to be so.

This lesson highlights some aspects of Americans' participation in the international arena. When you have completed the lesson, you should be able to identify the constitutional responsibilities of the three branches of the national government in shaping the involvement of the United States in world affairs. You should be able to describe globalization and to identify some of the challenges that globalization poses for citizenship and participation in world affairs. Finally, you should be able to evaluate, take, and defend positions on issues involving globalization and improving the image of the United States abroad.

TERMS AND CONCEPTS TO UNDERSTAND

collective security

globalization

international law

isolationism

letter of marque and reprisal

multinational corporation

treaty

United Nations

UNIT SIX | LESSON 38

WHAT ARE THE CHALLENGES OF THE PARTICIPATION OF THE UNITED STATES IN WORLD AFFAIRS?

wtpcompanion.civiced.org	LESSON PURPOSE + TERMS

Visit the We the People companion website for printable and downloadable Lesson Purposes and Terms and Concepts to Understand sections for each lesson. Audio readings of each Lesson Purpose and Term are also available online in MP3 format.

student page ▾ 286–287

WHY IS INTERNATIONAL ENGAGEMENT INEVITABLE?

Thucydides wrote, "Wars spring from unseen and generally insignificant causes, the first outbreak being often but an explosion of anger." And regarding both foreign and domestic politics Machiavelli argued, "A wise ruler ought never to keep faith when by doing so it would be against his interests."

ISOLATIONISM Isolationism is the theory and practice of noninvolvement in the affairs of other nations. Isolationism is the opposite of a policy of internationalism, which is the theory and practice of national involvement in collective efforts to solve economic, political, or security problems.

student page ▾ 287

CRITICAL THINKING EXERCISE

The following is background information on the foreign policies mentioned:

MONROE DOCTRINE In his 1823 State of the Union message President James Monroe warned against any European intervention in the affairs of the American continents. He reaffirmed the United States' intention to refrain from interfering in European affairs as well. Over the years the Monroe Doctrine has developed into one of the basic tenets of American foreign policy through restatement and corollaries.

"GOOD NEIGHBOR" POLICY In his first inaugural address on March 4, 1933, President Franklin D. Roosevelt declared, "I would dedicate this nation to the policy of the good neighbor." He meant that the United States would respect the rights and honor the obligations of the United States "in and with a world of neighbors." Although the policy was initially directed to the world at large, it soon came into general use to describe the American policy of treating Latin American nations as friends and equals.

ATLANTIC CHARTER   To clarify the aims of World War II President Franklin Roosevelt and Prime Minister Winston Churchill issued the Atlantic Charter on August 14, 1941. Its terms stipulated that neither Britain nor the United States sought territorial gains and both nations

- would cooperate to secure access to the world's raw materials for all states;

- would respect the right of all peoples to choose the form of government they wished;

- would encourage international cooperation to secure just labor standards and social security;

- were committed to securing freedom from fear and want for all peoples;

- favored unrestricted freedom of the seas; and

- sought disarmament of aggressor nations as a step toward permanent peace.

TRUMAN DOCTRINE   In an address to a joint session of Congress President Harry S. Truman called for American support for all free peoples resisting subjugation by internal or external forces. The doctrine was aimed specifically at halting communist expansion in southeastern Europe. It marked the official acceptance of a "containment" policy to halt communist expansion.

MARSHALL PLAN   In a speech at Harvard University Secretary of State George C. Marshall proposed an economic aid program for European countries devastated by World War II. The plan worked so well that the term *Marshall Plan* entered the lexicon. It means any massive use of federal funds to solve a major social problem.

DÉTENTE WITH THE USSR   The word *détente* is a diplomatic term that means to ease tensions and reduce confrontations between two or more countries. The term was used to describe Soviet-American relations in the 1970s. Summit meetings of heads of state, economic agreements leading to increased trade, and strategic arms limitations were the major ways in which the United States practiced détente.

student page ▼ 287–289

HOW DOES THE CONSTITUTION PROVIDE FOR THE UNITED STATES' ROLE IN THE WORLD?

One of the Federalists' most powerful arguments on behalf of ratification of the U.S. Constitution was the advantage of a strong union in the international arena. In

Why did the United States send Benjamin Franklin to France to serve as American ambassador in 1776?

WHY IS INTERNATIONAL ENGAGEMENT INEVITABLE?

The Greek historian Thucydides (c. 460–400 BC) argued in his *History of the Peloponnesian War* that in international affairs the strong dominate the weak: "The powerful exact what they can, and the weak yield what they must." Renaissance Italian political theorist Niccolò Machiavelli (1469–1527) added in *The Prince* that preparing for war or being at war is a constant political reality. Those who insist on consistently following conventional morality in political affairs, he counseled, are soon destroyed.

International relations today involve delicate interactions among the more than two hundred independent nations in the world, generally known as nation-states. Given the risks of international involvement, some ask why the United States does not remove itself as far as possible from global engagement. A brief review of U.S. history during the founding period demonstrates why involvement with other countries is an inescapable part of American life.

When the United States declared independence from Great Britain, it needed help to win the Revolutionary War. At the time France wished to avenge its loss to Britain in the Seven Years' War, which had cost it most of its North American colonial holdings. France therefore lent its support to the American cause. In return, in 1778 the United States agreed to help France defend its West Indian islands if they were ever attacked and to permit France to bring ships captured in war into American ports. Spain also declared war on Britain but suffered a serious naval defeat to the British fleet off Portugal in 1780 and was unable to render aid to the American cause.

Soon after the Revolutionary War America's relationship with France became problematic. Despite its agreement in 1778 to aid France, the United States did not endorse the radically democratic French Revolution of 1789. When France went to war with Great Britain, Americans were deeply divided about which side the United States should support. At the same time America's relationship with Spain deteriorated, as Spain sought to detach Kentucky and Tennessee from the

United States, refused to allow American ships to pass through New Orleans, and aided the Creek and Cherokee Indians in wars with the United States. Not much later the French Revolution's focus on human rights sparked slave uprisings in Saint Dominique (now Haiti) that led to Haitian independence from France in 1804. The success of the Haitian revolution caused slave owners in the United States to fear similar uprisings.

When he left office in March 1797, President George Washington had warned Americans never to expect "real favors from nation to nation." President Thomas Jefferson later advocated "peace, commerce and honest friendship with all nations—entangling alliances with none." However, world trade and the need for certain scarce natural resources have kept the United States actively involved with the rest of the world to the present day. So have the desire to export America's founding ideas to oppressed peoples and, perhaps above all, real and perceived threats to the United States and its allies from other countries. In a world today endangered by fanatical terrorists and predatory states seeking or possessing nuclear and other horrific weapons, **isolationism**, a policy of noninvolvement with the world, has not been viewed as a realistic option.

What are some of the benefits of world trade?

CRITICAL THINKING EXERCISE

Examining American Foreign Policy

National self-interest is the driving force in international relations. Work in one of six groups. Each group should study one of the following foreign policies of the United States, prepare responses to the questions below, and then compare responses with the other groups.

- Monroe Doctrine, 1823
- "Good Neighbor" policy, 1933–1945
- Atlantic Charter, 1941
- Truman Doctrine, 1947
- Marshall Plan, 1947
- Détente with the USSR, 1969–1980

❶ How did the policy seek to advance the interests of the United States?

❷ How did the policy reflect American values and principles?

❸ How did other nations respond to the policy?

❹ What factors led to changes in the policy?

❺ Was this the right policy for the time it was made? Why or why not?

HOW DOES THE CONSTITUTION PROVIDE FOR THE UNITED STATES' ROLE IN THE WORLD?

The need for a national government to deal with other nations was one of the reasons behind the call for the Philadelphia Convention. The Constitution gives the three branches of the national government important powers in the international arena.

Congress has power to

- **Regulate commerce among foreign nations and with the Indian tribes** Congress uses this power to regulate imports and exports, encourage or discourage various forms of foreign trade through tariffs and other restrictions, set standards for the health and safety of foreign goods, and regulate employment conditions.

- **Declare war, issue letters of marque and reprisal, and make rules for captures on land and water** Congress has not exercised the power to declare war since the advent of nuclear weapons near the end of World War II. Instead, it has authorized the president to use

Federalist 42 Madison wrote that the class of powers given to the national government to "regulate the intercourse with foreign nations" was "an obvious and essential branch of the federal administration. If we are to be one nation in any respect, it clearly ought to be in respect to other nations."

REGULATION OF COMMERCE AMONG FOREIGN NATIONS AND WITH THE INDIAN TRIBES The Supreme Court has held that Congress may delegate "very large grants of its power over foreign commerce to the President." Moreover, establishing international air routes, unlike other modes of commerce, is within the exclusive authority of the president (*Chicago and Southern Air Lines v. Waterman*, 1948).

In *Crosby v. National Foreign Trade Council* (2000) the Court invalidated a Massachusetts law barring state entities from buying goods from or doing business with Burma (now Myanmar) on the grounds that the state law interfered with both Congress's power to regulate foreign commerce and the president's power over foreign policy.

wtpcompanion.civiced.org | **COURT CASES**

Visit the We the People companion website for links to Supreme Court syllabi and opinions for each of the cases described above.

CONGRESS'S POWER OVER WAR Early drafts of the Constitution gave Congress the power "to make war." Some delegates argued that the power should be vested in the president alone, the Senate alone, or in the president and the Senate. James Madison and Elbridge Gerry believed that Congress should be given the power to declare war, which would leave the president with the power "to repel sudden attacks." Giving both branches war powers reflected a compromise between those who feared the British system of letting a single individual commit the nation to war and those who feared leaving questions of war too close to popular passions.

The last time a president asked Congress to declare war was December 8, 1941, after Japan attacked Pearl Harbor, Hawaii.

student page ▾ 288

LETTERS OF MARQUE AND REPRISAL The Continental Congress issued letters of marque and reprisal in 1780 to allow colonial privateers to loot British merchant ships during the Revolutionary War. The authority of the privateers was carefully limited to comply with international trade customs and conventions and to avoid hostile responses from neutral or friendly nations.

In 2001 the 107th Congress considered the Air Piracy Reprisal and Capture Act of 2001 and the Marque and Reprisal Act of 2001. These acts would have updated the definition of "piracy" to include acts committed in the skies and authorized the president to issue letters of marque and reprisal in response to acts of air piracy. The sponsor of the acts, Texas Representative Ron Paul, believed that giving the president power to issue letters of marque and reprisal to private individuals was preferable to going to war over the terrorist attacks of September 2001. He explained,

> A letter of marque and reprisal is a constitutional tool specifically designed to give the president the authority to respond with appropriate force to those non-state actors who wage war against the United States while limiting his authority to only those responsible for the atrocities of that day. Such a limited authorization is consistent with the doctrine of just war and the practical aim of keeping Americans safe while mini-mizing the costs in blood and treasure of waging such an operation.

The acts did not become law.

TREATY-MAKING POWER   Until ten days before the Philadelphia Convention adjourned the delegates assumed that treaty-making power would reside in the Senate. On September 7 Article II, Section 2, Clause 2, gave the treaty-making power to the president, subject to the concurrence of two-thirds of the Senate.

In 1789 President George Washington appeared before the Senate with Secretary of War Henry Knox to ask questions about treaties with various Indian tribes. The senators referred the questions to committee, rather than debating them in front of President Washington. President Washington thereafter initiated the tradition that all subsequent presidents have followed of communicating with the Senate in writing about treaties.

Conflicts between the president's treaty power and the rights of the states surfaced almost immediately after the Constitution was ratified. For example, the Treaty of Paris of 1783, which ended the Revolutionary War, gave British creditors the right to collect debts in the former colonies. In *Ware v. Hylton* (1796) the Supreme Court ruled that the Treaty of Paris trumped a Virginia statute that permitted anyone owing a debt to a British creditor to discharge the debt by instead paying into the Virginia treasury. That decision began a trend of using treaty-making powers to limit the powers of the states.

One of the best-known cases is *Missouri v. Holland* (1920), a case involving the validity of a statute Congress enacted to implement the Migratory Bird Treaty. The goal was to prevent large-scale hunting of particular species of birds during the spring breeding season. The state of Missouri argued that protecting birds was one of the police powers of the states. The Supreme Court rejected Missouri's argument. The court in this and later cases held that state law is preempted if a state rule interferes with the conduct of foreign affairs by the national government.

wtpcompanion.civiced.org   COURT CASES

Visit the We the People companion website for links to Supreme Court syllabi and opinions for each of the cases described above.

---

military force overseas. Congress must fund all military actions. Historically, Congress issued letters of marque and reprisal to auth-orize private raids on merchant ships of enemy nations. A **letter of marque and reprisal** is a warrant that authorizes an agent to go beyond the borders of the nation—*marque*, meaning frontier—to search, seize, or destroy assets or people—*reprisal*—of the hostile foreign party.

● **Raise and support armies, provide and maintain a navy, and regulate land and naval forces**   The Constitution does not pro-vide for a standing army. Appropriations for armies can last no longer than two years.

● **Define and punish piracies and felonies on the high seas and offenses against the law of nations**   There have been few examples of piracy involving the United States since the nineteenth century, but Congress has used its power to punish felonies by authorizing drug arrests on the high seas. The Supreme Court has held that international law (discussed later) is part of the law of the United States.

● **Ratify treaties**   The Senate must ratify treaties negotiated by the president by a two-thirds vote. Ratified treaties require Congress to provide the funds needed to implement them.

The president has power to

● **Negotiate treaties**   A **treaty** is a formal agreement with one or more other nations. Treaties are used to conclude wars, help maintain peace, and affect international commerce. The delicate task of negoti-ating treaties rests with the president. The Department of State assists the president in this ongoing work. Once ratified by the Senate, treaties are part of the "supreme Law of the Land."

● **Act as commander in chief of the army and navy**   This power reflects the need for concentrated military authority in wartime. The United States has been at war—declared or undeclared—so often that the role of com-mander in chief has contributed significantly to the growth of presidential power.

Under what conditions, if any, should American presidents meet or refuse to meet directly with leaders of other nation-states?

288

When Africans on the Spanish slave ship *Amistad* mutinied in 1839 and took over the ship while it was at sea, what laws, if any, did they violate?

- **Appoint ambassadors, other public ministers, and consuls** Ambassadors, public ministers, and consuls make up the nation's diplomatic corps. They are the country's face and presence throughout the world. International diplomacy lays the groundwork for commercial treaties and helps implement American foreign policy.

- **Receive ambassadors and other public ministers** Receiving ambassadors and other public ministers establishes diplomatic relations with other countries. This power is used to recognize new nations and to accept changes of government in existing nations. Refusing to receive an ambassador or other public minister means refusing to have diplomatic relations with that country.

The Supreme Court has power to

- **Exercise original jurisdiction over cases affecting ambassadors, other public ministers, and consuls** The activities of these officials are directly related to peace and to the nation's sovereignty.

- **Exercise appellate jurisdiction over admiralty and maritime cases** These cases affect the nation's involvement in international trade.

WHAT DO YOU THINK?

The Constitution is not completely clear about the power of each branch of the national government in foreign affairs. For example, Congress has the authority to regulate the army and the navy, but the president is the commander in chief of the army and the navy. The president has the power to negotiate treaties. But the Senate must ratify them, and Congress is responsible for providing the money required to implement treaties.

❶ What are the advantages and disadvantages of checks and balances in the area of foreign relations?

❷ Are principles of separation of powers and federalism as viable in the making and execution of foreign policy as they are in the making and execution of domestic policy? If not, what are the alternatives? Explain.

WHAT IS INTERNATIONAL LAW?

International law may be defined as the body of rules of conduct accepted as legally binding by countries in their relations with each other. The purpose of international law is to create and maintain international order. Sources of international law include international treaties and conventions and international customs. The practices of international organizations, especially the United Nations, often are cited as sources of international law, though this claim is disputed. International law may be said to reflect four overarching ideals:

- **Equality of sovereign nation-states** All nations have the authority to exercise governmental power over those within their territory. The equality of nations is the key factor in international law. A corollary, or logical extension, of this principle is the self-determination of peoples.

- **Noninterference in the affairs of other nations** This principle ensures that each nation respects the rights and powers of other members of the international community.

EXECUTIVE AGREEMENTS In addition to treaties the president may enter into executive agreements with other nations. These agreements are not subject to approval by the Senate. Since World War II executive agreements entered into in Cairo, Tehran, Yalta, and Potsdam have significantly shaped American diplomacy. By the 1960s executive agreements had committed the United States to defend more than half the nations of the world, leading the Senate in 1969 to pass S.R. 85, the National Commitments Resolution, stating as follows:

> Whereas accurate definition of the term "national commitment" in recent years has become obscured: Now, therefore, be it resolved, that a national commitment for the purpose of this resolution means the use of the armed forces on a foreign territory, or a promise to assist a foreign country, government or people by the use of armed forces or financial resources of the United States, either immediately or upon the happening of certain events, and that it is the sense of the Senate that a national commitment by the United States results only from affirmative action taken by the Legislative and Executive Branches of the United States Government by means of a treaty, statute, or concurrent resolution of both houses of Congress specifically providing for such commitment.

TREATY RATIFICATION Article II, Section 2, Clause 2, requires two-thirds of the Senators present to concur in the president's treaty-making power. Nonetheless, it is common to refer to Senate "ratification" of treaties.

wtpcompanion.civiced.org **LINKS**

Visit the We the People companion website for a link to a list of treaties in force to which the United States is a party.

COMMANDER IN CHIEF OF THE ARMY AND THE NAVY The debate over presidential power as commander in chief of the Army and the Navy goes back to Thomas Jefferson and Alexander Hamilton. Soon after Jefferson took office, the Bey of Tripoli declared war on the United States. Lacking a declaration of war by Congress, Jefferson sent a squadron of frigates to the Mediterranean to protect American ships. However, he limited its actions to defense in the narrowest sense of the term. Jefferson informed Congress of his actions, believing his authority was limited because of the lack of a declaration of war.

Alexander Hamilton, by contrast, argued that if another nation declares war on the United States, the nation is in a state of war and no declaration from Congress is needed for the United States to respond in whatever way the president deems appropriate.

wtpcompanion.civiced.org **PRIMARY SOURCES**

Visit the We the People companion website for a link to Jefferson's message to Congress and Hamilton's response.

SUPREME COURT   In *Ames v. Kansas ex rel. Johnston* (1884) the Supreme Court held that Congress could grant concurrent jurisdiction to inferior federal courts in cases where Article III of the Constitution grants the Supreme Court original jurisdiction. Thus lower federal courts today have authority to hear cases involving ambassadors and consuls.

> **wtpcompanion.civiced.org**   **COURT CASES**
>
> Visit the We the People companion website for a link to Supreme Court syllabi and opinions for *Ames v. Kansas ex rel. Johnston* (1884).

student page ▼ 289–290

WHAT IS INTERNATIONAL LAW?

Generally speaking, international law is derived from two sources:

- Customary international law, based on long-standing practices
- Treaties (sometimes called "conventions") negotiated between and among nations

The Vienna Convention on the Law of Treaties (1969) was an attempt to codify customary international law. It also contained provisions about how treaties are to be interpreted.

> **wtpcompanion.civiced.org**   **PRIMARY SOURCES**
>
> Visit the We the People companion website for a link to the Vienna Convention.

International law historically was understood to involve only relationships between and among nations represented by their governments. Individuals were not considered to be obligated to obey international laws, nor were they thought to benefit from those laws (including human rights declarations). However, it is generally accepted today that individuals have at least some legal status under international law.

Whether international law or the law of particular nations should play a role in the interpretation of the U.S. Constitution has been a topic of considerable controversy. Two cases demonstrate disagreement among the justices:

- *Roper v. Simmons* (2004). In a 5-4 decision the Court held that the Eighth and Fourteenth Amendments prohibit executing convicted felons who were under the age of eighteen when they committed their crimes. The majority cited the International Convention on Civil and

- **No use of force or threat of force**   This principle reflects the need to avoid armed conflict and has become especially important since the advent of nuclear weapons. A corollary to this principle is the peaceful resolution of disputes.
- **Respect for human rights**   This principle recognizes developments in international law since the end of World War II. This principle frequently comes into conflict with the principles of sovereign equality and noninterference.

One of the primary aspects of international law is self-help. For example, international law allows nations to defend themselves. Another aspect is that international law differs significantly from domestic law. In many situations there is no universal enforcement mechanism for international law. There is no international police force to enforce the law. And although there is an International Court of Justice, it functions only for those countries that wish to join it.

International law depends on the willingness of nations to obey it. International law is complicated by the fact that countries have distinctly different geographies, cultures, histories, and languages. These differences often lead to disagreements about the meaning of international law, the right of each country to enforce it, and the extent to which circumstances and under what circumstances it is obligatory.

HOW DO INTERNATIONAL ORGANIZATIONS HELP TO MAINTAIN INTERNATIONAL ORDER?

The League of Nations, created after World War I, was the first attempt among nations to create a large-scale international organization to maintain international order through **collective security**. That is, the collective force of all members was to come to the aid of any member that was attacked. However, the League was a failure, largely because the United States refused to join. After World War II another attempt was made to maintain international order through collective security. Abandoning its previous isolationism, in 1945 the United States was one of fifty countries that agreed to form the **United Nations** (UN).

The UN is composed of states, or countries. Neither organizations nor individuals are eligible for membership. The goals of the UN are to maintain peace through collective security, which obliges member states to come to the aid of other member states if they are attacked by a third party; to promote friendly relations among nations and international cooperation in solving problems; to resolve international disputes peacefully; and to encourage respect for human rights and fundamental freedoms for everyone. The UN has many administrative bodies and agencies, including the World Health Organization and the United Nations Children's Fund.

Why might nations with disagreements agree to have their cases heard by the International Court of Justice and abide by its decisions? Why might they refuse?

What are the purposes of the Security Council of the United Nations?

Political Rights, the United Nations Convention on the Rights of the Child, the American Convention on Human Rights, and the African Charter on Rights and Welfare of the Child as support for its decision. In dissent Justice Scalia rejected the Court's use of international law, stating, "Acknowledgement of foreign approval has no place in the legal opinion of this Court" (see Lesson 32).

- *Lawrence v. Texas* (2003). In a 6–3 opinion the Court struck down a Texas statute making it a crime for two persons of the same gender to engage in certain sexual conduct. The majority cited the European Court of Human Rights as support for its decision. Justice Scalia's dissent cautioned against imposing "foreign moods, fads, or fashions on Americans."

wtpcompanion.civiced.org   COURT CASES

Visit the We the People companion website for links to Supreme Court syllabi and opinions for each of the cases described above.

wtpcompanion.civiced.org   PRIMARY SOURCES

Visit the We the People companion website for a link to a 2005 debate between Justices Antonin Scalia and Stephen Breyer about the use of foreign law in interpreting the U.S. Constitution.

All countries, including the United States, are expected to provide financial support to these bodies.

In addition to being a leader in the creation of the United Nations, the United States houses the organization's headquarters in New York City. The United States also is one of five permanent members of the UN Security Council. The others are Britain, China, France, and Russia. The Security Council is charged with maintaining peace and security among the nations of the world. Each of the five permanent member nations of the council has veto power over council resolutions.

The UN was founded with the assumption that the five permanent members of the Security Council would come together in the face of threats to international order. This soon proved illusory when the Cold War between the western democracies and the Soviet Union broke out in the late 1940s. Continuing political divisions among the Security Council's permanent members often have compromised its effectiveness.

Other international organizations have emerged since the end of World War II, and the United States is a member of many, including the North Atlantic Treaty Organization, which focuses on regional security in Europe. The United States also plays an active role in organizations such as the International Monetary Fund, the World Trade Organization, and the World Bank.

HOW CAN AMERICANS INFLUENCE INTERNATIONAL RELATIONS?

Americans indirectly influence American foreign policy and the nation's international economic decisions. However, there are many opportunities for involvement, and there is considerable evidence that individuals and groups can have a significant effect on the United States' role in international affairs. Opportunities for involvement include the following:

- **Voting, lobbying, and contacting national officials** Candidates for national political office must take stands on issues facing the United States in the global arena. Informed public opinion is important before and after elections and in the course of deliberations about policy choices.

- **Joining nongovernmental organizations** There are more than forty-four thousand nongovernmental organizations in the international arena, in addition to those operating primarily within the United States. They focus on business, environment, health, poverty, education, children's issues, human rights, and other matters that cut across all aspects of international affairs.

THE *AMISTAD* CASE In 1839 a revolt erupted on a Spanish vessel, the *Amistad*, that was transporting Africans from the Port of Havana to Puerto Príncipe. The Africans killed the captain and took control of the vessel. American seamen found the vessel and took it to a port in Connecticut. Later the Americans claimed rights to the vessel as salvage. The Spanish owners argued that the Africans and the vessel should be returned to them under the terms of a 1795 treaty between the United States and Spain. The treaty provided that "all ships and merchandises of what nature soever, which shall be rescued out of the hands of pirates or robbers on the high seas…shall be restored, entire, to the true proprietor." The Africans contended that they had been kidnapped and petitioned for their freedom. In 1841 in *United States v. Amistad* the Supreme Court held that the treaty did not apply because the Africans had never been legal property of the Spanish. The Court ordered the Africans freed and awarded salvage from the vessel to the Americans.

wtpcompanion.civiced.org   COURT CASES

Visit the We the People companion website for links to information about *United States v. Amistad* (1841).

291

student page ▾ 290–291

HOW DO INTERNATIONAL ORGANIZATIONS HELP TO MAINTAIN INTERNATIONAL ORDER?

UNITED NATIONS   The United Nations developed directly from discussions among the Allies during World War II. Even before the United States entered the war President Franklin D. Roosevelt was encouraging the State Department to think about the relationships among nations after the war. Although the Allied leaders agreed in principle on the need for an international organization to prevent future aggression, Roosevelt was the most vigorous supporter of the idea.

Roosevelt died before the founding conference of the UN in San Francisco. Harry Truman, who succeeded Roosevelt, gave his first major speech as president at the signing of the UN Charter on June 26, 1945. The following month the U.S. Senate approved the charter by a vote of 89 to 2.

The General Assembly chose the United States as the site for the permanent headquarters of the UN. It accepted a gift from John D. Rockefeller Jr. to buy a tract of land on the East River in New York City, where the United Nations building now stands.

INTERNATIONAL COURT OF JUSTICE   Commonly known as the World Court this body was created in 1945 and is located in The Hague, Netherlands. It consists of fifteen judges elected by the UN General Assembly and UN Security Council.

wtpcompanion.civiced.org   LINKS

Visit the We the People companion website for a link to the website of the International Court of Justice.

Unlike the Supreme Court of the United States the World Court issues advisory opinions at the request of the UN Security Council, the General Assembly, or any other agency authorized by the Security Council.

The United States withdrew its agreement to recognize the jurisdiction of the court in 1986. The United States accepts the jurisdiction and decisions of the court only on a case-by-case basis. Among developing countries willingness to accept the jurisdiction of the court has been increasing.

wtpcompanion.civiced.org   LINKS

Visit the We the People companion website for a link to the websites of the United Nations, WHO, UNICEF, NATO, IMF, WTO, and the World Bank.

- **Traveling, exercising citizen diplomacy, and participating in international education**
  Traveling to other countries is a common way for individuals to develop knowledge and expertise in international affairs. Students can participate in foreign exchange and sister-city programs, study international relations, and become multilingual. Those who cannot travel can help host foreign exchange students and other visitors from abroad. Americans also can learn about, connect with, and converse with people from around the world on the Internet.

- **Making informed consumer decisions**
  In the world's increasingly interdependent economy consumer choices can have important ripple effects. Some consumers refuse to buy, or boycott, products that they believe are produced in conditions that violate human rights or violate copyright laws designed to protect inventors and creative entrepreneurs.

Before the United States entered World War II most Americans saw themselves and their country as isolationist—fundamentally inward-looking, rather than involved with the world. After World War II and the outbreak of the Cold War with the Soviet Union and its allies, Americans' attitudes toward the rest of the world changed. Since the 1940s Americans have largely accepted the necessity for America's worldwide involvements for the sake of the nation's security and the security of the free world. Nevertheless, many Americans are not well informed about other countries, world affairs, or how the United States is perceived in other parts of the world.

WHAT DO YOU THINK?

❶ How important is it for Americans to be informed about what is happening in the rest of the world? Explain your response.

❷ What suggestions do you have for (a) improving Americans' understanding of other countries, (b) improving other countries' understanding of the United States, and (c) fostering dialogue among citizens of different nations?

WHAT IS GLOBALIZATION?

The word *globalization* refers to the global economy and the effects of worldwide economic interdependence on cultures, social relations, and politics. The central features of globalization are trade and commerce, worker migration, capital, and information.

- **Trade and commerce**   In the last half of the twentieth century the volume of world trade increased twenty-fold. **Multinational corporations**, or enterprises that manage production or deliver services in two or more countries, often have budgets bigger than those of some countries. Globalization also involves massive exports of manufactured goods, particularly from Asia. Some national economies have prospered in the era of globalization. Others, such as those of many African nations, have not.

How might world trade enhance relations among nations?

What have been some of the positive and negative effects of globalization?

- **Worker migration** Workers throughout the world are proving to be remarkably mobile. People move from one country to another seeking better jobs, which can lead to disputes about immigration policies. At the same time many companies in industrialized nations such as the United States are outsourcing jobs— that is, sending work to other countries to take advantage of cheaper labor and to use workplaces that are relatively free from government regulation. Outsourcing also affects migration patterns within the United States as unemployed or underemployed workers move to different communities or states in search of jobs.

- **Capital** Investment patterns have changed dramatically in the past decade, as corporations explore new markets throughout the world. Creditor nations make loans to debtor nations, often giving the creditors leverage over the debtor nation's political decisions. Capital markets are increasingly volatile, as witnessed by the reactions of stock markets in one part of the world to news of events on the other side of the globe.

- **Information** Technology has had the greatest effect on globalization. The Internet and other innovations provide all economic actors—

consumers, investors, and businesses—with virtually instant access to important information for making decisions. New technologies also make it possible to transfer capital quickly and easily. Information technologies are being used to influence public opinion and to affect political decisions throughout the world.

WHAT DO YOU THINK?

❶ Make a list of the ways you and your family are affected by globalization at home, at school, and in the workplace. Compare your list with those of your classmates. Which effects are positive? Which are negative? Explain.

❷ Think about the following factors that you might consider in deciding whether to purchase a particular item of clothing or some other consumer good:

- The country in which it was made

- Whether the workers who produced the item earn a minimum or working wage

- Environmental costs of transporting the item for sale

293

student page ▼ 291–292

HOW CAN AMERICANS INFLUENCE INTERNATIONAL RELATIONS?

At the beginning of 2008 more than six million American citizens were living outside the United States. Their presence and daily interactions influence how people in other countries think about the United States.

Influence on international relations begins with knowledge. Former State Department official and columnist Robert Kagan laments,

> Americans have cherished an image of themselves as by nature inward-looking and aloof, only sporadically and spasmodically venturing forth into the world, usually in response to external attack or perceived threats. This self-image survives, despite four hundred years of steady expansion and an ever-deepening involvement in world affairs, and despite innumerable wars, interventions, and prolonged occupations of foreign lands. It is as if it were all an accident or odd twist of fate. Even as the United States has risen to a position of global hegemony, expanding its reach and purview and involvement across the continent and then across the oceans, Americans still believe their nation's natural tendencies are toward passivity, indifference, and insularity.

student page ▼ 292–293

WHAT IS GLOBALIZATION?

Globalization is not new. Peoples, nations, and corporations have been buying and selling from each other across great distances for centuries. However, recent economic and political policies, as well as technology, have spurred cross-border involvement, resulting in a new phase in economic and cultural development. *New York Times* foreign affairs columnist Thomas Friedman describes the current wave of globalization as "farther, faster, cheaper, and deeper."

wtpcompanion.civiced.org **LINKS**

Visit the We the People companion website for a link to websites about globalization.

An example of the pace of globalization can be found in China. In early 2008 the government of China reported the number of Internet users in that country had increased by more than fifty percent in only one year—to 210 million. The investment bank Morgan Stanley predicted that China soon would have more Internet users than the United States, the current leader. However, unlike in the United States the Internet is tightly controlled in China; access to many websites is restricted.

According to the 2007 Pew Global Attitudes Survey many Americans had begun to question the desirability of globalization. Only fifty-nine percent of those surveyed reported thinking international trade is benefiting the country, down from seventy-eight percent in 2002. Almost three-quarters of those surveyed wanted to see immigration further restricted.

wtpcompanion.civiced.org | **LINKS**

Visit the We the People companion website for a link to complete 2007 Pew Global Attitudes Survey results.

- Working conditions of the workers who made the item

- The price of the item

- The social desirability of owning the item

❸ Which of the above factors would influence your buying decisions? Why? What, if anything, would persuade you to consider factors that you do not now consider when making consumer choices?

CRITICAL THINKING EXERCISE

Assessing the Effects of Globalization on the United States

Work in small groups to respond to the following questions. Share your responses with the whole class.

❶ What are the economic and political benefits and drawbacks of globalization for the United States? Explain.

❷ Some observers claim that globalization of the world economy diminishes citizens' ability to monitor and influence actions that might affect their welfare. Do you agree with this position? Why or why not? If you do agree, what remedies should be used? Explain your reasoning.

REVIEWING AND USING THE LESSON

❶ Explain why the United States is involved in the international arena.

❷ Identify the three most important constitutional powers that Congress and the president have in the area of international relations. How do checks and balances and the separation of powers affect the exercise of those powers?

❸ What is globalization? How does globalization affect American society and the U.S. economy?

❹ Identify ways in which Americans can participate in and have an effect on international relations.

How are you affected by globalization?

39
WHAT DOES RETURNING TO FUNDAMENTAL PRINCIPLES MEAN?

UNIT SIX | LESSON 39

WHAT DOES RETURNING TO FUNDAMENTAL PRINCIPLES MEAN?

wtpcompanion.civiced.org   **LESSON PURPOSE + TERMS**

Visit the We the People companion website for printable and downloadable Lesson Purposes and Terms and Concepts to Understand sections for each lesson. Audio readings of each Lesson Purpose and Term are also available online in MP3 format.

wtpcompanion.civiced.org   **BIOGRAPHIES**

Visit the We the People companion website for brief printable and downloadable biographies of the people mentioned in the student and teacher's editions. Audio readings of each biography are also available online in MP3 format.

LESSON PURPOSE

One of the Founders, George Mason from Virginia, said, "No free government, or the blessings of liberty can be preserved to any people, but by frequent recurrence to fundamental principles." In this concluding lesson, you have the opportunity of relating some fundamental principles and ideas of our government to contemporary issues.

The format of this concluding lesson differs from the others. Critical Thinking Exercises similar to others throughout this text present a series of quotations that represent great ideas and principles that have shaped our constitutional heritage. Some of these ideas contradict each other. However, American constitutional history has witnessed many conflicts between competing principles of equal merit. Examples include the conflict between majority rule and minority rights, between sovereign power and fundamental rights, between liberty and order, and between unity and diversity.

Examples of conflicts appear in the following exercises. In each case you will be asked to apply the principles and ideas suggested in the quotations to a contemporary issue, to work through the issue on your own or in small groups, and to reach your own conclusions.

In so doing you will use the skills of citizenship—observation, analysis, debate, and careful selection of value judgments—to reach, express, and defend an opinion. These exercises provide practice for the responsibilities you will encounter in the years ahead.

WHY ARE FUNDAMENTAL PRINCIPLES IMPORTANT?

This book began with the observation that the American experiment in self-government was an adventure in ideas. The individuals who founded America's governments cherished and respected ideas. They were excited about them. The United States was created by ideas. It is not the product of a homogeneous common culture or centuries of tradition. The United States began as a test to see if certain ideas about government—many never before tried on such a scale or in such a way—would work.

The British economist John Maynard Keynes (1883–1946) once remarked that "in the long run it is ideas and not men who rule the world." If the upheavals of this century have taught Americans anything, it is that ideas have consequences, sometimes for good, sometimes for evil. Everyone likes to believe that in the end good ideas will prevail over bad, although there is nothing automatic or inevitable about this. Good ideas do matter. One of the twentieth century's most compelling images comes from the Chinese student democracy movement of 1989. It is a photograph of a young man, armed only with the moral authority of his cause, confronting a column of armored tanks. This image has moved and inspired the world.

Joseph Stalin, the Soviet dictator from 1929 to 1953, once disparaged the influence of religion by asking, "How many divisions does the Pope have?" One of the great ironies of the twentieth century was that the most influential movement to set in motion the fall of the Soviet empire began in Poland. It was impossible for Poland's communist regime to gain acceptance by a population that retained its deep Catholic faith and where the Catholic Church remained staunchly independent of the communist state.

It was in these circumstances that the independent Polish trade union Solidarity was founded in 1980. This movement was secular, that is, not specifically related to religion or a religious group, although allied with the Catholic Church and strongly aided by the moral influence of the papacy. Eventually Solidarity was able to form a free, noncommunist government in 1989. The victory of Solidarity over Polish communism inspired similar victories, known as the Revolutions of 1989, in neighboring Soviet satellites in Central and Eastern Europe.

These revolutions inaugurated democracy throughout much of the region and helped to weaken the Soviet state, which hastened the dissolution of the Soviet Union at the end of 1991. "An invasion of armies can be resisted," the eighteenth-century French novelist Victor Hugo once wrote, "but not an idea whose time has come."

WHAT DID THE FOUNDERS MEAN BY RETURNING TO FIRST PRINCIPLES?

When George Mason spoke of the importance of a "frequent recurrence to fundamental principles," he was invoking an old idea associated with republican government. The ancient Greeks and Romans believed that a government established with the purpose of serving the public good and involving the participation of all citizens could not survive unless each generation was reminded of that government's reason for being and the principles by which it operated.

Another of the Founders, probably Melancton Smith or Richard Henry Lee, writing in 1788 as the Anti-Federalist Federal Farmer (see Lesson 13), said,

> If a nation means its systems, religious or political, shall have duration, it ought to recognize the leading principles of them in the front page of every family book. What is the usefulness of a truth in theory, unless it exists constantly in the minds of the people and has their assent?

It is doubtful that these Founders had in mind an uncritical acceptance of the "wisdom of the past." In revisiting these principles each generation must examine and evaluate them anew. The Founders probably would be somewhat surprised at the reverence in which they and their writings have been held by subsequent generations of Americans.

What principles were Chinese demonstrators advocating when they passed out copies of the Declaration of Independence in Tiananmen Square in 1989?

Should residents of public housing projects be required to waive their Fourth Amendment rights so that law enforcement officers can search their apartments for illegal weapons or drugs without warrants?

The Founders themselves were vigorous critics of the wisdom that they had inherited and the principles in which they believed. They were articulate, opinionated individuals who loved to examine ideas—to analyze, argue, and debate them. They expected no less of future generations. They would expect no less of us. To go back in thought or discussion to first principles requires us to make principled arguments and to ground our opinions in ideas of enduring value. It is what citizenship in a free society is all about.

CRITICAL THINKING EXERCISE 1

Liberty versus Order

One of the most enduring and important challenges in our constitutional system of government is how to balance order with liberty. In this exercise the issue of crime demonstrates the challenge. Violent crime is widespread in the nation's inner cities, but few areas of our society feel safe. Violence even has become a problem in our schools.

In response to the crime problem in a housing project of one of the nation's largest cities, officials in that city proposed large-scale police "sweeps" of apartments to search for illegal weapons. These searches would not require search warrants or evidence of probable cause. After a judge struck down the proposal as an unconstitutional violation of the Fourth Amendment, the city proposed a new policy requiring prospective tenants in public housing projects to waive their Fourth Amendment rights as a condition of their leases.

❶ How do the following statements apply to the issue of sweeps for illegal weapons? What principles and ideals are implied in each statement? How, if at all, do these principles conflict with each other?

❝ The right of the people to be secure in their persons, houses, papers, and effects, against unreasonable searches and seizures, shall not be violated, and no Warrants shall issue, but upon probable cause.
    Fourth Amendment

❝ The good of the people is the highest law.
    Cicero

❝ Authority without wisdom is like a heavy axe without an edge, fitter to bruise than polish.
    Anne Bradstreet

❝ For a man's house is his castle.
    Edward Coke

❝ They that can give up essential liberty to obtain a little temporary safety deserve neither liberty nor safety.
    Benjamin Franklin

❝ Since the general civilization of mankind, I believe there are more instances of the abridgment of the freedom of the people, by gradual and silent encroachments of those in power, than by violent and sudden usurpations.
    James Madison

❝ Every successful revolution puts on in time the robe of the tyrant it has deposed.
    Barbara Tuchman

❝ Liberty, too, must be limited in order to be possessed.
    Edmund Burke

❝ The great and chief end, therefore, of men's uniting into Commonwealths, and putting themselves under Government, is the preservation of property [life, liberty, and estate].
    John Locke

❷ Which, if any, of these statements do you find most persuasive? Why?

❸ What is your position on this issue? Explain the reasons for your position in terms of the situation and the principles involved.

297

---

student page ▾ 297

CRITICAL THINKING EXERCISE 1

LIBERTY VERSUS ORDER

The following are brief biographical sketches of the people quoted.

Marcus Tullius Cicero (106–43 BC)   Born into a provincial, middle-class family, Cicero became the greatest lawyer and orator of his day. His speeches and philosophical works are models of Latin prose. One of the most versatile minds of his time, he thought about the law in ways that foreshadowed key aspects of Anglo-American common law. One of those ideas was that everyone in a country, even aliens, has an equal right to due process of law.

Anne Bradstreet (1612–1672)   Born in England, Bradstreet emigrated to America in 1630 with her Puritan husband, Simon Bradstreet. He later became governor of Massachusetts. She became one of the first poets to write English verse in the American colonies. Her sequence of religious poems, *Contemplations*, was written for her family and not published until the mid-nineteenth century. Her work won critical acceptance in the twentieth century.

Sir Edward Coke (1552–1639)   Coke was Queen Elizabeth's attorney general and then chief justice under King James I. A born advocate, he loved the courtroom and vigorously prosecuted Sir Walter Raleigh in 1603. In 1605 he prosecuted the Gunpowder Plot conspirators on charges that they had attempted to kill King James I. Later in life, as a judge and leader of the House of Commons, he risked his life for the principles he believed in—the right to a public trial, habeas corpus, and the right against self-incrimination. Coke helped draft the Petition of Right of 1628, which served as a model for the American founders. His writings on the English common law were the leading texts on the law for some three hundred years.

Benjamin Franklin (1706–1790)   Franklin was an American statesman, diplomat, printer, publisher, inventor, and scientist. A staunch advocate of colonial rights, he helped draft the Declaration of Independence and the Treaty of Paris (1783). He was the oldest member of the Philadelphia Convention in 1787.

James Madison (1751–1836)   Often called the "Father of the Constitution," Madison took an active part in the Philadelphia Convention and in the First Federal Congress, where he championed the Bill of Rights. He served as the fourth president of the United States (1809–1817).

Barbara Tuchman (1912–1989)   Tuchman was an American historian and journalist whose books are praised for their narrative force and illuminating detail. Her best-known book is *The Guns of August*, which details the history leading up to World War I and the first month of that conflict. It won the Pulitzer Prize in 1962.

Edmund Burke (1729–1797) British conservatives regarded Burke as the greatest of their political theorists. In Parliament from 1765 Burke opposed the government's attempts to coerce the American colonists. He supported the American Revolution but opposed the French Revolution.

John Locke (1632–1704) English philosopher John Locke's *Two Treatises of Government*, published anonymously in 1690, presented a theory of the social contract. It embodied a defense of natural rights and enjoyed great influence in America. Thomas Jefferson drew heavily on Locke in writing the Declaration of Independence.

---

wtpcompanion.civiced.org BIOGRAPHIES

Visit the We the People companion website for brief printable and downloadable biographies of the people mentioned in the student and teacher's editions. Audio readings of each biography are also available online in MP3 format.

---

student page ▼ 298

CRITICAL THINKING EXERCISE 2

UNITY VERSUS DIVERSITY

The following are brief biographical sketches of the people quoted.

Israel Zangwill (1864–1926) Zangwill was an English writer and political activist best known in the United States for his work *The Melting Pot*, dealing with issues of immigration and assimilation in America and praising the country's capacity to absorb and grow from the contributions of immigrants.

Mary Antin (1881–1949) Born in Poland, Antin immigrated to the United States in 1894. Her widely acclaimed autobiography, *Promised Land*, narrates the experiences of Jews in Europe in contrast with the experiences of Jewish immigrants in the United States.

Noah Webster (1758–1843) An ardent Federalist, Webster favored a strong national government. He was well known for his *Spelling Book*, first composed in 1782, which was issued under various titles well into the twentieth century. He wanted to standardize American spelling and grammar to show that the United States was a nation distinct from Britain and that it had a historical destiny. His life and work are celebrated in *Noah Webster, Schoolmaster to America*, written by Harry R. Warfel in 1936.

Theodore Roosevelt (1858–1919) The twenty-sixth president of the United States, Roosevelt was an immensely popular leader who wrote about American ideals, ranching, hunting, and zoology. He won the Nobel Peace Prize in 1906 for his part in ending the Russo-Japanese War by orchestrating meetings that led to the Treaty of Portsmouth in 1905.

CRITICAL THINKING EXERCISE 2

Unity versus Diversity

Is a common language essential to the survival of American democracy? One of the most controversial aspects of diversity in America has to do with language. Throughout American history English has been the principal language of the country. For millions of immigrants learning English has been an important first step to becoming a U.S. citizen.

Schools must teach immigrant children who speak languages other than English. Educators differ about how best to accomplish their tasks. A large percentage of recent immigrants speak Spanish as their first language. In certain areas of the country Spanish is as commonly spoken as English. Some believe that we are becoming a bilingual nation.

❶ How do the following statements apply to this situation? What principles and ideals are implied in each statement? How, if at all, do these principles conflict with each other?

   ❝ America is God's crucible, the great melting pot where all the races of Europe are melting and re-forming!
   Israel Zangwill

❝ [Immigrants are] not the refuse but the sinew and bone of all the nations.… [Education is] the essence of American opportunity, the treasure that no thief could touch, not even misfortune or poverty.
Mary Antin

❝ Our political harmony is therefore concerned in a uniformity of language.
Noah Webster

❝ We have room for but one language here, and that is the English language, and we intend to see that the crucible turns our people out as Americans, and not as dwellers of a polyglot boarding-house.
Theodore Roosevelt

❝ In world history, those who have helped to build the same culture are not necessarily of one race, and those of the same race have not all participated in one culture.
Ruth Fulton Benedict

❝ America is not a melting pot. It is a sizzling cauldron.
Barbara Mikulski

Under what conditions, if any, should government officials be allowed to confiscate literature or computer files they might consider evidence of terrorist activities or sympathies?

298

In order to become citizens, should people be required to be fluent in English?

> " We have become not a melting pot but a beautiful mosaic. Different people, different beliefs, different yearnings, different hopes, different dreams.
>
> Jimmy Carter

> " Here in America we are descended in blood and in spirit from revolutionaries and rebels—men and women who dared to dissent from accepted doctrines. As their heirs may we never confuse honest dissent with disloyal subversion.
>
> Dwight D. Eisenhower

> " I believe respect for diversity and encouragement of a plurality of communities have been among the glories of the best elements of the American political system.... But, like all other values, diversity has its problems and costs as well as its advantages and benefits. The problem is often simply referred to as the tension between unity and diversity, or order and liberty, or the public and the private.
>
> R. Freeman Butts

❷ Which, if any, of these statements do you find most persuasive? Why?

❸ Is a common language necessary to American citizenship? Explain your position in terms of the principles involved.

CRITICAL THINKING EXERCISE 3

Majority Rule versus Minority Rights

The rights and wrongs of majority rule have been the subject of debate for centuries. One scholar recently compared Americans' concern about the problem of majority tyranny to "a nagging tooth."

The term *majority* is derived from the Latin *major pars*, or the "weightier part." In medieval Europe the term referred to powerful nobles who were considered "weightier" than the common people. Today, in a democratic society that adheres to a principle of political equality—"each is to count for one and no more than one"—numbers rather than social position determine the meaning of majority.

The term *minority* may refer to those on the losing side of a vote of any kind. It also refers to a part of a population differing from others in some characteristic such as ethnicity, language, religion, or political party.

Majority rule is an essential concept of democratic government because there needs to be a way to settle disputes and decide issues. If unanimous agreement were necessary before a law could be enacted, a policy put in place, or an official elected, then nothing would get done.

However, majority rule is not an absolute principle. If it were, then the majority of voters or legislators could ignore the wishes of minorities and deprive them of their rights.

Today, most Americans believe themselves to be members, at least part of the time, of one or more minorities. Their views could be ignored and their goals threatened if

299

Ruth Fulton Benedict (1887–1948)   An American anthropologist, Benedict contended that every culture tends to predispose its members to adopt its distinctive ethos. Her best-known works include *Patterns of Culture* (1934) and *The Chrysanthemum and the Sword: Patterns of Japanese Culture* (1946).

Barbara Mikulski (1936–)   Mikulski, a U.S. senator from Maryland, was elected to a fourth term in 2002. A champion of civil rights and issues affecting women, she became the Senate's most senior female member. She served on the Baltimore City Council and in the House of Representatives before being elected to the Senate.

James Earl (Jimmy) Carter (1924–)   Carter was the thirty-ninth president of the United States and a champion of civil and human rights. He has served as a leader on international election observation teams and as a mediator of several international disputes. He won the Nobel Peace Prize in 2002.

Dwight D. Eisenhower (1890–1969)   Eisenhower was the thirty-fourth president of the United States, a decorated Army general in World War II, and president of Columbia University. He launched the space race and initiated the interstate highway system.

R. Freeman Butts (1910–)   Butts has been the William E. Russell Professor Emeritus in the Foundations of Education, Columbia Teachers College, Columbia University, a senior fellow of the Kettering Foundation, and a visiting scholar at the Hoover Institution, Stanford University.

wtpcompanion.civiced.org | **BIOGRAPHIES**

Visit the We the People companion website for brief printable and downloadable biographies of the people mentioned in the student and teacher's editions. Audio readings of each biography are also available online in MP3 format.

student page ▼ 299

CRITICAL THINKING EXERCISE 3

MAJORITY RULE VERSUS MINORITY RIGHTS

The following are brief biographical sketches of the people quoted.

Thomas Jefferson (1743–1826)   Third president of the United States and founder of the Democratic Republican Party, Jefferson is remembered as the author of the Declaration of Independence. He helped found the University of Virginia.

Abraham Lincoln (1809–1865)   Lincoln was the sixteenth president of the United States. In his Gettysburg Address he declared the aim of preserving a "nation conceived in liberty and dedicated to the proposition that all men are created equal."

Franklin D. Roosevelt (1882–1945) The thirty-second president of the United States, Roosevelt was the only person to be elected to the office four times. He served during the Great Depression of the 1930s and World War II.

Eugene Debs (1855–1926) A labor union leader, Debs helped found the Socialist Party of America and stood as its unsuccessful candidate in all the presidential elections between 1900 and 1920, except the election of 1916.

René Lévesque (1922–1988) A journalist and television commentator who also served as the twenty-third premier of Quebec, Lévesque founded the Parti Quebecois with the aim of making Quebec independent of English-speaking Canada. His proposal was rejected in a referendum in 1980.

Arthur James Balfour (1848–1930) Balfour was a British Conservative who served as prime minister (1902–1905) and foreign secretary (1916–1919). He issued the 1917 Balfour Declaration advocating a national home in Palestine for the Jews.

Adlai Stevenson (1900–1965) As governor of Illinois Stevenson campaigned vigorously against corruption in public life. He was defeated in his bid for the presidency in 1952 and again in 1956 by Dwight Eisenhower. He served as ambassador to the United Nations from 1961 to 1965.

Harlan Fiske Stone (1872–1946) Appointed to the U.S. Supreme Court in 1925, Stone served as chief justice from 1941 to 1946. The quotation is from the famous Footnote Four in *United States v. Carolene Products* (1938).

wtpcompanion.civiced.org **BIOGRAPHIES**

Visit the We the People companion website for brief printable and downloadable biographies of the people mentioned in the student and teacher's editions. Audio readings of each biography are also available online in MP3 format.

---

the will of majorities were legally unlimited. How to achieve the proper balance between majority rule and minority rights therefore remains a continuing challenge.

❶ How do the following statements address the problem of reconciling majority rule with minority rights? What principles and ideals are implied in each statement? How, if at all, do these principles conflict with each other?

❝ The first principle of republicanism is, that the *lex-majoris partis* is the fundamental law of every society of individuals with equal rights; to consider the will of society enounced by the majority of a single vote, as sacred as if unanimous, is the first of all lessons in importance.

Thomas Jefferson

What evidence is there in this picture of a minority exercising the right to freedom of expression? Should this particular form of expression be protected? Why or why not?

❝ Unanimity is impossible; the rule of a minority, as a permanent arrangement, is wholly inadmissible; so that, rejecting the majority principle, anarchy, or despotism, in some form is all that is left.

Abraham Lincoln

❝ No democracy can long survive which does not accept as fundamental to its very existence the recognition of the rights of minorities.

Franklin D. Roosevelt

❝ When great changes occur in history, when great principles are involved, as a rule the majority are wrong. The minority are right.

Eugene Debs

❝ A nation is judged by how it treats its minorities.

René Lévesque

❝ All, too, will bear in mind this sacred principle, that though the will of the majority is in all cases to prevail, that will to be rightful must be reasonable; that the minority possess their equal rights, which equal law must protect, and to violate would be oppression.

Thomas Jefferson

❝ I admit the tyranny of majorities may be as bad as the tyranny of kings ... and I do not think any rational or sober man will say that what is justifiable against a tyrannical king may not under certain circumstances be justifiable against a tyrannical majority.

Arthur James Balfour

❝ My definition of a free society is a society where it is safe to be unpopular.

Adlai Stevenson

❝ Nor need we enquire whether similar considerations enter into the review of statutes directed at particular religious ... or national ... or racial minorities ... whether prejudice against discrete and insular minorities may be a special condition, which tends seriously to curtail the operation of those political processes ordinarily to be relied upon to protect minorities, and which may call for correspondingly more searching judicial inquiry.

Harlan F. Stone, *United States v. Carolene Products*, 304 U.S. 144 (1938)

❷ Which, if any, of these statements do you find most persuasive? Why?

CRITICAL THINKING EXERCISE 4

Positive versus Negative Rights

A major issue in the United States is health care reform. Health care services comprise about one-seventh of the nation's economy. Millions of Americans are not covered by private health insurance; neither can many afford medical care. State or national health care plans would mean a substantial expansion of government involvement in the private sector.

Is health care a fundamental right? Do governments have a compelling interest in the health and well-being of their citizens?

❶ How do the following statements apply to this situation? What principles and ideals are implied in each statement? How, if at all, do these principles conflict with each other?

> ❝ [To] promote the general Welfare.
>
> Preamble to the Constitution

> ❝ To make all Laws which shall be necessary and proper for carrying into Execution the foregoing Powers.
>
> Constitution, Article I, Section 8

> ❝ If, my countrymen, you wait for a constitution which absolutely bars a power of doing evil, you must wait long, and when obtained it will have no power of doing good.
>
> Oliver Ellsworth

> ❝ A government ought to contain in itself every power requisite to the full accomplishment of the objects committed to its care, and to the complete execution of the trusts for which it is responsible, free from every other control, but a regard to the public good and to the sense of the people.
>
> Alexander Hamilton

> ❝ I own I am not a friend to a very energetic government. It is always oppressive.
>
> Thomas Jefferson

❷ Should health care be considered a private or a public matter? Why?

❸ Should states have a greater responsibility than the national government for assuring adequate health care? Why?

❹ What is your position on this issue? Explain the reasons for your position in terms of the situation and the principles involved.

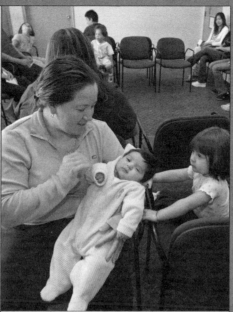

Should health care be considered a fundamental right of all Americans? Why or why not?

POSTSCRIPT

Our Constitution is a covenant running from the first generation of Americans to us and then to future generations. It is a coherent succession. Each generation must learn anew that the Constitution's written terms embody ideas and aspirations that must survive more ages than one.

U.S. Supreme Court Justices
Sandra Day O'Connor, Anthony
Kennedy, and David Hackett Souter,
Planned Parenthood v. Casey, 505
U.S. 833 (1992) (plurality opinion)

---

student page ▼ 301

CRITICAL THINKING EXERCISE 4

POSITIVE VERSUS NEGATIVE RIGHTS

The following are brief biographical sketches of the people quoted.

Oliver Ellsworth (1745–1807) A delegate to the Philadelphia Convention, Ellsworth helped to effect the Connecticut (Great) Compromise regarding representation in Congress. President George Washington appointed him chief justice of the United States. His opinions helped to shape admiralty and treaty law.

Alexander Hamilton (1757–1804) One of the authors of *The Federalist* and a leader in the Federalist Party, Hamilton served as the first secretary of the Treasury and put the nation's finances on a firm footing.

wtpcompanion.civiced.org BIOGRAPHIES

Visit the We the People companion website for brief printable and downloadable biographies of the people mentioned in the student and teacher's editions. Audio readings of each biography are also available online in MP3 format.

ENRICHMENT ACTIVITY

REFLECTING ON "CONSTITUTIONAL CITIZENSHIP"

Political scientist William F. Harris II has described "constitutional citizenship" as involving three dimensions:

- First is self-governance. This refers to the responsible exercise of private actions, such as making contracts, owning property, searching for and practicing a faith, and being a responsible family member.

- Second are activities associated with self-government, such as being informed about public issues, registering to vote, voting to elect representatives, participating directly in governance at the local, state, or national level, or serving on a jury or a public commission.

- Third is private activity that has positive public consequences, such as mentoring younger students or at-risk youth, volunteering at a youth or senior citizen center, or contributing time or money to civic causes.

Good constitutional citizenship requires devotion to all three.

Ask each student to write a letter to himself or herself in which the writer reflects on being a "constitutional citizen." The following are questions to guide the students' self-descriptions.

❶ Are you a "good" citizen? How might you be better?

❷ Do you excel at one or more particular aspects of constitutional citizenship but need to improve in others? Explain.

❸ What actions, if any, are you prepared to take to become a better constitutional citizen?

Ask students to put their letter away and promise to review it in ten years.

What are some of the fundamental responsibilities associated with the rights of citizens of the United States? What role should first principles play when citizens participate in politics and government?

302

Reference

THE VIRGINIA DECLARATION OF RIGHTS
JUNE 12, 1776

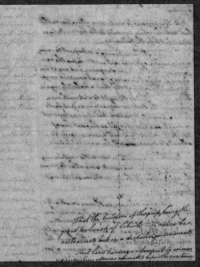

A DECLARATION OF RIGHTS made by the Representatives of the good people of VIRGINIA, assembled in full and free Convention; which rights do pertain to them and their posterity, as the basis and foundation of Government.

1 That all men are by nature equally free and independent, and have certain inherent rights, of which, when they enter into a state of society, they cannot, by any compact, deprive or divest their posterity; namely, the enjoyment of life and liberty, with the means of acquiring and possessing property, and pursuing and obtaining happiness and safety.

2 That all power is vested in, and consequently derived from, the People; that magistrates are their trustees and servants, and at all times amenable to them.

3 That Government is, or ought to be, instituted for the common benefit, protection, and security of the people, nation, or community; of all the various modes and forms of Government that is best which is capable of producing the greatest degree of happiness and safety, and is most effectually secured against the danger of maladministration; and that, whenever any Government shall be found inadequate or contrary to these purposes, a majority of the community hath an indubitable, unalienable, and indefeasible right, to reform, alter, or abolish it, in such manner as shall be judged most conducive to the publick weal.

4 That no man, or set of men, are entitled to exclusive or separate emoluments and privileges from the community, but in consideration of publick services; which, not being descendible, neither ought the offices of Magistrate, Legislator, or Judge, to be hereditary.

5 That the Legislative and Executive powers of the State should be separate and distinct from the Judicative; and, that the members of the two first may be restrained from oppression, by feeling and participating the burdens of the people, they should, at fixed periods, be reduced to a private station, return into that body from which they were originally taken, and the vacancies be supplied by frequent, certain, and regular elections, in which all, or any part of the former members, to be again eligible, or ineligible, as the law shall direct.

6 That elections of members to serve as Representatives of the people, in Assembly, ought to be free; and that all men, having sufficient evidence of permanent common interest with, and attachment to, the community, have the right of suffrage, and cannot be taxed or deprived of their property for publick uses without their own consent or that of their Representative so elected, nor bound by any law to which they have not, in like manner, assented, for the publick good.

7 That all power of suspending laws, or the execution of laws, by any authority, without consent of the Representatives of the people, is injurious to their rights, and ought not to be exercised.

8 That in all capital or criminal prosecutions a man hath a right to demand the cause and nature of his accusation, to be confronted with the accusers and witnesses, to call for evidence in his favour, and to a speedy trial by an impartial jury of his vicinage, without whose unanimous consent he cannot be found guilty, nor can he be compelled to give evidence against himself; that no man be deprived of his liberty except by the law of the land, or the judgment of his peers.

9 That excessive bail ought not to be required, nor excessive fines imposed, nor cruel and unusual punishments inflicted.

10 That general warrants, whereby any officer or messenger may be commanded to search suspected places without evidence of a fact committed, or to seize any person or persons not named, or whose offence is not particularly described and supported by evidence, are grievous and oppressive, and ought not to be granted.

11 That in controversies respecting property, and in suits between man and man, the ancient trial by Jury is preferable to any other, and ought to be held sacred.

12 That the freedom of the Press is one of the greatest bulwarks of liberty, and can never be restrained but by despotick Governments.

13 That a well-regulated Militia, composed of the body of the people, trained to arms, is the proper, natural, and safe defence of a free State; that Standing Armies, in time of peace, should be avoided as dangerous to liberty; and that, in all cases, the military should be under strict subordination to, and governed by, the civil power.

14 That the people have a right to uniform Government; and, therefore, that no Government separate from, or independent of, the Government of Virginia, ought to be erected or established within the limits thereof.

15 That no free Government, or the blessing of liberty, can be preserved to any people but by a firm adherence to justice, moderation, temperance, frugality, and virtue, and by frequent recurrence to fundamental principles.

16 That Religion, or the duty which we owe to our Creator, and the manner of discharging it, can be directed only by reason and conviction, not by force or violence; and, therefore, all men are equally entitled to the free exercise of religion, according to the dictates of conscience; and that it is the mutual duty of all to practice Christian forbearance, love, and charity, towards each other.

RALEIGH TAVERN
A painting depicts Patrick Henry, Thomas Jefferson, Richard Henry Lee, and Francis Lightfoot Lee establishing the Committee of Correspondence at Raleigh Tavern, Williamsburg, Virginia, in 1773. The tavern was a popular meeting place for Revolutionary patriots and the birthplace of the Virginia Declaration of Rights.

305

THE DECLARATION OF INDEPENDENCE
JULY 4, 1776

In CONGRESS, July 4, 1776.
The unanimous Declaration of the thirteen united States of America,

WHEN in the Course of human Events, it becomes necessary for one People to dissolve the Political Bands which have connected them with another, and to assume among the Powers of the Earth, the separate and equal Station to which the Laws of Nature and of Nature's God entitle them, a decent Respect to the Opinions of Mankind requires that they should declare the causes which impel them to the Separation.

We hold these Truths to be self-evident, that all Men are created equal, that they are endowed by their Creator with certain unalienable Rights, that among these are Life, Liberty, and the Pursuit of Happiness—That to secure these Rights, Governments are instituted among Men, deriving their just Powers from the Consent of the Governed, that whenever any Form of Government becomes destructive of these Ends it is the Right of the People to alter or to abolish it, and to institute new Government, laying its Foundation on such Principles, and organizing its Powers in such Form, as to them shall seem most likely to effect their Safety and Happiness. Prudence, indeed, will dictate that Governments long established should not be changed for light and transient Causes; and accordingly all Experience hath shewn, that Mankind are more disposed to suffer, while Evils are sufferable, than to right themselves by abolishing the Forms to which they are accustomed. But when a long Train of Abuses and Usurpations, pursuing invariably the same Object, evinces a Design to reduce them under absolute Despotism, it is their Right, it is their Duty, to throw off such Government, and to provide new Guards for their future Security. Such has been the patient Sufferance of these Colonies; and such is now the Necessity which constrains them to alter their former Systems of Government. The History of the present King of Great-Britain is a History of repeated Injuries and Usurpations, all having in direct Object the Establishment of an absolute Tyranny over these States. To prove this, let Facts be submitted to a candid World.

He has refused his Assent to Laws, the most wholesome and necessary for the public Good.

He has forbidden his Governors to pass Laws of immediate and pressing Importance, unless suspended in their Operation till his Assent should be obtained; and when so suspended, he has utterly neglected to attend to them.

He has refused to pass other Laws for the Accommodation of large Districts of People, unless those People would relinquish the Right of Representation in the Legislature, a Right inestimable to them, and formidable to Tyrants only.

He has called together Legislative Bodies at Places unusual, uncomfortable, and distant from the Depository of their public Records, for the sole Purpose of fatiguing them into Compliance with his Measures.

He has dissolved Representative Houses repeatedly, for opposing with manly Firmness his Invasions on the Rights of the People.

He has refused for a long Time, after such Dissolutions, to cause others to be elected; whereby the Legislative Powers, incapable of Annihilation, have returned to the People at large for their exercise; the State remaining in the mean time exposed to all the Dangers of Invasions from without, and Convulsions within.

He has endeavored to prevent the Population of these States; for that Purpose obstructing the Laws for Naturalization of Foreigners; refusing to pass others to encourage their Migrations hither, and raising the Conditions of new Appropriations of Lands.

He has obstructed the Administration of Justice, by refusing his Assent to Laws for establishing Judiciary Powers.

He has made Judges dependent on his Will alone, for the Tenure of their Offices, and the Amount and Payment of their Salaries.

He has erected a Multitude of new Offices, and sent hither Swarms of Officers to harass our People and eat out their Substance.

He has kept among us, in Times of Peace, Standing Armies, without the consent of our Legislatures.

He has affected to render the Military independent of and superior to the Civil Power.

He has combined with others to subject us to a Jurisdiction foreign to our Constitution, and unacknowledged by our Laws; giving his Assent to their Acts of pretended Legislation:

For quartering large Bodies of Armed Troops among us:

For protecting them, by a mock Trial, from Punishment for any Murders which they should commit on the Inhabitants of these States:

For cutting off our Trade with all Parts of the World:

For imposing Taxes on us without our Consent:

For depriving us, in many Cases, of the Benefits of Trial by Jury:

For transporting us beyond Seas to be tried for pretended Offenses:

For abolishing the free System of English Laws in a neighbouring Province, establishing therein an Arbitrary Government, and enlarging its Boundaries, so as to render it at once an Example and fit Instrument for introducing the same absolute Rule into these Colonies:

For taking away our Charters, abolishing our most valuable Laws, and altering fundamentally the Forms of our Governments:

For suspending our own Legislatures, and declaring themselves invested with Power to legislate for us in all Cases whatsoever.

He has abdicated Government here, by declaring us out of his Protection and waging War against us.

He has plundered our Seas, ravaged our Coasts, burnt our Towns, and destroyed the Lives of our People.

He is, at this Time, transporting large Armies of foreign Mercenaries to compleat the Works of Death, Desolation, and Tyranny, already begun with circumstances of Cruelty and Perfidy, scarcely paralleled in the most barbarous Ages, and totally unworthy the Head of a civilized Nation.

He has constrained our fellow Citizens taken Captive on the high Seas to bear Arms against their Country, to become the Executioners of their Friends and Brethren, or to fall themselves by their Hands.

He has excited domestic Insurrections amongst us, and has endeavoured to bring on the Inhabitants of our Frontiers, the merciless Indian Savages, whose known Rule of Warfare, is an undistinguished Destruction, of all Ages, Sexes and Conditions.

In every stage of these Oppressions we have Petitioned for Redress in the most humble Terms: Our repeated Petitions have been answered only by repeated Injury. A Prince, whose Character is thus marked by every act which may define a Tyrant, is unfit to be the Ruler of a free People.

Nor have we been wanting in Attentions to our British Brethren. We have warned them from Time to Time of Attempts by their Legislature to extend an unwarrantable Jurisdiction over us. We have reminded them of the Circumstances of our Emigration and Settlement here. We have appealed to their native Justice and Magnanimity, and we have conjured them by the Ties of our common Kindred to disavow these Usurpations, which, would inevitably interrupt our Connections and Correspondence. They too have been deaf to the Voice of Justice and of Consanguinity. We must, therefore, acquiesce in the Necessity, which denounces our Separation, and hold them, as we hold the rest of Mankind, Enemies in War, in Peace, Friends.

We, therefore, the Representatives of the UNITED STATES OF AMERICA, in GENERAL CONGRESS, Assembled, appealing to the Supreme Judge of the World for the Rectitude of our Intentions, do, in the Name, and by Authority of the good People of these Colonies, solemnly Publish and Declare, That these United Colonies are, and of Right ought to be, FREE AND INDEPENDENT STATES; that they are absolved from all Allegiance to the British Crown, and that all political Connection between them and the State of Great Britain, is and ought to be totally dissolved; and that as FREE AND INDEPENDENT STATES, they have full Power to levy War, conclude Peace, contract Alliances, establish Commerce, and to do all other Acts and Things which INDEPENDENT STATES may of right do. And for the support of this Declaration, with a firm Reliance on the Protection of divine Providence, we mutually pledge to each other our Lives, our Fortunes, and our sacred Honor.

307

Signed by ORDER and
in BEHALF of the CONGRESS,

JOHN HANCOCK, PRESIDENT.

New-Hampshire
Josiah Bartlett,
Wm. Whipple,
Matthew Thornton.

Massachusetts-Bay
Saml. Adams,
John Adams,
Robt. Treat Paine,
Elbridge Gerry.

Rhode-Island and Providence, &c.
Step. Hopkins,
William Ellery.

Connecticut
Roger Sherman,
Saml. Huntington,
Wm. Williams,
Oliver Wolcott.

New-York
Wm. Floyd,
Phil. Livingston,
Frans. Lewis,
Lewis Morris.

New-Jersey
Richd. Stockton,
Jno. Witherspoon,
Fras. Hopkinson,
John Hart,
Abra. Clark.

Pennsylvania
Robt. Morris,
Benjamin Rush,
Benja. Franklin,
John Morton,
Geo. Clymer,
Jas. Smith,
Geo. Taylor,

James Wilson,
Geo. Ross.

Delaware
Casar Rodney,
Geo. Read,
(Tho M.Kean.)

Maryland
Samuel Chase,
Wm. Paca,
Thos. Stone,
Charles Carroll,
    of Carrollton.

Virginia
George Wythe,
Richard Henry Lee,
Ths. Jefferson,
Benja. Harrison,
Thos. Nelson, jr.,
Francis Lightfoot Lee,
Carter Braxton.

North-Carolina
Wm. Hooper,
Joseph Hewes,
John Penn.

South-Carolina
Edward Rutledge,
Thos. Heyward, junr.,
Thomas Lynch, junr.,
Arthur Middleton.

Georgia
Button Gwinnett,
Lyman Hall,
Geo. Walton.

309

THE ARTICLES OF CONFEDERATION
NOVEMBER 15, 1777

**Agreed to by Congress November 15, 1777;
ratified and in force, March 1, 1781**

TO ALL TO WHOM these Presents shall come, we the undersigned Delegates of the States affixed to our Names send greeting. Whereas the Delegates of the United States of America in Congress assembled did on the fifteenth day of November in the Year of our Lord One Thousand Seven Hundred and Seventy seven, and in the Second Year of the Independence of America agree to certain articles of Confederation and perpetual Union between the States of Newhampshire, Massachusetts-bay, Rhodeisland and Providence Plantations, Connecticut, New York, New Jersey, Pennsylvania, Delaware, Maryland, Virginia, North-Carolina, South Carolina and Georgia in the Words following, viz. "Articles of Confederation and perpetual Union between the states of Newhampshire, Massachusetts-bay, Rhodeisland and Providence Plantations, Connecticut, New-York, New-Jersey, Pennsylvania, Delaware, Maryland, Virginia, North-Carolina, South-Carolina and Georgia.

ART. I.

The Stile of this confederacy shall be "The United States of America."

ART. II.

Each state retains its sovereignty, freedom and independence, and every Power, Jurisdiction and right, which is not by this confederation expressly delegated to the United States, in Congress assembled.

ART. III.

The said states hereby severally enter into a firm league of friendship with each other, for their common defence, the security of their Liberties, and their mutual and general welfare, binding themselves to assist each other, against all force offered to, or attacks made upon them, or any of them, on account of religion, sovereignty, trade, or any other pretence whatever.

ART. IV.

The better to secure and perpetuate mutual friendship and intercourse among the people of the different states in this union, the free inhabitants of each of these states, paupers, vagabonds and fugitives from Justice excepted, shall be entitled to all privileges and immunities of free citizens in the several states; and the people of each state shall have free ingress and regress to and from any other state, and shall enjoy therein all the privileges of trade and commerce, subject to the same duties, impositions and restrictions as the inhabitants thereof respectively, provided that such restriction shall not extend so far as to prevent the removal of property imported into any state, to any other state of which the Owner is an inhabitant; provided also that no imposition, duties or restriction shall be laid by any state, on the property of the united states, or either of them.

If any Person guilty of, or charged with treason, felony, or other high misdemeanor in any state, shall flee from Justice, and be found in any of the united states, he shall upon demand of the Governor or executive power, of the state from which he fled, be delivered up and removed to the state having jurisdiction of his offence.

Full faith and credit shall be given in each of these states to the records, acts and judicial proceedings of the courts and magistrates of every other state.

ART. V.

For the more convenient management of the general interests of the united states, delegates shall be annually appointed in such manner as the legislature of each state shall direct, to meet in Congress on the first Monday in November, in every year, with a power reserved to each state, to recal its delegates, or any of them, at any time within the year, and to send others in their stead, for the remainder of the Year.

No state shall be represented in Congress by less than two, nor by more than seven Members; and no person shall be capable of being a delegate for more than three years in any term of six years; nor shall any person, being a delegate, be capable of holding any office under the united states, for which he, or another for his benefit receives any salary, fees or emolument of any kind.

Each state shall maintain its own delegates in a meeting of the states, and while they act as members of the committee of the states.

In determining questions in the united states, in Congress assembled, each state shall have one vote.

Freedom of speech and debate in Congress shall not be impeached or questioned in any Court, or place out of Congress, and the members of congress shall be protected in their persons from arrests and imprisonments, during the time of their going to and from, and attendance on congress, except for treason, felony, or breach of the peace.

ART. VI.

No state without the Consent of the united states in congress assembled, shall send any embassy to, or receive any embassy from, or enter into any conference, agreement, or alliance or treaty with any King, prince or state; nor shall any person holding any office of profit or trust under the united states, or any of them, accept of any present, emolument, office or title of any kind whatever from any king, prince or foreign state; nor shall the united states in congress assembled, or any of them, grant any title of nobility.

No two or more states shall enter into any treaty, confederation or alliance whatever between them, without the consent of the united states in congress assembled, specifying accurately the purposes for which the same is to be entered into, and how long it shall continue.

No state shall lay any imposts or duties, which may interfere with any stipulations in treaties, entered into by the united states in congress assembled, with any king, prince or state, in pursuance of any treaties already proposed by congress, to the courts of France and Spain.

No vessels of war shall be kept up in time of peace by any state, except such number only, as shall be deemed necessary by the united states in congress assembled, for the defence of such state, or its trade; nor shall any body of forces be kept up by any state, in time of peace, except such number only, as in the judgment of the united states, in congress assembled, shall be deemed requisite to garrison the forts necessary for the defence of such state; but every state shall always keep up a well regulated and disciplined militia, sufficiently armed and accoutred, and shall provide and constantly have ready for use, in public stores, a due number of field pieces and tents, and a proper quantity of arms, ammunition and camp equipage.

No state shall engage in any war without the consent of the united states in congress assembled, unless such state be actually invaded by enemies, or shall have received certain advice of a resolution being formed by some nation of Indians to invade such state, and the danger is so imminent as not to admit of a delay, till the united states in congress assembled can be consulted: nor shall any state grant commissions to any ships or vessels of war, nor letters of marque or reprisal, except it be after a declaration of war by the united states in congress assembled, and then only against the kingdom or state and the subjects thereof, against which war has been so declared, and under such regulations as shall be established by the united states in congress assembled, unless such state be infested by pirates, in which case vessels of war may be fitted out for that occasion, and kept so long as the danger shall continue, or until the united states in congress assembled shall determine otherwise.

ART. VII.

When land-forces are raised by any state for the common defence, all officers of or under the rank of colonel, shall be appointed by the legislature of each state respectively by whom such forces shall be raised, or in such manner as such state shall direct, and all vacancies shall be filled up by the state which first made the appointment.

ART. VIII.

All charges of war, and all other expences that shall be incurred for the common defence or general welfare, and allowed by the united states in congress assembled, shall be defrayed out of a common treasury, which shall be supplied by the several states, in proportion to the value of all land within each state, granted to or surveyed for any Person, as such land and the buildings and improvements thereon shall be estimated according to such mode as the united states in congress assembled, shall from time to time direct and appoint. The taxes for paying that proportion shall be laid and levied by the authority and direction of the legislatures of the several states within the time agreed upon by the united states in congress assembled.

ART. IX.

The united states in congress assembled, shall have the sole and exclusive right and power of determining on peace and war, except in the cases mentioned in the sixth article—of sending and receiving ambassadors—entering into treaties and alliances, provided that no treaty of commerce shall be made whereby the legislative power of the respective states shall be restrained from imposing such imposts and duties on foreigners, as their own people are subjected to, or from prohibiting the exportation or importation of any species of goods or commodities whatsoever—of establishing rules for deciding in all cases, what captures on land or water shall be legal, and in what manner prizes taken by land or naval forces in the service of the united states shall be divided or appropriated—of granting letters of marque and reprisal in times of peace—appointing courts for the trial of piracies and felonies committed on the high seas and establishing courts for receiving and determining finally appeals in all cases of captures, provided that no member of congress shall be appointed a judge of any of the said courts.

The united states in congress assembled shall also be the last resort on appeal in all disputes and differences now subsisting or that hereafter may arise between two or more states concerning boundary, jurisdiction or any other cause whatever; which authority shall always be exercised in the manner following. Whenever the legislative or executive authority or lawful agent of any state in controversy with another shall present a petition to congress, stating the matter in question and praying for a hearing, notice thereof shall be given by order of congress to the legislative or executive authority of the other state in controversy, and a day assigned for the appearance of the parties by their lawful agents, who shall then be directed to appoint by joint consent, commissioners or judges to constitute a court for hearing and determining the matter in question: but if they cannot agree, congress shall name three persons out of each of the united states, and from the list of such persons each party shall alternately strike out one, the petitioners beginning, until the number shall be reduced to thirteen; and from that number not less than seven, nor more than nine names as congress shall direct, shall in the presence of congress be drawn out by lot, and the persons whose names shall be so drawn or any five of them, shall be commissioners or judges, to hear and finally determine the controversy, so always as a major part of the judges who shall hear the cause shall agree in the determination: and if either party shall neglect to attend at the day appointed, without shewing reasons, which congress shall judge sufficient, or being present shall refuse to strike, the congress shall proceed to nominate three persons out of each state, and the secretary of congress shall strike in behalf of such party absent or refusing; and the judgment and sentence of the court to be appointed, in the manner before prescribed, shall be final and conclusive; and if any of the parties shall refuse to submit to the authority of such court, or to appear to defend their claim or cause, the court shall nevertheless proceed to pronounce sentence, or judgment, which shall in like manner be final and decisive, the judgment or sentence and other proceedings being in either case transmitted to congress, and lodged among the acts of congress for the security of the parties concerned: provided that every commissioner, before he sits in judgment, shall take an oath to be administered by one of the judges of the supreme or superior court of the state, where the cause shall be tried, "well and truly to hear and determine the matter in question, according to the best of his judgment, without favour, affection or hope of reward:" provided also that no state shall be deprived of territory for the benefit of the united states.

All controversies concerning the private right of soil claimed under different grants of two or more states, whose jurisdictions as they may respect such lands, and the states which passed such grants are adjusted, the said grants or either of them being at the same time claimed to have originated antecedent to such settlement of jurisdiction, shall on the petition of either party to the congress of the united states, be finally determined as near as may be in the same manner as is before prescribed for deciding disputes respecting territorial jurisdiction between different states.

The united states in congress assembled shall also have the sole and exclusive right and power of regulating the alloy and value of coin struck by their own authority, or by that of the respective states—fixing the standard of weights and measures throughout the united states—regulating the trade and managing all affairs with the Indians, not members of any of the states, provided that the legislative right of any state within its own limits be not infringed or violated—establishing and regulating post-offices from one state to another throughout all the united states, and exacting such postage on the papers passing thro' the same as may be requisite to defray the expences of the said office—appointing all officers of the land forces, in the service of the united states, excepting regimental officers.—appointing all the officers of the naval forces, and commissioning all officers whatever in the service of the united states—making rules for the government and regulation of the said land and naval forces, and directing their operations.

The united states in congress assembled shall have authority to appoint a committee, to sit in the recess of congress, to be denominated "A Committee of the States," and to consist of one delegate from each state; and to appoint such other committees and civil officers as may be necessary for managing the general affairs of the united states under their direction—to appoint one of their number to preside, provided that no person be allowed to serve in the office of president more than one year in any term of three years; to ascertain the necessary sums of Money to be raised for the service of the united states, and to appropriate and apply the same for defraying the public expences—to borrow money, or emit bills on the credit of the united states, transmitting every half year to the respective states an account of the sums of money so borrowed or emitted,—to build and equip a navy—to agree upon the number of land forces, and to make requisitions from each state for its quota, in proportion to the number of white inhabitants in such state; which requisition shall be binding, and thereupon the legislature of each state shall appoint the regimental officers, raise the men and cloath, arm and equip them in a soldier like manner, at the expence of the united states, and the officers and men so cloathed, armed and equipped shall march to the place appointed, and within the time agreed on by the united states in congress assembled: But if the united states in congress assembled shall, on consideration of circumstances judge proper that any state should not raise men, or should raise a smaller number than its quota, and that any other state should raise a greater number of men than the quota thereof, such extra number shall be raised, officered, cloathed, armed and equipped in the same manner as the quota of such state, unless the legislature of such state shall judge that such extra number cannot be safely spared out of the same, in which case they shall raise officer, cloath, arm and equip as many of such extra number as they judge can be safely spared. And the officers and men so cloathed, armed and equipped, shall march to the place appointed, and within the time agreed on by the united states in congress assembled.

The united states in congress assembled shall never engage in a war, nor grant letters of marque and reprisal in time of peace, nor enter into any treaties or alliances, nor coin money, nor regulate the value thereof, nor ascertain the sums and expences necessary for the defence and welfare of the united states, or any of them, nor emit bills, nor borrow money on the credit of the united states, nor appropriate money, nor agree upon the number of vessels of war, to be built or purchased, or the number of land or sea forces to be raised, nor appoint a commander in chief of the army or navy, unless nine states assent to the same: nor shall a question on any other point, except for adjourning from day to day be determined unless by the votes of a majority of the united states in congress assembled.

The Congress of the United States shall have power to adjourn to any time within the year, and to any place within the united states, so that no period of adjournment be for a longer duration than the space of six Months, and shall publish the Journal of their proceedings monthly, except such parts thereof relating to treaties, alliances or military operations as in their judgement require secresy; and the yeas and nays of the delegates of each state on any question shall be entered on the Journal, when it is desired by any delegate; and the delegates of a state, or any of them, at his or their request shall be furnished with a transcript of the said Journal, except such parts as are above excepted, to lay before the legislatures of the several states.

ART. X.

The committee of the states, or any nine of them, shall be authorized to execute, in the recess of congress, such of the powers of congress as the United States in congress assembled, by the consent of nine states, shall from time to time think expedient to vest them with; provided that no power be delegated to the said committee, for the exercise of which, by the articles of confederation, the voice of nine states in the congress of the united states assembled is requisite.

ART. XI.

Canada acceding to this confederation, and joining in the measures of the united states, shall be admitted into, and entitled to all the advantages of this union: but no other colony shall be admitted into the same, unless such admission be agreed to by nine states.

ART. XII.

All bills of credit emitted, monies borrowed and debts contracted by, or under the authority of congress, before the assembling of the united states, in pursuance of the present confederation, shall be deemed and considered as a charge against the united states, for payment and satisfaction whereof the said united states, and the public faith are hereby solemnly pledged.

ART. XIII.

Every state shall abide by the determinations of the united states in congress assembled, on all questions which by this confederation are submitted to them. And the Articles of this confederation shall be inviolably observed by every state, and the union shall be perpetual; nor shall any alteration at any time hereafter be made in any of them; unless such alteration be agreed to in a congress of the united states, and be afterwards confirmed by the legislatures of every state.

AND WHEREAS it hath pleased the Great Governor of the World to incline the hearts of the legislatures we respectively represent in congress, to approve of, and to authorize us to ratify the said articles of confederation and perpetual union. KNOW YE that we the under-signed delegates, by virtue of the power and authority to us given for that purpose, do by these presents, in the name and in behalf of our respective constituents, fully and entirely ratify and confirm each and every of the said articles of confederation and perpetual union, and all and singular the matters and things therein contained: And we do further solemnly plight and engage the faith of our respective constituents, that they shall abide by the determinations of the united states in congress assembled, on all questions, which by the said confederation are submitted to them. And that the articles thereof shall be inviolably observed by the states we respectively represent, and that the union shall be perpetual. In Witness whereof we have hereunto set our hands in Congress. Done at Philadelphia in the state of Pennsylvania the ninth Day of July in the Year of our Lord one Thousand seven Hundred and Seventy-eight, and in the third year of the independence of America.

313

SIGNERS OF THE ARTICLES OF CONFEDERATION

Josiah Bartlett
John Wentworth, junr
August 8th 1778
On the part & behalf of
the State of New Hampshire

John Hancock
Samuel Adams
Elbridge Gerry
Francis Dana
James Lovell
Samuel Holten
On the part and behalf of
The State of Massachusetts Bay

William Ellery
Henry Marchant
John Collins
On the part and behalf of the State of
Rhode-Island and Providence Plantations

Roger Sherman
Samuel Huntington
Oliver Wolcott
Titus Hosmer
Andrew Adams
On the part and behalf of the State of Connecticut

Jas Duane
Fras Lewis
Wm Duer
Gouvr Morris
On the Part and Behalf of the State of New York

Jno Witherspoon
Nathl Scudder
On the Part and in Behalf of the State
of New Jersey, November 26, 1778.

Robert Morris
Daniel Roberdeau
Jon. Bayard Smith
William Clingan
Joseph Reed,
22d July 1778
On the part and behalf of the State
of Pennsylvania

Thos McKean,
Feby 12d, 1779
John Dickinson
May 5th, 1779
Nicholas Van Dyke
On the part & behalf of the State of Delaware

John Hanson,
March 1, 1781
Daniel Carroll, do
On the part and behalf of the State of Maryland

Richard Henry Lee
John Banister
Thomas Adams
Jno Harvie
Francis Lightfoot Lee
On the Part and Behalf of the State of Virginia

John Penn,
July 21st, 1778
Corns Harnett
Jno Williams
On the part and behalf of the State
of North Carolina

Henry Laurens
William Henry Drayton
Jno Mathews
Richd Hutson
Thos Heyward, Junr
On the part & behalf of the State
of South Carolina

Jno Walton,
24th July 1778
Edwd Telfair
Edwd Langworthy
On the part & behalf of the State of Georgia

JOHN DICKINSON
(1732–1808) Dickinson, one of the wealthiest of the British colonists, gained renown as the author of "Letters from a Farmer in Pennsylvania" supporting American liberty. The essay, composed of twelve letters, was widely read; this success contributed to the unification of the colonies against the Townshend Acts.

315

THE CONSTITUTION OF THE UNITED STATES OF AMERICA

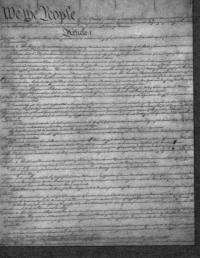

PREAMBLE

We the People of the United States, in Order to form a more perfect Union, establish Justice, insure domestic tranquility, provide for the common defense, promote the general Welfare, and secure the Blessings of Liberty to ourselves and our Posterity, do ordain and establish this Constitution for the United States of America.

ARTICLE I
THE LEGISLATIVE BRANCH

Section 1

All legislative Powers herein granted shall be vested in a Congress of the United States, which shall consist of a Senate and House of Representatives.

Section 2
House of Representatives:
Organization and Power of Impeachment

❶ The House of Representatives shall be composed of Members chosen every second Year by the People of the several States, and the Electors in each State shall have the Qualifications requisite for Electors of the most numerous Branch of the State Legislature.

❷ No Person shall be a Representative who shall not have attained to the Age of twenty five Years, and been seven Years a Citizen of the United States, and who shall not, when elected, be an Inhabitant of that State in which he shall be chosen.

❸ [Representatives and direct Taxes shall be apportioned among the several States which may be included within this Union, according to their respective Numbers, which shall be determined by adding to the whole Number of free Persons, including those bound to Service for a Term of Years, and excluding Indians not taxed, three fifths of all other Persons.]* The actual Enumeration shall be made within three Years after the first Meeting of the Congress of the United States, and within every subsequent Term of ten Years, in such Manner as they shall by Law direct. The number of Representatives shall not exceed one for every thirty Thousand, but each State shall have at Least one Representative; and until such enumeration shall be made, the State of New Hampshire shall be entitled to choose three, Massachusetts eight, Rhode Island and Providence Plantations one, Connecticut five, New York six, New Jersey four, Pennsylvania eight, Delaware one, Maryland six, Virginia ten, North Carolina five, South Carolina five, and Georgia three.

❹ When vacancies happen in the Representation from any State, the Executive Authority thereof shall issue Writs of Election to fill such Vacancies.

❺ The House of Representatives shall choose their Speaker and other Officers; and shall have the sole Power of Impeachment.

* Changed by Section 2 of the Fourteenth Amendment

Section 3
The Senate: Organization and Powers to Try Cases of Impeachment

❶ The Senate of the United States shall be composed of two Senators from each State, chosen [by the Legislature thereof,]** for six Years; and each Senator shall have one Vote.

❷ Immediately after they shall be assembled in Consequence of the first Election, they shall be divided as equally as may be into three Classes. The seats of the Senators of the first Class shall be vacated at the Expiration of the second Year, of the second Class at the Expiration of the fourth Year, and of the third Class at the Expiration of the sixth Year, so that one third may be chosen every second Year; [and if Vacancies happen by Resignation, or otherwise, during the Recess of the Legislature of any State, the Executive thereof may make temporary Appointments until the next Meeting of the Legislature, which shall then fill such Vacancies.]**

❸ No Person shall be a Senator who shall not have attained to the Age of thirty Years, and been nine Years a Citizen of the United States, and who shall not, when elected, be an Inhabitant of that State for which he shall be chosen.

❹ The Vice President of the United States shall be President of the Senate, but shall have no Vote, unless they be equally divided.

❺ The Senate shall choose their other officers, and also a President pro tempore, in the Absence of the Vice President, or when he shall exercise the Office of President of the United States.

❻ The Senate shall have the sole Power to try all Impeachments. When sitting for that Purpose, they shall be on Oath or Affirmation. When the President of the United States is tried, the Chief Justice shall preside; And no person shall be convicted without the Concurrence of two thirds of the Members present.

❼ Judgment in Cases of Impeachment shall not extend further than to removal from Office, and disqualification to hold and enjoy any Office of honor, Trust or Profit under the United States; but the Party convicted shall nevertheless be liable and subject to Indictment, Trial, Judgment and Punishment, according to Law.

Section 4
Elections and Meeting of Congress

❶ The Times, Places and Manner of holding Elections for Senators and Representatives shall be prescribed in each State by the Legislature thereof; but the Congress may at any time by Law make or alter such Regulations, except as to the Places of choosing Senators.

❷ The Congress shall assemble at least once in every Year, and such Meeting shall be [on the first Monday in December,]*** unless they shall by Law appoint a different Day.

Section 5
Congress's Rules of Procedure, Powers, Quorum, Journals, Meetings, Adjournments

❶ Each House shall be the Judge of the Elections, Returns and Qualifications of its own Members, and a Majority of each shall constitute a Quorum to do Business; but a smaller Number may adjourn from day to day, and may be authorized to compel the Attendance of absent Members, in such Manner, and under such Penalties as each House may provide.

❷ Each House may determine the Rules of its Proceedings, punish its members for disorderly Behavior, and, with the Concurrence of two thirds, expel a Member.

❸ Each House shall keep a Journal of its Proceedings, and from time to time publish the same, excepting such Parts as may in their Judgement require Secrecy; and the Yeas and Nays of the Members of either House on any question shall, at the Desire of one fifth of those Present, be entered on the Journal.

❹ Neither House, during the Session of Congress, shall, without the Consent of the other, adjourn for more than three days, nor to any other Place than that in which the two Houses shall be sitting.

Section 6
Pay, Privileges, Limitations

❶ The Senators and Representatives shall receive a Compensation for their Services, to be ascertained by Law, and paid out of the Treasury of the United States. They shall in all cases, except Treason, Felony and Breach of the Peace, be privileged from Arrest during their Attendance at the Session of their respective Houses, and in going to and returning from the same; and for any Speech or Debate in either House, they shall not be questioned in any other Place.

❷ No Senator or Representative shall, during the Time for which he was elected, be appointed to any civil Office under the Authority of the United States, which shall have been created, or the Emoluments whereof shall have been increased during such time; and no Person holding any Office under the United States, shall be a Member of either House during his Continuance in Office.

** Changed by the Seventeenth Amendment

*** Changed by Section 2 of the Twentieth Amendment

Section 7
Procedure in Passing Bills, President's Veto Power

① All Bills for raising Revenue shall originate in the House of Representatives; but the Senate may propose or concur with Amendments as on other Bills.

② Every Bill which shall have passed the House of Representatives and the Senate, shall, before it becomes a Law, be presented to the President of the United States; if he approves he shall sign it, but if not he shall return it, with his Objections, to that House in which it shall have originated, who shall enter the Objections at large on their Journal, and proceed to reconsider it. If after such Reconsideration two thirds of that House shall agree to pass the Bill, it shall be sent, together with the Objections, to the other House, by which it shall likewise be reconsidered, and if approved by two thirds of that House, it shall become a Law. But in all such Cases the Votes of both Houses shall be determined by Yeas and Nays, and the Names of the Persons voting for and against the Bill shall be entered on the Journal of each House respectively. If any Bill shall not be returned by the President within ten Days (Sundays excepted) after it shall have been presented to him, the Same shall be a Law, in like Manner as if he had signed it, unless the Congress by their adjournment prevent its Return, in which Case it shall not be a Law.

③ Every Order, Resolution, or Vote to which the Concurrence of the Senate and House of Representatives may be necessary (except on a question of Adjournment) shall be presented to the President of the United States; and before the Same shall take Effect, shall be approved by him, or being disapproved by him, shall be repassed by two thirds of the Senate and House of Representatives, according to the Rules and Limitations prescribed in the Case of a Bill.

Section 8
Powers Delegated to Congress

The Congress shall have Power

① To lay and collect Taxes, Duties, Imposts and Excises, to pay the Debts and provide for the common Defense and general Welfare of the United States; but all Duties, Imposts and Excises shall be uniform throughout the United States;

② To borrow Money on the credit of the United States;

③ To regulate Commerce with foreign Nations, and among the several States, and with the Indian Tribes;

④ To establish a uniform Rule of Naturalization, and uniform Laws on the subject of Bankruptcies throughout the United States;

⑤ To coin Money, regulate the Value thereof, and of foreign Coin, and fix the Standard of Weights and Measures;

⑥ To provide for the Punishment of counterfeiting the Securities and current Coin of the United States;

⑦ To establish Post Offices and post Roads;

⑧ To promote the Progress of Science and useful Arts, by securing for limited Times to Authors and Inventors the exclusive Right to their respective Writings and Discoveries;

⑨ To constitute Tribunals inferior to the Supreme Court;

⑩ To define and punish Piracies and Felonies committed on the high Seas, and Offenses against the Law of Nations;

⑪ To declare War, grant Letters of Marque and Reprisal, and make Rules concerning Captures on Land and Water;

⑫ To raise and support Armies, but no Appropriation of Money to that Use shall be for a longer Term than two Years;

⑬ To provide and maintain a Navy;

⑭ To make Rules for the Government and Regulation of the land and naval Forces;

⑮ To provide for calling forth the Militia to execute the Laws of the Union, suppress Insurrections and repel Invasions;

⑯ To provide for organizing, arming, and disciplining the Militia, and for governing such Part of them as may be employed in the Service of the United States, reserving to the States respectively, the Appointment of the Officers, and the Authority of training the Militia according to the discipline prescribed by Congress;

⑰ To exercise exclusive Legislation in all Cases whatsoever, over such District (not exceeding ten Miles square) as may, by Session of particular States, and the Acceptance of Congress, become the Seat of the Government of the United States, and to exercise like Authority over all Places purchased by the Consent of the Legislature of the State in which the Same shall be, for the Erection of Forts, Magazines, Arsenals, dock-Yards and other needful Buildings;—and

⑱ To make all Laws which shall be necessary and proper for carrying into Execution the foregoing Powers, and all other Powers vested by this Constitution in the Government of the United States, or in any Department or Officer thereof.

Section 9
Powers Denied to Congress

❶ The Migration or Importation of such Persons as any of the States now existing shall think proper to admit, shall not be prohibited by the Congress prior to the Year one thousand eight hundred and eight, but a Tax or duty may be imposed on such Importation, not exceeding ten dollars for each Person.

❷ The Privilege of the Writ of Habeas Corpus shall not be suspended, unless when in Cases of Rebellion or Invasion the public Safety may require it.

❸ No Bill of Attainder or ex post facto Law shall be passed.

❹ [No Capitation, or other direct, Tax shall be laid, unless in Proportion to the Census or Enumeration herein before directed to be taken.]*

❺ No Tax or Duty shall be laid on Articles exported from any State.

❻ No Preference shall be given by any Regulation of Commerce or Revenue to the Ports of one State over those of another; nor shall Vessels bound to, or from, one State, be obliged to enter, clear, or pay Duties in another.

❼ No Money shall be drawn from the Treasury, but in Consequence of Appropriations made by Law; and a regular Statement and Account of the Receipts and Expenditures of all public Money shall be published from time to time.

❽ No Title of Nobility shall be granted by the United States: And no Person holding any Office of Profit or Trust under them, shall, without the Consent of the Congress, accept of any present, Emolument, Office, or Title, of any kind whatever, from any King, Prince, or foreign State.

Section 10
Restrictions on States' Powers

❶ No State shall enter into any Treaty, Alliance, or Confederation; grant Letters of Marque and Reprisal; coin Money; emit Bills of Credit; make any Thing but gold and silver Coin a Tender in Payment of Debts; pass any Bill of Attainder, ex post facto Law, or Law impairing the Obligation of Contracts, or grant any Title of Nobility.

❷ No State shall, without the Consent of the Congress, lay any Imposts or Duties on Imports or Exports, except what may be absolutely necessary for executing its inspection Laws: and the net Produce of all Duties and Imposts, laid by any State on Imports or Exports, shall be for the Use of the Treasury of the United States; and all such Laws shall be subject to the Revision and Control of the Congress.

❸ No State shall, without the Consent of Congress, lay any Duty of Tonnage, keep Troops, or Ships of War in time of Peace, enter into any Agreement or Compact with another State, or with a foreign Power, or engage in War, unless actually invaded, or in such imminent Danger as will not admit of delay.

ARTICLE II
THE EXECUTIVE BRANCH
Section 1
President and Vice President: Election, Qualifications, and Oath

❶ The executive Power shall be vested in a President of the United States of America. He shall hold his Office during the term of four Years, and, together with the Vice President, chosen for the same Term, be elected, as follows.

❷ Each State shall appoint, in such Manner as the Legislature thereof may direct, a Number of Electors, equal to the whole Number of Senators and Representatives to which the State may be entitled in the Congress: but no Senator or Representative, or Person holding an Office of Trust or Profit under the United States, shall be appointed an Elector.

❸ [The Electors shall meet in their respective states, and vote by Ballot for two Persons, of whom one at least shall not be an Inhabitant of the same State with themselves. And they shall make a List of all the Persons voted for, and of the Number of Votes for each; which List they shall sign and certify, and transmit sealed to the Seat of the Government of the United States, directed to the President of the Senate. The President of the Senate shall, in the Presence of the Senate and House of Representatives, open all the Certificates, and the Votes shall then be counted. The Person having the greatest Number of Votes shall be the President, if such Number be a Majority of the whole Number of Electors appointed; and if there be more than one who have such Majority, and have an equal Number of Votes, then the House of Representatives shall immediately choose by Ballot one of them for President; and if no Person have a Majority, then from the five highest on the List the said House shall in like manner choose the President. But in choosing the President, the Votes shall be taken by States, the Representation from each State having one Vote; A quorum for this Purpose shall consist of a Member or Members from two thirds of the States, and a Majority of all the States shall be necessary to a Choice. In every Case, after the Choice of the President, the Person having the greatest Number of Votes of the Electors shall

* Changed by the Sixteenth Amendment

be the Vice President. But if there should remain two or more who have equal Votes, the Senate shall choose from them by Ballot the Vice President.]*

❹ The Congress may determine the Time of choosing the Electors, and the day on which they shall give their Votes; which Day shall be the same throughout the United States.

❺ No Person except a natural born Citizen, or a Citizen of the United States at the time of the Adoption of this Constitution, shall be eligible to the Office of the President; neither shall any person be eligible to that Office who shall not have attained to the Age of thirty five Years, and been fourteen Years a Resident within the United States.

❻ [In Case of the Removal of the President from Office, or of his Death, Resignation, or Inability to discharge the Powers and Duties of the said Office, the Same shall devolve on the Vice President, and the Congress may by Law provide for the Case of Removal Death, Resignation or Inability, both of the President and Vice President, declaring what Officer shall then act as President, and such Officer shall act accordingly, until the Disability be removed, or a President shall be elected.]**

❼ The President shall, at stated Times, receive for his Services, a Compensation, which shall neither be increased nor diminished during the Period for which he shall have been elected, and he shall not receive within that Period any other Emolument from the United States, or any of them.

❽ Before he enter the Execution of his Office, he shall take the following Oath or Affirmation:— "I do solemnly swear (or affirm) that I will faithfully execute the Office of President of the United States, and will to the best of my Ability, preserve, protect, and defend the Constitution of the United States."

Section 2
Powers of the President

❶ The President shall be Commander in Chief of the Army and Navy of the United States, and of the Militia of the several States, when called into the actual Service of the United States; he may require the Opinion, in writing, of the principal Officer in each of the executive Departments, upon any Subject relating to the Duties of their respective Offices, and he shall have Power to grant Reprieves and Pardons for Offenses against the United States, except in Cases of Impeachment.

❷ He shall have Power, by and with the Advice and Consent of the Senate, to make Treaties, provided two thirds of the Senators present concur; and he

shall nominate, and by and with the Advice and Consent of the Senate, shall appoint Ambassadors, other public Ministers and Consuls, Judges of the supreme Court, and all other Officers of the United States, whose Appointments are not herein otherwise provided for, and which shall be established by Law: but the Congress may by Law vest the Appointment of such inferior Officers, as they think proper, in the President alone, in the Courts of Law, or in the Heads of Departments.

❸ The President shall have Power to fill up all Vacancies that may happen during the Recess of the Senate, by granting Commissions which shall expire at the End of their next Session.

Section 3
Duties of the President

He shall from time to time give to the Congress Information of the State of the Union, and recommend to their Consideration such Measures as he shall judge necessary and expedient; he may, on extraordinary Occasions, convene both Houses, or either of them, and in Case of Disagreement between them, with Respect to the Time of Adjournment, he may adjourn them to such Time as he shall think proper; he shall receive Ambassadors and other public Ministers; he shall take Care that the Laws be faithfully executed, and shall Commission all the Officers of the United States.

Section 4
Impeachment and Removal from Office for Crimes

The President, Vice President and all civil Officers of the United States, shall be removed from Office on Impeachment for, and Conviction of, Treason, Bribery, or other high Crimes and Misdemeanors.

ARTICLE III
THE JUDICIAL BRANCH

Section 1
Federal Courts, Tenure of Office

The judicial Power of the United States, shall be vested in one supreme Court, and in such inferior Courts as the Congress may from time to time ordain and establish. The Judges, both of the supreme and inferior Courts, shall hold their Offices during good Behavior, and shall, at stated Times, receive for their Services a Compensation, which shall not be diminished during their Continuance in Office.

Section 2
Jurisdiction of Federal Courts

❶ The judicial Power shall extend to all Cases, in Law and Equity, arising under this Constitution, the Laws of the United States, and Treaties made, or which shall be made, under their Authority;— to all Cases affecting Ambassadors, other public Ministers and Consuls; —to all Cases of admiralty

*   Changed by the Twelfth Amendment
** Changed by the Twentieth-fifth Amendment

and maritime Jurisdiction;—to Controversies to which the United States shall be a Party;—to Controversies between two or more States; [between a State and Citizens of another State;]*** between Citizens of different States;—between Citizens of the same State claiming Lands under Grants of different States;—[and between a State, or the Citizens thereof, and foreign States, Citizens or Subjects.]***

❷ In all Cases affecting Ambassadors, other public Ministers and Consuls, and those in which a State shall be Party, the supreme Court shall have original Jurisdiction. In all the other Cases before mentioned, the supreme Court shall have appellate Jurisdiction, both as to Law and Fact, with such Exceptions, and under such Regulations as the Congress shall make.

❸ The Trial of all Crimes, except in Cases of Impeachment, shall be by Jury; and such Trial shall be held in the State where said Crimes shall have been committed; but when not committed within any State, the Trial shall be at such Place or Places as the Congress may by Law have directed.

Section 3
Treason: Conviction Of and Punishment For

❶ Treason against the United States shall consist only in levying War against them, or in adhering to their Enemies, giving them Aid and Comfort. No Person shall be convicted of Treason unless on the Testimony of two Witnesses to the same overt Act, or on Confession in open Court.

❷ The Congress shall have Power to declare the Punishment of Treason, but no Attainder of Treason shall work Corruption of Blood, or Forfeiture except during the Life of the Person attainted.

ARTICLE IV
RELATIONS AMONG THE STATES

Section 1
Full Faith and Credit

Full Faith and Credit shall be given in each State to the public Acts, Records, and judicial Proceedings of every other State; And the Congress may by general Laws prescribe the manner in which such Acts, Records and Proceedings shall be proved, and the Effect thereof.

Section 2
Rights of State Citizens; Right of Extradition

❶ The Citizens of each State shall be entitled to all Privileges and Immunities of Citizens in the several States.

❷ A Person charged in any State with Treason, Felony, or other Crime, who shall flee from Justice,

and be found in another State, shall on Demand of the executive Authority of the State from which he fled, be delivered up, to be removed to the State having Jurisdiction of the Crime.

❸ [No person held to Service or Labour in one State, under the Laws thereof, escaping into another, shall, in Consequence of any Law or Regulation therein, be discharged from such Service or Labour, but shall be delivered up on Claim of the Party to whom such Service or Labour may be due.]****

Section 3
Admission of New States

❶ New States may be admitted by the Congress into this Union; but no new State shall be formed or erected within the Jurisdiction of any other State; nor any State be formed by the Junction of two or more States, or parts of States, without the Consent of the Legislatures of the States concerned as well as of the Congress.

❷ The Congress shall have Power to dispose of and make all needful Rules and Regulations respecting the territory or other Property belonging to the United States; and nothing in this Constitution shall be so construed as to Prejudice any Claims of the United States, or of any particular State.

Section 4
Republican Government Guaranteed

The United States shall guarantee to every State in this Union a Republican Form of Government, and shall protect each of them against Invasion; and on Application of the Legislature, or of the Executive (when the Legislature cannot be convened) against domestic Violence.

ARTICLE V
AMENDMENT PROCEDURES

The Congress, whenever two thirds of both Houses shall deem it necessary, shall propose Amendments to this Constitution, or, on the Application of the Legislatures of two thirds of the several States, shall call a Convention for proposing Amendments, which, in either Case, shall be valid to all Intents and Purposes, as Part of this Constitution, when ratified by the Legislatures of three fourths of the several States, or by Conventions in three fourths thereof, as the one or the other Mode of Ratification may be proposed by the Congress; Provided that no Amendment which may be made prior to the Year One thousand eight hundred and eight shall in any Manner affect the first and fourth Clauses in the Ninth Section of the first Article; and that no State, without its Consent, shall be deprived of its equal Suffrage in the Senate.

*** Changed by the Eleventh Amendment

**** Changed by the Thirteenth Amendment

ARTICLE VI
SUPREMACY OF THE
CONSTITUTION AND FEDERAL LAWS

❶ All debts contracted and Engagements entered into, before the Adoption of this Constitution, shall be as valid against the United States under this Constitution, as under the Confederation.

❷ This Constitution, and the Laws of the United States which shall be made in Pursuance thereof; and all Treaties made, or which shall be made, under the Authority of the United States, shall be the supreme Law of the Land; and the Judges in every State shall be bound thereby, any Thing in the Constitution or Laws of any State to the Contrary notwithstanding.

❸ The Senators and Representatives before mentioned, and the Members of the several State Legislatures, and all executive and judicial Officers, both of the United States and of the several States, shall be bound by Oath or Affirmation, to support this Constitution; but no religious Test shall ever be required as a Qualification to any Office or public Trust under the United States.

ARTICLE VII
RATIFICATION

The Ratification of the Conventions of nine States, shall be sufficient for the Establishment of this Constitution between the States so ratifying the Same.

Done in Convention by the unanimous consent of the States present the seventeenth day of September in the year of our Lord one thousand seven hundred and eighty seven and of the Independence of the United States of America the Twelfth. In witness whereof we have hereunto subscribed our Names,

President and deputy from Virginia
George Washington

New-Hampshire
John Langdon
Nicholas Gilman

Massachusetts
Nathaniel Gorham
Rufus King

Connecticut
William Samuel Johnson
Roger Sherman

New York
Alexander Hamilton

New Jersey
William Livingston
David Brearley
William Paterson
Jonathan Dayton

Pennsylvania
Benjamin Franklin
Thomas Mifflin
Robert Morris
George Clymer
Thomas Fitzsimons
Jared Ingersoll
James Wilson
Gouverneur Morris

Delaware
George Read
Gunning Bedford, Jr.
John Dickinson
Richard Bassett
Jacob Broom

Maryland
James McHenry
Daniel of St. Tho. Jenifer
Daniel Carroll

Virginia
John Blair
James Madison, Jr.

North Carolina
William Blount
Richard Dobbs Spaight
Hugh Williamson

South Carolina
John Rutledge
Charles Cotesworth Pinckney
Charles Pinckney
Pierce Butler

Georgia
William Few
Abraham Baldwin

Attest:
William Jackson, Secretary

The Constitution was adopted in Philadelphia on September 17, 1787, by the Constitutional Convention and was declared ratified on July 2, 1788.

JAMES MADISON

(1751–1836) Madison is considered the "Father of the Constitution" for his role as principal author of the document, as well as "Father of the Bill of Rights" for drafting the first ten amendments to the U.S. Constitution. He served as Thomas Jefferson's secretary of state and eventually became the nation's fourth president, holding office from 1809 to 1817.

AMENDMENTS TO THE CONSTITUTION OF THE UNITED STATES OF AMERICA

AMENDMENT I

Congress shall make no law respecting an establishment of religion, or prohibiting the free exercise thereof; or abridging the freedom of speech, or of the press; or the right of the people peaceably to assemble, and to petition the Government for a redress of grievances.

AMENDMENT II

A well regulated Militia, being necessary to the security of a free State, the right of the people to keep and bear Arms, shall not be infringed.

AMENDMENT III

No Soldier shall, in time of peace be quartered in any house, without the consent of the Owner, nor in time of war, but in a manner to be prescribed by law.

AMENDMENT IV

The right of the people to be secure in their persons, houses, papers, and effects, against unreasonable searches and seizures, shall not be violated, and no Warrants shall issue, but upon probable cause, supported by Oath or affirmation, and particularly describing the place to be searched, and the persons or things to be seized.

AMENDMENT V

No person shall be held to answer for a capital, or otherwise infamous crime, unless on a presentment or indictment of a Grand Jury, except in cases arising in the land or naval forces, or in the Militia, when in actual service in time of War or public danger; nor shall any person be subject for the same offence to be twice put in jeopardy of life or limb; nor shall be compelled in any criminal case to be a witness against himself, nor be deprived of life, liberty, or property, without due process of law; nor shall private property be taken for public use, without just compensation.

AMENDMENT VI

In all criminal prosecutions, the accused shall enjoy the right to a speedy and public trial, by an impartial jury of the State and district wherein the crime shall have been committed, which district shall have been previously ascertained by law, and to be informed of the nature and cause of the accusation; to be confronted with the witnesses against him; to have compulsory process for obtaining witnesses in his favor, and to have the Assistance of Counsel for his defence.

AMENDMENT VII

In Suits at common law, where the value in controversy shall exceed twenty dollars, the right of trial by jury shall be preserved, and no fact tried by a jury, shall be otherwise re-examined in any Court of the United States, than according to the rules of the common law.

AMENDMENT VIII

Excessive bail shall not be required, nor excessive fines imposed, nor cruel and unusual punishments inflicted.

AMENDMENT IX

The enumeration in the Constitution, of certain rights, shall not be construed to deny or disparage others retained by the people.

AMENDMENT X

The powers not delegated to the United States by the Constitution, nor prohibited by it to the States, are reserved to the States respectively, or to the people. [The first ten amendments were ratified December 15, 1791.]

AMENDMENT XI

The Judicial power of the United States shall not be construed to extend to any suit in law or equity, commenced or prosecuted against one of the United States by Citizens of another State, or by Citizens or Subjects of any Foreign State. [Ratified February 1795.]

AMENDMENT XII

The Electors shall meet in their respective states and vote by ballot for President and Vice-President, one of whom, at least, shall not be an inhabitant of the same state with themselves; they shall name in their ballots the person voted for as President, and in distinct ballots the person voted for as Vice-President, and they shall make distinct lists of all persons voted for as President, and of all persons voted for as Vice-President, and of the number of votes for each, which lists they shall sign and certify, and transmit sealed to the seat of the government of the United States, directed to the President of the Senate;—the President of the Senate shall, in the presence of the Senate and House of Representatives, open all the certificates and the votes shall then be counted;—The person having the greatest number of votes for President, shall be the President, if such number be a majority of the whole number of Electors appointed; and if no person have such majority, then from the persons having the highest numbers not exceeding three on the list of those voted for as President, the House of Representatives shall choose immediately by ballot, the President. But in choosing the President, the votes shall be taken by states, the representation from each state having one vote; a quorum for this purpose shall consist of a member or members from two-thirds of the states, and a majority of all the states shall be necessary to a choice. [And if the House of Representatives shall not choose a President whenever the right of choice shall devolve upon them, before the fourth day of March next following, then the Vice-President shall act as President, as in the case of the death or other constitutional disability of the President .—]*
The person having the greatest number of votes as Vice-

President, shall be the Vice-President, if such number be a majority of the whole number of Electors appointed, and if no person have a majority, then from the two highest numbers on the list, the Senate shall choose the Vice-President; a quorum for the purpose shall consist of two-thirds of the whole number of Senators, and a majority of the whole number shall be necessary to a choice. But no person constitutionally ineligible to the office of President shall be eligible to that of Vice-President of the United States. [Ratified June 1804.]

AMENDMENT XIII

Section 1

Neither slavery nor involuntary servitude, except as a punishment for crime whereof the party shall have been duly convicted, shall exist within the United States, or any place subject to their jurisdiction.

Section 2

Congress shall have power to enforce this article by appropriate legislation. [Ratified December 1865.]

AMENDMENT XIV

Section 1

All persons born or naturalized in the United States and subject to the jurisdiction thereof, are citizens of the United States, and of the State wherein they reside. No State shall make or enforce any law which shall abridge the privileges or immunities of citizens of the United States; nor shall any State deprive any person of life, liberty, or property, without due process of law; nor deny to any person within its jurisdiction the equal protection of the laws.

Section 2

Representatives shall be apportioned among the several States according to their respective numbers, counting the whole number of persons in each State, excluding Indians not taxed. But when the right to vote at any election for the choice of electors for President and Vice-President of the United States, Representatives in Congress, the Executive and Judicial officers of a State, or the members of the Legislature thereof, is denied to any of the male inhabitants of such State, being twenty-one years of age,** and citizens of the United States, or in any way abridged, except for participation in rebellion, or other crime, the basis of representation therein shall be reduced in the proportion which the number of such male citizens shall bear to the whole number of male citizens twenty-one years of age in such State.

Section 3

No person shall be a Senator or Representative in Congress, or elector of President and Vice-President, or hold any office, civil or military, under the United States, or under any State, who, having previously taken

---

* Superseded by Section 3 of the Twentieth Amendment

** Changed by Section 1 of the Twenty-sixth Amendment

an oath, as a member of Congress, or as an officer of the United States, or as a member of any State legislature, or as an executive or judicial officer of any State, to support the Constitution of the United States, shall have engaged in insurrection or rebellion against the same, or given aid or comfort to the enemies thereof. But Congress may by a vote of two-thirds of each House, remove such disability.

Section 4

The validity of the public debt of the United States, authorized by law, including debts incurred for payment of pensions and bounties for services in suppressing insurrection or rebellion, shall not be questioned. But neither the United States nor any State shall assume or pay any debt or obligation incurred in aid of insurrection or rebellion against the United States, or any claim for the loss or emancipation of any slave; but all such debts, obligations and claims shall be held illegal and void.

Section 5

The Congress shall have the power to enforce, by appropriate legislation, the provisions of this article. [Ratified July 1868.]

AMENDMENT XV

Section 1

The right of citizens of the United States to vote shall not be denied or abridged by the United States or by any State on account of race, color, or previous condition of servitude.

Section 2

The Congress shall have the power to enforce this article by appropriate legislation. [Ratified February 1870.]

AMENDMENT XVI

The Congress shall have power to lay and collect taxes on incomes, from whatever source derived, without apportionment among the several States, and without regard to any census or enumeration. [Ratified February 1913.]

AMENDMENT XVII

The Senate of the United States shall be composed of two Senators from each State, elected by the people thereof, for six years; and each Senator shall have one vote. The electors in each State shall have the qualifications requisite for electors of the most numerous branch of the State legislatures. When vacancies happen in the representation of any State in the Senate, the executive authority of such State shall issue writs of election to fill such vacancies: *Provided*, That the legislature of any State may empower the executive thereof to make temporary appointments until the people fill the vacancies by election as the legislature may direct. This amendment shall not be so construed as to affect the election or term of any Senator chosen before it becomes valid as part of the Constitution. [Ratified April 1913.]

AMENDMENT XVIII

Section 1

After one year from the ratification of this article the manufacture, sale, or transportation of intoxicating liquors within, the importation thereof into, or the exportation thereof from the United States and all territory subject to the jurisdiction thereof for beverage purposes is hereby prohibited.

Section 2

The Congress and the several States shall have concurrent power to enforce this article by appropriate legislation.

Section 3

This article shall be inoperative unless it shall have been ratified as an amendment to the Constitution by the legislatures of the several States, as provided in the Constitution, within seven years from the date of the submission hereof to the States by the Congress. [Ratified January 1919.]*

AMENDMENT XIX

The right of citizens of the United States to vote shall not be denied or abridged by the United States or by any State on account of sex. Congress shall have power to enforce this article by appropriate legislation. [Ratified August 1920.]

AMENDMENT XX

Section 1

The terms of the President and the Vice President shall end at noon on the 20th day of January, and the terms of Senators and Representatives at noon on the 3rd day of January, of the years in which such terms would have ended if this article had not been ratified; and the terms of their successors shall then begin.

Section 2

The Congress shall assemble at least once in every year, and such meeting shall begin at noon on the 3rd day of January, unless they shall by law appoint a different day.

Section 3

If, at the time fixed for the beginning of the term of the President, the President elect shall have died, the Vice President elect shall become President. If a President shall not have been chosen before the time fixed for the beginning of his term, or if the President elect shall have failed to qualify, then the Vice President elect shall act as President until a President shall have qualified; and the Congress may by law provide for

---

* Repealed by the Twenty-first Amendment

the case wherein neither a President elect nor a Vice President elect shall have qualified, declaring who shall then act as President, or the manner in which one who is to act shall be selected, and such person shall act accordingly until a President or Vice President shall have qualified.

Section 4

The Congress may by law provide for the case of the death of any of the persons from whom the House of Representatives may choose a President whenever the right of choice shall have devolved upon them, and for the case of the death of any of the persons from whom the Senate may choose a Vice President whenever the right of choice shall have devolved upon them.

Section 5

Sections 1 and 2 shall take effect on the 15th day of October following the ratification of this article.

Section 6

This article shall be inoperative unless it shall have been ratified as an amendment to the Constitution by the legislatures of three-fourths of the several States within seven years from the date of its submission. [Ratified January 1933.]

AMENDMENT XXI

Section 1

The eighteenth article of amendment to the Constitution of the United States is hereby repealed.

Section 2

The transportation or importation into any State, Territory, or Possession of the United States for delivery or use therein of intoxicating liquors, in violation of the laws thereof, is hereby prohibited.

Section 3

This article shall be inoperative unless it shall have been ratified as an amendment to the Constitution by conventions in the several States, as provided in the Constitution, within seven years from the date of the submission hereof to the States by the Congress. [Ratified December 1933.]

AMENDMENT XXII

Section 1

No person shall be elected to the office of the President more than twice, and no person who has held the office of President, or acted as President, for more than two years of a term to which some other person was elected President shall be elected to the office of the President more than once. But this Article shall not apply to any person holding the office of President when this Article was proposed by the Congress, and shall not prevent any person who may be holding the office of President, or acting as President, during the term within which this Article becomes operative from holding the office of President or acting as President during the remainder of such term.

Section 2

This article shall be inoperative unless it shall have been ratified as an amendment to the Constitution by the legislatures of three-fourths of the several States within seven years from the date of its submission to the States by the Congress. [Ratified February 1951.]

AMENDMENT XXIII

Section 1

The District constituting the seat of Government of the United States shall appoint in such manner as the Congress may direct: A number of electors of President and Vice President equal to the whole number of Senators and Representatives in Congress to which the District would be entitled if it were a State, but in no event more than the least populous State; they shall be in addition to those appointed by the States, but they shall be considered, for the purposes of the election of President and Vice President, to be electors appointed by a State; and they shall meet in the District and perform such duties as provided by the twelfth article of amendment.

Section 2

The Congress shall have power to enforce this article by appropriate legislation. [Ratified March 1961.]

AMENDMENT XXIV

Section 1

The right of citizens of the United States to vote in any primary or other election for President or Vice President, for electors for President or Vice President, or for Senator or Representative in Congress, shall not be denied or abridged by the United States or any State by reason of failure to pay any poll tax or other tax.

Section 2

The Congress shall have power to enforce this article by appropriate legislation. [Ratified January 1964.]

AMENDMENT XXV

Section 1

In case of the removal of the President from office or of his death or resignation, the Vice President shall become President.

Section 2

Whenever there is a vacancy in the office of the Vice President, the President shall nominate a Vice President who shall take office upon confirmation by a majority vote of both Houses of Congress.

Section 3

Whenever the President transmits to the President pro tempore of the Senate and the Speaker of the House of Representatives his written declaration that he is unable to discharge the powers and duties of his office, and until he transmits to them a written declaration to the contrary, such powers and duties shall be discharged by the Vice President as Acting President.

Section 4

Whenever the Vice President and a majority of either the principal officers of the executive departments or of such other body as Congress may by law provide, transmit to the President pro tempore of the Senate and the Speaker of the House of Representatives their written declaration that the President is unable to discharge the powers and duties of his office, the Vice President shall immediately assume the powers and duties of the office as Acting President.

Thereafter, when the President transmits to the President pro tempore of the Senate and the Speaker of the House of Representatives his written declaration that no inability exists, he shall resume the powers and duties of his office unless the Vice President and a majority of either the principal office of the executive department or of such other body as Congress may by law provide, transmit within four days to the President pro tempore of the Senate and the Speaker of the House of Representatives their written declaration that the President is unable to discharge the powers and duties of his office. Thereupon Congress shall decide the issue, assembling within forty-eight hours for that purpose if not in session. If the Congress, within twenty-one days after receipt of the latter written declaration, or, if Congress is not in session, within twenty-one days after Congress is required to assemble, determines by two-thirds vote of both Houses that the President is unable to discharge the powers and duties of his office, the Vice President shall continue to discharge the same as Acting President; otherwise, the President shall resume the powers and duties of his office. [Ratified February 1967.]

AMENDMENT XXVI

Section 1

The right of citizens of the United States, who are eighteen years of age or older, to vote shall not be denied or abridged by the United States or by any State on account of age.

Section 2

The Congress shall have power to enforce this article by appropriate legislation. [Ratified July 1971.]

AMENDMENT XXVII

No law, varying the compensation for the services of the Senators or Representatives, shall take effect, until an election of Representatives shall have intervened. [Ratified May 1992.]

GEORGE MASON

(1725–1792) Mason, a delegate from Virginia at the U.S. Continental Congress, led the effort to include individual rights in the Constitution, refusing to sign until such rights were made explicit. The resulting Bill of Rights was based on Mason's own work: the Virginia Declaration of Rights.

329

CONGRESSIONAL HEARING

A congressional hearing is a meeting or session of a Senate, House, special, or joint committee. The purpose of a hearing can be to

❶ Obtain information and opinions about proposed legislation, including agency budgets

❷ Conduct an investigation

❸ Evaluate or oversee the activities of a government department of the implementation of a congressional law

❹ Acquire information about presidential nominees for purposes of confirmation

Hearings also may simply explore topics of current interest. Hearings usually are held in House or Senate committee hearing rooms in the U.S. Capitol, but they also can occur in other parts of the country. Hearings almost always are open to the public, except when hearings involve national security or classified information. Most congressional hearings are published two months to two years after they occur. A catalog of available House and Senate hearings is available online through the Government Printing Office (GPO) Access.

The usual steps in a congressional hearing are as follows:

❶ **NOTICE OF HEARING AND LIST OF TENTATIVE WITNESSES**

The press secretaries of the committee chair and committee members send out notices describing the purpose of the hearing, when it will be held, and a tentative list of witnesses. A person who wishes to be invited to testify can contact any member of the committee or the person's representative or Senator. If the committee wishes to hear from a witness, it invites that person's testimony.

❷ **OPENING STATEMENTS**

The chair convenes the hearing and usually makes a statement about the purpose of the hearing and what the committee hopes to accomplish. The ranking minority member of the committee also makes a brief opening statement. On rare occasions, such as during confirmation hearings of nominees to the United States Supreme Court, other committee members may also be allowed to make brief opening statements.

❸ **WITNESS TESTIMONY**

Before the hearing, committee staff informs witnesses about the desired time limit of their testimony. Witnesses usually are required to submit written copies of their testimony to staff at least two days before the hearing. Written testimony is entered into the official committee record. Rather than reading their entire testimony at the hearing, witnesses are encouraged to provide only a summary.

❹ AT THE HEARING, THE CHAIRS CALL ON WITNESSES WHO HAVE BEEN INVITED TO PRESENT TESTIMONY

Witnesses introduce themselves and explain their interest in the subject of the hearing. They then present a summary of their prepared testimony that describes the problem or issue and states what action they want the committee to take. Witnesses who share common interests frequently consult with one another about their written statements and testimony. They also often hold strategy meetings to discuss how to present their testimony effectively.

❺ COMMITTEE QUESTIONS

Members of the committee then may ask witnesses about their testimony. Chairs can invite questions from members of the majority party, then members of the minority party, or alternate between parties. Sometimes questions elicit further facts or information from the witness. Sometimes the questions reveal the member's views on the subject and criticize the witness's testimony. Witnesses frequently offer to provide additional information after the hearing in response to questions.

❻ CONCLUSION

Sometimes committee members wish to make statements at the conclusion of all the testimony. After these statements, the chair closes the hearing.

331

► EXECUTIVE ORDER 9981

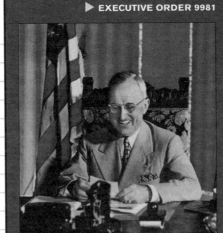

PRESIDENT HARRY S. TRUMAN
(1884–1972) During his term as thirty-third president of the United States from 1945 until 1953, Truman saw the end of World War II and the beginning of the Cold War.

▼ BRIEFING A SUPREME COURT OPINION

CHIEF JUSTICE JOHN MARSHALL
(1755–1835) A Federalist leader, John Marshall was the fourth chief justice of the U.S. Supreme Court, serving from 1801 until his death in 1835. Chief Justice Marshall presided over *Marbury v. Madison*, in which, for the first time, an act of Congress was ruled unconstitutional.

► EXECUTIVE ORDER

An executive order is a directive from the president to an administrative agency. The Constitution does not explicitly authorize such orders, but the power to issue them is assumed to come from the provision in Article II, Section 1, directing the president to "take Care that the Laws be faithfully executed." President George Washington issued the first executive order in 1789.

Below is an example of an executive order. It was issued by President Harry S. Truman on July 26, 1948.

EXECUTIVE ORDER 9981
DESEGREGATION OF THE ARMED FORCES

"WHEREAS it is essential that there be maintained in the armed services of the United States the highest standards of democracy, with equality of treatment and opportunity for all those who serve in our country's defense:

"NOW THEREFORE, by virtue of the authority vested in me as President of the United States, by the Constitution and the statutes of the United States, and as Commander in Chief of the armed services, it is hereby ordered as follows:

1. It is hereby declared to be the policy of the President that there shall be equality of treatment and opportunity for all persons in the armed services without regard to race, color, religion or national origin. This policy shall be put into effect as rapidly as possible, having due regard to the time required to effectuate any necessary changes without impairing efficiency or morale.

2. There shall be created in the National Military Establishment an advisory committee to be known as the President's Committee on Equality of Treatment and Opportunity in the Armed Services, which shall be composed of seven members to be designated by the President.

3. The Committee is authorized on behalf of the President to examine into the rules, procedures and practices of the Armed Services in order to determine in what respect such rules, procedures and practices may be altered or improved with a view to carrying out the policy of this order."

THE WHITE HOUSE
July 26, 1948

▼ BRIEFING A SUPREME COURT OPINION

Supreme Court decisions can be difficult to read. Some justices use specialized legal terms and write long sentences or paragraphs. They also make complicated arguments. Often legal citations are placed within sentences, making it necessary to read the sentence several times to understand the meaning. Opinions usually contain the following elements, although not always in the order presented below. Reading an opinion by looking for these elements makes it easier to understand the opinion.

❶ STATEMENT OF FACTS

Every case involves particular individuals or groups and is based on specific facts. Identify the parties, what led them to this lawsuit, and why they think they are entitled to win. Sometimes the facts are in one place, usually early in the opinion. Other times, the facts are scattered throughout the opinion.

❷ EXPLANATION OF LOWER COURT DECISIONS

The Supreme Court usually reviews the decisions of lower courts. Its opinion will explain how the trial court ruled, and whether the court of appeals or highest state court affirmed or reversed the decision of the trial court. Often the opinion will also state how other courts in the United States have ruled on the legal issue involved in the case.

❸ DESCRIPTION OF LEGAL ISSUE OR ISSUES

Legal issues often can be stated as questions. For example, "Does the state's requirement that trucks traveling through the state use mud flaps produced in the state violate the Commerce Clause?" Most issues focus on the meaning of a statute or a provision of the Constitution.

❹ HOLDING

This portion of an opinion describes how the court answers the legal issue. For example, "we hold that the Constitution was violated when [the] demand for a jury trial was refused."

❺ STATEMENT OF THE LAW

In deciding the case, the court announces a rule of law. The rule is statement about the meaning of a statute or a provision of the Constitution. For example, "The power of Congress over interstate commerce is... complete in itself, may be exercised to its utmost extent, and acknowledges no lim-

itations other than are prescribed in the Constitution." The rule of law is a broad statement that applies generally, not just to the facts of the particular case.

❻ APPLICATION OF THE LAW TO THE FACTS

After it has stated the law, the court explains how the law applies to the facts of the case. Sometimes this portion of the opinion is called the "holding," because it explains which party wins based on application of the law to the facts.

❼ CONCURRING AND/OR DISSENTING OPINIONS

A justice who agrees with the result but not with the majority's reasoning, can write an opinion explaining his or her reasoning. A justice who disagrees with the opinion can write a dissenting opinion. Sometimes a dissent disagrees with the statement of the law. Sometimes it argues that the majority did not correctly apply the law to the facts. Future courts sometimes look to concurring and dissenting opinions for guidance in changing their interpretations of the law. Justice Benjamin Curtis's dissent in *Dred Scott v. Sandford* (1857) is an example of an influential dissent.

Writing a summary of an opinion using this format is called "briefing" the case. Preparing a brief is a good way to make sure you understand the opinion.

THE UNIVERSAL DECLARATION OF HUMAN RIGHTS, 1948

JOHN PETERS HUMPHREY

(1905–1995) As the first director of the Human Rights Division of the United Nations Secretariat, Canadian professor John Peters Humphrey prepared the principal draft of the Universal Declaration of Human Rights, ratified on December 10, 1948. Eleanor Roosevelt, a co-creator of the declaration, deemed it "the international Magna Carta of all humankind."

PREAMBLE

Whereas recognition of the inherent dignity and of the equal and inalienable rights of all members of the human family is the foundation of freedom, justice and peace in the world,

Whereas disregard and contempt for human rights have resulted in barbarous acts which have outraged the conscience of mankind, and the advent of a world in which human beings shall enjoy freedom of speech and belief and freedom from fear and want has been proclaimed as the highest aspiration of the common people,

Whereas it is essential, if man is not to be compelled to have recourse, as a last resort, to rebellion against tyranny and oppression, that human rights should be protected by the rule of law,

Whereas it is essential to promote the development of friendly relations between nations,

Whereas the peoples of the United Nations have in the Charter reaffirmed their faith in fundamental human rights, in the dignity and worth of the human person and in the equal rights of men and women and have determined to promote social progress and better standards of life in larger freedom,

Whereas Member States have pledged themselves to achieve, in cooperation with the United Nations, the promotion of universal respect for and observance of human rights and fundamental freedoms,

Whereas a common understanding of these rights and freedoms is of the greatest importance for the full realization of this pledge,

Now, therefore,
THE GENERAL ASSEMBLY Proclaims
THIS UNIVERSAL DECLARATION OF HUMAN RIGHTS as a common standard of achievement for all peoples and all nations, to the end that every individual and every organ of society, keeping this Declaration constantly in mind, shall strive by teaching and education to promote respect for these rights and freedoms and by progressive measures, national and international, to secure their universal and effective recognition and observance, both among the peoples of Member States themselves and among the peoples of territories under their jurisdiction.

ARTICLE 1

All human beings are born free and equal in dignity and rights. They are endowed with reason and conscience and should act towards one another in a spirit of brotherhood.

ARTICLE 2

Everyone is entitled to all the rights and freedoms set forth in this Declaration, without distinction of any kind, such as race, colour, sex, language, religion, political or other opinion, national or social origin, property, birth or other status. Furthermore, no distinction shall be made on the basis of the political, jurisdictional or international status of the country or territory to which a person belongs, whether it be independent, trust, non-self-governing or under any other limitation of sovereignty.

ARTICLE 3

Everyone has the right to life, liberty and the security of person.

ARTICLE 4

No one shall be held in slavery or servitude; slavery and the slave trade shall be prohibited in all their forms.

ARTICLE 5

No one shall be subjected to torture or to cruel, inhuman or degrading treatment or punishment.

ARTICLE 6

Everyone has the right to recognition everywhere as a person before the law.

ARTICLE 7

All are equal before the law and are entitled without any discrimination to equal protection of the law. All are entitled to equal protection against any discrimination in violation of this Declaration and against any incitement to such discrimination.

ARTICLE 8

Everyone has the right to an effective remedy by the competent national tribunals for acts violating the fundamental rights granted him by the constitution or by law.

ARTICLE 9

No one shall be subjected to arbitrary arrest, detention or exile.

ARTICLE 10

Everyone is entitled in full equality to a fair and public hearing by an independent and impartial tribunal, in the determination of his rights and obligations and of any criminal charge against him.

ARTICLE 11

1. Everyone charged with a penal offence has the right to be presumed innocent until proved guilty according to law in a public trial at which he has had all the guarantees necessary for his defence.

2. No one shall be held guilty of any penal offence on account of any act or omission which did not constitute a penal offence, under national or international law, at the time when it was committed. Nor shall a heavier penalty be imposed than the one that was applicable at the time the penal offence was committed.

ARTICLE 12

No one shall be subjected to arbitrary interference with his privacy, family, home or correspondence, nor to attacks upon his honour and reputation. Everyone has the right to the protection of the law against such interference or attacks.

ARTICLE 13

1. Everyone has the right to freedom of movement and residence within the borders of each State.

2. Everyone has the right to leave any country, including his own, and to return to his country.

ARTICLE 14

1. Everyone has the right to seek and to enjoy in other countries asylum from persecution.

2. This right may not be invoked in the case of prosecutions genuinely arising from non-political crimes or from acts contrary to the purposes and principles of the United Nations.

ARTICLE 15

1. Everyone has the right to a nationality.

2. No one shall be arbitrarily deprived of his nationality nor denied the right to change his nationality.

ARTICLE 16

1. Men and women of full age, without any limitation due to race, nationality or religion, have the right to marry and to found a family. They are entitled to equal rights as to marriage, during marriage and at its dissolution.

2. Marriage shall be entered into only with the free and full consent of the intending spouses.

3. The family is the natural and fundamental group unit of society and is entitled to protection by society and the State.

ARTICLE 17

1. Everyone has the right to own property alone as well as in association with others.

2. No one shall be arbitrarily deprived of his property.

ARTICLE 18

Everyone has the right to freedom of thought, conscience and religion; this right includes freedom to change his religion or belief, and freedom, either alone or in community with others and in public or private, to manifest his religion or belief in teaching, practice, worship and observance.

ARTICLE 19

Everyone has the right to freedom of opinion and expression; this right includes freedom to hold opinions without interference and to seek, receive and impart information and ideas through any media and regardless of frontiers.

ARTICLE 20

1. Everyone has the right to freedom of peaceful assembly and association.

2. No one may be compelled to belong to an association.

ARTICLE 21

1. Everyone has the right to take part in the government of his country, directly or through freely chosen representatives.

2. Everyone has the right of equal access to public service in his country.

3. The will of the people shall be the basis of the authority of government; this will shall be expressed in periodic and genuine elections which shall be by universal and equal suffrage and shall be held by secret vote or by equivalent free voting procedures.

ARTICLE 22

Everyone, as a member of society, has the right to social security and is entitled to realization, through national effort and international co-operation and in accordance with the organization and resources of each State, of the economic, social and cultural rights indispensable for his dignity and the free development of his personality.

ARTICLE 23

1. Everyone has the right to work, to free choice of employment, to just and favourable conditions of work and to protection against unemployment.

2. Everyone, without any discrimination, has the right to equal pay for equal work.

3. Everyone who works has the right to just and favourable remuneration ensuring for himself and his family an existence worthy of human dignity, and supplemented, if necessary, by other means of social protection.

4. Everyone has the right to form and to join trade unions for the protection of his interests.

ARTICLE 24

Everyone has the right to rest and leisure, including reasonable limitation of working hours and periodic holidays with pay.

ARTICLE 25

1. Everyone has the right to a standard of living adequate for the health and well-being of himself and of his family, including food, clothing, housing and medical care and necessary social services, and the right to security in the event of unemployment, sickness, disability, widowhood, old age or other lack of livelihood in circumstances beyond his control.

2. Motherhood and childhood are entitled to special care and assistance. All children, whether born in or out of wedlock, shall enjoy the same social protection.

ARTICLE 26

1. Everyone has the right to education. Education shall be free, at least in the elementary and fundamental stages. Elementary education shall be compulsory. Technical and professional education shall be made generally available and higher education shall be equally accessible to all on the basis of merit.

2. Education shall be directed to the full development of the human personality and to the strengthening of respect for human rights and fundamental freedoms. It shall promote understanding, tolerance and friendship among all nations, racial or religious groups, and shall further the activities of the United Nations for the maintenance of peace.

3. Parents have a prior right to choose the kind of education that shall be given to their children.

ARTICLE 27

1. Everyone has the right freely to participate in the cultural life of the community, to enjoy the arts and to share in scientific advancement and its benefits.

2. Everyone has the right to the protection of the moral and material interests resulting from any scientific, literary or artistic production of which he is the author.

ARTICLE 28

Everyone is entitled to a social and international order in which the rights and freedoms set forth in this Declaration can be fully realized.

ARTICLE 29

1. Everyone has duties to the community in which alone the free and full development of his personality is possible.

2. In the exercise of his rights and freedoms, everyone shall be subject only to such limitations as are determined by law solely for the purpose of securing due recognition and respect for the rights and freedoms of others and of meeting the just requirements of morality, public order and the general welfare in a democratic society.

3. These rights and freedoms may in no case be exercised contrary to the purposes and principles of the United Nations.

ARTICLE 30

Nothing in this Declaration may be interpreted as implying for any State, group or person any right to engage in any activity or to perform any act aimed at the destruction of any of the rights and freedoms set forth herein.

ELEANOR ROOSEVELT

(1884–1962) As first lady of the United States during her husband Franklin Roosevelt's presidency (1933–1945), Eleanor Roosevelt worked to support his New Deal policies, became a champion of civil rights, and continued her work as speaker and writer despite some criticism. She began holding weekly press conferences and saw her role as that of buffer between victims of the Great Depression and the bureaucracy of government. She chaired the committee that drafted and approved the Universal Declaration of Human Rights in 1948 and was instrumental in the founding of the United Nations. President Truman called her "First Lady of the World."

337

GEORGE WASHINGTON

(1732–1799) Washington was described by Henry Lee, governor of Virginia and father of Robert E. Lee, as being "first in war, first in peace, and first in the hearts of his countrymen." Washington was also the first president of the United States under the U.S. Constitution (1789–1797) after having led the Continental Army as commander in chief in the Revolutionary War. He remains the only president to secure one hundred percent of the electoral vote. There is no evidence that as a boy he said, "I cannot tell a lie." Washington is referred to as the "Father of His Country."

abolitionists Opponents of slavery who wished to put an end to the institution.

abridging Limiting or reducing.

adversary system A system of justice in which court trials are essentially contests between accuser and accused that take place before an impartial judge or jury.

advice and consent The check on executive power granted to the U.S. Senate in Article II of the U.S. Constitution giving it the right to review and nullify proposed treaties and presidential appointments. A two-thirds vote of the Senate is required to approve treaties; a simple majority is needed for appointments.

advisory opinion In some judicial systems, a formal opinion on a point of law given by a judge or court when requested by a legislature or government official.

affidavit A formally sworn statement.

affirmative action A plan or program intended to remedy the effects of past discrimination in employment, education, or other activity and to prevent its recurrence. Such programs may or may not include preferential policies in which a group or groups are preferred over others in the award of some benefit.

alien A foreign-born resident.

Alien and Sedition Acts Laws passed during the administration of President John Adams that made it a crime for editors, writers, or speakers to criticize the government and its policies.

allegiance (1) Loyalty to a government, ruler, or nation. (2) Loyalty to a person, social group, or cause.

amendment A change in or addition to a legal document.

American Revolutionary War (1775–1783) The war fought by the American colonists and their allies to gain their independence from Great Britain.

Anti-Federalists Opponents to ratification of the U.S. Constitution who believed that it gave excessive power to the federal government and failed to protect the rights and liberties of the people.

appeal The bringing of a court case from a lower court to a higher court in an attempt to have the lower court's decision reversed. Grounds for appeal include errors of law, fact, or procedure.

appellate court A judicial body that hears cases appealed from a lower court. Appellate courts may be called courts of appeals, superior courts, or supreme courts.

appellate jurisdiction The legal authority of a court to hear appeals from a lower court.

apportion To allocate legislative seats.

Articles of Confederation (1781–1789) The first constitution of the United States, created to form a perpetual union and a firm league of friendship among the thirteen original states. It was adopted by the Second Continental Congress on November 15, 1777, and sent to the states for ratification.

assemble, right to *See* right to assemble

associate, right to *See* right to associate

association (1) An organized group of people joined for a common purpose. (2) A meeting or involvement of one person with others.

autocratic government A form of government in which a single ruler or group has unlimited power.

autonomy Independence, freedom, or the right to self-governance.

bail Money or other security given to obtain an arrested person's release from legal custody, which is forfeited if the individual subsequently fails to appear before the court for trial.

bailiff A court officer who carries out legal orders, makes arrests, keeps order in court, or serves as a messenger and doorkeeper.

balance of power In American constitutional arrangements, the division of governmental powers among different people or institutions in such a way that no one individual or group can dominate or control the exercise of power by others. *See also* checks and balances

basic rights Fundamental rights such as those to life, liberty, and property. These are called basic rights because they are considered more important than other, non-basic rights, such as the right to dispute a parking ticket.

bill A proposed law placed before a legislature for approval.

bill of attainder An act of the legislature that inflicts punishment on an individual or group without a judicial trial.

Bill of Rights The first ten amendments to the U.S. Constitution. The Bill of Rights lists many basic rights that the federal government may not interfere with and must protect. Nearly all these rights are now also protected from violation by state governments.

Black Codes Regulations passed by Southern state governments during Reconstruction to prevent African Americans from voting.

Boston Massacre (1770) The killing by British soldiers on March 5, 1770, of five members of a drunken mob of colonists who harassed and threatened the soldiers as they guarded the tax collector's office in Boston, Massachusetts. Six of the eight soldiers tried for murder were acquitted; two others received minor sentences.

Boston Tea Party (1773) An act of rebellion against British authority in response to the Tea Act (1773) in which a band of colonists boarded ships in Boston Harbor and destroyed thousands of dollars worth of tea by throwing it overboard. *See also* Tea Act (1773)

boycott To refuse to buy a manufacturer's product or make purchases from a merchant or company as an act of public protest.

broad interpretation The view that the First Amendment prevents government from providing any aid to any religion.

bully pulpit An expression coined by Theodore Roosevelt to mean a position of visibility and influence, often a political office such as the presidency, from which to advocate a particular point of view. The word "bully," in this case, means "very good" or "excellent."

bureaucracy Governmental departments and agencies and their staffs, principally civil service members and political appointees.

cabinet The group of advisors to the president composed of the heads of the departments of the executive branch and certain other officials. Cabinet advice to U.S. presidents is not binding, as opposed to parliamentary systems, where the consensus of cabinets is said to bind prime ministers.

capital punishment The use of the death penalty by a judicial system.

capitalism An economic system in which the means of producing and distributing goods are privately owned and operated for profit in competitive markets.

charter A written document from a government or ruler that grants certain rights to an individual, group, organization, or to people in general. In colonial times, a charter granted land to a person or company along with the right to found a colony on that land.

checks and balances In American constitutional thought, distributing and balancing the powers of government among different branches so that no one branch or individual can completely dominate the others. *See also* balance of power

chief justice The head of a court or a legal system. The Chief Justice of the United States is the highest-ranking judicial official in the nation and heads the U.S. Supreme Court.

citizen A person who is a legal member of a nation, country, or other organized, self-governing political community, such as any of the fifty U.S. states.

city-state A politically independent community consisting of a city and its surrounding territory.

civic life The public life of citizens; that which is concerned with citizens' interests and the common affairs and interests of their community and nation.

civic participation Taking part in formal political processes as well as formal or informal community activities outside of government.

civic virtue The dedication of citizens to the common welfare of their community or country, even at the cost of their individual interests. Traditionally considered most relevant to republics, since republican citizens are responsible for the well-being of their country.

civil (1) Related to citizens, particularly the relationship between citizens and government. (2) Polite: politeness is a principal virtue of civil society.

civil discourse Reasoned discussion as opposed to emotional display. *See* civility

civil disobedience The nonviolent refusal to obey laws that citizens regard as unjust or in protest of specific public policy.

civil rights The rights belonging to an individual by virtue of citizenship. In the United States, the term refers especially to the fundamental freedoms and privileges guaranteed by the Thirteenth and Fourteenth Amendments to the U.S. Constitution and by subsequent acts of Congress. These include civil liberties, due process, equal protection of the laws, and freedom from discrimination. *See* civil rights movement

Civil Rights Act of 1866 An act of Congress that attempted to protect the rights of African Americans following the Civil War. The act was ineffective because it was not enforced and the U.S. Supreme Court refused to hear cases about it.

Civil Rights Act of 1964 An act of Congress outlawing segregation in public places, including restaurants, movie theaters, and hotels. The law also stipulates that employers cannot unfairly discriminate against individuals because of their race, national origin, religion, or gender.

civil rights movement A social movement in the United States during the 1950s, 1960s, and 1970s in which concerned individuals and groups organized to demand equal rights for racial and ethnic minorities, especially African Americans in the South. Adherents to the movement sought to change unfair laws by making speeches, marching in the streets, and participating in economic boycotts, among other activities.

civil service Employment in federal, state or provincial, and local governmental agencies. The civil service was formed in an effort to reduce political patronage and promote professionalism in government.

Civil War (1861–1865) The war between the Federal Union, called "the Union" or "the North," and the states that had seceded from the Union and organized as the Confederate States of America, referred to as "the South."

Civil War Amendments The Thirteenth, Fourteenth, and Fifteenth Amendments to the U.S. Constitution ratified after the Civil War. The Thirteenth Amendment abolished slavery, the Fourteenth Amendment granted full citizenship to African Americans, and the Fifteenth Amendment prohibited federal and state governments from denying or abridging the right of anyone to vote on the basis of "race, color, or previous condition of servitude."

civility   The respectful treatment of others.

classical republicanism   The ideals and practices of ancient Greek or Roman city-states that emphasized civic participation and the responsibility of citizens for the well-being of their polity, or country. Acts by citizens that placed the public good, or common welfare, above private interest were especially prized.

cloture   A rule of the U.S. Senate stipulating that debate on a legislative proposal be cut off and the proposal voted upon by the full Senate if sixty members agree.

collective security   A system formed to maintain peace among nations in which participant members agree that a military attack on one is an attack on all and will result in a united response by all members.

commander in chief   Highest ranked person of the military forces. According to the U.S. Constitution, the president is commander-in-chief of the nation's armed forces.

commerce clause   Article I, Section 8, of the U.S. Constitution that gives Congress the power "to regulate Commerce with foreign Nations, and among the several States, and with the Indian Tribes." The clause has been used to regulate organizations engaged in interstate commerce by prohibiting them from engaging in racial discrimination.

committees of correspondence   Originating as voluntary associations during the era of the American Revolution, the committees were organized to ensure that news and the views of legislatures were accurately portrayed among and between the colonies. At first temporary, they became permanent by 1773 and helped to unite the colonists against the British.

common good   The good of the community as a whole, as contrasted with private interests that may conflict with public interest. Also known as the public good.

common law   The body of unwritten law developed in England from judicial decisions based on custom and earlier judicial decisions. Constitutes the basis of the English legal system and became part of American law, except in Louisiana, which inherited its civil law system from France.

commonwealth   A self-governing state or nation whose members are expected to help serve the good of all.

compact   A formal contract or agreement between or among two or more parties or states. The Mayflower Compact of 1620 was such a formal agreement.

compelling state interest   A public or common good claimed to take precedence over individual interests or, in some cases, rights.

confederation   A form of political organization in which the sovereign states combine for certain specified purposes, such as mutual defense. Member states can leave a confederation at any time. The United States was a confederation from 1776 to 1789.

congressional oversight   The implied power of Congress to monitor, supervise, inspect, and review the operations of the executive branch, particularly the agencies it creates.

consent of the governed   Agreement by citizens to obey the laws and the government they create. Consent is the foundation of government's legitimacy.

constituent   A person represented by an elected official.

constitution   A plan of government that sets forth the structures and powers of government. In democracies, a constitution is an authoritative law through which the sovereign people authorize a government to be established and grant it certain powers.

Constitutional Convention   *See* Philadelphia Convention

constitutional government   Limited government; the rule of law. A form of government in which a written, unwritten, or partly written constitution serves as a higher or fundamental law that everyone, including those in power, must obey. The rule of law is an essential feature of constitutional government.

constitutional law   A form of law in which a constitution serves as a source of rights. Distinguished from statutory and common law, which relate to matters subordinate to the constitution.

constitutional principle   An essential idea contained in the Constitution. For example, the idea that no branch of government should have a monopoly on power is a principle of the U.S. Constitution.

constitutionalism   The use of written, unwritten, or partly written constitutions and the use of rule of law to empower and limit government. Constitutions are superior to statutes, treaties, and executive and judicial actions.

Continental Congress   *See* First Continental Congress *and* Second Continental Congress

counsel, right to   *See* right to counsel

covenant   A binding agreement made by two or more persons or parties. In Protestant churches during the Reformation, a covenant was an agreement made in the sight of God. The Mayflower Compact was such a covenant.

cruel and unusual punishment   A criminal sanction or penalty that is not in accord with the moral standards of a humane and compassionate society. The Eighth Amendment prohibits such punishments.

Daughters of Liberty   An organization formed by women prior to the American Revolution to protest British policy.

Dawes Act (1887)   An act of Congress that granted American citizenship and small parcels of land to American Indians who would give up allegiance to their tribe, historical traditions, and ways of life.

Declaration of Independence   A proclamation passed by Congress on July 2, 1776, and issued on July 4, announcing the separation of the "United Colonies" from Britain and the formation of a new nation, the United States of America. The document listed reasons for the separation and a philosophical argument in defense of the action.

Declaratory Act (1766)   A British law that reaffirmed the right of Parliament to pass laws for the colonies in "all cases whatsoever." The purpose of the law was to remind the colonists that the authority of the king and Parliament was superior to colonial governments.

de facto segregation   Racial separation not mandated by law.

de jure segregation   Racial separation mandated by law.

delegate   (1) (*noun*) A person chosen to act for or represent others. (2) (*verb*) To entrust someone to represent your interests.

delegate theory of representation   The idea that a legislative representative should exactly mirror his or her constituents' views in deciding on public policy. *See also* trustee theory of representation

delegated powers   According to the natural rights philosophy, people always retain their basic rights, but provisionally entrust or assign certain powers to their government for certain, limited purposes. The powers of government are therefore "delegated powers" in that they are granted by the people, and the people can take them back if government fails to fulfill its purposes.

deliberative body   A legislative assembly that meets to debate issues.

democracy Literally defined as "rule of the people," democracy is a form of government in which all citizens exercise political power, either directly or through their elected representatives. *See also* representative democracy

Democratic-Republican Party Also known as the Republican Party (not related to the present-day Republican Party), founded by Thomas Jefferson and James Madison in 1792. It was the dominant American political party from 1800 until the 1820s, when it split into competing factions. One faction became the present-day Democratic Party.

denaturalization In the United States, a legal process by which native-born citizens may voluntarily divest themselves of citizenship or by which naturalized citizens found to have made fraudulent claims in applying for citizenship may be deprived of citizenship.

dictatorial government A political system in which rulers have unlimited power over the fundamental rights of the governed.

diplomacy The practice of carrying on formal relationships with governments of other countries through a corps of professionally trained persons known as diplomats.

direct democracy A type of government in which the citizens meet in person to make laws and decisions on public business.

discrimination Unfair treatment of people based on such factors as race, ethnicity, religion, or gender.

district court The court of original jurisdiction for most federal cases and the only federal court that holds trials in which juries and witnesses are used. Each state has at least one district court.

diversity Variation among the members of a community or society, such as age, geographical region, race, ethnicity, cultural origin, religion, and other factors that make people different from each other.

divine right The idea prevalent in early modern Europe that monarchs derive their authority directly from God. Adherents to this doctrine claimed that to disobey such monarchs, to attempt to replace them, or to limit their powers is contrary to the will of God. Also known as the divine right of kings.

domestic tranquility As used in the Preamble to the U.S. Constitution, peaceful conditions within the country.

double jeopardy The provision in the Fifth Amendment to the U.S. Constitution that a person may not be tried twice for the same crime.

dual national citizenship The status of a person who is a legal citizen of two or more nations.

due process of law A requirement stated in the Fifth and Fourteenth Amendments that treatment by state and federal governments in matters of life, liberty, or property of individuals be reasonable, fair, and follow known rules and procedures. *See* procedural due process *and* substantive due process

duty In economics, a tax on goods that are either imported or exported. Also known as a tariff.

E pluribus unum Latin: Out of Many, One.

economic reprisal An act or policy that injures the economic well-being of someone or something, such as a nation or corporation; an economic punishment undertaken in response to a perceived harm.

economic rights Those rights essential to citizens that allow them to earn a living, to acquire and transfer property, and to produce, buy, and sell goods and services in free markets.

elector (1) One of the 538 members of the Electoral College chosen by the political parties in a state. (2) Any qualified voter.

Electoral College The group of presidential electors who cast the official votes for president and vice president after a presidential election. Each state has a number of electors equal to the total of its members in the Senate and House of Representatives. The functioning of the Electoral College is provided for in Article II of the U.S. Constitution and amended by the Twelfth and Twenty-third Amendments.

eminent domain The inherent power of the state to seize a citizen's private property or to expropriate property or rights in property without the owner's consent. The Fifth Amendment to the U.S. Constitution provides for "just compensation" for private property taken for public use, known as the "takings clause".

enforcement powers The power of Congress to enforce laws.

enfranchisement Giving the right to vote to a person or category of persons.

English Bill of Rights An act passed by the English Parliament in 1689 that limited the power of the monarch. This document established Parliament as the most powerful branch of the English government.

enlightened self-interest A philosophy in ethics that states that persons who act to further the interests of others ultimately serve their own self-interest.

enumerated powers Those rights and responsibilities of the U.S. government specifically provided for and listed in the Constitution.

enumerated rights Those rights of U.S. citizens specifically provided for and listed in the Constitution.

enumeration A specific listing of elements.

equal protection clause Section 1 of the Fourteenth Amendment providing for "the equal protection of the laws." It has been used to prevent states from treating individuals unfairly because of their race, national origin, citizenship status, or gender. It prohibits laws that unreasonably and unfairly favor some groups over others or arbitrarily discriminate against persons.

equal protection of the law *See* equal protection clause

equal representation The idea that each state should have the same number of representatives in Congress. The number of representatives in the U.S. Senate is based on equal representation.

equality of condition Equality in all aspects of life, such as wealth, standards of living, medical care, and working conditions.

equality of opportunity A right guaranteed by both federal and many state laws against discrimination in employment, education, housing, or credit rights due to a person's race, color, sex and sometimes sexual orientation, religion, national origin, age, or handicap.

established church An official, state-sponsored religion, such as those in dozens of countries that have official state religions, including Roman Catholicism, Anglicanism, Lutheranism, Eastern Orthodox, Islam, Buddhism, and others. States with established churches include Argentina, Denmark, Indonesia, and Pakistan.

establishment clause The part of the First Amendment that prohibits the government from declaring an official religion.

ethnicity Ethnic classification or affiliation.

ex post facto **law** A law that criminalizes an act that was not a crime when committed, that increases the penalty for a crime after it was committed, or that changes the rules of evidence to make conviction easier. *Ex post facto* laws are forbidden by Article I of the Constitution.

excise A tax on goods produced within a certain country imposed by that country's government.

exclusionary rule The rule established by the U.S. Supreme Court that evidence unconstitutionally gathered by law enforcement officers may not be used against a defendant in a trial.

executive branch The branch of government that carries out the laws made by the legislative branch and undertakes other constitutionally provided functions.

executive departments Cabinet-level agencies in the federal government, such as the Departments of State, Defense, and the Treasury.

executive orders Directives issued by the president, including Presidential Directives, National Security Directives, and Homeland Security Presidential Directives. Presidents have issued such orders since 1789. Such orders are open to the public, except for National Security Directives.

executive power The authority to carry out and enforce the law.

faction (1) A small group within a larger group. (2) In its political sense, according to James Madison in Federalist 10, a faction is a "number of citizens, whether amounting to a majority or a minority of the whole, who are united…by some common impulse of passion, or of interest, adverse to the rights of other citizens or to the permanent and aggregate interests of the community."

federal courts The courts of the national government that deal with problems between states, with the U.S. Constitution, and with laws made by Congress.

federal district court The court of original jurisdiction for most federal cases. This is the only federal court that holds trials in which juries and witnesses are used. Each state has at least one district court.

federal government Another name for the national government of the United States.

federal system *See* federalism

federalism A form of government in which power is divided and shared between a central government and state and local governments.

Federalist, The A series of articles written for newspapers in 1787–88 by Alexander Hamilton, James Madison, and John Jay urging the adoption of the Constitution and supporting the need for a strong national government. The articles were published as a book, *The Federalist*, in 1788.

Federalists Advocates for a strong central government who urged ratification of the U.S. Constitution in 1787–88. They flourished as a political party in the 1790s under the leadership of Alexander Hamilton. The party disappeared from national politics in 1816.

felony A crime, such as murder or rape, considered more serious than a misdemeanor and subject to more severe punishment.

feudalism A system of social, economic, and political organization in Europe from the ninth to about the fifteenth century in which a politically weak monarch shared power with the nobility. The nobility required work and services from the common people, known as serfs, in return for allowing them to live on and make use of the noble's land and benefit from the noble's protection.

filibuster The practice of refusing to surrender the floor during a debate to prevent the Senate from voting on a proposal.

First Continental Congress The body of colonial delegates that convened in Philadelphia from September 5, 1774, to October 26, 1774, to represent the interests of the colonists and to protest British rule. The Congress drafted the Articles of Association, on the basis of which the colonies agreed to a highly successful boycott of British goods. It also provided for a Second Continental Congress, which eventually declared independence from Britain, to meet the following May.

forms of government (1) Aristotle's idea of three forms of government based on the number of people exercising power. Each has a "right" form and a "corrupt" form. The right form of government by a single person is a "monarchy." The right form of government by a few people is an "aristocracy." And the right form of government by many people is called "polity." (2) Types of democratic governments. For example, parliamentary systems, such as those of Britain and India; separation of powers systems, such as that of the United States; and presidential systems, such as that of France. (3) General forms of government, such as monarchies, republics, and autocracies.

Founders The political leaders of the thirteen original colonies during the era of the American Revolution and its aftermath. They were key figures in the establishment of the United States of America and in framing and ratifying the U.S. Constitution.

Framers The delegates to the Philadelphia Convention of 1787. They are the group of men who wrote the U.S. Constitution.

franchise A right or privilege. In the context of American politics, it means the right to vote.

free exercise clause The part of the First Amendment stating that Congress shall make no laws that prevent people from holding whatever religious beliefs they choose or that unfairly or unreasonably limit the right to practice religious beliefs.

freedom of assembly *See* right to assemble

freedom of belief or conscience The right to believe or not to believe as one chooses, including freedom from being coerced to believe in something one does not.

freedom of expression As provided for in the First Amendment, the right to make known one's attitudes, thoughts, or feelings in a variety of contexts, such as speech, writing, and the arts.

freedom of the press The right to read, write, and publish what you wish without government interference. Laws regarding libel and obscenity limit this right.

freedom of religion The right to hold whatever religious beliefs one wishes and to practice religious beliefs without unfair or unreasonable interference from government.

freedom of speech The right to express one's beliefs, ideas, or feelings. In the United States, this right is limited by laws regarding slander and by "time, place, and manner" restrictions. *See* time, place, and manner restrictions

French Constitution of 1791 A constitution adopted during the French Revolution that established a constitutional monarchy in France. Power was concentrated in the legislative assembly, and the power of the king was limited.

fugitive slave clause Article IV, Section 2, Clause 3 of the Constitution, which stated that slaves who escaped must be returned to their owners. It was later abolished by the Thirteenth Amendment (1865).

Fundamental Orders of Connecticut A series of laws adopted in 1639 that formed the first written constitution in North America.

fundamental principles A method of constitutional interpretation that seeks to identify the fundamental principles embodied in the Constitution as a way to determine the meaning of particular words, phrases, or clauses.

fundamental rights *See* basic rights

gag rule Any rule restricting open discussion or debate on a particular issue.

general warrant A legal search warrant that does not describe in detail the places to be searched or the things or persons to be seized. Opposition to the British government's use of general warrants played a role in the era of the American Revolution. *See also* writ of assistance

general welfare That which contributes to the overall well-being of the nation.

general welfare clause Article I, Section 8, Clause 1 of the U.S. Constitution that authorizes Congress to provide for the common defense of the country and for the common good, described as the "general Welfare of the United States."

George III (1738–1820; reigned 1760–1820) King of Great Britain during the American Revolution; widely reviled by the colonists.

gerrymandering Drawing the boundaries of an electoral district to favor a political party.

globalization The process of increasing interconnectedness and closer integration of the world's markets and businesses as a result of advances in transportation, communications, and information technologies. Such advances promote the flow of goods and services, ideas, capital, and people across borders.

Glorious Revolution (1688) The English Parliament's successful, bloodless overthrow of King James II, establishing Parliament's supremacy and independence from the monarchy.

government The people and institutions with authority to make and enforce laws and rules and manage disputes in a politically organized community.

grandfather clause Provisions of laws passed in the South after the Civil War stating that citizens could vote only if their grandfathers had been allowed to vote. The law made it impossible for African Americans to vote because their grandfathers had been excluded from voting.

grand jury A panel of jurors designated to inquire into alleged violations of the law in order to ascertain whether the evidence is sufficient to warrant trial. Contrasted with the "petite jury," usually composed of twelve people, of an ordinary trial.

Great Awakening Religious revival in the American colonies from the 1730s to the 1750s during which a number of new Protestant churches were established. This religious movement formed part of the backdrop to the American Revolutionary period that began soon afterwards.

Great Compromise A plan accepted at the Philadelphia Convention in 1787 that called for a Congress of two houses: in the upper house, or Senate, representation of the states would be equal, with each state having two senators; in the lower house, or House of Representatives, representation would be apportioned according to the population of each state, so that states with more people would have more representatives. Also called the Connecticut Compromise.

habeas corpus *See* writ of habeas corpus

hearing A meeting in which citizens present their views to public officials.

hierarchical Organized or classified according to rank, capacity, or authority, so that some are higher than others; contrasted with "egalitarian," in which the equality of those being considered is emphasized.

higher law As used in describing a legal system, this term refers to the superiority of one set of laws to another. For example, the U.S. Constitution is a higher law than any federal or state law. In the natural rights philosophy, "higher law" means that natural law and divine law are superior to laws made by human beings.

human rights Basic rights and freedoms said to belong to all people everywhere. *See* Universal Declaration of Human Rights

immigration The movement of people into one place from another.

immunity In legal terms, exemption from prosecution.

impeachment Charging a public official with a crime while in office and bringing him or her to trial. Convicted officials are removed from office.

implied powers Those powers authorized by a legal document that are not expressly stated but can be inferred from expressly stated powers. The power of Congress to do all things "necessary and proper" to carry out the powers delegated to it by Article I, Section 8, Clause 18 of the U.S. Constitution. The "necessary and proper" clause is also known as the "elastic clause," because it greatly expands the Constitution's enumeration of the powers of Congress. Implied powers can be distinguished from "inherent powers," those that are expressly provided for in the Constitution.

impost A tax or customs duty; a tariff.

inalienable rights Fundamental rights inherent to being human that every person therefore possesses that cannot be taken away by government or another entity. This phrase was used in the Virginia Declaration of Rights and the Declaration of Independence. *Inalienable* is sometimes spelled *unalienable*.

incorporation The process through which the U.S. Supreme Court has applied the due process clause of the Fourteenth Amendment to extend the reach of the Bill of Rights to include protection from interference by states.

indentured servant A person who voluntarily sold his or her labor for a set period of time in return for the cost of passage to the American colonies. Indentured servants provided the most important source of labor in the colonies in the seventeenth century and for a large part of the eighteenth century.

independent agencies Administrative organizations located outside the structure of executive departments.

independent judiciary An inviolate, or uncorrupted, judicial branch that serves to protect the U.S. Constitution and prevents the executive and legislative branches from disregarding it. An independent judiciary is necessary for the rule of law, because otherwise political interference could determine judicial decisions.

Indian Citizenship Act (1924) An act of Congress that recognized all American Indians as citizens of the United States and granted them the right to vote in federal elections.

indictment A formal charge by a grand jury accusing a person of having committed a crime.

individual rights Specific rights that belong to each person, such as those listed in the Bill of Rights.

inherent powers Those powers ingrained so deeply in an institution that they need not be stated. For example, what the "inherent powers of the presidency" might be is a hotly contested subject in American national politics.

initiative A proposed law placed on the ballots of some states for voter decision. Initiatives that pass immediately become law.

inquisitorial system A trial system in which a judicial official or set of officials acts as both prosecutor and judge, questioning witnesses, examining evidence, and reaching a verdict.

instrumentalism A method of interpreting the Constitution to help it adapt to changing circumstances and contemporary needs.

intermediate scrutiny In U.S. constitutional law, the middle level of scrutiny applied by courts deciding constitutional issues through judicial review.

international law Rules, usually the result of treaties but also from custom, that regulate how countries are to behave toward one another. International law differs from municipal, or domestic law, in that, in many cases, there is no enforcement mechanism and no universal authoritative interpretation. The rulings of international tribunals are binding on states that have agreed to adhere to tribunal findings, but such rulings are not binding on others.

international relations The purposeful interactions among sovereign nations in which they attempt to advance national interests and values, especially security and economic well-being.

isolationism The foreign policy of a nation that wishes to be inward-looking rather than involved with other countries. Historically, some cases of isolationism have combined a noninterventionist military policy with a protectionist economic policy.

Jim Crow laws Certain laws common in the American South from 1877 until the 1960s that required African Americans to use separate schools and other public facilities, prevented them from exercising the right to vote, and discriminated against them in public life.

Judeo-Christian Ideas, beliefs, and practices that have their historical roots in Judaism and Christianity.

judicial review The power of the courts to declare laws and actions of the local and state governments or the national government invalid if they are found to contradict the U.S. Constitution.

Judiciary Act of 1789 A law passed by the first Congress to establish the federal court system. The act determined the organization and jurisdiction of the courts.

jurisdiction The power or authority to hear cases and make decisions.

jus sanguines A right by which nationality or citizenship can be recognized to any individual born to a parent who is a national or citizen of that state.

jus soli The right by which nationality or citizenship can be recognized to any individual born in the territory of the related state.

justice (1) Fair treatment according to law. (2) A member of the U.S. Supreme Court or a state supreme court.

landmark decision A legal decision that constitutes a turning point or stage. *Brown v. Board of Education* (1954) is an example of a landmark decision.

landmark legislation A law that constitutes a turning point or stage. The Civil Rights Act of 1965 was landmark legislation.

law A rule established by government or other source of authority to regulate people's conduct or activities. In the United States, a bill that is passed by the legislature and signed by the executive, or that is passed over his or her veto, becomes a law.

law of nature In natural rights philosophy, moral rules found out by correctly applied reason or right reason, telling persons what they may and may not do in various circumstances. In philosophy, laws of nature have often referred to the rules that would prevail in the absence of man-made law. Natural law is conceived to contain standards of justice that apply to all people.

legal permanent resident A noncitizen living in a country with the permission of its government. Legal permanent residents of the United States enjoy most of the rights and obligations of citizens, though not the right to vote or the obligation to serve on juries. They have the same right to due process of law as citizens, must serve in the military, and pay taxes.

legislative supremacy A system of government in which the legislative branch has ultimate power. Parliamentary government is such a system.

legislature A group of elected government officials with authority to make and change laws.

Letter from Birmingham City Jail A letter written to fellow clergymen by Martin Luther King Jr. in Birmingham, Alabama, on April 16, 1963, after his arrest for violating a state court order against participating in protests. In his letter, King explains the reasons for his involvement in the civil rights movement and for his belief in nonviolent methods of protest.

letter of marque and reprisal A grant of authority from Congress to private citizens, not the president, to expressly authorize seizure and forfeiture of goods by such citizens in the context of undeclared hostilities with another country or countries. Without such authorization, citizens seizing such goods would be pirates in the eyes of international law.

libel Published words or pictures that falsely and maliciously defame a person.

liberty, right to The right to be free, within certain limits, in political, personal, and economic affairs. Some examples of liberties are the rights to vote for whom you wish, believe what you wish, read what you want, speak freely, and travel. In liberal democracies, the boundaries of liberty or freedom are defined by law. Those living under such governments are therefore said to enjoy "freedom under law."

life, right to The right to live without fear of being injured or killed by others or by government.

limited government In natural rights philosophy, a system restricted to protecting natural rights that does not interfere with other aspects of life. More generally, limited government is constitutional government governed by the rule of law. Written or unwritten constitutions are used to empower and limit government.

literacy test A test to prove a person's abilities to read and write. Until 1964, such tests were used in various states to prevent minorities from voting.

literal interpretation The view that the First Amendment prohibits only the establishment of an official government religion.

literalism *See* strict construction.

litigant A party involved in a lawsuit.

lobbying The practice of attempting to affect legislation by influencing legislators.

local government Government of a specific local area, such as state subdivisions authorized by states or governments of cities, counties, and towns. Also includes special government units, such as water districts.

loyalists Colonists opposed to American independence who remained loyal to Great Britain during the American Revolution.

magistrate A lower-level judicial officer, usually elected in urban areas, who handles traffic violations, minor criminal offenses, and civil suits involving small amounts of money. More generally, *magistrate* means public official.

Magna Carta Also known as the Great Charter, King John of England agreed to this document in 1215 at the demand of his barons. The Magna Carta granted certain civil rights and liberties to English nobles and to all "freemen," such as the right to a jury of one's peers and the guarantee against loss of life, liberty, or property except in accordance with law. Some rights were guaranteed for all the king's subjects, free or not free. In doing so, the Magna Carta limited the power of the king, who agreed that his will could be bounded by law, and became a landmark in the history of constitutional government.

majority rule A doctrine by which a numerical majority of an organized group holds the power to make decisions binding on all in the group. Majority rule is a foremost principle of democracy, but is not always practiced in societies that value consensus.

majority tyranny A situation in which a majority uses the principle of majority rule but fails to respect the rights and interests of the minority. *See also* majority rule

Massachusetts Body of Liberties (1641) The first American document to describe the rights of individuals.

Massachusetts constitution The state constitution ratified by Massachusetts voters in 1780. It is the oldest written constitution still in use in the world today.

Mayflower Compact An agreement to form a political body signed on November 21, 1620, by all adult males aboard the Mayflower before the ship landed in Plymouth, Massachusetts. The signers agreed to submit to "just and equal Laws" put into effect under the compact "for the general good of the Colony."

melting pot A term used to describe a society made up of diverse cultures or races that have merged or "melted" into each other. American society has often been called a melting pot.

methods of constitutional interpretation Interpretive methods employed by U.S. Supreme Court justices when considering constitutional issues of some cases. *See* strict construction, original intent, fundamental principles, and instrumentalism

Middle Ages A period of European history lasting roughly from the fifth to the fourteenth century during which the political, economic, and military structure of Europe was characterized by feudalism. The term *medieval* describes that which occurred during the Middle Ages.

Minutemen Civilian militias of the American Revolution, so called because of their readiness for battle.

misdemeanor A minor criminal offense that is less serious than a felony. The punishment for a misdemeanor is a fine or imprisonment for up to one year.

mixed constitution Traditionally, constitutions that include elements of the rule of one (monarchy), the few (aristocracy or oligarchy), and the many (democracy). Aristotle first wrote of mixed constitutions, although not always about all three elements simultaneously, stating that they are more stable than simple forms. Some American writers have argued that a mixed constitution is a hallmark of a republic. The idea influenced the writing of the U.S. Constitution.

modernism *See* instrumentalism

monarchy A form of government in which political power is held by a single ruler such as a king or queen. Historically, monarchies have been "absolute," or legally unlimited, or "constitutional," in which the powers of monarchs are limited by law.

multinational corporation An enterprise that operates in at least two countries.

narrow interpretation The view that the First Amendment prohibits only the establishment of an official government religion.

nation-state As currently used, a country; the standard unit of political organization in the world. The nation-state received its name from the idea of a people, or "nation," organizing itself politically for self-rule. Many countries today, however, are composed of two or more distinct peoples.

National Association for the Advancement of Colored People (NAACP) An interracial interest group founded in 1909 to advocate the rights of African Americans, primarily through legal and political action.

national government The organization having central political authority in a nation; the representative unit of political organization.

natural law *See* law of nature

natural rights The doctrine that people have basic rights, such as those to life, liberty, and property in a state of nature. Some writers, especially those influencing the American Founders, argued that certain of these rights are inalienable—inherent in being human—and that people create governments to protect those rights.

naturalization The legal process by which a foreign citizen becomes a citizen of the United States, concluding with an oath of allegiance.

naturalized citizens People who become citizens via the naturalization process rather than by birth. *See* naturalization

necessary and proper clause Article I, Section 8, Clause 18 of the Constitution that gives Congress the power to make all laws that are "necessary and proper" to carry out the powers specifically delegated to it by the Constitution. It is also known as the "elastic clause" because of the vagueness of the phrase "necessary and proper."

negative rights Those rights that prohibit government from acting in certain ways; rights that are not to be interfered with.

New Jersey Plan The plan presented at the Constitutional Convention in Philadelphia (1787) that called for a one-house national legislature, in which each state would have equal representation. This arrangement would favor small states. The New Jersey Plan followed the framework of the Articles of Confederation and favored a weak national government.

"new science of politics" James Madison's term in *The Federalist* for a study of politics utilizing reason, observation, and history that would help the Founders construct a new government on a rational and informed basis.

nongovernmental organization (NGO) An autonomous organization independent of direct governmental control that exists to perform any of a large variety of purposes, including those dealing with humanitarian, educational, or public policy problems and issues.

nonviolent social action Use of peaceful tactics, such as parades, demonstrations, rallies, and civil disobedience as means of furthering civil or political ends.

Northwest Ordinance (1787) Passed by Congress under the Articles of Confederation, the ordinance defined the process by which territories would become states, protected civil liberties in new territories, and was the first national legislation to set limits on the expansion of slavery.

Northwest Territory A governmental region within the early United States that included all the land west of Pennsylvania and northwest of the Ohio River.

Organization of American States (OAS) A regional organization headquartered in Washington, D.C., composed of thirty-five North, South, and Central American nations, formed in 1948 to promote economic, political, military, and cultural cooperation among its members.

original history *See* original intent

original intent A method of constitutional interpretation that seeks to understand what the Founders meant when they wrote the words of the Constitution.

original jurisdiction In some cases, such as those in which a state is a party, the Supreme Court has the right to consider the facts and the law in a case without it having first been passed on by a lower court.

orthodoxy The approved form of a belief or practice.

override To pass a bill after it has been vetoed. Congress may override the president's veto by a two-thirds vote of both houses.

Parliament The British legislature, which consists of two houses: the House of Lords, which once represented the nobility, and the House of Commons, which formally represents the common people. Most members of the House of Lords are appointed for life by the government of the day and are not members of the hereditary aristocracy, who once dominated it.

parliamentary government A system that gives governmental authority to a legislature or parliament, which in turn selects the head of government, the prime minister, from among its members. Parliament has continuing power to remove prime ministers by passing a vote of no confidence.

party system A concept in political science that political parties control government.

patronage Support, often financial, given by a person or institution to a person, group, or institution in need.

peer (1) A person of equal standing or rank. (2) In British government, a member of the House of Lords.

personal rights Those rights of individuals in their private capacity, such as the rights to life and liberty, as distinguished from the political rights of citizens, such as the rights to vote and to hold public office.

petition, right to *See* right to petition

petty offenses Those crimes for which the maximum penalty for conviction is six months or less.

Philadelphia Convention The meeting held in Philadelphia from May to September 1787 at which the U.S. Constitution was written. Also called the Constitutional Convention.

platform List of the policies and priorities of a political party; also known as a manifesto.

plea agreement Pleading guilty to a lesser crime than that charged by a prosecutor.

plenary powers Unlimited and undefined powers.

pocket veto A presidential practice that allows a bill to die if not signed within ten days and Congress is adjourned. The president is conceived as keeping the bill in his pocket rather than taking it out and signing it.

police powers The inherent authority of a government to impose restrictions on private rights for the sake of public welfare, order, and security within the boundaries of constitutional law.

political action Any organized attempt to influence the political process and affect public policy, from lobbying legislators to seeking the election or defeat of particular candidates.

political legitimacy Acceptance by the governed that the claim to authority by those who govern is justified. In democratic societies, legitimacy is achieved only when those who govern gain power through the free consent of the governed in free and fair elections.

political party An organization seeking to achieve political power by electing members to public office so that its political philosophy is reflected in public policy.

political philosophy A set of ideas about government and politics, such as the nature of justice and the role and proper limits of government.

political rights All rights of a citizen in a free society that are clearly expressed and guaranteed by the Constitution and implied by natural laws.

politics The processes by which groups of people make decisions. In politically organized societies, politics includes the processes of making authoritative rules known as laws.

poll tax A tax that voters in many states were required to pay in order to exercise their right to vote. These barriers were used until 1964 to prevent African Americans from voting.

popular sovereignty The natural rights concept that ultimate political authority rests with the people.

positive rights Those rights that require overt government action, as opposed to negative rights that require government not to act in specified ways. Examples of positive rights are those to public education and, in some cases, to medical care, old age pensions, food, or housing.

power to investigate The power of Congress to undertake formal inquiries into matters of public business and public policy.

Preamble Preface or introduction to the U.S. Constitution stating that "the People of the United States" are establishing the Constitution and enumerating the purposes for doing so.

precedent Previous court decisions upon which legal issues are decided.

prime minister The highest-ranking member of government in a parliamentary system. Both Britain and Japan, for example, have prime ministers.

primogeniture The condition of being the firstborn child. In law, it refers to the right of the eldest son at some times and places to inherit all of his parents' estates rather than sharing it with his male siblings.

principle Basic truth or underlying assumption regarding rules of conduct or behavior. Moral principles are statements of guiding ideas, often expressed as laws, of what is right and wrong, good and evil. Political principles are general statements of guiding ideas of what is right and wrong in matters of politics, government, and public policy.

privacy, right to *See* right to privacy

private morality An individual's ideas about right and wrong to be practiced in one's personal life. These are derived from religious, philosophical, familial, and other sources, including individual conscience.

probable cause Reasonable grounds for presuming that a crime has been or is in the process of being committed. Provided for in the Fourth Amendment.

procedural due process The principle that government must respect all, not some, of a person's legal rights. Government must not subject individuals to unreasonable, unfair, or arbitrary treatment.

procedure The steps taken to accomplish a task.

Proclamation of 1763 A British law that banned settlement in certain western lands to reduce tensions between the colonists and Native Americans. The law was unpopular among American frontiersmen and traders.

property, right to *See* right to property

proportional representation In the context of American government, the electoral system in which the number of representatives for a state is based on the number of people living in the state. Proportional representation is used to determine the number of each state's representatives in the U.S. House of Representatives.

public good *See* common good

public forum   Geographical places in a community, such as streets, parks, or virtual reality sites, where people can express and exchange their views.

public morality   The values and principles of right and wrong pertaining to public policies and actions.

pursuit of happiness   An "unalienable" right stated in the Declaration of Independence. It is the right of Americans to pursue personal fulfillment in their own way, so long as they do not infringe on the rights of others. Within certain limits, this right denies the legitimacy of government to decide what kind of happiness one ought to seek.

quasi-judicial   Actions of an agency, board, or other government entity in which there are hearings, orders, judgments, or other activities similar to those of courts.

quasi-legislative powers   Having a partly legislative character by possession of the right to make rules and regulations having the force of law.

Quartering Act (1765)   Also known as the Mutiny Act, a British law authorizing colonial governors to requisition certain buildings, including parts of people's homes, for the housing, or quartering, of British troops.

radical   (1) Going to the root of things in philosophical or political analysis. (2) Advocating extreme or revolutionary changes, especially in politics or government.

rational basis   In U.S. constitutional law, the lowest level of scrutiny applied by courts deciding constitutional issues through judicial review.

ratification   (1) Formal approval of some formal legal instrument such as a constitution or treaty. (2) In U.S. constitutional history, the approval of the U.S. Constitution in 1788 by the ratifying conventions held in each state, except for Rhode Island, which initially voted the Constitution down by popular referendum.

reasonableness   Quality of what a rational and fair-minded person might say.

recall   A process of using special or general elections for removing elected officials from office.

redress of grievances   The correction of complaints. The First Amendment protects the right of the people to petition government to obtain remedies for claimed wrongs.

referendum   Placing a measure approved by a legislature on a ballot for popular approval.

Reformation   Sixteenth-century religious movement aimed at reforming the Roman Catholic Church and resulting in the establishment of Protestant churches.

religious test   A requirement that a person swear to a belief in God or belong to a particular religion in order to qualify for a political office or to vote.

Renaissance   The great revival of art, literature, and learning in Europe during the fourteenth, fifteenth, and sixteenth centuries, based on classical sources and leading to a new confidence in the powers of human beings and in the potential of the individual. Attitudes formed in the Renaissance were later important in the development of democratic ideas and practices.

representative democracy   A system of government in which citizens elect officials to make and administer laws for their country; often combined with elements of direct democracy, such as the use of initiative and referendum elections. Involves free, fair, and regular competitive elections and requires freedom of speech, political association, and the rule of law. Because the citizenry is considered sovereign (*see* popular sovereignty), civilian control of the military is also required. Liberal versions of representative democracy further require protection of a full panoply of basic rights, such as freedom of religion, freedom of expression, and economic freedom.

republic   According to James Madison, a form of government that derives its powers directly or indirectly from the people, is administered by officials holding power for a limited time, and incorporates representative institutions.

republican government   *See* republic

republicanism   *See* republic

reserved powers   Those powers referred to in the Ninth and Tenth Amendments that are reserved to the states or to the people.

resident alien   A noncitizen legally residing in a country other than his or her birth country.

resolution   A formal statement of a decision or expression of opinion put before or adopted by an assembly such as the U.S. Congress.

reverse discrimination   The argument that preferential policies found in certain affirmative action programs discriminate against majority groups.

revolution, right to   *See* right to revolution

right against self-incrimination   A guarantee found in the Fifth Amendment against being compelled in any criminal case to be a witness against oneself.

right to assemble   The right or legal claim provided for in the First Amendment that allows people to meet to discuss and express their beliefs, ideas, or feelings, especially in a political context.

right to associate   The freedom to meet with others for political or any other lawful purposes.

right to counsel   Part of the right to a fair trial, allowing for the defendant to be assisted by an attorney, and if the defendant cannot afford counsel, requiring that the state appoint an attorney or pay the defendant's legal fees.

right to petition   The legal claim that allows citizens to urge their government to correct wrongs and injustices or to take some other action.

right to privacy   The constitutional right, founded upon U.S. Supreme Court decisions, that requires that people be free from unwarranted intrusion into their private lives by government officials.

right to property   The right or legal claim that allows a person to own things and to transfer them to others.

right to revolution   The right of the sovereign people of any democratic state or regime to depose a government after it has attacked citizens' basic rights for a significant period of time. This right, espoused by English philosopher John Locke, was asserted in the Declaration of Independence to justify separation from Britain and the overturning of the authority of King George III.

rights   Moral or legal claims justified in ways that are generally accepted within a society or the international community.

rights of Englishmen   Term prevalent in seventeenth-century England and America referring to certain historically established rights, beginning with the rights of the Magna Carta, that all English subjects were understood to have. These included the right not to be kept in prison without a trial, the right to trial by jury, security in one's home from unlawful entry, and no taxation without consent, among others.

rule of law   The principle that both those who govern and those who are governed must obey the law and are subject to the same laws. This principle is contrasted to the "rule of men," in which those in power make up the rules as they please. The rule of law requires an independent judiciary that is immune from political or other manipulation.

search In the context of American constitutional law, intrusion into someone's privacy.

secede Formal withdrawal by a constituent member from an alliance, federation, or association.

secession In U.S. history, the act of states leaving the Union in 1861 following the election of President Abraham Lincoln; precipitated the Civil War.

Second Continental Congress The body of delegates representing the colonies that met in 1775 shortly after the start of the Revolutionary War. The Congress organized the Continental Army, selected George Washington to lead it, appointed a committee to draft the Declaration of Independence, and adopted the Articles of Confederation.

Sedition Act of 1798 Endorsed by the Federalist administration of John Adams, the legislation provided penalties for writing, printing, or uttering "false, scandalous, or malicious" statements against the government or Congress.

sedition Incitement to rebellion.

seditious libel Written language that seeks to convince others to engage in the overthrow of a government.

segregation The separation or isolation of a race, class, or ethnic group from the rest of society, whether or not by a deliberate policy.

seizure In the context of U.S. constitutional law, interference with a person's property or freedom of movement.

selective incorporation The application of some parts but not others of the federal Bill of Rights to state law. This process is also known as absorption.

self-incrimination, right against *See* right against self-incrimination

self-interest Personal benefits; contrasted with the public interest or common good.

seniority Length of service. In the U.S. House of Representatives or the U.S. Senate, certain powers and responsibilities of congressional members, such as committee chairmanships, are granted on the basis of their time in office.

separate but equal The argument, upheld by the U.S. Supreme Court in *Plessy v. Ferguson* (1896) but later reversed, that racially segregated public facilities are constitutional if those facilities are of equal quality.

separation of church and state A basic principle of American government that no single religion should be favored by government over other religions, nor should government interfere with the right to practice or not practice religious beliefs. This term was used in 1802 by President Thomas Jefferson to explain his understanding of the protection of religious freedom afforded by the Constitution.

separated powers The division of the powers of government among the different branches. Separating powers is a primary strategy of promoting constitutional or limited government by ensuring that no one individual or branch has excessive power that can be abused. *See* checks and balances

serf A peasant under the medieval system of manorialism, which enforced the labor of serfs in the fields of landowners in return for protection and the right to work on their leased fields. Serfs were not free to leave the area in which they worked.

Seven Years' War A series of wars between England and France fought both in Europe and in North America. The American phase, fought between 1754 and 1763, is known as the French and Indian War. Costs of fighting the war and protecting the American colonies afterwards led Britain to levy taxes on the colonists that eventually led to the American Revolution.

shared powers Legislative powers not completely separated between the branches of government.

Shays' Rebellion (1786–1787) An armed revolt by Massachusetts farmers seeking relief from debt and mortgage foreclosures. The rebellion fueled support for amending the Articles of Confederation.

sit-in Nonviolent civil disobedience action in which people protesting certain conditions, laws, or public policies occupy an appropriate place and refuse to move until their demands are considered or met.

slave A person under the complete control of a master, with no legal rights, forced to work without compensation.

slave trade The commercial practice of forcibly taking people from their homes in Africa and selling them into slavery in the New World.

social action Attempts by groups or individuals to change society using a variety of means.

social contract theory Presumption of an imaginary or actual agreement among people to set up a government and obey its laws. The theory was developed by the English natural rights philosopher John Locke, among others, to explain the origin of legitimate government.

Sons of Liberty A secret organization of American colonists that originated in 1765 to express colonial opposition to the Stamp Act. The organization, or those using its name, existed in nearly every colony and was active in attacking British interests throughout the Revolutionary period.

sovereignty The ultimate, supreme power in a state. Democratic theory states that the people as a whole are sovereign (*See* popular sovereignty); the citizens of the United States constitute the sovereign people.

speech, freedom of *See* freedom of speech

Stamp Act (1765) A British law that required the payment of a tax through the purchase of stamps for documents such as newspapers, magazines, and legal and commercial papers of all kinds.

Stamp Act Congress A meeting in New York in 1765 of twenty-seven delegates from nine colonies. The congress was the first example of united colonial action in the developing struggle against Great Britain. The congress was successful in bringing about a repeal of the Stamp Act.

stare decisis Latin: "Let the precedent (decision) stand." The doctrine that a court should follow the previous decisions of other courts on cases in which the facts are substantially the same. This principle plays a key role in common law systems such as those of Britain and the United States.

state of nature The condition of people living in a situation without government; anarchy. Natural rights philosophy inquired about what rights, moral rules, or laws applied in such circumstances and what rights, if any, people retained after agreeing to leave the state of nature to form a politically organized society or state.

statutory law The body of law passed by legislatures; contrasted with common law in which the law is derived from court decisions.

strict construction A method of constitutional interpretation that focuses on the plain meaning of the words of the Constitution.

strict scrutiny Under U.S. constitutional law, the second highest level of scrutiny used by courts reviewing federal law for constitutional legitimacy. "Super strict scrutiny" is the highest level.

subject A person who is said to owe allegiance to a government or ruler but who does not necessarily have a voice in choosing those in power. Often contrasted with citizens, who do have such a voice.

substantive due process Judicial interpretations of the due process clauses of the U.S. Constitution requiring the content of law to be fair and reasonable.

suffrage The right to vote. *See* franchise

supremacy clause Article VI, Section 2 of the Constitution, which states that the U.S. Constitution, laws passed by Congress, and treaties of the United States "shall be the supreme Law of the Land" and binding on the states.

tariff A tax on imported or exported goods. Also known as a duty.

Tea Act (1773) The British law that granted the East India Company a monopoly on the importation of tea into the colonies, thus eliminating the profits of colonial importers and shopkeepers. *See also* Boston Tea Party

textualism *See* strict construction

Three-Fifths Compromise Article I, Section 2, Clause 3 of the U.S. Constitution, later eliminated by the Fourteenth Amendment. The clause provided that each slave should be counted as three-fifths of a person in determining the number of representatives a state might send to the House of Representatives. It also determined the amount of direct taxes Congress might levy on a state.

ticket The choice of candidates of a political party for president and vice president.

time, place, and manner restrictions Government regulations that place restrictions on free speech. These regulations, specifying when, where, and in what way speech is allowed, are applied when unrestricted free speech will conflict with the rights of others.

totalitarianism A form of government in which one person or party exercises absolute control over all aspects of life, demanding devotion to an official ideology and using terror and modern technology to ensure that no independent organizations, especially political opposition, can function.

treason Betrayal of one's country. In American constitutional law, treason consists of making war on the United States or in giving aid and comfort to its enemies. Treason is carefully defined in the U.S. Constitution, and requirements for conviction are spelled out to ensure against government abuse of its powers.

treaty An agreement under international law between states or international organizations.

Treaty of Paris The agreement signed on September 3, 1783, between Great Britain and the United States that ended the Revolutionary War. With the treaty, Great Britain recognized the independence of the United States. Also called the Peace of Paris.

trustee theory of representation The idea that a legislative representative should use his or her best judgment in making decisions on public policy, regardless of constituent opinion. *See also* delegate theory of representation

tyranny A government in which a ruler or rulers possess and abuse absolute power.

unalienable rights *See* inalienable rights

unconstitutional Not allowed by or contradicting the U.S. Constitution; illegal.

unitary government A centralized form of government in which states or local governments exercise only those powers delegated to them by the central or national government. Contrasted with federal government, such as in the United States. *See* federalism

United Nations An international organization created in 1945 to maintain peace through the collective security of its members.

Universal Declaration of Human Rights An advisory declaration adopted by the United Nations General Assembly on December 10, 1948, consisting of thirty articles outlining the views of the General Assembly on those rights conceived as guaranteed to all people.

unwritten constitution The body of political practices developed through custom and tradition. Only three of the world's major democracies have constitutions that are not single, written documents: Britain, Israel, and New Zealand. In each of these nations, the constitution is a combination of written laws and precedents.

use immunity A guarantee government prosecutors give to a witness to not use the witness's self-incriminating compelled testimony as evidence against the witness in a subsequent criminal prosecution. A witness who receives use immunity may still be prosecuted, but based only on evidence not gathered from the protected testimony.

vassal In feudal times, a person granted the use of land by a feudal lord in return for military or other service.

veto The right of a branch of government to reject a proposed law that has been passed by another branch in an effort to delay or prevent its enactment. Under the U.S. Constitution, it is the power of the president to refuse to sign a bill passed by Congress, thereby preventing it from becoming a law. The president's veto may be overridden by a two-thirds vote of both the Senate and House of Representatives.

Virginia Declaration of Rights The first state declaration of rights, adopted on June 12, 1776, which served as a model for other state declarations of rights and the Bill of Rights and influenced the Declaration of Independence.

Virginia Plan The plan presented at the Philadelphia Convention that provided for a national government composed of three branches. It proposed a Congress of two houses, both of which would be based on proportional representation. The Virginia Plan favored a strong national government.

voluntary associations Autonomous organizations founded and administered by private citizens, not elected officials, devoted to any number of purposes. Voluntary associations form an essential element of the social basis of democracy, especially American democracy.

voter registration The requirement in some democracies for citizens to enroll in voting rolls before being allowed to participate in elections.

Voting Rights Act (1965) An act to strengthen the protections of the right to vote for all U.S. citizens. It compels the states to obey the U.S. Constitution and makes clear that the right to vote cannot be denied because of a person's color or race.

warrant An order by a judge authorizing a police officer to make an arrest or search or perform some other designated act.

writ of assistance A document giving a governmental authority the power to search and seize property without restrictions. Abolished in American law, the use of such writs by the British government was a major issue during some phases of the American Revolution.

writ of certiorari A type of writ seeking judicial review of a legal decision.

writ of habeas corpus Latin: "You shall/should have the body." A court order directing that a prisoner be brought to court before a judge to determine whether that prisoner's detention is lawful.

JOHN HANCOCK

(1737–1793) An American Revolutionary politician, Hancock was President of the Second Continental Congress and of the Congress of the Confederation. From 1780–1785, he served as the first Governor of Massachusetts. Hancock was the first person to sign the United States Declaration of Independence.

LEGEND

RED page numbers indicate activities, debates, discussions, or exercises.
 indicates page where a definition of a term or phrase has been provided.

A

abolitionists 39, ▶118, 137, 217

Adams, John
  as Founder 2
  Jefferson and 68
  Massachusetts constitution 51, 136
  Philadelphia Convention and 69
  as president 113, 114

Adams, John Quincy 217

Adams, Samuel 46, 69

adversary system 125, ▶125, 128, 230, 235

advisory opinion ▶181

affidavit ▶226

affirmative action 133, 168

African Americans
  Brown v. Board of Education and 132, 134, 262, 263
  civil rights movement and 263–64
  discrimination against 131, 132, 147, 262–63
  equal protection clause and 130–31
  limitations on rights 121, 122, 122, 131, 137
  Plessy v. Ferguson and 131, 134
  population of 278
  voting rights 50, 121, 122, 137, 139

Age of Enlightenment 24–25, 26

Alien and Sedition Acts 113, 113

aliens ▶251

American Indian Movement (AIM) 267–68

American Indians *See* Native Americans

American Revolution
  Battle of Concord and 46
  debt resulting from 63, 65, 66
  foreign relations and 286
  as inspiration for French Revolution 270
  onset 46, 48
  postwar treatment of loyalists 64–65

Americans with Disabilities Act (1990) 157

Anthony, Susan B. 138, 138

Anti-Federalists
  Bill of Rights and 95, 95, 96
  Constitution and 92, 93, 93–94, 94–95, 95–96, 96, 101
  fears of national judiciary's powers 128
  importance of small communities to 93–94

Antigone 266

Antin, Mary 298

appeal ▶178, 179

appellate jurisdiction ▶178, 178–79, 182, 182, 289

aristocracy 7

Aristotle 6–7, 7, 10

armed forces
  desegregation of 168, 262
  presidential command of 164, 288
  religious freedom in 204, 205, 206

Nineteenth Amendment 106, 138, 147, 189, 268
  text of 326
Ninth Amendment 198, 198, 200
  text of 325
Nixon, Richard 160, 166, 167, 181
Nixon v. United States 179
No Child Left Behind Act (2002) 188
nongovernmental organizations (NGOs) ▶255, 257, 260, 291
nonviolent direct action 263, 263, 266
North Atlantic Treaty Organization 291
Northwest Ordinance (1787) 63, 65, 78, 118
Northwest Territory 63, 118

O

Oath of Allegiance 248, 248, 251
O'Connor, Sandra Day 301
original jurisdiction ▶178, 182, 289

P

Paine, Thomas 37, 46, 136, 137
Parks, Rosa 263–64, 264
Parliament, British
  American colonies and 45, 47–48, 224, 225
  compared to colonial legislatures 7, 41, 41–42, 42
  compared to U.S. Congress 79, 144–45, 150
  establishment of 28, 28
  strengths and weaknesses of 30–32, 32, 33, 80
parliamentary systems
  head of government 169, 271
party system ▶112, 116, 116
  See also political parties
Paterson, William 74, 75, 75
patronage ▶115, ▶174, 175
Peace of Westphalia 23, 23
Penn, William 36
Pennsylvania
  colonial government 38, 41
  Constitution and 68, 69, 98
  constitution of 51, 52–53
permanent residents 250–51
personal rights ▶195, 197
petition ▶216
Petition of Right (1628) 30, 31, 34
Philadelphia Convention
  Bill of Rights and 108, 108
  civil discourse in 93, 282
  committees 70
  compared to European Convention 271
  delegates to 68, 69, 69, 70, 72 (*See also* Framers)
  executive branch issues 81–83, 84
  idea for 65
  influence on other nations 271
  judicial branch issues 83
  legislative branch issues 80, 84
  rules of 70, 71, 282
  unaddressed issues 89–90, 136, 136

Pinckney, Charles 108
piracy 288
Planned Parenthood v. Casey 301
platform ▶115
Plato 21
plea agreements ▶234, 240
plenary powers ▶80
Plessy v. Ferguson 131, 134
pocket veto ▶156
police powers ▶184
political activity
  participation of civil servants in 175
political legitimacy 16, 17–18
political parties 112, 112–16, 113, 114, 115, 116, 153, 154, 257
  See also party system
political rights ▶196, 197, 199
poll tax ▶122, 137, 139, 265
popular sovereignty ▶17, 50, 56, 190, 270
positive rights ▶196, 197, 199, 200, 301
power to investigate 159–60, 160
Preamble to the U.S. Constitution 18
  text of 316
precedents ▶28
Pregnancy Discrimination Act 268
president
  appointment powers 83, 84, 172, 175, 181, 257
  cabinet 172
  checks and balances and 166–67, 167, 170, 170, 175
  as commander in chief 84, 86, 162, 288
  Congress and 82, 84, 156, 158, 158, 162, 163
  Constitution and 94, 162, 163, 199
  differences from prime ministers 145, 169, 169–70, 170, 271
  election of 81–83, 83, 100, 107
  expansion of powers 165–66, 170
  foreign relations role 84, 164–65, 165, 170, 288, 288–89, 289, 294
  Framers' vision of 163
  impeachment of 84, 167
  public opinion and 170, 170, 257
  qualifications for 164, 246
  succession 107, 172
  term length and limits 81, 81, 107, 166, 170, 170, 283
  wartime powers 120–21, 122, 165, 288
prime ministers 169, 169–70, 170
prisons
  religious freedom in 204, 205
private morality ▶20
private organizations
  right of association 219, 220, 221
probable cause 225, ▶226, 228, 229, 232
procedural due process ▶124, 126, 128
procedural rights 234, 234–35
Proclamation Act (1763) 44
prohibition 107
property rights 38, 119, 124, 283
proportional representation ▶71, 74, 76, 77, 78, 149
proprietors *See* royal proprietorships

Van Buren, Martin 114, 115

veto 51, 80, 84, 156, 162, 163

vice president 82–83, 107, 154

Virginia
Constitution ratification and 98, 101
Declaration of Rights 53–54, 54, 56,
   69, 194, 194–95
Philadelphia Convention delegates 69, 71,
   77, 86, 92, 108

Virginia Company of London 36, 38

Virginia Plan 69, 71, 71–72, 72,
   74, 74, 77, 78, 80, 81

Voltaire 200, 210

voluntary associations 254, 254,
   254–55, 255, 257, 260

voter registration 257, 257–58

voting rights
African Americans and 122, 137–38
age and 139, 140, 251
citizenship and 138, 250, 252
in colonial America 38, 39, 40
Constitution and 89–90, 106, 107, 121
exercise of 252, 258, 258, 260
felons and 250, 251
Native Americans and 139, 249
property requirements 39, 136, 136, 137, 137, 140
resident aliens and 251, 251
at state level 50, 136, 136–37, 140, 189
women and 137–38, 138, 189, 268

Voting Rights Act (1965) 139, 157, 264, 265, 265, 268

W

war
Constitution and 84, 165, 287–88

warrants 224, ▶224, 225, 226,
   226, 227, 228, 228, 229, 232, 297

Warren, Earl 132

Warren, Mercy Otis 92, 93, 95

Washington, George
civic virtue of 14
as Framer 66, 68–69, 69
as president 102, 108, 113, 163, 166, 287

Webster, Noah 298

Weeks v. United States 226

William of Orange, Prince (Netherlands) 32

William the Conqueror 28

Williams, Roger 202, 202

Williams v. Florida 237

Wilson, James 69, 74, 75, 76, 82

Wilson, Woodrow 138, 163, 165, 279

women
in colonial America 18, 38–39, 42
petitions to Congress 217
voting rights 107, 137–38, 138, 140, 189, 268
See also gender-based laws

World Court *See* International Court of Justice

writ of certiorari ▶178, 179

writ of habeas corpus ▶31, 32–33, 34, 86, 120–21

writs of assistance ▶45

written constitutions 8, 10, 40, 42, 271

Y

Yates, Robert 92, 93–94, 94, 98

Yick Wo v. Hopkins 130

Z

Zangwill, Israel 298

Zenger, John Peter 209, 209

THOMAS JEFFERSON

(1743–1826) Thomas Jefferson, principal author of the Declaration of Independence, served as the first U.S. secretary of state and as the nation's second vice president (1797–1801). He became the third president of the United States in a tie-breaking decision by the House of Representatives after thirty-six ballots. Jefferson was a strong proponent of a "wall of separation" between church and state. He included in his draft of the Northwest Ordinance that "there shall be neither slavery nor involuntary servitude" in any newly admitted states of the Union. Considered one of the greatest minds to occupy the office of the presidency, his interests included architecture, horticulture, and archaeology. He founded the University of Virginia.

PHOTO CREDITS

Cover
Howard Chandler Christy, *Signing of the Constitution*, Architect of the Capitol, House wing, east stairway.

Front Matter
P. i, Howard Chandler Christy, *Signing of the Constitution*, Architect of the Capitol, House wing, east stairway; vii, Warren Burger, Supreme Court Historical Society.

Preface
P. viii, National Archives and Records Administration.

Introduction
P. xiii, Gilbert Stuart, James Madison, © Burstein Collection/CORBIS; xv (l and r), National Archives and Records Administration; xvii, ©iStockphoto.com/Jacom Stephens, Avid Creative, Inc.; xviii, Alfred Eisenstaedt/Time & Life Pictures/Getty Images.

Unit One
P. 1, The Granger Collection, New York.

Lesson 1
P. 3, Prints and Photographs Division, Library of Congress, LC-USZC4-9904; 4, The Granger Collection, New York; 5, Prints and Photographs Division, Library of Congress, LC-USZC4-2536; 7, The Granger Collection, New York; 8–9, The Granger Collection, New York.

Lesson 2
P. 11, Snark/Art Resource, NY; 12, School of Giovanni Paolo Panini, *Capricci of Classical Ruins with the Arch of Septimus Severus, Trajan's Column, and the Maison Carree, with Philosophers Discoursing and Figures Strolling*, © Christie's Images/CORBIS; 14, Juan Antonio Ribera y Fernández, *Cincinnatus Abandons the Plow to Dictate Laws in Rome*, Museo Nacional del Prado, Madrid, Spain; 16 (l), The Granger Collection, New York; 16 (r), Bildarchiv Preussischer Kulturbesitz/Art Resource, NY; 18, The Granger Collection, New York.

Lesson 3
P. 19, Bildarchiv Preussischer Kulturbesitz/Art Resource, NY; 20, Erich Lessing/Art Resource, NY; 22, Foto Marburg/Art Resource, NY; 23, Erich Lessing/Art Resource, NY; 24, National Portrait Gallery, London; 25, Erich Lessing/Art Resource, NY; 26, The Granger Collection, New York.

Lesson 4
P. 27, © Ann Ronan Picture Library, London, Great Britain/HIP/Art Resource, NY; 28–29, The Granger Collection, New York; 30, © National Archives, London, Great Britain/HIP/Art Resource, NY; 31, *Coronation Procession of Charles II to Westminster from the Tower of London*, 1661/Dirck Stoop/The Bridgeman Art Library/Getty Images.

Lesson 5
P. 35, © Ann Ronan Picture Library, London, Great Britain/HIP/Art Resource, NY; 36, The Granger Collection, New York; 37, Courtesy of The Maryland Historical Society; 38, The Granger Collection, New York; 39, The Granger Collection, New York; 40, Museum of Connecticut History; 41, The Granger Collection, New York; 42, Getty Images.

Lesson 6
Pp. 43, 45–46, The Granger Collection, New York; 47, © 2008 Jupiterimages Corporation; 48, Prints and Photographs Division, Library of Congress, LC-USZC4-2959.

Lesson 7
P. 49, Courtesy of Picture History; 50, The New York Public Library/Art Resource, NY; 52–53, 55 (l), 55 (r), The Granger Collection, New York; 56, Scala/Art Resource, NY.

Unit Two
P. 57, Prints and Photographs Division, Library of Congress, LC-USZ62-995.

Lesson 8
P. 59, The Granger Collection, New York; 60, National Archives and Records Administration; 61, Smithsonian Institution, www.si.edu; 62, *American Colonies, circa 1780s*, by Mapping Specialists, www.mappingspecialists.com, © 2009 Center for Civic Education; 64, 66, The Granger Collection, New York.

Lesson 9
P. 67, The Granger Collection, New York; 68 (l), © Tom Grill/Corbis; 68 (r), Prints and Photographs Division, Library of Congress, HABS PA-1430, sheet 16 of 45; 69, Charles Willson Peale, *George Washington at the Battle of Princeton*, 1781, Given by the Associates in Fine Arts and Mrs. Henry B. Loomis in memory of Henry Bradford Loomis, B.A. 1875, 1942.319, Yale University Art Gallery/Art Resource, NY; 72, © 2008 Stock Connection, from Fotosearch.

Lesson 10
P. 73, Prints and Photographs Division, Library of Congress, LC-USZC4-2485; 75, Portrait by C. Gregory Stapko, Collection of the Supreme Court of the United States; 76, *The Connecticut Compromise*, by Bradley Stevens, U.S. Senate Collection; 78, The Granger Collection, New York.

Lesson 11
P. 79, Prints and Photographs Division, Library of Congress, POS-MIN-.H39, no. 1 (C size) <P&P>[P&P]; 81 (t), Art Resource, NY; 81 (b), National Portrait Gallery, Smithsonian Institution/Art Resource, NY; 82, The Granger Collection, New York; 84, AP Images/Gerald Herbert.

Lesson 12
P. 85, *Old State House* by James B. Marston, © Burstein Collection/CORBIS; 86, AP Images; 87, GREG DERR photos/The Patriot Ledger; 88, Mark Reinstein/© photolibrary. All rights reserved.; 89, Prints and Photographs Division, Library of Congress, LC-USZC2-3367; 90, The Granger Collection, New York.

Lesson 13
P. 91, Robert E. Goodier, *Delaware, The First State*, Artwork provided courtesy of PNC Bank, Delaware; 92, The Granger Collection, New York; 93 (l), *Mrs James Warren* (Mercy Otis) c.1763 (oil on canvas), Copley, John Singleton (1738–1815)/Museum of Fine Arts, Boston, Massachusetts, USA, Bequest of Winslow Warren/The Bridgeman Art Library International; 93 (r), National Portrait Gallery, Smithsonian Institution/Art Resource, NY; 96, Art Resource, NY.

Lesson 14
P. 97, National Portrait Gallery, Smithsonian Institution/Art Resource, NY; 98, Rare Books and Special Collections Division, Library of Congress; 101, The Granger Collection, New York; 102, SuperStock.

Unit Three
P. 103, © Elliott Teel, www.eteel.com.

Lesson 15
P. 105, National Archives and Records Administration; 107, Prints and Photographs Division, Library of Congress; 108, The Granger Collection, New York; 110, White House Historical Association (White House Collection).

Lesson 16
Pp. 111, 113–114, The Granger Collection, New York; 115, AP Images; 116, Dirck Halstead/Time & Life Pictures/Getty Images.

Lesson 17
Pp. 117, 119–120, The Granger Collection, New York.

Lesson 18
P. 123, © Joe Tresh 2007; 125, DANIEL JOUBERT/Reuters /Landov; 126, Time & Life Pictures/Getty Images; 128, Bill Wingell.

Lesson 19
P. 129, Prints and Photographs Division, Library of Congress, LC-USZ62-119343; 131, © Bettmann/CORBIS; 133, Andersen Ross/Digital Vision/Getty Images.

Lesson 20
P. 135, The Granger Collection, New York; 137, National Portrait Gallery, London; 138 (l), histopics–ullstein bild/The Granger Collection, New York; 138 (r), © 2008 JupiterImages Corporation; 139, Rick Scibelli/Getty Images News/Getty Images; 140, National Archives and Records Administration, Records of the U. S. Marine Corps.

Unit Four
P. 141, Provided courtesy HarpWeek., LLC (colorized).

Lesson 21
P. 143, U.S. Senate Historical Office; 144, Architect of the Capitol; 145, AP Photo/PA; 14, *Texas Congressional District 17*, by Mapping Specialists, www.mappingspecialists.com, © 2009 Center for Civic Education; 148, The Granger Collection, New York; 150, AP Images/ Mark Wilson.

Lesson 22
P. 151, Courtesy Senator Richard G. Lugar of Indiana; 152, AP Images/Pablo Martinez Monsivais; 153, Courtesy of Nancy Pelosi, Speaker of the House of Representatives; 155, AP Images/ Greg Wahl-Stephens; 156, AP Images/ Rick Bowmer; 157, AP Images/ Barry Thumma; 158, AP Images; 159, "Impeachment Parade," a 1999 Herblock Cartoon, copyright by The Herb Block Foundation; Library of Congress, Prints & Photographs Division, LC-USZ62-126913; 160, The Granger Collection, New York.

Lesson 23
P. 161, The Granger Collection, New York; 162, AP Images/Ruth Fremson; 164, Wisconsin Historical Society (WHS Image ID 55239); 165, AP Images; 166, AP Images/Federal Register; 167, George Skadding/Time & Life Pictures/Getty Images; 168, Thomas D. McAvoy/Time & Life Pictures/Getty Images; 169, AP Images/J. Scott Applewhite; 170, AP Images.

Lesson 24
P. 171, Department of Energy, Department of Homeland Security, Department of Defense, Department of the Treasury, Department of Veterans Affairs, Department of State, Department of Housing, Department of the Navy, Department of Health and Human Services; 173, Photo by Marvin Nauman/FEMA News Photo; 174 (l), © Joseph Sohm; Visions of America/CORBIS; 174 (c), © Peter Turnley/Corbis; 174 (r), Gery Jacobs/U.S. Mission to the European Union.

Lesson 25
P. 177, © Mark Karrass/Corbis; 178, AP Images/J. Scott Applewhite; 180, © 2006 American Constitution Society for Law and Policy; 181, The Granger Collection, New York; 182, Mark Wilson/Getty Images News/Getty Images.

Lesson 26
P. 183, REUTERS/Jason Reed/Landov; 184, AP Images/Robert E. Klein; 185 (t), AP Images/Rich Pedroncelli; 185 (c), AP Images/Ric Francis; 185 (b), AP Images, Eric Risberg; 186 (t), AP Images/Stefano Paltera; 186 (c), AP Images/Damian Dovarganes; 186 (b), AP Images/Matt Sayles; 189, Bill Greenblatt/Liaison Agency/ Getty Images News/Getty Images; 190, © 2008 Jupiterimages Corporation.

Unit Five
P. 191, AP Images/William Wilson Lewis III.

Lesson 27
P. 193, ©Spencer Grant/age fotostock; 194, The Granger Collection, New York; 196, AP Images/Carlos Osorio; 198, AP Images/Steve Helber; 199, George Doyle/Stockbyte/Getty Images.

Lesson 28
P. 201, ColorBlind/Digital Vision/Getty Images; 202, The Granger Collection, New York; 205, U.S. Air Force photo by Master Sgt. Jim Varhegyi.

Lesson 29
P. 207, Julian Wasser/Time & Life Pictures/Getty Images; 208, Art © Estate of Ben Shahn/Licensed by VAGA, New York, NY, Smithsonian American Art Museum, Washington, D.C./Art Resource, NY; 209, The Granger Collection, New York; 214, AP Images/Scott Dalton.

Lesson 30
P. 215, AP Images/Coke Whitworth; 216, The Granger Collection, New York; 217, AP Images/ Carlos Osorio; 218, AP Images/Corpus Christi Caller-Times/Todd Yates; 220, The Granger Collection, New York; 222, AP Images/Columbus Dispatch/Eric Albrecht.

Lesson 31
P. 223, Andersen Ross/Blend Images/Getty Images; 224, Shelly Katz/Time & Life Pictures/Getty Images; 228, © 2008 JupiterImages Corporation; 230, AP Images/Ron Edmonds; 232, MPI/Hulton Archive/Getty Images.

Lesson 32
P. 233, REUTERS/Davis Turner/POOL/Landov; 234, Elizabeth Williams/Bloomberg News/Landov; 235, Darrin Klimek/Digital Vision/Getty Images; 236, AP Images/Robert Galbraith; 239, The Granger Collection, New York; 240, Mike Fiala/Getty Images News/Getty Images.

Unit Six
P. 241, Stan Honda/AFP/Getty Images.

Lesson 33
Pp. 243–244, The Granger Collection, New York; 245, George Caleb Bingham/The Bridgeman Art Library/Getty Images; 247, Purestock/Getty Images; 248, National Portrait Gallery, Smithsonian Institution/Art Resource, NY; 250, AP Images/Don Ryan; 251, UPI Photo/Jim Ruymen/Landov; 252, AP Images/Middletown Journal, Pat Auckerman.

Lesson 34
P. 253, AP Images/Jim Cole; 254, Paul Burns/Photodisc/Getty Images; 255, Ed Edahl/FEMA; 256, Andersen Ross/Photodisc/Getty Images; 257, Courtesy Congressman Dale E. Kildee (MI-05); 260, © 2006 Corporation for National and Community Service, Office of Public Affairs/Corporation photo by M. T. Harmon, Office of Public Affairs.

Lesson 35
P. 261, Rue des Archives/The Granger Collection, New York; 262, Esther Bubley/© Corbis; 263, Copyright: Peter Ruhe/GandhiServe; 264 (l), Don Cravens/Time & Life Pictures/Getty Images; 264 (r), 266, AP Images; 267, AP Images/Al Grillo; 268, AP Images/Greg Smith.

Lesson 36
P. 269, Toshio Sakai/AFP/Getty Images; 270, AP Images/Michal Dolezal; 271, Johannes Eisele/AFP/Getty Images; 272, The Granger Collection, New York; 275, AP Images/Christian Lutz; 276, AP Images/Jerome Delay.

Lesson 37
P. 277, NASA/Getty Images News/Getty Images; 278, David Mclain/Aurora/Getty Images; 279, Grant Faint/Photographer's Choice/Getty Images; 280, AP Images/Pat Sullivan; 282, The New York Public Library/Art Resource, NY; 283, Jonathan Nourok/Stone/Getty Images; 284, AP Images/Steve Mitchell.

Lesson 38
P. 285, De Agostini/De Agostini Picture Library/Getty Images; 286, Prints and Photographs Division, Library of Congress, LC-USZC4-3804; 287, Rue des Archives/The Granger Collection, New York; 288, Credit: Picture History; 289, The Granger Collection, New York; 290, AP Images/Fred Ernst; 291, AP Photo/Gregory Bull; 292, AP Images/Maersk/PA, HO; 293, Peter Harmsen/AFP/Getty Images.

Lesson 39
P. 295, The Granger Collection, New York; 296, AP Images/Jeff Widener; 297, AP Images/Mark Duncan; 298, AP Images/Daniel Hulshizer; 299, AP Images/Marcio Jose Sanchez; 300, AP Images; 301, AP Images/Paul Sakuma; 302, AP Images/Toby Talbot.

Reference
P. 303, The Granger Collection, New York; 304, Manuscript Division, Library of Congress; 305, The Granger Collection, New York; 306, National Archives and Records Administration; 308–309, The Granger Collection, New York; 310, National Archives and Records Administration; 315, The Granger Collection, New York; 316, National Archives and Records Administration; 323, The Granger Collection, New York; 324, National Archives and Records Administration; 329, The Granger Collection, New York; 330, AP Images/Gerald Herbert, Pool; 332 (t), MPI/Hulton Archive/Getty Images; 332 (b), National Portrait Gallery, Smithsonian Institution/Art Resource, NY; 334, Portrait of John Peters Humphrey, Circa 1950, McGill University Archives, MG 4127, Humphrey Images; 337, UN Photo; 338, 350, 364, The Granger Collection, New York.

SUGGESTED READING LIST FOR STUDENTS AND TEACHERS

UNIT 1

Bailyn, Bernard. *The Ideological Origins of the American Revolution*. Cambridge, MA: The Belknap Press of Harvard University, 1992. 416pp. ISBN: 978-0-67444-302-0. Winner of the Pulitzer and Bancroft Prizes. Chapters on the sources of colonists' thought and their understanding of the concepts of power and liberty are especially helpful.

Ellis, Joseph J. *What Did the Declaration Declare?* Boston: Bedford/St. Martin's, 1999. 110pp. ISBN: 978-0-31219-063-7. Five leading scholars discuss the meaning and larger implications of the Declaration of Independence. "Questions for Closer Reading" follow each selection. Brief and thought provoking.

Holton, Woody. *Unruly Americans and the Origins of the Constitution*. New York: Hill and Wong, 2007. 384pp. ISBN: 978-0-80908-061-8. Although a traditional reading of the reason for calling the Philadelphia Convention focuses on the weaknesses of the Articles of Confederation, Holton maintains that the economic slump of the 1780s was the primary reason. He contends that the decade following the Revolutionary War was as disastrous as the Great Depression of the 1930s. Americans—especially debtors and farm families—blamed state governments for high taxes and tight money. They demanded something be done for their relief. Shays' Rebellion and other protests were one result. The Constitution yielded tremendous economic benefits but, the author argues, they came at a political cost. The Constitution made the national government less responsive to the public than its state-level counterparts.

King, Anthony. *The British Constitution*. 428pp. ISBN: 978-0-19923-232-1. Oxford: Oxford University Press, 2007. King begins by answering the question "What is a constitution?" He then describes and discusses Britain's traditional constitution. He concludes by looking at "Britain's new constitution," or the great changes and reforms of the twentieth and twenty-first centuries.

Sandoz, Ellis, ed. *The Roots of Liberty: Magna Carta, Ancient Constitutions and the Anglo-American Tradition of the Rule of Law*. Indianapolis, IN: Liberty Fund, 1993. 363pp. ISBN: 978-0-86597-709-9. This collection of essays explores the Magna Carta, the ancient constitution of medieval England, and the contexts in which they developed. It looks for how ideas of liberty and the rule of laws in earlier times came to maturity. It examines how these issues sharpened during the eighteenth-century conflict that led to American independence and the framing of the U.S. Constitution.

Tuck, Richard. *Hobbes: A Very Short Introduction*. Oxford: Oxford University Press, 2002. 168pp. ISBN: 978-0-19280-255-2. A very readable, short account of Hobbes's life and his work as both a philosopher and a scientist. The book emphasizes the importance of Hobbes not only in the debates of his own time but in the debates of today.

Wood, Gordon. *The Creation of the American Republic 1776–1787*. Chapel Hill: University of North Carolina Press, 1998. 675pp. ISBN: 978-0-80784-723-7. Winner of the Bancroft and John H. Dunning Prizes, this book focuses on the ideology of the American Revolution and the influence of the English constitution on the colonists. Part Two, which discusses the period leading up to the Philadelphia Convention, is especially helpful. Wood's focus on major concepts—social contract, representation, republicanism, and constitutionalism—contribute to the reader's better understanding of the founding era.

UNIT 2

Broadwater, Jeff. *George Mason: Forgotten Founder*. Chapel Hill: University of North Carolina Press, 2006. 352pp. ISBN: 978-0-80783-053-6. A sympathetic but balanced portrait of an underappreciated Founder.

Conley, Patrick T., and John P. Kaminski, eds. *The Bill of Rights and the States: The Colonial and Revolutionary Origins of American Liberties*. Madison, WI: Madison House, 1992. 568pp. ISBN: 978-0-94561-229-2. These introductory essays provide a concise overview of the evolution of American individual rights. The state-by-state chapters that follow look to the foundation and development of liberty in each of the first fourteen states.

Kaminski, John P., ed. *A Necessary Evil? Slavery and the Debate Over the Constitution*. Madison, WI: Madison House Publishers, 1995. 301pp. ISBN: 978-0-94561-233-9. A superb collection of primary sources regarding slavery from the Constitutional Convention through the ratification debates in the New England, Middle, and Southern Colonies.

Ketcham, Ralph, ed. *The Anti-Federalist Papers and the Constitutional Convention Debates*. New York: Mentor, 1986. 416pp. ISBN: 978-0-45152-884-1. This volume includes complete texts of selected Anti-Federalist writings, the Constitutional Convention debates, commentaries, and a very useful index of the ideas discussed and debated during the ratification debates. The introduction helps to put Anti-Federalists and their thoughts in a larger context.

Larson, Edward J., and Michael P. Winship. *The Constitutional Convention: A Narrative History from the Notes of James Madison*. New York: The Modern Library, 2005. 256pp. ISBN: 978-0-81297-517-8. The authors' goal was to make the deliberations of the Constitutional Convention accessible to modern readers. They have edited out materials deemed extraneous to the main debates while maintaining the integrity of the historical record. The delegates' arguments speak for themselves and will afford the reader insight into the controversies and compromises of the Philadelphia Convention.

Levy, Leonard W., and Dennis J. Mahoney, eds. *The Framing and Ratification of the Constitution*. New York: Macmillan, 1987. 395pp. ISBN: 978-0-02918-790-6. Short selections on major events and issues of the time written by leading scholars. Writing accessible to diligent students.

Myerson, Michael I. *Liberty's Blueprint: How Madison and Hamilton Wrote the Federalist Papers, Defined the Constitution, and Made Democracy Safe for the World*. New York: Basic Books, 2008. 336pp. ISBN: 978-0-46500-264-1. Legal scholar Michael Myerson has provided a short, fresh look at how and why the *Federalist Papers* were written. He examines the collaboration of two very different individuals, Alexander Hamilton and James Madison, and explains why the two friends became political enemies. The *Federalist Papers*, Myerson contends, remain as relevant today as they were during the founding era. They are a guide to understanding current contentious constitutional issues.

Rakove, Jack N. *Original Meanings: Politics and Ideas in the Making of the Constitution*. New York: Alfred A. Knopf, 1996. 464pp. ISBN: 978-0-67978-121-9. Pulitzer Prize–winning reexamination of principal issues that the Framers of the Constitution grappled with: federalism, representation, executive power, and rights. In examining the sources of contention, the author reveals the character of the central actors in the Philadelphia Convention.

Rossiter, Clinton, ed. *The Federalist Papers*. New York: Signet Classics, 2003. 688pp. ISBN: 978-0-45152-881-0. Complete text of the *Federalist Papers* aided by a brief introduction and very helpful notes. Also contains a copy of the Constitution collated with the papers.

St. John, Jeffrey. *Constitutional Journal: A Correspondent's Report from the Convention of 1787*. Ottawa, IL: Jameson Books Inc., 1987. 302pp. ISBN: 978-0-91546-355-8. Written as a journalist's eyewitness day-to-day account of the Philadelphia Convention. Praised as "lively, gripping, and informative," it makes the debates at the Convention come alive. The Bicentennial Commission donated a copy to every high school in the United States.

Storing, Herbert J. *What the Anti-Federalists Were For: The Political Thought of the Opponents of the Constitution*. Chicago: University of Chicago Press, 1981. 120pp. ISBN: 978-0-22677-574-6. Exploration of Anti-Federalist criticisms of the Constitution and their pertinence today. Storing argues that Anti-Federalists are entitled to be counted among the Founders.

Webster, Mary E., ed. *The Federalist Papers in Modern Language Indexed for Today's Political Issues*. Bellevue, WA: Merrill Press, 1999. 408pp. ISBN: 978-0-93678-321-5. Extended index, glossary, and translation into modern language are aids to reading and understanding the original texts.

Winik, Jay. *The Great Upheaval: America and the Birth of the Modern World 1788–1800*. New York: HarperCollins, 2007. 688pp. 978-0-06008-313-7. Highly acclaimed and very readable, comparative history of three countries—the United States, France, and Russia—in the throes of revolutionary change. Winik captures the men, women, and tumultuous events of the late eighteenth century, and shows how they are interrelated and how they have affected the modern world.

Wood, Gordon S. *Revolutionary Characters: What Made the Founders Different*. New York: Penguin Press, 2006. 336pp. ISBN: 978-0-14311-208-2. Pulitzer Prize winner. A delight to read, fresh, and insightful. See especially the epilogue, "The Founders and the Creation of Modern Public Opinion." Wood's first Pulitzer book, *Radicalism of the American Revolution*, is still useful and incomparable.

UNIT 3

Farber, Daniel A. *Lincoln's Constitution*. Chicago: University of Chicago Press, 2004. 256pp. ISBN: 978-0-22623-796-1. The Civil War brought some of the deepest, most critical constitutional questions to the fore. Farber examines those issues and pays special attention to their relevance to today. A well-written work by a fine scholar.

Fehrenbacher, Don E. *The Dred Scott Case: Its Significance in American Law and Politics*. New York: Oxford University Press, 1978. 741pp. ISBN: 978-0-19514-588-5. Winner of the Pulitzer Prize, it remains one of the best histories of a landmark constitutional case. Very readable and very interesting.

Friedman, Leon, ed. *Brown v. Board: The Landmark Oral Argument Before the Supreme Court*. New York: The New Press, 2004. 416pp. ISBN: 978-1-56584-913-6. The *Brown* transcripts provide an opportunity for teachers and students to read for themselves everything that happened in oral argument of a case that's been called "the most important American act of government…since the Emancipation Proclamation." The questioning of Justices Thurgood Marshall, Hugo Black, Felix Frankfurter, and Robert Jackson are of special interest.

Keyssar, Alexander. *The Right to Vote: The Contested History of Democracy in the United States*. New York: Basic Books, 2000. 496pp. ISBN: 978-0-46502-969-3. Examines how states and the nation have expanded—and at times curtailed—the right to vote, from colonial times to the present. An extraordinary appendix includes twenty tables that track the right to vote, state by state, across categories such as race, gender, property requirements, and much more.

Kluger, Richard. *Simple Justice: The History of Brown v. Board of Education*. New York: Random House, 1975. 864pp. ISBN: 978-0-39472-255-9. Surveys the history of American slavery, the evolution and passage of the Fourteenth Amendment, and the famous Supreme Court case ordering desegregation of the public schools. One of the best case studies of a Supreme Court decision and the context in which it was set.

Miller, William Lee. *President Lincoln: The Duty of a Statesman*. New York: Alfred A. Knopf, 2008. 512pp. ISBN: 978-1-40004-103-9. An award-winning scholar, Miller explores the decisions "of utmost gravity" Lincoln made as a wartime president. The sections on Lincoln and the Declaration of Independence and on Lincoln's view of the Constitution and his interpretation of the powers it grants to the executive are illuminating.

Orth, John V. *Due Process of Law: A Brief History*. Lawrence: University Press of Kansas, 2003. 116pp. ISBN: 978-0-70061-242-0. Brief but accessible history of due process from its origins in medieval England to its applications in recent cases. Covers both procedural and substantive due processes.

Wilson, Douglas L. *Lincoln's Sword: The Presidency and the Power of Words*. New York: Vintage Books, 2006. 352pp. ISBN: 978-1-40003-263-1. A fascinating study of the origins, writing, and rewriting of Lincoln's most important presidential papers. Very helpful for understanding Lincoln's views on slavery and secession. Chapter Five, "Proclaiming Emancipation," is especially good.

UNIT 4

Aberbach, Joel D., and Mark A. Peterson, eds. *Institutions of American Democracy: The Executive Branch*. New York: Oxford University Press, 2005. 640pp. ISBN: 978-0-19530-915-7. Another volume in the series *Institutions of American Democracy*. Essays by leading scholars and practicing politicians deal with the invention and evolution of the presidency and with the executive agencies. Essays on the relationships between and among the other institutions of government are especially insightful. Available in paperback.

Gerston, Larry N. *American Federalism: A Concise Introduction*. Armonk, NY: M.E. Sharpe, 2007. 197pp. ISBN: 978-0-76561-672-2. Short, readable introduction to federalism. Examines historical and philosophical underpinnings of federalism, how federalism works in the United States, and how it affects the lives of Americans. Concludes with consideration of the international dimensions of federalism and how it might change in the twenty-first century.

Gould, Lewis L. *The Most Exclusive Club: A History of the Modern United States Senate*. New York: Basic Books, 2005. 402pp. ISBN: 978-0-465-02778-1. An analysis of the Senate in the twentieth century. Gould focuses on personalities, controversies, and current concerns. Chapter Five, on the Senate and the League of Nations, and Chapter Eleven, on "The Age of McCarthy," are worth special attention.

Hall, Kermit L., and Kevin T. McGuire, eds. *Institutions of American Democracy: The Judicial Branch*. New York: Oxford University Press, 2005. 624pp. ISBN: 978-0-19530-917-1. Another volume in the series *Institutions of American Democracy*. Essays by leading scholars deal with the impact of courts on American life and the role of courts in the constitutional system. Section IV, on rights, liberties, and democracy, as well as Section V, on property rights, are particularly noteworthy. Available in paperback.

Jones, Charles O. *The American Presidency: A Very Short Introduction*. New York: Oxford University Press, 2007. 192pp. ISBN: 978-0-19530-701-6. A concise, readable survey of the American presidency. Jones considers not only how the presidency was invented and how federal power has grown, but how the presidency might change in the future.

Quirk, Paul J., and Sarah A. Binder, eds. *Institutions of American Democracy: The Legislative Branch*. New York: Oxford University Press, 2006. 624pp. ISBN: 978-0-19530-916-4. One of the volumes in the outstanding series *Institutions of American Democracy*. Essays by leading political scientists and scholars of public policy examine the historical development of Congress and its current organization along with its strengths and weaknesses. Available in paperback.

Remini, Robert V., and Library of Congress. *The House: The History of the House of Representatives*. Washington, DC: Smithsonian Books in association with Harper-Collins Publishers, 2006. 624pp. ISBN: 978-0-06134-111-3. Winner of the National Book Award. A very readable account of the controversies and characters that have figured in the history of what some have called "the finest deliberative body in human history."

UNIT 5

Dershowitz, Alan M. *America on Trial: Inside the Legal Battles That Transformed Our Nation*. New York: Warner Books, 2004. 608pp. ISBN: 978-0-44652-058-4. Dershowitz, a professor of law at Harvard University, has written short sketches of the most influential trials in America from the Peter Zenger and Boston Massacre trials of the colonial era to the cases of the terrorist detainees at Guantanamo and on the United States mainland.

Foster, James C., and Susan M. Leeson. *Constitutional Law: Cases in Context. Vol. II: Civil Rights and Civil Liberties. Parts A and B*. Upper Saddle River, NJ: Prentice Hall, 1998. 184pp. ISBN: 978-0-13568-759-8. Each case in this volume begins with the setting or context in which the case arose. Highlights of the Supreme Court arguments as well as summaries of the briefs and the Court's decisions are presented for each case. An opening section, "Understanding the Supreme Court," is very helpful. This volume deals with religion, speech, press, and assembly cases. It also deals with Fourteenth Amendment cases. Part B is concerned with voting rights, privacy, and personal autonomy rights as well as the constitutional rights of the criminally accused. Very readable and accessible for high school students. Available in paperback.

Hall, Kermit L. *The Oxford Companion to the Supreme Court of the United States*. New York: Oxford University Press, 2005. 272pp. ISBN: 978-0-19517-661-2. This invaluable reference guide contains brief articles about justices, constitutional topics, and landmark Supreme Court decisions. Articles appear alphabetically.

Klarman, Michael J. *From Jim Crow to Civil Rights: The Supreme Court and the Struggle for Racial Equality*. New York: Oxford University Press, 2006. 672pp. ISBN: 978-0-19531-018-4. Traces the social and political history, as well as legal interpretations of civil rights issues, from the 1880s through the civil rights movement of the 1960s. Insightful and interesting.

Lewis, Anthony. *Gideon's Trumpet*. New York: Random House, 1964. 288pp. ISBN: 978-0-67972-312-7. A very readable and widely acclaimed account of *Gideon v. Wainwright* (1963). Gideon's case reflected the emergence of a nationwide concern for equal justice of the poor. In a unanimous ruling, the Supreme Court established the right to counsel in every felony or potentially lengthy imprisonment case.

Lewis, Anthony. *Make No Law: The Sullivan Case and the First Amendment*. New York: Random House, 1991. 368pp. ISBN: 978-0-67973-939-5. Another important case study of a landmark Supreme Court case. The book provides background and context for the decision in *New York Times v. Sullivan*, in which the Supreme Court adopted a new legal standard governing the law of libel as it relates to public officials.

O'Connor, Sandra Day. *The Majesty of the Law: Reflections of a Supreme Court Justice*. New York: Random House, 2004. 352pp. ISBN: 978-0-81296-747-0. The high court's first female justice reflects on her experience, some landmark cases, and the Constitution. Very readable.

Perry, Michael J. *We the People: The Fourteenth Amendment and the Supreme Court*. Oxford: Oxford University Press, 2001. 288pp. ISBN: 978-0-19515-125-1. Historical background of the Fourteenth Amendment and an examination of the norms the Fourteenth Amendment established. Separate chapters deal with race and affirmative action, sexual orientation, abortion, and physician-assisted suicide.

UNIT 6

Brookhiser, Richard. *What Would the Founders Do? Our Questions, Their Answers.* New York: Basic Books, 2006. 261pp. ISBN: 978-0-46500-819-3. With his characteristic wit and insight, Brookhiser uses his knowledge of the Founders and of modern politics to apply their views to today's issues. An early chapter is titled "Their World, Our World." Brookhiser then looks at what the Founders might think about current concerns, such as war and peace, race and identity, and education and the media. A brief work, but it is provocative and enjoyable.

Clapham, Andrew. *Human Rights: A Very Short Introduction.* New York: Oxford University Press, 2007. 144pp. ISBN: 978-0-19920-552-3. A very readable introduction to human rights. After a brief review of the historical development of international human rights, the book focuses on specific concerns, including torture, privacy, discrimination and equality, education, and the death penalty.

Dahl, Robert A., Ian Shapiro, and Jose Antonio Cheibub, eds. *The Democracy Sourcebook.* Cambridge, MA: The MIT Press, 2003. 568pp. ISBN: 978-0-26254-147-3. A superb collection of classic and contemporary readings. The book is divided into nine self-contained chapters. The final chapter, "Democracy and the Global Order," expands on ideas presented in Unit Six.

Kagan, Robert. *Dangerous Nation: America's Place in the World from Its Earliest Days to the Dawn of the Twentieth Century.* New York: Alfred A. Knopf, 2006. 544pp. ISBN: 978-0-37572-491-6. In this very readable book, Kagan refutes what he calls "the myth of America's isolationist tradition." The Declaration of Independence firmly established America's conviction that the inalienable rights of all humankind transcended territorial borders and blood ties. A reexamination of early American foreign policy, Kagan contends, will show that the United States has been regarded not only as a wellspring of political and social revolution, but as an ambitious and, at times, a "dangerous" nation.

Koser, Khalid. *International Migration: A Very Short Introduction.* New York: Oxford University Press, 2007. 138pp. ISBN: 978-0-19929-801-3. A balanced, thoughtful introduction to migration, a matter of worldwide concern. Koser puts migration to the United States in a global perspective.

Power, Timothy J., and Nicol C. Rae, eds. *Exporting Congress? The Influence of the U.S. Congress on World Legislatures.* Pittsburgh: Pittsburgh University Press, 2006. 248pp. ISBN: 978-0-82295-921-2. Analysis of how the U.S. Congress has influenced elected assemblies in both old and new democracies. The essay comparing the U.S. House of Representatives with the European Parliament is especially insightful.

Sabato, Larry J. *A More Perfect Constitution: 23 Proposals to Revitalize Our Constitution and Make America a Fairer Country.* New York: Walker and Company, 2007. 352pp. ISBN: 978-0-80271-621-7. Twenty-three proposals, ranging from reforming Congress and the Electoral College to requiring national service and holding a new constitutional convention, are intended to stimulate discussion and debate.

BIBLIOGRAPHY ON AMERICAN INDIANS

Calloway, Colin G. *First Peoples: A Documentary Survey of American Indian History*. Boston: Bedford/St. Martin's, 2007. 672pp. ISBN: 978-0-31245-373-2. Includes documents spanning from pre-1492 through the 1990s, with brief introductions. Timelines, References, and Additional Suggested Readings.

Cronon, William. *Changes in the Land: Indians, Colonists, and the Ecology of New England*. New York: Hill and Wang, 2003. 242pp. ISBN: 978-0-80901-643-1. Environmental history of colonial New England. Compares ecological relationships of precolonial Indians and colonial Europeans, especially conceptions of land ownership.

Davis, Mary B., Joan Berman, Mary E. Graham, and Lisa A. Mitten, eds. *Native America in the Twentieth Century: An Encyclopedia*. New York: Garland, 1996. 787pp. ISBN: 978-0-81532-583-3.

Debo, Angie. *A History of the Indians of the United States*. Reprint edition: Norman: University of Oklahoma Press, 1984. 450pp. ISBN: 978-0-80611-888-8.

Debo, Angie. *And Still the Waters Run: The Betrayal of the Five Civilized Tribes*. Princeton, NJ: Princeton University Press, 1940. 472pp. ISBN: 978-069104-615-0.

Deloria, Vine, Jr. *American Indian Policy in the Twentieth Century*. Reprint edition: Norman: University of Oklahoma Press, 1992. 266pp. ISBN: 978-0-80612-424-7.

Deloria, Vine, Jr., and Raymond J. Demallie, eds. *Documents of American Indian Diplomacy: Treaties, Agreements, and Conventions, 1775–1979*. Norman: University of Oklahoma Press, 1999. 1,536pp. ISBN: 978-0-80613-118-4.

Deloria, Vine, Jr., and Clifford M. Lytle. *The Nations Within: The Past and Future of American Indian Sovereignty*. Reprint edition: Austin: University of Texas Press, 1998. 296pp. ISBN: 978-0-29271-598-1.

Deloria, Vine Jr., and David E Wilkins. *Tribes, Treaties, and Constitutional Tribulations*. Austin: University of Texas Press, 2000. 221pp. ISBN: 978-0-29271-608-7.

Grounds, Richard, George E. Tinker, and David E. Wilkins, eds. *Native Voices: American Indian Identity and Resistance*. Lawrence: University Press of Kansas, 2003. 362pp. ISBN: 978-0-70061-259-8.

Iverson, Peter, ed. *The Plains Indians of the Twentieth Century*. Norman: University of Oklahoma Press, 1986. 277pp. ISBN: 978-0-80611-959-5.

Mohawk, John C. *Utopian Legacies: A History of Conquest and Oppression in the Western World*. Santa Fe, NM: Clear Light, 2000. 256pp. ISBN: 978-1-57416-040-6.

O'Brien, Sharon. *American Indian Tribal Governments*. Norman: University of Oklahoma Press, 1989. 368pp. ISBN: 978-0-80612-564-0.

Prucha, Francis Paul. *American Indian Treaties: The History of a Political Anomaly*. Berkeley: University of California Press, 1997. 562pp. ISBN: 978-0-52020-895-7.

Prucha, Francis Paul. *The Great Father: The United States Government and the American Indians*. Two volumes. Lincoln: University of Nebraska Press, 1984. 1,355pp. ISBN: 978-0-80328-734-1. History of United States–American Indian relations from the early republic through the 1970s.

Robinson, Jennifer, Susan Olson, and Daniel McCool. *Native Vote: American Indians, the Voting Rights Act, and the Right to Vote*. New York: Cambridge University Press, 2007. 232pp. ISBN: 978-0-52183-983-9.

Thomas, David Hurst. *Skull Wars: Kennewick Man, Archeology, and the Battle for Native American Identity*. New York: Basic, 2000. 368pp. ISBN: 978-0-46509-224-6.

Waldman, Carl. *Atlas of the North American Indian*. Revised ed. New York: Checkmark, 2000. 385pp. ISBN: 978-0-81603-975-3.

APPENDICES

APPENDIX LIST

APPENDIX A

TEST MATERIALS ON THE CONSTITUTION AND THE BILL OF RIGHTS

A 1   Multiple-Choice Test—Teacher's Instructions for Administering

A 2   Multiple-Choice Test—Test on the History and Principles of the United States Constitution

A 3   Multiple-Choice Test—Answer Guide

A 4   Multiple-Choice Test—Text Correlation

APPENDIX B

CERTIFICATES

B 1   We the People: The Citizen and the Constitution Certificates

Certificate of Achievement

Certificate of Appreciation

APPENDIX C

CONDUCTING A SIMULATED CONGRESSIONAL HEARING –
GUIDELINES AND HANDOUTS

C 1   Teacher Instructions

C 2   Steps for Organizing

C 3   Rules for High School Competition

C 4   Congressional District-Level Hearing Questions

C 5   Judges' Instructions

C 6   Judges' Score Sheet

C 7   Scorekeeper's Summary Score Sheet

C 8   Event Report Form

APPENDIX D

STUDENT HANDOUTS

D 1   Student Handout for Lesson 2—Charting Classical Republicanism and Natural Rights Philosophy

D 2   Student Handout for Lesson 14—The Anti-Federalist Position on Ratification of the Constitution

D 3   Student Handout for Lesson 14—The Federalist Position on Ratification of the Constitution

D 4   Student Handout for Lesson 17—Comparing the South Carolina Declaration of Causes with Lincoln's First Inaugural Address

D 5   Student Handout for Lesson 25—United States Courts of Appeal

D 6   Student Answer Sheet for the Multiple-Choice Test

D 7   Student Multiple-Choice Test—The History and Principles of the United States Constitution

MULTIPLE-CHOICE TEST – TEACHER'S INSTRUCTIONS FOR ADMINISTERING

1. This test is based on the *We the People: The Citizen & the Constitution* Level 3 high school text and is designed as an integral part of the instructional program.

2. Teachers should instruct students to take the test without the aid of notes or their books and to select the best possible answer.

3. A reproducible answer sheet for students is included in the student handout section as Appendix D 6.

4. The teacher's answer guide for the test is in this section as Appendix A 3.

5. Teachers who have not taught the entire curriculum should refer to the test–text correlation, Appendix A 4, to determine which questions pertain to lessons they have covered. They should instruct students to answer only the questions that were covered. In evaluating performance, a student's percentage should be based only on the questions used. Students may retake the test to achieve an acceptable score.

6. Certificates of achievement may be awarded to students at the teacher's discretion. Certificates of appreciation may be awarded to those individuals who contribute to the success of your program. Sample certificates are included as Appendix B. Additional free color certificates may be obtained by calling the Center toll-free at 800-350-4223 or by emailing your request to wethepeople@civiced.org.

MULTIPLE-CHOICE TEST – TEACHER'S COPY

Name _____

Class _____

Date _____

Test on the History and Principles of the United States Constitution

Instructions

For each question, select the one best answer.

Mark your answers on a separate answer sheet as instructed by your teacher.

1. **According to the natural rights philosophy, the main purpose of government is to**
   a. create a democracy.
   b. protect individual rights.
   c. create a system of separation of powers.
   d. promote the rights of the ruling class.

2. **To say that the rights to life, liberty, and property are unalienable means that they**
   a. cannot be given up or taken away.
   b. belong only to citizens.
   c. are subject to governmental approval.
   d. are protected by the Constitution.

3. **Which of the following statements describes a constitution?**
   a. A list of obligations of citizens.
   b. A priority for achieving particular policies.
   c. A plan that sets forth the structure and powers of government.
   d. A compilation of statutes that have been in effect at least fifty years.

4. **One major issue left unresolved by the Philadelphia Convention in 1787 was**
   a. the power of the states to coin money.
   b. the power of the House to initiate revenue bills.
   c. the definition of national citizenship.
   d. the power of the national government to regulate commerce with the Indian tribes.

5. **Civic virtue is best defined as**
   a. giving authority to government in exchange for protection of natural rights.
   b. putting the common good above individual interests.
   c. giving up some natural rights to create a strong government.
   d. separating power among groups to maintain balanced government.

6. **The Founders believed that the separation of powers was important to**
   a. make the government more efficient.
   b. allow more people to hold office.
   c. prevent the misuse of power.
   d. provide for legislative supremacy.

7. **In comparison with the Greek and Roman ideals of civic virtue, the Judeo-Christian tradition**
   a. advocates enlightened self-interest.
   b. emphasizes the common good.
   c. stresses the dignity and worth of each individual.
   d. reduces the importance of individual rights.

8. **The Enlightenment inspired America's Founders by**
   a. endorsing executive supremacy.
   b. making society more rigidly structured.
   c. justifying divine right of kings.
   d. emphasizing what could be achieved through the exercise of human reason.

9. **The distribution of powers between the national government and the states in the U.S. is known as**
   a. federalism.
   b. feudalism.
   c. separation of powers.
   d. delegation of powers.

10. **The Magna Carta included the important constitutional principle that established**
    a. freedom of religion.
    b. equal rights for all citizens.
    c. government based on the rule of law.
    d. the supremacy of Parliament.

11. **The purpose of a writ of habeas corpus is to protect the individual against**
    a. accusation of treason.
    b. unlawful detention.
    c. cruel and unusual punishment.
    d. self-incrimination.

12. **In colonial America, the right to vote most often depended on a person's gender and**
    a. national origin.
    b. social class.
    c. ancestry.
    d. property ownership.

13. **The Declaration of Independence asserted that**
    a. a "candid world" would emerge from the American revolution.
    b. the colonies were now free and independent states.
    c. Parliament had oppressed the colonies through the Townsend Acts.
    d. American independence respected "the opinions of mankind."

14. **The idea that political power is derived from the people is called**
    a. popular sovereignty.
    b. judicial review.
    c. unitary government.
    d. executive supremacy.

15. **Many of the first state constitutions included**
    a. unrestricted voting rights.
    b. the right of initiative and referendum.
    c. executive supremacy.
    d. bills of rights.

16. **Some Founders believed that majority rule could be a threat to**
    a. states' rights.
    b. local self-government.
    c. individual rights.
    d. constitutional government.

17. **A major weakness of the national government under the Articles of Confederation was its**
    a. lack of authority to regulate interstate trade.
    b. unequal representation of the states.
    c. power to violate individual rights.
    d. plural executive.

18. **The delegates to the Philadelphia Convention were authorized to**
    a. draft treaties governing international trade.
    b. write a new constitution for the nation.
    c. amend the Articles of Confederation.
    d. develop a plan for admitting new states to the union.

19. **In the debate over representation in Congress, the Virginia Plan advocated**
    a. equal representation of the states.
    b. proportional representation.
    c. bipartisan representation.
    d. limited representation.

20. **According to the supremacy clause of the U.S. Constitution, "supreme law of the land" refers to**
    a. acts of the president.
    b. decisions of the Supreme Court.
    c. the Constitution, laws enacted by Congress, and treaties.
    d. laws passed by state legislatures.

21. **The right of the Senate to ratify or reject a treaty made by the president is an example of**
    a. the "general welfare" clause.
    b. checks and balances.
    c. proportional representation.
    d. federalism.

22. **The Framers adopted the Electoral College method of choosing the president because**
    a. they wanted to assure a wise consideration in the choice of president.
    b. they were afraid women would vote.
    c. the colonies had used that system.
    d. it was used successfully in the French system.

23. **Anti-Federalists objected to the proposed Constitution because they believed that it**
    a. placed too much power in the national government.
    b. established the supremacy of Congress.
    c. enumerated individual rights in too many places.
    d. authorized the Supreme Court to exercise judicial review.

24. **The "establishment clause" of the First Amendment**
    a. prohibits the press from inquiring into government operations.
    b. prohibits Congress from establishing a national religion.
    c. prohibits the government from requiring individuals to house soldiers.
    d. places limits on an individual's right to free expression.

25. **The most persuasive objection to the Constitution by George Mason and other Anti-Federalists was that**
    a. the judicial branch lacked sufficient power.
    b. it gave too much power to the House of Representatives.
    c. certain actions required more than a simple majority vote.
    d. it did not contain a bill of rights.

26. **In comparison with the executive branch as organized by the First Congress, the executive branch today has**
    a. lost much of its original power.
    b. asked Congress to be more active in developing federal regulations.
    c. allowed the cabinet to dominate the presidency.
    d. grown larger and more complex.

27. **The primary method Congress uses to consider proposed legislation is**
    a. open debate on the floor of the House.
    b. the committee system.
    c. public opinion polls.
    d. executive orders from the president.

28. **The Tenth Amendment was included in the Bill of Rights**
    a. over the objections of Anti-Federalists.
    b. to protect rights that were not specifically listed.
    c. so that the states could not violate individual rights.
    d. in an effort to reserve powers not specifically stated in the Constitution, to the states or to the people.

29. **Which of the following is an example of a "positive right" found in the U.S. Bill of Rights?**
    a. The First Amendment, which states, "Congress shall make no law" that violates fundamental rights to freedom of religion, speech, press, assembly, and petition.
    b. The Sixth Amendment, which guarantees criminal defendants in criminal cases the right to speedy and public trials.
    c. The Third Amendment, which states, "No Soldier shall, in time of peace be quartered in any house, without the consent of the Owner, nor in time of war, but in a manner to be prescribed by law."
    d. The Second Amendment, which requires the government to refrain from infringing upon the "right of the people to keep and bear Arms."

30. **Congress represents both the people and the states by**
    a. gerrymandering electoral districts.
    b. proportional representation in the House and equal state representation in the Senate.
    c. requiring consensus on all bills approved by the House and Senate.
    d. having the power to override presidential vetoes.

31. **Political parties in the United States**
    a. were created by Article IV of the U.S. Constitution.
    b. are examples of narrow factions and interests.
    c. have their rules approved by the U.S. Supreme Court.
    d. generally reflect broad coalitions of interests.

32. **Critics of judicial review claim that it conflicts with principles of**
    a. original jurisdiction.
    b. the supremacy clause.
    c. executive supremacy.
    d. legislative supremacy.

33. **In the American federal system, the scope of the national government's authority grew significantly because of the Supreme Court's interpretation of the**
    a. "privileges and immunities" clause.
    b. "free exercise" clause.
    c. "commerce" clause.
    d. "full faith and credit" clause.

34. **The Federalists defended the proposed Constitution because it would**
    a. be easy to amend.
    b. rely on separation of powers and checks and balances.
    c. provide for a highly educated people.
    d. allow all adult males the right to vote.

35. **A fundamental difference between the Articles of Confederation and the Virginia Plan was that**
    a. the Articles of Confederation allowed the national government to collect taxes from individuals.
    b. the Virginia Plan called for a strong national government.
    c. the Virginia Plan recommended a weak legislative branch.
    d. the Articles of Confederation called for a strong national government.

36. **When Southern states seceded from the Union, they justified their actions by arguing that the United States is a**
    a. sovereign nation.
    b. constitutional democracy.
    c. democratic republic.
    d. federation of sovereign states.

37. **Black Codes were passed in some states to**
    a. help African Americans find employment.
    b. limit the newly won freedoms of former slaves.
    c. help local governments protect African Americans.
    d. deny state citizenship to freed slaves.

38. **In the decades immediately following their ratification, the Civil War Amendments did little to protect the rights of African Americans because**
    a. freed slaves refused to support the amendments.
    b. U.S. Congress passed laws preventing the amendments from taking effect.
    c. state government officials did little to enforce the provisions of the amendments.
    d. the U.S. Supreme Court declared state civil rights laws unconstitutional.

39. **The guarantee of equal protection of the laws in the Fourteenth Amendment means that government**
    a. is responsible for seeing that Americans have the same opportunities.
    b. may not unfairly or unreasonably treat people differently.
    c. is responsible for ensuring that people have a decent standard of living.
    d. may not conduct unreasonable searches and seizures of private property.

40. **The Fourteenth Amendment changed the Constitution by**
    a. defining national and state citizenship.
    b. making national citizenship unavailable to Confederate officials.
    c. defining the period of residence required to become a naturalized citizen.
    d. giving the states exclusive power over citizenship.

41. **The power of Congress to investigate is an example of its**
    a. delegated powers.
    b. reserved powers.
    c. inherent powers.
    d. implied powers.

42. **The leaders of civil rights movements are significantly aided by the Constitution's protection of**
    a. freedom to assemble and petition.
    b. the privileges and immunities of citizenship.
    c. property rights.
    d. the separate but equal doctrine.

43. **The struggle to extend voting rights to women was made especially difficult by**
    a. the increase in women entering the workforce.
    b. fears that it would set back the cause for former slaves.
    c. constitutional questions over whether women are citizens.
    d. the failure of states to grant women voting rights.

44. **Citizenship of Native Americans was resolved by the**
    a. Indian Citizenship Act of 1924.
    b. *Dred Scott* decision of 1857.
    c. Missouri Compromise of 1821.
    d. Northwest Ordinance of 1787.

45. **Nations try to maintain international order by**
    a. collective security, in which nations agree to protect one another from attack.
    b. participating in the League of Nations.
    c. participating in the international police force to enforce international law.
    d. enforcing trade agreements.

46. **Americans can influence Congress in all the following ways except**
    a. petitioning.
    b. testifying before committees.
    c. lobbying on behalf of pending legislation.
    d. voting on pending legislation.

47. **"The right of the people peaceably to assemble" means that government may**
    a. forbid assemblies based on their content, subject, or theme.
    b. prohibit the use of public property for assemblies or demonstrations.
    c. apply restrictions to some groups but not to others.
    d. make reasonable "time, place, and manner" restrictions.

48. **The due process clause of the Fourteenth Amendment is important because it**
    a. changed the emphasis of the Magna Carta on procedural rights of subjects.
    b. has been used to extend the protections of most of the provisions of the Bill of Rights.
    c. provides a referendum on pending national legislation.
    d. modifies the commerce clause of Article I of the U.S. Constitution.

49. **Time, place, and manner restrictions of free expression generally are upheld by the courts if they**
    a. give local authorities adequate discretion to limit the rights of unpopular groups.
    b. apply only to obscene material or libelous statements.
    c. are authorized by Congress or a majority of state legislatures.
    d. are applied in a nondiscriminatory manner toward particular groups or individuals.

50. **Which of the following situations might violate a First Amendment right?**
    a. Police search a high school student's locker for drugs.
    b. A state legislature passes a law prohibiting the possession of firearms.
    c. Prisoners are not allowed to consult their attorneys.
    d. A city council refuses to grant a controversial group's permit to march.

51. **Individuals and groups that lobby government officials are exercising their constitutional rights of**
    a. due process.
    b. petition and association.
    c. habeas corpus.
    d. privilege against self-incrimination.

52. **The Fourth Amendment protects an individual's privacy from government intrusion in which of the following ways?**
    a. It requires a general warrant to be issued before search or seizure.
    b. It requires absolute proof of a crime committed before issuing a warrant for arrest.
    c. It prohibits general warrants because they allow indiscriminate searches.
    d. It prohibits general warrants because they limit government power.

53. **Procedural due process is based on the idea that**
    a. defendants' rights must be considered over the needs of society.
    b. systems of criminal justice must be affordable.
    c. police officers must have necessary authority to enforce the law.
    d. government officials must follow recognized procedures when making or enforcing the law.

54. **Which of the following is an important characteristic of an adversary legal system?**
    a. Cross-examination of witnesses conducted by the judge.
    b. Two opposing sides present their cases to an impartial judge or jury.
    c. There are no jury trials.
    d. Cases are presented by the parties themselves, without assistance of counsel.

55. **Nongovernmental organizations (NGOs) are examples of ways Americans can**
    a. advance the common good without relying on government.
    b. receive charters from Congress to perform quasi-legislative duties.
    c. avoid other civic responsibilities.
    d. avoid registering for the draft.

56. **States are called "laboratories of democracy" because they**
    a. test the validity of executive orders at the local level
    b. issue advisory opinions to Congress.
    c. implement novel social and economic policies.
    d. place limits on the federal government.

57. **Administrative agencies are important because they**
    a. make rules to implement laws passed by Congress.
    b. are elected by the people.
    c. are provided for in Article VII of the Constitution.
    d. are not required to exercise judgment.

58. **A fundamental difference between citizens and resident aliens is that only citizens may**
   a. enjoy the protections of the Bill of Rights and the Fourteenth Amendment.
   b. engage in social and political actions.
   c. serve on juries.
   d. buy and sell real estate.

59. **Because many Americans believe that their own opportunity to succeed is related to the well-being of society, they**
   a. act for the common good out of enlightened self-interest.
   b. put aside civic virtue for the sake of their families.
   c. respect and accept the opinions of elected public officials.
   d. reject classical republicanism in favor of the natural rights philosophy.

60. **In American constitutional democracy, citizens are expected to**
   a. promote their individual rights without regard to the common good.
   b. allow government to assume responsibility for solving social problems.
   c. ignore their own personal interests when making political choices.
   d. think critically about public issues and participate in public affairs.

61. **Which of the following is not a fundamental principle of the American constitutional system?**
   a. checks and balances
   b. popular sovereignty
   c. rule of law
   d. executive supremacy

62. **Civil disobedience differs from mere lawbreaking in which of the following ways?**
   a. Civil disobedience is not breaking the law because the First Amendment protects it.
   b. Civil disobedience is a spontaneous act.
   c. Civil disobedience is not breaking the law because it has been an important tool in civil and voting rights movements.
   d. Civil disobedience seeks to justify its actions by reference to higher moral laws.

63. **A basic difference between the Bill of Rights and the Universal Declaration of Human Rights is that the Bill of Rights**
   a. is enforceable by an authorized government.
   b. enumerates more rights.
   c. is more recent.
   d. contains only "positive" rights.

64. **The Supreme Court's power to declare the meaning of the U.S. Constitution is known as**
   a. judicial restraint.
   b. judicial activism.
   c. judicial review.
   d. judicial inquiry.

65. **The "exclusionary rule" enforces protections found in the Fourth Amendment in which of the following ways?**
   a. It requires the police to read individuals their rights.
   b. It requires the government to show "probable cause" before a warrant is issued.
   c. It prohibits the police from searching or seizing property at a school.
   d. It prohibits the government from using evidence obtained in an illegal search.

1.	b	16.	c	31.	d	46.	d	61.	d
2.	a	17.	a	32.	d	47.	d	62.	d
3.	c	18.	c	33.	c	48.	b	63.	a
4.	c	19.	b	34.	b	49.	d	64.	c
5.	b	20.	c	35.	b	50.	d	65.	d
6.	c	21.	b	36.	d	51.	b		
7.	c	22.	a	37.	b	52.	c		
8.	d	23.	a	38.	c	53.	d		
9.	a	24.	b	39.	b	54.	b		
10.	c	25.	d	40.	a	55.	a		
11.	b	26.	d	41.	d	56.	c		
12.	d	27.	b	42.	a	57.	a		
13.	b	28.	d	43.	b	58.	c		
14.	a	29.	b	44.	a	59.	a		
15.	d	30.	b	45.	a	60.	d		

MULTIPLE-CHOICE TEST – TEXT CORRELATION

Question 1. **LESSON 2**	Question 18. **LESSON 8**	Question 35. **LESSON 28**	Question 52. **LESSON 31**
Question 2. **LESSON 6**	Question 19. **LESSON 9**	Question 36. **LESSON 17**	Question 53. **LESSON 18**
Question 3. **LESSON 1**	Question 20. **LESSON 12**	Question 37. **LESSON 17**	Question 54. **LESSON 18**
Question 4. **LESSON 12**	Question 21. **LESSON 11**	Question 38. **LESSON 17**	Question 55. **LESSON 34**
Question 5. **LESSON 4**	Question 22. **LESSON 14**	Question 39. **LESSON 17**	Question 56. **LESSON 26**
Question 6. **LESSON 14**	Question 23. **LESSON 14**	Question 40. **LESSON 17**	Question 57. **LESSON 24**
Question 7. **LESSON 3**	Question 24. **LESSON 28**	Question 41. **LESSON 21**	Question 58. **LESSON 33**
Question 8. **LESSON 3**	Question 25. **LESSON 14**	Question 42. **LESSON 30**	Question 59. **LESSON 33**
Question 9. **LESSON 21**	Question 26. **LESSON 23**	Question 43. **LESSON 20**	Question 60. **LESSON 34**
Question 10. **LESSON 4**	Question 27. **LESSON 22**	Question 44. **LESSON 20**	Question 61. **LESSON 39**
Question 11. **LESSON 4**	Question 28. **LESSON 27**	Question 45. **LESSON 38**	Question 62. **LESSON 35**
Question 12. **LESSON 7**	Question 29. **LESSON 27**	Question 46. **LESSON 22**	Question 63. **LESSON 36**
Question 13. **LESSON 7**	Question 30. **LESSON 21**	Question 47. **LESSON 30**	Question 64. **LESSON 16**
Question 14. **LESSON 7**	Question 31. **LESSON 16**	Question 48. **LESSON 33**	Question 65. **LESSON 31**
Question 15. **LESSON 7**	Question 32. **LESSON 15**	Question 49. **LESSON 29**	
Question 16. **LESSON 8**	Question 33. **LESSON 21**	Question 50. **LESSON 30**	
Question 17. **LESSON 8**	Question 34. **LESSON 14**	Question 51. **LESSON 30**	

UNIT 1	LESSON	QUESTION
	1	3
	2	1
	3	7, 8
	4	5, 10, 11
	5	—
	6	2
	7	12, 13, 14, 15

UNIT 2	LESSON	QUESTION
	8	16, 17, 18
	9	19
	10	—
	11	21
	12	4, 20
	13	—
	14	6, 22, 23, 25, 34

UNIT 3	LESSON	QUESTION
	15	32
	16	31, 64
	17	36, 37, 38, 39, 40
	18	53, 54
	19	—
	20	43, 44

UNIT 4	LESSON	QUESTION
	21	9, 30, 33, 41
	22	27, 46
	23	26
	24	57
	25	—
	26	56

UNIT 5	LESSON	QUESTION
	27	28, 29
	28	24, 35
	29	49
	30	42, 47, 50, 51
	31	52, 65
	32	—

UNIT 6	LESSON	QUESTION
	33	48, 58, 59
	34	55, 60
	35	62
	36	63
	37	—
	38	45
	39	61

CERTIFICATE OF ACHIEVEMENT

Certificates of achievement may be awarded to students at the teacher's discretion. A sample certificate is provided.

CERTIFICATE OF APPRECIATION

Certificates of appreciation may be awarded to those persons who contribute to the success of your program. A sample certificate is provided.

FREE COLOR CERTIFICATES

Additional certificates of achievement and appreciation may be obtained from the Center by calling 800-350-4223 or by emailing your request to wethepeople@civiced.org.

WE THE PEOPLE
THE CITIZEN & THE CONSTITUTION

For the study of the history and principles of the United States Constitution and Bill of Rights

PRESENTED TO

_____

PRESENTED BY

_____

Certificate
of
Achievement

Funded by the U.S. Department of Education under the Education for Democracy Act approved by the United States Congress

Permission for reproduction is granted by the Center for Civic Education for hearings and classroom use

WE THE PEOPLE

THE CITIZEN & THE CONSTITUTION

Certificate

of

Appreciation

For outstanding contributions to civic education

PRESENTED TO

_____

PRESENTED BY

_____

Funded by the U.S. Department of Education under the Education for Democracy Act approved by the United States Congress

Permission for reproduction is granted by the Center for Civic Education for hearings and classroom use

What is a simulated congressional hearing?

A simulated congressional hearing is the culminating activity for We the People: The Citizen and the Constitution. The simulated hearing is an authentic, performance-based assessment where students demonstrate their understanding of the U.S. Constitution and the Bill of Rights.

During the simulated hearing, students assume the role of constitutional experts. Students present prepared oral statements before a panel of judges, usually adults from the community. Following the formal presentations, students respond to follow-up questions from the panel of judges. The purpose of the follow-up questions is to give students the opportunity to demonstrate the depth of their understanding of the Constitution and Bill of Rights and to allow students time to clarify issues they may have raised in their formal statements.

This teacher's edition provides all the materials you need to prepare your class to participate in a simulated congressional hearing:

- A test on the Constitution and Bill of Rights
- Hearing questions for each of the six units of the student text
- Instructions for how to organize and prepare your students
- Instructions for the panel of judges
- Scoring sheets for the panel of judges
- Certificates of achievement and appreciation

What is a competitive hearing?

Each state has adopted a geographic organizational plan for the simulated congressional hearing. This is known as the congressional district-level hearing. Every congressional district has a district coordinator for the We the People program. The district coordinator is responsible for the organization of district hearings for elementary, middle, and high school students.

High school classes may compete at the congressional district and state levels. The winner of the district competition progresses to the state level, and the winner of the state competition progresses to the prestigious national competition in Washington, D.C., in late April or early May.

District-level competitions are held under the supervision and authority of the district coordinators. They have the final word on all decisions regarding rules and logistics.

For the complete Rules for High School Competition, see Appendix C 3. Rules are reviewed annually. For the most up-to-date rules, check with your district coordinator or visit the We the People website, wethepeople.civiced.org.

To inquire about participation in your congressional district hearing, contact your district coordinator. If you do not know who your coordinator is, visit wethepeople.civiced.org, contact your state coordinator from the list provided in the We the People brochure, or contact the Center for Civic Education at 800-350-4223.

Should a district coordinator be involved in my class's noncompetitive simulated hearing?

It is your decision whether to involve your district coordinator in noncompetitive hearings. You should notify the district coordinator about your hearing. You may want to ask your district coordinator for support, for help in finding judges, or even to participate as a judge.

If your class participates in a hearing, please complete the Event Report Form, Appendix C 8.

How do students prepare for participating in a simulated congressional hearing?

Studying the *We the People* text is the best preparation for participating in the simulated congressional hearing. The instructional activities in each lesson require students to analyze, evaluate, take, and defend positions on a variety of constitutional issues. Each lesson is designed to help students acquire the knowledge, critical-thinking skills, and participation skills necessary to successfully take part in a hearing.

All students in the class must participate in the simulated congressional hearing. All students study the entire text. The teacher then divides the class into six equal groups (if possible) corresponding to the units of the text. Student preparation is based on topical questions provided by the Center. Each group assumes responsibility for preparing and presenting the question related to their unit.

Students may use the text or any other reference materials to prepare a formal response to their question. Students are encouraged to investigate related topics in preparation for the follow-up questions that the panel of judges may ask during the actual hearing.

You may want to attend one or more of the Center's professional development opportunities. Please see the Center's website, www.civiced.org, for more details.

What criteria will the panel of judges use to evaluate student performance?

The panel of judges will score each group of students on six criteria:

- Understanding of constitutional principles
- Application of constitutional principles
- Reasoning
- Supporting evidence
- Responsiveness to questions from the panel of judges
- Cooperation and participation among the members of the group

At the conclusion of each presentation, the panel of judges provides oral feedback. Judges generally speak to the strengths of the presentation; they may offer suggestions for improvement. Judges give the teacher or designated volunteer the score sheets.

Who are the participants in a simulated congressional hearing and what should each do?

Students

The class is organized into groups, one group of students for each unit of the text. It is expected that every student in the class will participate in the activity. The number of students in each group should be as equal as possible, but each group should include at least three students. For the competitive hearing, no student may be in more than one group unless a class has fewer than eighteen students. (See C 3, Rules for High School Competition.)

Students should prepare a four-minute presentation responding to the question for their unit. Responses may be written on note cards and read aloud or memorized and recited. No other materials or references may be used.

Each group of students meets with the teacher to decide how responsibilities will be divided among the members of the group. Each group member should have a speaking role during the opening statement before the panel of judges. Each group member should also participate in the six-minute follow-up questioning period after the formal presentation. Evidence of cooperation and full participation by all members of the group is one criterion that will be evaluated.

After the four-minute opening statement, judges will ask follow-up questions for six minutes (each hearing lasts a total of ten minutes). Suggested follow-up questions are provided for the panel of judges. Students are not permitted to see the follow-up questions in advance of the hearing. The purpose of the follow-up questions is to probe students' understanding of the material. It is also an opportunity for the judges to engage in discussion with students. Suggested follow-up questions should encompass only the material in the group's unit. Judges may decide to formulate their own questions; they are encouraged to do so.

Judges

Eighteen judges, three for each group of students, is ideal but not always practical. Minimally, three judges are needed to listen to and evaluate the presentations from all six groups.

People who serve as judges usually are recruited from the community. Suggestions for invitations include, but should not be limited to, the following:

- District social studies supervisors
- Professors from local colleges or universities
- Members of Congress or staffers from your congressional representative's local office
- Members of state legislatures or staffers
- Members of the city council or mayor's office
- Leaders of community groups or service organizations
- Attorneys and judges
- Social studies teachers
- We the People alumni

Once you have selected your panel of judges, provide each member of the panel with the following items:

- *We the People* text
- Appendix C 4, Congressional District-Level Hearing Questions
- Appendix C 5, Judges' Instructions
- Appendix C 6, Judges' Score Sheet
- Follow-up questions provided annually by the Center to district coordinators

It is best to send the judges these materials a couple of weeks in advance of the event. You should also schedule a pre-event meeting with the judges. During the meeting review the procedures for the hearing and respond to questions that the judges may have. Remember that judges may have little or no classroom experience. You may want to share some of the characteristics of your class and tactfully remind the judges of your students' ages and level of education. Also, emphasize the importance of comments to students at the end of each presentation. Judges and students should have a good experience interacting with each other.

Remind judges that at the conclusion of the hearing they have additional time to tabulate scores. Judges should consult each other but need not agree among themselves before completing their written comments and tabulating final scores. Judges must return their scoring sheets to the teacher before leaving the hearing site.

Timekeeper

Each hearing should have a timekeeper to officially keep and enforce time limits during each presentation. This person should be someone other than one of the judges.

The timekeeper should allot ten minutes for each group's presentation: four minutes for the formal statement and six minutes for follow-up questioning from the judges. Timing should start when students begin their opening statement. In the event that the full four minutes are not used for the opening statement, the remaining time should be allotted to the follow-up period. Judges may allow a student to speak beyond the time limit so that the student may finish a sentence or thought. Be mindful, however, that fairness is always an issue and exceptions to the rule should be applied judiciously.

The timekeeper should give notice when one minute remains for the opening statement. The timer may do this by holding up a card showing that one minute remains. At the end of the four minutes, the timekeeper calls time. Repeat the process during the follow-up questioning period.

SIMULATED CONGRESSIONAL HEARING – TEACHER INSTRUCTIONS

Audience

A simulated hearing is an excellent opportunity for your students to demonstrate to the community what they know and what they can do. Having an audience lends formality and excitement to the event. In addition, it helps to publicize the program, both in your school and in the community.

Suggestions for those you might want to invite to the simulated congressional hearing include the following:

- Parents
- Your We the People congressional district, regional, and state coordinators
- District superintendent
- Curriculum coordinators
- Building principal and staff
- Members of Congress or staffers from your congressional representative's local office
- State legislators or staffers
- City officials
- Journalists from both the print and electronic media
- Community organizations
- Other teachers in your school
- Other classes in your school

It is best to send invitations at least two weeks in advance of the event. The invitation should briefly describe the program and specify time and location. On the day of the hearing, someone should be available to greet guests and direct them to the site where the event will occur.

How can I recognize student achievement in the program?

You will likely want to hold an awards ceremony immediately after the simulated hearing. Certificates of achievement may be given to students, and certificates of appreciation may be given to people who have supported the program in your school or district. You may want to invite a distinguished guest to present the awards or to speak to the assembled group.

Often, a reception for students and guests follows the awards ceremony. The reception need not be elaborate. The important thing is to create an opportunity for your students and the adults to interact.

How can I organize a simulated congressional hearing?

To ensure a successful hearing and a good experience for your students, follow these steps (appropriate modifications should be made to suit individual situations):

Step 1. Prepare students

After students have studied the entire curriculum, administer and score the multiple-choice test.

Divide the class into six groups and assign each group to a unit. Explain to your students the purposes and procedures of a real congressional hearing. Explain the roles students will play and the procedures that will be followed.

Distribute the appropriate hearing question to each group. Students need to prepare a four-minute presentation addressing the issues raised in the question. Answers to the questions are in their *We the People* textbook. Encourage students to phrase answers in their own words and not to recite verbatim from the text. Questions may require students to gather additional information and form their own opinions.

Inform students about the following guidelines for the formal presentations:

- Students may use notes during their prepared presentations
- All students in each group should be prepared to speak during the formal presentation
- Students may not use visual aids such as posters, videos, computer presentations, pictures, or charts

Allow class time for groups to meet and prepare for the hearing. If desired, arrange for one or more outside experts to assist students in preparing their presentations. Subject matter experts, speech or debate specialists, attorneys, other community representatives, and We the People alumni can be helpful and stimulating.

Students also should prepare for six minutes of spontaneous follow-up questioning from the judges. Inform students about the guidelines for responding to the follow-up questions:

- Students may not use notes during this period
- All students in the group should participate in responding to the judges' questions
- Students may assist each other during the response period
- Students may politely disagree with the responses of other members of the group

Note: These guidelines are intended to be flexible and may be modified to meet the needs of individual teachers and their classes.

Step 2. Determine the time and location for the hearing

Under the most favorable circumstances, the hearing would be conducted in an auditorium or other facility that can accommodate an audience. If it is not feasible to conduct the hearing in such a space, it may be conducted in a classroom with a smaller audience.

The simulated hearing may be held either during the school day or during evening hours when more parents are able to attend.

You may want to involve a cosponsoring organization to help in planning and running the hearing. Possible cosponsors might include local bar associations, judges' associations, historical societies, or community service groups. Cosponsors may help provide a site for the hearing, help students prepare for the hearing, donate refreshments, etc.

Each congressional district has a coordinator. You should attempt to involve your We the People congressional district coordinator in your program. This person is available to help you organize your simulated hearing. Please call your state coordinator or the Center for Civic Education at 800-350-4223 to identify your district coordinator. A list of state coordinators is also available at wethepeople.civiced.org.

Step 3. Select and invite judges

Step 4. Invite guests

Step 5. Invite a member of Congress to participate

The Center recommends that a member of Congress (or staff representative) in whose district the school is located be invited to participate by

- signing certificates,
- visiting classes,
- speaking to students and teachers,
- observing or participating in simulated congressional hearings, or
- presenting certificates or speaking at awards ceremonies

Step 6. Prepare certificates of achievement and certificates of appreciation

Each student earns a certificate of achievement by passing the test on the principles and history of the Constitution and participating in the simulated congressional hearing. The Center for Civic Education will provide free certificates of achievement for each student and certificates of appreciation for those who assist with the program.

You may order your certificates by calling the Center at 800-350-4223 or by sending an email request to wethepeople@civiced.org. You may also download certificates from the Center's website. Another choice may be to make photocopies of the sample certificate that is included with this set of materials.

Your member of the House of Representatives or someone on her or his staff should sign the certificates. An official of your school district also may sign the certificates.

Step 7. Organize your awards ceremony and reception

Step 8. Arrange the hearing room

If the hearing is held in a school auditorium or other large meeting room, arrange tables and chairs in a "V" shape at the front of the room. The open end of the "V" should face the audience. The panel of judges sits along one arm of the "V." Each group of students should be seated along the other arm when it is their turn to present their unit. If needed, provide microphones for both the panel of judges and the students.

Arrange an area of the room with seating for students waiting their turn to present.

If the hearing is to be held in a classroom, arrange the space so that a set of chairs faces the judges, in a "V" shape if possible. These chairs are for students who will be presenting to the judges; other students will remain at their desks.

Arrange seating for the timekeeper in a location where he or she can be seen by both students and the judges.

Step 9. Meet with the judges

Instruct the judges that student groups will have prepared statements to present. Each group of students will be prepared to respond to a hearing question for their assigned unit. During the follow-up question period, panel members may ask students to explain or expand upon their prepared statement. Follow-up questions should not raise topics with which students are not familiar. Rather, they should help students demonstrate their knowledge and understanding of the basic constitutional principles they have studied.

Judges may ask follow-up questions that allow students to apply historical or contemporary events to their unit topic. Judges should address the entire group when asking a specific question.

Review the procedures for conducting the simulated hearing with the panels of judges. Be prepared to respond to the judges' questions and concerns.

Step 10. Conduct the hearing

What procedures should be followed during the simulated hearing?

1. Start the session by giving a brief overview of the We the People curriculum and a rationale for studying the Constitution and Bill of Rights. You may want to share some examples of student work and offer some anecdotes related to what students did during their study of the curriculum.

2. Introduce any dignitaries who are present in the audience. Parents and people from cosponsoring organizations should also be introduced.

3. Acknowledge the judges and others who are present at the hearing.

4. You may call upon designated judges or other guests to make some brief opening remarks.

5. Call the first student group forward. Students sit in the chairs facing the judges.

6. The chairperson of the panel of judges should direct the introduction. The judges should introduce themselves first and tell students their professions. Then the students should introduce themselves. Name cards for students and the judges are helpful.

7. The chairperson should read aloud the unit question in its entirety.

8. Students then present their prepared statement in response to the designated question for their unit. Timekeeping begins at this moment.

9. At the conclusion of the prepared statement, the judges begin their follow-up questions.

10. After each group's presentation and the follow-up period, each judge on the panel should offer brief feedback to students on their performance. The judges may use their scoring sheet as a guide. This evaluation period is not timed.

11. At the conclusion of the evaluation feedback, students return to the audience and you may call the next group forward.

We the People: The Citizen and the Constitution is intended for all students. High schools with classes competing in the We the People simulated congressional hearings must comply with the following rules:

1. Teachers must provide a copy of their official class roster, signed by their school principal or other appropriate school administrator, as a confirmation that the class meets the competition rules.

2. The Center is committed to encouraging the widest possible participation from a broad range of students with the continued emphasis on the involvement of all members of a class. For purposes of the competition a "class" must

   - be constituted according to the school's normal policies and procedures for student admittance to a class;

   - be designated on the school's master program (schedule of class offerings) as a required or elective class;

   - be in session during the regular hours of the school day;

   - have all enrollees entered in the teacher's record book; and

   - provide graduation credits to students for satisfactory course completion.

3. In addition to meeting during regularly scheduled class periods, students are permitted to meet for extended study and preparation for simulated congressional hearings. If a class ends before the scheduled dates for holding district, regional, state, and national competitions it is understood that preparation for the competition will take place after the class has ended.

4. Students who have previously participated in the high school competitive option at the congressional district, regional, state, or national level will not be allowed to compete in the oral presentation or questioning at any subsequent competition at congressional district, regional, state, or national levels. However, students who are rostered in a class participating in the competition and who have previously competed may attend hearings as teaching assistants or spectators. Students who have participated in elementary or middle school hearings are eligible to participate in the high school competition.

5. Teachers agree to teach the entire six units of the curriculum. The Center provides a multiple-choice test that teachers may use to evaluate students' knowledge acquisition. The test may help teachers assess the readiness of students for participation in the competition. Teachers may use an alternate test if they choose, or readminister the Center test and remedy weaknesses until a desired score is attained.

Permission for reproduction is granted by the Center for Civic Education for hearings and classroom use

Permission for reproduction is granted by the Center for Civic Education for hearings and classroom use

6. Each class must be divided into six groups, and each group will be responsible for "testifying" on their assigned unit of the text. Each group must have at least three members, and the number of students in each group should be as equal as possible. No student may be in more than one group unless a class has fewer than eighteen students.

7. When a class has fewer than eighteen students, teachers may allow some students to participate in two groups but not more than two. The number of students allowed to participate in more than one group is determined by the total number of students in the class.

Number of students in class	Number of different students participating in two groups
17	1
16	2
15	3
14	4
13	5
12	6
11	7
10	8
9	9

8. The class roster shall identify the unit to which each student is assigned. A class roster is required for each level of competition (district, regional, state, and national). Teachers may change student unit assignments for each level of competition, if they so desire. New students, however, may not be added to a roster after a class enters its first level of competition without permission from the We the People state coordinator and the national program director. Once a class is defined by its roster as being composed of specific students, the same students must participate in all levels of competition. If a student drops out of a class for reasons beyond his or her control, verification by the school's principal must be sent to the We the People state coordinator and the national program director. No class with fewer than nine students will be eligible to compete.

9. Two high school classes may be combined in order to participate in the competition if the total number of students in the combined class does not exceed thirty-five students. The combining of two classes must have the approval of both the district and state coordinator, and both classes must meet the definition of a "class." All students in both classes must be listed on the class roster, and all students must participate in the hearing competition.

UNIT INSTRUCTIONS

As you know from studying your *We the People: The Citizen & the Constitution* textbook, members of Congress make laws. These laws should protect our rights and promote our welfare. To make good decisions about which laws they want to pass, members of Congress need to gather information. This information will help them understand how to address our nation's problems and pass good laws.

One way that members of Congress get the information they need is by holding congressional hearings. At these hearings, they ask experts to answer questions about important issues that affect proposed laws.

For this activity, you will play the role of an expert who has been asked to speak at a congressional hearing. Each unit group will act as a team of experts on one of the six units of your text.

You will need a good understanding of your unit. You will also have to prepare answers to the questions assigned to your unit. At the hearing, committee members might ask you other questions about the information you have presented.

Your unit group should meet before the congressional hearing to prepare answers to your assigned questions. Most of the information you need for preparing good answers is in your text. In some cases, you might want to ask parents, teachers, and friends for their ideas about government in the United States today. Each member of your group should contribute to the presentation and speak at the hearing.

Permission for reproduction is granted by the Center for Civic Education for hearings and classroom use

Permission for reproduction is granted by the Center for Civic Education for hearings and classroom use

UNIT 1

WHAT ARE THE PHILOSOPHICAL AND HISTORICAL FOUNDATIONS OF THE AMERICAN POLITICAL SYSTEM?

1. **How did both classical republicans and the natural rights philosophers influence the Founders' views about government?**

   - What are the essential differences between classical republicanism and natural rights philosophy?

   - Why do both classical republicans and natural rights philosophers stress the need for education and preparation for citizenship?

2. **What are the fundamental characteristics of a constitutional government?**

   - In what ways does constitutional government mean limited government?

   - Describe at least three provisions of the Constitution that provide a means of preventing the abuse or misuse of governmental power. Explain how these provisions work in our system of government today.

3. **What effect did colonial experiences have on the Founders' views about rights and government?**

   - In what ways were eighteenth-century American and British societies similar or dissimilar in terms of the rights of individual liberty, equality of opportunity, and property?

   - How did early state constitutions reflect colonial experiences as well as the ideas of classical republicanism and natural rights philosophy?

UNIT 2

HOW DID THE FRAMERS CREATE THE CONSTITUTION?

1. **How does the Constitution limit government power to protect individual rights while promoting the common good?**

   - Why did the Federalists and Anti-Federalists disagree on whether the Constitution sufficiently protected individual rights and promoted the common good?

   - What responsibilities, if any, do citizens have for seeing that individual rights are protected and the common good is promoted?

2. **What were the major conflicts at the Philadelphia Convention and how were they resolved?**

   - What arguments can you make for and against giving each state the right to send the same number of members to the Senate?

   - What arguments can you make for and against including the three-fifths clause and the fugitive slave clause in the Constitution?

3. **What were the major differences between the Federalists and the Anti-Federalists?**

   - How did the arguments of the Federalists and the Anti-Federalists reflect their points of view regarding natural rights, republicanism, and the powers of the states?

   - Why are the Federalist and Anti-Federalist debates still relevant today?

Permission for reproduction is granted by the Center for Civic Education for hearings and classroom use

Permission for reproduction is granted by the Center for Civic Education for hearings and classroom use

UNIT 3

HOW HAS THE CONSTITUTION BEEN CHANGED TO FURTHER THE IDEALS CONTAINED IN THE DECLARATION OF INDEPENDENCE?

1. **What are the basic purposes of the Fourteenth Amendment?**

   - How are questions left unresolved at the Philadelphia Convention addressed in the Fourteenth Amendment?

   - How are the due process and equal protection clauses of the Fourteenth Amendment related to principles of limited government?

2. **How and why has suffrage been expanded in the United States?**

   - Why has the expansion of suffrage been controversial?

   - How have advocates of expanded suffrage used their rights under the First Amendment to achieve their goals?

3. **What are the major arguments for and against judicial review?**

   - Alexander Hamilton claimed in Federalist No. 78 that "the interpretation of the laws is the proper and peculiar province of the courts." Do you agree or disagree? Why?

   - What are the advantages and disadvantages of an appointed, life-tenured branch of government overturning laws passed by a democratically elected body of government?

UNIT 4

HOW HAVE THE VALUES AND PRINCIPLES EMBODIED IN THE CONSTITUTION SHAPED AMERICAN INSTITUTIONS AND PRACTICES?

1. **In the Constitution, why are the powers of and limits on Congress addressed first and in greater detail than those of other branches?**

   ● In addition to the powers granted to Congress in Article I, what other provisions in the Constitution address legislative powers? Why?

   ● How have the "enforcement" provisions of amendments adopted since the Civil War increased congressional power?

2. **How and why has presidential power expanded since the ratification of the Constitution?**

   ● How have wars, emergencies, and the media contributed to the expansion of presidential powers?

   ● How have the other branches of government responded to the expansion of presidential power? Do you think they have done so adequately? Explain.

3. **How and why did the founders create America's system of federalism?**

   ● How does federalism limit the powers of both the national government and the states?

   ● How does federalism extend opportunities for citizen participation?

Permission for reproduction is granted by the Center for Civic Education for hearings and classroom use

Permission for reproduction is granted by the Center for Civic Education for hearings and classroom use

UNIT 5

WHAT RIGHTS DOES THE BILL OF RIGHTS PROTECT?

1. **Why have First Amendment rights been viewed as essential to the functioning of a free society?**

   - In what ways have these rights been of particular importance to women and minorities?

   - Although First Amendment rights are considered essential in a constitutional democracy, it is sometimes argued that these rights must be limited. Under what circumstances, if any, do you think limitations are justified? Explain your answer.

2. **How are individual rights protected in the body of the Constitution?**

   - Given the protection of rights in the body of the Constitution, would you have agreed or disagreed with the Anti-Federalists' argument for the addition of a bill of rights? Why?

   - What additional rights, if any, do you think should be added to the Constitution? Why?

3. **What fundamental American values are embodied in the Fourth Amendment?**

   - Why have Fourth Amendment issues been a persistent concern from colonial times until today?

   - How and why does modern technology raise new concerns about the Fourth Amendment?

UNIT 6

WHAT CHALLENGES MIGHT FACE AMERICAN CONSTITUTIONAL DEMOCRACY IN THE TWENTY-FIRST CENTURY?

1. **Why does the United States' commitment to the rule of law appeal to other peoples?**

   ● How would you explain the meaning of the rule of law?

   ● How do America's founding documents express the nation's commitment to the rule of law?

2. **What do you think are the greatest challenges of American citizenship today?**

   ● Why and how does constitutional democracy in the United States depend on the active participation of its citizens?

   ● What are the advantages and disadvantages, if any, of being a citizen of both the United States and the state in which you reside?

3. **What do you think are the best ways to achieve constitutional change?**

   ● Thomas Jefferson argued that the Constitution should be revised every generation. The Founders provided instead for an amendment process to take place only if and when revisions may be deemed necessary. Which method do you think is better? Why?

   ● In what ways, if any, have constitutional amendments helped the United States become "a more perfect union"? Explain.

Permission for reproduction is granted by the Center for Civic Education for hearings and classroom use

Permission for reproduction is granted by the Center for Civic Education for hearings and classroom use

Structure of the Hearings

During simulated congressional hearings on the U.S. Constitution and Bill of Rights, students appear before a panel of judges role-playing a congressional committee. The panels are composed of three knowledgeable people from the community. The panel of judges questions students who are representing constitutional experts called on to answer questions about the U.S. Constitution and Bill of Rights. The panel listens to oral presentations from small groups of students on selected constitutional issues chosen from one unit of the *We the People: The Citizen & the Constitution* text. Students should be treated as experts who have been asked to testify before the congressional committee on their particular topic.

The panel selects one member to act as chair. The chair begins the proceedings. On entering the hearing room, the chair introduces the judges and asks students to introduce themselves. One judge reads the entire question. Students have four minutes to respond. A group should not be penalized for using less than their allotted time during prepared statements. Any excess time will be added to the six-minute follow-up period.

The classes are divided into groups, one group for each of the six units in the text. Each group has been given questions in advance to prepare for questioning on its topic.

Students will respond to their group's question with a four-minute prepared presentation. They may use notes during this presentation. Then they respond for six minutes to follow-up questions by the judges. During the follow-up questioning period, they cannot use notes. Each of the six groups will thus appear before the judges for a total of ten minutes.

The judges listen to each group's presentation, question the group on its topic, and score the group. The class's total score consists of the combined scores received by its six groups.

Students might be nervous. Therefore, it is the task of the judges to encourage them to feel at ease so that they may demonstrate their knowledge. The simulated hearing serves as the culmination of their classroom learning.

Hearing Questions

After hearing a group's prepared presentation, there is a six-minute follow-up question-and-answer period. The follow-up questioning constitutes the judges' most challenging task. The Center for Civic Education provides suggested follow-up questions. Judges are encouraged to use these questions whenever appropriate. Follow-up questions should be addressed to the entire group; singling out a particular student to answer should be avoided. Judges should focus much of their questioning on what students said in their four-minute prepared presentations. Therefore, judges may want to formulate their own questions.

Judges should phrase follow-up questions concisely. It is best not to ask multipart follow-up questions. During the final minute—indicated by a signal from the official timer—questions should be brief.

Timing

For each hearing, there will be an official timekeeper. The timekeeper keeps strictly to the framework of ten minutes per group: four minutes for the initial oral presentation and six minutes for the follow-up questioning. Timekeepers will silently notify groups by holding up a card when they have one minute left in their initial oral presentation time and will silently notify judges and students when there is one minute left in the follow-up question period. When time expires, the timekeeper stops all participants by saying "Time" and by holding up a card with the word printed on it.

Every effort should be made to observe time limits. At the discretion of judges, however, extra time may be allowed to compensate a group for any situation that significantly reduces their allowed response time. For example, if a judge has taken inordinate time to phrase a question, extra time may be granted to allow students to adequately respond.

Use of Notes or Materials

Students may use written aids on note cards or on paper not larger than 8½ by 11 inches during their four-minute presentation period. No other materials or references may be used. Neither notes nor any other materials may be used during the follow-up questioning period.

Judging Criteria

Judges score each student group on six criteria: understanding, constitutional application, reasoning, supporting evidence, responsiveness, and participation. These criteria are fully explained on the Judges' Score Sheet (Appendix C 6). Throughout their assessment of student performance, judges should be careful to base their scores on the six established criteria, not on their agreement or disagreement with students' positions.

For each criterion listed, each judge scores the group on a scale of 1 to 10, with 10 being the highest score. Judges must use a separate form for each group. Before beginning a hearing, judges should ascertain that they have the appropriate score sheet (correct teacher name, school name, and unit number). The scorekeeper will total class scores on a separate summary form.

Special care must be taken in judging a group on participation. Groups in which most members speak should be rated higher than those in which one or two students dominate the entire ten minutes. Because it is recognized that certain students have an especially difficult time with speaking in public, it is the policy of the We the People program that a group not be penalized if one or two students do not participate because of shyness, language problems, handicaps, etc. In rating participation, judges should evaluate the extent to which most students respond.

Judges may keep score sheets for all groups seen during one session. Score sheets may be revised during that session. For example, if after judging two or three groups, the judges think they were too harsh or too easy on the first group, they may adjust their scores. Once scores have been turned in, it is no longer possible to make revisions. Judges may consult with one another about scoring; however, they do not need to agree on their scores.

Feedback

Although students should be given some oral feedback, they should not be told how their presentations were scored. Feedback should include comments on the group's strengths and suggestions for improvement. Time constraints require that feedback be brief.

Permission for reproduction is granted by the Center for Civic Education for hearings and classroom use

Permission for reproduction is granted by the Center for Civic Education for hearings and classroom use

C 6

SIMULATED CONGRESSIONAL HEARING – JUDGES' SCORE SHEET   UNIT _____

Teacher _____

School _____

Congressional District _____

State _____

Date _____

For each criterion listed, score the group on a scale of 1 to 10, with 10 being the best score.
Use a separate form for each group.

1-2 = Poor   **3-4** = Fair   **5-6** = Average   **7-8** = Above Average   **9-10** = Excellent

		SCORE	NOTES
1	**UNDERSTANDING** — To what extent did participants demonstrate a clear understanding of the basic issues involved in the question?		
2	**CONSTITUTIONAL APPLICATION** — To what extent did participants appropriately apply knowledge of constitutional history and principles?		
3	**REASONING** — To what extent did participants support positions with sound reasoning?		
4	**SUPPORTING EVIDENCE** — To what extent did participants support positions with historical or contemporary evidence, examples, and/or illustrations?		
5	**RESPONSIVENESS** — To what extent did participants' answers address the question asked?		
6	**PARTICIPATION** — To what extent did most group members contribute to the group's presentation?		
	GROUP TOTAL		

JUDGE	TIEBREAKER*

*Tiebreaker

Designate a score of any number between 0 and 100 that reflects this group's OVERALL performance. (This score will be used only in the event of a tie.) Use the following scale:

Outstanding	**90 to 100**	points
Very Good	**80 to 89**	points
Above Average	**70 to 79**	points
Average	**50 to 69**	points
Below Average	**30 to 49**	points
Poor	**0 to 29**	points

SCOREKEEPER'S SUMMARY SCORE SHEET

Teacher _____

School _____

Congressional District _____

State _____

Date _____

For each group, record the totals from the Simulated Congressional Hearing—Judges' Score Sheets (one per judge) in the spaces provided.

Then, add the group totals to determine the Combined Group Total. For example, if Group 1 received scores of 48, 46, and 51 from the three judges, you would record a 145 for Unit 1's group.

Add all Combined Group Totals to obtain the Class Grand Total.

Unit Group Number	JUDGE 1		JUDGE 2		JUDGE 3		Combined Group Total
UNIT 1		+		+		=	
UNIT 2		+		+		=	
UNIT 3		+		+		=	
UNIT 4		+		+		=	
UNIT 5		+		+		=	
UNIT 6		+		+		=	

CLASS GRAND TOTAL =

Scorekeeper

Make sure that you retain all Simulated Congressional Hearing — Judges' Score Sheets to use in case of ties. When two or more classes have the same grand totals, the tiebreaker points from all the judges should be added together to determine the winner. A tiebreaker compilation score sheet is available at wethepeople.civiced.org.

Permission for reproduction is granted by the Center for Civic Education for hearings and classroom use

Permission for reproduction is granted by the Center for Civic Education for hearings and classroom use

C 8
EVENT REPORT FORM

Center for Civic Education • 5145 Douglas Fir Road • Calabasas, CA 91302 • (800) 350.4223

Please print with ballpoint pen

Date of event ___ - ___ - ___

Location of event ___

Organizer ___

State/District Coordinator? ☐ yes ☐ no

Address ___

City ___ State ___ Zip ___ Country ___ Language of event ___

☐ We the People: The Citizen and the Constitution
(circle one)   elementary   middle   high school

☐ We the People: Project Citizen
(circle one)   portfolio   hearing   both

☐ School Violence Prevention Demonstration Program

☐ Foundations of Democracy

Level   ☐ state   ☐ school
        ☐ region   ☐ class
        ☐ congressional district   ☐ youth organization
        ☐ other

Winning class/youth organization ___

Number of volunteers (judges, trainers, timers, facilitators, and others) ___

Funding source (International program only) ___

Type of event   ☐ competitive   ☐ noncompetitive/showcase

Participating Teachers or Youth Organization Leaders   Use multiple forms if necessary

Teacher/Leader Mr. / Mrs. / Ms. ___

School/Organization Name ___

☐ Public   ☐ Private   ☐ Parochial   ☐ Youth Org.   ☐ Other

School/Organization Address ___

Email ___

Phone ( ) ___   Fax ( ) ___

Grade level ___ Course ___

Number of classes participating ___   Number of students per class/organization ___

Teacher/Leader Mr. / Mrs. / Ms. ___

School/Organization Name ___

☐ Public   ☐ Private   ☐ Parochial   ☐ Youth Org.   ☐ Other

School/Organization Address ___

Email ___

Phone ( ) ___   Fax ( ) ___

Grade level ___ Course ___

Number of classes participating ___   Number of students per class/organization ___

Teacher/Leader Mr. / Mrs. / Ms. ___

School/Organization Name ___

☐ Public   ☐ Private   ☐ Parochial   ☐ Youth Org.   ☐ Other

School/Organization Address ___

Email ___

Phone ( ) ___   Fax ( ) ___

Grade level ___ Course ___

Number of classes participating ___   Number of students per class/organization ___

Teacher/Leader Mr. / Mrs. / Ms. ___

School/Organization Name ___

☐ Public   ☐ Private   ☐ Parochial   ☐ Youth Org.   ☐ Other

School/Organization Address ___

Email ___

Phone ( ) ___   Fax ( ) ___

Grade level ___ Course ___

Number of classes participating ___   Number of students per class/organization ___

STUDENT HANDOUT FOR LESSON 2

Name _____

Class _____

Date _____

CHARTING CLASSICAL REPUBLICANISM AND NATURAL RIGHTS PHILOSOPHY

INSTRUCTIONS

FILL OUT THE CHART BELOW BY RESPONDING TO THE FOLLOWING QUESTIONS.

1. What is the primary goal of humans living together?

2. What ought to motivate human behavior?

3. What is the relationship between the public sphere and the private sphere?

4. How important is participation in civic activities?

	CLASSICAL REPUBLICANISM	NATURAL RIGHTS PHILOSOPHY
1		
2		
3		
4		

Permission for reproduction is granted by the Center for Civic Education for hearings and classroom use

Permission for reproduction is granted by the Center for Civic Education for hearings and classroom use

Name

Class

Date

THE ANTI-FEDERALIST POSITION ON RATIFICATION OF THE CONSTITUTION

The following information summarizes some of the arguments presented by opponents of the Constitution—known today as the Anti-Federalists—in speeches, pamphlets, and newspaper articles.

I. REPUBLICAN GOVERNMENT

Republican government is the only form of government suited to the United States. Most writers on republicanism agree that republican government is possible only when the people have roughly the same economic status, pursue similar economic activities, live their lives in similar ways, and have the same religious and moral points of view.

Writers such as Montesquieu explain that a large republic is contrary to the experience of mankind. Republican government thrives only in small communities where people know one another and care about one another's needs. This is clearly not the case in the United States. "The idea of a... republic on an average one thousand miles in length and eight hundred in breadth, and containing six millions of white inhabitants...is in itself an absurdity, and contrary to the whole experience of mankind."

Republican government also requires virtuous citizens who are committed to the common good. The proposed Constitution does not emphasize the common good. Instead, it allows people and groups to be selfish and concentrate only on their personal interests, which it controls with checks and balances.

Moreover, republican government requires the active support of the people. The government created by the Constitution is too distant from the people to gain this support. The country will quickly sink into monarchy, then despotism.

wtpcompanion.civiced.org | **PRIMARY SOURCES**

Visit the We the People companion website for links to Centinel No. 1, Brutus No. 1, and Melancton Smith's speech to the New York Ratifying Convention on June 21, 1787.

II. FEDERALISM

The proposed Constitution creates a national, or consolidated, government. It will destroy the states. The states are the governments closest to the people and are vital to political liberty.

The lust for power knows no limits. If the people give the national government great powers, it will always expand and abuse that power. Four provisions of the Constitution demonstrate its dangerous tendency toward consolidated government.

❶ ARTICLE I, SECTION 8, GIVES CONGRESS THE POWER TO LEVY TAXES

Congress does not have this power under the Articles of Confederation. Giving Congress the power of the purse makes it dangerously independent of the people. The power to tax is the power to destroy and creates horrible images of the people being bled dry. The taxing power of the national government will be used to destroy state governments. One Pennsylvanian has warned that "the Congress may monopolize every source of revenue, and thus indirectly demolish the state government, for without funds they could not exist."

❷ ARTICLE I, SECTION 8, ALSO GIVES CONGRESS THE POWER TO RAISE AND SUPPORT ARMIES

This is the ultimate means of suppression. A standing army is "that grand engine of oppression." There is no question that the national government will be willing to use that engine.

❸ ARTICLE I, SECTION 8, CONTAINS TWO CLAUSES THAT ARE ESPECIALLY DANGEROUS

One is the "general welfare" clause. Congress can decide that anything is necessary to further the general welfare, and it will seize every opportunity to raise revenue on behalf of the general welfare. The second dangerous clause is the "necessary and proper" clause. That clause gives Congress such a sweeping grant of power that there are no logical limits to the powers of the national government.

❹ ARTICLE VI CONTAINS A "SUPREMACY CLAUSE" THAT MAKES LAWS ENACTED BY CONGRESS AND TREATIES THE SUPREME LAW OF THE LAND

This clause leaves no doubt: if this system is adopted, the citizens of every state will be forced to surrender all their rights and privileges to the national government.

wtpcompanion.civiced.org   PRIMARY SOURCES

Visit the We the People companion website for links to Brutus No. 1 and Brutus No. 6.

Permission for reproduction is granted by the Center for Civic Education for hearings and classroom use

Permission for reproduction is granted by the Center for Civic Education for hearings and classroom use

III. SEPARATION OF POWERS AND CHECKS AND BALANCES

The proposed Constitution does not adequately separate legislative, executive, and judicial powers. Separation of powers is essential for maintaining political liberty. The blending of powers, such as between the president and the Senate in making executive and judicial appointments and treaties, makes the president and Senate "partners in crime" in pursuit of unlimited power. The blending of powers, which occurs throughout the proposed Constitution, demonstrates a breakdown of checks and balances, and will destroy liberty.

History demonstrates that no country can remain free when governmental powers are blended. All the states assured the separation of powers in their constitutions, thereby guaranteeing liberty. The legislative and executive powers are too closely united in the proposed Constitution. Where legislative and executive powers are united, in either the same body of magistrates or the same person, there can be no liberty.

> **wtpcompanion.civiced.org**   **PRIMARY SOURCES**
>
> Visit the We the People companion website for links to Brutus No. 16 and Centinel No. 1.

IV. THE CONGRESS

Representatives ought to mix with the people, think as they think, feel as they feel, and know their interests and situations. The Congress created in the proposed Constitution will be unrepresentative and aristocratic. This is so for several reasons.

❶ ONE OF THE FIRST PRINCIPLES OF DEMOCRATIC GOVERNMENT IS ANNUAL ELECTIONS

The members of the House will be elected only every two years, and senators stand for election only every six years.

❷ ROTATION OF OFFICE IS IMPORTANT TO PREVENTING ARISTOCRATIC GOVERNMENT

By allowing elected officials to be reelected, without limit, the proposed Constitution invites corruption. Once men have tasted power, they do not want to give it up, and they become dangerous.

❸ THE PROPOSED CONSTITUTION PROVIDES REPRESENTATION FOR EVERY 30,000 INHABITANTS; IT IS NOT POSSIBLE TO ADEQUATELY REPRESENT THAT MANY PEOPLE

The best form of government is one in which people govern themselves in a town meeting. Representative government is a substitute for self-government. Therefore, representatives should act to the greatest possible degree as the individual citizen would act if representing himself. This is possible only if there are frequent elections and each representative represents a small number of people.

❹ **A SMALL NUMBER OF REPRESENTATIVES REPRESENTING LARGE DISTRICTS OR, LIKE SENA-
TORS, REPRESENTING ENTIRE STATES WILL MOST LIKELY COME FROM THE UPPER CLASSES.**

Only the rich will be able to afford to run for election and be motivated to do so. Very few people from the middle class will choose to run for Congress because the institution will not be staffed by people who have been used to living plain and frugal lives.

Representatives ought to mix with the people, think as they think, feel as they feel, and know their interests and situations.

PRIMARY SOURCES

wtpcompanion.civiced.org

Visit the We the People companion website for links to "The Federal Farmer," October 8–9, 1787, and the speeches of Patrick Henry at the Virginia Ratifying Convention, June 5–7, 1788.

V. THE PRESIDENCY

At best, a president elected for a four-year term, eligible for reelection, and given all the powers the proposed Constitution gives to the president will be an "elective monarch." Once a monarchy is established, the monarch's family will continue in office for generation after generation.

At worst, the proposed Constitution creates an arbitrary aristocracy. The president will have the worst characteristics of the British monarchy and the royal governors.

The president will surround himself with those who flatter him, are subservient to him, and do what he wants them to do.

PRIMARY SOURCES

wtpcompanion.civiced.org

Visit the We the People companion website for links to Centinel No. 1 and the Pennsylvania Ratifying Convention Minority, December 18, 1787.

Permission for reproduction is granted by the Center for Civic Education for hearings and classroom use

Permission for reproduction is granted by the Center for Civic Education for hearings and classroom use

VI.   THE JUDICIARY

The proposed Constitution gives unelected judges power for life. It creates a judicial branch that will absorb and swallow up the judicial systems of the states.

The national judiciary no doubt will claim the power to declare what the Constitution means ("judicial review"). The power to declare what the Constitution means belongs to the Congress.

The Constitution also fails to guarantee trial by jury in civil cases and does not contain adequate protections for those who are accused of crimes.

The judiciary under the proposed Constitution also is flawed because it is not as independent as it should be from the other branches. The judges will be too willing to reflect the political biases of those on whom they depend for their power.

wtpcompanion.civiced.org   **PRIMARY SOURCES**

Visit the We the People companion website for links to Brutus Nos. 11 and 12 (Part 2).

VII.   THE BILL OF RIGHTS

The proposed Constitution creates a powerful national government that will have authority directly over the people. It is true that it protects some rights. For example, Article I, Section 9, prohibits Congress from enacting bills of attainder and ex post facto laws.

However, the Constitution does guarantee other important liberties and rights. Those rights are protected only in state constitutions. The lust for power that infects all officeholders will threaten the basic rights of the people. The proposed Constitution is dangerous to the liberties of Americans because it does not have a bill of rights. This alone justifies not ratifying the proposed Constitution.

wtpcompanion.civiced.org   **PRIMARY SOURCES**

Visit the We the People companion website for a link to John DeWitt Essay No. 2 and the Pennsylvania Ratifying Convention Minority, December 18, 1787.

D 3

STUDENT HANDOUT FOR LESSON 14

Name

Class

Date

THE FEDERALIST POSITION ON RATIFICATION OF THE CONSTITUTION

The following information summarizes some of the arguments presented in favor of the Constitution by Alexander Hamilton, John Jay, and James Madison using a common pen name, Publius, in a series of essays titled *The Federalist.*

I. REPUBLICAN GOVERNMENT

Republican government is possible in a territory as large as the thirteen states even if the people lack civic virtue. History demonstrates that reliance on civic virtue in small communities does not work. Republics have been destroyed because people prefer their own interests to the good of the community.

The proposed Constitution addresses in a realistic manner the problem of factions. Factions are groups of people who share interests or beliefs who try to get the government to do what they want, not what is good for the community as a whole.

In a large republic, people and factions are dispersed over a large territory. A larger number of people creates greater numbers of factions. Factions scattered over a large territory will find it impossible to cooperate with one another to form majorities, get the government to do what they want it to do, and obtain laws that are favorable to their own interests rather than the good of the community.

Furthermore, the system of representation and checks and balances created by the Constitution helps to ensure that interests opposed to the good of the community will not be able to determine public policy. Proposals for laws and policies based only on selfish interests are not likely to survive the deliberative process created by the Constitution.

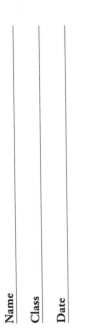

wtpcompanion.civiced.org **PRIMARY SOURCES**

Visit the We the People companion website for links to Federalist 9 and 10.

Permission for reproduction is granted by the Center for Civic Education for hearings and classroom use

Permission for reproduction is granted by the Center for Civic Education for hearings and classroom use

II. FEDERALISM

The Articles of Confederation led to a crisis in the United States because they created a situation in which the central government had very little authority, making the United States weak in the eyes of other nations and disunited at home. America needs a national government to deal with problems that are common to all states, as well as in the area of foreign affairs.

The proposed Constitution does not eliminate the states. Nor does it make the states inferior to the national government on matters that affect only the states and their communities. Article I, Section 8, lists the powers of Congress. It does not give Congress all legislative power, only legislative power "herein granted." All other legislative power remains with the states. People will always be more loyal to their states than to the national government because state governments are closest to them. In a contest between state and national powers, states are most likely to win. In fact, the greatest problem under the proposed Constitution probably will come from the powers retained by the states, not from the powers of the national government.

wtpcompanion.civiced.org   PRIMARY SOURCES

Visit the We the People companion website for links to Federalist 9, 37, and 46.

III. SEPARATION OF POWERS AND CHECKS AND BALANCES

It is well understood that the accumulation of all governing powers in the same hands is tyranny. Republican government therefore requires separation of powers. Each branch of the government must have a will of its own.

Each branch also must have the power to resist the efforts of the other branches to exercise powers that do not belong to them. Merely spelling out the powers of each branch in the Constitution and instructing each branch to exercise its own powers and not to invade the powers of the other branches is not enough. Each branch of government must jealously guard its powers, check the exercise of power by the other branches, and be able to resist the efforts of the other branches to take away its powers.

The proposed Constitution achieves separation of powers through a system of shared powers that gives each branch of government the power to check the exercise of power by the other branch. For example, the executive can check the legislature through the veto power. The legislative branch can check the executive by overriding a veto with a two-thirds majority vote or by failing to concur in presidential appointments.

By blending powers, the proposed Constitution assures that each branch will aggressively protect its own powers and make sure that the other branches do not exceed theirs.

wtpcompanion.civiced.org   PRIMARY SOURCES

Visit the We the People companion website for links to Federalist 47–51.

IV. THE CONGRESS

Elections every two years for members of the House are sufficient to protect the political liberty and safety of the people. Two years in office also gives representatives an opportunity to get legislative experience without making them dangerously independent of the people's judgment.

The limited powers given to Congress make it safe to have members of the House represent relatively large numbers of people. Moreover, if Congress becomes too large, which it would if there were more representatives, the House would be an unwieldy deliberative body. Large bodies are more likely to respond to the appeal of emotion and be swayed by potential dictators.

The office of senator requires more knowledge and greater stability of character. Therefore, senators need to be older and have more experience than members of the House. Having senators selected by state legislatures is an important way to assure that the national government is linked to state governments. It is true that allowing each state to have two senators was a compromise at the Constitutional Convention. It was a good compromise. The composition of the Senate assures that all laws Congress enacts will reflect the will of both the people and the states. The relatively small size of the Senate will give the government both stability and dignity because senators will engage in more sober, deliberative debate than is possible in large bodies. The stability the Senate brings to Congress will be advantageous for both domestic and foreign relations.

---

wtpcompanion.civiced.org **PRIMARY SOURCES**

Visit the We the People companion website for links to Federalist 52, 53, 55, 56, and 62–65.

V. THE PRESIDENT

The method in the proposed Constitution for selecting the president (the Electoral College) removes the selection of the president from tumult and disorder. Having the House resolve ties in the Electoral College guarantees that the person selected to be president will have the ability and virtue to serve the country well.

Energy and strength in the executive is essential to protecting the United States against foreign attacks. It also is essential to the steady administration of the laws, to protection of private property, and to the protection of liberty against those with ambitions to destroy personal liberty and against self-interested faction and anarchy.

Having a single rather than a plural executive is an important strength of the proposed Constitution. Plural executives are weak executives. Plural executives also lack responsibility, they usually lack secrecy, and they are not decisive.

Permission for reproduction is granted by the Center for Civic Education for hearings and classroom use

The president's four-year term gives the executive a certain independence from the passing whims and opinions of the people. The people are easily led astray by momentary passions. A statesman, and especially the executive, should be able to resist fleeting passions and act instead on long-term calculations of the public good. These same reasons support permitting the president to be reelected. Having the president stand for election every four years assures responsiveness to the people. Being eligible for reelection provides a degree of continuity in administration, which is desirable for both domestic and foreign policy.

The executive power created by the proposed Constitution protects against the risk of monarchy. The president must stand for election every four years. The Electoral College, which is chosen by the people, assures that the president is a person of wisdom and excellence. The president is also subject to impeachment, trial, and removal from office if he exceeds his power. Moreover, the Constitution places many checks on the exercise of executive power. For example, the president makes treaties and appointments, but they are subject to the advice and consent of the Senate. Congress can override presidential vetoes. The system of checks and balances assures that executive power will not be abused.

wtpcompanion.civiced.org | **PRIMARY SOURCES**

Visit the We the People companion website for links to Federalist 69–72.

VI. THE JUDICIARY

The proposed Constitution provides for a national judiciary made up of appointed judges who serve lifetime terms during good behavior. This assures that the judges will be independent. An independent judiciary is especially important under a constitution that creates a government of limited powers. Life tenure assures judges who have the knowledge and experience to perform the arduous task of deciding cases and protecting the Constitution. The appointment process, which involves both the president and the Senate, will guard against foolish appointments.

As important as it is to have an independent judiciary, the judiciary is the weakest of the three branches. It has access to neither the purse (controlled by Congress) nor the sword (controlled by the president). It is therefore the least dangerous of the branches.

The proposed Constitution creates a limited government. For example, Article I, Section 9, prohibits Congress from enacting ex post facto laws. In practice, the only way to preserve such limitations is through the courts. It is their duty to declare laws that violate the Constitution null and void. If courts did not have this power, people's rights and privileges would mean nothing.

wtpcompanion.civiced.org | **PRIMARY SOURCES**

Visit the We the People companion website for links to Federalist 78 and 81.

VII. BILL OF RIGHTS

The proposed Constitution protects many of the rights usually mentioned in bills of rights. These include the guarantee of habeas corpus, the prohibition against ex post facto laws, the guarantee of trial by jury in criminal cases in the state where the crime was committed, protection for those accused of treason, and the prohibition against titles of nobility.

Bills of rights, such as the Magna Carta, usually are limitations on monarchs. They are not needed in a political system where sovereignty resides in the people and the government is merely the servant of the people. Moreover, the proposed Constitution delegates only limited powers to the national government. Other powers remain with the states, or with the people. Bills of rights in state constitutions can protect the people against the arbitrary exercise of power by their state governments.

Finally, it would be dangerous to try to list all the rights retained by the people. Listing their rights would imply that the national government had power over anything not listed. This might cause the national government in the future to assume that it has powers over the people that the proposed Constitution does not give it.

wtpcompanion.civiced.org   **PRIMARY SOURCES**

Visit the We the People companion website for a link to Federalist 84.

Permission for reproduction is granted by the Center for Civic Education for hearings and classroom use

Permission for reproduction is granted by the Center for Civic Education for hearings and classroom use

D 4
STUDENT HANDOUT FOR LESSON 17

Name

Class

Date

COMPARING THE SOUTH CAROLINA DECLARATION OF CAUSES WITH LINCOLN'S FIRST INAUGURAL ADDRESS

INSTRUCTIONS

Read both the South Carolina Declaration of Causes and Lincoln's First Inaugural Address. Then fill out the chart below by answering the following questions. Answer each question using arguments from each document.

1. What is the nature of the union formed by the Constitution?

2. Who formed the union: the people or the states?

3. What are the rights of the states under the Constitution?

4. Do states have the right to secede from the union?

5. What is the significance of the Declaration of Independence?

	SOUTH CAROLINA DECLARATION OF CAUSES	LINCOLN'S FIRST INAUGURAL ADDRESS
1		
2		
3		
4		
5		

D 5

STUDENT HANDOUT FOR LESSON 25

Name

Class

Date

UNITED STATES COURTS OF APPEAL___KEY

1 **FIRST CIRCUIT**   Maine, Massachusetts, New Hampshire, Puerto Rico, Rhode Island

2 **SECOND CIRCUIT**   Connecticut, New York, Vermont

3 **THIRD CIRCUIT**   Delaware, New Jersey, Pennsylvania, Virgin Islands

4 **FOURTH CIRCUIT**   Maryland, North Carolina, South Carolina, Virginia, West Virginia

5 **FIFTH CIRCUIT**   Louisiana, Mississippi, Texas

6 **SIXTH CIRCUIT**   Kentucky, Michigan, Ohio, Tennessee

7 **SEVENTH CIRCUIT**   Illinois, Indiana, Wisconsin

8 **EIGHTH CIRCUIT**   Arkansas, Iowa, Minnesota, Missouri, Nebraska, North Dakota, South Dakota

9 **NINTH CIRCUIT**   Alaska, Arizona, California, Hawaii, Idaho, Nevada, Oregon, Washington, Guam, Northern Mariana Islands

10 **TENTH CIRCUIT**   Colorado, Kansas, New Mexico, Oklahoma, Utah, Wyoming

11 **ELEVENTH CIRCUIT**   Alabama, Florida, Georgia

12 **UNITED STATES COURT OF APPEALS FOR THE FEDERAL CIRCUIT**

Permission for reproduction is granted by the Center for Civic Education for hearings and classroom use

Permission for reproduction is granted by the Center for Civic Education for hearings and classroom use

UNITED STATES COURTS OF APPEAL__MAP

D 6

STUDENT ANSWER SHEET

Name _____

Class _____

Date _____

Instructions

For each question, select the one best answer. Mark your answers on this answer sheet as instructed by your teacher.

Cross off the correct answer with an X.

1. a b c d	18. a b c d	35. a b c d	52. a b c d
2. a b c d	19. a b c d	36. a b c d	53. a b c d
3. a b c d	20. a b c d	37. a b c d	54. a b c d
4. a b c d	21. a b c d	38. a b c d	55. a b c d
5. a b c d	22. a b c d	39. a b c d	56. a b c d
6. a b c d	23. a b c d	40. a b c d	57. a b c d
7. a b c d	24. a b c d	41. a b c d	58. a b c d
8. a b c d	25. a b c d	42. a b c d	59. a b c d
9. a b c d	26. a b c d	43. a b c d	60. a b c d
10. a b c d	27. a b c d	44. a b c d	61. a b c d
11. a b c d	28. a b c d	45. a b c d	62. a b c d
12. a b c d	29. a b c d	46. a b c d	63. a b c d
13. a b c d	30. a b c d	47. a b c d	64. a b c d
14. a b c d	31. a b c d	48. a b c d	65. a b c d
15. a b c d	32. a b c d	49. a b c d	
16. a b c d	33. a b c d	50. a b c d	
17. a b c d	34. a b c d	51. a b c d	

Permission for reproduction is granted by the Center for Civic Education for hearings and classroom use

Permission for reproduction is granted by the Center for Civic Education for hearings and classroom use

D 7

STUDENT MULTIPLE-CHOICE TEST

Name _____

Class _____

Date _____

THE HISTORY AND PRINCIPLES OF THE UNITED STATES CONSTITUTION

Instructions

For each question, select the one best answer. Mark your answers on a separate answer sheet as instructed by your teacher.

1. **According to natural rights philosophy, the main purpose of government is to**

   a. create a democracy.
   b. protect individual rights.
   c. create a system of separation of powers.
   d. promote the rights of the ruling class.

2. **To say that the rights to life, liberty, and property are unalienable means that they**

   a. cannot be given up or taken away.
   b. belong only to citizens.
   c. are subject to governmental approval.
   d. are protected by the Constitution.

3. **Which of the following statements describes a constitution?**

   a. A list of obligations of citizens.
   b. A priority for achieving particular policies.
   c. A plan that sets forth the structure and powers of government.
   d. A compilation of statutes that have been in effect at least fifty years.

4. **One major issue left unresolved by the Philadelphia Convention in 1787 was**

   a. the power of the states to coin money.
   b. the power of the House to initiate revenue bills.
   c. the definition of national citizenship.
   d. the power of the national government to regulate commerce with the Indian tribes.

5. **Civic virtue is best defined as**

   a. giving authority to government in exchange for protection of natural rights.

   b. putting the common good above individual interests.

   c. giving up some natural rights to create a strong government.

   d. separating power among groups to maintain balanced government.

6. **The Founders believed that the separation of powers was important to**

   a. make the government more efficient.

   b. allow more people to hold office.

   c. prevent the misuse of power.

   d. provide for legislative supremacy.

7. **In comparison with the Greek and Roman ideals of civic virtue, the Judeo-Christian tradition**

   a. advocates enlightened self-interest.

   b. emphasizes the common good.

   c. stresses the dignity and worth of each individual.

   d. reduces the importance of individual rights.

8. **The Enlightenment inspired America's Founders by**

   a. endorsing executive supremacy.

   b. making society more rigidly structured.

   c. justifying divine right of kings.

   d. emphasizing what could be achieved through the exercise of human reason.

9. **The distribution of powers between the national government and the states in the U.S. is known as**

   a. federalism.

   b. feudalism.

   c. separation of powers.

   d. delegation of powers.

10. **The Magna Carta included the important constitutional principle that established**

    a. freedom of religion.

    b. equal rights for all citizens.

    c. government based on the rule of law.

    d. the supremacy of Parliament.

Permission for reproduction is granted by the Center for Civic Education for hearings and classroom use

Permission for reproduction is granted by the Center for Civic Education for hearings and classroom use

11. **The purpose of a writ of habeas corpus is to protect the individual against**

   a. accusation of treason.

   b. unlawful detention.

   c. cruel and unusual punishment.

   d. self-incrimination.

12. **In colonial America, the right to vote most often depended on a person's gender and**

   a. national origin.

   b. social class.

   c. ancestry.

   d. property ownership.

13. **The Declaration of Independence asserted that**

   a. a "candid world" would emerge from the American revolution.

   b. the colonies were now free and independent states.

   c. Parliament had oppressed the colonies through the Townsend Acts.

   d. American independence respected "the opinions of mankind."

14. **The idea that political power is derived from the people is called**

   a. popular sovereignty.

   b. judicial review.

   c. unitary government.

   d. executive supremacy.

15. **Many of the first state constitutions included**

   a. unrestricted voting rights.

   b. the right of initiative and referendum.

   c. executive supremacy.

   d. bills of rights.

16. **Some Founders believed that majority rule could be a threat to**

   a. states' rights.

   b. local self-government.

   c. individual rights.

   d. constitutional government.

17. **A major weakness of the national government under the Articles of Confederation was its**

    a. lack of authority to regulate interstate trade.
    b. unequal representation of the states.
    c. power to violate individual rights.
    d. plural executive.

18. **The delegates to the Philadelphia Convention were authorized to**

    a. draft treaties governing international trade.
    b. write a new constitution for the nation.
    c. amend the Articles of Confederation.
    d. develop a plan for admitting new states to the union.

19. **In the debate over representation in Congress, the Virginia Plan advocated**

    a. equal representation of the states.
    b. proportional representation.
    c. bipartisan representation.
    d. limited representation.

20. **According to the supremacy clause of the U.S. Constitution, "supreme law of the land" refers to**

    a. acts of the president.
    b. decisions of the Supreme Court.
    c. the Constitution, laws enacted by Congress, and treaties.
    d. laws passed by state legislatures.

21. **The right of the Senate to ratify or reject a treaty made by the president is an example of**

    a. the "general welfare" clause.
    b. checks and balances.
    c. proportional representation.
    d. federalism.

22. **The Framers adopted the Electoral College method of choosing the president because**

    a. they wanted to assure a wise consideration in the choice of president.
    b. they were afraid women would vote.
    c. the colonies had used that system.
    d. it was used successfully in the French system.

Permission for reproduction is granted by the Center for Civic Education for hearings and classroom use

Permission for reproduction is granted by the Center for Civic Education for hearings and classroom use

23. **Anti-Federalists objected to the proposed Constitution because they believed that it**

a. placed too much power in the national government.

b. established the supremacy of Congress.

c. enumerated individual rights in too many places.

d. authorized the Supreme Court to exercise judicial review.

24. **The "establishment clause" of the First Amendment**

a. prohibits the press from inquiring into government operations.

b. prohibits Congress from establishing a national religion.

c. prohibits the government from requiring individuals to house soldiers.

d. places limits on an individual's right to free expression.

25. **The most persuasive objection to the Constitution by George Mason and other Anti-Federalists was that**

a. the judicial branch lacked sufficient power.

b. it gave too much power to the House of Representatives.

c. certain actions required more than a simple majority vote.

d. it did not contain a bill of rights.

26. **In comparison with the executive branch as organized by the First Congress, the executive branch today has**

a. lost much of its original power.

b. asked Congress to be more active in developing federal regulations.

c. allowed the cabinet to dominate the presidency.

d. grown larger and more complex.

27. **The primary method Congress uses to consider proposed legislation is**

a. open debate on the floor of the House.

b. the committee system.

c. public opinion polls.

d. executive orders from the president.

28. **The Tenth Amendment was included in the Bill of Rights**

a. over the objections of Anti-Federalists.

b. to protect rights that were not specifically listed.

c. so that the states could not violate individual rights.

d. in an effort to reserve powers not specifically stated in the Constitution, to the states or to the people.

29. **Which of the following is an example of a "positive right" found in the U.S. Bill of Rights?**

    a. The First Amendment, which states, "Congress shall make no law" that violates fundamental rights to freedom of religion, speech, press, assembly, and petition.

    b. The Sixth Amendment, which guarantees criminal defendants in criminal cases the right to speedy and public trials.

    c. The Third Amendment, which states, "No Soldier shall, in time of peace be quartered in any house, without the consent of the Owner, nor in time of war, but in a manner to be prescribed by law."

    d. The Second Amendment, which requires the government infringing upon the "right of the people to keep and bear Arms."

30. **Congress represents both the people and the states by**

    a. gerrymandering electoral districts.

    b. proportional representation in the House and equal state representation in the Senate.

    c. requiring consensus on all bills approved by the House and Senate.

    d. having the power to override presidential vetoes.

31. **Political parties in the United States**

    a. were created by Article IV of the U.S. Constitution.

    b. are examples of narrow factions and interests.

    c. have their rules approved by the U.S. Supreme Court.

    d. generally reflect broad coalitions of interests.

32. **Critics of judicial review claim that it conflicts with principles of**

    a. original jurisdiction.

    b. the supremacy clause.

    c. executive supremacy.

    d. legislative supremacy.

33. **In the American federal system, the scope of the national government's authority grew significantly because of the Supreme Court's interpretation of the**

    a. "privileges and immunities" clause.

    b. "free exercise" clause.

    c. "commerce" clause.

    d. "full faith and credit" clause.

Permission for reproduction is granted by the Center for Civic Education for hearings and classroom use

Permission for reproduction is granted by the Center for Civic Education for hearings and classroom use

34. The Federalists defended the proposed Constitution because it would

a. be easy to amend.

b. rely on separation of powers and checks and balances.

c. provide for a highly educated people.

d. allow all adult males the right to vote.

35. A fundamental difference between the Articles of Confederation and the Virginia Plan was that

a. the Articles of Confederation allowed the national government to collect taxes from individuals.

b. the Virginia Plan called for a strong national government.

c. the Virginia Plan recommended a weak legislative branch.

d. the Articles of Confederation called for a strong national government.

36. When Southern states seceded from the Union, they justified their actions by arguing that the United States is a

a. sovereign nation.

b. constitutional democracy.

c. democratic republic.

d. federation of sovereign states.

37. Black Codes were passed in some states to

a. help African Americans find employment.

b. limit the newly won freedoms of former slaves.

c. help local governments protect African Americans.

d. deny state citizenship to freed slaves.

38. In the decades immediately following their ratification, the Civil War Amendments did little to protect the rights of African Americans because

a. freed slaves refused to support the amendments.

b. U.S. Congress passed laws preventing the amendments from taking effect.

c. state government officials did little to enforce the provisions of the amendments.

d. the U.S. Supreme Court declared state civil rights laws unconstitutional.

39. **The guarantee of equal protection of the laws in the Fourteenth Amendment means that government**

   a. is responsible for seeing that Americans have the same opportunities.
   b. may not unfairly or unreasonably treat people differently.
   c. is responsible for ensuring that people have a decent standard of living.
   d. may not conduct unreasonable searches and seizures of private property.

40. **The Fourteenth Amendment changed the Constitution by**

   a. defining national and state citizenship.
   b. making national citizenship unavailable to Confederate officials.
   c. defining the period of residence required to become a naturalized citizen.
   d. giving the states exclusive power over citizenship.

41. **The power of Congress to investigate is an example of its**

   a. delegated powers.
   b. reserved powers.
   c. inherent powers.
   d. implied powers.

42. **The leaders of civil rights movements are significantly aided by the Constitution's protection of**

   a. freedom to assemble and petition.
   b. the privileges and immunities of citizenship.
   c. property rights.
   d. the separate but equal doctrine.

43. **The struggle to extend voting rights to women was made especially difficult by**

   a. the increase in women entering the workforce.
   b. fears that it would set back the cause for former slaves.
   c. constitutional questions over whether women are citizens.
   d. the failure of states to grant women voting rights.

44. **Citizenship of Native Americans was resolved by the**

   a. Indian Citizenship Act of 1924.
   b. *Dred Scott* decision of 1857.
   c. Missouri Compromise of 1821.
   d. Northwest Ordinance of 1787.

Permission for reproduction is granted by the Center for Civic Education for hearings and classroom use

Permission for reproduction is granted by the Center for Civic Education for hearings and classroom use

45. **Nations try to maintain international order by**

a. collective security, in which nations agree to protect one another from attack.

b. participating in the League of Nations.

c. participating in the international police force to enforce international law.

d. enforcing trade agreements.

46. **Americans can influence Congress in all the following ways except**

a. petitioning.

b. testifying before committees.

c. lobbying on behalf of pending legislation.

d. voting on pending legislation.

47. **"The right of the people peaceably to assemble" means that government may**

a. forbid assemblies based on their content, subject, or theme.

b. prohibit the use of public property for assemblies or demonstrations.

c. apply restrictions to some groups but not to others.

d. make reasonable "time, place, and manner" restrictions.

48. **The due process clause of the Fourteenth Amendment is important because it**

a. changed the emphasis of the Magna Carta on procedural rights of subjects.

b. has been used to extend the protections of most of the provisions of the Bill of Rights.

c. provides a referendum on pending national legislation.

d. modifies the commerce clause of Article I of the U.S. Constitution.

49. **Time, place, and manner restrictions of free expression generally are upheld by the courts if they**

a. give local authorities adequate discretion to limit the rights of unpopular groups.

b. apply only to obscene material or libelous statements.

c. are authorized by Congress or a majority of state legislatures.

d. are applied in a nondiscriminatory manner toward particular groups or individuals.

50. **Which of the following situations might violate a First Amendment right?**

   a. Police search a high school student's locker for drugs.

   b. A state legislature passes a law prohibiting the possession of firearms.

   c. Prisoners are not allowed to consult their attorneys.

   d. A city council refuses to grant a controversial group's permit to march.

51. **Individuals and groups that lobby government officials are exercising their constitutional rights of**

   a. due process.

   b. petition and association.

   c. habeas corpus.

   d. privilege against self-incrimination.

52. **The Fourth Amendment protects an individual's privacy from government intrusion in which of the following ways?**

   a. It requires a general warrant to be issued before search or seizure.

   b. It requires absolute proof of a crime committed before issuing a warrant for arrest.

   c. It prohibits general warrants because they allow indiscriminate searches.

   d. It prohibits general warrants because they limit government power.

53. **Procedural due process is based on the idea that**

   a. defendants' rights must be considered over the needs of society.

   b. systems of criminal justice must be affordable.

   c. police officers must have necessary authority to enforce the law.

   d. government officials must follow recognized procedures when making or enforcing the law.

54. **Which of the following is an important characteristic of an adversary legal system?**

   a. Cross-examination of witnesses conducted by the judge.

   b. Two opposing sides present their cases to an impartial judge or jury.

   c. There are no jury trials.

   d. Cases are presented by the parties themselves, without assistance of counsel.

55. **Nongovernmental organizations (NGOs) are examples of ways Americans can**

   a. advance the common good without relying on government.

   b. receive charters from Congress to perform quasi-legislative duties.

   c. avoid other civic responsibilities.

   d. avoid registering for the draft.

Permission for reproduction is granted by the Center for Civic Education for hearings and classroom use

Permission for reproduction is granted by the Center for Civic Education for hearings and classroom use

56. **States are called "laboratories of democracy" because they**

  a. test the validity of executive orders at the local level.

  b. issue advisory opinions to Congress.

  c. implement novel social and economic policies.

  d. place limits on the federal government.

57. **Administrative agencies are important because they**

  a. make rules to implement laws passed by Congress.

  b. are elected by the people.

  c. are provided for in Article VII of the Constitution.

  d. are not required to exercise judgment.

58. **A fundamental difference between citizens and resident aliens is that only citizens may**

  a. enjoy the protections of the Bill of Rights and the Fourteenth Amendment.

  b. engage in social and political actions.

  c. serve on juries.

  d. buy and sell real estate.

59. **Because many Americans believe that their own opportunity to succeed is related to the well-being of society, they**

  a. act for the common good out of enlightened self-interest.

  b. put aside civic virtue for the sake of their families.

  c. respect and accept the opinions of elected public officials.

  d. reject classical republicanism in favor of the natural rights philosophy.

60. **In American constitutional democracy, citizens are expected to**

  a. promote their individual rights without regard to the common good.

  b. allow government to assume responsibility for solving social problems.

  c. ignore their own personal interests when making political choices.

  d. think critically about public issues and participate in public affairs.

61. **Which of the following is not a fundamental principle of the American constitutional system?**

  a. checks and balances

  b. popular sovereignty

  c. rule of law

  d. executive supremacy

62. **Civil disobedience differs from mere lawbreaking in which of the following ways?**

   a. Civil disobedience is not breaking the law because the First Amendment protects it.

   b. Civil disobedience is a spontaneous act.

   c. Civil disobedience is not breaking the law because it has been an important tool in civil and voting rights movements.

   d. Civil disobedience seeks to justify its actions by reference to higher moral laws.

63. **A basic difference between the Bill of Rights and the Universal Declaration of Human Rights is that the Bill of Rights**

   a. is enforceable by an authorized government.

   b. enumerates more rights.

   c. is more recent.

   d. contains only "positive" rights.

64. **The Supreme Court's power to declare the meaning of the U.S. Constitution is known as**

   a. judicial restraint.

   b. judicial activism.

   c. judicial review.

   d. judicial inquiry.

65. **The "exclusionary rule" enforces protections found in the Fourth Amendment in which of the following ways?**

   a. It requires the police to read individuals their rights.

   b. It requires the government to show "probable cause" before a warrant is issued.

   c. It prohibits the police from searching or seizing property at a school.

   d. It prohibits the government from using evidence obtained in an illegal search.

Permission for reproduction is granted by the Center for Civic Education for hearings and classroom use

American Legacy

American Legacy: The United States Constitution and Other Essential Documents of American Democracy is an 80-page, pocket-sized (3.5 × 6.5″) booklet that includes the U.S. Constitution and the Declaration of Independence together with passages from 27 other documents that encompass essential ideas of American democracy. The documents are arranged chronologically, beginning with the Mayflower Compact.

Included are excerpts from documents such as *The Federalist*, Chief Justice John Marshall's decision in *Marbury v. Madison*, George Washington's Farewell Address, Thomas Jefferson's first inaugural address, Sojourner Truth's "Ain't I a Woman?," Abraham Lincoln's first inaugural address, the Gettysburg Address, the Emancipation Proclamation, Learned Hand's "The Spirit of Liberty," Martin Luther King Jr.'s "I Have a Dream," and the Civil Rights Act of 1964.

The booklet has an extensive index to the Constitution. It also contains the Oath of Allegiance for New Citizens and the Pledge of Allegiance.

To order *American Legacy*, visit the Center for Civic Education's online store at http://civiced-store.stores.yahoo.net/index.html or email our sales department at sales@civiced.org.

American Legacy was produced with the assistance of the U.S. Department of Education under the Education for Democracy Act approved by the United States Congress.

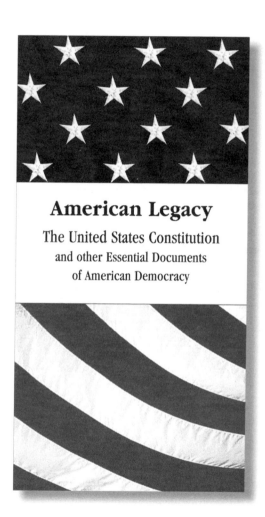

American Legacy
The United States Constitution
and other Essential Documents
of American Democracy

We the People: Project Citizen

Project Citizen is a curricular program for middle, high, and postsecondary school students and youth groups that promotes competent and responsible participation in local, state, and federal government. The program is designed to help students learn how to monitor and influence public policy. In the process, they develop support for democratic values and principles, tolerance, and feelings of political efficacy.

Entire classes of students or members of youth organizations work cooperatively to identify a public policy problem in their community. They then research the problem, evaluate alternative solutions, develop their own solution, and create a political action plan to enlist local or state authorities to adopt their proposed policy. Participants develop a portfolio of their work and present their project to a panel of civic-minded community members.

Project Citizen is administered with the assistance of a national network of coordinators in every state in the nation and conducted with the assistance of the National Conference of State Legislatures.

We the People: Project Citizen is funded by the U.S. Department of Education under the Education for Democracy Act approved by the United States Congress. Additional funding at the state level is also provided by an increasing number of state legislatures.

To contact your state coordinator or to request free instructional materials, visit the Center for Civic Education's website at www.civiced.org/project_citizen.php. Order the *Project Citizen* text from the Center for Civic Education's online store at http://civiced-store.stores.yahoo.net/index.html or email our sales department at sales@civiced.org.

Representative Democracy in America: Voices of the People

This six-part video series introduces citizens, particularly young people, to the representatives, institutions, and processes that realize the goal of a government of, by, and for the people. Developed with the involvement of students, teachers, scholars, and other educational leaders, the videos help students understand the essential elements of representative democracy and encourage their commitment to becoming responsible participants. The video series is accompanied by an instructional package.

The programs are best integrated at the high school level. They are designed to be used as a complete series but may also be used independently. The six programs, each approximately 15 minutes in length, address the following topics:

- The roots of representative democracy
- Federalism and the separation of powers
- The roles of representatives, executives, and justices in our democracy
- Our representatives and how they are chosen
- The role of the citizen in a representative democracy

Representative Democracy in America: Voices of the People is a five-year national project to reinvigorate and educate Americans on the critical relationship between government and the people it serves. The Center for Civic Education, the Center on Congress at Indiana University, and the Trust for Representative Democracy of the National Conference of State Legislatures are implementing the project.

Representative Democracy in America: Voices of the People was funded by the U.S. Department of Education under the Education for Democracy Act approved by the United States Congress. To order *Representative Democracy in America: Voices of the People*, email our sales department at sales@civiced.org.

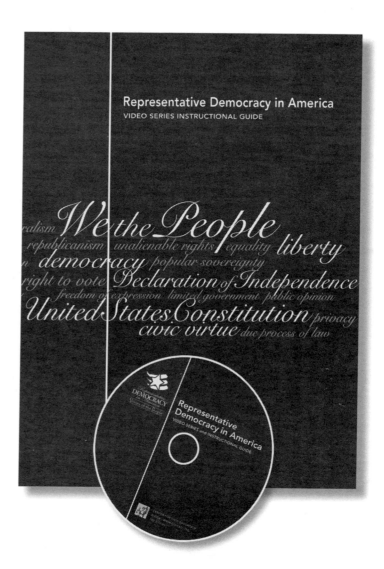

Foundations of Democracy

Foundations of Democracy is a K–12 curricular program based on concepts fundamental to an understanding of politics and government, such as Authority, Privacy, Responsibility, and Justice. This multi-disciplinary program draws upon such fields as political philosophy, political science, law, history, literature, and environmental studies.

The Foundations curricular materials are designed to progress sequentially in scope and complexity through four levels: Grades K–2, 3–5, 6–9, and 10–12. The primary goal of the Foundations of Democracy program is to promote civic competence and responsibility among the nation's elementary and secondary students.

In this course of study, students are challenged to discuss and debate situations involving such topics as the use of authority, the protection of privacy, and the choices that need to be made between competing values and interests. Students are asked to decide how responsibilities should be fulfilled and how justice could be achieved in a number of situations. The methodology employed helps students develop their own positions and support their positions with reasons.

Foundations of Democracy curricular materials are developed and disseminated with support from the Office of Juvenile Justice and Delinquency Prevention (OJJDP) of the U.S. Department of Justice and the U.S. Department of Education.

To order books from our Foundations of Democracy Series, visit the Center for Civic Education's online store at http://civiced-store.stores.yahoo.net/index.html or email our sales department at sales@civiced.org. The Center also offers sample lessons online at www.civiced.org/lessons_index.php.

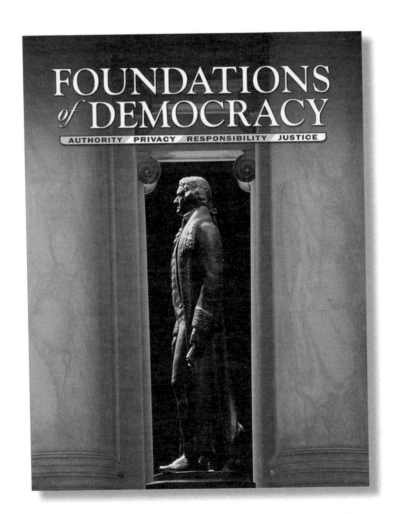

Elements of Democracy

Elements of Democracy is intended to bring a sense of clarity to the meanings of fundamental terminology surrounding the theory and practice of democracy. In this attempt to facilitate the understanding of the complex terms required to comprehend and discuss democracy, the authors expect and encourage the readers to inquire further into their significance of these terms and the controversies that underlie them.

The ideas that surround the practice of democracy are among the most consequential of the modern world and destined only to become more so. *Elements of Democracy* is an attempt to explore the range of ideas that make up the vocabulary of democracy. For example, the section titled "Concepts and Fundamental Principles of Democracy" encompasses such subjects as democracy and equality, the common good, and the role of law in democracy; other sections include "The Political Processes of Democracy" and "Democracy and Citizenship." This text is an excellent resource for high school, college level, and adult audiences.

Elements of Democracy was developed by the Center for Civic Education and funded by the U.S. Department of Education under the Education for Democracy Act approved by the United States Congress. *Elements of Democracy* is a project of the Alliance for Representative Democracy, a consortium of the Center for Civic Education, the Trust for Representative Democracy of the National Conference of State Legislatures, and the Center for Congress at Indiana University.

To order *Elements of Democracy*, visit the Center for Civic Education's online store at http://civicedstore.stores.yahoo.net/index.html or email our sales department at sales@civiced.org. The Center also offers sample lessons online at www.civiced.org/lessons_index.php.

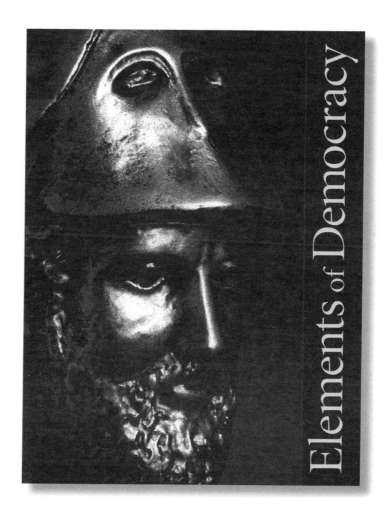

WE THE PEOPLE COMPANION WEBSITE

wtpcompanion.civiced.org

The We the People companion website, wtpcompanion.civiced.org, provides a variety of resources students and teachers can use to facilitate comprehension of the concepts mentioned in the text. The companion website for the *We the People* high school student text contains the following features:

- An overview of the student edition, the Preface, and the Introduction

- Full text of all unit and lesson purposes

- Each Term and Concept to Understand with definitions

- The complete glossary

- Brief biographies of each Founder and Framer

- Links to Supreme Court syllabi and opinions for each case described in the student edition

- Links to the full text of primary sources mentioned in the text

- Annotated bibliographies for each unit

- Links to specially selected websites that illuminate concepts mentioned in the student text

- Descriptions of each image contained in the student edition

- Links to films and podcasts related to the book's content

In addition, the unit and lesson purposes, terms, glossary, and biographies are printable, downloadable, and can be downloaded in MP3 format.

Resources are added constantly, so be sure to visit wtpcompanion.civiced.org frequently for the latest dynamic content.

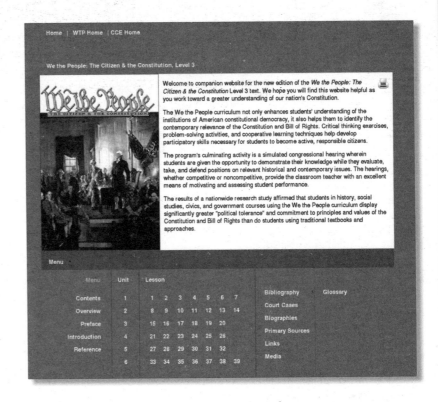